France

Vintage	Red Bordeaux		White Bordeaux		Alsace
	Médoc/Graves	Pom/St-Em	Sauternes & sw	Graves & dry	
2010	7–10	6–10	8–10	7–8	8–9
2009	7–10	7–10	8–10	7–9	8–9
2008	6–9	6–9	6–7	7–8	7–8
2007	5–7	6–7	8–9	8–9	6–8
2006	7–8	7–9	8–9	8–9	6–8
2005	9–10	9–10	8–10	8–10	8–9
2004	7–8	7–9	5–7	6–7	6–8
2003	5–9	5–8	7–8	6–7	6–7
2002	6–8	5–8	7–8	7–8	7–8
2001	6–8	7–8	8–10	7–9	6–8
2000	8–10	7–9	6–8	6–8	8–10
1999	5–7	5–8	6–9	7–10	6–8
1998	5–8	6–9	5–8	5–9	7–9
1997	5–7	4–7	7–9	4–7	7–9
1996	6–8	5–7	7–9	7–10	8–10
1995	7–9	6–9	6–8	5–9	6–9
1994	5–8	5–8	4–6	5–8	6–9
1993	4–6	5–7	2–5	5–7	6–8
1992	3–5	3–5	3–5	4–8	5–7

France continued

Vintage	Burgundy			Rhône	
	Côte d'Or red	Côte d'Or white	Chablis	Rhône (N)	Rhône (S)
2010	7–8	6–7	7–9	8–9	7–8
2009	7–10	7–8	7–8	7–9	7–8
2008	7–9	7–9	7–9	6–7	5–7
2007	7–8	8–9	8–9	6–8	7–8
2006	7–8	8–10	8–9	7–8	7–9
2005	7–9	7–9	7–9	7–8	6–8
2004	6–7	7–8	7–8	6–7	6–7
2003	6–7	6–7	6–7	5–7	6–8
2002	7–8	7–8	7–8	4–6	5–5
2001	6–8	7–9	7–8	7–8	7–9
2000	7–8	6–9	7–8	6–8	7–9
1999	7–10	5–7	5–8	7–9	6–9
1998	5–8	5–7	7–8	6–8	7–9
1997	5–8	5–8	7–9	7–9	5–8

Beaujolais 2010, 09, 08, 07. Crus will keep. **Mâcon–Villages** (white). Drink 10, 09, 08. **Loire** (Sweet Anjou and Touraine) best recent vintages: 10, 09, 07, 05, 02, 97, 96, 93, 90, 89; Bourgueil, Chinon, Saumur–Champigny: 10, 09, 06, 05, 04, 02, 00, 99. **Upper Loire** (Sancerre, Pouilly–Fumé): 10, 09, 08 **Muscadet** 10 DYA.

MITCHELL BEAZLEY

HUGH JOHNSON'S

POCKET WINE BOOK

2012

Hugh Johnson's Pocket Wine Book 2012

Edited and designed by Mitchell Beazley, an imprint of
Octopus Publishing Group Limited, Endeavour House,
189 Shaftesbury Avenue, London WC2 8JY

An Hachette Livre UK Company
www.hachettelivre.co.uk

Distributed in the USA and Canada by Octopus Books
USA: c/o Hachette Book Group USA,
237 Park Avenue, New York, NY 10017

www.octopusbooksusa.com

Copyright © Octopus Publishing Group Ltd 2011

First edition published 1977

Revised editions published 1978, 1979, 1980, 1981,
1982, 1983, 1984, 1985, 1986, 1987, 1988, 1989, 1990,
1991, 1992, 1993, 1994, 1995, 1996, 1997, 1998,
1999, 2000, 2001, 2002 (twice), 2003, 2004, 2005,
2006 (twice), 2007, 2008, 2009, 2010, 2011

A CIP record for this book is available from
the British Library.

ISBN (UK): 978 1 845 33632 5

ISBN (US): 978 1 84533602 8

The author and publishers will be grateful for any
information that will assist them in keeping future
editions up to date. Although all reasonable care
has been taken in preparing this book, neither the
publishers nor the author can accept any liability for
any consequences arising from the use thereof, or
from the information contained herein.

General Editor **Margaret Rand**
Editoral Director **Tracey Smith**
Commissioning Editor **Hilary Lumsden**
Project Editor **Jo Wilson**
Proofreader **Jamie Ambrose**
Deputy Art Director **Yasia Williams-Leedham**
Designer **Ashley Western**
Production Manager **Peter Hunt**
Printed and bound in China

Picture credits in page order
1 Fotolia/Stefano Neri; 3 Fotolia/Mikko Pitkänen; 4 Fotolia/
Elenathewise; 6 Octopus Publishing Group/Adrian Pope; 305
Photolibrary/Eye Ubiquitous; 306 Scope; 308 Fotolia/Phillip
Minnis; 309 Monty Waldin; 311c Alamy/Per Karlsson/BKWine.
com; 311b Corbis/Owen Franken; 311a Photolibrary/Michael
Busselle/Robert Harding Travel; 312 Getty Images/Louis-Laurent
Grandadam; 315a Alamy/Sue Heaton; 315b Corbis/Peter Adams/
JAI; 315c SuperStock/Hemis.fr; 316l SuperStock/age footstock;
316r Cephas/Mick Rock; 317l Scope Image/J L Barde; 317r Ryan
O'Connell; 318r courtesy Mas Amiel; 318l courtesy Domaine de
Trevallon; 319r Alamy/Per Karlsson/BKWine.com; 319l courtesy
Mas de Daumac Gassac; 320r Ludovic Molinier; 320l Domaine de
la Rectorie/Pierre Parce

HUGH JOHNSON'S

POCKET WINE BOOK

GENERAL EDITOR
MARGARET RAND

2012

Acknowledgements

This store of detailed recommendations comes partly from my own notes and mainly from those of a great number of kind friends. Without the generous help and cooperation of innumerable winemakers, merchants and critics, I could not attempt it. I particularly want to thank the following for help with research or in the areas of their special knowledge:

Sarah Ahmed
Helena Baker
Nicolas Belfrage MW
Philipp Blom
Jim Budd
Michael Cooper
Terry Copeland
Michael Edwards
Sarah Jane Evans MW
Rosemary George MW
Caroline Gilby MW

Anthony Gismondi
Annie Kay
Chandra Kurt
James Lawther MW
Konstantinos Lazarakis MW
John Livingstone-Learmonth
Campbell Mattinson
Adam Montefiore
Jasper Morris MW
Shirley Nelson
Margaret Rand

Daniel Rogov
Ulrich Sautter
Eleonora Scholes
Stephen Skelton MW
Paul Strang
Marguerite Thomas
Larry Walker
Simon Woods
Philip van Zyl

Contents

Agenda 2012

Do you remember the years – not so long ago – when the wine world was like watching an airport arrivals board? New wines from Chile, Argentina, Oregon, New Zealand, South Africa, Uruguay were landing ("Baggage on carousel number...") at such a rate that drinkers felt cheated if there was no new region, country or continent to explore. Sommeliers loved it. "You mean you haven't seen the Mexican Merlot, or the Viognier from Venezuela?" Novelty is fun, and it gave us the sense that the world was a level-playing vineyard: one man's Cab was (or soon would be) as good as another's.

That phase pretty much obliged every winemaker to have a go at everything, or at least at the internationally valid varieties, all French, that held the unwieldy world of wine together. Standardization was the threat, or was deemed to be: wine from everywhere would taste the same, made by itinerant gurus from the same grape varieties, with price-points ("premium" means drinkable; "super-premium"– you might want a second glass) the only differentiation.

In fact, the opposite is happening. Far from becoming more alike, the contributions of the world's new or newish regions are slowly growing more distinct. Ten years ago "Anything but Chardonnay" was the slogan. You don't hear it now – for several reasons. Rookie winemakers have gone past the stage of slathering their wine with oak ("Anything but oak" was the slogan we really needed). Farmers are getting smarter about the characteristics of their land. Competition makes specialization a more and more tempting option. And the knee-jerk notion that a single grape variety was somehow superior to a blend is giving way to intelligent blending. Not for all varieties, for sure: the Fourth Circle of the *Inferno* is reserved for people

who blend Riesling or Pinot Noir. But the truth has
dawned that matching the variety or varieties to
the soil and climate is the one prime factor in making
a wine that will catch on.

To start with, multitasking is your insurance policy.
All big Californian wineries used to offer "a full range".
If the dry red didn't work out, you could always sell
your customers "Chablis" or "Sherry". Years down the
track you've dropped the fortifieds and made a name for
Cab and Chard and Sauv Blanc. You find the mailing
list is buying, and the critics talking about, your red
and ignoring your whites. You create a Reserve label:
punchier wine aged longer in oak. Next step, you make
separate wines from the slopes with the healthiest and
ripest grapes, christen them Gravel Gulch or Red Rock
Canyon and start charging serious money. You have
been, in fact, through the whole process of evolution that
created Chambertin or the Grand Vin de Château Latour
– only it took the French centuries rather than decades.

Judging the right moment to become a specialist,
to put your eggs in one basket, is a big decision. Whole
countries or regions do it for simple reasons. New
Zealand became a near-monoculture of Sauvignon Blanc
because its wine is almost alarmingly recognizable,
and simplicity sells. Winemakers follow their fancies,
keep up with the Joneses, or even follow a star invisible
to anyone else. More than you might think are plain
cussed, and plant Pinot Noir because they're told they
shouldn't – hugely to our benefit. If we still believed
Burgundy was the only place it would grow, just think of
all the lovely, juicy bottles we wouldn't have from New
Zealand, from Oregon, from Australia, from Germany...

If this sounds like unmitigated good news for wine,
the sunlit uplands in sight, perhaps I should blow a little
raspberry, too. It has not been, and never will be, plain
sailing. The wine industry is famous for its booms and
busts. Australia overplanted absurdly in the 1990s – as
much to dodge tax as anything – then discounted its
produce to destruction. For an industry to prosper, each
of its members has to keep good accounting discipline.

Wine is cursed, too, by being an obvious and attractive loss-leader for supermarkets. Supermarket buyers are not famously charitable to their suppliers, but they see wine-producers as particularly soft targets. Even a winery with money can't store its wine until a good moment to sell; it is in its nature to charge as it matures, and the tanks are needed for the next harvest. What supermarkets call a "promotional budget" is in reality a painful price cut for the producers, who are consequently obliged to cut corners in production – hence the dreary industrial nature of much of the wine they sell.

At the other extreme there is a world in which, literally, the higher the price, the better. That is from the point of view of a Chinese businessman entertaining a government official. The bureaucrat knows only that Château Lafite is the most expensive wine. He feels short-changed if asked to toast in anything else. Guess where the contract goes?

Low price and top price need little interpretation. Knowledge of the product is irrelevant. Gauging value in the middle ground is more challenging. My personal benchmark, portable and memorable, is the price of Champagne. I'm fond of Champagne. Many excellent wines cost about the same as good NV Champagne (in Britain currently, say, £25–£30 a bottle). Less than that and I feel I'm not really splashing out, so I get experimental. More than that and I want reassurance; I play relatively safe.

Most of all I look for precise flavours that mean something to me; a grape variety, or better a grape plus terroir, a cellar-style, above all a good, fresh drink that suits my mood and my food. With wine-geek friends, comparing several wines, a theme or argument. With normal human friends, some familiar reminder of past meetings or fun discovery for the future. Without the appropriate taste and the satisfaction it brings, there is no such thing as a bargain.

Where do I look? I investigate the fringes of famous regions. Some have physical, often geological boundaries, others merely political ones that make no impact on their flavour. "Bordeaux" on a bottle, for example, simply means coming from the *département* of the Gironde. Not everything in the Gironde is special, and not everything from its neighbours is inferior. St-Emilion is world-famous, Castillon less so; the same with Corton and Auxey-Duresses, with Napa and, say, Mendocino, or with Châteauneuf and a wider stretch of the southern Rhône.

I look for producers who understand blending, who add Sémillon to Sauvignon, Mourvèdre to Grenache, Viognier to Syrah, Merlot to Sangiovese, or cultivate a bit of Petit Verdot – not because a mixture is inherently better, but because they taste and *think*. I look for producers who have grasped the nettle and bottle fresh wines with screwcaps. I settle, more and more often, for rosé; not because it's fashionable, but because it can be delicious, and it can solve so many knotty what-goes-with-what and who's-having-the-fish problems.

And I look – oh, how I look! – for wines with moderate alcohol content. A few styles do need more than 14%, but they also need a damn good excuse.

gers on

ve indicated within entries 200 or so of the wines
pecially (and in some cases regularly) enjoyed
that is, early 2009–10). It can be no guide
ny alternatives on offer one has to start
ries seem the best place. Lest anyone
o Best Wines", let me restate my
what I like – and so should you.
this way: **Clos de Chênes**

How to use this book

The top line of most entries consists of the following information:

① **③**

Aglianico del Vulture Bas | r dr (s/sw sp) | ★★★ | 96' 97 98 99' 00 01' 02 (03)

② **④**

① Wine name and the region the wine comes from.

② Whether it is red, rosé or white (or brown/amber), dry, sweet or sparkling, or several of these (and which is most important):

r	red
p	rosé
w	white
br	brown
dr	dry*
sw	sweet
s/sw	semi-sweet
sp	sparkling

( ) brackets here denote a less important wine
* assume wine is dry when dr or sw are not indicated

③ Its general standing as to quality: a necessarily rough-and-ready guide based on its current reputation as reflected in its prices:

★	plain, everyday quality
★★	above-average
★★★	well known, highly reputed
★★★★	grand, prestigious, expensive

So much is more or less objective. Additionally there is a subjective rating:

★ etc	Stars are coloured for any wine which, in my experience, is usually especially good within its price range. There are good everyday wines as well as good luxury wines. This system helps you find them.

④ Vintage information: which of the recent vintages can be recommended; of these, which are ready to drink this year, and which will probably improve with keeping. Your choice for current drinking should be one of the vintage years printed in **bold** type. Buy light-type years for further maturing.

00 etc	recommended years that may be currently available
96' etc	vintage regarded as particularly successful for the property in question
97 etc	years in bold should be ready for drinking (those not in bold will benefit from keeping)
98 etc	vintages in colour are those recommended as first choice drinking in 2010. (*See also* Bordeaux introduction, p.84
(02) etc	provisional rating

The German vintages work on a different principle again: see p.14

Other abbreviations

DYA	Drink the youngest available.
NV	Vintage not normally shown on label; in Champ: means a blend of several **vintages** for continuity
CHABLIS	Properties, areas or terms cross-referenced wi
Aiguilloux	Type so styled within entries indicates wine (especially enjoyed by Hugh Johnson.

Vintage report 2010

Vintage 2010 had its fair share of eventfulness, but in some places it was a year of blessed peace. In Australia, it was the calm after (and before) the storm: the drought was succeeded by pretty normal rainfall, dams were replenished and growers looked a little less terrified. The balance of the wines is good: plenty of acidity, and pure, intense fruit. New Zealand, too, had good weather and good wines, but rather more of them than it wanted. Glut is the current problem, and falling prices: NZ does not want to find itself following Australia into mass discounting. Growers were urged to cap yields (most of them did), celebrating Marlborough's 30th Sauvignon Blanc harvest with decent concentration.

Argentina is reporting a cooler year than usual and (hooray!) slightly lower alcohol in wines that have no shortage of concentration or flavour. And Chile, where the main event was the earthquake, which struck just when the harvest should have been beginning, nevertheless managed to produce wines of lovely balance. It was a cool year, and cool-climate spots such as Leyda, Limarí and San Antonio have produced some really elegant wines. The vintage was helped, paradoxically, by a cold winter that delayed ripening, thus allowing producers some crucial extra time to sort out their damaged wineries before having to deal with the grapes.

The cool weather extended north to California, with 2010 offering great concentration and plenty of elegance; not an easy vintage, and not the sort of style that Californians really go for. It was flavour development before sugar. The same applies in Oregon, where, again, 2010 is about elegance and slightly lower alcohol, plus good concentration.

So what of Europe? The 2009 vintage was a tough one to follow in many places, and first tastings in Bordeaux suggest it's a Cabernet and Left Bank vintage there with huge power and tannin. In Burgundy, yields were down, and hail in the southern Côte de Beaune on September 12, followed by cold, rainy weather, necessitated swift picking as rot set in. Overall acidity seems good, as does tannin in the reds. It may not be a year to buy the more basic wines, however. In Beaujolais, which began its renaissance with 2009, 2010 seems to be an earlier-maturing, but worthy follow-up vintage. The Loire has produced fabulous sweet wines and very good reds and dry whites, and the Rhône is potentially outstanding. Yields were down, but both north and south report supple tannins, sumptuous fruit and good concentration. In Alsace it's a similar picture: good acidity and low yields enabled the grapes to ripen in spite of a cool summer, saved by a warm September. In Champagne it seems to have been a Chardonnay year; the Pinots fell victim to rot and vintage declarations will depend on how much good Pinot any given house needs, or can find.

And in Germany, with its unbroken run of good vintages, nobody is saying that 2010 is the equal of 2009, but low quantities (it's the smallest vintage for 25 years) meant beautifully ripe grapes, especially when October brought warm sunshine. In Austria, a small crop was often the result of an enormous amount of rain, and the disease that followed. Clever viticulture and a lot of grape sorting at the wineries was needed. The wines are attractive, but probably not for keeping. And grape prices in both Austria and Germany have risen. Every silver lining has a cloud.

A closer look at 2009

The test of a great year is that the wines get better on further acquaintance; and 2009, in the main, is doing rather well so far.

Bordeaux claimed to have produced its best vintage, thus relegating all previous vintage-of-the-decade or -century claims to second place. Logically they should be right, because viticulture and winemaking both become more accurate year by year. Combine that with near-ideal weather, and if they didn't do better than ever we should be demanding to know why. Prices for the top wines inevitably followed the hyperbole upwards, but there will be lots of delicious lesser wines at affordable prices. You could argue that some of these lesser wines are as good as the great wines were in the past; not completely right, but you could put up a decent case – a comforting thought.

The reputation of the 2009 Bordeaux has been driving demand for the 2009 burgundies, too, even though 2008 was a better year in Burgundy. Lack of acidity is the main problem: the wines can feel a little flat, a little lacking in drive. But they're certainly seductive, and will give great pleasure. Some of the reds will probably turn out to be more powerful than they appeared in youth. In the Rhône, 2009 is looking superb: wines of great verve and concentration that will last well. In the south it's very good, though 2007 might have the edge; but in the north the wines are outstanding: they're big, but they wear their weight lightly, with elegance and precision. A vintage to buy and drink for many years.

In the Loire, the picture is more mixed. Sauvignon was better in 2008: the extra warmth and alcohol of 2009 sit awkwardly on these wines. And though the reds are good, there can be a touch of alcoholic heat here as well. In parts of Spain, too – Ribera del Duero, Priorat, Rioja in some places – 2009 was on the edge of being too hot and the wines were rescued from jamminess by timely rain. When people talk about great wines being made at the margin, it's the other margin, the margin of being too cool, that they mean. Portugal looks rather the same this year: sometimes a bit too much weight, a bit too much alcohol. When it works, the effect is opulent; when the balance is wrong, it's just too much. Germany is less marginal than it was, but warmer summers here still mean better quality – and 2009 here was superb. It is hard to imagine that Riesling can get any better. The 2008s have more acidity, but the 2009s have magnificent depth.

In Italy, Amarone looks terrific, and is benefitting from tighter regulation, although the top growers still reckon the regulations are nowhere near enough (a familiar story, this). Sangiovese in Tuscany looks like another star.

In California, the wines have a classic richness (classic for California, that is) and are weightier and lusher than the 2010s. And Australia, that land of survivors, has survived the drought, heat and bushfires of 2009 to produce wines that are at least good and often very good. Smoke-tainted wines should have been weeded out before bottling. There's no cure for it except to throw it away: once grapes have been tainted by smoke the wine will be acrid, and reds are more affected than whites because the skins are in contact with the juice during winemaking. But Aussies are not exactly novices at dealing with it.

If you like this, try this...

Why should wines from different grapes and different climates taste alike? Sometimes they just do: there can be similarities of structure, with high acidity or low, with brick-like tannins or supple ones, or fruit reminiscent of apricots or limes or straw. It doesn't make them interchangeable, and though you might adore the aromas of both Hermitage and Barolo there will still be days, and dinners, when you want one and not the other. What I want to underline here is that thinking about wines in terms of grapes or regions is not the only way; to think of similarities of flavour and style across continents and hemispheres can make you see wines differently.

If you like Clare Riesling, try Petit and Gros Manseng

Clare is the region of Australia that has reintroduced Riesling to wine-lovers uncertain about the complications of European Riesling. It has clear, singing flavours of lime cordial and toast, and it ages every bit as well as you'd expect, gaining layers of spiced honey without any hint of sweetness. Its high acidity keeps it company while it ages; it's linear, pure, and clean as a whistle. Petit and Gros Manseng are grapes from southwest France, down near the Pyrénées: think of limes and apricots, picked ripe, with vibrant acidity. It doesn't age as well as Riesling (not many grapes do) but if you love those intense, lime-cordial flavours, this is the way to go. Petit Manseng has the more extreme style, and both can be made dry or sweet.

If you like Chablis, try Saar Riesling

Chablis – good Chablis – is searingly mineral; tight and deceptively light in youth, it fills out with age to become immensely complex. It's a terroir wine to its toes: never especially fruity, it instead reflects the chalk and clay, sun and wind of its northerly hills. Saar Riesling is a northern wine, too. The leanest and most intense of German Rieslings, it comes from a chilly tributary of the Mosel, more marginal in climate than the great Mittelmosel yet reaching surprisingly high ripeness levels to balance its taut acidity. A mature Saar Riesling demands one's full attention: its layers of complexity emerge slowly, with smoke and earth, peaches and lemon zest and the minerality of this breezy hillside all arranged with Germanic precision.

If you like Grüner Veltliner, try Verdicchio

There's more minerality here, too – it's the secret weapon of great dry whites. Grüner Veltliner comes at all levels of ripeness and quality, from light, quaffing styles to powerful, structured, single-vineyard wines from the best sites of the Wachau and Kamptal. It's not particularly aromatic, but there'll be a note of white pepper and bayleaf there, with some celery and, in the biggest wines, some ripe apricot and peach flavours. The same structure can be found in Verdicchio: it's the wine Italians choose when they want a white wine that reminds them of a red. Verdicchio doesn't boast much aroma; instead, there's acidity, weight and a certain nuttiness to balance the quince-like fruit. Neither it nor Grüner Veltliner are showy: subtle power is what they're about.

If you like Muscat, try Gewürztraminer

There's far less subtlety about these two. Muscat smells and tastes over-whelmingly of grapes: the most aromatic, flower-scented, crunchy grapes you can imagine. It's the platonic ideal of grapiness. It covers a vast selection of wines, from the lightness of Asti to the caramelized weight of Victorian fortified Muscat from Australia. But imagine something in the middle: something dry or dryish, delicate but not evanescent, perhaps from Italy or Austria; and then imagine a Gewurztraminer from Alsace (spelled here without the ü): all spice and perfume, roses and lychees, probably off-dry but creamy enough to taste off-dry even if it's not. It's a natural step.

If you like red burgundy, try Malbec
The fascination of red burgundy is hard to imitate: the incense notes of youth, the mineral spiciness, the perfect focus. Describing Pinot in terms of flavours, be they strawberry or cherry, game or leather, gives very little idea of what it's actually like on the palate. But the flavours of Malbec are not so far away, and the structure is similar, too: acidity, firmness, some silky flesh. If Malbec is overripe, or worked too hard, or overoaked, it can be made into something resembling Frankenstein's monster. We're talking here about light- to middleweight Malbec from high-altitude sites in Argentina: elegant, aromatic and always with that trademark silkiness. There's a strong similarity of style.

If you like red Rioja, try Alentejo
The keynote here is bright, red fruit, though with a rounded, friendly profile: red Rioja slips down very easily. Tempranillo has the strawberry fruit and the acidity; Garnacha adds some toffee sweetness, and there may be some Mazuelo there for colour, or Graciano for violet perfume. The fruit is more accentuated than in the past: the wines are fresh, concentrated, silky. Portugal's Alentejo is a more recent addition. It makes masses of wine, but only recently has it developed a definite style of its own. Bright, spicy, balanced; not overripe, but pure, fresh and juicy. So far it's not hitting the heights that Rioja at its best can reach, but as an everyday red it should be right on the button for Rioja-lovers.

If you like Merlot, try Carmenère
This is a no-brainer, really: for years growers in Chile thought they were the same vine. They were mixed up together in the vineyards, and they look very similar: the differences are as subtle as the colour of the underside of the young leaves. But they ripen at different times, so have to be treated differently. And they taste different. Merlot's flavour can be a little hard to pin down, it's true: anything from lush, juicy and toffeeish in much of the New World to the darkly spicy complexities of Pomerol. But it tends to be low in acidity, and there's that seductive mouthfeel... Carmenère is low in acidity, too, and has a chocolatey fleshiness to its fruit. There's black-pepper spice, and the tannins are supple and silky. Some Chilean Carmenère is just too much: carved from American oak and almost impenetrable. Less expensive wines can be a safer bet.

If you like northern Rhône reds, try Barolo
Great Northern Rhône Syrah tastes wild, almost dangerous: there's something untamed and feral about its gamy spice and herbs. You can taste the granite and the heat of the sun and the herbs of the *garrigue*. Syrah is a potential blockbuster, but a deeply aromatic one. Barolo is not exactly a pussycat, either: its tannins, like those of the Northern Rhône, need careful vinification to domesticate them. And then the aromas are let loose. Barolo smells and tastes of tar and dead roses, delicate and deep, feminine and macho at the same time. Neither is a wine to be drunk frivolously; they need thought and patience and some game or a rich, dark, beef stew.

Grape varieties

In the past two decades a radical change has come about in all except the most long-established wine countries: the names of a handful of grape varieties have become the ready-reference to wine. In senior wine countries, above all France and Italy, more complex traditions prevail. All wine of old prestige is known by its origin, more or less narrowly defined – not just the particular fruit-juice that fermented.

For the present, the two notions are in rivalry. Eventually the primacy of place over fruit will become obvious, at least for wines of quality. But for now, for most people, grape tastes are the easy reference-point – despite the fact that they are often confused by the added taste of oak. If grape flavours were really all that mattered, this would be a very short book.

But of course they do matter, and a knowledge of them both guides you to flavours you enjoy and helps comparisons between regions. Hence the originally Californian term "varietal wine", meaning, in principle, from one grape variety.

At least seven varieties – Cabernet Sauvignon, Pinot Noir, Riesling, Sauvignon Blanc, Chardonnay, Gewürztraminer and Muscat – taste and smell distinct and memorable enough to form international categories of wine. To these you can add Merlot, Malbec, Syrah, Sémillon, Chenin Blanc, Pinots Blanc and Gris, Sylvaner, Viognier, Nebbiolo, Sangiovese, Tempranillo. The following are the best and/or most popular wine grapes.

Grapes for red wine

Agiorgitiko (St George) Versatile Greek (Nemea) variety with juicy damson fruit and velvety tannins. Sufficient structure for serious ageing.

Aglianico Southern Italian, dark, deep and fashionable.

Baga Bairrada grape. Dark and tannic. Great potential but hard to grow.

Barbera Widely grown in Italy, at its best in Piedmont, giving dark, fruity, often sharp wine. Fashionable in California and Australia; promising in Argentina.

Blaufränkisch Mostly Austrian; can be light and juicy but at best (in Burgenland) a considerable red. LEMBERGER in Germany, KÉKFRANKOS in Hungary.

Brunello Alias for SANGIOVESE, splendid at Montalcino.

Cabernet Franc, alias Bouchet (Cab Fr) The lesser of two sorts of Cabernet grown in Bordeaux but dominant in St-Emilion. The Cabernet of the Loire, making Chinon, Saumur-Champigny and rosé. Used for blending with CAB SAUV, etc., or alone, in California, Australia, South Africa and elsewhere.

Cabernet Sauvignon (Cab Sauv) Grape of great character: spicy, herby, tannic, with characteristic blackcurrant aroma. The first grape of the Médoc; grown almost everywhere. Its wine almost always needs ageing; usually benefits from blending with eg. MERLOT, CAB FR, SYRAH, TEMPRANILLO, SANGIOVESE, etc. Makes aromatic rosé.

Cannonau GRENACHE in its Sardinian manifestation; can be very fine, potent.

Carignan Newly fashionable as the focus swings towards local and indigenous vines. Old-vine versions are best. Common in southern France, Spain; sought-after in Chile.

Carmenère An old Bordeaux variety that is now a star, rich and deep, in Chile. Bordeaux is looking at it again.

Cinsault/Cinsaut A staple of southern France, very good, if low-yielding, wine-lake stuff if not. Makes good rosé. One of the parents of PINOTAGE.

Dolcetto Source of soft, seductive dry red in Piedmont. Now high fashion.

Gamay The Beaujolais grape: light, very fragrant wines, at their best young. Makes even lighter wine in the Loire Valley, in central France, and in Switzerland and Savoie. Known as "Napa Gamay" in California.

Grenache, alias Garnacha, Cannonau Becoming ultra-fashionable with *terroiristes*, who admire the way it expresses its site. Also good for rosé and *vin doux naturel* (especially South of France, Spain, California). Mainstay of beefy Priorato. Old-vine versions are prized in South Australia. Usually blended with other varieties.

Grignolino Makes one of the good everyday table wines of Piedmont.

Kadarka, alias Gamza Makes healthy, sound, agreeable reds in East Europe.

Kékfrankos Hungarian BLAUFRÄNKISCH; similar lightish reds.

Lambrusco Productive grape of the lower Po Valley, giving quintessentially Italian, cheerful, sweet and fizzy red.

Lemberger *See* BLAUFRÄNKISCH. Württemberg's Red.

Malbec, alias Côt Minor in Bordeaux, major in Cahors (alias Auxerrois) and the star in Argentina. Dark, dense, tannic wine capable of real quality. High-altitude versions in Argentina are the bee's knees.

Mencía Making waves in Spain with fresh, aromatic wines.

Merlot The grape behind the great fragrant and plummy wines of Pomerol and (with CAB FR) St-Emilion, an important element in Médoc reds, soft and strong (and à la mode) in California, Washington, Chile, Australia. Lighter but often good in north Italy, Italian Switzerland, Slovenia, Argentina, South Africa, New Zealand, etc. Perhaps too adaptable for its own good: can be very dull indeed.

Montepulciano A good central-eastern Italian grape, and a Tuscan town.

Morellino Alias for SANGIOVESE in Scansano, southern Tuscany.

Mourvèdre, alias Mataro A star of southern France and Australia and, as Monastrell, Spain. Excellent dark, aromatic, tannic grape, good for blending. Enjoying new interest in, for example, South Australia and California.

Nebbiolo, alias Spanna and Chiavennasca One of Italy's best red grapes; makes Barolo, Barbaresco, Gattinara and Valtellina. Intense, nobly fruity, perfumed wine but very tannic: improves for years.

Negroamaro Dark, pungent grape of southern Italy. Quality can be excellent.

Nerello Mascalese Characterful Sicilian grape, good acidity, good quality.

Periquita Ubiquitous in Portugal for firm-flavoured reds. Often blended with CAB SAUV and also known as Castelão.

Petit Verdot Excellent but awkward Médoc grape, now increasingly planted in Cabernet areas worldwide for extra fragrance.

Pinotage Singular South African grape (PINOT N X CINSAUT). Can be very fruity and can age interestingly, but often jammy. Good rosé.

Pinot Noir (Pinot N) The glory of Burgundy's Côte d'Or, with scent, flavour and texture that are unmatched anywhere. Makes light wines rarely of much distinction in Switzerland and Hungary. Improving in Germany and Austria. But now also splendid results in California's Sonoma, Carneros and Central Coast, as well as Oregon, Ontario, Yarra Valley, Adelaide Hills, Tasmania, New Zealand's South Island (Central Otago) and South Africa's Walker Bay.

Primitivo Southern Italian grape making big, rustic wines, now fashionable because genetically identical to ZIN.

Refosco In northeast Italy, possibly a synonym for Mondeuse of Savoie. Deep, flavoursome and age-worthy wines, especially in warmer climates.

Sagrantino Italian grape found in Umbria for powerful, cherry-flavoured wines.

Sangiovese (or Sangioveto) Main red grape of Chianti and much of central Italy. Aliases include BRUNELLO and MORELLINO. Interesting in Australia.

Saperavi Makes good, sharp, very long-lived wine in Georgia, Ukraine, etc. Blends very well with CAB SAUV (eg. in Moldova).

Spätburgunder German for PINOT N. Quality is variable, seldom wildly exciting.

St-Laurent Dark, smooth and full-flavoured Austrian specialty. Also in the Pfalz.

Syrah, alias Shiraz The great Rhône red grape: tannic, purple, peppery wine that matures superbly. Important as Shiraz in Australia, and under either name in California, Washington State, South Africa, Chile, New Zealand and elsewhere.

Tannat Raspberry-perfumed, highly tannic force behind Madiran, Tursan and other firm reds from southwest France. Also rosé. Now the star of Uruguay.

Tempranillo Aromatic, fine Rioja grape, called Ull de Llebre in Catalonia, Cencibel in La Mancha, Tinto Fino in Ribera del Duero, Tinta Roríz in Douro, Aragonez in southern Portugal. Now Australia, too. Very fashionable; elegant in cool climates, beefy in warm. Early-ripening.

Touriga Nacional Top Port grape grown in the Douro Valley. Now being pushed for Portuguese table wines too; best in blends.

Zinfandel (Zin) Fruity, adaptable grape of California (though identical to PRIMITIVO) with blackberry-like, and sometimes metallic, flavour. Can be structured and gloriously lush, but also makes "blush" white wine.

Zweigelt Popular in Austria for aromatic, dark, supple wines.

Grapes for white wine

Airén Anonymous grape of La Mancha, Spain: fresh if made well.

Albariño The Spanish name for north Portugal's Alvarinho, making excellent fresh and fragrant wine in Galicia. Both fashionable and expensive in Spain.

Aligoté Burgundy's second-rank white grape. Crisp (often sharp) wine needs drinking in 1–3 years. Perfect for mixing with cassis (blackcurrant liqueur) to make Kir. Widely planted in East Europe, especially Russia.

Arinto White central Portuguese grape for crisp, fragrant, dry whites.

Arneis Aromatic, high-priced grape, DOC in Roero, Piedmont.

Bourboulenc This and the rare Rolle make some of the Midi's best wines.

Bual Makes top-quality sweet Madeira wines, not quite so rich as Malmsey.

Chardonnay (Chard) The white grape of Burgundy and Champagne, now ubiquitous worldwide, partly because it is one of the easiest to grow and vinify. The fashion for overoaked butterscotch versions now thankfully over.

Chasselas Prolific early-ripening grape with little aroma, mainly grown for eating. Aka Fendant in Switzerland (where it is supreme), Gutedel in Germany.

Chenin Blanc (Chenin Bl) Great white grape of the middle Loire (Vouvray, Layon, etc). Wine can be dry or sweet (or very sweet), but with plenty of acidity. Bulk wine in California, but increasingly serious in South Africa.

Clairette A low-acid grape, part of many southern French blends.

Colombard Slightly fruity, nicely sharp grape, makes everyday wine in South Africa, California and southwest France. Often blended.

Falanghina Ancient grape of Campanian hills. Excellent dense, aromatic dry whites.

Fiano High-quality grape giving peachy, spicy wine in Campania, south Italy.

Folle Blanche High acid/little flavour make this ideal for brandy. Called Gros Plant in Brittany, Picpoul in Armagnac. Also respectable in California.

Furmint A grape of great character: the trademark of Hungary, both as the principal grape in Tokaji and as vivid, vigorous table wine with an appley flavour. Called ipon in Slovenia. Some grown in Austria.

Garganega Best grape in the Soave blend. Top wines, especially sweet, age well.

Gewürztraminer, alias Traminer (Gewürz) One of the most pungent grapes, spicy with aromas such as rose petals and grapefruit. Wines are often rich and soft, even when fully dry. Best in Alsace (Gewurztraminer); also good in Germany, east Europe, Australia, California, the Pacific Northwest and New Zealand.

Glera Uncharismatic new name for the Prosecco vine: Prosecco is now only a wine, no longer a grape.

Grechetto or Greco Ancient grape of central and south Italy noted for the vitality and stylishness of its wine.

Grüner Veltliner Austria's signature grape, making everything from fresh, inexpensive young wines to serious, concentrated, single-site versions. The best can age well.

Hárslevelu Other main grape of Tokaji (with FURMINT). Adds softness and body.

Kéknyelu Low-yielding, flavourful grape giving one of Hungary's best whites. Has the potential for fieriness and spice. To be watched.

Kerner Quite successful German crossing. Early ripening, flowery (but often too blatant) wine with good acidity.

Loureiro The best and most fragrant Vinho Verde variety in Portugal.

Macabeo The workhorse white grape of north Spain, widespread in Rioja (alias viura) and in Catalan Cava country. Good quality potential.

Malvasia A family of grapes rather than a single variety, found all over Italy and Iberia. May be red, white, or pink. Usually plump, soft wine. Malvoisie in France is unrelated.

Marsanne Principal white grape (with ROUSSANNE) of the northern Rhône (eg. in Hermitage, St-Joseph, St-Péray). Also good in Australia, California, and (as Ermitage Blanc) the Valais. Soft, full wines that age very well.

Moschofilero Good, aromatic pink Greek grape. Makes white or rosé wine.

Müller-Thurgau (Müller-T) Soft, aromatic wines for drinking young. Makes good sweet wines but usually dull, often coarse, dry ones. Should have no place in top vineyards.

Muscadelle Adds aroma to white Bordeaux, especially Sauternes. In Victoria it is used (with MUSCAT, to which it is unrelated) for Rutherglen Muscat.

Muscadet, alias Melon de Bourgogne Makes light, refreshing, very dry wines with a seaside tang around Nantes in Brittany.

Muscat (Many varieties; the best is Muscat Blanc à Petits Grains.) Widely grown, easily recognized, pungent grapes, mostly made into perfumed sweet wines, often fortified (as in France's *vins doux naturels*). Superb in Australia. The third element in Tokaji Aszú. Occasionally (eg. Alsace) made dry.

Palomino, alias Listán Great for Sherry; of local appeal (on a hot day) for table wine.

Pedro Ximénez, alias PX Makes sweet Sherry under its own name, and used in Montilla and Málaga. Also grown in Argentina, the Canaries, Australia, California and South Africa.

Petit (and Gros) Manseng The secret weapon of the French Basque country: vital for Jurançon; increasingly blended elsewhere in the southwest.

Pinot Blanc (Pinot Bl) A cousin of PINOT N, similar to but milder than CHARD: light, fresh, fruity, not aromatic, to drink young. Good for Italian *spumante*. Grown in Alsace, northern Italy, south Germany and eastern Europe. Weissburgunder in Germany.

Pinot Gris (Pinot Gr) Light and fashionable as Pinot Grigio in northern Italy, even for rosé; best in Alsace for full-bodied whites with a certain spicy style. In Germany can be alias Ruländer (sweet) or Grauburgunder (dry). Also found in Hungary, Slovenia, Canada, Oregon, New Zealand...

Pinot Noir (Pinot N) Superlative black grape used in Champagne and elsewhere (eg. California, Australia) for white, sparkling, or very pale-pink *vin gris*.

Prosecco *See* GLERA.

Riesling (Ries) Making its re-entrance on the world stage. Riesling stands level with CHARD as the world's best white wine grape, though diametrically opposite in style. CHARD gives full-bodied but aromatically discreet wines; Riesling offers a range from steely to voluptuous, always positively perfumed, and with more ageing potential than CHARD. Germany makes the greatest Riesling in all styles.

Gives lime-cordial and toast flavours in South Australia, convincing Germanic styles in New Zealand, elegance and power in Alsace. Holding the middle ground, with forceful but still-steely wines, is Austria, while lovers of light and fragrant, often piercingly refreshing Rieslings have the Mosel as their exclusive playground. Also grown in the Pacific Northwest, Ontario, California and South Africa.

Roussanne Rhône grape of finesse, now popping up in California and Australia. Can age well.

Sauvignon Blanc (Sauv Bl) Makes distinctive aromatic, grassy wines, pungent in New Zealand, often minerally in Sancerre, riper in Australia; good in Rueda, Austria, north Italy, Chile's Casablanca Valley and South Africa. Blended with Sémillon in Bordeaux. Can be austere or buxom (or indeed nauseating).

Savagnin The grape of *vin jaune* of Savoie: related to Traminer?

Scheurebe Spicy-flavoured German RIES X SILVANER (possibly), very successful in Pfalz, especially for Auslese. Can be weedy: must be very ripe to be good.

Sémillon (Sem) Contributes the lusciousness to Sauternes but decreasingly important for Graves and other dry white Bordeaux. Grassy if not fully ripe, but can make soft dry wine of great ageing potential. Superb in Australia; New Zealand and South Africa promising.

Sercial Makes the driest Madeira (where myth used to identify it with RIES).

Seyval Blanc (Seyval Bl) French-made hybrid of French and American vines. Very hardy and attractively fruity. Popular and reasonably successful in eastern states and England but dogmatically banned by EU from "quality" wines.

Silvaner, alias Sylvaner Germany's former workhorse grape, can be excellent in Franken, Rheinhessen, Pfalz. Very good (and powerful) as Johannisberg in the Valais, Switzerland.

Tocai Friulano North Italian grape with a flavour best described as "subtle". Now to be called plain Friulano.

Torrontés Strongly aromatic, MUSCAT-like Argentine specialty, usually dry.

Trebbiano Important but mediocre grape of central Italy (Orvieto, Soave, etc.). Also grown in southern France as Ugni Blanc, and Cognac as St-Emilion. Mostly thin, bland wine; needs blending (and more careful growing).

Ugni Blanc (Ugni Bl) *See* TREBBIANO.

Verdejo The grape of Rueda in Castile, potentially fine and long-lived.

Verdelho Great quality in Australia, and in Spain as Godello: probably Spain's best white grape. Rare but good (and medium-sweet) in Madeira.

Verdicchio Potentially good, muscular dry wine in central-eastern Italy.

Vermentino Italian, sprightly with satisfying texture and ageing capacity.

Vernaccia Name given to many unrelated grapes in Italy. Vernaccia di San Gimignano is crisp, lively; Vernaccia di Oristano is Sherry-like.

Viognier Ultra-fashionable Rhône grape, finest in Condrieu, less fine but still aromatic in the Midi. Good examples from California and Australia.

Viura *See* MACABEO.

Welschriesling Light and fresh to sweet and rich in Austria; ubiquitous in central Europe, with aliases including Laski Rizling, Riesling Italico, Olaszriesling.

Wine & food

Food these days is becoming almost as complicated as wine. We take Japanese for granted, Chinese as staple, look to Italian for comfort and then stir the pot with this strange thing called "fusion rules". Don't try to be too clever; wine you like with food you like is safest.

Before the meal – apéritifs

The conventional apéritif wines are either sparkling (epitomized by Champagne) or fortified (epitomized by Sherry in Britain, Port in France, vermouth in Italy, etc.). A glass of table wine before eating is an alternative.
Warning Avoid peanuts; they destroy wine flavours. Olives are too piquant for many wines; they need Sherry or a Martini. Eat almonds, pistachios, cashews, or walnuts, plain crisps or cheese straws instead.

First courses

Aïoli A thirst-quencher is needed for its garlic heat. Rhône, sparkling dry white; Provence rosé, Verdicchio. And *marc* or *grappa*, too, for courage.

Antipasti Dry, medium white: Italian (Arneis, Soave, Pinot Grigio, Prosecco, Vermentino); light but gutsy red (Vapolicella, straight or *ripasso* handles most).

Artichoke vinaigrette An incisive dry white: New Zealand Sauv Bl; Côtes de Gascogne or a modern Greek; young red: Bordeaux, Côtes du Rhône.
    with hollandaise Full-bodied, slightly crisp dry white: Pouilly-Fuissé, Pfalz Spätlese, or a Carneros or Yarra Valley Chard.

Asparagus A difficult flavour for wine, being slightly bitter, so the wine needs plenty of its own. Sauv Bl echoes the flavour. Sem beats Chard, especially Australian, but Chard works well with melted butter or hollandaise. Alsace Pinot Gr, even dry Muscat is gd, or Jurançon Sec.

Aubergine purée (*melitzanosalata*) Crisp New World Sauv Bl, eg. from South Africa or New Zealand; or modern Greek or Sicilian dry white. Or try Bardolino red or Chiaretto. Baked aubergine dishes can need sturdier reds: Shiraz, Zin.

Avocado and tiger prawns Dry-to-medium or slightly sharp white: Rheingau or Pfalz Kabinett, Grüner Veltliner, Wachau Ries, Sancerre, Pinot Gr; Sonoma or Australian Chard or Sauv Bl, or a dry rosé. Or *premier cru* Chablis.
    with mozzarella and tomato Crisp but ripe white with acidity: Soave, Sancerre, Greek white.

Carpaccio, beef Seems to work well with most wines, including reds. Top Tuscan is appropriate, but fine Chards are good. So are vintage and pink Champagnes.
    salmon Chard or Champagne.
    tuna Viognier, California Chard or New Zealand Sauv Bl.

Caviar Iced vodka. Champagne, if you must, full-bodied (eg. Bollinger, Krug).

Ceviche Australian Ries or Verdelho, New Zealand Sauv Bl.

Charcuterie/salami Young Beaujolais-Villages, Loire reds, ie. Saumur, New Zealand or Oregon Pinot N. Lambrusco or young Zin. Young Argentine or Italian reds. Bordeaux Blanc and light Chard like Côte Chalonnaise can work well, too.

Chorizo Fino, Austrian Ries, good white Graves, Grüner Veltliner.

Crostini Morellino di Scansano, Montepulciano d'Abruzzo, Valpolicella, or a dry Italian white, such as Verdicchio or Orvieto.

Crudités Light red or rosé: Côtes du Rhône, Minervois, Chianti, Pinot N; or Fino Sherry. For whites: Alsace Sylvaner or Pinot Bl.

Dim sum Classically, China tea. For fun: Pinot Gr or Ries; light red (Bardolino or Loire). NV Champagne or good New World fizz.

Eggs *See also* SOUFFLÉS. These present difficulties: they clash with most wines and can ruin good ones. But local wine with local egg dishes is a safe bet, so ★→★★ of whatever is going. Try Pinot Bl or not too oaky Chard. As a last resort I can bring myself to drink Champagne with scrambled eggs.

    quail's eggs Blanc de Blancs Champagne.

    seagull's (or gull's) eggs Mature white burgundy or vintage Champagne.

    oeufs en meurette Burgundian genius: eggs in red wine with glass of the same.

Escargots Rhône reds (Gigondas, Vacqueyras), St-Véran, Aligoté. In the Midi, very good Petits-Gris go with local white, rosé, or red. In Alsace, Pinot Bl or dry Muscat.

Fish terrine Pfalz Ries Spätlese Trocken, Grüner Veltliner, *premier cru* Chablis, Clare Valley Ries, Sonoma Chard; or Manzanilla.

Foie gras Sweet white. In Bordeaux they drink Sauternes. Others prefer a late-harvest Pinot Gr or Ries (including New World), Vouvray, Montlouis, Jurançon Moelleux, or Gewürz. Tokaji Aszú 5 Puttonyos is a Lucullan choice. Old, dry Amontillado can be sublime. With hot foie gras, mature vintage Champagne. But not on any account Chard or Sauv Bl.

Goat's cheese, warm Sancerre, Pouilly-Fumé, or New World Sauv Bl.

    chilled Chinon, Saumur-Champigny, or Provence rosé. Or strong red: Château Musar, Greek, Turkish, Australian sparkling Shiraz.

Guacamole California Chard, Sauv Blanc, dry Muscat, or NV Champagne. Or Mexican beer.

Haddock, smoked, mousse, or brandade Wonderful for showing off any stylish, full-bodied white, inc *grand cru* Chablis or Sonoma, South African or New Zealand Chard.

Ham, raw or cured *See also* PROSCIUTTO. Alsace Grand Cru Pinot Gr or gd, crisp Italian Collio white. With Spanish *pata negra* or *jamón*, Fino Sherry, or tawny Port. *See also* HAM, COOKED (Meat, poultry, game).

Herrings, raw or pickled Dutch gin (young, not aged) or Scandinavian *akvavit*, and cold beer. If wine essential, try Muscadet.

Mackerel, smoked An oily wine-destroyer. Manzanilla Sherry, proper dry Vinho Verde or Schnapps, peppered or bison-grass vodka. Or good lager.

Mayonnaise Adds richness that calls for a contrasting bite in the wine. Côte Chalonnaise whites (eg. Rully) are good. Try New Zealand Sauv Bl, Verdicchio, or a Spätlese Trocken. Or Provence rosé.

Mezze A selection of hot and cold vegetable dishes. Sparkling is a good all-purpose choice, as is rosé. Fino Sherry is in its element.

Mozzarella with tomatoes, basil Fresh Italian white, eg. Soave, Alto Adige. Vermintino from the coast. Or simple Bordeaux Blanc. *See also* AVOCADO.

Oysters, raw NV Champagne, *premier cru* Chablis, Muscadet, white Graves, Sancerre, or Guinness. Or even light, cold Sauternes.

    cooked Puligny-Montrachet; gd New World Chard. Champagne good with either.

Pasta Red or white according to the sauce or trimmings:

    cream sauce Orvieto, Frascati, Alto Adige Chard.

    meat sauce Montepulciano d'Abruzzo, Salice Salentino, Merlot.

    pesto (basil) sauce Barbera, Ligurian Vermentino, New Zealand Sauv Bl, Hungarian Furmint.

    seafood sauce (eg. vongole) Verdicchio, Soave, white Rioja, Cirò, Sauv Bl.

    tomato sauce Chianti, Barbera, south Italian red, Zin, south Australian Grenache.

Pastrami Alsace Ries, young Sangiovese or Cab Fr.

Pâté, chicken liver Calls for pungent white (Alsace Pinot Gr or Marsanne), a smooth red like a light Pomerol, Volnay, or New Zealand Pinot N, or even Amontillado Sherry. More strongly flavoured pâté (duck, etc.) needs Châteauneuf-du-Pape, Cornas, Chianti Classico, Franciacorta, or good white Graves.

Pipérade Navarra *rosado*, Provence or southern French rosés. Or dry Australian Ries. For a red: Corbières.

Prawns, shrimps, or langoustines Fine dry white: burgundy, Graves, New Zealand Chard, Washington Ries, Pfalz Ries, Australian Ries – even fine mature Champagne. ("Cocktail sauce" kills wine, and in time, people.)

Prosciutto (also with melon, pears, or figs) Full, dry or medium white: Orvieto, Lugana, Sauv Bl, Grüner Veltliner, Tokaji Furmint, white Rioja, Australian Sem, or Jurançon Sec.

Risotto Pinot Gr from Friuli, Gavi, youngish Sem, Dolcetto or Barbera d'Alba.
　with *fungi porcini* Finest mature Barolo or Barbaresco.

Salads Any dry and appetizing white or rosé wine.
　NB Vinegar in salad dressings destroys the flavour of wine. If you want salad at a meal with fine wine, dress the salad with wine or a little lemon juice instead of vinegar.

Salmon, smoked A dry but pungent white: Fino (especially Manzanilla) Sherry, Alsace Pinot Gr, *grand cru* Chablis, Pouilly-Fumé, Pfalz Ries Spätlese, vintage Champagne. If you must have a red, try a lighter one such as Barbera. Vodka, schnapps, or *akvavit*.

Soufflés As show dishes these deserve ★★★ wines.
　cheese Red burgundy or Bordeaux, Cab Sauv (not Chilean or Australian), etc. Or fine white burgundy.
　fish Dry white: ★★★ Burgundy, Bordeaux, Alsace, Chard, etc.
　spinach (tougher on wine) Mâcon-Villages, St-Véran, Valpolicella. Champagne can also be good with the texture of soufflé.

Tapas Perfect with Fino Sherry, which can cope with the wide range of flavours in both hot and cold dishes.

Tapenade Manzanilla or Fino Sherry, or any sharpish dry white or rosé.

Taramasalata A rustic southern white with personality; not necessarily *retsina*. Fino Sherry works well. Try white Rioja or a Rhône Marsanne. The bland supermarket version submits to fine, delicate whites or Champagne.

Tempura The Japanese favour oaked Chardonnay with acidity.

Tortilla Rioja *crianza*, Fino Sherry, or white Mâcon-Villages.

Trout, smoked Sancerre; California or South African Sauv Bl. Rully or Bourgogne Aligoté, Chablis, or Champagne. Light German Ries Kabinett.

Vegetable terrine Not a great help to fine wine, but Chilean Chard makes a fashionable marriage, Chenin Bl such as Vouvray a lasting one.

Whitebait Crisp, dry whites, eg. Furmint, Greek, Touraine Sauv Bl, Verdicchio, Fino.

Fish

Abalone Dry or medium white: Sauv Bl, Côte de Beaune *blanc*, Pinot Gr, Grüner Veltliner. Chinese-style: vintage Champagne.

Anchovies, marinated The marinade will clash with pretty well everything. Keep it light, white, dry and neutral.
　in olive oil or salted A robust wine: red, white, rosé – try Rioja.

Bass, sea Weissburgunder from Baden or Pfalz. Very good for any fine/delicate white, eg. Clare dry Ries, Chablis, white Châteauneuf-du-Pape. But strengthen the flavours of the wine according to the flavourings of the fish:
　ginger, spring onions more powerful Ries; **porcini** top Alsace Pinot Bl.

Beurre blanc, fish with A top-notch Muscadet sur lie, a Sauv Bl/Sem blend, *premier cru* Chablis, Vouvray, or a Rheingau Ries.

Brandade *Premier cru* Chablis, Sancerre Rouge, or New Zealand Pinot N.

Brill Very delicate: hence a top fish for fine old Puligny and the like.

Cod, roast Gd neutral background for fine dry/medium whites: Chablis, Meursault,

Corton-Charlemagne, *cru classé* Graves, Grüner Veltliner, German Kabinett or *grosses gewächs*, or a good lightish Pinot N.

Crab Crab and Ries are part of the Creator's plan.

Chinese, with ginger and onion German Ries Kabinett or Spätlese Halbtrocken. Tokaji Furmint, Gewürz.

cioppino Sauv Bl; but West Coast friends say Zin. Also California sparkling.

cold, dressed Alsace, Austrian or Rhine Ries; dry Australian Ries, or Condrieu.

softshell Chard or top-quality German Ries Spätlese.

Thai crabcakes Pungent Sauv Bl (Loire, South Africa, Australia, New Zealand) or Ries (German Spätlese or Australian).

with black bean sauce A big Barossa Shiraz or Syrah. Even Cognac.

with chilli and garlic Quite powerful Ries, perhaps German *grosses gewächs*.

Curry A generic term for a multitude of flavours. Too much heat makes wine problematic: rosé is a good bet. Hot-and-sour flavours (with tamarind tomato, eg.) need acidity (perhaps Sauv Bl); mild, creamy dishes need richness of texture (dry Alsace Ries).

Eel, smoked Ries, Alsace, Austrian, according to the other ingredients. Or Fino Sherry, Bourgogne Aligoté. Schnapps.

Fish and chips, *fritto misto*, **tempura** Chablis, white Bordeaux, Sauv Bl, Pinot Bl, Gavi, Fino, Montilla, Koshu, tea; or NV Champagne and Cava.

Fish baked in a salt crust Full-bodied white or rosé: Albariño, Sicily, Greek, Hungarian. Côtes de Lubéron or Minervois.

Fish pie (with creamy sauce) Albariño, Soave Classico, Alsace Pinot Gr or Ries, Spanish Godello.

Haddock Rich, dry whites: Meursault, California Chard, Marsanne, Grüner Veltliner.

Hake Sauv Bl or any fresh fruity white: Pacherenc, Tursan, white Navarra.

Halibut As for *turbot*.

Herrings, fried/grilled Need a white with some acidity to cut their richness. Rully, Chablis, Bourgogne Aligoté, Greek, dry Sauv Bl. Or cider.

Kedgeree Full white, still or sparkling: Mâcon-Villages, South African Chard, Grüner Veltliner, German *grosses gewächs*, or (at breakfast) Champagne.

Kippers A good cup of tea, preferably Ceylon (milk, no sugar). Scotch? Dry Oloroso Sherry is surprisingly good.

Lamproie à la Bordelaise 5-yr-old St-Emilion or Fronsac. Or Douro reds with Portuguese lampreys.

Lobster, richly sauced Vintage Champagne, fine white burgundy, *cru classé* Graves, California Chard or Australian Ries, *grosses gewächs*, Pfalz Spätlese.

cold NV Champagne, Alsace Ries, *premier cru* Chablis, Condrieu, Mosel Spätlese, or a local fizz.

Mackerel, grilled Hard or sharp white: Sauv Bl from Touraine, Gaillac, Vinho Verde, white Rioja, or English white. Or Guinness.

with spices White with muscle: Austrian Ries, Grüner Veltliner, German *grosses gewächs*.

Monkfish Often roasted, which needs fuller rather than leaner wines. Try New Zealand Chard, New Zealand/Oregon Pinot N, or Chilean Merlot.

Mullet, grey Verdicchio, Rully, or unoaked Chard.

Mullet, red A chameleon, adaptable to gd white or red, espcially Pinot N.

Mussels Muscadet-sur-lie, *premier cru* Chablis, Chard.

stuffed, with garlic See escargots.

with chorizo Unoaked white: Grüner Veltliner, southern French. Dry rosé.

Paella, shellfish Full-bodied white or rosé, unoaked Chard.

Perch, sandre Exquisite fish for finest wines: top white burgundy, *grand cru* Alsace Ries, or noble Mosels. Or try top Swiss Fendant or Johannisberg.

Prawns With garlic, keep the wine light, white or rosé, and dry. With spices, up to and including chilli, go for a bit more body, but not oak: dry Ries good.

Salmon, seared or grilled Pinot N is the fashionable option. Merlot or light claret not bad. Or fine white burgundy: Puligny- or Chassagne-Montrachet, Meursault, Corton-Charlemagne, *grand cru* Chablis; Grüner Veltliner, Condrieu, California, Idaho or New Zealand Chard, Rheingau Kabinett/ Spätlese, Australian Ries.
    fishcakes Call for similar (as for above), but less grand, wines.

Sardines, fresh grilled Very dry white: Vinho Verde, Muscadet, or modern Greek.

Sashimi The Japanese preference is for white wine with body (*premier cru* Chablis, Alsace Ries) with white fish, Pinot N with red. Both need acidity: low-acidity wines don't work. Simple Chablis can be a bit thin. If soy is involved, then low-tannin red (again, Pinot).

Scallops An inherently slightly sweet dish, best with medium-dry whites.
    in cream sauces German Spätlese, Montrachet, or top Australian Chard.
    grilled or seared Hermitage Blanc, Grüner Veltliner, Entre-Deux-Mers, vintage Champagne, or Pinot N.
    with Asian seasoning New Zealand, Chenin Bl, Verdelho, Godello, Gewürz.

Shellfish Dry white with plain boiled shellfish, richer wines with richer sauces.
    with *plateaux de fruits de mer* Chablis, Muscadet, Picpoul de Pinet, Alto Adige Pinot Bl.

Skate/raie with brown butter White with some pungency (eg. Pinot Gr d'Alsace), or a clean, straightforward wine like Muscadet or Verdicchio.

Snapper Sauv Bl if cooked with oriental flavours; white Rhône or Provence rosé with Mediterranean flavours.

Sole, plaice, etc., plain, grilled, or fried Perfect with fine wines: white burgundy or its equivalent.
    with sauce According to the ingredients: sharp, dry wine for tomato sauce, fairly rich for creamy preparations.

Sushi Hot wasabi is usually hidden in every piece. German QbA Trocken wines, simple Chablis, or NV *brut* Champagne. Or, of course, sake or beer.

Swordfish Full-bodied, dry white of the country. Nothing grand.

Tagine, with couscous North African flavours need substantial whites to balance – Austrian, Rhône – or crisp, neutral whites that won't compete. Preserved lemon demands something with acidity. Go easy on the oak.

Trout, grilled or fried Delicate white wine, eg. Mosel (esp Saar or Ruwer), Alsace Pinot Bl.

Tuna, grilled or seared Generally served rare, so try a red: Cab Fr from the Loire, or Pinot N. Young Rioja is a possibility.

Turbot Serve with your best rich, dry white: Meursault or Chassagne-Montrachet, Corton-Charlemagne, mature Chablis or its California, Australian or New Zealand equivalent. Condrieu. Mature Rheingau, Mosel or Nahe Spätlese or Auslese (not Trocken).

Meat, poultry, game

Barbecues The local wine: Australian, South African, Argentina are right in spirit.
    Asian flavours (lime, coriander, etc.) Rosé, Pinot Gr, Ries.
    chilli Shiraz, Zin, Pinotage, Malbec.
    Middle Eastern (cumin, mint) Crisp, dry whites, rosé.
    oil, lemon, herbs Sauv Bl.
    red wine Cab Sauv, Merlot, Malbec, Tannat.
    tomato sauces Zin, Sangiovese.

Beef Stroganoff Dramatic red: Barolo, Valpolicella Amarone, Cahors, Hermitage, late-harvest Zin – even Moldovan Negru de Purkar.

Beef, boiled Red: Bordeaux (Bourgogne or Fronsac), Roussillon, Gevrey-Chambertin, or Côte-Rôtie. Medium-ranking white burgundy is gd, eg. Auxey-Duresses. Or top-notch beer. Mustard softens tannic reds, horseradish kills everything – but can be worth the sacrifice.

    roast An ideal partner for fine red wine of any kind. *See* above for mustard.

    stew Sturdy red: Pomerol or St-Emilion, Hermitage, Cornas, Barbera, Shiraz, Napa Cab Sauv, Ribera del Duero, or Douro red.

Boudin blanc (white pork sausage) Loire Chenin Bl, especially when served with apples: dry Vouvray, Saumur, Savennières; mature red Côtes de Beaune if without.

Boudin noir (blood sausage) Local Sauv Bl or Chenin Bl – especially in the Loire. Or Beaujolais *cru*, especially Morgon. Or light Tempranillo.

Cabbage, stuffed Hungarian Cab Fr/Kadarka; *village* Rhônes; Salice Salentino, Primitivo and other spicy south Italian reds. Or Argentine Malbec.

Cajun food Fleurie, Brouilly, or New World Sauv Bl.

    with gumbo Amontillado.

Cassoulet Red from southwest France (Gaillac, Minervois, Corbières, St-Chinian, or Fitou) or Shiraz. But best of all Beaujolais *cru* or young Tempranillo.

Chicken/turkey/guinea fowl, roast Virtually any wine, including very best bottles of dry to medium white and finest old reds (especially burgundy). The meat of fowl can be adapted with sauces to match almost any fine wine (eg. *coq au vin* with red or white burgundy). Sparkling Shiraz with strong, spicy stuffing.

Chicken Kiev Alsace Ries, Collio, Chard, Bergerac *rouge*.

Chilli con carne Young red: Beaujolais, Tempranillo, Zin, Argentine Malbec.

Chinese food

    Canton or Peking style Rosé or dry to medium-dry white – Mosel Ries Kabinett or Spätlese Trocken – can be good throughout a Chinese banquet. Gewürz often suggested but rarely works (but brilliant with ginger), yet Chasselas and Pinot Gr are attractive alternatives. Dry or off-dry sparkling (especially Cava) cuts the oil and matches sweetness. Eschew sweet/sour dishes but try St-Emilion ★★, New World Pinot N or Châteauneuf-du-Pape with duck. I often serve both white and red wines concurrently during Chinese meals. Champagne becomes a thirst-quencher.

    Szechuan style Verdicchio, Alsace Pinot Bl or very cold beer.

Choucroute garni Alsace Pinot Bl, Pinot Gr, Ries, or beer.

Cold roast meat Generally better with full-flavoured white than red. Mosel Spätlese or Hochheimer and Côte Chalonnaise are very good, as is Beaujolais. Leftover cold beef with leftover vintage Champagne is bliss.

Confit d'oie/de canard Young, tannic red Bordeaux, California Cab Sauv and Merlot, and Priorato cut richness. Alsace Pinot Gr or Gewurz match it.

Coq au vin Red burgundy. Ideal: bottle of Chambertin in the dish, two on the table.

Duck or goose Rather rich white: Pfalz Spätlese or off-dry *grand cru* Alsace. Or mature, gamy red: Morey-St-Denis, Côte-Rôtie, Bordeaux, burgundy. With oranges or peaches, the Sauternais propose drinking Sauternes, others Monbazillac or Ries Auslese. Mature, weighty vintage Champagne is good, too, and handles red cabbage surprisingly well.

    Peking *See* CHINESE FOOD.

    wild duck Big-scale red: Hermitage, Bandol, California or South African Cab Sauv, Australian Shiraz – Grange if you can afford it.

    with olives Top-notch Chianti or other Tuscans.

    with pomegranate molasses Young red burgundy of good quality.

    roast breast & confit leg with Puy lentils Mid-weight red with some richness.

Frankfurters German, NY Ries, Beaujolais, light Pinot N. Or Budweiser (Budvar).

Game birds, young, plain-roasted The best red wine you can afford.

    older birds in casseroles Red (Gevrey-Chambertin, Pommard, Santenay, or *grand cru classé* St-Emilion, Napa Valley Cab Sauv or Rhône).

    well-hung game Vega Sicilia, great red Rhône, Château Musar.

    cold game Mature vintage Champagne.

Game pie, hot Red: Oregon Pinot N.

    cold Gd-quality white burgundy, *cru* Beaujolais, or Champagne.

Goulash Flavoursome young red: Hungarian Kékoportó, Zin, Uruguayan Tannat, Morellino di Scansano, Mencía, young Australian Shiraz.

Grouse *See* GAME BIRDS – but push the boat right out.

Haggis Fruity red, eg. young claret, young Portuguese red, New World Cab Sauv or Malbec, or Châteauneuf-du-Pape. Or, of course, malt whisky.

Ham, cooked Softer red burgundies: Volnay, Savigny, Beaune; Chinon or Bourgueil; sweetish German white (Rhine Spätlese); Tokaji Furmint or Czech Frankovka; lightish Cab Sauv (eg. Chilean), or New World Pinot N. And don't forget the heaven-made match of ham and Sherry. *See* HAM, RAW OR CURED.

Hamburger Young red: Australian Cab Sauv, Chianti, Zin, Argentine Malbec, Tempranillo. Or full-strength colas (not diet).

Hare Jugged hare calls for flavourful red: not-too-old burgundy or Bordeaux, Rhône (eg. Gigondas), Bandol, Barbaresco, Ribera del Duero, Rioja *reserva*. The same for saddle, or for hare sauce with pappardelle.

Indian dishes Medium-sweet white, very cold: Orvieto *abboccato*, South African Chenin Bl, Alsace Pinot Bl, Torrontés, Indian sparkling, Cava or NV Champagne. Rosé can be a safe all-rounder. Tannin – Barolo or Barbaresco, or deep-flavoured reds such as Châteauneuf-du-Pape, Cornas, Australian Grenache or Mourvèdre, or Valpolicella Amarone – will emphasize the heat. Soft reds can be easier. Hot-and-sour flavours need acidity.

Kebabs Vigorous red: moderate Greek, Corbières, Chilean Cab Sauv, Zin, or Barossa Shiraz. Sauv Bl, if lots of garlic.

Kidneys Red: St-Emilion or Fronsac, Nuits-St-Georges, Cornas, Barbaresco, Rioja, Spanish or Australian Cab Sauv, top Alentejo.

Lamb, roast One of the traditional and best partners for very good red Bordeaux – or its Cab Sauv equivalents from the New World. In Spain, the partner of the finest old Rioja and Ribera del Duero *reservas*.

    cutlets or chops As for roast lamb, but a little less grand.

    slow-cooked roast Flatters top reds, but needs less tannin than pink lamb.

Liver Young red: Beaujolais-Villages, St-Joseph, Médoc, Italian Merlot, Breganze Cab Sauv, Zin, Tempranillo, Portuguese Bairrada.

    calf's Red Rioja *crianza*, Salice Salentino *riserva*, Fleurie.

Meatballs Tangy, medium-bodied red: Mercurey, Crozes-Hermitage, Madiran, Morellino di Scansano, Langhe Nebbiolo, Zin, Cab Sauv.

    spicy Middle-Eastern style Simple, rustic red.

Moussaka Red or rosé: Naoussa from Greece, Sangiovese, Corbières, Côtes de Provence, Ajaccio, New Zealand Pinot N, young Zin, Tempranillo.

Mutton A stronger flavour than lamb, and not served pink. Robust but elegant red and top-notch. Mature Cab Sauv, Syrah. Some sweetness of fruit suits it.

Osso bucco Low-tannin, supple red such as Dolcetto d'Alba or Pinot N. Or dry Italian white such as Soave and Lugana.

Ox cheek, braised Superbly tender and flavoursome, this flatters the best reds: Vega Sicilia, Bordeaux. Best with substantial wines.

Oxtail Rather rich red: St-Emilion, Pomerol, Pommard, Nuits-St-Georges, Barolo, or Rioja *reserva*, Ribera del Duero, California or Coonawarra Cab Sauv, Châteauneuf-du-Pape, mid-weight Shiraz, Amarone.

Paella Young Spanish wines: red, dry white, rosé: Penedès, Somontano, Navarra, or Rioja.

Pigeon Lively reds: Savigny, Chambolle-Musigny, Crozes-Hermitage, Chianti Classico, Argentine Malbec, or California Pinot N. Or Franken Silvaner Spätlese.

Pork, roast A good, rich, neutral background to a fairly light red or rich white. It deserves ★★ treatment – Médoc is fine. Portugal's suckling pig is eaten with Bairrada Garrafeira; Chinese is good with Pinot N.

    pork belly Slow-cooked and meltingly tender, this needs a red with some acidity. Italian would be gd: Dolcetto or Barbera. Or Loire red, or lightish Argentine Malbec.

Pot au feu, bollito misto, cocido Rustic red wines from the region of origin; Sangiovese di Romagna, Chusclan, Lirac, Rasteau, Portuguese Alentejo, or Yecla and Jumilla from Spain.

Quail Carmignano, Rioja *reserva*, mature claret, Pinot N.

Rabbit Lively, medium-bodied young Italian red or Aglianico del Vulture; Chiroubles, Chinon, Saumur-Champigny, or Rhône rosé.

    with prunes Bigger, richer, fruitier red.

    as ragu Medium-bodied red with acidity.

Satay Australia's McLaren Vale Shiraz, or Alsace or New Zealand Gewürz. Peanut sauce is a problem with wine.

Sauerkraut (German) Lager or Pils. (But *see also* CHOUCROUTE GARNI.)

Sausages *See also* CHARCUTERIE, FRANKFURTERS. The British banger requires a young Malbec from Argentina (a red wine, anyway), or British ale.

Shepherd's pie Rough-and-ready red seems most appropriate, eg. Sangiovese di Romagna, but either beer or dry cider is the real McCoy.

Steak

    au poivre A fairly young Rhône red or Cab Sauv.

    filet or tournedos Any red (but not old wines with Béarnaise sauce: top New World Pinot N or Californian Chard is better).

    Fiorentina (bistecca) Chianti Classico *riserva* or Brunello. The rarer the meat, the more classic the wine; the more well-done, the more you need New World, fruit-driven wines. Argentina Malbec is the perfect partner for steak Argentine style, ie. cooked to death.

    Korean *yuk whe* (the world's best steak tartare) Sake.

    tartare Vodka or light young red: Beaujolais, Bergerac, Valpolicella.

    T-bone Reds of similar bone structure: Barolo, Hermitage, Australian Cab Sauv or Shiraz.

Steak-and-kidney pie or pudding Red Rioja *reserva* or mature Bordeaux.

Stews and casseroles Burgundy, such as Chambolle-Musigny or Bonnes-Mares, if fairly simple; otherwise lusty, full-flavoured red: young Côtes du Rhône, Toro, Corbières, Barbera, Shiraz, Zin, etc.

Sweetbreads A grand dish, so grand wine: Rhine Ries or Franken Silvaner Spätlese, *grand cru* Alsace Pinot Gr, or Condrieu, depending on sauce.

Tagines These vary enormously, but fruity young reds are a gd bet: Beaujolais, Tempranillo, Sangiovese, Merlot, Shiraz.

Tandoori chicken Ries or Sauv Bl, young red Bordeaux, or light north Italian red served cool. Also Cava and NV Champagne.

Thai dishes Ginger and lemon grass call for pungent Sauv Bl (Loire, Australia, New Zealand, South Africa) or Ries (Spätlese or Australian).

    coconut milk Hunter Valley and other ripe, oaked Chards; Alsace Pinot Bl (refreshing); Gewürz or Verdelho. Of course, Prosecco or NV Champagne.

Tongue Good for any red or white of abundant character, especially Italian. Also Beaujolais, Loire reds, Tempranillo, and full, dry rosés.

Veal, roast Good for any fine old red that may have faded with age (eg. a Rioja *reserva*) or a German or Austrian Ries, Vouvray, Alsace Pinot Gr.

Venison Big-scale reds, including Mourvèdre, solo as in Bandol, or in blends. Rhône, Bordeaux or California Cab Sauv of a mature vintage; or rather rich white (Pfalz Spätlese or Alsace Pinot Gr). With a sharp berry sauce, try a German *grosses gewächs* Ries, or a New World Cab Sauv.

Vitello tonnato Full-bodied whites: Chard; light reds (eg. Valpolicella) served cool.

Wild boar Serious red: top Tuscan or Priorat.

Vegetarian dishes (*see also* FIRST COURSES)

Baked pasta dishes *Pasticcio*, lasagne and cannelloni with elaborate vegetarian fillings and sauces: an occasion to show off a grand wine, especially finest Tuscan red, but also claret and burgundy. Also Gavi from Italy.

Beetroot A medium-weight red with some softness: Southern Rhône, Tempranillo. Or white.

and goat's cheese gratin Sauv Bl.

Cauliflower cheese Crisp, aromatic white: Sancerre, Ries Spätlese, Muscat, English Seyval Bl, Godello.

Couscous with vegetables Young red with a bite: Shiraz, Corbières, Minervois; or well-chilled rosé from Navarra or Somontano; or a robust Moroccan red.

Fennel-based dishes Sauv Bl: Pouilly-Fumé or one from New Zealand; English Seyval Bl, or young Tempranillo.

Grilled Mediterranean vegetables Brouilly, Barbera, Tempranillo, or Shiraz.

Lentil dishes Sturdy reds such as southern French, Zin, or Shiraz.

dhal, with spinach Tricky. Soft, light red or rosé is best – and not top-flight.

Macaroni cheese As for CAULIFLOWER CHEESE.

Mushrooms (in most contexts) Fleshy red: Pomerol, California Merlot, Rioja *reserva*, top burgundy, or Vega Sicilia. On toast, best claret. Ceps/porcini, Ribera del Duero, Barolo, Chianti Rufina, top claret: Pauillac or St-Estèphe.

Onion/leek tart Fruity, off-dry or dry white: Alsace Pinot Gr or Gewürz, Canadian or New Zealand Ries, English whites, Jurançon, Australian Ries. Or Loire red.

Peppers or aubergines (eggplant), stuffed Vigorous red wine: Nemea, Chianti, Dolcetto, Zin, Bandol, Vacqueyras.

Pumpkin/squash ravioli or risotto Full-bodied, fruity dry or off-dry white: Viognier or Marsanne, *demi-sec* Vouvray, Gavi, or South African Chenin.

Ratatouille Vigorous young red: Chianti, New Zealand Cab Sauv, Merlot, Malbec, Tempranillo; young red Bordeaux, Gigondas, or Coteaux du Languedoc.

Spanacopitta Young Greek or Italian red or white.

Spiced vegetarian dishes See INDIAN DISHES, THAI DISHES (Meat, poultry, game).

Watercress, raw This makes every wine on earth taste revolting. Soup is slightly easier, but doesn't require wine.

Wild garlic leaves, wilted Tricky: a fairly neutral white with acidity will cope best.

Desserts

Apple pie, strudel or tarts Sweet German, Austrian or Loire white, Tokaji Aszú or Canadian Icewine.

Apples, Cox's Orange Pippins Vintage port (and sweetmeal biscuits).

Bread-and-butter pudding Fine 10-yr-old Barsac, Tokaji Aszú, or Australian botrytized Sem.

Cakes and gâteaux *See also* CHOCOLATE, COFFEE, GINGER, and RUM. Bual or Malmsey Madeira, Oloroso, Cream Sherry.

cupcakes Prosecco presses all the right buttons.

Cheesecake Sweet white: Vouvray, Anjou, or fizz – refreshing, nothing special.

Chocolate Generally only powerful flavours can compete. Bual, California Orange Muscat, Tokaji Aszú, Australian Liqueur Muscat, 10-yr-old tawny Port; Asti for light, fluffy mousses. Experiment with rich, ripe reds: Syrah, Zin, even sparkling Shiraz. Banyuls for a weightier partnership. Médoc can match bitter black chocolate. Or a tot of good rum.

and olive oil mousse 10-yr-old tawny, or as for black chocolate, above.

Christmas pudding, mince pies Tawny Port, Cream Sherry, or liquid Christmas pudding itself: Pedro Ximénez Sherry. Asti or Banyuls.

Coffee desserts Sweet Muscat, Australia Liqueur Muscats, Tokaji Aszú.

Creams, custards, fools, syllabubs *See also* CHOCOLATE, COFFEE, GINGER, RUM. Sauternes, Loupiac, Ste-Croix-du-Mont, or Monbazillac.

Crème brûlée Sauternes or Rhine Beerenauslese, best Madeira or Tokaji Aszú. (With concealed fruit, a more modest sweet wine.)

Crêpes Suzette Sweet Champagne, Orange Muscat, or Asti.

Fruit

blackberries Vintage Port.

dried fruit (and compotes) Banyuls, Rivesaltes, Maury.

flans and tarts Sauternes, Monbazillac, sweet Vouvray or Anjou.

fresh Sweet Coteaux du Layon or light, sweet Muscat.

poached, ie. apricots, pears, etc. Sweet Muscatel: try Muscat de Beaumes-de-Venise, Moscato di Pantelleria, or Spanish dessert Tarragona.

salads, orange salad A fine sweet Sherry or any Muscat-based wine.

Ginger flavours Sweet Muscats, New World botrytized Ries and Sem.

Ice-cream and sorbets Fortified wine (Australian Liqueur Muscat, Banyuls); sweet Asti or sparkling Moscato. Pedro Ximénez, Amaretto liqueur with vanilla; rum with chocolate.

Lemon flavours For dishes such as tarte au citron try sweet Ries from Germany or Austria, or Tokaji Aszú; v. sweet if lemon is very tart.

Meringues Recioto di Soave, Asti, or Champagne *doux*.

Mille-feuille Delicate sweet sparkling white, such as Moscato d'Asti or *demi-sec* Champagne.

Nuts Finest Oloroso Sherry, Madeira, vintage or tawny Port (nature's match for walnuts), Tokaji Aszú, *vin santo*, or Setúbal Moscatel.

salted nut parfait Tokaji Aszú, Vin Santo.

Orange flavours Experiment with old Sauternes, Tokaji Aszú or California Orange Muscat.

Panettone Jurançon *moelleux*, late-harvest Ries, Barsac, Tokaji Aszú.

Pears in red wine A pause before the Port. Or try Rivesaltes, Banyuls, or Ries Beerenauslese.

Pecan pie Orange Muscat or Liqueur Muscat.

Raspberries (no cream, little sugar) Excellent with fine reds, which themselves taste of raspberries: young Juliénas, Regnié.

Rum flavours (baba, mousses, ice-cream) Muscat – from Asti to Australian Liqueur, according to weight of dish.

Salted caramel mousse/parfait Late-harvest Ries, Tokaji Aszú.

Strawberries and cream Sauternes or similar sweet Bordeaux, Vouvray *moelleux* or *vendange tardive* Jurançon.

Strawberries, wild (no cream) Serve with red Bordeaux (most exquisitely Margaux) poured over.

Summer pudding Fairly young Sauternes of a good vintage.

Sweet soufflés Sauternes or Vouvray *moelleux*. Sweet (or rich) Champagne.

Tiramisú *Vin santo*, young tawny Port, Muscat de Beaumes-de-Venise, Sauternes, or Australian Liqueur Muscat.

Trifle Should be sufficiently vibrant with its internal Sherry.

Zabaglione Light-gold Marsala or Australian botrytized Sem, or Asti.

Wine & cheese

The notion that wine and cheese were married in heaven is not borne out by experience. Fine red wines are slaughtered by strong cheeses; only sharp or sweet white wines survive. Principles to remember (despite exceptions): first, the harder the cheese, the more tannin the wine can have; second, the creamier the cheese is the more acidity needed in the wine. Cheese is classified by its texture and the nature of its rind, so its appearance is a guide to the type of wine to match it. Below are examples, I try to keep a glass of white wine for my cheese.

Bloomy rind soft cheeses, pure-white rind if pasteurized, or dotted with red: Brie, Camembert, Chaource, Bougon (goats milk "Camembert") Full, dry white burgundy or Rhône if the cheese is white and immature; powerful, fruity St-Emilion, young Australian (or Rhône) Shiraz/ Syrah, or Grenache if it's mature.

Blue cheeses Roquefort can be wonderful with Sauternes, but don't extend to other blues. It's Sauternes' sweetness, especially old, that complements the saltiness. Stilton and Port, preferably tawny, is a classic. Intensely flavoured old Oloroso, Amontillado, Madeira, Marsala, and other fortified wines go with most blues.

Fresh, no rind – cream cheese, crème fraîche, mozzarella Light crisp white: simple Bordeaux Blanc, Bergerac, English unoaked whites; rosé: Anjou, Rhône; very light, young, fresh red: Bordeaux, Bardolino, or Beaujolais.

Hard cheeses, waxed or oiled, often showing marks from cheesecloth – Gruyère family, Manchego and other Spanish cheeses, Parmesan, Cantal, Comté, old Gouda, Cheddar and most "traditional" English cheeses Particularly hard to generalize here; Gouda, Gruyère, some Spanish, and a few English cheeses complement fine claret or Cab Sauv and great Shiraz/Syrah wines. But strong cheeses need less refined wines, preferably local ones. Sugary, granular old Dutch red Mimolette or Beaufort are good for finest mature Bordeaux. Also for Tokaji Aszú. But try white wines, too.

Natural rind (mostly goats cheese) with bluish-grey mould (the rind becomes wrinkled when mature), sometimes dusted with ash – St-Marcellin Sancerre, Valençay, light, fresh Sauv Bl, Jurançon, Savoie, Soave, Italian Chard, lightly oaked English whites.

Semi-soft cheeses, thickish grey-pink rind – Livarot, Pont l'Evêque, Reblochon, Tomme de Savoie, St-Nectaire Powerful white Bordeaux, Chard, Alsace Pinot Gr, dryish Ries, southern Italian and Sicilian whites, aged white Rioja, dry Oloroso Sherry. But the strongest of these cheeses kills most wines.

Washed-rind soft cheeses, with rather sticky, orange-red rind – Langres, mature Epoisses, Maroilles, Carré de l'Est, Milleens, Munster Local reds, especially for Burgundy cheeses; vigorous Languedoc, Cahors, Côtes du Frontonnais, Corsican, southern Italian, Sicilian, Bairrada. Powerful whites: Alsace Gewurz and Muscat.

Food and finest wines

With very special bottles, the wine guides the choice of food rather than the other way around. The following are based largely on the gastronomic conventions of the wine regions producing these treasures, plus much diligent research. They should help bring out the best in your best wines.

Red wines

Barolo, Barbaresco Risotto with white truffles; pasta with game sauce (eg. *pappardelle alla lepre*); porcini mushrooms; Parmesan.

Red Bordeaux and other Cab Sauv-based wines (very old, light and delicate: eg. pre-1959, with exceptions such as 1945). Leg or rack of young lamb, roast with a hint of herbs (but not garlic); *entrecôte*; roast partridge or grouse; sweetbreads; or cheese soufflé after the meat has been served.

Côte d'Or red burgundy Consider the weight and texture, which grow lighter/more velvety with age. Also the character of the wine: Nuits is earthy, Musigny flowery, great Romanées can be exotic, Pommard renowned for its four-squareness. Roast chicken or capon is a safe standard with red burgundy; guinea-fowl for slightly stronger wines, then partridge, grouse, or woodcock for those progressively more rich and pungent. Hare and venison (*chevreuil*) are alternatives.

great old burgundy The Burgundian formula is cheese: Epoisses (unfermented); a fine cheese but a terrible waste of fine old wines.

vigorous younger burgundy Duck or goose roasted to minimize fat.

Fully mature great vintages (eg. Bordeaux 59 61 82) Shoulder or saddle of lamb, roast with a touch of garlic, roast ribs, or grilled rump of beef.

Mature but still vigorous (eg. 89 90) Shoulder or saddle of lamb (inc kidneys) with rich sauce. Fillet of beef *marchand de vin* (with wine and bone-marrow). Avoid beef Wellington: pastry dulls the palate.

Merlot-based Bordeaux (Pomerol, St-Emilion) Beef as above (fillet is richest) or well-hung venison.

Rioja *gran reserva*, Pesquera... Richly flavoured roasts: wild boar, mutton, saddle of hare, whole suckling pig.

Great Syrahs: Hermitage, Côte-Rôtie, Grange; Vega Sicilia Beef, venison, well-hung game; bone marrow on toast; English cheese (especially best farm Cheddar), also hard goats milk and ewes milk cheeses, ie. England's Berkswell and Ticklemore.

Great vintage Port or Madeira Walnuts or pecans. A Cox's Orange Pippin and a digestive biscuit is a classic English accompaniment.

White wines

Beerenauslese/Trockenbeerenauslese Biscuits, peaches, greengages. Desserts made from rhubarb, gooseberries, quince, apples.

Supreme white burgundy (le Montrachet, Corton-Charlemagne) or equivalent Graves Roast veal, farm chicken stuffed with truffles or herbs under the skin, or sweetbreads; richly sauced white fish or scallops as above. Or lobster or wild salmon.

Very good Chablis, white burgundy, other top-quality Chards White fish simply grilled or *meunière*. Dover sole, turbot, halibut best; brill, drenched in butter, can be excellent. (Sea bass is too delicate; salmon passes but does little for the finest wine.)

Condrieu, Château-Grillet, Hermitage Blanc Very light pasta scented with herbs and tiny peas or broad beans.

Grand cru Alsace: Riesling *Truite au bleu*, smoked salmon, or *choucroute garni*. **Pinot Gris** Roast or grilled veal. **Gewurztraminer** Cheese soufflé (Münster cheese). *Vendange tardive* Foie gras or tarte tatin.

Old vintage Champagne (not Blanc de Blancs) As an apéritif, or with cold partridge, grouse, woodcock.

Sauternes Simple crisp, buttery biscuits (eg. *langues de chat*), white peaches, nectarines, strawberries (without cream). Not tropical fruit. Pan-seared foie gras. Experiment with blue cheeses.

Supreme Vouvray *moelleux*, etc. Buttery biscuits, apples, apple tart.

Tokaji Aszú (5–6 puttonyos) Foie gras recommended. Fruit desserts, cream desserts, even chocolate can be wonderful. So is the naked sip.

France

More heavily shaded areas are
the wine-growing regions.

Abbreviations used in the text:

Al	Alsace
Beauj	Beaujolais
Burg	Burgundy
B'x	Bordeaux
Champ	Champagne
Cors	Corsica
C d'O	Cote d'Or
L'doc	Languedoc
Lo	Loire
Mass C	Massif Central
Prov	Provence
Pyr	Pyrenees
N/S Rh	Northern/Southern Rhône
Rouss	Roussillon
Sav	Savoie
SW	Southwest
AC	*appellation contrôlée*
ch, chx	château(x)
dom, doms	domaine(s)

Le Havre

Caen

Brest

LOIRE

Loire

Nantes
Muscadet

Anjou-Saumur

La Rochelle

BORDEAU

Médoc

Bordeaux
Graves

Pomerol
St-Emili
Entre
Deux

Sauternes
Côtes du
Marmand
Buzet

Biarritz

Tursan
Côtes
St-Mo
Madir
Jurançon

Fashion seems to be turning France's way. After a decade or more that
voted for the wines of the New World, in which ever-greater power,
extraction and alcohol were lauded, now most winemakers in most parts
of the world are seeking balance and elegance again. This doesn't mean
they want underpowered, insipid wines; they want concentration, but
with drinkability. And this is what France is so good at delivering.
Overalcoholic wines are not favoured in France – or indeed, among
wine-drinkers anywhere that treat wine as part of their daily diet.

Nevertheless, France has constantly to look to its laurels. Will its
superstars fetch the world's highest prices forever? Other countries
challenge it on quality and style: New Zealand's Hawke's Bay can produce

Syrahs and Bordeaux blends that give the best of the Rhône and Médoc a run for their money; Champagne no longer has the sparkling wine sector sewn up; great Pinot Noirs can be made outside the Côte d'Or (and the Côte d'Or long ago proved it could make some pretty miserable ones). Partly this is because France's native grapes seem to travel so well compared to, say, Italy's; nobody has yet succeeded in making a Nebbiolo to rival Barolo or a Sangiovese to upstage Chianti. But then they haven't been trying for so long.

The result has been to make the best producers up their game. Terroir expression is the goal worldwide now. Suddenly France has a head start.

Recent vintages of the French classics

Red Bordeaux

Médoc/red Graves For some wines, bottle age is optional; for these it is indispensable. Minor châteaux from light vintages need only two or three years, but even modest wines of great years can improve for 15 or so, and the great châteaux of these years can profit from double that time.

2010 Another outstanding year. Difficult flowering and tiny berries so smaller crop. One of the driest summers ever has produced magnificent Cab Sauv – deeply coloured, concentrated, firmly structured.

2009 Outstanding year, touted as "The Greatest". Hot, dry summer and extended sunny harvest have made structured wines with an exuberance of fruit.

2008 Much better than expected; fresh classic flavours. Cab Sauv ripened in late-season sunshine. Yields down due to poor fruit set, mildew and frost in places. Prices initially down but have risen on the back of 2009.

2007 Miserable summer; huge attack of mildew spelled a difficult year. Easy drinking; best are structured for ageing. Variable, so be selective.

2006 Cab Sauv had difficulty ripening; best are long-ageing. Good colour and acidity. Be selective.

2005 Perfect weather conditions throughout the year. Rich, balanced, long-ageing wines from an outstanding vintage. Keep all major wines.

2004 Mixed bag, but top wines good in a classic mould. Starting to drink.

2003 Hottest summer on record. Cab Sauv can be great (St-Estèphe, Pauillac). Atypical but rich, powerful at best (keep), unbalanced at worst (drink).

2002 Saved by a dry, sunny September. Later-ripening Cab Sauv benefited most. Some good wines if selective. Drink now–2018.

2001 A cool September and rain at vintage meant Cab Sauv had difficulty in ripening fully. Some excellent fresh wines to drink now–2015.

2000 Superb wines throughout. Start tentatively on all but the top wines.

1999 Vintage rain diluted ripe juice; so-so wines; drink now, but try to keep.

1998 Good (especially Pessac-Léognan), but the Right Bank is clearly the winner this year. Drink now–2015.

1997 Uneven flowering and summer rain were a double challenge. Top wines still of some interest, but the rest have faded.

1996 Cool summer, fine harvest. Good to excellent. Drink now–2020.

Older fine vintages: 95 90 89 88 86 85 82 75 70 66 62 61 59 55 53 49 48 47 45 29 28

St-Emilion/Pomerol

2010 Outstanding. Powerful wines again with high alcohol. Small berries so a lot of concentration.

2009 Outstanding. Powerful wines (high alcohol) but seemingly balanced. Hail in St-Emilion cut production at certain estates.

2008 Similar conditions to the Médoc. Late harvest into November. Tiny yields helped quality, which is surprisingly good.

2007 Same pattern as the Médoc. Huge disparity in picking dates (up to five weeks). Extremely variable.

2006 Rain and rot at harvest. Earlier-ripening Pomerol a success but St-Emilion and satellites variable.

2005 Same conditions as the Médoc. An overall success. Start to drink.

2004 Merlot often better than 2003 (Pomerol). Good Cab Fr. Variable.

2003 Merlot suffered in the heat; exceptional Cab Fr. Very mixed. Top St-Emilion on the plateau good. Experiment; some need drinking.

2002 Problems with rot and ripeness. Modest to good. Drink.

2001 Less rain than Médoc during vintage. Some powerful Merlot, sometimes better than 2000. Drinking now–2015.

2000 Similar conditions to Médoc. Less kind to Merlot, but a very good vintage.

1999 Careful, lucky growers made good wines; rain a problem. Now–2015.

1998 Earlier-ripening Merlot largely escaped the rain. Some excellent wines.

1997 Merlot suffered in the rain. Only a handful of wines still of interest.

1996 Cool, fine summer. Vintage rain. Less consistent than Médoc. Now–2015.

Older fine vintages: 95 90 89 88 85 82 71 70 67 66 64 61 59 53 52 49 47 45

Red Burgundy

Côte d'Or Côte de Beaune reds generally mature sooner than bigger wines of Côte de Nuits. Earliest drinking dates are for lighter commune wines – eg. Volnay, Beaune; latest for biggest wines, eg. Chambertin, Romanée. Even the best burgundies are more attractive young than equivalent red Bordeaux.

2010 Short crop of potentially exciting wines in Côte de Nuits but may be tougher going in Côte de Beaune (more rain).

2009 Glorious middle and late summer make beautiful, ripe, plump reds that will be accessible before the 2005s.

2008 Fine wines from those who avoided fungal diseases oidium and mildew, disaster for others. Pick and choose carefully.

2007 Small crop of attractive, perfumed wines. Buy to drink, not lay down.

2006 An attractive year in Côte de Nuits (less rain) with power to develop in medium term. Start drinking Côte de Beaune reds.

2005 The best for more than a generation, outstanding wines everywhere. Top wines must be kept, however tempting.

2004 Lighter wines, some pretty, others with herbaceous flavours. Drink soon.

2003 Reds coped with the heat better than the whites. Muscular, rich wines. Best wines outstanding, others short and hot.

2002 Middleweight wines of great class with an attractive point of freshness. Now showing real class. No hurry.

2001 Just needed a touch more sun for excellence. Good to drink now.

2000 Gave more pleasure than expected, but drink up now.

1999 Big, ripe vintage; good colour, bags of fruit, steely tannins, most ready now, but top wines will improve.

1998 Ripe fruit but dry tannins. Those in balance look good now.

Older fine vintages: 96 95 93 90 88 85 78 71 69 66 64 62 61 59

White Burgundy

Côte de Beaune White wines now rarely made for ageing as long as they used to be. Top wines should still improve for up to ten years.

2010 September rain problematic – but there may be some good wines.

2009 Fine crop of healthy grapes; definitely charming; enough acidity to age?

2008 Small crop, ripe flavours yet high acidity. Very fine; keep best. 2012–20.

2007 Big crop – those who picked late did very well. Drink soon.

2006 Plentiful crop of charming, aromatic wines. Drink now.

2005 Small, outstanding crop of dense, concentrated wines. Don't wait too long.

2004 Aromatic, sometimes herbaceous whites. Drink soon.

2003 Hot vintage; all but the best are falling over fast.

2002 Stylish wines showing very well.

2000 A big crop of ripe, healthy grapes. Drink now.

Mâconnais (Pouilly-Fuissé, St-Véran, Mâcon-Villages) follow a similar pattern, but don't last as long – appreciated more for their freshness than their richness.

Chablis *Grand cru* Chablis of vintages with both strength and acidity can age superbly for up to ten years; *premiers crus* less, but give them three years at least.
2010 Pretty good weather late on suggests another fine vintage.
2009 Rich, accessible wines, less mineral than 2007 or 2008. 2012–16.
2008 Excellent. Small crop: powerful, juicy wines, ageing potential 2012–20.
2007 Brilliant *grands crus* and *premiers crus* where not damaged by hail. Basic Chablis more modest. 2012–17.
2006 An early harvest of attractive, aromatically pleasing wines. But drink up.
2005 Small but outstanding crop of dense, concentrated wines. 2012–17.
2004 Difficult vintage, with mildew a problem. Not for keeping.
2003 Small crop of ripe wines, but acidity is low. Drink up.

Beaujolais 10 promising follow-on to 09. 09 Wonderful, the best for years, has reignited interest in Beaujolais. 08 Tough going with widespread hail. 07 Attractive but without the heart of a really great year. 06 Tricky vintage with some rot. 05 Concentrated wines.

Southwest France
2010 Poor spring caused widespread *coulure*, reducing yields. Dry and finally hot summer has raised expectations of a fine year.
2009 Very good, if not great. Certainly the best since 2005. Reds and dry whites uniformly excellent, ultra-sweet whites prejudiced by late rain.
2008 Expectations salvaged by late sunshine. A rescued but not notable year.
2007 The omens were terrible, but the wines have turned out better than expected. Average. Sweet whites bucked the trend.
2006 Reds are now drinking rather well. The whites won't keep much longer.
2005 Great year. Mostly drinking now but best reds and sweet whites will keep.

The Midi
2010 Cool, damp spring. Summer late; grapes ripened well. Fine quality throughout the region; yields lower thanks to summer drought.
2009 A cool spring, a hot, dry summer. Quality is excellent.
2008 A similar year to 2007, with sufficient sunshine to produce some elegant wines from unstressed vines. Severe hail damage in Faugères.
2007 Damp spring, cooler-than-average summer, fine September produced some beautifully balanced wines with some ageing potential.
2006 Fine results from the best winemakers.

Northern Rhône
2010 Extremely promising. Marvellous fruit in Syrahs (balanced, fresh). Very good Condrieu, fresher than recent years. Whites also full of potential.
2009 Excellent. Some fantastically rich Hermitage reds, very full Côte-Rôties. Good, lively Crozes and St-Joseph. Sound, rather big whites that can live.
2008 Tricky, rain-hit vintage. Select top names only. Some fine Côte-Rôties, Hermitage fair. Good whites – will live (Condrieu). Reds: 8–12 years.
2007 Depth and quality as wines age. Best Hermitage, Côte-Rôtie, Cornas, St-Joseph already attractive, age 18+ years. Good whites, depth to live well.
2006 Big crop, rich, clear fruit, sound stuffing. Have improved well, especially at Côte-Rôtie. Good acidity in robust whites, heady Condrieu.
2005 Exceptional. Tight flavours, long ageing potential for Hermitage, Cornas, fullest Côte-Rôties. St-Joseph reds have lovely tangy fruit. Whites are full.
2004 Mid-weight, mid-term year, with Côte-Rôtie showing well over time; fine reds from top vineyards. Superb whites really singing now.

2003 Intense sun gave cooked "southern" flavours. Best reds show genuine richness, and are coming together. 25+ yrs for best.

2002 Heavy rain. Stick to best growers. Drink up red St-Josephs, small-grower Côte-Rôtie. Hermitage, Cornas until 2015–18. Good whites (Condrieu).

2001 Lovely vintage. Reds ageing well, now stylish, fresh. Top year at Côte-Rôtie. Often very good whites. Good value if available.

Southern Rhône

2010 Small crop, good quality. Lovely, clear-fruited wines (1999 similarities). Successful Gigondas, Vacqueyras, Vinsobres. Interesting, full whites, too.

2009 Full reds in best cases; drought – grainy tannins. Châteauneuf reds very ripe. Good Côtes du Rhône/Villages. Sound whites.

2008 Rain, mildew. Many suppressed prestige wines. Best have body, drinking well to 2012–13; life 15 years or so. Stick to top names. Very good whites.

2007 Very good. Grenache-only wines can lack tannin. Exceptional Châteauneuf from top names. Very good Gigondas. Drink up Côtes du Rhônes, whites.

2006 Underrated; some very good reds. Rich Châteauneuf: more open than 2005s, less potent than 2007s. Full whites, ideal for food.

2005 Very good. Slow ageing year. Tight-knit, concentrated. Will age well, 20+ years for top Châteauneufs. Whites best drunk young.

2004 Good, but variable. Minerally, intricate flavours in Châteauneufs. Best names are profound. Starting to drink now. Complex whites will age well.

2003 Slowly coming together, a surprise. Chunky, high-octane wines. Less daunting textures now. Best can live long. Pick best names, best areas.

2002 Drink up. Simply fruited, early reds, acceptable whites. Gigondas best.

2001 Excellent classic vintage. Complex reds, lots of life ahead, be patient for top areas. Cracking Châteauneufs on great form now.

2000 Tasty, open wines, led by fruit, singing now. 15–18-year longevity. Go for leading names. Gigondas may edge Châteauneuf in quality.

1999 Very good, underestimated wines from the best names. Châteauneuf reds have moved up a gear with age. Very good Gigondas, best names at Lirac.

Champagne

2010 Heavy rain mid-August – extensive rot and loss of black grapes crop (Pinot Meunier in Marne Valley). A year for Blanc de Blancs (Chard).

2009 A fine year of ripeness, charm and refined aromas; will give great pleasure earlier than 08s. Sumptuous Pinot N from the Aube.

2008 A likely to be slow-developing classic vintage that might be great, but with very high acidity that will need mastering. Better for Pinot N than Chard.

2006 Topsy-turvy growing season but fine September made for ripe, expressive wines, especially Pinot N. Could be underrated by some houses.

2005 Not a great year overall in Champagne: a bit hot for real class, wines lacking dash and verve. Vintage wines from Bollinger and Jacquesson.

2004 Classic finesse and "tension". A vintage year to look forward to.

2002 A great, graceful year for superb Pinot N and sumptuous Chard. Best of early 21st century. Very fine Dom Pérignon and Piper Rare. No hurry.

Older fine vintages: 2000 99 98 96 95 90 89 88 85 82

The Loire

2010 Challenging and classic year. Big climatic variations. Muscadet, Anjou (fine sweets), Touraine, Central V'yds good. Montlouis, Vouvray – rot.

2009 Generally very good, but drought in Anjou-Touraine, severe hail damage in Menetou-Salon and Sancerre. High alcohol problem in some Sauv Bl.

2008 Small harvest, especially Muscadet. Healthy grapes, high acidity. Good age-worthy reds, excellent dry whites (Chenin Bl), sweets hit by late rain.

2007 Vintage saved by fine September and October. Producer's name crucial. Austere dry whites, exceptional Anjou sweets. Reds for early drinking.

2006 Only the conscientious succeeded. Dry whites fared well, good reds, some age-worthy. Not great for sweet whites.

2005 Excellent. Buy without fear, though some reds quite tannic.

Alsace

2010 Extreme: -26ffflC (-14.8fflF) Christmas to scorched July. V. small crop, down as much as 70%. Excellent wines for long keeping, most naturally dry.

2009 A mild winter, warm July, blistering August. Drought affected heat-stressed Ries. Great Pinot Gr, Gewurz, some fine late-harvest wines.

2008 Cool, dry August, good September – healthy vintage of dry, crisp wines.

2007 Hot spring, cold, wet summer, sunny autumn gave ripe grapes. Promise.

2006 Hottest recorded July, coolest August. Top names made subtle, fine Ries.

2005 Indian summer; large crop of healthy grapes. Ripe, balanced mineral.

2004 Those who picked early, kept low yields, made classic wines. Subtle year.

Abymes Sav w ★ DYA Hilly area nr Chambéry; light, mild Vin de Savoie AC from Jacquère grape has alpine charm. SAVOIE has many such *crus*.

Ackerman Lo w (dr sw sp) p r (sp) ★→★★ Major négociants. Founded in 1811 – first SAUMUR sparkling wine house. Major négociants with Alliance Loire (eight CAVE-CO-OPS) a shareholder. Ackerman group, inc Rémy-Pannier, has sparkling SAUMUR and CRÉMANT and still wines from throughout Loire, often made at its own wineries. Bought Monmousseau (TOURAINE) in 2010. *See* their blog: Xnoir.

Agenais SW r p w ★ DYA IGP of Lot-et-Garonne. Independents, eg. DOMS Lou Gaillot and Campet, better than moderate co-ops, and cost only a little more.

Aligoté Burg DYA Fresh, sharpish secondary grape from Burgundy with own appellation at BOUZERON. Base wine for apéritif Kir or *blanc cassis*.

Alliet, Philippe Lo r w ★★→★★★ 02 04 05' 06 08 09' (10) Top CHINON producer making concentrated CUVÉES to age. Best inc barrel-aged steeply sloped Coteau du Noire and VIEILLES VIGNES from flat, gravel vineyards and new hill v'yd L'Huisserie. A little CHINON *blanc*.

Aloxe-Corton Burg r w ★★→★★★ 99' 02' 03 05' 06 07 08 09' Famous for its GRANDS CRUS (CORTON, CORTON-CHARLEMAGNE) but less interesting at village or PREMIER CRU level. Reds can be attractive if not overextracted. Best producers: Follin-Arbelet, Pierre André, Senard.

Alquier, Jean-Michel L'doc r w Leading FAUGÈRES producer. Do not confuse with brother Frédéric. White Marsanne/Grenache Bl IGP blend; also Sauvignon Les Pierres Blanches IGP, red CUVÉES Les Premières, Maison Jaune and age-worthy single-v'yd Les Bastides.

Alsace Al w (r sw sp) ★★ →★★★★ 00' 02' 04 05' 06 07 08 09' 10 The sheltered east slope of the Vosges Mts makes France's Rhine wines: aromatic, fruity, full-strength, mostly dry and expressive of variety. Sugar levels vary widely: dry wines now easier to find. Much sold by variety (Pinot Bl, Ries, Gewurz). Matures well (except Pinot Bl, MUSCAT) 5–10 yrs; GRAND CRU even longer. Gd-quality and -value CRÉMANT. Formerly fragile Pinot N improving fast, esp in 2010. *See* VENDANGE TARDIVE, SÉLECTION DES GRAINS NOBLES.

Alsace Grand Cru Al w ★★★ →★★★★ 90' 95 96 97 98 99 00' 02' 04 05' 06 07 08 09' 10' AC restricted to 51 (KAEFFERKOPF added in 2006) of the best-named v'yds (approx 1,600 ha, 800 in production) and four noble grapes (Ries, PINOT GR,

Gewurz, MUSCAT) mainly dry, some sweet. New, much-needed production rules inc higher minimum ripeness, suppression of *chaptalization*.

Amiel, Mas Rouss r w sw ★★★ The pioneering MAURY domaine. Others following. Warming CÔTES DU ROUSSILLON *Carérades* red, white Altaïr, *vin de liqueur* Plénitude from Maccabeu. Vintage and cask-aged VDN. Prestige 15 yrs a star. STÉPHANE DERENONCOURT (B'x) consults.

Amirault, Yannick Lo r ★★→★★★★ 02 03 **04** 05' 06 08' 09' (10) Meticulous, first-rate producer of both BOURGUEIL and ST-NICOLAS-DE-BOURGUEIL – amongst the Loire's finest reds. Top CUVÉES La Petite Cave and Les Quartiers in BOURGUEIL and Malagnes and La Mine in ST-NICOLAS – all age-worthy.

André, Pierre C d'O ★★ Négociant at CH Corton-André, ALOXE-CORTON; 5 ha of v'yds in and around CORTON plus wide range from purchased grapes. Significant improvement since purchase by Ballande Group in 2003. One to watch.

Anjou Lo r p w (dr sw sp) ★→★★★★ Both region and umbrella AC covering ANJOU and SAUMUR. Many styles: Chenin Bl dry whites range from light quaffers to potent agers; juicy reds, inc Gamay; juicy Cab Fr-based Anjou *rouge*; structured ANJOU-VILLAGES; also strong, mainly dry SAVENNIÈRES; lightly sweet to luscious COTEAUX DU LAYON Chenin Bl; dry and sweet rosé and sparkling. AC Anjou suffers from historically poor image but can be excellent and v.gd value.

Anjou-Coteaux de la Loire Lo w sw s/sw ★★→★★★ 02 03 05' 07 09' (10) Small (40 ha) westernmost ANJOU AC for sweet whites from Chenin Bl; less rich but nervier than COTEAUX DU LAYON. Esp DOMS du Fresche, Musset-Roullier, CH de Putille.

Anjou-Villages Lo r ★→★★★★ 02 03 05' 06 08 09' (10) Superior central ANJOU AC for reds (Cab Fr/Cab Sauv, but a few pure Cab Sauv). Quality tends to be high and prices reasonable, esp DOM de Brizé, DOM Philippe, DOM CADY, Clos de Coulaine, Philippe Delesvaux, DOM de la Bergerie, Ogereau, CH PIERRE-BISE. Sub-AC Anjou-Villages-Brissac covers the same zone as COTEAUX DE L'AUBANCE; look for Bablut, DOM de Haute Perche, Montigilet, Richou, Rochelles, CH de Varière.

Appellation Contrôlée (AC or AOC) Government control of origin and production (not quality) of all the best French wines; about 45% of the total.

Apremont Sav w ★★ DYA One of the best villages of SAVOIE for pale, delicate whites, mainly from Jacquère grapes, but recently inc CHARD.

Arbin Sav r ★★ Deep-coloured, lively red from MONDEUSE grapes, rather like a gd Loire Cab Sauv. Ideal après-ski. Drink at 1–2 yrs.

Arbois Jura r p w (sp) ★★→★★★ Various gd and original light but tasty wines; specialty is VIN JAUNE. On the whole, DYA except Vin Jaune.

Ariège SW r ★ 08 09 (10) VDP from south of Toulouse. DOM des Coteaux d'Engravies is the best of the new Ariège wines. Will keep, esp if Syrah-based.

Arlaud C d'O ★★→★★★★ MOREY-ST-DENIS estate with CHARMES-CHAMBERTIN, CLOS DE LA ROCHE, etc. Fine wine at all levels in relatively easy, modern style.

Arlot, Dom de l' C d'O ★★★ Leading exponent in CÔTE DE NUITS of whole-bunch fermentation. Wines pale but aromatic and full of fruit. Best v'yds ROMANÉE-ST-VIVANT and NUITS-ST-GEORGES, esp Clos de l'Arlot. Gd whites, too.

Armand, Comte C d'O ★★★ Sole owner of exceptional Clos des Epeneaux in POMMARD, as well as other v'yds in AUXEY and VOLNAY. On top form since 1999.

Aube Southern extension of CHAMPAGNE, known as Côte des Bar. Ever-better Pinot N.

Auxey-Duresses C d'O r w ★★→★★★ 99' 02' 03 05' **06** 07 08 09' CÔTE DE BEAUNE village tucked away out of sight. Slightly tough wines but gd things to be had, esp mineral whites. Best examples (red): COMTE ARMAND, MAISON LEROY, Prunier; (white): Lafouge, Maison Leroy (Les Boutonniers).

Aveyron SW r p w Nascent IGP with some exciting NATURAL growers. ★★ Nicolas Carmarans uses local rare Négret de Banhars grape, DYA; ★★ Patrick Rols more conventional Merlot and Cab Sauv, which will keep.

Avize Champ One of the top Côte des Blancs villages. Most complete wines.

Aÿ Champ One of the best Pinot N-growing villages. Velvety wines.

Ayala Champ Revitalized AŸ-based house, owned by BOLLINGER. Fine Brut Nature Zéro Dosage and racy Rosé. Excellent Prestige Perle d'Ayala (02' 04 05 06 08).

Bandol Prov r p (w) ★★★ 96 97 98 99 00 01 02 03 04 05 06 07 08 Small coastal AC; PROVENCE's finest. Long-lasting oak-aged reds, mainly Mourvèdre with Grenache and Cinsault; elegant rosé from young vines; a little white from CLAIRETTE, Ugni Bl, occasionally Sauv Bl. Stars: DOMS de la Laidière, Lafran Veyrolles, La Suffrène, TEMPIER, CH'X Pibarnon, Mas de la Rouvière, La Bégude, La Bastide Blanche.

Banyuls Rouss br sw ★★→★★★ Wonderfully original VDN, mainly Grenache (Banyuls GRAND CRU: over 75% Grenache, aged for 2 yrs+). Newer vintage style resembles ruby Port; far better are traditional RANCIOS, aged for yrs. Think fine old tawny Port, or even Madeira. Best: DOMS du Mas Blanc (★★★), la Rectorie (★★★), Vial Magnères, Coume del Mas (★★), la Tour Vieille(★★★). *See also* MAURY.

Barrique The BORDEAUX (and Cognac) term for an oak barrel holding 225 litres. Barrique-ageing to flavour almost any wine with oak was a craze in late 1980s. These days taste and price (of barrels) inspire caution.

Barsac Saut w sw ★★→★★★★ 83' 86' 88' 89' 90' 95 96 97' 98 **99'** 01' 02 **03' 05'** 07' 09' 10 Neighbour of SAUTERNES with similar superb golden wines from lower-lying limestone soil; fresher, less powerful and with more finesse. Repays long ageing. Top: CLIMENS, COUTET, DOISY-DAËNE, DOISY-VÉDRINES, NAIRAC.

Barthod, Ghislaine C d'O ★★★→★★★★ Impressive range of archetypal CHAMBOLLE-MUSIGNY. Marvellous poise and delicacy, yet with depth and concentration. Nine PREMIER CRUS, such as Les Cras, Les Fuées and Beaux Bruns.

Barton & Guestier B'x BORDEAUX négociant now part of the group Castel (2010).

Bâtard-Montrachet C d'O w ★★★★ **99'** 00 02' **04'** 05' 06' 07 08 09' 12-ha GRAND CRU down-slope from LE MONTRACHET itself. Powerful, rich wines, occasionally a touch chunky. Also worthy siblings Bienvenues-B-M and Criots B-M. Seek out: Bachelet-Monnot, BOILLOT, CARILLON, GAGNARD, FAIVELEY, LATOUR, DOM LEFLAIVE, MOREY, Pernot, Ramonet, SAUZET.

Baudry, Dom Bernard Lo r p w ★★→★★★ 02 03 04 05 06 08 09' (10) Excellent CHINON across the range, from Chenin Bl-based whites to Cab Fr-based rosés and excellent CHINON CUVÉES of red, from juicy Les Granges to structured Clos Guillot and Croix Boissées. Now joined by son Matthieu.

Baudry-Dutour Lo r p w ★★→★★★ 02 03 05' 06 08 09' (10) A merger in 2003 of DOMS de la Perrière and de la Roncée. Now CHINON's largest producer with 120 ha, inc CHX de St Louand and latest acquisition de la Grille. Reliable quality from light, early drinking to age-worthy reds. Modern winery in Panzoult.

Baumard, Dom des Lo r p w sw sp ★★→★★★★ 02 03 04 05' 06 07' (sw) 08 09 (10) Leading family producer of ANJOU wine, esp Chenin Bl-based whites, inc SAVENNIÈRES (Clos St Yves, Clos du Papillon), QUARTS DE CHAUME and Clos Ste Catherine (COTEAUX DU LANGUEDOC). Makes a tangy VIN DE TABLE from Verdelho. The Loire's brave screwcap pioneer and proponent of cryoextraction: freezing grapes to concentrate the sugars for sweet wine.

Baux-en-Provence, Les Prov r p ★★→★★★ 03 **04** 05 06 07 08 09 Dramatic bauxite outcrop of the Alpilles topped by village of Les Baux. AC in own right (r p). White is COTEAUX D'AIX. Most v'yds organic. Best: TRÉVALLON, Cab Sauv/Syrah blend (IGP for lack of Grenache). Also Mas de la Dame, Dom Hauvette, Sainte Berthe.

Béarn SW r p w ★→★★ w p DYA r **08** 09' 10 Rosés from MADIRAN and JURANÇON producers and Béarn co-op. Good reds from DOM Lapeyre/Guilhémas ★★. Whites less successful.

Beaujolais Beauj r (p w) ★ DYA The most basic appellation of the huge Beaujolais region, producing five million cases a yr. Some from the hills can be excellent.

Beaujolais Primeur (or Nouveau) The Beaujolais of the new vintage, made in a hurry (often only 4–5 days' fermenting) for release at midnight on the third Wednesday in Nov. Ideally soft, pungent, fruity and tempting; too often crude, sharp, too alcoholic. More of an event than a drink.

Beaujolais-Villages Beauj r ★★ 05' 06 09' 10 The middle category between straight BEAUJOLAIS and the ten named *crus* such as MOULIN-À-VENT. Best locations around Beaujeu and Lantigné, worth waiting for.

Beaumes-de-Venise S Rhô r br (p w) ★★ 05' 06 07' 09' 10' for reds. DYA for MUSCAT. Long-established VDN MUSCAT, from southeast CÔTES DU RHÔNE; musky, aromatic, peach/apricot/caramel flavours, more elegance recently (eg. DOMS Beaumalric, Bernardins, Coyeux, Durban, JABOULET, Pigeade (v.gd), VIDAL-FLEURY, co-op), gd with melon, soft cheese, chocolate. Direct, punchy, bit austere reds, best ripe yrs. (CH Redortier, DOMS Cassan, de Fenouillet, Durban, St-Amant.) Leave for 2–3 yrs. Fresh whites, jolly rosés are CÔTES DU RHÔNE.

Beaumont des Crayères Champ Côte d'Épernay co-op making excellent Pinot Meunier-based Grande Réserve NV and v. fine Fleur de Prestige 98 02 04. Exceptional CHARD-led Cuvée Nostalgie 02'. Fleur de Rosé 02 04 05.

Beaune C d'O r (w) ★★★ 02' 03 05' 07 08 09' Historic wine capital of Burgundy and home to many merchants: BOUCHARD, CHAMPY, CHANSON, DROUHIN, JADOT, LATOUR as well as HOSPICES DE BEAUNE. No GRAND CRU v'yds but sound red PREMIERS CRUS eg. Avaux, Bressandes, Cras, Grèves, Teurons, Clos du Roi and an increasing amount of white, of which DROUHIN'S CLOS DES MOUCHES stands out.

Bellet Prov r p w ★★ DYA Local wine of Nice; expensive, original but ignored in city. White from Rolle grape is best; unexpected ageing potential. Braquet and Folle Noire for red. V. few producers: CH de Bellet is oldest and best, Les Coteaux de Bellet, CH de Crémat.

Bellivière, Dom de Lo r w sw ★★→★★★ 02 03 05' 06 07 08 09' (10) Now biodynamic – conversion started 2008. Precise Chenin Bl in JASNIÈRES and COTEAUX DU LOIR and revelatory Pineau d'Aunis.

Bergerac SW r p w dr sw ★→★★★ 00'(sw) 05' 06 07'(sw) 08 09' (10) Neighbour and inexpensive alternative to BORDEAUX from the same grapes. Look for ★★★ DOMS l'Ancienne Cure, Clos des Verdots, *La Tour des Gendres*, Jonc Blanc, Les Marnières. ★★ CHX Belingard-Chayne, Clos de la Colline, les Eyssards, les Fontenelles, Grinou, de la Mallevieille, les Miaudoux, Monastier la Tour, le Paradis, Thénac. *See also* MONBAZILLAC, MONTRAVEL, PÉCHARMANT, ROSETTE, SAUSSIGNAC.

Bertrand, Gérard L'doc r p w ★★ Now one of biggest v'yd owners in south, with 325 ha; Villemajou in CORBIÈRES *cru* Boutenac, Laville-Bertou in MINERVOIS-LA LIVINIÈRE, l'Hospitalet in La Clape, l'Aigle in LIMOUX, and IGP PAYS D'OC. Best wines: La Viala (MINERVOIS), La Forge (CORBIÈRES), l'Hospitalet (La Clape).

Besserat de Bellefon Champ Épernay house specializing in gently sparkling styles (old CRÉMANT style). Now owned by Boizel Chanoine group. Improved quality.

Beyer, Léon Al ★★→★★★ V. fine, intense, dry wines often needing 10 yrs+. Superb Ries. Comtes d'Eguisheim, but no mention on label of GRAND CRU PFERSIGBERG (originating v'yd). Natural wines for great cuisine; listed by many top restaurants.

Bichot, Maison Albert Burg ★★→★★★ Dynamic merchant and owner/distributor of LONG-DEPAQUIT (CHABLIS), Clos Frantin and more. Quality on the rise.

Billecart-Salmon Champ Family house makes exquisite long-lived wines, vintage CUVÉES partly fermented in wood. Superb Clos St-Hilaire Blanc de Noirs (96' 98' 99), NF Billecart (97' 98 99 00), top BLANC DE BLANCS (98' 99 00) and new BRUT 04 and Extra Brut NV. Exquisite *Cuvée Elisabeth Salmon rosé* 02.

Bize, Simon C d'O ★★→★★★★ Key producer in SAVIGNY-LÈS-BEAUNE with wide range of PREMIER CRU v'yds, esp Vergelesses, also exciting gd-value BOURGOGNE, both colours. Top wine is LATRICIÈRES-CHAMBERTIN.

Blagny C d'O r w ★★→★★★ (r) 99′ 02′ 03′ 05′ 07 08 09′ 10 Austere reds now out of fashion; replanting CHARD in the manner of MEURSAULT. Best v'yds: Pièce sous le Bois, Sous le Dos d'Ane. AMPEAU, Jobard, Matrot, Martelet de Cherisey best.

Blanc de blancs Any white wine made from white grapes only, esp CHAMPAGNE. An indication of style, not of quality.

Blanc de noirs White (or slightly "blush") wine from red grapes, esp CHAMPAGNE.

Blanck, Paul & Fils Al ★★→★★★ Grower at Kientzheim, producing huge range of wines. Finest from 6 ha GRAND CRU Furstentum (Ries, Gewurz, PINOT GR) and GRAND CRU SCHLOSSBERG (Great Ries 02′ **06** 08). Also gd Pinot Bl.

Blanquette de Limoux L'doc w sp ★★ Gd-value creamy fizz from cooler area nr Carcassonne; claims older history than CHAMPAGNE. Basic Mauzac much improved by CHARD, Chenin Bl and, more recently, Pinot N, esp in newer AC CRÉMANT DE LIMOUX. Large co-op with Sieur d'Arques label. Also Rives-Blanques, Martinolles, Antech, Laurens, Fourn.

Blaye B'x r w ★→★★ 01 03 04 05′ **06** 08 09′ Designation for top, concentrated reds (lower yields, etc.) from what used to be Premières Côtes de Blaye, now new AC (2008) BLAYE-CÔTES DE BORDEAUX (*see* box p. 89).

Blaye-Côtes de Bordeaux B'x r w ★→★★ 00′ 01 03 04 05′ **06** 08 09′ Mainly red AC east of the Gironde. Formerly Premières Côtes de Blaye but new designation in 2008. Greatly improved quality. Best CHX: Bel Air la Royère, Gigault (Cuvée Viva), Haut-Bertinerie, Haut-Colombier, Haut-Grelot, Jonqueyres, Monconseil-Gazin, Mondésir-Gazin, Montfollet, Roland la Garde, Segonzac, des Tourtes.

Boillot C d'O Interconnected Burgundy growers. Look for Jean-Marc (POMMARD) ★★★ for fine oaky reds and whites, Henri (DOM in VOLNAY, merchant in MEURSAULT) ★★★ and Louis (CHAMBOLLE, married to GHISLAINE BARTHOD) ★★→★★★.

Boisset, Jean-Claude Burg New kid on the Burgundy block, now respectable after 40 yrs. Own wines and v'yds. DOM DE LA VOUGERAIE excellent. Also owns other businesses, latest Rodet. Projects in Canada, California, Chile, Uruguay looked after by son Jean-Charles, now married to Gina Gallo of eponymous US giant.

Boizel One of CHAMPAGNE's surest values: brilliant, aged BLANC DE BLANCS NV and *prestige* Joyau de France (95 96 98 00), Joyau Rosé (00 02′). Also Grand Vintage Brut (98 99 00 02′ 04) and Cuvée Sous Bois. New v.gd Brut Ultime *zero dosage*.

Bollinger Great individualistic CHAMPAGNE house, on a roll in recent vintages (viz Grande Année 95′ **99** 00 02). New non-vintage rosé. Luxury wines: RD (90 95 96′ 97), Vieilles Vignes Françaises (98 99) from ungrafted Pinot N vines, La Côte aux Enfants, AŸ (02′ 05). *See also* LANGLOIS-CH.

Bonneau du Martray, Dom C d'O r w ★★★★ (w) ★★ (r) Scintillating, mineral CORTON-CHARLEMAGNE from hyper-meticulous producer with top holding in the heart of the AC. Red CORTON fine but pricey.

Bonnes-Mares C d'O r ★★★→★★★★ 90′ **91** 95 96′ 98 99′ 00 02′ 03 05′ **06 07** 08 09′ 10 GRAND CRU (15 ha) between CHAMBOLLE-MUSIGNY and MOREY-ST-DENIS. Sturdy, long-lived wines, less fragrant than MUSIGNY. Best: Drouhin-Laroze, DUJAC, Groffier, JADOT, ROUMIER, de VOGÜÉ, VOUGERAIE.

Bonnezeaux Lo w sw ★★★→★★★★ 88 89′ 90′ 95′ 96′ 97′ 02 03′ 05′ 07′ 09 (10) Magnificently rich, almost everlasting sweet Chenin Bl with QUARTS DE CHAUME top site in COTEAUX DU LAYON. Esp: CHX de Fesles, la Fresnaye, de Varière, DOMS les Grandes Vignes, du Petit Val (Goizil).

Bordeaux B'x r w (p) ★→★★ 05′ 08 09′ Catch-all AC for generic Bordeaux (represents nearly half the region's production). Mixed quality but usually recognizable. Most brands are in this category.

Bordeaux Supérieur B'x r ★→★★ 00′ 01 03 04 05′ 08 09′ Superior denomination to above. Higher min alcohol, lower yield and longer ageing. 75% of production bottled at the property, the reverse of AC BORDEAUX.

Borie-Manoux B'x Admirable BORDEAUX shipper, CH-owner. CHX inc BATAILLEY, BEAU-SITE, Croix du Casse, DOM DE L'EGLISE, HAUT-BAGES-MONPELOU, TROTTEVIEILLE.

Bouchard Père & Fils Burg ★★→★★★★ Huge v'yd owner – largest in CÔTE D'OR? Whites esp strong in MEURSAULT and CHEVALIER-MONTRACHET. Flagship red is BEAUNE Grèves, Vigne de L'Enfant Jésus. Part of Henriot Burgundian interests with WILLIAM FÈVRE, CHABLIS and Villa Ponciago, BEAUJOLAIS.

Bouches-du-Rhône Prov r p w ★ IGP from Marseille environs. Simple, fruit-filled reds from southern varieties, plus Cab Sauv, Syrah and Merlot.

Bourgeois, Henri Lo ★★→★★★ 02 03 05 06 07 **08** 09 (10) Leading SANCERRE grower/merchant in Chavignol. Overall 70 ha. Also POUILLY-FUMÉ, MENETOU-SALON, QUINCY, COTEAUX DU GIENNOIS, CHÂTEAUMEILLANT and IGP Petit Bourgeois. Top wines: MD de Bourgeois, La Bourgeoise (r w), Jadis, Sancerre d'Antan. Also CLOS Henri (r w) in Marlborough, NZ.

Bourgogne Burg r w (p) ★★ (r) 05' **07 08** 09' 10 (w) **07 08** 09' 10 Catch-all AC, with higher standards than basic BORDEAUX. Light, often gd flavour, best at 2–4 yrs. Top growers make bargain beauties from fringes of CÔTE D'OR villages; do not despise. BEAUJOLAIS crus (except REGNIÉ) may be labelled Bourgogne.

Bourgogne Grand Ordinaire Burg r (w) ★ DYA Who invented this crazy name for the most basic of Burgundy? It is about to become Coteaux Bourguignons instead. Gamay for red, CHARD, Aligoté, or Melon de Bourgogne for white.

Bourgogne Passe-Tout-Grains Burg r (p) ★ Age 1–2 yrs. The name suggests you can put any grape in, but in fact it must be a mix of Pinot N (min 33%) and Gamay. Can be fun from CÔTE D'OR DOMS.

Bourgueil Lo r (p) ★★→★★★(★) 96' 02 03 05' 06 08 09' (10) Burly, full-flavoured TOURAINE reds and big, fragrant rosés based on Cab Fr. Gd vintages can age 15 yrs. Esp AMIRAULT, Audebert, DOM de la Butte, DOM de la Chevalerie, Delaunay, Druet, Jamet, Lamé Delisle Boucard, Nau Frères. See ST-NICOLAS-DE-BOURGUEIL.

Bouvet-Ladubay Lo ★→★★★ Major sparkling SAUMUR house owned by United Breweries (India). Best is the barrel-fermented Cuvée Trésor – both white and rosé. Also still wines mainly from ANJOU-SAUMUR. Large art centre at premises at St-Hilaire-St-Florent (SAUMUR).

Bouzereau C d'O ★★→★★★ Family in MEURSAULT making gd whites at gd prices and improving reds. Jean-Baptiste (son of Michel B) and Vincent B are the two best.

Bouzeron Burg w ★★ CÔTE CHALONNAISE AC since 1998 for ALIGOTÉ, with stricter rules and greater potential than straight BOURGOGNE AC. Best from A&P de Villaine.

Bouzy Rouge Champ r ★★★ 90 95 96 97 99 02 05 Still red of famous Pinot N village. Like v. light burgundy, but can last well in sunny vintages.

Brocard, J-M Chab ★★→★★★ One of the recent success stories of CHABLIS with a fine range of wines at all levels. Also on offer: a range of BOURGOGNE blancs from different soil types (Kimmeridgian, Jurassic, Portlandian).

Brouilly Beauj r ★★ 05' **08** 09' 10 Biggest of the ten crus of BEAUJOLAIS: fruity, round, refreshing wine, can age 3–4 yrs. CH de la Chaize is largest estate. Top growers: Michaud, DOMS de Combillaty, des Grandes Vignes, Dubost, de Pierreux.

Brumont, Alain SW ★★★ Manages still to keep his nose in front (just) in MADIRAN. His oaked 100% Tannat wines, Le Tyre, CH MONTUS, Bouscassé needs long keeping. Torus brand quicker, easier-drinking. IGPS inc 100% Gros Manseng, Tannat/Cab blends.

Brut Term for the dry classic wines of CHAMPAGNE.

Brut Ultra/Zéro Term for bone-dry wines in CHAMPAGNE – many term variations on the theme – back in fashion and improved, with precision and weight.

Bugey Sav r p w sp ★→★★ DYA VDQS for light sparkling, still, or half-sparkling wines from Roussette (or Altesse) and CHARD (gd). Best from Montagnieu; also Rosé de Cerdon, mainly Gamay.

Burguet, Alain C d'O ★★→★★★ Compact VIGNERON for outsize GEVREY-CHAMBERTIN, esp Mes Favorites. Sons Eric and Jean-Luc now taking over.

Buxy Burg w Village in AC MONTAGNY with gd co-op for CHARD and Pinot N.

Buzet SW r (p w) ★★ 06 07 08 09' (10) Nr BORDEAUX, dominated by powerful co-op. Note its prize-winning ★★ CH de Mazelières. Biodynamic independent ★★★ Dom du Pech outclasses the field. Try ★★ CHX du Frandat, Tournelles.

Cabardès L'doc r (p w) ★ →★★ 03 04 05 06 07 08 09 BORDEAUX Cab and Merlot meet Midi Syrah and Grenache for original blends. Best is DOM de Cabrol with Vin de l'Est, Vin d'Ouest; also Jouclary, Font Juvénal. Cazaban. CH Pennautier is largest.

Cabernet d'Anjou Lo p s/sw ★ →★★ Traditionally sweet DEMI-SEC, often derided, rosé enjoying renaissance, especially strong local demand. Can be age-worthy. CH PIERRE-BISE; DOMS de Bablut, CADY, Clau de Nell, les Grandes Vignes, Ogereau, de Sauveroy, Varière.

Cabrières L'doc p (r) ★★ DYA Traditionally full-bodied rosé; also sound reds, mostly from energetic village co-op.

Cadillac-Côtes de Bordeaux B'x r w dr sw (p) ★ →★★★ 98 00' 01 03 05' 08 09' Long, narrow, hilly zone on the right bank of the Garonne opposite GRAVES. Formerly Premières Côtes de Bordeaux but renamed from 2008 vintage (*see* box p. 89). Medium-bodied, fresh reds. Quality extremely varied. Best: Alios de Ste-Marie, Carignan, *Carsin*, Clos Ste-Anne, Le Doyenné, Grand-Mouëys, Lezongars, Mont-Pérat, Plaisance, Puy Bardens, REYNON, Suau.

Cady, Dom Lo r p sw ★★→★★★ 02 03 04 05' 06 07' (sw) 09 (10) Excellent ANJOU family grower of everything from dry whites and off-dry rosés to lusciously sweet COTEAUX DU LAYON and CHAUME. Sweet wines are strongest suit. Alexandre has now joined his father, Philippe.

Cahors SW r ★★→★★★ 01' 02 04 05' 06 08 (09') (10) Historic but chameleon all-red AC, must contain at least 70% Malbec. Easy styles from ★★ CH Latuc, Clos Coutale, DOM Boliva; more weight from ★★★ *Clos de Gamot* (esp ★★★★ Cuvée Vignes Centenaires and ★★★★ Clos St Jean), Triguedina, ★★ CHX Armandière, la Coustarelle, Croze de Pys, Gaudou, Clos d'un Jour, DOMS de la Bérengeraie, Paillas, Pineraie, les Rigalets, Savarines (organic); modern styles from ★★★ CHX DU CÈDRE, Lamartine, la Caminade, Eugénie, La Reyne; best of all worlds from cult ★★★★ DOM Cosse-Maisonneuve.

Cailloux, Les S Rhô r (w) ★★★ 78' 79' 81' 85' 89' 90 95' 96' 98' 99 00' 01 03' 04' 05' 06' 07' 09' 10' 18-ha CHÂTEAUNEUF 2012; deft, stylish, hand-made reds of breeding, elegance foremost. Very consistent, sound value. Special wine Centenaire, with oldest Grenache 1889, pure and refined. Also André Brunel and Féraud-Brunel CÔTES DU RHÔNE merchant range, sound, not more.

Cairanne S Rhô r p w ★★ →★★★ 01' 03 04' 05' 06' 07' 09' 10' Best of the 17 CÔTES DU RHÔNE-VILLAGES: direct, bristling fruit, live tannins, esp DOMS Alary, Ameillaud, Armand, Brusset, Escaravailles, Grosset, Hautes Cances (trad), Oratoire St-Martin (classy), Présidente, Rabasse-Charavin, Richaud (great fruit), Perrin et Fils. Food-friendly, robust whites.

Canard-Duchêne Champ CHAMPAGNE house. Improving under ALAIN THIÉNOT. Brut Vintage 02 04 Fine Cuvée Charles VII.

Canon-Fronsac B'x r ★★ →★★★ 98 00' 01 03 05' 06 08 09' 260-ha enclave within FRONSAC, otherwise same wines. Best rich, full, finely structured. Try CHX Barrabaque, Canon Pécresse, Cassagne Haut-Canon la Truffière, la Fleur Cailleau, DU GABY, Grand-Renouil, Haut-Ballet, Haut-Mazeris, MOULIN-PEY-LABRIE, Pavillon, Vrai Canon Bouché.

Carillon, Louis C d'O ★★★ Sensibly priced and consistently fine PULIGNY producer, esp Combettes, Perrières, Referts. From 2009 brothers Jacques and François are going their separate ways.

Cassis Prov w (r p) ★★ DYA Fashionable pleasure Port east of Marseille with traditional reputation for dry whites based on CLAIRETTE and MARSANNE. Delicious with bouillabaisse, but expensive (DOM de la Ferme Blanche, Clos Ste Magdeleine, Clos d'Albizzi, Paternel, Fontcreuse). Growers fighting rear-guard action with property developers. Do not confuse with the blackcurrant liqueur.

Castillon-Côtes de Bordeaux B'x r ★★ →★★★ 00' 01 02 03 04 05' 08 09' Previously Côtes de Castillon, renamed 2008. Flourishing region east of ST-EMILION; similar wines. Ageing potential; much recent investment. Top: de l'A, d'Aiguilhe, Ampélia, Cap de Faugères, La Clarière-Laithwaite, Clos l'Eglise, Clos Les Lunelles, Clos Puy Arnaud, Joanin Bécot, Montlandrie, Poupille, Robin, Veyry, Vieux CH Champs de Mars.

Cathiard C d'O ★★★ Brilliant VOSNE-ROMANÉE producer on top form since late 1990s. Perfumed, sensual wines; charming young but will age. Vosne Malconsorts best.

Cave Cellar, or any wine establishment.

Cave coopérative Wine-growers' co-op winery; over half of all French production. Often well-run, well-equipped, and wines gd value for money, but many disappearing in the economic crisis.

Cazes, Dom Rouss r p w sw ★★ Large producer in ROUSSILLON. IGP pioneer, with Merlot and Cab Sauv, esp for brand Le Canon du Maréchal and Le Crédo, also CÔTES DU ROUSSILLON-VILLAGES and delicious aged RIVESALTES. Now part of Jeanjean group, but still run by family. Excellent value.

Cérons B'x w dr sw ★★ 97' 98 99' 01' 02 03' 05' 07 09' 60-ha neighbour of SAUTERNES. Less intense wines, eg. CHX de Cérons, CHANTEGRIVE, Grand Enclos.

Chablis Chab w ★★→★★★ 05' 06' 07 08 09 10 So famous that it has been widely imitated round the world, this lean but lovely northern Burgundy is mostly unoaked. But too much is just mass-produced, early bottled, anonymous CHARD.

Chablis Grand Cru Chab w ★★★ →★★★★ 95' 96' 98 99 00' 02' 03 05' 06 07' 08' 09 10 Small block of seven v'yds on steep slope on right bank of Serein. The richest Chablis is comparable to fine CÔTE DE BEAUNE whites. Needs age for minerality and individual style to develop. V'yds: Blanchots, Bougros, Clos, Grenouilles, Preuses, Valmur, Vaudésir. Clos and Vaudésir best.

Chablis Premier Cru Chab w ★★★ 99 00' 02' 05' 06 07 08' 09 10 Better sites on the rolling hillsides; more white flowers on left bank of the river Serein (Vaillons, Montmains, Côte de Léchet), yellow fruit on right bank (Fourchaume, Mont de Milieu, Montée de Tonnerre). Well worth small premium over straight CHABLIS.

Chablis

There is no better expression of the all-conquering CHARD than the full but tense, limpid but stony wines it makes on the heavy limestone soils of Chablis. Chablis terroir divides into three quality levels (four, inc PETIT CHABLIS) with great consistency. Best makers use little or no new oak to mask the precise definition of variety and terroir: Barat, Bessin ★, Billaud-Simon ★, BOUCHARD PÈRE & FILS, Boudin ★, J-M BROCARD, J Collet ★, D Dampt, R/V DAUVISSAT ★, J Dauvissat, B, D et E and J Defaix, Droin, DROUHIN ★, Duplessis, DURUP, FÈVRE ★, Geoffroy, J-P Grossot ★, LAROCHE, LONG-DEPAQUIT, DOM des Malandes, L Michel, Christian Moreau ★, Picq ★, Pinson, RAVENEAU ★, G Robin ★, Servin, Tribut, Vocoret. Simple, unqualified "Chablis" may be thin; best is PREMIER or GRAND CRU. The co-op, La Chablisienne, has high standards (esp Grenouille ★) and many different labels (it makes one in every three bottles). (★ = outstanding)

FRANCE

Chambertin C d'O r ★★★★ 88 89 90' 93 95 96' 98 99' 01 02' 03 05' 06 07 08 09' 10 13-ha (or 28-ha inc Clos de Bèze) of Burgundy's most imperious wine; amazingly dense, sumptuous, long-lived and expensive. Not everybody up to standard, but try from BOUCHARD PÈRE ET FILS, Charlopin, Damoy, DROUHIN, DOM LEROY, MORTET, PRIEUR, Rossignol-Trapet, ROUSSEAU, TRAPET.

Chambertin-Clos de Bèze C d'O r ★★★★ 88 89 90' 93 95 96' 98 99' 01 02' 03 05' 06 07 08 09' 10 May be sold under the name of neighbouring CHAMBERTIN. Splendid wines, may be more accessible in youth. 16 growers, inc CLAIR, Damoy, DROUHIN, Drouhin-Laroze, FAIVELEY, Groffier, JADOT, Prieuré-Roch, ROUSSEAU.

Chambolle-Musigny C d'O r ★★★ → ★★★★ 90' 93 95' 96' 98 99' 02' 03 05' 06 07 08 09' 10 CÔTE DE NUITS village (170 ha): fragrant, complex but never heavy wine. Best v'yds: Amoureuses, BONNES-MARES, Charmes, Cras, Fuées, MUSIGNY. Growers to note: Amiot-Servelle, BARTHOD, Digoia-Royer, DROUHIN, Groffier, Hudelot-Baillet, JADOT, MUGNIER, RION, ROUMIER, DE VOGÜÉ.

Champagne Champ Sparkling wines of Pinots N and Meunier and/or CHARD, and its region (34,000-ha, 145-km east of Paris); made by *méthode traditionnelle*. Bubbles from elsewhere, however gd, cannot be Champagne.

Champagne growers to watch in 2011

Edmond Barnaut Bouzy. Complex, fine CHAMPAGNES mainly from Pinot N culminate in first-rate Sélection Ultra Brut Grand Cru (02 04 06 08') and delicious COTEAUX CHAMPENOIS Rosé.

Francis Boulard et Fille Visionary Massif St-Thierry grower making v.gd multi-vintage Cuvée Petraea and superb all-CHARD Les Rachais 02 ★★★★★ 04 05 06).

Claude Cazals Exciting Extra-Brut Blanc de Blancs (99 02' 04) and exceptional Clos Cazals (96★★★★ 99 02).

Richard Cheurlin One of best grower-winemakers of the Aube. Rich but balanced Carte d'Or and vintage-dated Cuvée Jeanne (99 02 05). New Cuvée Coccinelle & Papillon, natural and chemical-free.

Pierre Cheval-Gatinois Impeccable Aÿ producer of *mono-cru* CHAMPAGNES and excellent still COTEAUX CHAMPENOIS (99 02 05).

Collard-Picard Rising Marne Valley and Côte des Blancs grower. Impressive Cuvée Prestige (all three grapes), two gd vintages, part oak-fermented.

Benoît Lahaye Fine organic Bouzy grower: excellent Essentiel NV Brut, BLANC DE NOIRS and 02 vintage for long ageing.

Jean- Luc Lallement Exceptional Verzenay grower making muscular yet exquisitely refined BLANC DE NOIRS. His first vintage wines will be available in 2012. Great Rosé, too.

Lilbert et fils Scion of blue-chip Cramant DOM takes his GRAND CRU CHARDONNAY CHAMPAGNES to higher level: great purity of flavours, with kinetic energy. Text-book 04 Cramant Grand Cru.

V. Testulat Great-value Épernay DOM and merchant. First rate BLANC DE NOIRS and elegant Paul Vincent Vintage (99 02 04).

J-L Vergnon Fine restored LE MESNIL estate making exquisite all CHARD extra-BRUT CUVÉES, esp Confidence (02' 03 04 05).

Veuve Fourny Rising Côte des Blancs star at Vertus: ★★★★★ Extra-Brut 02' 04 and superb single-v'yd Clos du Faubourg Notre Dame 99 00 02'.

Champagne le Mesnil Champ Top-flight co-op in greatest GRAND CRU CHARD village. Exceptional Cuvée Sublime (02' 04) from finest sites. Real value.

Champs-Fleuris, Dom des Lo r p w sw ★★→★★★ 02 03 05' **06 07** 08 (09) Go-ahead 34-ha DOM. Top-notch SAUMUR *blanc*; SAUMUR-CHAMPIGNY; fine CRÉMANT; pretty rosé; when vintage warrants, succulent COTEAUX DU SAUMUR called Cuvée Sarah.

Champy Père & Cie Burg ★★→★★★ Ancient négociant house revitalized by Meurgey family. Own DOM of 17 ha now biodynamic, centred on BEAUNE v'yds. Still improving. Acquisition of DOM Laleure-Piot brings 10 ha more.

Chandon de Briailles, Dom C d'O ★★→★★★ Unfashionable but fine, light reds, esp PERNAND-VERGELESSES, Île de Vergelesses and CORTON. Biodynamic farming, lots of stems, no new oak define the style.

Chanson Père & Fils Burg ★→★★★ Unpushy BEAUNE-based merchant of increasing quality. Look for Clos des Fèves red and Corton-Vergennes white. Wines to follow for value.

Chapelle-Chambertin C d'O r ★★★ 90' 93 95 96' 98 99' 01 02' 03 05' 07 08 09' 10 A 5.2-ha neighbour of CHAMBERTIN. Wine more "nervous", less meaty. V.gd in cooler yrs. Top producers: Damoy, Drouhin-Laroze, JADOT, Rossignol-Trapet, TRAPET, Tremblay.

Chapoutier N Rhô ★★→★★★★ Owner of great N Rhône vineyards, esp HERMITAGE, also merchant. Intense wines; biodynamic. Note low-yield, special plot-specific CUVÉES, full, gourmand CHÂTEAUNEUF: Barbe Rac, Croix de Bois (r), CÔTE-RÔTIE La Mordorée, HERMITAGE: L'Ermite, Le Pavillon (r), L'Ermite, Cuvée de l'Orée, Le Méal (w). Also ST-JOSEPH Les Granits (r w). Fab Marsanne N Rhône whites, great with food. Gd-value *Meysonniers Crozes*. Also holdings in BANYULS, Garde-Adhémar, COTEAUX D'AIX-EN-PROVENCE, CÔTES DU ROUSSILLON-VILLAGES (gd DOM Bila-Haut), RIVESALTES. Michel has ALSACE venture (Schieferkopf). Active Australian joint ventures (DOMS Tournon, Terlato & Chapoutier); Portugal (Estremadura).

Charbonnière, Dom de la S Rhô r (w) ★★★ 95' 98 99' 00 01' 03 04 05' 06' 07' 09' 10 Gd 17-ha CHÂTEAUNEUF estate. Solid Tradition wine, notable, authentic Mourre des Perdrix, also Hautes Brusquières, VIEILLES VIGNES from northern zones. Steady white, sound VACQUEYRAS red also.

Chardonnay As well as a white wine grape, also the name of a MÂCON-VILLAGES commune. Hence Mâcon-Chardonnay.

Charmes-Chambertin C d'O r ★★★ 90' 93 95 96' 98 99' 01 02' 03 05' 06 07 08 09' 10 31 ha inc neighbour MAZOYÈRES-CHAMBERTIN of mixed quality. Best has intense, ripe, dark-cherry fruit and fragrant finish. Try Arlaud, Bachelet, DROUHIN, DUGAT, DUJAC, LEROY, Perrot-Minot, ROTY, ROUMIER, ROUSSEAU, VOUGERAIE.

Chassagne-Montrachet C d'O w r ★★★→★★★★ (w) 99 00 02' 04 05' 06' 07 08 09' 10 Large village at south end of CÔTE DE BEAUNE. Reds can be tough so now more whites, esp from Caillerets, La Romanée, Blanchots and GRANDS CRUS. Best reds: Morgeot, Clos St Jean. Production dominated by inter-related families Coffinet, COLIN, GAGNARD, MOREY, Pillot. Top domaines Niellon, Ramonet, CH de Maltroye.

Château (Ch/x) Means an estate, big or small, gd or indifferent, particularly in Bordeaux (*see* Chx of Bordeaux). In France, château tends to mean, literally, castle or great house. In Burgundy, DOMAINE is the usual term.

Château d'Arlay Jura ★→★★★ Major Jura estate; 65 ha in skilful hands. Wines inc v.gd VIN JAUNE, VIN DE PAILLE, Pinot N, and MACVIN.

Château de Beaucastel S Rhô r w ★★★★ 78' 79 81' 83 85 86' 88 89' 90' 94' 95' 96' 97 98' 99' 00' 01' 03' 04 05' 06' 07' 08 09' 10' Long-time organic top CHÂTEAUNEUF estate, grower of old Mourvèdre, v. old Roussanne. Also excellent Perrin & Fils S Rhone business (320+ ha). Deep, smoky, complex wines, drink at 2 yrs or from 7–8 yrs. Recent vintages softer. Top-quality 60% Mourvèdre Hommage à Jacques Perrin red. *Wonderful old-vine Roussanne*: keep 5–25 yrs. Superior CÔTES DU RHÔNE Coudoulet de Beaucastel red (lives

8+ yrs). Perrin et Fils CAIRANNE, GIGONDAS, RASTEAU, VINSOBRES v.gd, great value. V.gd organic Perrin Nature CÔTES DU RHÔNE (r w). (*See also* Tablas Creek, California.)

Château du Cèdre SW r w ★★★ 01' 02 04 **06** (08) (09') (10) Much-admired modern CAHORS. Le Prestige quicker-maturing than hefty top growths which need ageing. Delicious white IGP from Viognier.

Château de la Chaize Beauj r ★★★ Magnificent recently restored CH, home to leading 98-ha BROUILLY estate.

Château-Chalon Jura w ★★★ Not a CH but AC and village. Unique dry, yellow, Sherry-like wine (Savagnin grape). Develops *flor* (*see* "Port, Sherry & Madeira") while ageing in barrels for min 6 yrs. Ready to drink when bottled (62-cl *clavelin* bottle), but ages almost forever. A curiosity.

Château Fuissé Burg w ★★→★★★ Substantial producer with some of the best terroirs of POUILLY-FUISSÉ. Esp Les Clos, Combettes. Also négociant lines.

Château-Grillet N Rhô w ★★ 91' 95' 98' 00' **01' 04'** 05 06' **07'** 08 09 3.6-ha terraced granite v'yd, own AC. Bought by F Pinault of CH LATOUR (spring 2011). Better recently. Subtle Viognier, can be big, usually needs food. Elegance sought since mid-2000s. Can take 3+ yrs to open. Decant.

Châteaumeillant Lo r p ★→★★ DYA A small new AC area (82 ha), Nov 2010, southwest of Bourges in Georges Sand country. Gamay, Pinot N for light reds, *gris*, rosés. 100% Pinot N not permitted. Look for: Chaillot, Geoffrenet-Morval.

Château de Meursault C d'O r w ★★ 61-ha estate owned by PATRIARCHE; gd v'yds and wines in BEAUNE, MEURSAULT, POMMARD, VOLNAY. Cellars open to public.

Chateau Montus r w ★★★ 00 01' 02 04 05' 06 (08) (09') (10) Still precariously perched at the top of the MADIRAN tree, ALAIN BRUMONT'S top wine still commands critical respect as well as long ageing.

Château la Nerthe S Rhô r w ★★★ 78' 81' 89' 90' 95' 96' 97 **98'** 99' 00 01 03 **04'** 05' **06'** 07' 09' 10' V.gd 90-ha CHÂTEAUNEUF estate. Modern, polished wines, more international of late. Special CUVÉES delicious Cadettes (r), oaked Beauvenir (w). Also runs v.gd TAVEL Prieuré Montézargues, gd-value DOM de la Renjarde CÔTES DU RHÔNE, CH Signac CHUSCLAN.

Châteauneuf-du-Pape S Rhô r (w) ★★★ 78' 81' 83 85 86 88 89' 90' 94 **95'** 96 98' 99' 00' 01' 03' 04' 05' **06'** 07' 09' 10' 3,230 ha nr Avignon with about 45 DOMS for best wines (remaining 85 inconsistent). Up to 13 red, white varieties, led by Grenache, plus Syrah, Mourvèdre, Counoise. Intense, heady, v. long-lived. Too many sweet-fruit, sip-only wines (RP Jr's taste) lately. Tradition wines, small names can be gd value. Prestige wines (old vines, late harvest, new oak) often too expensive. Whites fresh, fruity, or sturdy, best can age 15 yrs. Top growers inc: CHX DE BEAUCASTEL, Fortia, Gardine, Mont-Redon, LA NERTHE, RAYAS, Vaudieu; DOMS de Beaurenard, Bois de Boursan, Bosquet des Papes, LES CAILLOUX, Chante Cigale, CHARBONNIÈRE, Charvin, Cristia, Font-de-Michelle, Grand Veneur, Marcoux (fantastic VIEILLES VIGNES), Monpertuis, Pegaü, Roger Sabon, VIEUX TÉLÉGRAPHE, Henri Bonneau, Clos du Mont-Olivet, CLOS DES PAPES, Clos St-Jean, Cuvée du Vatican, P Usseglio, Vieux Donjon.

Château Pierre-Bise Lo r p w ★★→★★★★ 02 03 04 05 06 07' (sw) **08** 09 (10) Claude Papin – terroir specialist COTEAUX DU LAYON, inc Chaume, QUARTS DE CHAUME, and SAVENNIÈRES, esp Clos de Grand Beaupréau and ROCHE-AUX-MOINES. V.gd concentrated ANJOU Gamay, ANJOU-VILLAGES – both Cuvée Schist and Spilite, and Anjou Blanc Haut de la Garde.

Château Rayas S Rhô r w ★★★→★★★★★ 78' 79 81' 85 86 88' 89 90' 93 94 95' **96' 98'** 99 00 01 03 **04'** 05' 06' 07' 08 09' 10' Fantastic, v. traditional 12-ha CHÂTEAUNEUF estate. Subtle, complex, delicious reds (100% Grenache) age v. well. White Rayas (Grenache Blanc, Clairette) v.gd over 18+ yrs. Gd-value second wine: *Pignan*. V.gd CH Fonsalette, CÔTES DU RHÔNE. Decant all. Gd CH des Tours VACQUEYRAS.

Château Simone Prov r p w ★★→★★★ Historic estate where Winston Churchill painted Mont St-Victoire. Same family for over two centuries. Virtually synonymous with AC PALETTE nr Aix-en Provence. Warming soft reds; white repays bottle-ageing. Full-bodied rosé. Original but traditional.

Château de Villeneuve Lo r w ★★→★★★★ 96 99 02 03 05 **06 07** 08 09' (10) Meticulous producer. Wonderful SAUMUR *blanc* (esp barrel-fermented Les Cormiers) and SAUMUR-CHAMPIGNY (esp VIEILLES VIGNES, Grand Clos). Superb COTEAUX DE SAUMUR in 2003. Top CUVÉES only released in gd vintages.

Chave, Dom Jean-Louis N Rhô r w ★★★★ Top grade HERMITAGE DOM. Astute blending from prime hillside sites. Classy, generous, long-lived wines, esp white (mainly Marsanne), also v.gd occasional VIN DE PAILLE. Improving DOM ST-JOSEPH red (bought 6+ ha DOM Florentin 2009), fruity J-L Chave brand St-Joseph Offerus, fine merchant HERMITAGE red and white.

Chavignol Lo SANCERRE village with famous steep v'yds: Les Monts Damnés, Cul de Beaujeu. Full-bodied, minerally wines that age 7–10 yrs (or longer); esp Boulay, BOURGEOIS, Cotat, DAGUENEAU, Yves and Pierre Martin and Thomas Laballe.

Chénas Beauj r ★★★ **05' 06 07 08** 09 10 Smallest BEAUJOLAIS CRU, one of the weightiest; neighbour to MOULIN-À-VENT and JULIÉNAS. Growers: Aufranc, Champagnon, Charvet, DUBOEUF, Lapierre, Piron, Robin, Trichard, co-op.

Chevalier-Montrachet C d'O w ★★★★ 99' 00' 01 02' 04 05' 06' 07 08 09' 10 Just above MONTRACHET geographically, just below in quality, though still capable of brilliant, long-lived, mineral wines. Best sectors are Les Demoiselles (JADOT, LATOUR) and La Cabotte (BOUCHARD). Other top growers: Colin-Deleger, Dancer, LEFLAIVE, Niellon, CH de Puligny.

Cheverny Lo r p w ★→★★ 05' 06 07 08 09' (10) Loire AC (534 ha) nr Chambord. Pungent dry white from Sauv Bl and CHARD. Generally light reds, mainly Gamay, Pinot N (also Cab Fr, Côt). Richer, rarer and more age-worthy *Cour-Cheverny* uses local Romorantin grape only. Sparkling uses Crémant de Loire and TOURAINE ACS. Esp Cazin, Clos Tue-Boeuf, Gendrier, Huards, Philippe Tessier; DOMS de la Desoucherie, du Moulin, Veilloux, Villemade.

Chevillon, R C d'O ★★★ Delicious, approachable NUITS-ST-GEORGES with v'yds in the best sites, esp Les St-Georges, Cailles, Vaucrains, Roncières.

Chidaine, François Lo w dr sw sp (r) ★★★ 02' 05' 07 08' 09 Producer of ambitious, v. pure, v. precise MONTLOUIS. In 2002 took over Clos Baudoin (formerly Prince Poniatowski) – now renewing vineyard – making similarly styled VOUVRAY. Concentrates on dry and DEMI-SEC styles. AC TOURAINE at Chissay in the Cher Valley. Biodynamic producer.

Chignin Sav w ★ DYA Light, soft white from Jacquère grapes for alpine summers. Chignin-Bergeron (with Roussanne grapes) is best and liveliest.

Chinon Lo r p (w) ★★→★★★ 89' 90' 95 96' 97 02 03 05' 06 08 **09'** (10) Juicy, light to rich TOURAINE Cab Fr from 2,300 ha. 10% rosé. Drink young; top vintages from top growers can age 10+ yrs. Some taut, dry Chenin Bl from 36 ha. ALLIET, BAUDRY, Baudry-Dutour, Couly-Dutheil, Couly (Pierre and Bertrand), Grosbois; CHX de la Bonnelière, de Coulaine, DOM de la Noblaie.

Chiroubles Beauj r **05' 08** 09' 10 Rarely seen BEAUJOLAIS CRU in the hills above FLEURIE; fresh, fruity, silky wine for early drinking (1–3 yrs). Growers: Cheysson, DUBOEUF, Fourneau, Métrat, Passot, Raousset, Trenel.

Chorey-lès-Beaune C d'O r (w) ★★ 99' 02' 05' **06 07 08** 09' 10 Gd, affordable burgundy adjoining BEAUNE: CH de Chorey (Germain), Loichet, *Tollot Beaut*.

Chusclan S Rhô r p w ★→★★ 06' 07' 09' 10 CÔTES DU RHÔNE-VILLAGES with gd-quality co-op. Soft reds, bright rosés. Best co-op labels Cuvée de Marcoule, Seigneurie de Gicon. Also gd CH Signac (can age) and special CUVÉES from *André Roux*. Drink most young.

Clair, Bruno C d'O ★★→★★★ Terrific MARSANNAY estate with major holdings in GEVREY-CHAMBERTIN (esp Clos de Bèze, Clos St Jacques, Cazetiers), FIXIN, MOREY-ST-DENIS and old vine SAVIGNY La Dominode.

Clairet B'x Between rosé and red. BORDEAUX Clairet is AC. Try CHX Fontenille, Penin.

Clairette Traditional white grape of the Midi. Its low-acid wine was a vermouth base. Improvements in winemaking produce easy-drinking glassfuls.

Clairette de Bellegarde L'doc w ★ DYA AC nr Nîmes: elegant, dry white from CLAIRETTE, esp stylish Mas Carlot.

Clairette de Die S Rhô w dr s/sw sp ★★ NV Dry or (better) semi-sweet, easy-drinking. Underrated, traditional, sweetly fruited, MUSCAT sparkling wine from low Alps in east Rhône; or flinty, dry CLAIRETTE, can age 3–4 yrs. Excellent aperitif. Achard-Vincent, A Poulet, J-C Raspail.

Clairette du Languedoc L'doc w ★ DYA Small white AC of the Midi. Original identity was soft and creamy; now some oak-ageing and even late-harvest and RANCIO.

Clape, Auguste and Pierre N Rhô r (w) ★★★→★★★★ 90' 95' 97 98' 99' 00 01' 02 03' 04' 05' 06' 07' 08 09' 10' *The kings of Cornas*. Supreme 5+ ha Syrah central v'yd at CORNAS, many old vines. Deep, backward, consistent reds, need 6+ yrs. Gd young vines Renaissance. Gd CÔTES DU RHÔNE, ST-PÉRAY, VIN DE TABLE.

Clape, la L'doc r p w ★★→★★★ *Cru* of note in former AC COTEAUX DU LANGUEDOC. Set to become GRAND CRU du Languedoc for 2011 vintage. Warming, spicy reds from sun-soaked hills between Narbonne and the Mediterranean. *Tangy, salty whites* age surprisingly well. Gd: CHX l'Hospitalet, Moyau, La Négly, Pech-Céléyran, Pech-Redon, Rouquette-sur-Mer, Ricardelle, Anglès, Mas du Soleila, Complazens.

Climat Burgundian word for individually named v'yd, eg. Meursault Tesson.

Clos A term carrying some prestige, reserved for distinct (walled) v'yds, often in one ownership (esp Burgundy and ALSACE).

Clos de Gamot SW ★★★ 90' 95 96 98' 00 01' 02' 04 05' 06 08 (09)'(10) Some say that this is what CAHORS is/should be all about. The Jouffreaux' long-living ★★★★ Cuvée Vignes Centenaires (made best yrs only) and micro-CUVÉE ★★★★ Clos St Jean fear no competition from the modern styles of the region.

Clos de la Roche C d'O r ★★★ 90' 93' 95 96' 98 99' 01 02' 03 05' 06 07 08 09' 10 Arguably the finest GRAND CRU of MOREY-ST-DENIS, with as much grace as power. Best: Amiot, ARLAUD, DUJAC, LEROY, LIGNIER, PONSOT, ROUSSEAU.

Clos de Tart C d'O r ★★★★ 90' 96' 99' 02' 03 05' 06 07 08 09' 10 MOREY-ST-DENIS GRAND CRU upgraded in quality and price on the watch of Sylvain Pitiot.

Clos de Vougeot C d'O r ★★★ 90' 93' 95 96' 98 99' 01 02' 03' 05' 06 07 08 09' 10 A 50-ha CÔTE DE NUITS GRAND CRU with many owners. Occasionally sublime. Maturity depends on grower's philosophy, technique and position. Top growers inc CH de la Tour, DROUHIN, EUGÉNIE, FAIVELEY, GRIVOT, GROS, Hudelot-Noëllat, JADOT, LEROY, LIGER-BELAIR, MÉO-CAMUZET, MUGNERET, *Vougeraie*.

Clos des Lambrays C d'O r ★★★ 90' 95 99' 00 02 03 05' 06 07 09' 10 GRAND CRU v'yd (6 ha) at MOREY-ST-DENIS. A virtual monopoly of the DOM du Clos des Lambrays, recently more severe in selecting best grapes. Spicy, stemmy style.

Clos des Mouches C d'O r w ★★★ Splendid PREMIER CRU BEAUNE v'yd, largely owned by DROUHIN. Whites and reds, spicy and memorable – and consistent. Little-known v'yds of the same name exist in SANTENAY and MEURSAULT, too.

Clos des Papes S Rhô r w ★★★★ 90' 95 98' 99' 00 01' 03' 04' 05' 06' 07' 08 09' 10' Top 32-ha (18 plots) CHATEAUNEUF estate of Avril family for centuries. Rich, complex red, more sweet and ripe recently (mainly Grenache, Mourvèdre, drink from 6 yrs) and *great white* (deserves fine cuisine; 5–18 yrs), both merit patience.

Clos du Roi C d'O r ★★→★★★ The best v'yd in GRAND CRU CORTON, PREMIER CRU v'yd in BEAUNE and top site in MARSANNAY. The king usually chose well.

Clos Rougeard Lo r w (sw) ★★★★ 02 03 04 05' **06** 07 08 09' (10) Small, long-established, influential DOM run by Foucault brothers – benchmark SAUMUR-CHAMPIGNY fine SAUMUR *blanc*, and, when possible, luscious COTEAUX DE SAUMUR.

Clos St-Denis C d'O r ★★★ 90' **93** 95 96' 98 **99' 01** 02' 03 05' 06 07 08 09' 10 GRAND CRU at MOREY-ST-DENIS (6.4 ha). Splendid sturdy wine growing silky with age. Growers inc: ARLAUD, Bertagna, DUJAC and PONSOT.

Clos St-Jacques C d'O r ★★★ 90' 93 95' 96' 98 99' 01 02' 03 05' 06 07 08 09' 10 6.7-ha hillside PREMIER CRU in GEVREY-CHAMBERTIN with perfect southeast exposure. Five excellent producers: CLAIR, ESMONIN, FOURRIER, JADOT, ROUSSEAU; powerful, velvety reds often ranked above many GRANDS CRUS.

Clos Ste-Hune Al w ★★★★ Greatest Ries in ALSACE (00' 02' 04 05 06 08' 09' 10'). V. fine, initially austere; needs 5–10+ yrs' ageing. A TRIMBACH wine from GRAND CRU ROSACKER.

Coche-Dury C d'O ★★★★ Superb 11.5-ha MEURSAULT DOM led by Jean-François Coche and son Raphaël. Exceptional whites from ALIGOTÉ to CORTON-CHARLEMAGNE and v. pretty reds, too. Hard to find.

Colin C d'O ★★★ Leading CHASSAGNE-MONTRACHET and ST-AUBIN family, several members of the next generation succeeding either Marc Colin (Pierre-Yves) or Michel Colin-Deleger (Bruno, Philippe).

Collines Rhodaniennes N Rhô r w ★★ Quality Rhône IGP, clear-fruited, granite-derived reds v.gd value. Also young-vine CÔTE-RÔTIE, recent v'yds at Seyssuel. Mainly red, mainly Syrah (best), also Merlot, Gamay. Authentic Viognier (best), CHARD. Reds: Barou, Bonnefond, L Cheze, J-M Gérin, Jamet (v.gd), Jasmin, Monier, S Ogier. Whites: Barou, Y Cuilleron, Perret (v.gd), G Vernay.

Collioure Rouss r w ★★ The table-wine twin of BANYULS, with most producers making both. Gutsy red, mainly Grenache, from dramatic terraces overlooking the Med. Also rosé and, since 2002, white, based on Grenache Blanc. Top growers: Le Clos des Paulilles, DOMS du Mas Blanc, de la Rectorie, La Tour Vieille, Vial-Magnères, Madeloc.

Comté Tolosan SW r p w ★ Mostly DYA VDP found all over the SW, but surprising quality from ★★★ CH de Cabidos (Béarn) for a range of wines, esp a *moelleux* from Petit Manseng, ★★ DOM DE RIBONNET (south of Toulouse) for experimental use of non-indigenous grape varieties. Otherwise you take pot luck.

Condrieu N Rhô w ★★★ 04' 05 07 08' 09 10' Full, freesia-fragrant white from seat of Viognier, many granite slopes. Best are mineral-tinted, pure. Lot of young vines, new vineyard (now 125 ha; 75 growers) mean quality varies (except marvellous 2004, v.gd 2008, 2010); oak, alcohol can be excessive. Best: CHAPOUTIER, Y Cuilleron, DELAS, Gangloff, GUIGAL, F Merlin, Niéro, A Perret, C Pichon, ROSTAING, G Vernay (esp classy, long-lived Coteau de Vernon), F Villard.

Corbières L'doc r (p w) ★★ →★★★ 02 03 04 05' 06 07' 08 09 The biggest AC of the LANGUEDOC, with *cru* of Boutenac. Wild scenery dominated by Mont Tauch and Mont d'Alaric. Wines like the scenery: sun-soaked and rugged. Best estates inc CHX Aiguilloux, de Cabriac, Les Clos Perdus, Lastours, Ollieux Romanis, Les Palais, Pech-Latt, de la Voulte Gasparet, DOMS du Grand Crès, de Fontsainte, du Vieux Parc, de Villemajou, Villerouge. Co-ops: Camplong, Embrès-et-Castelmaure, Tuchan.

Cornas N Rhô r ★★★ 78' 83' 85' 88' 89' 90' 91' 94' **95' 96** 97 **98' 99'** 00' 01' 02 03' 04 05' 06' 07' 08 09' 10' Exciting Syrah. Deep, mineral-tinted, needs to age 5–15 yrs. Younger growers making more accessible wines. Top: Allemand, Balthazar (traditional), *Clape* (benchmark), Colombo (new oak), Courbis (modern), *Delas*, J & E Durand, JABOULET (St-Pierre CUVÉE), Lemenicier, V Paris, Tardieu-Laurent (modern), *Dom du Tunnel*, Voge (oak).

Corsica (Vin de Corse) Cors r p w ACS Ajaccio, PATRIMONIO, better *crus* Coteaux du

Cap Corse, Sartène and Calvi. IGP: Île de Beauté. Light, spicy reds from Sciacarello and more structured, tannic wines from Nielluccio; gd rosés; *tangy, herbal whites from Vermentino*. Top growers: Abbatucci, Antoine Arena, Clos d'Alzeto, Clos Capitoro, Gentile, Yves Leccia, Montemagni, Peraldi, Vaccelli, Saperale, Fiumicicoli, Torraccia. Wines almost worth the journey.

Corton C d'O r (w) ★★★ 90' 95 96' 98 99' 01 02' 03' 05' 06 07 08 09' 10 The 160 ha classified as GRAND CRU is much too much – only a few Corton v'yds such as CLOS DU ROI, Bressandes, Le Rognet deserve it. These have weight and structure; others make appealing, softer reds. DRC involvement since 2009 will increase interest. Look for d'Ardhuy, BONNEAU DU MARTRAY, CHANDON DE BRIAILLES, Dubreuil-Fontaine, FAIVELEY, Camille Giroud, MÉO-CAMUZET, Senard, TOLLOT-BEAUT. Occasional whites, eg. HOSPICES DE BEAUNE.

Corton-Charlemagne C d'O w ★★★★ 99' 00' 02' 03 04 05' 06 07 08 09' 10 Southwest and west exposure of hill of Corton, plus a band round the top, all more suited to white wines. Intense minerality and great ageing potential, often insufficiently realized. Top growers: BONNEAU DU MARTRAY, COCHE-DURY, FAIVELEY, HOSPICES DE BEAUNE, JADOT, P Javillier, LATOUR, Rapet, Rollin, VOUGERAIE.

Costières de Nîmes S Rhô r p w ★→★★ 06 07' 09' 10 Underrated region. Red: full, spiced, ages 6–8 yrs, gd value. Main names: CHX de Campuget, Grande Cassagne, Mas des Bressades, Mas Carlot, Mas Neuf, Mourgues-du-Grès, Nages, d'Or et des Gueules, Roubaud, de la Tuilerie; DOMS de la Patience, Tardieu-Laurent, du Vieux Relais. Lively rosés, stylish whites from Roussanne.

Côte Chalonnaise Burg r w sp ★★ Region south of CÔTE D'OR vineyards; lower prices. BOUZERON for ALIGOTÉ, *Mercurey* and GIVRY for structured reds and interesting whites, RULLY for lighter wines in both colours, MONTAGNY for its leaner CHARD.

Côte d'Or Burg *Département* name applied to the central and principal Burgundy v'yd slopes: CÔTE DE BEAUNE and CÔTE DE NUITS. Not used on labels. BOURGOGNE Côte d'Or AC under discussion.

Côte de Beaune C d'O r w ★★→★★★★ Used geographically: the southern half of the CÔTE D'OR. Applies as an AC only to top of hill above BEAUNE itself.

Côte de Beaune-Villages C d'O r ★★ 05' 07 08 09' 10 Red wines from the lesser villages of the southern half of the CÔTE D'OR. Rarely exciting.

Côte de Brouilly Beauj r ★★ 05' 07 08 09' 10 Flanks of the hillside above BROUILLY, one of the richest BEAUJOLAIS *cru*. Try from J-P Brun, L Martray or CH Thivin.

Côte de Nuits r (w) ★★→★★★★ Northern half of CÔTE D'OR. Mostly red wine.

Côte de Nuits-Villages C d'O r (w) ★★ 02' 03 05' 06 07 08 09' 10 Junior AC for extreme north and south ends of CÔTE DE NUITS; well worth investigating for bargains. Single-v'yd versions appearing. Try Ardhuy, Jourdan, Chopin, Gachot-Monot.

Côte Roannaise Lo r p ★→★★ 05' 06 08 09' (10) Small AC (215 ha) on lower slopes of the high granite hills west of Roanne, northwest of Lyon. Silky, focused Gamay. DOMS du Fontenay, Lapandéry, des Millets, du Pavillon, Robert Sérol, Vial. Also white IGP from CHARD and Viognier.

Côte-Rôtie N Rhô r ★★★→★★★★ 78' 85' 88' 89' 90' 91' 94' 95' 98' 99' 00 01' 03' 04 05' 06' 07' 08 09' 10' Finest Rhône red, mainly Syrah, touch of Viognier. Aromatic, floral, complex, very fine with age (esp 5–10+ yrs). Top: Barge (traditional), Bernard, Bonnefond (oak), Bonserine (GUIGAL-owned), CHAPOUTIER, Clusel-Roch (organic), DELAS, Duclaux, Gaillard (oak), J-M Gérin (oak), GUIGAL (own oaked style), Jamet (wonderful), Jamin, Monteillet, S Ogier (oak), ROSTAING, J-M Stéphan (organic), VIDAL-FLEURY (La Chatillonne).

Coteaux Champenois Champ r w (p) ★★★ DYA (whites). AC for non-sparkling CHAMPAGNE. Vintages follow those for CHAMPAGNE. Not worth inflated prices.

Coteaux d'Aix-en-Provence Prov r p w ★★→★★★ Sprawling AC from hills north of Aix and on plain around Etang de Berre. A fruit salad of grape varieties, both Bordelais and Midi. Reds are best, esp from CHX Beaupré, Calissanne, Revelette, les Bastides, la Realtière, les Béates, Bas. See also LES BAUX-EN-PROVENCE. Sometimes lacks real identity.

Coteaux d'Ancenis Lo r p w (sw) ★ Generally DYA VDQS (180 ha) – slopes on both banks of the Loire, east of Nantes. Chiefly for dry, DEMI-SEC and sweet Chenin Bl whites plus age-worthy Malvoisie; also light reds and rosés, mainly Gamay plus Cab Fr and Cab Sauv. Esp Guindon but also Athimon et ses Enfants. Promotion to AC status expected in 2011.

Coteaux de Glanes SW r ★★ DYA Lively, gd-value IGP, nr Beaulieu-sur-Dordogne. Eight growers run their own co-op. Merlot/Gamay/Ségalin blend local best-seller.

Coteaux de l'Ardèche S Rhô r p (w) ★ ★★★ Streams and valleys area west of Rhône, plenty of choice, gd value. New DOMS; fresh reds, some oaked; Viognier (eg. Mas de Libian, CHAPOUTIER) and Marsanne. Best from Syrah, also Gamay, Cab Sauv (Serret). Burgundian-style CHARD Ardèche by LOUIS LATOUR; Grand Ardèche from mature vines, but oaked. DOMS du Colombier, J & E Durand, Favette, Flacher, Grangeon, Mazel, Vigier, CH de la Selve.

Coteaux de l'Aubance Lo w sw ★★→★★★★ 89' 90' 95' 96' 97' 02 03 **05**' 06' 07' 09 (10) Small AC for sweet whites from Chenin Bl. Nervier, less sumptuous than COTEAUX DU LAYON except when SÉLECTIONS DES GRAINS NOBLES. Overall slopes more gentle than in Layon. Often gd value. Esp Bablut, Haute-Perche, Montgilet, CH Princé, Richou, Rochelles.

Coteaux de Pierrevert Prov r p w ★ Cool area producing quaffable wines from high v'yds nr Manosque. DOM la Blaque, CH Régusse, CH Rousset. AC since 1998.

Coteaux de Saumur Lo w sw ★★ →★★★ 03 05 07 (10) Sweet Chenin Bl. A tradition revived since 1989 – resembles COTEAUX DU LAYON but less rich. Often citric flavours. Esp DOM DES CHAMPS FLEURIS/Retiveau-Retif, CLOS ROUGEARD, Régis Neau (Dom de Nerleux), Vatan (CH de Hureau).

Coteaux des Baronnies S Rhô r p w ★ DYA Rhône VDP hills nr VINSOBRES. Syrah, Cab Sauv, Merlot, CHARD, plus traditional grapes. Light reds, also Viognier. Note DOMS du Rieu-Frais, Rosière.

Coteaux du Giennois Lo r p w ★ DYA Small appellation (190 ha) north of POUILLY. Scattered v'yds (Cosne to Gien). Light reds hampered by unconvincing, imposed blend of Gamay and Pinot N; Sauv Bl like junior SANCERRE (better than the reds). Best: Emile Balland, BOURGEOIS, Catherine & Michel Langlois, Paulat, Villargeau.

Coteaux du Languedoc L'doc r p w ★★ →★★★ **03 04 05 06** 07 08 09 10 A sprawling AC from Narbonne to Nîmes, with various crus and sub-divisions. Newer names are GRÈS DE MONTPELLIER, TERRASSES DU LARZAC and PÉZENAS, and Sommières. New estates galore demonstrating exciting potential of the MIDI. Destined to disappear in 2012 as larger AC LANGUEDOC, created 2007, is established, Hierachy of grands vins and GRANDS CRUS being created for 2011.

Coteaux du Layon Lo w sw s/sw ★★ →★★★★ 89 90 95 96 97 02 03 **05**' 07' 09 (10) Heart of ANJOU: sweet Chenin Bl, lush with admirable acidity, best almost everlasting. New SÉLECTION DES GRAINS NOBLES. Seven villages (300 ha) can add name to AC. Top ACS: BONNEZEAUX, QUARTS DE CHAUME. Growers: Baudouin, BAUMARD, Delesvaux, des Forges, DOM les Grands Vignes, Guegniard, DOM de Juchepie, Ogereau, Papin (CH PIERRE-BISE), Pithon-Paillé.

Coteaux du Loir Lo r p w dr sw→★★★ 02 03 04 05' 07 08 09 (10) Northern tributary of the Loire, Le Loir is small but dynamic region with Coteaux du Loir (80 ha) and JASNIÈRES (65 ha). Potentially fine, apple-scented Chenin Bl, Gamay, peppery Pineau d'Aunis that goes well with pungent cheeses, Grolleau (rosé), Cabernet and Côt. Top growers: Ange Vin, DOM DE BELLIVIERE, Le Briseau, Fresneau, Vins Gigou, Les Maisons Rouges, de Rycke.

Coteaux du Lyonnais Beauj r p (w) ★ DYA Junior BEAUJOLAIS. Best *en primeur*.

Coteaux du Quercy SW r ★ 05' 06 08 (09') (10) VDQS south of CAHORS. Cab Fr-based wines; best from ★★ DOM du Merchien, ★ DOMS de la Combarade, de Guyot, de Lafage, Lagarde. Successful and go-ahead ★ co-op.

Coteaux du Tricastin S Rhô *See* GRIGNAN-LES-ADHÉMAR.

Coteaux du Vendômois Lo r p w ★→★★ DYA Marginal Loire AC west of Vendôme (152 ha). The most characteristic wines are VINS GRIS from Pinot d'Aunis grape, which also gives peppery notes to red blends alongside Cab Fr, Pinot N, Gamay. Whites based on Chenin Bl and Chard. Producers: Patrice Colin, DOMS du Four à Chaux, J Martellière, Montrieux, Cave du Vendôme-Villiers.

Coteaux et Terrasses de Montauban SW r p w ★→★★ DYA ★★ Led by pioneering DOM de Montels, which invented this appellation single-handed. Local co-op at Lavilledieu-du-Temple has folded.

Coteaux Varois-en-Provence Prov r p w ★→★★★ 01 02 03 04 05' 06 07 08 Sandwiched between COTEAUX D'AIX and CÔTES DE PROVENCE. Gd source of warming reds and fresh rosés; deserves better reputation but still lacks a leader. Try CHX la Calisse, Miraval, DOM les Alysses, du Deffends.

Côtes Catalanes Rouss r p w ★→★★ The best IGP of ROUSSILLON, covering most of area. Exciting source of innovation and investment. Growers: Matassa, La Préceptorié Centernach, CH de Casenove, DOMS Gérard Gauby, Olivier Pithon, Padié, des Soulanes, le Soula.

Côtes d'Auvergne Mass C r p (w) ★→★★ Generally DYA Small new AC (412 ha), Nov 2010. Mainly Gamay, though some Pinot N (blend only) and CHARD. Best reds improve 2–3 yrs. Best villages: Boudes, Chanturgue, Châteaugay, Madargues (reds); Corent (rosé). Producers: Cave St-Verny, Jean Maupertuis, Sauvat.

Côtes de Bordeaux B'x 09 New appellation launched in 2008 (*see* box p. 89). Mainly red. Embraces and permits cross-blending between CASTILLON, FRANCS, BLAYE and CADILLAC (formerly Premières Côtes de Bordeaux).

Côtes de Bourg B'x r w ★→★★ 00' 01 02 03 04 05' 08 09' AC for robust red and (v. little) white from east of the Gironde. Steady quality. Top CHX: Brûlesécaille, Bujan, Civrac, *Falfas*, Fougas, Grand-Maison, Guerry, Haut-Guiraud, Haut-Maco, Haut Mondésir, Macay, Mercier, Nodoz, *Roc de Cambes*, Rousset, Sociondo.

Côtes de Duras SW r p w ★→★★★ 06 08 (09') (10) BORDEAUX satellite. Injection of new talent from ★★★ DOMS Chator, Mouthes-les-Bihan, Petit Malromé, and CHX Condom Perceval, also more established ★★ des Allegrets, Lafon and Laulan. Co-op (Berticot) dull, despite help from star consultant MICHEL ROLLAND.

Côtes de Gascogne SW w (r p) ★ DYA IGP. Exports from here exceed those of the rest of the SW put together. Quaffable style led by Plaimont co-op and Grassa family (CH de Tariquet). Try ★★ DOMS d'Arton, Chiroulet, Millet, Pellehaut, de San Guilhem. Otherwise ★ CH Monluc, des Cassagnoles, Higiuière, de Jöy, de Laballe, de Lauroux, de Magnaut, Papolle, St Lannes, Sédouprat. Also from MADIRAN growers, notably BRUMONT. And IGPS Gers and Terroirs Landais, which adjoin and often use the Gascon name.

Côtes de Millau SW r p w DYA Six independents inc ★★ DOM du Vieux Noyer work alongside co-op, their promotion assisted by Norman Foster's famous Tarn viaduct.

Côtes de Montravel SW w dr sw ★★ 04 05' 07 09 (10) Sub-division of BERGERAC; the indigenous medium-sweet style is being sadly squeezed between MONTRAVEL SEC and HAUT-MONTRAVEL, which is really sweet.

Côtes de Provence Prov r p w ★→★★★ r 04 05 06 07 08 09 10 (p w DYA) Large AC known mainly for rosé; enjoying a huge leap in quality, thanks to investment. Satisfying reds and herbal whites. STE-VICTOIRE, Fréjus and La Londe subzones, Pierrefeu coming soon. Leaders inc Castel Roubine, Commanderie de Peyrassol,

DOMS Bernarde, de la Courtade, Léoube, *Gavoty* (superb), CH'X *d'Esclans*, de Selle and Clos Mireille, des Planes, Rabiéga, *Richeaume*, Rimauresq. *See* COTEAUX D'AIX, BANDOL.

Côtes de St-Mont SW r w p ★★ (r) 06 08 (09') (10) (p w) DYA Gers VDQS the fiefdom of *Producteurs Plaimont*, the most successful co-op in the southwest. Gd red from DOM des Maouries on MADIRAN borders. Same grapes as MADIRAN and PACHERENC.

Côtes de Thongue L'doc r w ★★ (DYA p w) Dynamic IGP, aspiring AOP (*see* box p. 65) from Hérault. Intriguing blends preferable to single varietals. Reds age. DOMS Arjolle, les Chemins de Bassac, la Croix Belle, Magellan, Monplézy, des Henrys.

Côtes de Toul Al r p w ★ DYA V. light wines from Lorraine; mainly VIN GRIS.

Côtes du Brulhois SW r p (w) ★→★★ 06 08 (09') (10) Nr Agen. Reds better than others from this growing area. Co-op works with independents Le Bois de Simon, CH la Bastide, Clos Pountet, DOMS Coujétou-Peyret and des Thermes. Some Tannat (obligatory) gives weight and character.

Côtes du Couchois Burg ★→★★ 05' 08 09' Subdistrict of BOURGOGNE rouge at southern end of CÔTE D'OR v'yds. Powerful reds, on the tannic side. Best grower: Alain Hasard.

Côtes du Forez Lo r p (sp) ★ DYA Loire AC (200 ha) nr St-Etienne for Gamay reds and rosés. Les Vignerons Foréziens, also Le Clos de Chozieux, Verdier et Logel. IGP: CHARD, PINOT GR, Viognier.

Côtes du Jura Jura r p w (sp) ★→★★ DYA Many light tints/tastes. ARBOIS more substantial.

Côtes du Rhône S Rhô r p w ★→★★ 09' 10' Vast zone across 170 communes in S Rhône. Big split between handmade quality and mass-produced. Mainly Grenache, also Syrah, Carignan. Best drunk young, even as PRIMEUR. Vaucluse area best, then Gard (Syrah). 2009, 2010 both well-fruited.

Côtes du Rhône-Villages S Rhô r p w ★→★★ 05' 06' 07' 09' 10' Punchy wine from 7,700 ha, inc the 17 best southern Rhône villages. Deliver fruit, spice, tannin, gd value; keen growers behind them. Red core is Grenache, with Syrah, Mourvèdre support. Improving whites, often with Viognier, Roussanne added to CLAIRETTE, Grenache Blanc – gd with food. *See* CAIRANNE, CHUSCLAN, LAUDUN, ST-GERVAIS, SABLET, SÉGURET, VISAN. New villages (2005): MASSIF D'UCHAUX (gd), PLAN DE DIEU (robust), PUYMÉRAS, SIGNARGUES. Try: CHX Fontségune, Signac, DOMS Cabotte, Chaume-Arnaud, Deforge, Grand Moulas, Grand Veneur, Jérome, Montbayon, DOMS de *Mourchon*, Rabasse-Charavin, Renjarde, Romarins, Ste-Anne, St Siffrein, Saladin, Valériane, Vieux Chêne, Viret, Mas de Libian, Cave Estézargues, Cave Rasteau.

Top Côtes du Rhône producers
La Courançonne, Domazan, l'Estagnol, Fonsalette (sheer class), Grand Moulas, Haut-Musiel, Hugues, Montfaucon, St-Estève, Trignon (inc Viognier); Co-ops CAIRANNE, Chantecotes (Ste-Cécile-les-Vignes), Puyméras, RASTEAU, Villedieu (esp white); Cave Estézargues, DOMS Bramadou, Charvin, Combebelle, Coudoulet de BEAUCASTEL (classy r), Cros de la Mûre (gt value), M Dumarcher, Espiguette, Ferrand, Gourget, Gramenon (biodynamic), Janasse, Jaume, Perrin & Fils, Réméjeanne, Romarins, Rouge-Bleu, Soumade, Vieille Julienne, Vieux Chêne; DUBOEUF, GUIGAL, JABOULET.

Côtes du Roussillon Rouss r p w ★→★★ 04 05' 06 07' 08 09 10 East Pyrénées AC, covers v'yds of Pyrénées-Orientales behind Perpignan. Dominated by co-ops, notably Vignerons Catalans. Warming red is best, predominantly from Carignan and Grenache.

Côtes du Roussillon des Aspres Rouss AC since 2003 for reds only. Similar to basic CÔTES DU ROUSSILLON. Rarely found outside area. Based on Grenache Noir, Carignan, Syrah and Mourvèdre.

Côtes du Roussillon-Villages Rouss r ★★ 04 05 06 07 08 09 10 28 villages form best part of region. Dominated by Vignerons Catalans. Best labels: DOMS des Chênes, CAZES, la *Cazenove*, GAUBY (also characterful white IGP), Piquemal, CH de Jau, Mas Crémat.

Côtes du Tarn SW r p w ★ DYA IGP overlaps GAILLAC; but ★★ DOM d'en Segur outside GAILLAC area v. serious producer, esp off-dry Sauv Bl.

Coulée de Serrant Lo w dr sw (★★★) 95 96 97 98 99 02 03 **04** 05 07 08 09 (10) A 7-ha Chenin Bl v'yd at SAVENNIÈRES. High priest of biodynamics Nicolas Joly's wines now below par (fail to match theory), but daughter Virginie now taking charge. Decant two hours ahead; don't chill. Old vintages can be sublime.

Courcel, Dom de C d'O ★★★ Leading POMMARD estate; top PREMIERS CRUS Rugiens and Epenots, plus interesting Croix Noires. Wines age well.

Crémant In CHAMPAGNE, meant "creaming" (half-sparkling). An AC for quality classic-method sparkling from ALSACE, Loire, BORDEAUX (1990), BOURGOGNE, and most recently LIMOUX – often a bargain. Term no longer used in CHAMPAGNE.

Crépy Sav w ★★ DYA Light, soft, Swiss-style white from south shore of Lake Geneva. *Crépitant* has been coined for its faint fizz.

Crozes-Hermitage N Rhô r w ★★ 05 06 07 09' 10' Syrah hill/plain v'yds (1,355 ha) flank the HERMITAGE hill. Plain zone gives fruity, early drinking (2–5 yrs). Best (simple CUVÉES) have dashing black fruit. Some oaked, gritty techno wines, all costing more. Top: Belle, Y Chave, CH Curson, Darnaud, DOMS du Colombier, Combier, des Entrefaux (oak), *A Graillot*, Hauts-Chassis, Lises, Mucyn, du Pavillon-Mercurol, de Thalabert of JABOULET, *Chapoutier, Delas* (Tour d'Albon, Le Clos v.gd). Drink white (Marsanne) early.

Cuve close Short-cut method of making sparkling wine in a tank. Sparkle dies away in glass much quicker than with *méthode traditionnelle* wine.

Cuvée Wine contained in a *cuve*, or vat. A word of many uses, inc synonym for "blend" and first-press wines (as in CHAMPAGNE); in Burgundy, interchangeable with *cru*. Often just refers to a "lot" of wine.

d'Angerville, Marquis C d'O ★★★★ One of VOLNAY's superstar DOMS with brilliant PREMIERS CRUS, inc Clos des Ducs (MONOPOLE), Champans and Taillepieds. Quality rising yet further of late. Biodynamic.

d'Eguisheim, Cave Vinicole Al ★★ V.gd ALSACE co-op for its size. Excellent value: fine GRANDS CRUS Hatschbourg, HENGST, Ollwiller, Spiegel. Owns Willm. Top label: WOLFBERGER. Best: Grande Réserve, Sigillé, Armorié. Gd CRÉMANT and Pinot N (esp 09 10').

Dagueneau, Didier Lo ★★★→★★★★ 02 03 04 05' 07 08' 09 (10) Best producer of POUILLY-FUMÉ by far and a master of stunningly pure Sauv Bl. Died in plane crash Sept 2008. Son Louis-Benjamin now in charge – very impressive. Top CUVÉES: Pur Sang, Silex and ungrafted and astronomically priced Asteroide. Also SANCERRE; small v'yd in CHAVIGNOL; JURANÇON

Dauvissat, Vincent Chab ★★★ Great producer using old methods for v. long-lived CHABLIS. Cousin of RAVENEAU. Best: Forest, Preuses, Les Clos.

Degré alcoolique Degrees of alcohol, ie. % by volume.

Deiss, Dom Marcel Al ★★★ High-profile grower at Bergheim. Favours blended wines from individual v'yd sites. Gewurz and Ries Schoenenbourg are his best wines. Less inconsistency than before. Now biodynamic.

Delamotte Champ BRUT; BLANC DE BLANCS (**99** 02 04); CUVÉE Nicholas Delamotte. Fine small CHARD-dominated CHAMPAGNE house at LE MESNIL. V.gd saignée Rosé.

Managed with SALON by LAURENT-PERRIER. "Library" stock of old vintages: **superb Blanc de Blancs (85')**.

Delas Frères N Rhô ★→★★★ Precise quality, v. deep range N Rhône merchant with CONDRIEU, CROZES-HERMITAGE, CÔTE-RÔTIE, HERMITAGE v'yds. Top wines: CONDRIEU (Clos Boucher), CÔTE-RÔTIE Landonne, HERMITAGE M de la Tourette (r, w), Les Bessards (v. fine, long life). Owned by ROEDERER.

Demi-sec Half-dry: in practice more like half-sweet (eg. of CHAMPAGNE).

Deutz Champ Brut Classic NV; Rosé NV; BRUT (00 02 04). Top-flight CHARD CUVÉE Amour de Deutz (02). One of top small houses, ROEDERER-owned. V. dry, classic wines. **Superb Cuvée William Deutz (98 02)**.

Dom Pérignon Champ CUVÉE 98 superb 02'; rosé 98 00 02' Luxury CUVÉE of MOËT ET CHANDON, named after legendary cellarmaster who first blended CHAMPAGNE. Astonishingly **consistent quality** and creamy character, esp with 10-15 yrs' bottle age. Late-disgorged *Oenothèque* releases 95' and magical DP rosé 90'.

Domaine (Dom) Property, particularly in Burgundy and rural France. *See* under name, eg. TEMPIER, Dom.

Dopff & Irion Al ★→★★ 17th-century ALSACE firm at Riquewihr, now part of PFAFFENHEIM. MUSCAT Les Amandiers, Gewurz Les Sorcières. Also gd CRÉMANT D'ALSACE.

Dopff au Moulin Al ★★★ Ancient top-class family wine house at Riquewihr. Best: Gewurz GRANDS CRUS Brand, Sporen; Ries Schoenenbourg; **Sylvaner de Riquewihr**. Pioneers of ALSACE CRÉMANT; gd CUVÉES: Bartholdi, Julien. All wines esp gd in natural dry-style vintages.

Dourthe, Vins & Vignobles BORDEAUX merchant; wide range, quality emphasis: gd, notably CHX BELGRAVE, LE BOSCQ, LA GARDE. Beau-Mayne, Pey La Tour, Dourthe No 1 are well-made generic BORDEAUX. Essence is concentrated and modern.

Drappier, André Champ Outstanding family-run AUBE CHAMPAGNE house. **Pinot-led** NV, Brut Zéro, Rosé Saignée, Signature Blanc de Blancs (02 04), Millésime d'Exception (02 04), superb Prestige Cuvée Grande Sendrée (99 02 04). New unsulphured BLANC DE NOIRS. Superb older vintages 95 85 82.

DRC C d'O The wine geek's shorthand for DOM DE LA ROMANÉE-CONTI.

Drouhin, J & Cie Burg ★★★→★★★★ Deservedly prestigious grower (61 ha) and merchant. Cellars in BEAUNE; v'yds in BEAUNE, CHABLIS, CLOS DE VOUGEOT, MUSIGNY, etc., and Oregon, USA. Best inc (white) Beaune **Clos des Mouches**, CHABLIS LES CLOS, CORTON-CHARLEMAGNE, PULIGNY-MONTRACHET, Les Folatières, (red) GRIOTTE-CHAMBERTIN, MUSIGNY, GRANDS-ÉCHÉZEAUX.

Duboeuf, Georges Beauj ★★→★★★ Most famous name of the BEAUJOLAIS, proponent of *nouveau*. Huge range of CUVÉES and *crus*, but has the lustre faded?

Duclot BORDEAUX négociant; top-growth specialist. Owner Jean-François MOUEIX.

Dugat C d'O ★★★ Cousins Claude and Bernard (Dugat-Py) make excellent, deep-coloured GEVREY-CHAMBERTIN, respective labels. Tiny volumes, huge prices.

Dujac, Dom C d'O ★★★→★★★★ MOREY-ST-DENIS grower now with exceptional range of GRANDS CRUS. Lighter colours but intense fruit, smoky, strawberry character from use of stems. Also DOM Triennes in COTEAUX VAROIS.

Dulong BORDEAUX merchant. Part of Grands Chais de France.

Durup, Jean Chab ★★ Volume producer as DOM de l'Eglantière and CH de Maligny now allied by marriage to DOM Colinot in IRANCY.

Duval-Leroy Champ Dynamic Côte des Blancs CHAMPAGNE house. 200 ha of family-owned v'yds source of gd Fleur de Champagne NV, fine Blanc de Chard (99 00 02 04), and excellent prestige **Femme** de Champagne (96' 02). New single-village/v'yd bottlings, esp Authentis Cumière (04 05 09).

Échézeaux C d'O r ★★★ 90' 93 96' 99' 02' 99' 02' 03 05' 06 07 08 09' 10 GRAND CRU (37.7 ha) next to CLOS DE VOUGEOT. Middling weight, can have exceptionally intricate flavours and startling persistence. Best from Arnoux, DRC, DUJAC, EUGNIE, GRIVOT, GROS, Lamarche, LIGER-BELAIR, Mugneret-Gibourg, ROUGET.

Ecu, Dom de l' Lo dr w r ★★★ 89 90 95 96 97 02 03 04 05 06 09' (10) Guy Bossard is a superb producer of biodynamic MUSCADET-SÈVRE-ET-MAINE (esp mineral-rich CUVÉE Granite) and GROS PLANT, inc sparkling from GROS PLANT, plus excellent Cab Fr. Tiny production 2007 (mildew) and 2008 (frost). Estate now for sale.

Edelzwicker Al w ★ DYA Blended light white. Delicious CH d'Ittenwiller (09).

Entraygues et du Fel and Estaing SW r p w DYA ★ Minerally, cool twin VDQS. Diminutive mountain appellations. Zinging white ★★ DOM Méjannassère and Laurent Mousset's reds, esp La Pauca (would keep). W from Nicolas Carmarans eagerly awaited. Alaux (r) and Fages (w) best Estaing growers.

Entre-Deux-Mers B'x w ★→★★ DYA Improved dry white BORDEAUX from between rivers Garonne and Dordogne (aka E-2-M). Only 1,500 ha. Best CHX BONNET, Castenet Greffier, Fontenille, Landereau, Marjosse, Nardique-la-Gravière, Sainte-Marie, *Tour de Mirambeau*, Toutigeac, Turcaud.

Esmonin, Dom Sylvie C d'O ★★★ Rich, dark wines from fully ripe grapes, esp since 2000. Notable GEVREY-CHAMBERTIN VIEILLES VIGNES and CLOS ST-JACQUES. Cousin Frédéric has Estournelles St-Jacques.

Eugénie, Dom C d'O New owners of former DOM Engel, bought by François Pinault of CH LATOUR in 2006. Now more concentrated wines at higher prices. CLOS VOUGEOT and GRANDS-ÉCHÉZEAUX best.

Faiveley, J Burg ★★→★★★★ More growers now than merchants with big holdings in CÔTE CHALONNAISE plus top v'yds in CHAMBERTIN-CLOS DE BÈZE, CHAMBOLLE-MUSIGNY, CORTON, NUITS and recent acquisitions in MEURSAULT and PULIGNY. Hugely revitalised since 2007.

Faller, Théo/Dom Weinbach Al ★★→★★★★ Founded by Capuchin monks in 1612, now run by Colette Faller and two daughters. Outstanding wines now often drier, esp GRANDS CRUS SCHLOSSBERG (Ries esp 02 **06**), Furstentum (Gewurz 05). Wines of great *character and elegance*. Great Cuvée Sainte Catherine Sélection des Grains Noble Gewurz 02.

Fèvre, William Chab ★★★ Star in CHABLIS since HENRIOT purchase in 1998. Biggest owner of GRANDS CRUS. Les Clos outstanding. No expense spared but it costs.

Fiefs Vendéens Lo r p w ★→★★★ Mainly DYA AC (460 ha). Easy-drinking wines from the Vendée close to Sables d'Olonne. CHARD, Chenin Bl, Sauv Bl, Melon (whites), Grolleau Gris, Cab Fr, Cab Sauv, Gamay, Negrette, Pinot N (reds and rosés). Top CUVÉES, esp from Michon/DOM St-Nicolas, are serious and age-worthy. Also Aloha, Coirier, CH Marie du Fou.

Fitou L'doc r w ★★ 04 05' 06 07' 08 09 10 Powerful red, from wild hills south of Narbonne as well as coastal v'yds. The Midi's oldest AC for table wine, created in 1948, 11 mths' barrel-ageing and benefits from bottle age. Co-op at Tuchan a pacesetter among co-ops. Experiments with Mourvèdre. Gd estates inc CH de Nouvelles, DOMS Bertrand Bergé, Lerys, de Rolland.

Fixin C d'O r (w) ★★★ **99'** 02' 03 **05'** 06 07 08 09' 10 Worthy and undervalued northern neighbour of GEVREY-CHAMBERTIN. Sometimes splendid reds. Best v'yds: Clos de la Perrière, Clos du Chapitre, Clos Napoléon. Growers inc CLAIR, FAIVELEY, Gelin, Guyard and revitalized Manoir de la Perrière.

Fleurie Beauj r ★★★ 05' 07 08 09' 10 Top BEAUJOLAIS *cru* for perfumed, strawberry fruit and silky texture to tingle the pleasure centres. Racier from La Madone hillside, richer below. Look for Chapelle des Bois, Chignard, Clos de la Roilette, Depardon, Desprès, DUBOEUF, CH de Fleurie, Métrat, Villa Ponciago, co-op.

Fourrier, Jean-Claude C d'O ★★★ Jean-Marie F has taken this quiet GEVREY-CHAMBERTIN DOM to new heights for profound yet succulent reds, esp Combe aux Moines, CLOS ST JACQUES.

Francs-Côtes de Bordeaux B'x r w ★★ oo' oɪ o3 o4 o5' o8 o9' Fringe BORDEAUX next to CASTILLON. Previously Côtes de Francs but new AC name from 2008. Mainly red but some white: tasty and attractive. Reds can age a little. Top CHX: Charmes-Godard, Francs, Laclaverie, Marsau, Pelan, La Prade, PUYGUERAUD.

Fronsac B'x r ★★ →★★★ 96 98 oo' oɪ o3 o5' o6 o8 o9' Underrated, hilly AC west of ST-EMILION; one of the best-value reds in BORDEAUX. Top CHX: DALEM, *la Dauphine*, Fontenil, la Grave, Haut-Carles, Mayne-Vieil, *Moulin-Haut-Laroque*, Richelieu, *la Rivière*, la Rousselle, Tour du Moulin, les Trois Croix, LA VIEILLE CURE, Villars. *See also* CANON-FRONSAC.

Fronton SW r p ★★ o8 (o9') (ɪo) Local speciality grape (Négrette) gives these wines a fruitier-scented nose and palate than many. The ideal wine for cassoulet (not too heavy; Toulouse is nearby). Watch for DOMS de Caze, Joliet, du Roc, CHX Baudare, *Bellevue-la-Forêt*, Boissel, Boujac, Cahuzac, Cransac, Plaisance, Viguerie de Belaygues.

Gagnard C d'O ★★★ Well-known clan in CHASSAGNE-MONTRACHET. Long-lasting wines, esp Caillerets, Bâtard from Jean-Noël Gagnard while Blain-G and Fontaine G have full range as far as MONTRACHET itself.

Gaillac SW r p w d sw sp ★→★★★ AC at last finding its feet. p dr w DYA. Reds (esp oaked) o5' o6 o8 (o9') (ɪo). sw w o5' o7' o8 (o9') (ɪo). ★★★ PLAGEOLES, Causse-Marines, de la Ramaye, L'Enclos des Roses, ★★ DOMS de Brin, Cailloutis, la Chanade, d'Escausses, Gineste, Larroque, Mayragues (biodynamic), Peyres-Roses (biodynamic), Rotier, Salmes, Sarrabelle, CHX Bourguet, Palvié. Gd all-rounders ★★ DOMS de Labarthe, Mas Pignou, La Vayssette, Mas d'Aurel.

Garage B'x *Vins de garage* are (usually) BORDEAUX made on a v. small scale. Rigorous winemaking, but a bottle costs much the same as a full service.

Gard, Vin de Pays du L'doc ★ The Gard *département* west of the Rhône estuary gives sound IGP reds, inc Cévenne, du Pont du Gard, SABLES DU GOLFE DU LION. Duché d'Uzès an aspiring AOP.

Gauby, Dom Gérard Rouss r w ★★★ Pioneering producer. *L'histoire, c'est moi!* White VIN DE PAYS DES CÔTES CATALANES Les Calcinaires; Coume Ginestre; red CÔTES DU ROUSSILLON-VILLAGES called Muntada; Les Calcinaires VIELLES VIGNES. Associated with IGP Le Soula. Dessert wine: Le Pain du Sucre: biodynamic. Son Lionel following in father's footsteps.

Gevrey-Chambertin C d'O r ★★→★★★ 90' 96' 98 99' oɪ o2' o3 o5' o6 o7 o8 o9' ɪo Village containing the great CHAMBERTIN, its GRAND CRU cousins and many other noble v'yds eg. PREMIERS CRUS Cazetiers, Combe aux Moines, Combottes, CLOS ST-JACQUES. Top growers inc Bachelet, L BOILLOT, BURGUET, Damoy, DROUHIN, Drouhin-Laroze, DUGAT, Dugat-Py, ESMONIN, FAIVELEY, FOURRIER, Géantet-Pansiot, Harmand-Geoffroy, JADOT, LEROY, MORTET, Rossignol-Trapet, ROTY, ROUSSEAU, SÉRAFIN, TRAPET, Varoilles.

Gigondas S Rhô r p ★★ →★★★ 78' 89' 90' 95' 98' 99' oo' oɪ' o3' o4' o5' o6' o7' o8 o9' ɪo' Hill-and-plain 1,200-ha vy'ds east of Avignon; Grenache, plus Syrah, Mourvèdre. Robust, peppery wines, best gd clear fruit. Increase of oak, esp for US market. Genuine local feel in many. Try: CH de Montmirail, St-Cosme (oak), Clos du Joncuas, P Amadieu, DOM Boissan, Bouïssière, Brusset, Cassan, Espiers, Goubert, Gour de Chaulé, Grapillon d'Or, Oustet Fauquet, les Pallières, Raspail-Ay, Roubine, St-Gayan, Santa Duc, Perrin & Fils. Rosés often heavy.

Ginestet B'x Go-ahead BORDEAUX négociant. Quality controls for grape suppliers. Principal brands G de Ginestet, Marquis de Chasse, Mascaron.

Girardin, Vincent C d'O r w ★★→★★★ Small grower turned dynamic négociant reconverting to grower on larger scale, esp whites from MEURSAULT and PULIGNY. Modern but fine.

FRANCE

Givry Burg r (w) ★★ 05' 06 07 08 09' 10 Unsung village of CÔTE CHALONNAISE, with tasty reds for medium-term ageing. JOBLOT, Clos Salomon, F Lumpp best.

Gosset Champ Old house founded in 16th century, making CHAMPAGNES in vinous style. Now works out of new premises in Épernay. V.gd Cuvée Elegance NV. Tradtional Grand Millésime (**99** 02). Gosset Celebris (**98 99** 02) is finest CUVÉE. Remarkable Celebris Rosé (03).

Gouges, Henri C d'O ★★★ Grégory G continuing success of previous generation with rich, meaty, long-lasting NUITS-ST-GEORGES from a range of PREMIER CRU v'yds. Try Vaucrains, Les St Georges, or Chaignots. Interesting white, too.

Grand Cru Means different things in different areas. One of top Burgundy v'yds with its own AC. In ALSACE, one of the 51 top v'yds covered by ALSACE GRAND CRU AC. In ST-EMILION, 60% of the production is covered by the ST-EMILION *grand cru* AC. In the MÉDOC there are five tiers of Grands Crus Classés. In CHAMPAGNE the top villages are *grand cru*. Now a new designation for best bits of LANGUEDOC.

Grande Champagne SW The AC of the best area of Cognac. Nothing fizzy about it.

Grande Rue, La C d'O ★★★ 90' **95 96'** 98 00 02' 03 05' 06 07 08 09' 10 Narrow strip of VOSNE-ROMANÉE GRAND CRU (since 1991). MONOPOLE of DOM Lamarche now starting to make fine wines again.

Grands-Échézeaux C d'O r ★★★★ **90' 93 95 96'** 99' 00 02' 03 05' 06 07 08 09' 10 Superlative 9-ha GRAND CRU next to CLOS DE VOUGEOT may be more akin to MUSIGNY. Wines not weighty but aromatic. Viz: DRC, DROUHIN, EUGÉNIE, GROS, Lamarche, Mongeard-Mugneret.

Grange des Pères, Dom de la L'doc r w ★★★ IGP Pays de l'Hérault. Cult estate neighbouring MAS DE DAUMAS GASSAC, created by Laurent Vaillé for first vintage 1992. Red from Syrah, Mourvèdre, Cab Sauv; white Roussanne 80% plus Marsanne, CHARD. Original wines; well worth seeking out.

Gratien, Alfred and Gratien & Meyer Champ ★★→★★★ Brut NV; BRUT **97' 98** 00 02 04. Superb Prestige Cuvée Paradis Brut and Rosé (blend of fine yrs). Excellent quirky house, now German-owned. Fine, v. dry, lasting barrel-fermented wine inc *The Wine Society's house Champagne*. Gratien & Meyer is counterpart at SAUMUR. (Gd Cuvée Flamme.)

Graves B'x r w ★ →★★ 00 01 04 05' **06 08** 09' South of BORDEAUX city with soft, earthy red; dry white more consistent. Gd value. Top CHX: ARCHAMBEAU, CHANTEGRIVE, *Clos Floridène*, Crabitey, l'Hospital, Léhoul, Respide, *Respide-Médeville*, St-Robert CUVÉE Poncet Deville, Venus, Vieux CH Gaubert, Villa Bel Air.

Graves de Vayres B'x r w ★ DYA Tiny AC within E-2-M. Mainly red, drunk locally.

Grès de Montpellier L'doc r p w Recently recognized subzone of AC LANGUEDOC sprawling v'yds in the hills behind Montpellier, inc St-Georges d'Orques, La Méjanelle, St-Christol, St-Drézery. Try Clavel, Terre Megère, St Martin de la Garrigue, Prose, Grès St Paul, CH de Flaugergues.

Grignan-les-Adhémar S Rhô r (p) w ★→★★ **07' 09'** 10 Change of name from Coteaux de Tricastin due to nearby nuclear-plant troubles 2008–9. Mid-Rhône AC, narrow focus of quality, best reds full, tangy. Leaders: DOMS de Bonetto-Fabrol, Grangeneuve best (esp VIEILLES VIGNES), de Montine (gd white), St-Luc and CH La Décelle (inc white CÔTES DU RHÔNE).

Griotte-Chambertin C d'O r ★★★★ 90' **95 96' 97** 99' 00 02' 03 05' 06 07 08 09' 10 Small GRAND CRU next to CHAMBERTIN. Less weight but brisk red fruit and ageing potential, at least from DUGAT, DROUHIN, FOURRIER, PONSOT.

Grivot, Jean C d'O ★★★→★★★★ Huge improvements at this VOSNE-ROMANÉE DOM in the past decade. Superb range topped by GRANDS CRUS CLOS DE VOUGEOT, ÉCHÉZEAUX, RICHEBOURG.

Gros Plant du Pays Nantais Lo w ★ DYA AC. From Gros Plant (Folle Blanche in

Cognac), best crisply citric – great with oysters but v'yds diminishing (1,400 ha). Try: DOM Basse Ville, Bâtard, Luneau-Papin, CH de la Preuille.

Gros, Doms C d'O ★★★→★★★★ Fine family in VOSNE-ROMANÉE comprising (at least) DOMS Jean, Michel, Anne, Anne-Françoise Gros and Gros Frère & Soeur. Wines range from HAUTES CÔTES DE NUITS to RICHEBOURG.

Guelasses, Dom des r w Pretty nasty overoaked production happily less common than formerly.

Guffens-Heynen Burg ★★★★ Belgian MÂCON and POUILLY-FUISSÉ grower. Tiny quantity, top quality. Also négociant operation for rest of Burgundy as VERGET.

Guigal, E N Rhô ★★→★★★★ World-famous grower-merchant: 31-ha CÔTE-RÔTIE is base, plus CONDRIEU, CROZES-HERMITAGE, HERMITAGE, ST-JOSEPH. Merchant: CONDRIEU, CÔTE-RÔTIE, CROZES-HERMITAGE, HERMITAGE, S Rhône. Owns DOM de Bonserine, VIDAL-FLEURY (improving). Top CÔTE-RÔTIE La Mouline, La Landonne, La Turque (v. rich, new oak for 42 mths, so atypical); all reds seek scale. Standard wines: gd value, consistent, esp v.gd-value red, also white, rosé CÔTES DU RHÔNE. Also fat, oaky CONDRIEU La Doriane, sound HERMITAGE white.

Haut-Médoc B'x r ★★→★★★ 96 98 00' 01 02 03 04 05' 06 08 09' 4,600 ha. Source of gd-value, minerally, digestible wines. Some variation in soils and wines: sand and gravel in south; finer, heavier clay and gravel in north; sturdier. Five classed growths (eg. CANTEMERLE, LA LAGUNE, LA TOUR-CARNET). Other top CHX: D'AGASSAC, Belle-Vue, SÉNÉJAC, SOCIANDO-MALLET.

Haut-Montravel SW w sw ★★★ 03 05' 06 07 (08) (09') (10) Small but fine sub-AC of BERGERAC with different terroir from MONBAZILLAC or SAUSSIGNAC. Best (esp when kept): CH Puy-Servain-Terrement and DOMS Moulin Caresse and Libarde.

Haut-Poitou Lo r w p sp ★→★★ Top age 3–4 yrs. Promoted AC (Nov 2010; 800 ha) from Cab Sauv, Cab Fr, Gamay, CHARD, Pinot N, Sauv Bl. Cave du Haut-Poitou is largest producer (60%+; top wine: CH La Fuye); now 32 individual growers, with Ampelidae top producer (but using IGP).

Hautes-Côtes de Beaune/Nuits C d'O r w ★→★★ r 05' 06 07 08 w 05' 06' 07 08 09' ACS for the villages in the hills behind the CÔTE DE BEAUNE. Attractive, lighter reds and whites for early drinking. Best: Cornu, Devevey, Duband, DOMS Carré, GROS, Jacob, Jayer-Gilles, Mazilly. Also useful large co-op nr BEAUNE.

Heidsieck Monopole Champ Once-illustrious house. Silver Top (2002) best wine.

Heidsieck, Charles Champ Major house giving top quality but now up for sale. Buy mature stocks now. Brut Reserve NV. Vintage 95' & Rosé 96'. Outstanding Blanc des Millénaires (95'). *See also* PIPER-HEIDSIECK.

Hengst Al ALSACE GRAND CRU. Excels with top Gewurz from ZIND-HUMBRECHT and JOSMEYER; also Pinot-Auxerrois, Chasselas and Pinot N (not GRAND CRU).

Henriot Champ BRUT Souverain NV; Blanc de Blancs de Chard NV; BRUT 95 96 98; BRUT Rosé 99 02. Fine family house. Elegant, fresh, creamy style. Outstanding Prestige Cuvée Les Enchanteleurs (88' 95' 96). Also owns BOUCHARD PÈRE ET FILS (since 1995) and FÈVRE.

Hermitage N Rhô r w ★★★→★★★★ 61' 66' 78' 83' 85' 88 89' 90' 91' 95' 96 97' 98' 99' 00 01' 03' 04 05' 06' 07' 09' 10' Lingering, rich Syrah from mighty 133-ha granite-based hill, east bank of Rhône. Red, white repay ageing over 20+ yrs. Abundant, fascinating white (Marsanne, some Roussanne) best left for 6–7 yrs or more. Best: Belle, CHAPOUTIER, J-L CHAVE, Colombier, DELAS, Desmeure (oak), Faurie (pure wines), GUIGAL, Habrard (white), JABOULET, M Sorrel, Tardieu-Laurent (oak). TAIN co-op gd (esp Epsilon, Gambert de Loche).

Hortus, Dom de l' L'doc r p w ★★★ Pioneering producer of PIC ST-LOUP. Also IGP Val de Montferrand. Stylish wines; reds Bergerie and oak-aged Grande Réserve. Also red Clos du Prieur in Terrasses du Larzac.

Hospices de Beaune C d'O Grand charity auction on 3rd Sunday in Nov, revitalized since 2005 by Christie's. Individuals can now buy as well as trade. Standards should be more consistent, but excellent buys among BEAUNE CUVÉES or expensive GRANDS CRUS, eg. CLOS DE LA ROCHE, CORTON (r), BÂTARD-MONTRACHET (w).

Hudelot C d'O ★★★ VIGNERON family in CÔTE DE NUITS. New life breathed into H-Noëllat (VOUGEOT) while H-Baillet (CHAMBOLLE) challenging hard. Former more stylish, latter more punchy.

Huet Lo ★★★→★★★★ 88 89' 90' 95' 96' 97' 02' 03' 05' **06** 07 08' 09' Biodynamic estate in VOUVRAY. Anthony Hwang (owner), who also has the Királyudvar estate in Tokaj. Noël Pinguet, Gaston Huet's son-in-law, continues to run the estate. Three single v'yds: Le Haut Lieu, Le Mont, Clos du Bourg. Wonderful precision and great agers: look for ancient vintages such as 1919, 1924, 1947, 1959 and 1964. Also *pétillant*. A world benchmark for Chenin Bl.

Hugel & Fils Al ★★→★★★ Big house, making superb late-harvest wines. Three quality levels: Classic, Tradition, Jubilee. Top wines from GRANDS CRUS but never mentioned on label.

IGP Indication Géographique Protegée: the successor to VIN DE PAYS. No difference in status, only in name.

Irancy Burg r (p) ★★ 05' **06** 08 09' Light red made nr CHABLIS from Pinot N and local César. More interest in single-v'yd wines. Best: *Colinot*, Richoux, Goisot.

Irouléguy SW r p (w) ★→★★★ 04 05' **06** 08 (09') (10) Big production of rosé (DYA) to satisfy summer visitors to this Basque AC. Tannat-based reds are cultural match for *pelota*, bull-fighting and rugby. Note gd white ★★★ Xuri d Ansa from pioneering co-op and ★★★ Ameztia, Arretxea, Brana, Ilarria and ★★ Abotia, Bordathio, Etchegaraya and Mourguy.

Jaboulet Aîné, Paul N Rhô 19th-century owner-merchant at TAIN, sold to Swiss investor early 2006, wines are international, prices up. Once leading maker of HERMITAGE (esp La Chapelle ★★★, quality varies 1990s on), CORNAS St-Pierre, CROZES Thalabert, Roure; merchant of other Rhônes, notably CÔTES DU RHÔNE Parallèle 45, CONDRIEU, VENTOUX, VACQUEYRAS. Whites low on body, drink most young. Branded goods now the game, inc new v. expensive La Chapelle white.

Jacquart Champ Brut NV; Brut Rosé NV (Carte Blanche and Cuvée Spéciale); BRUT 00 02 04. Co-op-based CHAMPAGNE brand; in quantity the sixth largest. Improving quality. Luxury brands: Cuvée Nominée Blanc 00 02 04. Fine Mosaïque Blancs de Blancs 02 04 and Rosé 02 04. *Oenothèque* older vintages now launched.

Jacquesson Champ Bijou Dizy house. Superb Avize GRAND CRU 96' now relaunched as single-vineyard Champ Caïn 02': white (90 95 96'), new *saignée* skin-contact rosé Terre Rouge (04). Corne Bautray, Dizy 02 04 and *excellent numbered NV Cuvées* 728, 729, 730', 731, 732, 733, 734.

Jadot, Louis Burg ★★→★★★★ High-performance merchant house across the board with significant v'yd holdings in CÔTE D'OR and expanding fast in MÂCON and BEAUJOLAIS; esp POUILLY FUISSÉ (DOM Ferret) and MOULIN-À-VENT (CH des Jacques, Clos du Grand Carquelin). Mineral whites as gd as structured reds.

Jasnières Lo w dr (sw) ★★→★★★ 97 02 03 05' 06 07 08' 09' (10) VOUVRAY-like wine (Chenin Bl), both dry and off-dry from a tiny (65 ha) but v. dynamic v'yd north of Tours on south-facing slopes around La Chartre-sur-le-Loir. Top growers: L'Ange Vin, Aubert la Chapelle, DOMS DE BELLIVIÈRE, le Briseau, Freseneau, Gigou, les Maisons Rouges, Ryke.

Jobard C d'O VIGNERON family in MEURSAULT. Antoine, son of François, for long-lived Genevrières, etc. Cousin Rémi for more immediate class. Both ★★★.

Joblot Burg ★★★ Outstanding GIVRY DOM with v. high viticultural standards. Try PREMIER CRU La Servoisine in both colours.

Joseph Perrier Champ Improved Cuvée Royale Brut NV with lower *dosage*; Cuvée Royale Blanc de Blancs NV; Cuvée Royale Rosé NV; BRUT 99 00 02. Excellent smaller house at Châlons with gd v'yds in Marne Valley. Supple, fruity style; top Prestige Cuvée Joséphine 98 02 ★★★★.

Josmeyer Al ★★ →★★★ Specializes in fine, elegant, long-lived organic wines in dry style. Superb Ries Grand Cru Hengst. Also v.gd wines from lesser varietals, esp Auxerrois. Exceptional wines 2002, 2009. Intelligent biodynamists.

Juliénas Beauj r ★★★ 05' 07 08 09' 10 Leading *cru* of BEAUJOLAIS: vigorous, fruity wine to keep 2–3 yrs. Growers inc CHX du Bois de la Salle, des Capitans, de Juliénas, des Vignes; DOMS Bottière, du Chapon, Monnet, Michel Tête, co-op.

Jurançon SW w dr sw ★ →★★★ (sw) 97' 03 04' 05' 06 07' (09) (10) (dr) 04' 05' 06 (08') (09') (10) Great Pyrénéan success-story. Sweet and dry have separate ACS. Boutique ★★★★ Jardins de Babylon (Benjamin DAGUENEAU) in class (and price) of its own. ★★★ DOMS Bellegarde, Bordenave, Castéra, Cauhapé, Lapeyre, Larrédya, Girouilh, de Souch, Uroulat, Vignau-la-Juscle, ★★ DOMS Capdevielle, Nigri, Bellevue, Guirardel and Thou. Gd-value dry whites from co-op.

Kaefferkopf Al w dr (sw) ★★★ Since 2006 the 51st GRAND CRU of ALSACE at Ammerschwihr. Permitted to make blends as well as varietal wines.

Kientzler, Andre Al ★★ →★★★ Small, v. fine ALSACE grower at Ribeauvillé. V.gd Ries from GRANDS CRUS Osterberg and Geisberg (02 06) and aromatic Gewurz from Grand Cru Kirchberg (05). Rich, aromatic sweet wines.

Kreydenweiss, Marc Al ★★ →★★★ Fine ALSACE grower: 12 ha at Andlau, esp for PINOT GR (v.gd Grand Cru Moenchberg), Pinot Bl and Ries. Top wine: Grand Cru Kastelberg (ages 20 yrs); also fine Auxerrois Kritt Klevner and gd VENDANGE TARDIVE. One of first in Alsace to use new oak – now older casks, too. Gd Ries/ PINOT GR blend Clos du Val d'Eléon. Biodynamic here and in Rhône valley.

Krug Champ Grande Cuvée; Vintage 88 90 95 96 98'; Rosé; Clos du Mesnil (BLANC DE BLANCS) 88 90 95'; Krug Collection 76 81 85. Small, supremely prestigious CHAMPAGNE house. Rich, nutty wines, oak-fermented: long ageing, superlative quality and soaring price. Vintage Brut assemblage great in 98', a challenging year. Clos d'Ambonnay (95' 96) is for billionaires.

Kuentz-Bas Al ★ →★★ Famous grower/merchant at Husseren-les-Châteaux, esp PINOT GR, Gewurz. Gd VENDANGES TARDIVES. Owned by Caves J-B Adam.

L'Etoile Jura w dr sp (sw) ★★ Subregion known for stylish whites, inc VIN JAUNE, similar to CH-CHALON; gd sparkling.

Ladoix C d'O r (w) ★★ 02' 03 05' 07 08 09' 10 Village at north end of CÔTE DE BEAUNE, inc some CORTON and CORTON-CHARLEMAGNE. After yrs in shadow of ALOXE, now undergoing revival in the hands of Claude Chevalier, Michel Mallard, Sylvain Loichet. Exuberant whites of interest, too.

Ladoucette, de Lo w (p,r) ★★ →★★★ 05 06 07 08 09 (10) Largest individual producer of POUILLY-FUMÉ, based at CH de Nozet. Expensive luxury brand Baron de L. Sancerre Comte Lafond, La Poussie (vineyard severely eroded); Vouvray Marc Brédif. Owns Albert Pic (CHABLIS).

Lafarge, Michel C d'O ★★★★ Classic VOLNAY estate with great PREMIERS CRUS *Clos des Chênes*, Caillerets, Clos du Château des Ducs. Other fine BEAUNE and POMMARD wines made biodynamically by run by Frédéric L, son of ever-present Michel.

Lafon, Dom des Comtes Burg ★★★ →★★★★ Long famous for whites, MEURSAULT and MONTRACHET while red VOLNAY now outstanding. Also in Mâconnais while Dominique L has started own label in BEAUNE.

Laguiche, Marquis de C d'O ★★★ →★★★★ Largest owner of LE MONTRACHET and a fine PREMIER CRU CHASSAGNE, both made by DROUHIN.

Lalande de Pomerol B'x r ★★★ 95 96 98 99 00' 01' 04 05' 06 07 08 09' Northerly neighbour of POMEROL. Wines similar, but less structured and refined. New investors and younger generation: improving quality. Top CHX: des Annereaux, BERTINEAU-ST-VINCENT, Chambrun, Les Cruzelles, La Fleur de Boüard, Garraud,

Grand Ormeau, Jean de Gué, Haut-Chaigneau, Les Hauts Conseillants, Perron (La Fleur), La Sergue, Siaurac, TOURNEFEUILLE.

Landron (Doms) Lo w dr sp ★★→★★★ 05 06 09 (10) First-rate producer (48 ha); organic MUSCADET-SÈVRE-ET-MAINE, several CUVÉES bottled by terroir, inc Amphibolite age-worthy Fief du Breil, Clos de la Carizière; good sparkling (Gros Plant/Pinot N).

Langlois-Château Lo ★★→★★★ Top SAUMUR sparkling (CRÉMANT) house, BOLLINGER-owned. Also still wines, esp v.gd age-worthy Saumur Blanc Vielles Vignes.

Languedoc L'doc r p w General term for the MIDI and now AC enlarging COTEAUX DU LANGUEDOC to inc MINERVOIS and CORBIÈRES, and also ROUSSILLON. Rules the same as for COTEAUX DU LANGUEDOC, with 5-yr period for name-changing, up to April 2012. The bottom of the pyramid of MIDI ACS. A hierachy of *grands vins* and even better GRANDS CRUS planned for the 2011 vintage.

Lanson Champ Black Label NV; Rosé NV; BRUT 99 02. Important improving CHAMPAGNE house now part of Boizel Chanoine group. Long-lived luxury brand: Noble Cuvée as BLANC DE BLANCS, rosé and vintage blend (98'). New single-vyd Clos Lanson (07 08). New Extra Age (a blend of 99 02 03).

Lapierre, Marcel Beauj ★★ Late Marcel L was pioneer of sulphur-free winemaking for his top-end BEAUJOLAIS wines, esp MORGON.

Laroche Chab ★★ Change of ownership in 2009 for large-scale grower and merchant with interests in south of France, Chile and South Africa. Majority owner now Groupe Jeanjean. Try Grand Cru Réserve de l'Obédiencerie.

Latour de France Rouss r (w) ★→★★★ Theoretically superior village in CÔTES DE ROUSSILLON-VILLAGES. Esp Clos de l'Oum, Clos des Fées. Best wines often IGP CÔTES CATALANES.

Latour, Louis Burg ★★→★★★ Famous traditional family merchant; sound white wines from CÔTE D'OR v'yds (esp CORTON and CORTON-CHARLMAGNE), Mâconnais and the ARDÈCHE (all CHARD) and less exciting reds (all Pinot) from CÔTE D'OR and Coteaux du Verdon. Now also owns Henry Fessy in BEAUJOLAIS.

Latricières-Chambertin C d'O r ★★★ 90' **93 95 96'** 99' 02' 03 05' 06 **07** 08 09' 10 GRAND CRU (7.35 ha) next to CHAMBERTIN, rich if not quite as intense. Best from BIZE, Drouhin-Laroze, Duband, FAIVELEY, LEROY, Rossignol-Trapet, TRAPET.

Laudun S Rhô r p w ★→★★ 07' 09' **10'** West bank CÔTES DU RHÔNE-VILLAGE. Forward, clear reds (lots of Syrah), bright rosés, stylish whites. Drink early wines from Serre de Bernon co-op. DOM Pelaquié best, esp fab white. Also CHX de Bord, Courac, Marjolet, St-Maurice, DOM Duseigneur, Prieuré St-Pierre.

Laurent-Perrier Champ V.gd Brut NV; Rosé NV; BRUT **98** 02 Dynamic family owned house at Tours-sur-Marne. Fine, minerally NV; excellent luxury brands: Grand Siècle la Cuvée Lumière du Millésime (90 96), Cuvée Grand Siècle Alexandra Brut Rosé (98' 02). But Ultra Brut fails to impress.

Leflaive, Dom Burg ★★★★ Top biodynamic white burgundy producer at PULIGNY-MONTRACHET with a clutch of GRANDS CRUS, inc LE MONTRACHET and CHEVALIER. Fabulous PREMIERS CRUS: Pucelles, Combettes, Folatières. MÂCON since 2004.

Leflaive, Olivier C d'O ★★→★★★ High-quality négociant at PULIGNY-MONTRACHET, cousin of the above. Reliable wines, mostly white, but drink them young. V'yd holdings now expanded with Olivier's share from family DOM.

Leroy, Dom C d'O ★★★★ DOM built around purchase of Noëllat in VOSNE-ROMANÉE in 1988. Extraordinary quality (and prices) from tiny biodynamic yields. Also original Leroy family holdings, DOM d'Auvenay.

Leroy, Maison C d'O ★★★★ Burgundy's ultimate NÉGOCIANT-ÉLEVEUR at AUXEY-DURESSES. Small parcels of grand old wines at prices to make you rub your eyes.

Liger-Belair C d'O ★★★→★★★★ Two recently re-established DOMS of high quality. Vicomte Louis-Michel L-B makes brilliantly ethereal wines in VOSNE-ROMANÉE, while cousin Thibault makes plump red wines in NUITS-ST-GEORGES.

Lignier C d'O ★★→★★★ Family in MOREY-ST-DENIS. Best is Hubert (eg. CLOS DE LA ROCHE), but watch Virgile L-Michelot and DOM Lucie & Auguste L.

Limoux Rouss r w ★★ AC for great-value sparkling BLANQUETTE DE LIMOUX or better *Crémant de Limoux*, also unusual *méthode ancestrale*. Oak-aged CHARD for white Limoux AC. Set to become GRAND CRU du LANGUEDOC from 2011 vintage. Red AC since 2003 based on Merlot, plus Syrah, Grenache, Cabernets, Carignan. Pinot N in CRÉMANT and for IGP. Growers: DOMS de Fourn, Laurens, des Martinolles, de Mouscaillou, Rives Blanques. Gd whites (5 yrs). Sound co-op: Sieur d'Arques.

Lirac S Rhô r p w ★★ 03 04 05' 06' 07' 09' 10' Low-profile v'yd next to TAVEL. Lacks depth of quality. Fair-value red (can age 5+ yrs), helped by CHÂTEAUNEUF-DU-PAPE owners who bring better fruit, cleaner wines. Reds best, esp DOMS Beaumont, Joncier, Lafond Roc-Epine, Lorentine, Maby (Fermade), André Méjan, de la Mordorée (best), Rocalière, R Sabon, CHX Bouchassy, Manissy, Mont-Redon, St-Roch, Ségriès. Gd whites (5 yrs).

Listrac-Médoc H-Méd r ★★→★★★ 95 96 98 00' 01 03 05' 06 08 09' Neighbour of MOULIS in south MÉDOC. Grown-up clarets with tannic grip now rounded out with more Merlot. A little white. Best CHX: Cap Léon Veyrin, CLARKE, DUCLUZEAU, FONRÉAUD, FOURCAS-DUPRÉ, FOURCAS-HOSTEN, Mayne-Lalande, Reverdi.

Long-Depaquit Chab ★★★ BICHOT-owned DOM; flagship GRAND CRU brand La Moutonne.

Lorentz, Gustave ★★ ALSACE grower and merchant at Bergheim. Esp Gewurz, Ries from GRAND CRUS Altenberg de Bergheim, Kanzlerberg. Also owns Jerome Lorentz. Equally gd for top estate and volume wines.

Lot SW Growing IGP often from CAHORS growers not conforming to AC rules seeking wider market. Also from newly planted surrounding countryside, eg. ★★ DOMS de Sully and Belmont. Sometimes quite pricey.

Loupiac B'x w sw ★★ 96 97' 98 99' 01' 02 03' 05' 07 09' Across river from SAUTERNES. Lighter, fresher. Top Clos-Jean, Loupiac-Gaudiet, Noble, Ricaud, Les Roques.

Lubéron S Rhô r p w ★ →★★ 09' 10 Flashy, new-money area, 2,500-ha v'yds in southeast of Rhône. So-so terroir, modern methods. Syrah popular. Many new wannabes. Bright star is CH de la Canorgue. Also good: Cellier de Marrenon, DOM de la Citadelle, CH Clapier, Edem, Fontvert, O Ravoire, St-Estève de Neri (improving), Tardieu-Laurent (oak), Val-Joanis, LA VIEILLE FERME (w).

Lussac-St-Emilion B'x r ★★ 95 98 00' 01 03 05' 08 09' The lightest of the ST-EMILION satellites. Co-op the main producer. Top CHX: Barbe Blanche, Bel Air, Bellevue, Courlat, la Grenière, LUSSAC, LYONNAT, Mayne-Blanc.

AOP and IGP: what's happening in France
The appellations and VDPS of France will eventually convert to Appellation d'Origine Protegée (AOP) and Indication Géographique Protegée (IGP). This means that anywhere aspiring to an appellation is likely to become AOP rather than AOC. IGP will become more specific when the all-embracing category of Vin de Table de France finally comes on-stream; it allows wines to state their vintage and grape variety – information that was previously denied to VIN DE TABLE. For the sake of simplicity and brevity, the book now uses IGP for all former VDP.

Macération carbonique Traditional fermentation technique: whole bunches of unbroken grapes in a closed vat. Fermentation induced inside each grape eventually bursts it, giving vivid, fruity, mild wine, not for ageing. Esp in BEAUJOLAIS; now much used in the MIDI and elsewhere, even CHÂTEAUNEUF.

Mâcon Burg r w (p) DYA Sound, usually unremarkable reds (Gamay), tasty CHARD.

Mâcon-Lugny Burg w ★★ 09' 10 Leading Mâconnais village. Try Les Charmes from excellent co-op or Genevrières from LATOUR.

Mâcon-Villages Burg w ★★ →★★★ 07 08 09' 10 Catch-all name for better Mâconnais wines, which may also use their own names eg. MÂCON-LUGNY, La Roche Vineuse, etc. Quality individual growers emerging. Try Bonhomme, Guillot-Broux, LAFON, Maillet, Merlin, co-ops at Lugny, Prissé, Viré.

Macvin Jura w sw ★★ AC for "traditional" MARC and grape-juice apéritif.

Madiran SW r ★★ →★★★ 00' 01 02 04 05' 06 08 (09') (10) Many growers seek to lighten the style of these once-macho reds, making entry-style wines, but tradition lingers. ★★★ CHX *Montus* and Boucassé now chased hard by Barréjat, Berthoumieu, Capmartin, Chapelle Lenclos. Clos Basté, Crampilh, Damiens, dou Bernés, Labranche-Laffont, Laffitte-Teston and *Laplace* all need ageing.

Mähler-Besse B'x First-class Dutch négociant in BORDEAUX. Loads of old vintages. Has share in CH PALMER.

Mailly-Champagne Champ ★★★ Top co-op, all GRAND CRU grapes. Prestige Cuvée des Echansons (97 98') great wine for long ageing. Real value.

Maire, Henri Jura ★ →★★ The biggest grower/merchant of Jura wines, with half of the entire AC. Some top wines, many cheerfully commercial. Fun to visit.

Malepère L'doc r ★ DYA Originally Côtes de la Malepère, now plain Malepère AC near LIMOUX for reds that combine BORDEAUX and the MIDI. Fresh reds with a touch of rusticity provide original drinking, esp CH Guilhem.

Mann, Albert Al ★ →★★★ Top growers at Wettolsheim: rich, elegant wines. V.gd Pinot Bl, Auxerrois, Pinot N, and gd range of GRANDS CRU wines from SCHLOSSBERG, HENGST, Furstentum and Steingrubler. Immaculate biodynamic v'yds.

Maranges C d'O r (w) ★★ 02' 03' 05' 07 08 09' 10 Southernmost AC of CÔTE DE BEAUNE with relatively tannic reds. Gd value from PREMIERS CRUS. Best growers: Bachelet-Monnot, Contat-Grangé, Chevrot.

Marc Grape skins after pressing; the strong-smelling brandy made from them.

Marcillac SW r p ★★ 20-yr-old AC from precipitous Aveyron hillside terraces. Unmistakable blue-tinged, spicy, soft-fruit character from Mansois (aka Fer Servadou). DOMS du Cros, Costes, Mioula, Vieux Porche, gd co-op. Best at 3 yrs.

Margaux H-Méd r ★★ →★★★★ 89 90' 95 96 98 00' 01 02 04 05' 06 08 09' (10) Largest communal AC in south MÉDOC, grouping v'yds from five villages. Known for its elegant, fragrant style. 21 classed growths. Top CHX: BRANE-CANTENAC, FERRIÉRE, GISCOURS, MALESCOT-ST-EXUPÉRY, MARGAUX, PALMER, RAUZAN-SÉGLA.

Marionnet, Henry Lo r w ★★ →★★★ 05' 08' 09' (10) Influential grower at eastern extremity of TOURAINE fascinated by grape varieties. Wines inc Sauv Bl (top is Le M de Marionnet) and *Gamay*, esp the unsulphured Première Vendange, Provignage (from ungrafted Romorantin vines planted 1850). Range of ungrafted wines, inc juicy *Côt* and mineral Chenin Bl.

Marmande SW r p w ★ →★★★ 04 05' 06 08 (09') (10) ★★★ DOM Elian da Ros heads small band of independents, inc CH de Beaulieu, ★★ DOM Bonnet et Laborde and CH Lassolle. Co-op well-meaning and well-equipped but let down by unenthusiastic membership.

Marne & Champagne CHAMPAGNE house, and many smaller brands, inc BESSERAT DE BELLEFON. Alfred Rothschild brand v.gd CHARD-based wines. Improving quality under BOIZEL CHANOINE ownership.

Marque déposée Trademark.

Marsannay C d'O r p (w) ★★ 05' 06 08 09' 10 (rosé DYA) Easy-to-drink wines, all three colours. Little of note, except reds from gifted producers: Audoin, Charlopin, CLAIR, Fournier, *Pataille*, TRAPET. No PREMIERS CRUS yet, but plans afoot.

Mas de Daumas Gassac L'doc r p w ★★ 98 99 00 01 02 03 04 05 06 07 08 09 Pioneering IGP set new standards in the MIDI, with Cab-based reds from apparently unique wind-borne glacial soil. Quality now rivalled and surpassed by many, eg. neighbouring GRANGE DES PÈRES. Wines inc super-CUVÉE Emile Peynaud, rosé Frizant, delicious, rich, *fragrant white blend* to drink at 2–3 yrs. IGP status. Intriguing sweet wine: Vin de Laurence (MUSCAT, Sercial).

Mas, Doms Paul L'doc r p w ★★ Big player in the south; own estates and négociant wine, IGP and AC. Innovative marketing. Known for Arrogant Frog IGP range; also La Forge and Les Vignes de Nicole. Recent purchase of Dom Crès Ricards.

Massif d'Uchaux S Rhô r ★★ Cool-zone Rhône village with talented growers, stylish, clear-fruited wines. Note: CH St Estève, DOMS La Cabotte, Chapoton, Cros de la Mûre (v.gd), de la Guicharde, Renjarde.

Mau, Yvon B'x Négociant, now part of Freixenet. Original Mau-family owners kept CHX Brown (PESSAC-LÉOGNAN) and Preuillac (MÉDOC).

Maury Rouss r sw ★★ NV red VIN DOUX NATUREL from ROUSSILLON. From Grenache grown on island of schist in limestone hills. Much recent improvement, esp at *Mas Amiel*. Several new estates; sound co-op. RANCIOS age beautifully. Also gd red table wines.

Mazis- (or Mazy-) Chambertin C d'O r ★★★ 90' 93 95 96' 99' 02' 03 05' 06 07 08 09' 10 Northernmost GRAND CRU (9 ha) of GEVREY-CHAMBERTIN, top class in upper part; *heavenly wines*. Best from DUGAT-PY, FAIVELEY, HOSPICES DE BEAUNE, LEROY, Maume, ROUSSEAU.

Mazoyères-Chambertin C d'O *See* CHARMES-CHAMBERTIN.

Médoc B'x r ★★ 98 00' 02 03 04 05' 06 08 09' AC for reds in the flatter, northern part of the MÉDOC peninsula. Gd if you're selective. Earthy, with Merlot adding flesh. Top CHX: Goulée, GREYSAC, LOUDENNE, Lousteauneuf, LES ORMES-SORBET, POTENSAC, Rollan-de-By (HAUT-CONDISSAS), LA TOUR-DE-BY, TOUR HAUT-CAUSSAN.

Meffre, Gabriel S Rhô ★★ Big Rhône merchant under Boisset/Eric Brousse control since 2009. Owns GIGONDAS DOM Longue-Toque. Recent progress, quality can vary, sleek wines sought. Also bottles, sells small CHÂTEAUNEUF DOMS. Worthy N Rhône Laurus (new oak) range, esp CROZES-HERMITAGE, ST-JOSEPH.

Mellot, Alphonse Lo r p w ★★→★★★ 02 03 04 05 06 07 08' 09' (10) V. fine range of SANCERRE (white and esp reds) from leading grower, biodynamic since 2009: La Moussière (w r), barrel-fermented Cuvée Edmond, Génération XIX (w r), Les Demoiselles and En Grands Champs (r). Since 2005 in Les Pénitents (Côtes de La Charité IGP) CHARD and Pinot N.

Menetou-Salon Lo r p w ★★ 05 06 07 08 (10) AC (465 ha) southwest of SANCERRE; similar if lighter wines. Best producers: BOURGEOIS, Clement (DOM de Chatenoy), Jacolin, *Henry Pellé*, Jean-Max Roger, Teiller, Tour St-Martin. V. severely hit by hail in 2009 – ironically the 50th anniversary of the AC.

Méo-Camuzet C d'O ★★★★ V. fine DOM in VOSNE-ROMANÉE (NB Brûlées & Cros Parantoux) plus GRANDS CRUS CORTON, CLOS DE VOUGEOT, RICHEBOURG. Also less expensive négociant CUVÉES.

Mercier & Cie, Champagne Champ Brut NV, Brut Rosé NV, DEMI-SEC BRUT. One of biggest houses at Épernay. Controlled by MOËT & CHANDON. Sold mainly in France. Full-bodied, Pinot N-led CUVÉE Eugene Mercier.

Mercurey Burg r (w) ★★→★★★ 03 05' 06 07 08 09' 10 Leading red-wine village of CÔTE CHALONNAISE. *Gd middle-rank burgundy*, inc improving whites. Try CH de Chamirey, FAIVELEY, M Juillot, Lorenzon, Raquillet, de Suremain.

Mesnil-sur-Oger, Le Champ ★★★★ One of the top Côte des Blancs villages. Structured CHARD for v. long ageing.

Méthode champenoise Traditional method of putting bubbles into CHAMPAGNE by refermenting wine in its bottle. Outside CHAMPAGNE region, makers must use terms "classic method" or "*méthode traditionnelle*".

Meursault C d'O w (r) ★★★→★★★★ 99' 00' 02' 04 05' 06' 07 08 09' 10 CÔTE DE

BEAUNE village with some of world's greatest whites: savoury, dry, nutty, mellow. Best v'yds: Charmes, Genevrières, Perrières. Also: Goutte d'Or, Meursault-Blagny, Poruzots, Narvaux, Tesson, Tillets. Producers inc: Ampeau, J-M BOILLOT, M BOUZEREAU, V BOUZEREAU, Boyer-Martenot, CH DE MEURSAULT, COCHE-DURY, Ente, Fichet, GIRARDIN, *Javillier*, JOBARD, **Lafon**, Latour-Labille, Martelet de Cherisey, Matrot, Mikulski, P MOREY, Prieur, G ROULOT. See also BLAGNY.

Midi Broad term covering L'DOC, ROUSS, even PROV. A melting-pot; quality improves with every vintage. Brilliant promise, but of course no guarantee.

Minervois L'doc r bw sw (p w) ★★ 03 04 05' 06 07' 08 09 Hilly AC; gd, lively reds, esp CHX Bonhomme, Coupe-Roses, la Grave, Oupia, St Jacques d'Albas, La Tour Boisée, Villerembert-Julien, Clos Centeilles, Borie-de-Maurel, Ste Eulalie, Faiteau; co-ops La Livinière, de Peyriac, Pouzols. *See* ST-JEAN DE MINERVOIS.

Minervois-La Livinière L'doc r ★★→★★★ Quality village, GRAND CRU of L'DOC from 2011 vintage. Stricter selection and longer ageing. Best growers: Abbaye de Tholomies, Borie de Maurel, Combe Blanche, CH de Gourgazaud, Clos Centeilles, Laville-Bertrou, Ste-Eulalie, Vipur. Co-op La Livinière.

Mis en bouteille au ch/dom Bottled at the CH, property, or estate. NB *dans nos caves* (in our cellars) or *dans la région de production* (in the area of production) are often used but mean little.

Moët & Chandon Champ By far the largest house and enlightened leader of v'yd research and development. Now owns 1,500 ha, often in the best sites. Greatly improved Brut NV, recent fine run of grand vintages, esp 90 95 and an awesome 02'. Impressive CUVÉE DOM PÉRIGNON. Branches across Europe and New World.

Mommessin, J Burg Family own CLOS DE TART in MOREY-ST-DENIS, but sold BEAUJOLAIS-based merchant business to BOISSET. CH de Pierreux, BROUILLY, a specialty.

Monbazillac SW w sw ★★→★★★★ 90' 95' 01' 03' 05' 06 07' (09') (10) As in days gone by, this BERGERAC AC now rivals many fashionable Sauternes. Top producers inc ★★★★ Tirecul-la-Gravière, ★★★ L'Ancienne Cure, Clos des Verdots, La Grande Maison and Les Hauts de Caillavel; ★★ CHX de Belingard-Chayne, Le Fagé, Poulvère, Theulet. Also the co-op's *Ch de Monbazillac*.

Mondeuse Sav r ★★ DYA SAVOIE red grape. Potentially gd, deep-coloured wine. Possibly same as Italy's Refosco. Don't miss a chance, eg. *G Berlioz*.

Monopole A v'yd that is under single ownership.

Montagne-St-Emilion B'x r ★★ 95 98 00' 01 03 05' 08 09' Largest and possibly best satellite of ST-EMILION (1,600 ha). Similar style of wine. Top CHX: Beauséjour, Calon, La Couronne, Croix Beauséjour, Faizeau, La Fleur-Carrère, Haut Bonneau, Maison Blanche, Roudier, Teyssier, *Vieux Ch St-André*.

Montagny Burg w ★★ 07 08 09' 10 CÔTE CHALONNAISE village. Between MÂCON and MEURSAULT, both geographically and gastronomically. Top producers: Aladame, J-M BOILLOT, Cave de Buxy, Michel, CH de la Saule.

Monthélie C d'O r (w) ★★→★★★ 99' 02' 03' 05' 07 08 09' 10 Uphill from VOLNAY, touch more rustic. Best: Champs Fulliot, Duresses. Best: BOUCHARD PÈRE ET FILS, COCHE-DURY, Darviot-Perrin, Garaudet, LAFON, CH de Monthélie (Suremain).

Montille, de C d'O ★★★ Hubert de Montille made long-lived VOLNAY, POMMARD. Son Etienne has expanded DOM with purchases in BEAUNE, NUITS-ST-GEORGES and potentially outstanding Vosne-Romanée Malconsorts. Etienne also runs CH de Puligny. Also Deux Montille (white wines) négociant venture with sister Alix.

Montlouis Lo w dr sw (sp) ★★→★★★★ 89' 90' 95' 96' 97' 02' 03' 05' 07 08' 09 Sister AC to VOUVRAY on south side of Loire making similar range of wines from Chenin Bl. 370 ha. Currently *one of the Loire's most exciting ACS*. Top growers inc Berger, Chatenay, CHIDAINE, Damien Delecheneau, Deletang, Jousset, Moyer, Frantz Saumon, TAILLE-AUX-LOUPS, WEISSKOPF.

Montrachet C d'O w ★★★★ 92' 93 95 96' 97 99 00' 01 02' 04 05' 06 07 08 09' 10

GRAND CRU v'yd (8.01 ha) in both PULIGNY- and CHASSAGNE-MONTRACHET. Potentially the greatest white burgundy: strong, perfumed, intense, dry yet luscious. Top wines: LAFON, LAGUICHE (DROUHIN), LEFLAIVE, Ramonet, ROMANÉE-CONTI. DOM THÉNARD disappoints.

Montravel SW ★★ p w dr DYA (w p) r 02' 04 05' **06** (08) (09') (10). Part of BERGERAC with its own AC. Oaked reds (mostly Merlot) in modern style. Best are ★★ DOMS de Bloy, de Krevel, CHX Jonc Blanc, Laulerie, Masburel, Masmontet, Moulin-Caresse. Sweet whites from CÔTES DE MONTRAVEL, HAUT-MONTRAVEL.

Morey-St-Denis C d'O r (w) ★★★ 90' 93 95 96' 98 99' 02' 03 05' 06 07 08 09' 10 Small village with four GRANDS CRUS between GEVREY-CHAMBERTIN and CHAMBOLLE-MUSIGNY. Glorious wine often overlooked. Amiot, ARLAUD, CLOS DE TART, CLOS DES LAMBRAYS, DUJAC, LIGNIER, Perrot-Minot, PONSOT, ROUMIER, Taupenot-Merme.

Morey, Doms C d'O ★★★ VIGNERON family in CHASSAGNE-MONTRACHET, esp Jean-Marc, Marc, Thomas, Vincent, Michel M-Coffinet. Also Pierre Morey in MEURSAULT. All better known for whites than reds.

Morgon Beauj r ★★★ 03 05' **06 07 08** 09' 10 Firm, tannic BEAUJOLAIS *cru*, esp from Côte du Py hillside. Becomes meaty with age. Les Charmes is softer for earlier drinking. Try Desvignes, Foillard, Gaget, Lafont, LAPIERRE, CH de Pizay.

Mortet, Denis C d'O ★★★→★★★★ Arnaud M adding a touch of elegance to late father's powerful, deep-coloured wines from BOURGOGNE ROUGE to GRAND CRU CHAMBERTIN. Various GEVREY-CHAMBERTIN CUVÉES to look out for.

Moueix, J-P et Cie B'x Libourne-based merchant and proprietor named after legendary founder. Son Christian runs company. CHX inc: LA FLEUR-PÉTRUS, HOSANNA, MAGDELAINE, Providence, TROTANOY. BELAIR-MONANGE acquired in 2008. Distributes PÉTRUS. Also in California: see Dominus.

Moulin-à-Vent Beauj r ★★★ 99 03 05' **07 08** 09' 10 Biggest and potentially best wine of BEAUJOLAIS. Can be powerful, meaty, long-lived; can even taste like fine Rhône or burgundy. Many gd growers, esp CHX du Moulin-à-Vent, *des Jacques*, DOM des Hospices, JADOT, Janodet, Merlin.

Moulis H-Méd r ★★→★★★ **98** 00' 01 02 03 04 05' 06 08 09' Tiny inland AC in the south MÉDOC, with many honest, gd-value wines. Top CHX: Anthonic, Biston-Brillette, Branas Grand Poujeaux, Duplessis, Dutruch Grand Poujeaux, BRILLETTE, CHASSE-SPLEEN, MAUCAILLOU, POUJEAUX.

Mouton Cadet Biggest-selling red BORDEAUX brand (12 million bottles). Revamped, fruitier since 2004. Also white, rosé, Rés GRAVES, MÉDOC, ST-EMILION and SAUTERNES.

Mugneret C d'O ★★★ VIGNERON family in VOSNE-ROMANÉE. Dr. Georges M-Gibourg best (esp ÉCHÉZEAUX); Gérard M, Dominique M; DOM Mongeard-M improving.

Mugnier, J-F C d'O ★★★→★★★★ Outstanding grower of CHAMBOLLE-MUSIGNY Les Amoureuses and MUSIGNY at CH de Chambolle. Winery rebuilt to accommodate 9-ha NUITS-ST-GEORGES Clos de la Maréchale since 2004.

Mumm, G H & Cie Champ Cordon Rouge NV; Mumm de Cramant NV; Cordon Rouge 98 00 02 04; Rosé NV. Major CHAMPAGNE grower/merchant. Owned by Pernod-Ricard. Reclamation of quality under new winemaker, esp in CUVÉE R Lalou 98' and Grand Cru Verzenay.

Muré, Clos St-Landelin Al ★★→★★★ Great name; 16 ha of GRAND CRU Vorbourg, esp fine in full-bodied Ries and PINOT GR. The Pinot N Cuvée "V" (04 05 09 10'), truly ripe and vinous, is the region's best. Sumptuous 2009s from 2011/12.

Muscadet Lo w ★→★★★ DYA (but see below) 3,600 ha Popular, gd-value, often delicious bone-dry wine from nr Nantes. Should never be sharp, but always refreshing. Perfect with fish, seafood. Choose a SUR LIE. Best from zonal ACS: MUSCADET-COTEAUX DE LA LOIRE, MUSCADET CÔTES DE GRAND LIEU, MUSCADET-SÈVRE-ET-MAINE. 2009 first normal-volume vintage since 2005; money troubles in 2010.

Muscadet Côtes de Grand Lieu Lo ★→★★ 05 09 (10) Most recent (1995) of

MUSCADET's zonal ACS (300 ha) and the closest to Atlantic coast. Best are SUR LIE from eg. Bâtard, Eric Chevalier, Choblet (DOM des Herbauges), Malidain.

Muscadet-Coteaux de la Loire Lo w ★→★★ 05 09 (10) Small MUSCADET (200 ha) zone east of Nantes (best SUR LIE). Esp Guindon, CH du Ponceau, Les Vignerons de la Noëlle.

Muscadet-Sèvre-et-Maine Lo ★→★★★ 02 03 04 05' 06 09' (10) Largest and best of MUSCADET's delimited zones (8,800 ha). Top Guy Bossard (DOM DE L'ECU), Bernard Chereau, Bruno Cormerais, Michel Delhommeau, Douillard, Gadais, DOM de la Haute Fevrie, Joseph Landron, Luneau-Papin, Louis Métaireau, Marc Olivier, Sauvion. Wines from these properties can age beautifully – try 1989 or 1999.

Muscat Distinctively perfumed and usually sweet wine from the grape of same name, often fortified as VDN. Dry table wine in ALSACE.

Muscat de Frontignan L'doc golden sw ★★ NV Small AC outside Sète for sweet, fortified MUSCAT. Experiments with late-harvest unfortified and oak-aged IGP wines. Quality steadily improving. Leaders: CHX la Peyrade, de Stony.

Muscat de Lunel L'doc golden sw ★★ NV Tiny AC based on MUSCAT, fortified, luscious and sweet. Some experimental late-harvest IGP wines. Look for DOM de Bellevue, CH du Grès St Paul.

Muscat de Mireval L'doc sw ★★ NV Tiny fortified MUSCAT AC nr Montpellier. A handful of producers. DOM La Capelle the best.

Muscat de Rivesaltes Rouss Golden sw ★★ NV Sweet, fortified MUSCAT AC wine nr Perpignan. Popularity waning; Muscat Sec IGP instead; best from DOM CAZES, CH de Jau, Baixas co-op.

Musigny C d'Or (w) ★★★★ (★) 85' 88' 89' 90' 91 93 95 96' 98 99' 01 02' 03 05' 06 07 08 09' 10 GRAND CRU in CHAMBOLLE-MUSIGNY (11 ha). Can be the most beautiful, if not the most powerful, of all red burgundies. Best growers: DROUHIN, JADOT, LEROY, MUGNIER, PRIEUR, ROUMIER, DE VOGÜE, VOUGERAIE.

Napoléon Champ Brand name of PRIEUR family's Vertus CHAMPAGNE house now owned by British wine merchant. Seek out mature vintages 90 95 96.

Nature "Natural" or "unprocessed" – esp of still CHAMPAGNE.

Négociant-éleveur Merchant who "brings up" (ie. matures) the wine.

Nuits-St-Georges C d'Or r ★★→★★★★ 90' 93 96' 98 99' 02' 03 05' 06 07 08 09' 10 Important wine town: underrated wines, typically sturdy, tannic, need time. Best v'yds: Cailles, Vaucrains, Les St Georges south of Nuits; Boudots, Murgers by VOSNE; Clos de la Maréchale, Clos St Marc in Prémeaux. Try: Ambroise, L'ARLOT, J Chauvenet, R CHEVILLON, Confuron, *Faiveley*, GOUGES, GRIVOT, Lechéneaut, LEROY, *Liger-Belair*, Machard de Gramont, Michelot, MUGNIER, *Rion*.

Pacherenc du Vic-Bilh SW w dr sw ★★→★★★ The white wine from MADIRAN-producers, ranging from dry (DYA) to sweet (oaked versions need ageing); esp ★★★ CHX MONTUS and Bouscassé, ★★ CH Laffitte-Teston, DOMS Barréjat, Berthoumieu, Capmartin, Crampilh, Damiens, Labranche-Laffont.

Paillard, Bruno Champ Brut Première Cuvée NV; Rosé Première Cuvée; Chard Réserve Privé, BRUT 96' 98. New vintage BLANC DE BLANCS 95' 96. Superb Prestige Cuvée Nec-Plus-Ultra (90 95 96). Youngest grand CHAMPAGNE house. Fine quality. Refined, v. dry style best expressed in Blanc de Blancs Réserve Privée and Nec-Plus-Ultra, the 90' only now fully mature. Bruno Paillard heads BOIZEL CHANOINE group and owns CH de Sarrin, Provence.

Palette Prov r p w ★★★ Tiny AC nr Aix-en-Provence. Full reds, fragrant rosés and intriguing whites, traditional CH SIMONE, now challenged by CH Henri Bonnaud.

Patriarche Burg ★→★★ One of the bigger Burgundy merchants. Cellars in BEAUNE; also owns CH DE MEURSAULT (61 ha), sparkling Kriter, etc.

Patrimonio Cors r p w ★★→★★★ AC for some of the island's best, from dramatic limestone hills in north CORSICA. Characterful reds from Nielluccio, intriguing whites, even late harvest, from Vermentino. Top growers: Antoine Arena, Clos de Bernardi, Gentile, Yves Leccia at E Croce, Pastricciola.

Pauillac H-Méd r ★★★→★★★★ 89' 90' 94 95' 96' 98 00' 01 02 03' 04' 05' 06 08' 09' (10) Communal AC in the MÉDOC with three First Growths (LAFITE, LATOUR, MOUTON). Famous for its powerful, long-lived wines, stressing Cabernet Sauvignon. Other top CHX inc GRAND-PUY-LACOSTE, LYNCH-BAGES, PICHON-LONGUEVILLE, PICHON-LALANDE and PONTET-CANET.

Pays d'Oc, IGP L'doc r p w ★→★★ Largest IGP, formerly Vin de Pays d'Oc, covering LANGUEDOC-ROUSSILLON with focus on varietal wines. Tremendous recent technical advances. Main producers: Jeanjean, Val d'Orbieu, DOMS PAUL MAS, village co-ops, plus numerous small individual growers. Encompasses both the best and the worst of the MIDI.

Pécharmant SW r ★★→★★★ 01' 04 05' 06 (08) (09')(10) Inner appellation of BERGERAC; wines are noted for firmness and minerality derived from ferrous subsoil. Best: DOM du Haut-Pécharmant, Les Chemins d'Orient, Clos des Côtes, Terre Vieille, CH de Tiregand. Modern style from DOM des Costes. Former stars La Métairie, DOM des Bertranoux and CH de Biran undergoing renaissance.

Pernand-Vergelesses C d'O r w ★★★ (r) 99' 02' 03' 05' 06 07 08 09' 10 Village next to ALOXE-CORTON containing part of the great CORTON-CHARLEMAGNE and CORTON v'yds. Île des Vergelesses also first rate. Growers: CHANDON DE BRIAILLES, CHANSON, Delarche, Dubreuil-Fontaine, JADOT, LATOUR, Rapet, Rollin.

Perrier-Jouët Champ Brut NV; Blason de France NV; Blason de France Rosé NV; BRUT 98 Historic CHAMPAGNE house at Épernay, one of first to make dry CHAMPAGNE, once the smartest name of all; now best for respectable vintage wines. De luxe Belle Epoque 85' 95' 96 98 02' (Rosé 02) in a painted bottle.

Pessac-Léognan B'x r w ★★★→★★★★ 90' 95 96 98 00' 01 02 04 05' 06 08 09' (10) AC (1987) for the best part of north GRAVES, inc all the GRANDS CRUS: HAUT-BRION, LA MISSION-HAUT-BRION, PAPE-CLÉMENT, DOM DE CHEVALIER, etc. Plump, minerally reds with plenty of Merlot and BORDEAUX's finest barrel-fermented dry whites.

Petit Chablis Chab w ★ DYA Fresh and easy, lighter almost-CHABLIS from outlying v'yds. La Chablisienne co-op is gd.

Pézenas L'doc r p w ★★→★ LANGUEDOC subregion from v'yds around Molière's town, set to become GRAND CRU du LANGUEDOC from the 2011 vintage. Try Prieuré de St-Jean-de-Bébian, DOMS du Conte des Floris, des Aurelles, Stella Nova and Monplézy.

Pfaffenheim Al ★→★★ Respectable ALSACE co-op. Rather four-square wines.

Pfersigberg ALSACE GRAND CRU with two parcels; v. aromatic wines. Gewurz does v. well. Ries, esp Paul Ginglinger, BRUNO SORG and LÉON BEYER Comtes d'Eguisheim. Top grower: KUENTZ-BAS.

Philipponnat Champ NV; Rosé NV; BRUT 99 02 Cuvée 1522 00; Clos des Goisses 85' 91 95 96 98 99 Small house known for well-structured wines and now owned by BOIZEL CHANOINE group. Remarkable single-v'yd *Clos des Goisses* and charming rosé.

Pic St-Loup L'doc ★★→★★★★ r (p) 03 04 05 06 07 08 09 10 northernmost LANGUEDOC v'yds and from 2011 vintage a GRAND CRU du LANGUEDOC. Growers: Cazeneuve, Clos Marie, de Lancyre, Lascaux, Mas Bruguière, Mas Mortiès, DOM DE L'HORTUS, Valflaunès. Some of the MIDI's best: stylish and long-lasting.

Picpoul de Pinet L'doc w ★→★★ DYA From 2011 vintage a *grand vin* du LANGUEDOC, exclusively from the old variety Picpoul. Best growers: AC St Martin de la Garrigue, Félines-Jourdan, co-ops Pomerols and Pinet. Good *with an oyster*.

Pineau des Charentes SW Strong, sweet apéritif: white grape juice and Cognac.

Pinon, François Lo w sw sp ★★★ 89 90 95 96 97 02 03 04 05 06 08 09 Excellent organic producer of v. pure VOUVRAY in all its expressions, inc a v.gd *pétillant*.

Pinot Gris ALSACE grape formerly called Tokay d'Alsace: full, rich white, a subtler match for foie gras than usual *moelleux*.

Piper-Heidsieck CHAMPAGNE house in need of a new owner. Much-improved Brut NV, fruit-driven Brut Rosé Sauvage; BRUT 00 02 04. V.gd CUVÉE. Sublime DEMI-SEC, rich yet balanced. Piper Heidsieck Rare (esp 99 02') is a best-kept secret.

Plageoles, Robert and Bernard SW Bernard continues father's pioneering work with traditional Gaillac grapes. Ondenc yields ★★★★ Vin d'Autan (one of France's great stickies); ★★★ Prunelard, a deep, fruity red; Verdanel, a modern, dry white of unusual personality; and Mauzac Nature, a gentle sparkler.

Plan de Dieu S Rhô r ★→★★ Recent Rhône village, heady mainly Grenache wines from v. stony, windy plain next to RASTEAU. Try: CH la Courançonne, DOMS Durieu, Espiguette, Pasquiers, Saint-Pierre, Vieux-Chêne.

Pol Roger Champ Brut White Foil renamed Brut Réserve NV; BRUT 96' 98 99 00 02; Rosé 99; Blanc de Chard 98' ★★★★ Supreme, family-owned Épernay house now with vines in AVIZE joining 85 ha of family v'yds. V. fine, floral NV, new Pure Brut (*zero dosage*) great with seafood. Sumptuous Cuvée Sir Winston Churchill (96' 98 02).

Pomerol B'x r ★★★→★★★★ 88 89' 90' 94 95 96 98' 00' 01 04 05' 06' 08 09' (10) Tiny 800-ha AC bordering ST-EMILION but no limestone; only clay, gravel, sand. Famed Merlot-dominated, rich, unctuous style. Top estates: LA CONSEILLANTE, L'ÉGLISE-CLINET, L'ÉVANGILE, LA FLEUR-PÉTRUS, HOSANNA, LAFLEUR, PÉTRUS, LE PIN, TROTANOY, VIEUX-CH-CERTAN.

Pommard C d'O r ★★★ 90' 96' 98 99' 02' 03 05' 06 07 08 09' 10 The biggest CÔTE D'OR village. Few superlative wines, but many potent, tannic ones to age 10+ yrs. Best v'yds: Epenots, Rugiens. Growers inc Comte ARMAND, Billard-Gonnet,J-M BOILLOT, COURCEL, HOSPICES DE BEAUNE, Huber-Vedereau, LEROY, Machard de Gramont, DE MONTILLE, CH de Pommard, Pothier-Rieusset.

Pommery Champ Brut NV; Rosé NV; BRUT 82' 98 00 02 Historic CHAMPAGNE house; brand now owned by Vranken. Outstanding Cuvée Louise (89' 90' 98) and supple wintertime BLANC DE NOIRS.

Ponsot C d'O ★★→★★★★ Idiosyncratic top-quality MOREY-ST-DENIS DOM with great range of GRANDS CRUS, esp CLOS DE LA ROCHE. Extra kudos for Laurent P's fight against fraudulent bottles.

Potel, Nicolas C d'O ★★→★★★ Brand belonging to Cottin Frères (Labouré Roi) but since 2009 without eponymous Nicolas, who now has own businesses, Dom de Bellene and Maison Roche de Bellene in BEAUNE.

Pouilly-Fuissé Burg w ★★→★★★ 02' 04 05' 06 07 08 09' 10 Top AC of MÂCON region now exploring PREMIER CRU classification. Stylistic differences according to location. Wines from Chaintré the softest, Fuissé the most powerful, Vergisson for minerality. Top names: Barraud, de Beauregard, Cornin, Ferret, Forest, CH DE FUISSE, Merlin, CH des Rontets, Saumaize, VERGET.

Pouilly-Fumé Lo w ★→★★★★ 04 05' 06 07 08 09' (10) Often disappointing white (1,201 ha). Best is round and full-flavoured. Must be Sauv Bl. Top CUVÉES can improve 5–6 yrs. Growers inc BOURGEOIS, Alain Cailbourdin, Chatelain, DIDIER DAGUENEAU, Serge Dagueneau & Filles, CH de Favray, Edmond and André Figeat, Masson-Blondelet, Jean Pabiot, Michel Redde,Tabordet, CH de Tracy.

Pouilly-Loché Burg w ★★ 07 08 09' 10 Usually sold as POUILLY-VINZELLES. Clos des Rocs, Tripoz, Bret Bros offer Loché bottlings. Co-op dominant for volume.

Pouilly-sur-Loire Lo w ★ DYA Historic but neutral, non-aromatic wine from same v'yds as POUILLY-FUMÉ but different grape: Chasselas. Now only 33 ha in production. Best: Serge Dagueneau & Filles, Landrat-Guyollot, Michel Redde.

Pouilly-Vinzelles Burg w ★★ 05' 06' 07 09' 10 Superior neighbour to POUILLY-LOCHÉ. Best v'yd Les Quarts. Best producers: Bret Bros, Valette.

Premier Cru (1er Cru) First growth in BORDEAUX; second rank of v'yds (after GRAND CRU) in Burgundy.

Premières Côtes de Bordeaux B'x w sw ★→★★ 01 02 03 05 07 09' Same geographical zone as CADILLAC-CÔTES DE BORDEAUX but for sweet white wines only. Usually *moelleux* or gently sweet in style rather than full-blown, noble-rotted *liquoreux*. Quality varied. Best CHX: Crabitan-Bellevue, du Juge, Suau.

Prieur, Dom Jacques C d'O ★★★ MEURSAULT estate with fine range of GRANDS CRUS from MONTRACHET to MUSIGNY. Style aims at weight more than finesse.

Primeur "Early" wine for refreshment and uplift; esp from BEAUJOLAIS; VDP, too. Wine sold *en primeur* is still in barrel, for delivery when bottled – only buy from established and reputable companies.

Producteurs Plaimont SW This brilliant co-op goes from strength to strength. It uses only authentic Gascon grapes, Tannat and Fer Servadou for the reds, and the two Mansengs, Petit Courbu and Arrufiac for the whites.

Propriétaire récoltant Owner-operator, literally owner-harvester.

Provence *See* CÔTES DE PROVENCE, CASSIS, BANDOL, PALETTE, LES BAUX-EN-PROVENCE, BOUCHES-DU-RHÔNE, COTEAUX DE PIERREVERT, COTEAUX D'AIX-EN-PROVENCE, COTEAUX VAROIS-EN-PROVENCE, IGP Méditerranée.

Puisseguin St-Emilion B'x r ★★ 98 00' 01 03 05' 08 09' Satellite neighbour of ST-EMILION; wines firm and solid in style. Top CHX: Bel Air, Branda, Durand-Laplagne, Fongaban, Guibot la Fourvieille, DES LAURETS, La Mauriane, Soleil. Also Roc de Puisseguin from co-op.

Puligny-Montrachet C d'O w (r) ★★★→★★★★ 00 02' 04 05' 06 07 08 09' 10 Smaller neighbour of CHASSAGNE-MONTRACHET: potentially even finer, more vital and complex wine (apparent finesse can be result of overproduction). V'yds: BÂTARD-MONTRACHET, Bienvenues-Bâtard Montrachet, Caillerets, CHEVALIER-MONTRACHET, Combettes, Folatières, MONTRACHET, Pucelles. Producers: Ampeau, J-M BOILLOT, BOUCHARD PÈRE ET FILS, CARILLON, CH de Puligny, Chavy, DROUHIN, JADOT, LATOUR, DOM LEFLAIVE, OLIVIER LEFLAIVE, Pernot, Sauzet.

Pyrénées-Atlantiques SW DYA IGP for wines not qualifying for local ACS MADIRAN, PACHERENC DU VIC-BILH, TURSAN, or JURANÇON. Esp BRUMONT varietals. Also some wines from non-AC areas.

Quarts de Chaume Lo w sw ★★★→★★★★ 89' 90' 95' 96' 97' 02 03 04 05' 07' 09 (10) Tiny (40 ha), exposed slopes close to Layon devoted to Chenin Bl. Can be Loire's greatest sweet wine with strong mineral character. Esp BAUMARD, Branchereau, Yves Guegniard, CH PIERRE-BISE, Suronde. Stunning 2007s.

Quatourze L'doc r w (p) ★★ DYA Tiny *cru* of LANGUEDOC by Narbonne. Reputation kept almost single-handedly by CH Notre Dame du Quatourze.

Quincy Lo w ★→★★ Drink within 3 yrs. Small area (224 ha) on gravel west of Bourges in Cher Valley. SANCERRE-style Sauv Bl. Worth trying. Growers: Mardon, Portier, Jacques Rouzé, Tatin-Wilk (DOMS Ballandors, Tremblay).

Rancio Rouss The most original, lingering and delicious style of VDN, reminiscent of tawny Port, in BANYULS, MAURY, RIVESALTES, RASTEAU, wood-aged and exposed to oxygen and heat. Same flavour is a fault in table wine.

Rangen Al Most southerly GRAND CRU at Thann. 18.8 ha, extremely steep slopes, volcanic soils. Top wines: powerful Ries and PINOT GR from ZIND-HUMBRECHT (Clos St Urbain 02 05 06) and SCHOFFIT.

Rasteau S Rhô r br sw (w p dr) ★★ 06 07' 09' 10' Since 09 vintage has own red-wine appellation, now must deliver. Big-bodied, chewy reds, mainly Grenache, esp Beaurenard, *Cave des Vignerons* (gd), CH du Trignon, DOMS Beau Mistral, Didier Charavin, Collière, Escaravailles, Girasols, Gourt de Mautens (low yields), Rabasse-Charavin, Soumade, St-Gayan, Perrin & Fils (gd white, too). Grenache dessert wine VDN improving quality.

Ratafia de Champagne Sweet apéritif made in CHAMPAGNE of 67% grape juice and 33% brandy. Not unlike PINEAU DES CHARENTES.

Raveneau Chab ★★★★ Great CHABLIS producer using old methods for extraordinary long-lived wines. Cousin of DAUVISSAT. Vaillons, Blanchots, Les Clos best.

Regnié Beauj r ★★ 08 09' 10 Former BEAUJOLAIS VILLAGES turned *cru*. Sandy soil makes for lighter wines than other *crus*, wonderful in 2009. Try Aucoeur, DOM des Braves, DUBOEUF, Laforest, Pechard.

Reuilly Lo w p r ★→★★★ 05' 06 07 08 09' (10) Small AC (186 ha) west of Bourges for Sauv Bl whites plus rosés and *Vin Gris* made from Pinot N and/ or PINOT GR as well as reds from Pinot N. Best: Claude *Lafond*, DOM de Reuilly, Rouze, Sorbe.

Ribonnet, Dom de SW ★★ Against a Pyrenean backdrop, rebel Christian Gerber uses grape varieties from all over Europe to produce a fascinating range of IGP varietals and blends in all colours.

Riceys, Rosé des Champ p ★★★ DYA Minute AC in AUBE for a notable Pinot N rosé. Principal producers: *A Bonnet*, Jacques Defrance.

Richeaume, Dom Prov r ★★ Gd Cab Sauv/Syrah. Organic; a model.

Richebourg C d'O r ★★★★ 90' 93' 95 96' 98 99' 00 02' 03 05' 06 07 08 09' 10 VOSNE-ROMANÉE GRAND CRU. (8 ha) Fabulous, magical Burgundy; vastly expensive. Growers: DRC, GRIVOT, GROS, HUDELOT-Noëllat LEROY, LIGER-BELAIR, MÉO-CAMUZET.

Rimage Rouss Modern trend for a vintage VDN. Early drinking; think gd ruby Port.

Rion, Patrice C d'O ★★★★ Premeaux-based DOM with excellent NUITS-ST-GEORGES holdings, esp Clos des Argillières, Clos St Marc and CHAMBOLLE. Cousins B & B Rion in Vosne-Romanée also gd.

Rivesaltes Rouss r w br dr sw ★★ NV Fortified wine made nr Perpignan. Struggling but rewarding tradition. Top producers worth seeking out: DOM CAZES, CH de Jau, Sarda-Malet, des Schistes, Vaquer. Best are delicious and original, esp old RANCIOS. *See* MUSCAT DE RIVESALTES.

Roche-aux-Moines, La Lo w sw ★★→★★★ 89' 90' 95' 96' 97' 99 02 03 04 05' 06 07 08' 09 (10) A 33-ha *cru* of SAVENNIÈRES, ANJOU. Potentially powerful, intensely minerally wine; age or drink young "on the fruit". Growers inc: Le Clos de la Bergerie (Joly), DOM des Forges, Damien Laureau, CH PIERRE-BISE.

Roederer, Louis Champ Brut Premier NV; Rich NV; BRUT 97 99 00 02; BLANC DE BLANCS 97 99 00 02; Brut Rosé 99 02 Top-drawer family-owned house with enviable 218-ha estate of top v'yds. Magnificent Cristal (can be greatest of all Prestige Cuvées, viz 88' 90' 95 02' 04) and Cristal Rosé (90' 95 96 02). New Brut Nature from 2010. Also owns DEUTZ, DELAS, CH DE PEZ, CH PICHON-LALANDE. *See also* California.

Rolland, Michel B'x Ubiquitous and fashionable consultant winemaker and Merlot specialist working in BORDEAUX and worldwide, favouring super-ripe flavours as recommended by RP, Jr.

Rolly Gassmann Al ★★ Distinguished grower at Rorschwihr, esp for Auxerrois and MUSCAT from Moenchreben v'yds. Off-dry house style culminates in great rich Gewurz Cuvée Yves (00 02 05 06 08 09 10'). Now biodynamic.

Romanée-Conti C d'O r ★★★★ 71 76 78' 85' 88' 89' 90' 93' 95 96' 97 98 99' 00 01 02' 03 04 05' 06 07 09' 10 A 1.8-ha MONOPOLE GRAND CRU in VOSNE-ROMANÉE; 450 cases per annum. The most celebrated and expensive red wine in the world, with reserves of flavour beyond imagination.

Romanée-Conti, Dom de la C d'O (DRC) ★★★★ Grandest estate in Burgundy. Includes the whole of ROMANÉE-CONTI and LA TÂCHE, major parts of ÉCHÉZEAUX, GRANDS-ÉCHÉZEAUX, RICHEBOURG, ROMANÉE-ST-VIVANT and a tiny part of MONTRACHET. Crown-jewel prices (if you can buy them at all). Keep top vintages for decades.

Romanée-St-Vivant C d'O r ★★★★ 90' 93 95 96' 99' 02' 03 05' 06 07 08 09' 10

GRAND CRU in VOSNE-ROMANÉE (9.4 ha). Downslope from ROMANÉE-CONTI, perfumed but less sumptuous. Growers: ARLOT, CATHIARD, JJ Confuron, DRC, DROUHIN, HUDELOT-Nöellat, LATOUR, LEROY.

Romanée, La C d'O r ★★★★ 96' 98 99' 00 01 02' 03 05' 06 07 08 09 10 Tiniest GRAND CRU in VOSNE-ROMANÉE (0.85 ha), MONOPOLE of Comte LIGER-BELAIR. Exceptionally fine, perfumed, intense and understandably expensive.

Rosacker ALSACE GRAND CRU of 26 ha at Hunawihr. Produces best Ries in ALSACE (see CLOS STE-HUNE, SIPP-MACK).

Rosé d'Anjou Lo p ★→★★ DYA Pale, slightly sweet rosé (Grolleau dominates) enjoying a comeback in the hands of young VIGNERONS; look for Mark Angeli, Clau de Nell, DOMS de la Bergerie, les Grandes Vignes, des Sablonnettes.

Rosé de Loire Lo p ★→★★ DYA The driest of ANJOU's rosés – six permitted varieties esp Gamay and Grolleau. AC technically covers SAUMUR and TOURAINE, too. Best: Bablut, Ogereau, CH PIERRE-BISE, Richou.

Rosette SW w s/sw ★★ DYA Pocket-sized AC nr BERGERAC, becoming mildly fashionable for its *moëlleux* apéritif wines; sensational with foie gras or mushrooms. Try Clos Romain, CH Puypezat-Rosette, DOMS de la Cardinolle, de Coutancie.

Rostaing, René N Rhô ★★★ CÔTE-RÔTIE 8-ha DOM, top-grade plots, three v. precise wines, all v. fine, wait 4–5 yrs. Enticing Côte Blonde (5% Viognier) leads, also La Landonne (darker fruits, 15–20 yrs). Style approaches breeding of gd burgundy, pure fruit at heart; some new oak. Shapely CONDRIEU, also LANGUEDOC DOM Puech Noble (r, w).

Roty, Joseph C d'O ★★★ Small grower of classic GEVREY-CHAMBERTIN, esp CHARMES-CHAMBERTIN and MAZIS-CHAMBERTIN. Long-lived wines.

Rouget, Emmanuel C d'O ★★★★ Inheritor of the legendary Henri Jayer estate in ÉCHÉZEAUX, NUITS-ST-GEORGES, VOSNE-ROMANÉE. Top: VOSNE-ROMANÉE Cros Parantoux.

Roulot, Dom G C d'O ★★★ Outstanding MEURSAULT; fine range of v'yd sites, esp Tessons Clos de Mon Plaisir and PREMIERS CRUS eg. Bouchères, Perrières.

Roumier, Georges C d'O ★★★★ Reference DOM for BONNES-MARES and other *brilliant Chambolle* wines in capable hands of Christophe R. Long-lived wines but still attractive early.

Rousseau, Dom Armand C d'O ★★★★ Unmatchable GEVREY-CHAMBERTIN DOM, with thrilling CLOS ST-JACQUES and GRANDS CRUS. Unchanging, fragrant Pinot of extraordinary intensity.

Roussette de Savoie Sav w ★★ DYA Tastiest fresh white from south of Lake Geneva.

Roussillon Rouss Main region for VDN (eg. MAURY, RIVESALTES, BANYULS). Younger vintage RIMAGE wines are competing with aged RANCIO wines. See CÔTES DU ROUSSILLON (and CÔTES DU ROUSSILLON-VILLAGES), COLLIOURE, for table wines and IGP CÔTES CATALANES. Region included under AC LANGUEDOC.

Ruchottes-Chambertin C d'O r ★★★★ 90' 93' 95 96' 98 99' 00 02' 03 05' 06 07 08 09' 10 Tiny (3.3-ha) GRAND CRU neighbour of CHAMBERTIN. Less weighty but ethereal, intricate, lasting wine of great finesse. Top growers: MUGNERET-GIBOURG, ROUMIER, ROUSSEAU.

Ruinart Champ "R" de Ruinart Brut NV; Ruinart Rosé NV; "R" de Ruinart Brut (98 99). Oldest CHAMPAGNE house, owned by Moët-Hennessy. Already high standards should go higher still with talented new cellarmaster (since 2007). Prestige Cuvée *Dom Ruinart* is one of the two best vintage BLANC DE BLANCS in CHAMPAGNE (viz. 88' 90 95' 96 98). DR Rosé also v. special (88' 90' 02).

Rully Burg r w ★★ (r) 05' 07 08 09' 10 (w) 07 08 09' 10 CÔTE CHALONNAISE village. Whites are light, fresh and gd value. Reds fruit-forward. Delorme, Devevey, Dureuil-Janthial, FAIVELEY, Hasard, DOMS de la Folie, Jacqueson, Ninot, Rodet, Sounit.

Sables du Golfe du Lion L'doc r p w ★ DYA IGP from Mediterranean coastal sand-dunes: esp pink Gris de Gris from Carignan, Grenache, Cinsault. Giant Listel dominates production.

Sablet S Rhô r w (p) ★★ 07' 09 10' Best DOMS improving at this CÔTES DU RHÔNE VILLAGE. Sandy soils, often pliant, red-berry-fruited reds, esp DOMS de Boissan, Espiers, Les Goubert, Piaugier, Roubine. Gd full whites for apéritif and food.

Salon Champ ★★★★ The original BLANC DE BLANCS, from LE MESNIL in the Côte des Blancs. Awesome reputation for long-lived wines, in truth sometimes inconsistent but on song recently, viz. 90 96' 97' 99 02'

Sancerre Lo w (r p) ★→★★★ 03 05' 06 07 08' 09 (10) 2808 ha. Benchmark for Sauv Bl, often more aromatic and vibrant than POUILLY-FUMÉ. Best wines can age 10+ yrs. Top growers now making memorable reds (Pinot N). Sancerre rosé rarely worth the money. Best inc: Gérard Boulay, BOURGEOIS, Cotat, François Crochet, Lucien Crochet, André Dezat, Fouassier, Michel Girard, Thomas Laballe, ALPHONSE MELLOT, Mollet, Vincent Pinard, Pascal & Nicolas Reverdy, Claude Riffault, Jean-Max Roger, Vacheron, André Vatan.

Santenay C d'O r (w) ★★★ 99' 02' 03 05' 06 07 08 09' Sturdy reds from south of CHASSAGNE-MONTRACHET. Best v'yds more succulent: La Comme, Les Gravières, Clos de Tavannes. Try: GIRARDIN, *Jessiaume*, Lequin-Colin, Muzard, Vincent.

Saumur Lo r w p sp ★→★★★ 05' 06 07 08 09' (10) Umbrella AC for light whites plus more serious, particularly from SAUMUR-CHAMPIGNY zone; mainly easy-drinking reds, pleasant rosés, pungent CRÉMANT and SAUMUR MOUSSEUX. Saumur-Le-Puy-Notre-Dame new AC for Cab Fr reds but covers wide area – 17 communes. Producers inc: BOUVET-LADUBAY, Antoine Foucault, CLOS ROUGEARD, René-Hugues Gay, Guiberteau, DOMS DES CHAMPS FLEURIS/Retiveau-Retif, Paleine, St-Just; CH DE VILLENEUVE, Cave des Vignerons de Saumur.

Saumur-Champigny Lo r ★★→★★★ 95 96' 97 02' 03 04 05' 06 07 08' 09' (10) Popular nine-commune AC (1,500 ha); quality Cab Fr, ages well in gd yrs. Try: Bruno Dubois, CHX de Targé, DE VILLENEUVE; Clos Cristal, CLOS ROUGEARD; DOMS CHAMPS FLEURIS, de la Cune, Filliatreau, Legrand, Nerleux, Roches Neuves, St-Just, Antoine Sanzay, Val Brun; Cave des Vignerons de Saumur-St-Cyr-en-Bourg.

Saussignac SW w sw ★★→★★★ 05' 06 07' (09') Adjoins MONBAZILLAC; similar style, shade more acidity perhaps. Best: ★★★ DOM de Richard, Lestevénie, La Maurigne, Les Miaudoux, Clos d'Yvigne, ★★ CHX Le Chabrier, Court-les-Mûts, Le Payral, Le Tap, Tourmentine.

Sauternes B'x w sw ★★→★★★★ 83' 86' 88' 89' 90' 95 96 97' 98 99' 01' 02 03' 05' 07' 09' District of five villages (inc BARSAC) that make France's best sweet wine. Strong, luscious, golden, demanding 10+ yrs age. Still underpriced compared to red equivalents. Top CHX: d'YQUEM, GUIRAUD, LAFAURIE-PEYRAGUEY, RIEUSSEC, SUDUIRAUT, LA TOUR BLANCHE, etc. Dry wines cannot be sold as Sauternes.

Sauzet, Etienne C d'O ★★★ Once again leading PULIGNY DOM with superb PREMIERS CRUS (Combettes) and GRANDS CRUS (BÂTARD, etc). Fresh, lively wines.

Savennières Lo w dr sw ★★★ →★★★★ 89' 90' 93 95 96' 97' 99 02' 03 04 05' 06 07 08' 09 (10) Small (150 ha) ANJOU district for pungent, extremely minerally, long-lived whites. BAUMARD, Closel, Clos de Coulaine (*see* CH PIERRE-BISE), CH d'Epiré, DOM FL, Yves Guigniard, DOM Damien Laureau, Eric Morgat, Vincent Ogereau, CH Soucherie, Mathieu-Tijou. Top sites: COULÉE DE SERRANT, ROCHE-AUX-MOINES, Clos du Papillon.

Savigny-lès-Beaune C d'O r (w) ★★★ 99' 02' 03 05' 07 08 09' 10 Important village next to BEAUNE; similar mid-weight wines, should be delicious and lively; can be rustic. Top v'yds: Dominode, Guettes, Lavières, Marconnets, Vergelesses; growers inc: *Bize*, Camus, CHANDON DE BRIAILLES, CLAIR, Ecard, Girard, Guyon, LEROY, Pavelot, TOLLOT-BEAUT.

Savoie Sav r w sp ★★ DYA Alpine area with light, dry wines like some Swiss or minor Loires. APREMONT, CRÉPY and SEYSSEL are best-known whites; ROUSSETTE is more interesting. *Also gd Mondeuse red.*

Schlossberg ALSACE GRAND CRU of 80 ha at Kientzheim famed since 15th century. Glorious Ries from FALLER.

Schlumberger, Doms Al ★→★★★ Vast and top-quality DOM at Guebwiller owning approx 1% of all ALSACE v'yds. Holdings in GRANDS CRUS Kitterlé, Kessler, Saering and Spiegel. Range inc rare Ries, signature Cuvée Ernest and, latest addition, PINOT GR Grand Cru Kessler.

Schoenenbourg Al V. rich, successful Riquewihr GRAND CRU: PINOT GR, Ries, v. fine VENDANGE TARDIVE and SÉLECTION DES GRAINS NOBLES, esp from DEISS and DOPFF AU MOULIN. Also v.gd MUSCAT.

Schoffit, Dom Al ★★→★★★ Eclectic Colmar grower. Excellent VENDANGE TARDIVE Gewurz GRAND CRU RANGEN Clos St Theobald (00 05) on volcanic soil. Also rare, good Chasselas and fine Ries Sonnenberg (06 08 09')

Schröder & Schÿler Old BORDEAUX merchant, owner of CH KIRWAN.

Sciacarello Cors Indigenous grape variety, for original red and rosé.

Sec Literally means dry, though CHAMPAGNE so called is medium-sweet (and better at breakfast, teatime and weddings than BRUT).

Séguret S Rhô r w p ★★ 05' 06' 07' 09' 10' Postcard hillside village nr GIGONDAS. Mainly Grenache, peppery reds; clear-fruited whites. Esp CH la Couançonne, DOMS de l'Amauve, de Cabasse, J David (organic), Garancière, *Mourchon* (robust), Pourra, Soleil Romain.

Sélection des Grains Nobles Term coined by HUGEL for ALSACE equivalent to German Beerenauslese, and since 1984 subject to ever stricter regulations. *Grains nobles* are individual grapes with "noble rot".

Sérafin C d'O ★★★ Christian S has gained a cult following for his intense GEVREY-CHAMBERTIN VIEILLES VIGNES, CHARMES-CHAMBERTIN. Plenty of new wood here.

Seyssel Sav w sp ★★ NV Delicate white, pleasant sparkling. eg. Corbonod.

Sichel & Co One of BORDEAUX's most respected merchant houses (Sirius: top brand): interests in CHX D'ANGLUDET, PALMER and in CORBIÈRES.

Sipp-Mack Al ★★→★★★ Excellent DOM of 20 ha at Hunnawihr. Great Ries from GRANDS CRUS ROSACKER (02 06 08 10') and Osterberg; also v.gd PINOT GR.

Sipp, Jean & Louis Al ★★ Growers in Ribeauvillé (Louis also a négociant). Both make v.gd Ries Grand Cru Kirchberg. Jean's is youthful elegance; Louis's is firmer when mature. V.gd Gewurz from Louis, esp Grand Cru Osterberg.

Sorg, Bruno Al ★★→★★★ First-class small grower at Eguisheim for Grand Cru Florimont (Ries) and PFERSIGBERG (MUSCAT). Immaculate eco-friendly vyds. Winemaking with feeling.

St-Amour Beauj r ★★ 06 07 08 09' 10 Northernmost *cru*: light, fruity, resistible (except on 14 Feb). Growers to try: Janin, *Patissier*, Revillon.

St-Aubin C d'O r w ★★★ (w) 05' 06 07 08 09' 10 (r) 02' 03 05' 06 07 08 09' 10 Now front-line CÔTE DE BEAUNE white-wine village, also pretty reds. Best v'yds: En Remilly, Murgers Dents de Chien. Best: J C Bachelet, COLIN, Lamy, Prudhon.

St-Bris Burg w ★ DYA Neighbour to CHABLIS. Unique AC for Sauv Bl in Burgundy. Fresh, lively, worth keeping from J-H Goisot.

St-Chinian L'doc r ★→★★★★ 03 04 05' 06 07' 08 09' 10 Hilly area of growing reputation. AC for red (1982), white (2005). From 2011 vintage a *grand vin du* LANGUEDOC, with existing *crus*, Berlou and Roquebrun, becoming GRAND CRU du LANGUEDOC. Warm, spicy southern reds, based on Syrah, Grenache, Carignan. Gd co-ops Berlou, Roquebrun; CH de Viranel, DOMS Canet Valette, Madura, Rimbaud, Navarre, Borie la Vitarèle, Mas Champart.

St-Emilion B'x r ★★ →★★★★★ 89' 90' 94 95 96 98' 00' 01 03 **04** 05' 08 09' (10) Large, Merlot-dominated district on BORDEAUX's Right Bank. 5,500-ha. ST-EMILION

GRAND CRU AC the top designation. Warm, full, rounded style; the best firm and long-lived. Top CHX: ANGÉLUS, AUSONE, CANON, CHEVAL BLANC, FIGEAC, MAGDELAINE, PAVIE. Also *garagistes* LA MONDOTTE and VALANDRAUD. Gd co-op.

St-Estèphe H-Méd r ★★ →★★★★ 88′ 89′ 90′ 94 95′ 96′ **98** 00′ 01 02 03 04 05′ 06 08 09′ (10) Most northerly communal AC in the MÉDOC. Solid, structured wines. Top CHX: COS D'ESTOURNEL, MONTROSE, CALON-SÉGUR. Also many gd unclassified estates eg. HAUT-MARBUZET, ORMES-DE-PEZ, DE PEZ, PHÉLAN-SÉGUR.

St-Gall Champ BRUT NV; Extra Brut NV; Brut Blanc de Blancs NV; Brut Rosé NV; BRUT BLANC DE BLANCS **99 00** 02; Cuvée Orpale Blanc de Blancs **95** 96′ **98**. Brand used by Union-Champagne co-op: top CHAMPAGNE growers' co-op at AVIZE. Fine-value Pierre Vaudon NV and excellent Orpale (**95**′ 96).

St-Georges-St-Emilion B'x r ★★ **98** 00′ 01 03 05′ 08 09′ Tiny 200-ha ST-EMILION satellite. Usually gd quality. Best CHX: Calon, MACQUIN-ST-GEORGES, ST-GEORGES, TOUR DU PAS-ST-GEORGES, Vieux Montaiguillon.

St-Gervais S Rhô r (w p) ★ 07′ 09′ 10′ West bank Rhône village. Steady co-op, but star is top-grade, long-lived (10+ yrs) DOM Ste-Anne red (marked Mourvèdre licorice flavours); gd Viognier. Also DOM Clavel.

St-Jean de Minervois L'doc w sw ★★ Fine sweet VDN MUSCAT. Recent improvement, esp DOM de Barroubio, Michel Sigé, Clos du Gravillas, village co-op.

St-Joseph N Rhô r w ★★ 99′ 01′ 03′ 05′ 06′ 07′ **09′** 10′ AC all along west bank N Rhône (65 km). Syrah reds. Around Tournon, agreeably red-fruited wines; elsewhere darker flavours, more new oak. More complete, structured wines than CROZES-HERMITAGE, esp from CHAPOUTIER (Les Granits), Gonon (top class), **B Gripa**, GUIGAL (*lieu-dit* St-Joseph); also J–L CHAVE, Chèze, Courbis, Coursodon, Cuilleron, **Delas**, J & E Durand, B Faurie, P Faury, Gaillard, Nicolas Perrin, JABOULET, Monier-Perréol, A Perret, Vallet, F Villard. Gd food-friendly white (mainly Marsanne), esp Barge, CHAPOUTIER (Les Granits), Cuilleron, Gonon (fab), B Gripa, Faury, A Perret.

St-Julien H-Méd r ★★★ →★★★★ 88′ 89′ 90′ 94 95′ **96′** 98 00′ 01 **02 03 04** 05′ 06 08 09′ (10) Mid-MÉDOC communal AC with 11 classified (1855) estates, inc three LÉOVILLES, BEYCHEVELLE, DUCRU-BEAUCAILLOU, GRUAUD-LAROSE, etc. The epitome of harmonious, fragrant and savoury red wine.

St-Nicolas-de-Bourgueil Lo r p ★ →★★★ 89′ 90′ 95 96′ 97 02′ 03 05′ 06 08 09′ (10) Companion appellation to BOURGUEIL producing identical wines from Cab Fr. High proportion of gravel soils. Ranges from easy-drinking to age-worthy. More tannic and less supple than CHINON. Try: Yannick Amirault, Cognard, Lorieux, Frédéric Mabileau, Mabileau-Rezé, Taluau-Foltzenlogel, Gerard Vallée.

St-Péray N Rhô w sp ★★ 04′ 05′ 06′ 07′ 08′ 09′ 10′ Underrated white Rhône (mostly Marsanne) from tiny 60-ha granite v'yds nr Valence. A little *méthode Champenoise – worth trying*. Still white has a full minerality, is stylish, some are fat from v. ripe fruit. Best: S Chaboud, CHAPOUTIER, CLAPE, Colombo, B Gripa (v.gd), J-L Thiers, TAIN co-op, du Tunnel, Voge (oak).

St-Pourçain Mass C r p w ★→★★ DYA 2009 promoted to AC (600 ha). Light red and rosé from Gamay and Pinot N, white from local Tressalier and/or CHARD (v. popular), or Sauv Bl. Growers: DOM de Bellevue, Grosbot-Barbara, Nebout, Pétillat, Ray and gd co-op (Vignerons de St-Pourçain) with range of styles, inc drink-me-up Cuvée Ficelle. AC rules 100% Pinot N.

St-Romain C d'O r w ★★ (w) 05′ 06 07 08 09′ 10 *Crisp, mineral whites* and clean-cut reds from vines tucked away in the back of the CÔTE DE BEAUNE. PREMIER CRU v'yds expected soon. Alain Gras best. Also Buisson, De Chassorney.

St-Sardos SW r p w VDQS nr Montauban DYA ★ DOM de la Tucayne's owner founded ambitious co-op in remote area west of Toulouse. Gd-value Syrah-based wines.

St-Véran Burg w ★★ 07 08 09′ 10 AC loosely surrounding POUILLY-FUISSÉ with variable results, depending on soil and producer. DUBOEUF, Deux Roches, Poncetys for value, Cordier, Corsin, Merlin for top quality.

Southwest growers to watch in 2012

Patrick Rols (VDP Aveyron). Characterful biodynamic vines from nr Conques. Local sensation.

Dom Peyres-Roses (Gaillac). Passionately biodynamic family, working the vines with a horse.

Dom de Brin (Gaillac). Brilliant newcomer, esp for reds. Stole the show in recent Gaillac wine shows.

Dom de la Higuière (Côtes de Gascogne). Making gd wines here before Plaimont was thought of, or Grassa born.

Dom des Thermes (Côtes du Brulhois). Increasingly popular in local restaurants. No spa here. Delicious easy-drinking reds.

Ch Viguerie de Belaygues (Fronton). Multi-medal-winner all of a sudden. Now ranks with the best.

Ch Neyrac (Pécharmant). Young Bouché, scion of CH Champarel nearby, is making a fine reputation locally .

Dom Latapy (Jurançon). Mme. Guilhendou is at the southernmost end of the appellation, making lovely crisp wines.

Dom dou Bernès (Madiran). A notable step up in quality recently.

Dom L'Escudé (VDP Pyrénées-Atlantiques). Former *maître de chai* at CH Cabidos has struck out on his own. Wide range from local grapes as well as Merlot and Sauv Bl.

Dom Haut-Campagnau (Côtes de Gascogne). Conventional range of high quality complemented by eccentric oxydized styles. For the adventurous.

La Métairie, Dom des Bertranoux and Ch Biran. All once-distinguished PÉCHARMANT estates now having a makeover.

Ste-Croix-du-Mont B'x w sw ★★ 97' 98 99' 01' 02 03' **05' 07** 09' Sweet white AC facing SAUTERNES across the river Garonne. Well worth trying, esp CHX Crabitan-Bellevue, *Loubens*, du Mont, Pavillon, la Rame.

Ste-Victoire Prov r p ★★ New subzone of CÔTES DE PROVENCE from the southern slopes of the Montagne Ste-Victoire. Dramatic scenery goes with gd wine. Try Mas de Cadenet, Mauvan.

Sur lie "On the lees". MUSCADET is often bottled straight from the vat, for max zest, body and character.

Tâche, La C d'O r ★★★★ 90' 93' **95** 96' **97** 98 99' **00** 01 02' 03 05' 06 07 09 10 A 6-ha (1,500-case) GRAND CRU of VOSNE-ROMANÉE. One of best v'yds on earth: big, perfumed, luxurious wine. MONOPOLE of DOM ROMANÉE-CONTI.

Taille-aux-Loups, Dom de la Lo w sw sp ★★★ 02' 03' 05' **06** 07' 08' 09 (10, r) Jacky Blot, former wine broker, is one of the Loire's leading producers (60+ ha). Barrel-fermented MONTLOUIS and VOUVRAY, from dry to richly sweet; excellent Triple Zéro MONTLOUIS *pétillant* and fine reds from DOM de la Butte (14 ha) in BOURGUEIL. Triple Zéro Rosé Pétillant (Grolleau/Gamay) launched Dec 2010.

Tain, Cave de N Rhô ★★ Top co-op, 290 members, gd, mature v'yds, inc 25% of HERMITAGE. Improving quality. Decent red HERMITAGE, esp Epsilon, Gambert de Loche; modern style, esp CROZES. Marsanne whites gd value; great VIN DE PAILLE.

Taittinger Champ Brut NV; Rosé NV; BRUT **00 02** 04; Collection Brut **90 95** 96. Once-fashionable Reims grower and merchant sold to Crédit Agricole group in 2006. Distinctive silky, flowery touch, though not always consistent, often noticeably dosed. Excellent luxury brand: Comtes de Champagne Blanc de Blancs (96' 98' 02), Comtes de Champagne Rosé (96 02), also gd, rich Pinot Prestige Rosé NV. New CUVÉES Nocturne and Prélude. Also excellent new single-v'yd La Marquetterie. (*See also* California: Dom Carneros.)

Tavel S Rhô p ★★ DYA Once robust, big-flavoured rosé, now copying Provence style: pale, modern, easy apéritif. Best growers: DOM Corne-Loup, GUIGAL, Lafond Roc-Epine, Maby, DOM de la Mordorée (full), Prieuré de Montézargues (fine), Moulin-la-Viguerie, Rocalière (fine), CH de Manissy, Trinquevedel.

Tempier, Dom Prov r p w ★★★★ Once the pioneering grower of BANDOL. Wines of considerable elegance and longevity. Quality now challenged by several others.

Terrasses du Larzac L'doc r p w ★★→★ Northern part of AC LANGUEDOC. Wild, hilly region: Lac du Salagou towards Aniane. Cooler temperatures, fresher wines. From 2011 vintage a GRAND CRU du Languedoc. Stars/rising stars: Mas de l'Ecriture, Clos des Serres, Ca Delmoura, Montcalmès, *Mas Jullien*. Aspiring AOP (*see* p. 65).

Thénard, Dom Burg Major grower of the GIVRY appellation, but best known for his substantial portion (1.6 ha) of LE MONTRACHET. Should be better.

Thévenet, Jean Burg ★★★ Mâconnais purveyor of rich, some semi-botrytized, wines eg. Cuvée Levrouotée at DOM de la Bongran. Also DOM Emilian Gillet.

Thézac-Perricard SW r p ★★ 06 08 09' (10) Westward extension of CAHORS. MALBEC-based IGT; made for early drinking. Co-op good but ★★ DOM de Lancement better.

Thiénot, Alain Champ Broker-turned-merchant; dynamic force for gd in CHAMPAGNE. Ever-improving quality across the range. Impressive, fairly priced Brut NV. Rosé NV Brut. Vintage Stanislas (02 04) and Voluminous Vigne aux Gamins (single-v'yd Avize 99 02). Top Grande Cuvée 96' 98 02'. Also owns Marie Stuart and CANARD-DUCHÊNE in Champagne, CH Ricaud in LOUPIAC.

Thomas, André & Fils Al ★★★ V. fine grower at Ammerschwihr attached to rigorous biological methods. An artist-craftsman in the cellar: v.gd Ries Kaefferkopf and magnificent Gewurz VIEILLES VIGNES (05 06 08).

Thorin, J Beauj ★ Major BEAUJOLAIS négociant owned by BOISSET.

Tollot-Beaut C d'O ★★★ Stylish, consistent Burgundy grower with 20 ha in CÔTE DE BEAUNE, inc v'yds at BEAUNE (Grèves, Clos du Roi), CORTON, SAVIGNY (Les Champs Chevrey), and at its CHOREY-LÈS-BEAUNE base.

Touraine Lo r p w dr sw sp ★→★★★★ 05' 06 08 09' (10) Huge region (5,500 ha) with many ACS (eg. VOUVRAY, CHINON, BOURGUEIL) as well as umbrella AC of variable quality. Zesty reds (Cab Fr, Côt, Gamay, Pinot N), pungent whites (Sauv Bl, Chenin Bl), rosés and *mousseux*. Many gd bistro wines, often gd value. Producers: CH de Petit Thouars, Clos Roussely, DOMS des Bois-Vaudons, Corbillières, Joël Delaunay, de la Garrelière (François Plouzeau), de la presle; Clos Roche Blanche, Mandard, Jacky Marteau, *Marionnet*; Oisly & Thésée, Thierry Puzelat, Clos de Tue-Boeuf, Vincent Ricard. Ill-conceived reforms proposed.

Touraine-Amboise Lo r p w ★→★★ TOURAINE sub-appellation (220 ha). François 1er is entry-level tasty, food-friendly local blend (Gamay/Côt/Cab Fr). Chenin Bl for whites. Closerie de Chanteloup, Damien Delecheneau, DOM des Bessons, Dutertre, Xavier Frissant, de la Gabillière.

Touraine-Azay-le-Rideau Lo w p ★→★★ Small TOURAINE sub-appellation (60 ha) for Chenin Bl-based dry, off-dry white and Grolleau-dominated rosé. Producers: CH de l'Aulée, Nicolas Paget, Pibaleau.

Touraine-Mesland Lo r p w ★→★★ small TOURAINE sub-appellation (90 ha) best represented by its user-friendly red blends (Gamay/Côt/Cab Fr). Whites are mainly Chenin with a little CHARD. CH Gaillard, Clos de la Briderie.

Touraine-Noble Joué Lo p ★→★★ DYA Ancient but now revived rosé from three Pinots (N, Gr, Meunier) just south of Tours. Esp from ROUSSEAU and Sard. Became separate AC in 2001 and now totals 28 ha.

Trapet C d'O ★★→★★★ A long-established GEVREY-CHAMBERTIN DOM now enjoying new life and sensual wines with biodynamic farming. Ditto cousins Rossignol-Trapet – slightly more austere wines.

Trévallon, Dom de Prov r w ★★★ 95 96 97 98 99 00' 01 03 04 05 06 07 08 09 In Les Baux, but IGP Bouches du Rhône fully deserving its huge reputation. Intense Cab Sauv/Syrah to age. BARRIQUE-aged white from Marsanne and Roussanne, a drop of CHARD and now Grenache Bl. Well worth seeking out.

Trimbach, F E Al ★★★→★★★★ Supreme growers of Ries on limestone soils around Ribeauvillé, esp magnificent Clos Ste Hune (02') and almost-as-good *Frédéric Emile* (02 06 08). Wines for great cuisine in dry, elegant style.

Tursan SW r p w ★★→★★★ (Most DYA) Master chef Michel Guérard makes lovely ★★★ wines, but hardly typical of the appellation. More authentic ★★ DOM de Perchade gd. Lively ★ co-op, now twinned with Coteaux de Chalosse, is not bad.

Vacqueyras S Rhô r (p) w ★★ 95' 98' 99' 00' 01 03 04' 05' 06' 07' 09' 10' Direct, full, peppery, Grenache-led neighbour of GIGONDAS, hotter v'yds – can be potent. Lives 10+ yrs. NB: Arnoux Vieux Clocher, JABOULET, CHX de Montmirail, des Tours (v. fine), VIDAL-FLEURY; Clos des Cazaux (gd value), DOMS Amouriers, Archimbaud-Vache, Charbonnière, Couroulu (traditional), Font de Papier, Fourmone, Garrigue, Grapillon d'Or, Monardière (v.gd), Montirius (organic), Montvac, Perrin & Fils, Roucas Toumba (organic), Sang des Cailloux (v.gd).

Val de Loire Lo r p w DYA One of France's four regional IGPS, formerly Jardin de la France. Wide range of single varietals, inc CHARD, Cab Fr, Gamay and Sauv Bl.

Valençay Lo r p w ★ AC in east TOURAINE, 139 ha; light, sometimes rustic and sharp wines from similar range of grapes as TOURAINE, esp Sauv Bl. Clos Delorme (Minchin), Jacky Preys, Hubert & Olivier Sinson, Sébastien Vaillant.

Val d'Orbieu, Vignerons du L'doc ★★ Association of some 200 growers and co-ops in CORBIÈRES, LANGUEDOC, MINERVOIS, ROUSSILLON, etc., marketing a sound range of AC and IGP wines. Red Cuvée Mythique is flagship.

Valréas S Rhô r (p w) ★★ 07' 09' 10 Modest CÔTES DU RHÔNE village in northern Vaucluse black-truffle area; large co-op, but lacks range of gd DOMS. Fair-depth red (mainly Grenache), improving white. Esp Emmanuel Bouchard, DOM des Grands Devers, CH la Décelle.

Varichon & Clerc Sav Principal makers and shippers of sparkling wines.

VDQS *Vins délimité de qualité supérieure.* Due to be phased out at end of 2011.

Vendange Harvest. **Vendange tardive**: late harvest; ALSACE equivalent to German Auslese but usually higher alcohol.

Venoge, de Champ Venerable house now revitalized under BOIZEL Chanoine group management. Gd. niche blends: Cordon Bleu Extra-Brut, Vintage Blanc de Blancs (00 02), CUVÉE 20 ans and Prestige Cuvée Louis XV, a 10-yr-old BLANC DE NOIRS. Fine collection of old labels and posters.

Ventoux S Rhô r p (w) ★★ 07' 09' 10' Sprawling 6,000+ ha AC around Mont Ventoux between Rhône and PROVENCE for gluggable, clear red (Grenache-Syrah, café-style to richer, deeper), rosé and gd white (use of oak is growing). Altitude supplies welcome cool flavours for some. Best: LA VIEILLE FERME (r) owned by BEAUCASTEL, co-op Bédoin, Goult, St-Didier, DOMS Anges, Berane, Brusset, Cascavel, Champ-Long, Croix de Pins, Fondrèche, Font-Sane, Grand Jacquet, JABOULET, Martinelle, Murmurium, Pesquié (excellent), Pigeade, Terres de Solence, Valcombe, Verrière, VIDAL-FLEURY.

Verget Burg ★★→★★★★ Jean-Marie GUFFENS' Mâconnais-based white-wine merchant venture, nearly as idiosyncratic as his own DOM. Fine quality, plans for reds, too.

Veuve Clicquot Champ Yellow Label NV; White Label Demi-Sec NV; Vintage Réserve 98' 99 02'; Rosé Reserve 95 96 98 99' 02'. Historic house of highest standing (owner LVMH). Full-bodied, almost rich: one of Champagne's surest things. Reims cellars. Luxury brands: La Grande Dame (90' **95'**), Rich Réserve (**96** 99 02), La Grande Dame Rosé (**95** 96). Oak-fermented vintages from 2010. New Cave Privée re-release of old vintages in several formats: superb 85, 78 Rosé.

Veuve Devaux Premium CHAMPAGNE of powerful Union Auboise co-op. Excellent aged Grande Réserve NV, Oeil de Perdrix Rosé, Prestige Cuvée D (96). Also excellent Brut Vintage (02)

Vézelay Burg r w Age 1–2 yrs. Rising subdistrict of BOURGOGNE. Flavoursome whites from CHARD or Melon (BOURGOGNE GRANDE ORDINAIRE); local BOURGOGNE Pinot. Try DOM de la Cadette, des Faverelles, Maria Cuny, Elise Villiers.

Vidal-Fleury, J N Rhô ★★ Big moves at GUIGAL-owned merchant of Rhône wines and grower of CÔTE-RÔTIE, top-notch, v. elegant La Chatillonne (12% Viognier; wait min 5 yrs). Range sharply improving. Gd CÔTES DU RHÔNE Viognier, VENTOUX, MUSCAT DE BEAUMES-DE-VENISE, VACQUEYRAS.

Vieille Ferme, La S Rhô r w ★★ Often a star buy brand of esp VENTOUX (r) and LUBÉRON (w) made by Perrin family of CH DE BEAUCASTEL. Lots of fruit, gd value.

Vieilles Vignes Old vines: which should make the best wine. Eg. DE VOGÜÉ MUSIGNY Vieilles Vignes. But no rules about age and can be a tourist trap.

Vieux Télégraphe, Dom du S Rhô r w ★★★ 78' 81' 85 88 89' 90 94' 95' 96' 97 98' 99' 00 01' 03' 04' 05' **06'** 07' 09' 10' Top name, maker of complex, long-lived red CHÂTEAUNEUF, and rich white (more *gourmand* since 1990s, excellent with food, always gd in lesser yrs). Second DOM: de la Roquète, gd fruit, reds gaining depth, fresh whites, both on the rise. Owns gd, slow-ageing, understated *Gigondas Dom Les Pallières* with US importer Kermit Lynch.

Vigne or vignoble Vineyard (v'yd), vineyards (v'yds).

Vigneron Vine-grower.

Vin de paille Wine from grapes dried on straw mats, so v. sweet, like Italian *passito*. Esp in the Jura. *See also* CHAVE and VIN PAILLÉ DE CORRÈZE.

Vin de Pays (VDP) The most dynamic category in France (with over 150 regions). Renamed Indication Géographique Protegée (IGP) for 2009 vintage, but position unchanged and new terminology not accepted by every area. The zonal names are most individual: eg. CÔTES DE GASCOGNE, CÔTES DE THONGUE, Haute Vallée de l'Orb, Duché d'Uzès, among others. Enormous variety in taste and quality but never ceases to surprise.

Vin de table Category of standard everyday table wine, not subject to particular regulations about grapes and origin. Can be source of unexpected delights if a talented winemaker uses this category to avoid bureaucratic hassle. Regulations about to change to include vintage and grape variety.

Vin doux naturel (VDN) Sweet wine fortified with wine alcohol, so the sweetness is natural, not the strength. The specialty of ROUSSILLON, based on Grenache or MUSCAT. Top wines, esp RANCIOS, can be remarkable.

Vin gris "Grey" wine is v. pale pink, made of red grapes pressed before fermentation begins – unlike rosé, which ferments briefly before pressing. "Œil de Perdrix" means much the same; so does "blush".

Vin jaune Jura w ★★★ Specialty of ARBOIS: odd yellow wine like fino Sherry. Normally ready when bottled (after at least 6 yrs). Best is CH CHALON. *See also* PLAGEOLES. A halfway-house oxidized white is sold locally as *vin typé*.

Vin paillé de Corrèze SW r w Recently revived VIN DE PAILLE from Beaulieu-sur-Dordogne made by 25 growers and small co-op. Recommendation no longer limited (folklore) to breast-feeding mothers. Modern grape varieties preferred by most growers, esp ★ Christian Tronche (gd initiation to this style).

Vinsobres S Rhô r (p w) ★→★★ 06' 07' 09' 10' Syrah-accentuated appellation, helped by fresh breezes, altitude, nr Nyons. Top reds show live fruit, punchy body. Leaders: Cave la Vinsobraise, DOMS les Aussellons, Bicarelle, Chaume

Arnaud, Constant-Duquesnoy, Coriançon, Deurre (traditional), Jaume, Moulin (traditional), Perrin & Fils (v.gd value), Peysson, CH Rouanne.

Viré-Clessé Burg w ★★ 07 08 09' 10 AC based around two of best white villages of MÂCON. Extrovert style, though residual sugar originally forbidden. Try A Bonhomme, Bret Bros, Chaland, LAFON (from 2009), Michel, THÉVENET, co-op.

Visan S Rhô (p) (w) ★★ 07' 09' 10' Fast-improving Rhône village for medium-depth reds laced with fruit and freshness. Young grower momentum. Acceptable whites. Best: DOMS Coste Chaude, Florane, Fourmente (esp Nature), des Grands Devers, Roche-Audran.

Vogüé, Comte Georges de C d'O ★★★★ Iconic CHAMBOLLE estate inc lion's share of MUSIGNY. Heralded vintages from 1990s taking time to come round.

Volnay C d'O r ★★★ →★★★★ 90' 95 96' 98 99' 02' 03 05' 06 07 08 09' 10 Village between POMMARD and MEURSAULT: often the best reds of the CÔTE DE BEAUNE; structured and silky. Best v'yds: Caillerets, Champans, Clos des Chênes, Santenots, Taillepieds, etc. Best growers: D'ANGERVILLE, J-M BOILLOT, HOSPICES DE BEAUNE, LAFARGE, LAFON, DE MONTILLE, Rossignol.

Volnay-Santenots C d'O r ★★★ Best red-wine v'yds of MEURSAULT sold under this name. Indistinguishable from other PREMIER CRU VOLNAY, unless more body, less delicacy. Best growers: Ampeau, HOSPICES DE BEAUNE, LAFON, LEROY, PRIEUR.

Vosne-Romanée C d'O r ★★★ →★★★★ 90' 93 95 96' 98 99' 02' 03 05' 06 07 08 09' 10. Village with Burgundy's grandest *crus* (eg. ROMANÉE-CONTI, LA TÂCHE) and outstanding PREMIERS CRUS Malconsorts, Suchots, Brûlées, etc. There are (or should be) no common wines in Vosne. Many gd growers, inc: Arnoux, CATHIARD, Clavelier, DRC, EUGÉNIE, GRIVOT, GROS, Lamarche, LEROY, LIGER-BELAIR, MÉO-CAMUZET, MUGNERET, ROUGET, Tardy.

Vougeot C d'O r w ★★★ 90' 93 95' 96' 98 99' 02' 03 05' 06 07 08 09' 10 Mostly GRAND CRU as CLOS DE VOUGEOT but also village and PREMIER CRU, inc outstanding white MONOPOLE, Clos Blanc de V. HUDELOT-Noellat and VOUGERAIE best.

Vougeraie, Dom de la C d'O r w ★★ →★★★ DOM uniting all BOISSET's v'yd holdings since 1999. Gd-value BOURGOGNE *rouge* up to fine MUSIGNY GRAND CRU and unique white Clos Blanc de Vougeot.

Vouvray Lo w dr sw sp ★★ →★★★★ For sweet Vouvray: 89' 90' 95' 96' 97' 03' 05' 08 09'. For dry Vouvray: 89 90 96' 97 02' 03 05' 06 07 08' 09. Important AC east of Tours: still wines increasingly gd and reliable. DEMI-SEC is classic style, but in gd yrs *moelleux* can be intensely sweet, almost immortal. Variable sparkling (60% of production): look out for *pétillant*. Best producers: Allias, Bonneau, Carême, *Champalou*, Clos Baudoin (CHIDAINE), Dhoye-Deruet (DOM de la Fontanerie), Foreau, Fouquet (DOM des Aubuisières), CH Gaudrelle, *Huet*, DOM DE LA TAILLE-AUX-LOUPS, Vigneau-Chevreau. If you find ancient vintages – such as 1921, 1924, 1947 or 1959 – don't hesitate.

Vranken Ever more powerful CHAMPAGNE group created in 1976. Sound quality. Leading brand: Demoiselle. Owns HEIDSIECK MONOPOLE and POMMERY.

Wolfberger Al ★★ Principal label of Eguisheim co-op. Exceptional quality for such a large-scale producer. V. important for CRÉMANT.

"Y" B'x (pronounced "ygrec") 80' 85 86 88 94 96 00 02 04 05 06 07 08 Intense, dry white wine produced at CH D'YQUEM, lately with more regularity. Enticing young but interesting with age. Dry style in 2004, otherwise in classic off-dry mould, but recently purer and fresher than in the past.

Zind Humbrecht, Dom Al ★★★★ ALSACE growers since 1620. Now leading biodynamic DOM sensitively run by Olivier Humbrecht, great winemaker and scholar: rich, powerful yet balanced wines, using v. low yields. Top wines from single v'yds *Clos St-Urbain*, Jebsal (superb PINOT GR 02' 06 09 10) and Windsbuhl (esp Gewurz 05), and GRANDS CRUS RANGEN, HENGST, Brand, Goldert.

Châteaux of Bordeaux

Abbreviations used in the text:

B'x	Bordeaux
Bar	Barsac
E-2-M	Entre-Deux-Mers
Grav	Graves
H-Méd	Haut-Médoc
L de P	Lalande de Pomerol
List	Listrac
Mar	Margaux
Méd	Médoc
Mou	Moulis
Pau	Pauillac
Pe-Lé	Pessac-Léognan
Pom	Pomerol
St-Em	St-Emilion
St-Est	St-Estèphe
St-Jul	St-Julien
Saut	Sauternes
AC	*appellation contrôlée*
ch, chx	château(x)
dom, doms	domaine(s)

More heavily shaded areas are the wine-growing regions.

Bordeaux managed a hat-trick of golden vintages with 1988, 1989 and 1990, and 20 years on has done it again with 2008, 2009 and 2010. The first was saved by an Indian summer and has a classic touch (a bit like 1988 – one for those who think exuberance can be overdone); the second an explosion of fruit that may transcend even 1982, and the last an unbelievable depth of colour and virile structure to match. They've all got their own characters but all are top-grade, age-worthy vintages. Price is the only dampener; and yes, the elite are destined for investment funds and millionaires. But humbler Bordeaux is still not that easy to sell.

In the middle and lower reaches there are bargains, if not in restaurants. So if 2008, 2009 and 2010 are due to be cellared for a number of years (as 2005 and 2006), what is there for drinking over the coming year? Well, 2007 has a fruity immediacy; 2002 and 2004 classicism – beginning to drink well now – and 2001 (best between 2010–2015) the balance and charm that make Bordeaux our favourite daily drink. 2003 is an odd vintage; too hot. Set your expectations on the low side and you might be very happy. Otherwise look at some of the older vintages you might have saved (2000, 1999, 1998). Work on them. Don't forget dry white Bordeaux (2010 is another excellent year); stunning Sauternes vintages (2009, 2007, 2005, 2003, 2002, 2001).

d'Agassac H-Méd r ★★ 00' 02 03 04 05 06 07 08 09' "Sleeping Beauty" 14th-century moated fort. 42 ha nr BORDEAUX suburbs. Modern, accessible MÉDOC.

Andron-Blanquet St-Est r ★★ 96 98 00' 03 04 05' 06 08 09 16-ha sister CH to COS-LABORY. Unfashionable but gd value.

Angélus St-Em r ★★★★ 89' 90' 92' 95 96 98' 99 00' 01 02 03' 04 05 06 07 08 09' 10 Leading PREMIER GRAND CRU CLASSÉ on ST-EMILION CÔTES. Pioneer of the modern style; dark, rich, sumptuous. Manual destemming since 2009, laser-optical sorter in 2010. Second wine: Le Carillon de L'Angélus. Fleur de Boüard in LALANDE DE POMEROL and Bellevue in ST-EMILION same ownership.

d'Angludet Marg r ★★★ 90 95 96' 98' 00 02 04 05 06 08 09' 10 34-ha estate owned and run by SICHEL. Lively, fragrant gd value MARGAUX of great style popular in UK.

Archambeau Grav r w dr (sw) ★★ (r) 98 00 02 04 05 06 08 09 (w) 01 02 04 05 06 07 08 09 Up-to-date 27-ha property at Illats. Gd fruity, dry white; fragrant barrel-aged reds. Same ownership as improving BARSAC classed growth CH Suau.

d'Arche Saut w sw ★★ 96 97' 98 99 00 00' 01' 02 03' 05 07 09' Much-improved 29-ha classed growth. Top vintages are creamy. CH d'Arche-Lafaurie is a richer micro-CUVÉE. Also bed-and-breakfast in 17th-century chapter house.

d'Armailhac Pau r ★★★ 89 90' 94 95' 96' 98 99 00 01 02 03 04 05' 06 07 08 09' 10 Formerly CH Mouton Baronne Philippe. Substantial Fifth Growth under Rothschild ownership. 51 ha: top-quality PAUILLAC with more finesse than sister CLERC MILON. On top form since 2004 and well priced.

l'Arrosée St-Em r ★★★ 98' 00 01 02 03 04 05' 06' 07 08 09' 10 A 9.7-ha côtes estate opposite ST-EMILION co-op. Progressed under new ownership since 2003. Aromatic, structured wines with plenty of Cab Fr and Cab Sauv (40%).

Ausone St-Em r ★★★★ 85 86' 88 89' 90 95 96' 97 98' 99 00' 01' 02 03' 04 05' 06' 07 08 09' 10 Illustrious First Growth with 7 ha (approx 1,500 cases); best position on the CÔTES with famous rock-hewn cellars. On superb form since 1996, hence the astronomical price. Long-lived wines, with volume, texture and finesse. Second wine: Chapelle d'Ausone (500 cases) also excellent.

Balestard La Tonnelle St-Em r ★★ 96 98' 00' 01 03 04 05 06 09 Historic classed growth, 11-ha. Associate of MICHEL ROLLAND consults. Richer and riper since 2003.

Barde-Haut St-Em r ★★ 98 99 00 01 02 03 05' 06 07 08 09 10 The 17-ha sister property of CLOS L'EGLISE and HAUT-BERGEY. Rich, modern and opulent in style.

Bastor-Lamontagne Saut w sw ★★ 96' 97' 98 99 01' 02 03' 05 07 09' Large (56 ha) Preignac sister to BEAUREGARD. Gd value; pure, harmonious style. Second label: Les Remparts de Bastor. Fruity Caprice (from 2004) for early drinking. Also CH St-Robert at Pujols: red and white GRAVES.

Batailley Pau r ★★★ 95 96 98 00' 02 03 04 05' 06 08 09' Fifth Growth property (55 ha) bordering PAUILLAC and ST-JULIEN. Fine, firm, strong-flavoured. *Gd-value Pauillac* on steady form. Denis Dubourdieu consults.

Beaumont Méd r ✰✰ 98 00' 02 04 05' 06 07 08 09 One of the largest (114 ha) estates in the MÉDOC; large volume, *easily enjoyable wines.* Second label: CH Moulin d'Arvigny. In the same hands as BEYCHEVELLE.

Beauregard Pom r ✰✰✰ 95' 96' 98' 00' 01 02 03 04 05' 06 08 09' 10 Large (for POMEROL) estate: 17 ha; fine 17th-century CH nr LA CONSEILLANTE. Harmonious rather than full style. Consistent. Second label: Benjamin de Beauregard.

Beau-Séjour-Bécot St-Em r ✰✰✰ 89' 90' 95' 96 98' 99 00' 01 02 03 04 05' 06 07 08 09' 10 18-ha estate on the limestone plateau. Demoted in class in 1986 but re-promoted to PREMIER GRAND CRU CLASSÉ in 1996. Seductive wines with more finesse from 2001. GRAND-PONTET and LA GOMERIE in same family hands.

Beauséjour-Duffau St-Em r ✰✰✰ 95 96 98 99 00 01 02 03 04 05' 06 08 09' 10 7-ha PREMIER GRAND CRU CLASSÉ estate on west slope of the CÔTES owned by Duffau-Lagarrosse family. New winemaking and management from 2009: Nicolas Thienpont and STÉPHANE DERENONCOURT at the helm.

Beau-Site St-Est r ✰✰ 96 98 00 03 04 05 06 08 09 40-ha property in same hands as BATAILLEY, etc. 70% Cab Sauv. Average wine but more flesh in recent yrs.

Belair-Monange St-Em r ✰✰✰ 89' 90' 94 95' 96 98 99 00' 01 02 03 04 05' 06 08 09' 10 Classed-growth neighbour of AUSONE. Name change 2008 from plain Belair. J-P MOUEIX owner since 2008, new investment. Fine, fragrant, elegant style; more concentration since 2002. Second wine: CH Haut Roc Blanquant.

Belgrave H-Méd r ✰✰ 96' 98' 00' 02' 03 04' 05' 06 07 08 09' 60-ha Fifth Growth well managed by CVBG-DOURTHE (*see* LA GARDE, REYSSON). Modern-classic in style. Reasonable value. Second label: Diane de Belgrave.

Bellefont-Belcier St-Em r ✰✰ 00 01 02 03 04 05' 06 07 08 09' 14-ha GRAND CRU CLASSÉ justifiably promoted in 2006. Neighbour of LARCIS-DUCASSE on the *côtes* at St-Laurent-des-Combes. Suave, fresh and refined. Recent vintages v.gd.

Bel-Orme-Tronquoy-de-Lalande H-Méd r ✰✰ 96 98' 00 02 03 04 05 08 09 28-ha estate north of ST-ESTÈPHE. Clay-limestone soils, so Merlot (60%) dominates. Firm, muscular style. Same owner as CROIZET-BAGES, RAUZAN-GASSIES.

Berliquet St-Em r ✰✰ 96 98' 99 00' 01 02 04 05' 06 08 09 A 9.3-ha GRAND CRU CLASSÉ on the *côtes*. DERENONCOURT consultant from 2008, new approach.

Bernadotte H-Méd r ✰✰ 99 00' 01 02 03 04 05' 06 07 08 09 30-ha estate managed by PICHON-LALANDE team since 1997. ROEDERER owner since 2006. Structured wines. Recent vintages have more finesse.

Bertineau St-Vincent r ✰✰ 98 99 00' 01 04 05 06 08 09 Top oenologist MICHEL ROLLAND owns this 5.6-ha estate in Lalande-de-Pomerol. Old vines, fairly consistent. (*See also* LE BON PASTEUR.)

Beychevelle St-Jul r ✰✰✰ 96 98 99 00' 01 02 03 04 05' 06 07 08 09' 10 Fourth Growth (90 ha) with eye-catching boat label. Insurance company and Suntory (LAGRANGE) owners. Wines of consistent elegance rather than power. On top form since late 1990s. Second wine: Amiral de Beychevelle.

Biston-Brillette Mou r ✰✰ 00 01 02 03 04 05' 06 08 09 Attractive, fruit-bound, gd-value, family-owned MOULIS. 25 ha in production.

Bonalgue Pom r ✰✰ 96' 98' 99 00 01 04 05 06 08 09 Dark, rich, meaty POMEROL. As gd-value as it gets. MICHEL ROLLAND consults. Sister estate: Clos du Clocher.

Bonnet r w ✰✰ (r) 04 05 06 08 09 (w) DYA Owned by octogenarian André Lurton. Big producer (270 ha!), some of the best E2-M and red BORDEAUX. *Prestige* red CUVÉE, Divinus. LA LOUVIÈRE, COUHINS-LURTON, ROCHEMORIN same stable.

Bon Pasteur, le Pom r ✰✰✰ 95 96' 98' 99 00 01 02 03 04 05' 06 08 09' 10 Excellent 7-ha property on ST-EMILION border, owned by MICHEL ROLLAND. Ripe, opulent, seductive wines guaranteed. (*See also* BERTINEAU ST-VINCENT.)

Boscq, le St-Est r ✰✰ 98 00 01 03 04 05' 06 08 09' Quality-driven 18-ha estate owned by CVBG-DOURTHE. Merlot-dominated (60%). Excellent value.

Bourgneuf-Vayron Pom r ★★ 96' 98' 99 00 01' 03 04 05' 06 08 09 10 Ample, firm-edged POMEROL from this 9-ha estate on sandy/gravel soils.

Bouscaut Pe-Lé r w ★★ (r) 90 95 98 00 01 02 04 05' 06 07 08 09 (w) 00 01 02 03 04 05' 06 07 08 09 46-ha classed growth owned by sister of BRANE-CANTENAC's Henri Lurton. Merlot-based reds. Sappy white wines.

Boyd-Cantenac Marg r ★★★ 95 96' 98' 00 01 02 03 04 05' 06 07 08 09' Little-known 18-ha Third Growth in better form since 2000. Cab Sauv-dominated with a little peppery Petit Verdot. Second wine: Jacques Boyd. *See also* POUGET.

Branaire-Ducru St-Jul r ★★★ 90' 93' 94 95 96 98 99 00' 01 02 03 04 05' 06 08 09' 10 Fourth Growth ST-JULIEN, 51 ha scattered around AC. "Fruit, freshness, finesse" the motto here. Less power, concentration than its peers. Second label: Duluc.

Brane-Cantenac Marg r ★★★ 89' 95 96 98 99 00' 01 02 03 04 05' 06 07 08 09' 10 Big (74-ha) Second Growth. Dense, fragrant MARGAUX. Improvements under Henri Lurton since 1995. Second label: Baron de Brane.

Brillette Mou r ★★ 98 99 00 02 03 04 05 06 08 09 MOULIS estate (40 ha). Wines of gd depth and fruit. MICHEL ROLLAND consults. Second label: Berthault Brillette.

Cabanne, La Pom r ★★ 95 96 98' 00 04 05 06' 08 09 10-ha property west of the POMEROL plateau. Rustic in style; finer and fleshier in 2006 but could do better. Second wine: DOM de Compostelle.

Cadet-Piola St-Em r ★★ 95 98 00 01 03 04 05 06 08 09 Small (7-ha) GRAND CRU CLASSÉ under same ownership/management as SOUTARD and LARMANDE from 2009. Fresh, firm, long-lived wines.

Caillou Saut w sw ★★ 89' 90' 95 96 97 98 99 01' 02 03' 05' 07 09' Well-run second-rank 13-ha BARSAC v'yd for firm, fruity wine. Cuvée Reine (99 01' 03') is a top selection, *prestige cuvée* another.

Calon-Ségur St-Est r ★★★ 90' 94 95 96' 98 99 00' 01 02 03' 04 05' 06 07 08 09' 46-ha Third Growth with great historic reputation. Mme. Capbern-Gasqueton the matriarchal owner. Former CH MARGAUX quality controller the new winemaker from 2006. Now really flying. Second label: Marquis de Calon.

Cambon la Pelouse H-Méd r ★★ 98' 99 00 01 02 03 04 05' 06 07 08 09 Big, supple, accessible southern HAUT-MÉDOC *cru*. L'Aura, a micro-CUVÉE from MARGAUX.

Camensac H-Méd r ★★ 95 96' 98 01 02 03 05 06 08 09 75-ha Fifth Growth. New owner (2005) has CHASSE-SPLEEN connection; change for the better from 2006; riper fruit. Second label: La Closerie de Camensac.

Canon St-Em r ★★★ 96 98' 99 00 01 02 03 04 05' 06 07 08' 09' 10 Famous first-classed growth; walled-in 22 ha on plateau west of the town; bought in 1996 by owners of RAUZAN-SÉGLA. Investment and restructuring of v'yd (70% replanted) has paid off. Elegant, long-lived wines. 2009 best ever. Second label: Clos Canon.

Canon-de-Brem r ★★ 00 01 03 04 05' RIP from 2006. Bought by Jean Halley of Carrefour supermarkets (2000), wine now absorbed into CH DE LA DAUPHINE. Massive recent investment. Firm, pure expression.

Canon la Gaffelière St-Em r ★★★ 95 96' 98' 99 00' 01 02 03 04 05' 06 08 09' 10 Leading 19-ha GRAND CRU CLASSÉ on the lower slopes of the *côtes*. Same ownership as CLOS DE L'ORATOIRE, LA MONDOTTE and Aiguilhe in Castillon. Stylish, upfront, impressive wines with 40% Cab Fr and 5% Cab Sauv.

Cantegril Grav r Saut w sw ★★ (r) 00 02 04 05 06 08 09 (w) 02 03 04 05' 06 07 09 Supple red; fine BARSAC-SAUTERNES from DOISY-DAËNE AND CLOS FLORIDÈNE connection. Value.

Cantemerle H-Méd r ★★★ 90 95 96' 98 00 01 02 03 04 05' 06' 07 08 09' 10 Large 90-ha property in south MÉDOC. Now merits its Fifth Growth status. Sandy/gravel soils give finer style. Second label: Les Allées de Cantemerle.

Cantenac-Brown Marg r ★★→★★★ 94 95 96' 98 99 00 01 02 03 04 05' 06 08 09' 10 42-ha Third Growth sold in 2006 to private investor; owned since late

1980s by AXA Millésimes. Previously robust style being steadily refined (v.gd 09). Second label: Brio du CH Cantenac Brown.

Capbern-Gasqueton St-Est r ★★ 98 00 02 03 04 05 06 08 09' 38-ha property offering solid fare; same owner as CALON-SÉGUR. Highly rated 2009.

Cap de Mourlin St-Em r ★★→★★★ 96 98' 99 00 01 03 04 05 06 08 09 Well-known 15 ha owned by Capdemourlin family, also owner of CH BALESTARD LA TONNELLE and CH Roudier, MONTAGNE-ST-EMILION. Riper and more concentrated than in the past.

Carbonnieux Pe-Lé r w ★★★ 95 96 98 99 00 02 04 05' 06 07 08 09' 10 Large (90-ha), historic estate at Léognan for sterling red and white. Charismatic owner Antony Perrin died 2008; sons Eric and Philibert now in charge. The whites, 65% Sauv Bl (eg. 98 99 00 01 02 03 04 05 06 07 08 09 10), can age up to 10 yrs. CHX Le Pape and Le Sartre are also in the family. Second label: La Tour-Léognan.

Carles, de r St-Em r ★★→★★★ 99 00 01 02 03 04 05' 06' 07 08 09 10 FRONSAC. Haut Carles (★★★) is top selection here with its own modern, gravity-fed cellars. Investment and aspirations of a top growth. Superb from 2006. Second label: de Carles.

Carmes Haut-Brion, les Pe-Lé r ★★★ 90' 94 95 96 98 99 00 01 02 03 04 05' 06 07 08 09 10 Small (4.7-ha) neighbour of HAUT-BRION with classed-growth standards. 55% Merlot. New ownership in 2010.

Caronne-Ste-Gemme H-Méd r ★★ 00 01 02 03 04 05 06 08 09' 40-ha MÉDOC estate. Olivier Dauga consults. Recent vintages show more class.

Carruades de Château Lafite Pau 10 Second wine of CH LAFITE; a relatively easy-drinker (40% Merlot). Its price continues to go ballistic thanks to Chinese demand.

Carteau Côtes-Daugay St-Em r ★★ 00 01 02 03 04 05 08 09 Consistent 16-ha ST-EMILION GRAND CRU; full-flavoured wines maturing fairly early.

Certan-de-May Pom r ★★★ 95 96 98 00' 01' 04 05' 06 08 09' 10 5-ha property on the POMEROL plateau opposite VIEUX-CH-CERTAN. Generous but lacks a little finesse.

Certan-Marzelle Pom Little J-P MOUEIX estate for *fragrant, light, juicy Pomerol.*

Chantegrive Grav r w ★★→★★★ 99' 00 01 02 03 04 05' 06 07 08 09 10 With 92 ha, the largest estate in the AC; modern GRAVES of v.gd quality. Reds rich and finely oaked. Cuvée Caroline is top white (00 01 02 03 04 05' 06 07 08 09 10).

Chasse-Spleen Mou r (w) ★★★ 98 99 00 01 02 03 04 05' 06 07 08 09' 10 104-ha estate; classed-growth level. Consistently gd, often outstanding (90' 00' 05'), long-maturing wine. Second label: L'Heritage de Chasse Spleen. One of Bordeaux's surest things. A little white. *See also* CAMENSAC and GRESSIER-GRAND-POUJEAUX.

Chauvin St-Em r ★★ 98' 99 00 01 03 04 05 06 08 09 15-ha GRAND CRU CLASSÉ. Steady performer; increasingly serious. New winemaker in 2008.

Cheval Blanc St-Em r ★★★★ 88 89 90' 93 94 95 96' 97 98' 99 00' 01' 02 03 04 05' 06 07 08 09' 10 37-ha PREMIER GRAND CRU CLASSÉ of ST-EMILION. High percentage of Cab Fr (60%). Rich, fragrant, vigorous wines with some of the voluptuousness of neighbouring POMEROL. Delicious young; lasts a generation. Same ownership and management as YQUEM and Quinault L'Enclos (ST-EMILION). 1947 Imperial (six litres) sold at auction for record $304,375 in 2010. New eco-friendly winery for 2011 vintage. Second wine: Le Petit Cheval.

Chevalier, Domaine de Pe-Lé r w ★★★ →★★★★ 89 90' 95 96' 98' 99' 00' 01' 02 03 04' 05' 06 07 08 09' 10 Superb 47-ha estate. Impressive since 1998, the red has gained in finesse, fruit, texture. Complex, long-ageing white: consistent, develops richness (89 90' 93 94 95 96' 97 98' 99 00 01 02 03 04 05' 06 07' 08' 09 10). Second wine: Esprit de Chevalier. Try DOM de la Solitude, PESSAC-LÉOGNAN.

Cissac H-Méd r ★★ 95 96' 98 00 02 03 04 05 08 09 50-ha MÉDOC cru west of PAUILLAC. Firm, tannic wines that need time. More weight since 2001. Second wine: Reflet du CH Cissac.

Citran H-Méd r ★★ 96 98 99 00 02 03 04 05' 06 08 09 90-ha estate owned by Villars-Merlaut (patriarch Jacques Merlaut died in 2008) family since 1996

> **Côtes de Bordeaux – it's official**
> From 2009 the new appellation CÔTES DE BORDEAUX (14,000 ha) became obligatory on labels replacing Côtes de Castillon, Côtes de Francs, Premières Côtes de Blaye and Premières Côtes de Bordeaux. Cross-blending of wines from these regions is allowed but for those wanting to maintain the identity of a single terroir, stiffer controls permit the mention BLAYE, CASTILLON, FRANCS and CADILLAC (for the Premières Côtes de Bordeaux) before Côtes de Bordeaux. The CÔTES DE BOURG is not part of the new designation.

BORDEAUX

(*see* CHASSE-SPLEEN, GRUAUD-LAROSE). Since 2001, ripe, supple; accessible early. Second label: Moulins de Citran.

Clarence de Haut-Brion, le Pe-Lé r ★★★ 89′ 90 93 94 95 96′ 98 99 00 01 02 03 04 05′ 06 07 08 09 10 The second wine of CH HAUT-BRION, known as Bahans Haut-Brion until 2007. Blend changes considerably with each vintage but style follows that of the *grand vin*.

Clarke List r (p w) ★★ 98′ 99 00 01 02 03 04 05′ 06 08 09 Large (54-ha) estate. Massive (Edmond) Rothschild investment. Now v.gd Merlot-based red. Greater progress from 2000: dark fruit and fine tannins. Also a dry white: Le Merle Blanc du CH Clarke. CH Malmaison in MOULIS same connection.

Clerc Milon Pau r ★★★ 89′ 90′ 94 95 96′ 98′ 99 00 01 02 03 04 05′ 06 07 08 09 10 Once-forgotten Fifth Growth owned by (MOUTON) Rothschilds. More Merlot so a lot broader and weightier than sister ARMAILHAC.

Climens Saut w sw ★★★★ 85′ 86′ 88′ 89 90′ 95 96 97′ 98 99′ 00 01′ 02 03′ 04 05′ 06 07 09 A 30-ha BARSAC classed growth making some of the world's most stylish wine. Concentrated, with vibrant acidity giving balance; ageing potential guaranteed. Going biodynamic. Second label: Les Cyprès. Owned by Bérénice Lurton (sister of Henri at BRANE-CANTENAC). Pricier than in the past.

Clinet Pom r ★★★★ 95 96 98′ 99 00 01 02 03 05′ 06 07 08 09′ 10 Made a name for intense, sumptuous wines in the 1980s ('89 and '90 legendary). Back on same form with 2008 and 2009. MICHEL ROLLAND consults. Second label: Fleur de Clinet introduced in 1997 but now a négociant brand.

Clos l'Eglise Pom r ★★★ 96 98 99 00′ 01 02 03 04 05′ 06 07 08 09′ 10 A 6-ha v'yd on one of the best sites in POMEROL. Rich, round and modern style since 1998. Same family owns HAUT-BERGEY and BARDE-HAUT.

Clos Floridène Grav r w ★★ (r) 00 01 02 03 04 05 06 08 09′ (w) 00 01′ 02 03 04′ 05′ 06 07 08 09 *A sure thing* from one of BORDEAUX's most famous white-winemakers, Denis Dubourdieu. Sauv Bl/Sém from limestone allows the wine to age well; much-improved red. *See also* CHX CANTEGRIL, DOISY-DAËNE and REYNON.

Clos Fourtet St-Em r ★★★ 89 90 94 95 96 98 99 00 01 02 03 04 05′ 06 07 08 09′ 10 First Growth on the limestone plateau, cellars almost in town. New owner/investment 2001; on stellar form. DERENONCOURT and former PÉTRUS winemaker (J-C Berrouet) consult. Also owns POUJEAUX. Second label: DOM de Martialis.

Clos Haut-Peyraguey Saut w sw ★★★ 88′ 89 90′ 95′ 96 97′ 98 99 00 01′ 02 03′ 04 05′ 06 07 09 Family DOM. 12 ha "upper" part of the original Peyraguey estate. Elegant, harmonious wines. Haut-Bommes (5 ha) same stable.

Clos des Jacobins St-Em r ★★ ·★★★ 95 96 98 00 01 02 03 04 05′ 06 07 08 09′ 8.5-ha classed growth; greater stature since 2000. New owners (2004); new creamy style. ANGÉLUS owner consults. Also owns CH La Commanderie, FLEUR CARDINALE.

Clos du Marquis St-Jul r ★★ ·★★★ 98 99 00 01 02 03 04 05′ 06 07 08 09′ 10 As of 2007 no longer considered the second wine of LÉOVILLE-LAS-CASES but a separate wine and v'yd (as has always been the case). As good as many classed growths.

Clos de l'Oratoire St-Em r ★★ 95 96 98 99 00' 01 03 04 05' 06 07 08 09 10 Serious performer on northeastern slopes of ST-EMILION. Same stable as CANON-LA-GAFFELIÈRE, LA MONDOTTE; polished and reasonable value. Small crop in 2009 (hail).

Clos Puy Arnaud r ★★ 00 01' 02 03 04 05' 06 08 09 10 Biodynamic; one of best in Castillon. 11 ha; depth and distinction. Owner formerly connected to PAVIE.

Clos René Pom r ★★ 95 96 98' 00' 01 04 05' 06 08 09 Merlot-dominated wine with a little spicy Malbec from sandy/gravel soils. Less sensuous than top POMEROL but gd value. Alias CH Moulinet-Lasserre.

Clotte, la St-Em r ★★ 96 98' 99 00' 01 02 03 04 05 06 08 09' Tiny (4-ha) *côtes* GRAND CRU CLASSÉ: fine, perfumed, supple wines. Confidential but gd value.

Colombier-Monpelou Pau r ★★ 98 99 00' 02 03 04 05 06 09 24-ha PAUILLAC estate nr PONTET-CANET. Underperforming; light and easy style.

Conseillante, la Pom r ★★★★ 88 89 90' 94 95' 96' 98' 99 00' 01 02 03 04 05' 06' 07 08 09' 10 Historic 12-ha property on plateau between PÉTRUS and CHEVAL BLANC. Some of the noblest and most fragrant POMEROL; almost Médocain in style; long ageing. Second wine (from 2007): Duo de Conseillante.

Corbin St-Em r ★★ 98 99 00' 01 02 04 05 08 09 Much-improved 12-ha GRAND CRU CLASSÉ on sand and clay soils. Improvements in the new millennium. Round and supple with soft red fruit.

Corbin-Michotte St-Em r ★★ 98' 99 00 01 02 04 05 06 08 09 Competent rather than exciting classed growth located close to POMEROL. Medium-bodied, fruity, early-drinking wines. In same hands as CHX Calon and Cantelauze.

Cordeillan-Bages Pau r ★★→★★★ A mere 1,000 cases of savoury PAUILLAC made by the LYNCH-BAGES team. Rarely seen outside BORDEAUX. Better known for its luxury restaurant and hotel.

Cos d'Estournel St-Est r ★★★★ 88' 89' 90' 94 95 96' 98' 00 01 02 03 04 05' 06 07 08 09' Fashionable 89-ha Second Growth with eccentric pagoda *chai*. Most refined ST-ESTÈPHE; more Cab Sauv in blend since 2007. New (wildly expensive) cellars in 2008. Pricey white from 2005. Second label: Les Pagodes de Cos (and CH MARBUZET for some markets). Same owner as super-modern Goulée (MÉDOC).

Cos-Labory St-Est r ★★ 90' 94 95 96' 98' 99 00 02 03 04 05' 06 07 08 09 10 Inconsistent Fifth Growth neighbour of COS D'ESTOURNEL with 18 ha. Recent vintages have more depth and structure. Gd value. ANDRON-BLANQUET is sister CH.

Coufran H-Méd r ★★ 98 99 00 01 02 03 04 05 06 08 09 76 ha Coufran and VERDIGNAN, in extreme north of the HAUT-MÉDOC, are co-owned. Coufran is mainly Merlot for supple wine. SOUDARS is another, smaller sister.

Couhins-Lurton Pe-Lé w r ★★→★★★ (w) 98' 99 00 01 02 03 04 05 06 07 08 09 (r) 02 03 04 05 06 09 Fine, minerally, long-lived classed-growth white from Sauv Bl. Now a supple, Merlot-based red from 2002 (17 ha). Same family as LA LOUVIÈRE and BONNET.

Couspaude, la St-Em r ★★★ 95 96 98 99 00' 01 02 03 04 05 06 08 09' Classed growth well-located on the ST-EMILION plateau. Modern style; rich and creamy with lashings of spicy oak. MICHEL ROLLAND consults.

Coutet Saut w sw ★★★ 88' 89' 90' 95 96 97' 98' 99 01' 02 03' 04 05 07 09' Traditional rival to CLIMENS but zestier style. 38-ha in BARSAC. Consistently v. fine. Cuvée Madame is a v. rich selection in certain yrs (89 90 95).

Couvent des Jacobins St-Em r ★★ 95 96 98' 99 00' 01 03 04 05 06 08 09' 10.7-ha GRAND CRU CLASSÉ vinified within the walls of ST-EMILION. Splendid cellars. Light, easy style. Denis Dubourdieu consults. Second label: Le Menut des Jacobins.

Crock, le St-Est r ★★ 96 98 99 00' 01 02 03 04 05 06 07 08 09' V. fine property (32 ha) in the same family (Cuvelier) as LÉOVILLE-POYFERRÉ. Fruit-packed ST-ESTÈPHE.

Croix, la Pom r ★★ 95 96 98 99 00 01 04 05 06 07 08 09 10-ha property owned by négociant Janoueix. Appealing rich, plummy POMEROL. Also LA CROIX-ST-GEORGES and other properties in POMEROL and ST-EMILION.

Croix-de-Gay, la Pom r ★★★ 90 94' 95 96 98 99 00' 00' 01' 02 04 05 06 09' 10 ha in the best part of the commune. Round, elegant style. LA FLEUR-DE-GAY is made from the best parcels. Same family as Faizeau (MONTAGNE ST-EMILION).

Croix du Casse, la Pom r ★★ 98 99 00' 01' 04 05 06 08 09 A 9-ha property on sandy/gravel soils in the south of POMEROL. Since 2005 owned by BORIE-MANOUX; investment and improvement from 2008. Medium-bodied; better value now.

Croizet-Bages Pau r ★★→★★★ 95 96' 98 00' 03 04 05 06 07 08 09 A 30-ha Fifth Growth. Same owners as RAUZAN-GASSIES. A new regime in the cellar is producing richer, more serious wines, especially from 2006.

Croque-Michotte St-Em r ★★ 96 98 00 01 03 04 05 08 09 A 14-ha estate on the sandy-gravel soils of the POMEROL border. Standard ST-EMILION.

Cru Bourgeois *See* Cru Bourgeois box, below.

Cruzeau, de Pe-Lé r w sw ★★ (r) 98 00 01 02 04 05 06 08 09 (w) 01 02 03 04 05 06 07 08 09 Large 97-ha (two-thirds red) PESSAC-LÉOGNAN v'yd developed by André Lurton of LA LOUVIÈRE. Gd-value wines. Sauv Bl-dominated white.

Dalem r ★★ 96' 98' 99 00 01 02 03 04 05' 06 08 09' Was full-blooded FRONSAC, now a feminine touch has added vibrancy and charm. 15 ha: 85% Merlot.

Dassault St-Em r ★★ 96 98' 99 00 01 02 03 04 05' 06 08 09 Consistent, modern, juicy 24-ha GRAND CRU CLASSÉ. Owning family of Dassault aviation fame. Also La Fleur in ST-EMILION and ventures in Chile and Argentina.

Dauphine, de la ★★→★★★ 98' 99 00 01 03 04 05 06' 08 09 10 FRONSAC. Total makeover since purchased by new owner in 2000. Renovation of CH and v'yds plus new, modern winery in 2002. Stablemate CANON-DE-BREM integrated in 2006; more refined and structured since. Second wine: Delphis (from 2006).

Dauzac Marg r ★★→★★★ 89' 90' 94 95 96 98' 99 00' 01 02 04 05 06 08' 09 10 A 49-ha Fifth Growth south of MARGAUX; now dense, rich, dark wines. Owned by an insurance company; managed by Christine Lurton, daughter of André, of LA LOUVIÈRE. Second wine: La Bastide Dauzac.

Derenoncourt, Stéphane Leading consultant winemaker; self-taught, focused on terroir, balance, elegance. Own property, DOM de l'A in CASTILLON.

Desmirail Marg r ★★→★★★ 00' 01 02 03 04 05 06 07 08 09 Third Growth (30 ha) owned by Denis Lurton, brother of Henri (BRANE-CANTENAC). Fine, delicate style.

Destieux St-Em r ★★ 98 99 00' 01 03' 04 05' 06 07 08 09' Promotion to GRAND CRU CLASSÉ in 2006. 8-ha estate to the east of ST-EMILION at St-Hippolyte. ROLLAND consults. Bold, powerful style; consistent.

Doisy-Daëne Bar w dr sw (r) ★★★ 88' 89' 90' 95 96 97' 98' 99 01' 02 03 04 05' 06 07 09 10 Family-owned (Dubourdieu) 17-ha estate; age-worthy, dry white and

---

Cru Bourgeois – some misgivings

The new Cru Bourgeois label – now a certificate awarded on a yearly basis, administered by an independent body, Bureau Véritas – was officially launched in 2010 with the 2008 vintage. Out of 290 hopefuls from appellations within the MÉDOC, 243 CHX were rubber-stamped for this vintage. The HAUT-MÉDOC and MÉDOC ACS provided the lion's share with 177 CHX. Those who failed will not be compromised from applying in subsequent vintages. Quality standards vary and there is clearly the need for a hierarchy to be introduced. A number of well-known names have also been unattracted by the new system and have withdrawn from the selection process. These include the nine CHX designated Cru Bourgeois Exceptionnel in the annulled 2003 classification.

CH CANTEGRIL, but above all renowned for its notably *fine, sweet Barsac*. L'Extravagant (90 96 97 01 02 03 04 05 06 07 09) is an intensely rich and expensive CUVÉE.

Doisy-Dubroca Bar r sw ★★ 90' 95 96 97' 99 01 03' 04 05 07 09 Tiny (3.4-ha) BARSAC classed growth allied to CH CLIMENS.

Doisy-Védrines Saut w sw ★★★ 89' 90 95 96 97' 98 99 01' 03' 04 05 07 09 10 A 27-ha classed growth at BARSAC owned by Casteja family (Joanne négociant). Delicious, sturdy, rich: ages well. A sure thing for many yrs.

Dôme, le St-Em r ★★★ 04 05 06 08 09 10 Micro-wine that used to be super-oaky but is now aimed at elegance and terroir expression (from 2004). Two-thirds old-vine Cab Fr. Owned by Jonathan Maltus, who has a string of other ST-EMILIONS (eg. CH Teyssier, Le Carré, Les Astéries), Australia's Barossa Valley (Colonial Estate) and California's Napa Valley (World's End).

Dominique, la St-Em r ★★★ 89' 90' 94 95 96 98 99 00' 01 04 05' 06 08 09' 10 23-ha classed growth adjacent to CHEVAL BLANC. Solid value until '96, then went off the boil. Back on form since 2006. Renovated cellars in 2011. To watch. Second label: St Paul de Dominique.

Ducluzeau List r ★★ 95 96 00 01 03 04 05 06 08 09 Tiny sister property of DUCRU-BEAUCAILLOU. 10 ha, 50/50 Merlot/Cab Sauv. Round, well-balanced wines.

Ducru-Beaucaillou St-Jul r ★★★★ 85' 94 95' 96' 98 99 00' 01 02 03 04 05' 06 07 08 09' 10 Outstanding Second Growth, excellent form except for a patch in the late 1980s; 75 ha overlooking the river. Added impetus from owner Bruno Borie from 2003. Classic cedar-scented claret suited to long ageing. *See also* LALANDE-BORIE. Second wine: Croix de Beaucaillou.

Duhart-Milon Rothschild Pau r ★★★ 95 96' 98 00' 01 02 03 04' 05' 06 07 08 09' 10 Fourth Growth stablemate of LAFITE. Greater precision from 2002; increasingly fine quality. Price surge with Chinese hunger for the Rothschild (Lafite) brand. Second label: Moulin de Duhart.

Durfort-Vivens Marg r ★★★ 89' 90 94 95 96 98 99 00 02 03 04 05' 06 08 09' 10 Second Growth owned and being improved by Gonzague Lurton, president of the MARGAUX winegrowers' association. Recent wines have structure (lots of Cab Sauv) and finesse.

Echo de Lynch-Bages Pau r ★★ 00 01 02 03 04 05 08 09 Second wine of LYNCH-BAGES. Pre-2008 known as Haut-Bages-Averous. Tasty and fairly consistent.

l'Eglise, Domaine, de Pom r ★★ 90 95 96 98 99 00 01 02 03 04 05' 06 07 08 09 10 Small property on the clay-gravel plateau: stylish, resonant wine. Denis Dubourdieu consults. Same stable as TROTTEVIEILLE and CROIX DE CASSE.

l'Eglise-Clinet Pom r ★★★→★★★★ 89 90' 93' 94 95 96 98' 99 00' 01' 02 03 04 05' 06 07 08 09' 10 6-ha estate. Top-flight POMEROL with great consistency; full, concentrated, fleshy wine. Owner-winemaker Denis Durantou excels. Expensive and limited quantity. Second label: La Petite Eglise.

l'Evangile Pom r ★★★★ 88' 89 90 95 96 98' 99 00' 01 02 03 04' 05' 06 07 08 09' 10 13 ha between PÉTRUS and CHEVAL BLANC. Rich, opulent style. Investment by owners (LAFITE) Rothschild has greatly improved quality. 2009 best of the modern era. Second wine: Blason de l'Evangile.

Fargues, de Saut w sw ★★★ 85' 86 88 89 90 95 96 97 98 99' 01 02 03' 04 05' 06 07 09' 10 A 15-ha v'yd by ruined castle owned by Lur-Saluces, ex-owner of YQUEM. Same techniques. Rich, unctuous, but balanced. Long ageing potential.

Faugères St-Em r ★★ 98 99 00' 02 03 04 05 06 07 08 09' A 49-ha property. Dark, fleshy, modern ST-EMILION. Cuvée Péby (100% Merlot) is the *garage* wine. Stunning new Mario Botta-designed winery opened in 2009. Sister to Cap de Faugères in CASTILLON and Chambrun in LALANDE DE POMEROL.

Faurie-de-Souchard St-Em r ★★ 95 96 98' 00 03 04 05 06 07 08 09 Previously underperforming CH on the *côtes*. Escaped declassification in 2006. Recent investment and greater effort from new generation. STÉPHANE DERENONCOURT consults. To watch.

de Ferrand St-Em r ★★ 98 00 01 03 04 05 06 08 09 10 Big (30-ha) St-Hippolyte estate owned by Baron Bich (Bic pens) family. Recent investment and improvement. Wines released with 5 yrs' age.

Ferrande Grav r (w) ★★ 00 01 02 04 05 06 08 09 Major estate at Castres owned by négociant Castel: over 40 ha. Easy, enjoyable red and reasonable white wine; at their best at 1–4 yrs.

Ferrière Marg r ★★→★★★ 96' 98 **99** 00' 02 03 04 05 06 08 09 10 Tiny 8-ha Third Growth with a CH in MARGAUX village restored by same capable hands as LA GURGUE and HAUT-BAGES-LIBÉRAL. Dark, firm, perfumed, need time. To watch.

Feytit-Clinet Pom r ★★ **95 96** 98 99 00 01 03 04 05' 06 07 08 09' 10 Tiny 6.5-ha property. Once managed by J-P MOUEIX; back with owning Chasseuil family since 2000. Improvements since. Rich, full POMEROL with ageing potential.

Fieuzal Pe-Lé r (w) ★★★ (r) 98' 00 01 06 07 08 09' 10 (w) 98' 99 01 02 03 05 06 07 08 09 10 Classed growth. Red form dipped from the heights of the mid-1980s but improvements from 2006. White more consistent. New Irish owner from 2001. ANGÉLUS owner now consults for reds. One to watch.

Figeac St-Em r ★★★★ 95' 96 98' **99** 00' 01 02 03 04 05' 06 07 08 09' 10 First growth, 40-ha gravelly v'yd with unusual 70% Cabs Fr and Sauv. Rich but always elegant wines; deceptively long-ageing. Legendary owner Thierry Manoncourt (63 vintages) died in 2010. Son-in-law Eric d'Aramon continues the good work. Second wine: Grange Neuve de Figeac.

Filhot Saut w dr sw ★★ 90 95 96' 97' 98 **99** 00' 01' 02 03' 04 05 07 09 10 Second-rank classed growth with splendid CH, 60-ha v'yd. Difficult young, more complex with age. Medium-sweet with a minerally finish.

Fleur Cardinale St-Em r ★★ 98 **99** 00 01 02 03 04 05' 06 07 08 09 10 18-ha property east of ST-EMILION. Gd from the 1980s, into overdrive since 2001 with new owner and *chai*. Promoted to GRAND CRU CLASSÉ in 2006. Ripe, unctuous, modern.

Fleur-de-Gay, la Pom r ★★★ 1,000-case super-CUVÉE of CH LA CROIX-DE-GAY. 100% Merlot.

Fleur-Pétrus, la Pom r ★★★★ 90' 94 95 96 98' **99** 00' 01 02 03 04 05' 06 08 09' 10 A 13-ha v'yd flanking PÉTRUS; same J-P MOUEIX management. Lazer-optical sorter used from 2009. Finer style than PÉTRUS or TROTANOY. Needs time.

Fombrauge St-Em r ★★→★★★ **96** 98 99 00' 01 02 03 04 05 06 08 09 A Bernard Magrez wine (*see* PAPE-CLÉMENT), so don't expect restraint. Big estate: 52 ha east of ST-EMILION. Since 1999, rich, dark, chocolatey, full-bodied wines. Magrez-Fombrauge is its *garage* wine.

Fonbadet Pau r ★★ 95 96' **98' 00'** 01 02 03 04 05' 06 08 09 20-ha family-owned estate. Reliable, gd value and typical of PAUILLAC style. Potential to age.

Fonplégade St-Em r ★★ **96 98** 00' 01 03 04 05 06' **07** 08 09 A 19-ha GRAND CRU CLASSÉ. New American owner from 2004 and progression since: riper, with more elegance than in the past. MICHEL ROLLAND consults. CH L'Enclos in POMEROL same owner since 2007.

Fonréaud List r ★★ 98 00' 02 03 04 05 06 08 09' One of the bigger (39 ha) and better LISTRACS producing savoury, mouth-filling wines. Investment since 1998. 2 ha of dry white: Le Cygne, barrel-fermented. *See* LESTAGE. Gd value.

Fonroque St-Em r ★★★ 96 98 01 03 04 05 06 08 09' 19 ha on the plateau north of ST-EMILION. Biodynamic (2008). Firm, a touch austere; more elegance recently. Managed by Alain Moueix (*see* MAZEYRES). MOULIN DU CADET sister estate.

Fontenil r ★★★ 98' **99** 00' 01' 02 03 04 05 06 08 09' Leading FRONSAC started by ROLLAND (1986). Ripe, opulent, balanced. *Garage*: Défi de Fontenil.

Forts de Latour, les Pau r ★★★→★★★★ 88 89' 90' 94 95' 96' 98 **99** 00' 01 02 03

04' 05' 06 07 08 09' 10 The (worthy) second wine of CH LATOUR; the authentic flavour in slightly lighter format at Second Growth price. From enlarged v'yds outside the central *Enclos*.

Fourcas-Dupré List r ★★ **95 96' 98' 99** 00' 01 02 03 04 05 06 08 09 Well-run 46-ha estate making fairly consistent wine in tight LISTRAC style. Second label: CH Bellevue-Laffont. Complete renovation in 2000.

Fourcas-Hosten List r ★★ ·★★★ **98' 00 01 02** 03 05 06 08 09 A 48-ha estate with new owners (Hermès fashion connection) from 2006: considerable investment and improvement from this date. More precision and finesse. To watch.

France, de Pe-Lé r w ★★ (r) 98 **99 00 02 03 04 05 06** 08 09 (w) 96 98 99 01' 02 03 04 05 06 07 08 09 40-ha PESSAC-LÉOGNAN neighbour of CH DE FIEUZAL making consistent wines in a ripe, modern style. MICHEL ROLLAND consults.

Franc-Mayne St-Em r ★★ 95 96 98' **99 00' 01 03 04 05 06 08 09** A 7.2-ha GRAND CRU CLASSÉ on the *côtes*. New owners in 2004 (sister properties CH DE LUSSAC and Vieux Maillet in POMEROL). Investment and renovation. Luxury accommodation as well. Fresh, fruity and structured style. Round but firm wines.

Gaby, du r ★★ 00' 01' 03 04 05 06 **07** 08 09 10 Splendid south-facing slopes in FRONSAC. New owners in 1999 and again in 2006 (Canadian). Serious wines.

Gaffelière, la St-Em r ★★★ 89' 90' **94 95 96 98' 99 00'** 01 03 04 05' 06 07 08 09' 10 A 22-ha First Growth at foot of the *côtes*. Elegant, long-ageing wines. More precision and purity from 2000. DERENONCOURT consulting from 2004.

Galius St-Em r ★★ Oak-aged selection from ST-EMILION co-op, usually to a high standard. Formerly called Haut Quercus.

Garde, la Pe-Lé r w ★★ (r) 98' **99** 00 01' 02 **04 05** 06 07 08 09' (w) **01 02 04 05** 06 07 08 09 Substantial property of 58 ha owned by négociant CVBG-DOURTHE; reliable, supple reds. Tiny production of Sauv Bl/Sauv Gris-based white.

Gay, le Pom r ★★★ 95 96 98 **99 00** 01 03 **04 05'** 06 07 08 09 10 Fine 10.5-ha v'yd on northern edge of POMEROL. Major investment, with MICHEL ROLLAND consulting. Now v. ripe and plummy in style. Improvements from 2003. CH Montviel and La Violette same stable and AC. Owner has Cristal d'Arques glassware origins.

Gazin Pom r ★★★ 90' **94'** 95 96 98' **99 00'** 01 02 03 04 05' 06 07 08 09' 10 Large (for POMEROL) 24-ha, family-owned (de Bailliencourt dit Courcol) neighbour of PÉTRUS. Well-distributed, now on v.gd form. Second label: L'Hospitalet de Gazin.

Gilette Saut w sw ★★★ 53 55 59 61 67 70 71 75 76 78 79 81 82 83 85 86 88 89 Extraordinary small Preignac CH stores its sumptuous wines in concrete vats for 16–20 yrs. Only about 5,000 bottles of each. Some bottle age still advisable. CH Les Justices is its sister (96 97 99 01 02 03' 05 07 09).

Giscours Marg r ★★★ 89' 90 **95** 96' **98 99** 00' 01 02 03 04 05' 06 07 08' 09' 10 Splendid 85-ha Third Growth south of Cantenac. V.gd, vigorous wine in 1970s and now. 1980s were v. wobbly; new (Dutch) ownership from 1995 and revival since 1999. Cellar-door operation as well. Second label: La Sirène de Giscours. CH La Houringue is baby sister, DU TERTRE stablemate.

Glana, du St-Jul r ★★ **98 99** 00 02 03 04 **05** 06 08 09 Large, 44-ha ST-JULIEN estate. Expansion through the acquisition of parcels of land from CH LAGRANGE. Undemanding; undramatic; value. Same owner as Bellegrave in PAUILLAC. Second wine: Pavillon du Glana.

Why Bordeaux?

People ask whether Bordeaux still justifies its own separate section of this international guide. The answer: it remains the motor of the fine wine world, by far its biggest producer, stimulating debate, investment, and collectors worldwide. Besides, there are few better drinks.

Gloria St-Jul r ★★ ‣★★★ 96 98 99 00' 01 02 03 04 05' 06 07 08 09' 10 A 45-ha ST-JULIEN estate with v'yds among the classed growths. Same ownership as ST-PIERRE. Regularly overperforms. Second label: Peymartin.

Gomerie, la St-Em 09 10 1,000 cases, 100% Merlot, *garagiste*. See BEAU-SÉJOUR-BÉCOT.

Grand-Corbin-Despagne St-Em r ★★‣★★★ 90' 94 95 96 98 99 00' 01 03 04 05 06 08 09 10 Demoted from GRAND CRU CLASSÉ in 1996 but reinstated in 2006. In between: investment and hard graft. Aromatic wines now with a riper, fuller edge. Still gd value. Also CH Maison Blanche, MONTAGNE ST-EMILION and CH Ampélia, CASTILLON. Second label: Petit Corbin-Despagne.

Grand Cru Classé See ST-EMILION classification box, p. 104.

Grand-Mayne St-Em r ★★★ 89' 90' 94 95 96 98 99 00' 01' 02 03 04 05' 06 07 08 09 Leading 16-ha GRAND CRU CLASSÉ on western *côtes*. Consistent, firm, full, savoury wines. New generation of Nony family at the helm.

Grand-Pontet St-Em r ★★★ 96 98' 99 00' 01 02 03 04 05 06 08 09 10 A 14-ha GRAND CRU CLASSÉ. Generous, fruity wines. Same family and team as BEAU-SÉJOUR-BÉCOT.

Grand-Puy-Ducasse Pau r ★★ 95 96' 98' 99 00 01 02 03 04 05' 06 07 08 09' 10 Fifth Growth owned by a bank; more consistent since 2005. New winemaker 2010. Denis Dubourdieu consults. Second label: CH Artigues-Arnaud.

Grand-Puy-Lacoste Pau r ★★★ 86' 88' 89' 90' 94 95' 96' 98 99 00' 01 02 03 04 05' 06 07 08' 09' 10 50-ha Fifth Growth famous for Cab Sauv-driven PAUILLAC to age. Same owner HAUT-BATAILLEY. Recent investment. Second label: Lacoste-Borie.

Grave à Pomerol, la Pom r ★★★ 95 96 98' 00 01 02 04 05 06 08 09' 10 Small 9-ha v'yd facing LALANDE-DE-POMEROL. Owned by Christian MOUEIX. Fine POMEROL of medium richness. Formerly known as La Grave Trigant de Boisset.

Gressier-Grand-Poujeaux Mou r ★★ 90 94 95 96 98 00 01 04 05 09 Since 2003, same owner as CHASSE-SPLEEN. 5,000 cases average. Little visibility. Solid in the past and in need of ageing.

Greysac Méd r ★★ 98 00' 02 03 04 05 06 08 09 10 Elegant 70-ha MÉDOC estate. Same management as CANTEMERLE. Fine, consistent quality and style.

Gruaud-Larose St-Jul r ★★★★ 86' 88 89' 90' 95' 96' 98 99 00' 01 02 04 05' 06 07 08 09' 10 One of biggest, best-loved Second Growths. 82 ha. Smooth, rich, vigorous; ages 20+ yrs. More finesse from 2007. Second wine: Sarget de Gruaud-Larose.

Guadet St-Em ★★ 01 04 05 06 08 09 10 Known as Guadet-St-Julien until 2005. Narrowly missed demotion from GRAND CRU CLASSÉ in 2006. DERENONCOURT now consulting and some improvement.

Guiraud Saut w sw (r dr) ★★★ 88' 89' 90' 95 96' 97' 98 99 01' 02 03 04 05' 06 07 09' 10 Top-quality classed growth with 100-ha v'yd. New owning consortium from 2006 includes long-time manager, Xavier Planty. More Sauv Bl than most. Dry white G de CH Guiraud. Second label: Le Dauphin de Guiraud.

Gurgue, la Marg r ★★ 98 00' 01 02 03 04 05' 06 08 09 Well-placed 10-ha property, for fine MARGAUX. Same management as FERRIÈRE.

Hanteillan H-Méd Cissac r ★★ 00' 02 03 04 05' 06 09 Huge 82-ha HAUT-MÉDOC v'yd: v. fair wines, early drinking. 50% Merlot. Second wine: CH Laborde.

Haut-Bages-Libéral Pau r ★★★ 96' 98 99 00 01 02 03 04 05' 06 08 09 10 Lesser-known Fifth Growth of 28 ha (next to LATOUR) in same stable as LA GURGUE. Results are excellent, full of PAUILLAC vitality. Usually gd value.

Haut-Bages-Monpelou Pau r ★★ 95 96 98 99 00 03 04 05 06 08 09 A 15-ha stablemate of CH BATAILLEY on former DUHART-MILON land. Could improve.

Haut-Bailly Pe-Lé r ★★★★ 89' 90' 95 96 98' 99 00' 01 02 03 04 05' 06 07 08 09' 10 Over 30 ha at Léognan. Since 1979 some of best savoury, intelligently made red GRAVES. New US ownership and investment from 1998 have taken it to greater heights. Denis Dubourdieu consults. Second label: La Parde de Haut-Bailly.

> **Rothschild craze in China**
> The ongoing love affair between the Chinese and CH LAFITE-ROTHSCHILD
> was further enhanced with the announcement that bottles of the 2008
> vintage will be embossed with the Chinese figure eight (a lucky number
> in China). Not to be outdone, CH MOUTON-ROTHSCHILD then unveiled
> the artist responsible for the 2008 (artists' series) label, the Chinese
> painter Xu Lei. Needless to say, prices for both wines have galloped.

Haut-Batailley Pau r ★★★ 95 96′ 98 99 00 02 03 04 05′ 06 07 08 09 Smaller
part of divided Fifth Growth BATAILLEY: 20 ha. Gentler than sister CH GRAND-PUY-
LACOSTE. New cellar in 2005; more precision. Second wine: La Tour-d'Aspic.

Haut-Beauséjour St-Est r ★★ 98 99 00 01 03 04 05 08 09 18-ha property revitalized
by owner CHAMPAGNE house ROEDERER. Lots of Merlot (60%). *See also* DE PEZ.

Haut-Bergey Pe-Lé r (w)★★ (r) 98 99 00 01 02 04 05 06 07 08 09 (w) 03 04 05
06 07 08 09 A 29-ha estate now producing a denser, more modern GRAVES with
oak overlay. Also a little dry white. Completely renovated in the 1990s. Same
ownership as BARDE-HAUT and CLOS L'EGLISE. Sister CH Branon.

Haut-Brion Pe-Lé r ★★★★ (r) 82′ 83′ 85′ 86′ 88′ 89′ 90′ 93 94 95′ 96′ 97 98′ 99
00′ 01 02 03 04 05′ 06 08 09′ 10 Oldest great CH of B'X and only non-MÉDOC
First Growth of 1855; owned by American Dillon family since 1935. 51 ha. Deeply
harmonious, never aggressive wine with endless, honeyed, earthy complexity.
Consistently great since 1975. A little dry, sumptuous *white*: 90 93 94 95 96
98 99 00′ 01 02 03 04′ 05′ 06 07 08′ 09 10. *See* LE CLARENCE DE HAUT-BRION,
LA MISSION-HAUT-BRION, LAVILLE-HAUT-BRION.

Haut Condissas Méd r ★★★ 99 00 01 02 03 04 05 06 07 08 09 MÉDOC with an
international flavour. Sister to CH Rollan-de-By. Rich, concentrated and oaky.
Merlot (60%) and Petit Verdot (20%) the essential components. ★

Haut-Marbuzet St-Est r ★★ ·★★★ 95 96′ 98 99 00′ 01 02 03 04 05′ 06 07 08
09 Leading non-classified estate. Rich, unctuous, ages well. M Duboscq has
reassembled ancient DOM de Marbuzet (71 ha). Also owns Chambert-Marbuzet,
MacCarthy, Tour de Marbuzet. This wine is 60% Merlot, seductive and
consistent. CH Layauga-Duboscq in AC MÉDOC is new venture (2005).

Haut-Pontet St-Em r ★★ 98 00 01 03 04 05 09 Tiny 4.8-ha Merlot v'yd of the *côtes*.
New owner (Janoueix – *see* HAUT-SARPE) from 2007.

Haut-Sarpe St-Em r ★★ 95 96 98 00′ 01 04 05 06 08 09 21-ha GRAND CRU CLASSÉ
with elegant CH and park, 70% Merlot. Same owner (Janoueix) as CH LA CROIX,
POMEROL. Rich, dark, modern style.

Hosanna Pom r ★★★★ 99 00 01 03 04 05′ 06 07 08 09′ 10 Formerly Certan-
Guiraud until purchased and renamed by J-P MOUEIX in 1999. Only best
4.5 ha retained. First vintages confirm power, complexity and class. New cellar in
2008, shared with Providence. Stablemate of PÉTRUS and TROTANOY.

d'Issan Marg r ★★★ 96′ 98 99 00′ 01 02 03 04′ 05′ 06 07 08 09′ 45-ha Third
Growth v'yd with moated CH. Fragrant wines; more substance since late 90s.
Owner Emmanuel Cruse is the new grand master of the Commanderie de
Bontemps Confrérie. Second label: Blason d'Issan.

Kirwan Marg r ★★★ 94 95 96 98 99 00′ 01 02 03 04 05′ 06 07 08 09 10
A 35-ha Third Growth; from 1997 majority-owned by SCHRÖDER & SCHŸLER. Pre-
2007 MICHEL ROLLAND influenced (rich, ripe and oaky); now more classic MARGAUX.
Second label: Les Charmes de Kirwan.

Labégorce Marg r ★★ ·★★★ 98 99 00 01 02 03 04 05′ 07 08 09 10 In 2009
absorbed neighbouring LABÉGORCE-ZÉDÉ, making one 55-ha estate. Solid, long-
lived MARGAUX. CH MARQUIS-D'ALESME same stable.

Labégorce-Zédé Marg r ★★ ·★★★ 95 96′ 98 99 00′ 01 02 03 04 05′ 06 07 RIP. From 2009, part of CH LABÉGORCE. Old vintages classic and fragrant in style.

Lafaurie-Peyraguey Saut w sw ★★★ 83′ 85 86′ 88′ 89′ 90′ 95 96′ 97 98 99 01′ 02 03′ 04 05′ 06 07 09′ 10 Fine 36-ha classed growth at Bommes; owners Groupe Banque Suez. One of best buys in SAUTERNES. New manager in 2006, formerly at PAPE-CLÉMENT. Second wine: La Chapelle de Lafaurie.

Lafite-Rothschild Pau r ★★★★ 82′ 83 85 86′ 88′ 89′ 90′ 93 94 95 96′ 97 98′ 99 00′ 01′ 02 03′ 04′ 05′ 06 07 08′ 09′ 10 First Growth; famous elusive perfume and style, never huge weight but more density and sleeker texture from 1996. Great vintages need keeping for decades; insatiable demand from China has driven the price sky-high. Joint ventures in Chile (1988), California (1989), Portugal (1992), Argentina (1999), now the MIDI, Italy, even China. Second wine: CARRUADES DE CH LAFITE. 91 ha. Also owns CHX DUHART-MILON, L'EVANGILE, RIEUSSEC.

Lafleur Pom r ★★★★ 85′ 86 88′ 89′ 90′ 93 94 95 96 98′ 99′ 00′ 01′ 02 03 04′ 05′ 06 07 08 09′ 10 Superb 4.8-ha family-owned and -managed property cultivated like a garden. Elegant, intense wine for maturing. 50% Cab Fr. Second wine: *Pensées de Lafleur*.

Lafleur-Gazin Pom r ★★ 98 00 01 04 05 06 08 09 10 Small 8-ha J-P MOUEIX estate on the northeastern border of POMEROL. Lighter style of POMEROL.

Lafon-Rochet St-Est r ★★★ 88′ 89′ 90′ 94 95 96′ 98 99 00′ 01 02 03′ 04 05′ 06 08 09′ 10 Fourth Growth neighbour of COS D'ESTOURNEL, 45 ha with distinctive yellow cellars (and label). Investment, selection and a higher percentage of Merlot have made this ST-ESTÈPHE more opulent since 1998. Gd value. Second label: Les Pèlerins de Lafon-Rochet.

Lagrange St-Jul r ★★★ 89′ 90′ 94 95 96 98 99 00′ 01 02 03 04 05′ 06 08 09 10 Formerly neglected Third Growth owned since 1983 by Suntory. 117 ha now in tip-top condition with wines to match. Marcel Ducasse oversaw the resurrection until retirement in 2007. More investment since. Dry white Les Arums de Lagrange since 1997. Second wine: Les Fiefs de Lagrange (gd value).

Lagrange Pom r ★★ 95 96 98 00 01 04 05 06 09 Tiny 5-ha v'yd in the centre of POMEROL run by the ubiquitous house of J-P MOUEIX. Gd value but not in the same league as HOSANNA, LA FLEUR-PÉTRUS, LATOUR-À-POMEROL, etc.

Lagune, la H-Méd r ★★★ 90′ 95 96′ 98 00′ 02 03 04 05′ 08 09 80-ha Third Growth in southern MÉDOC with sandy/gravel soils. Dipped in 1990s but on form from 2001. Fine-edged, now with added structure and depth. Owned by J-J Frey; recently acquired JABOULET AÎNÉ. Daughter Caroline the winemaker.

Lalande-Borie St-Jul r ★★ 98 00 01 02 03 04 05 06 07 08 09′ A baby brother (25 ha) of the great DUCRU-BEAUCAILLOU, created from part of the former v'yd of CH LAGRANGE. Gracious, easy-drinking wine.

Lamarque, de H-Méd r ★★ 95 96 98 99 00′ 02 03 04 05 06 08 09 Splendid medieval fortress in central MÉDOC with 35-ha v'yd; competent, mid-term wines. Second wine: Donjon de L.

Lamothe Bergeron H-Méd r ★★ 98′ 00 02 03 04 05 09 Large 67-ha estate in Cussac-Fort-Médoc. Same stable as GRAND-PUY-DUCASSE and RAYNE VIGNEAU. Reliable if unexceptional; but improving.

Lanessan H-Méd r ★★ 95 96′ 98 00′ 02 03 04 05 08 09′ Distinguished 44-ha property, south of ST-JULIEN. Former Calvet and Cordier-Mestrezat winemaker, Paz Espejo, now in charge (2009) so watch for change. Horse museum, tours.

Langoa-Barton St-Jul r ★★★ 90′ 94 95′ 96′ 98 99 00′ 01 02 03 04′ 05′ 06 07 08 09′ 10 Third Growth sister CH to LÉOVILLE-BARTON. Home to Anthony Barton; impeccable standards, gd value. Second wine: Réserve de Léoville-Barton.

Larcis-Ducasse St-Em r ★★★ 89′ 90′ 94 95 96 98 00 02 03 04 05′ 06 07 08 09′ 10 11-ha GRAND CRU CLASSÉ of St-Laurent, eastern neighbour of ST-EMILION, on the *côtes*. Spectacular rise in quality (and price) since 2002. Same management as PAVIE-MACQUIN.

Larmande St-Em r ★★ 95' 96 98' 00' 01 03 04 05 07 08 09 Substantial 24-ha property owned by Le Mondiale insurance (as is SOUTARD). Replanted, re-equipped, and now making consistently solid wines. All-female winemaking and management team. Second label: CH des Templiers.

Laroque St-Em r ★★→★★★ 89 90 94 95 96 98 99 00' 01 03 04 05 06 08 09 27-ha GRAND CRU CLASSÉ, 17th-century CH. Fresh, terroir-driven. Cellar renovated 2007.

Larose-Trintaudon H-Méd r ★★ 00 01 02 03 04 05 06 07 09' The biggest v'yd in the MÉDOC: 190 ha. Sustainable viticulture. Previously light and easy-drinking but improved quality from 2007. Second label: Larose St-Laurent. Special CUVÉE (from 1996) – Larose Perganson – from 35-ha parcel.

Laroze St-Em r ★★ 96' 98' 99 00 01 05 06 07 08 09' 10 Large v'yd (30-ha) west of ST-EMILION. Lighter-framed wines from sandy soils, more depth from 1998; approachable when young. New *tribaie* grape-sorting machine (v. ingenious, sorts according to specific gravity, and thus ripeness) in use. Second label: La Fleur Laroze.

Larrivet-Haut-Brion Pe-Lé r w ★★★ (r) 96' 98' 00 01 02 03 04 05' 06 07 08 09 Substantial 72-ha Léognan property with classed-growth aspirations. Rich, modern red. Also Sauv Bl/Sém barrel-fermented white (00 01 02 04' 05 06 07 08 09). New barrel cellar and tasting room. Former MONTROSE manager in charge since 2007. Second wine: Les Demoiselles de Larrivet-Haut-Brion.

Lascombes Marg r (p) ★★★ 90' 96' 98' 99 00 01 02 03 04 05' 06 07 08 09' 10 A 97-ha Second Growth owned by US pension fund. Wines were wobbly, but real improvements from 2001. MICHEL ROLLAND consults. Winemaker previously with LAFITE-ROTHSCHILD. Modern style. Second label: Chevalier de Lascombes.

Latour Pau r ★★★★ 78' 82' 85 86 88' 89 90' 91 93 94 95' 96' 97 98 99 00' 01 02 03' 04' 05' 06 07 08 09' 10 First Growth considered the grandest statement of the MÉDOC. Profound, intense, almost immortal wines in great yrs; even weaker vintages have the characteristic note of terroir and run for many yrs. Recently enlarged: 80+ ha, inc 48 ha "Enclos" for the *grand vin*. Latour always needs 10 yrs to show its hand. New state-of-the-art *chai* (2003) allows more precise vinification. About 10% of the v'yd now organic. Second wine: LES FORTS DE LATOUR; *third wine: Pauillac.*

Latour-Martillac Pe-Lé r w ★★ (r) 98 00 01 02 03 04 05' 06 08 09' 10 46-ha family-owned classed-growth property in Martillac. Regular quality (r w); gd value at this level. White can age as well (00 01 02 03 04 05 06 07 08 09).

Latour-à-Pomerol Pom r ★★★ 88' 89' 90' 94 95 96 98' 99 00' 01 02 04 05' 06 07 08 09' 10 Top growth of 7.6 ha on POMEROL plateau under J-P MOUEIX management. Rich, well-structured wines that age. Rarely disappoints.

Laurets, des St-Em r ★★ 00 01 03 04 05 06 08 09 Major property in PUISSEGUIN-ST-EMILION and MONTAGNE-ST-EMILION, with 72 ha of v'yd evenly split on the *côtes* (40,000 cases). Owned by Benjamin de Rothschild of CH CLARKE (2003).

Laville-Haut-Brion Pe-Lé w ★★★★ 92 93' 94 95' 96' 98 00' 01 02 03 04' 05' 06 07 08' 09 Former name for LA MISSION HAUT-BRION BLANC (renamed in 2009). Only 8,000 bottles/yr of v. best white GRAVES for long, succulent maturing. Great consistency. Mainly Sém. Second wine: La Clarté de Haut-Brion (formerly Les Plantiers); also includes wine from HAUT-BRION.

Léoville-Barton St-Jul r ★★★★ 88' 89' 90' 94' 95' 96' 98 99 00' 01 02 03' 04 05' 06 07 08' 09' 10 A 48-ha portion of great Second Growth Léoville v'yd in Anglo-Irish hands of the Barton family for over 180 yrs (Anthony Barton is present incumbent). Harmonious, classic claret; traditional methods, fair prices. Investment raised v. high standards to Super Second. *See* LANGOA-BARTON.

Léoville-las-Cases St-Jul r ★★★★ 83' 85' 86' 88 89' 90' 93 94 95' 96' 97 98 99 00' 01 02 03' 04' 05' 06 07 08 09' 10 The largest Léoville; 97 ha but the heart is the 53-ha *grand enclos*. Elegant, complex, powerful wines, for immortality. Second wine: Le Petit Lion (2007); previously CLOS DU MARQUIS but now considered a separate wine. Laser-optical grape sorting from 2009.

Léoville-Poyferré St-Jul r ★★★ 86' 88 89' 90 94 95 98 99 00' 01 02 03' 04 05' 06 07 08 09' 10 The best part of the v'yd lies opposite the *grand enclos* of LÉOVILLE-LAS-CASES. Now at Super Second level with dark, rich, spicy, long-ageing wines. ROLLAND consults at the 80-ha estate. Second label: CH Moulin-Riche.

Lestage List r ★★ 96 98 00 02 03 04 05 06 08 09 42-ha; same hands as CH FONRÉAUD. Firm, slightly austere. Second wine: La Dame du Coeur de CH Lestage.

Lilian Ladouys St-Est r ★★ 95 96 98 00 02 03 04 05 06 07 08 09 Created in the 1980s, the v'yd now covers 45 ha with 100 parcels of vines. Firm, sometimes robust wines; recent vintages more finesse. New owner in 2008 (owner of rugby club Racing Métro 92 and, since 2009, PEDESCLAUX). Same management as Belle-Vue in HAUT-MÉDOC.

Liot Bar w sw ★★ 89' 90' 95 96 97' 98 99 01' 02 03 05 07 09 Consistent, fairly light, golden wines from 20 ha. Simple, easy-drinking and inexpensive.

Liversan H-Méd r ★★ 95 96 98 00 02 03 04 05 07 09 A 47-ha estate inland from PAUILLAC. Same owner – Jean-Michel Lapalu – as PATACHE D'AUX. Quality oriented. Second wine: Les Charmes de Liversan.

Loudenne Méd r ★★ 00' 01 02 03 04 05 06 09' Beautiful pink riverside CH owned for a century by Gilbeys, since 2000 by Lafragette family. ROLLAND consults. Ripe, round reds. Also an oak-scented Sauv Bl white best at 2–4 yrs (02 04 05 06 07 08 09). Accommodation as well.

Loupiac-Gaudiet w sw ★★ 97 98 99 01 02 03' 05 07 09 A reliable source of gd-value "almost-SAUTERNES", just across river Garonne.

Louvière, la Pe-Lé r w ★★★(r) 98 99 00' 01 02 04 05 06 07 08 09 (w) 00 01 02 03 04' 05' 06 07 08 09 10 André Lurton's pride and joy. CH classed as historical monument (61-ha v'yd). Excellent *white*, classed-growth standard red. New barrel cellar (2009). *See also* BONNET, COUHINS-LURTON, DE CRUZEAU, DE ROCHEMORIN.

Lussac, de St-Em r ★★ 99 00 03 04 05 06 07 08 09 One of the best estates in LUSSAC-ST-EMILION. New owners and technical methods since 2000. Same stable as FRANC-MAYNE and Vieux Maillet in POMEROL.

Lynch-Bages Pau r (w) ★★★★ 82' 85' 86' 88' 89' 90' 94 95' 96' 98 99 00' 01 02 03 04' 05' 06 07 08 09' 10 Always popular, now a regular star. Priced higher than its Fifth Growth status. 96 ha. Rich, robust wine: deliciously dense; aspiring to greatness. *See* ECHO DE LYNCH-BAGES. Fresher-styled white, Blanc de Lynch-Bages, since 2007. Same owners (Cazes family) as LES ORMES-DE-PEZ and Villa Bel-Air.

Lynch-Moussas Pau r ★★ 95' 96' 98 00' 01 02 03 04 05' 07 08 09 Fifth Growth restored by director of BATAILLEY. On the up since 2000: more fruit and flavour.

Lyonnat, du St-Em r ★★ 00' 01 03 04 05 06 08 09 49-ha estate in LUSSAC-ST-EMILION. Reliable wine. The Rhône's J-L Colombo is the consulting oenologist.

Macquin-St-Georges St-Em r ★★ 96 98 99 00 01 03 04 05 06 09 Producer of delicious, not weighty, satellite ST-EMILION at ST-GEORGES. 30-ha v'yd.

Magdelaine St-Em r ★★★ 89' 90' 94 95 96 98' 99 00 01 03 04 05 06 08 09' Leading *côtes* First Growth: 11 ha owned by J-P MOUEIX. Delicate, fine, deceptively long-lived. Denser weight from 2008.

Malartic-Lagravière Pe-Lé r (w) ★★★ (r) 95 96 98 99 00' 01 02 03 04' 05' 06 08 09' 10 (w) 99 00 01' 02 03 04' 05' 06 07 08 09' 10 Léognan classed growth of 53 ha (majority red). Rich, modern red wine since late 1990s; a little lush Sauv Bl white. Belgian owner (since 1997) has revolutionized the property. ROLLAND advises. CH Gazin Rocquencourt (PESSAC-LÉOGNAN) new acquisition in 2006.

Malescasse H-Méd r ★★ 00 01 02 03 04 05 **06 07** 08 09 Renovated property with 40 ha well-situated nr MOULIS. Second label: La Closerie de Malescasse. Supple, inexpensive wines, accessible early.

Malescot-St-Exupéry Marg r ★★★ **94** 95 96 **98 99** 00' **01** 02 03 04 05' 06 07 08' 09' Third Growth of 24 ha returned to fine form in the 1990s. Now ripe, fragrant and finely structured. MICHEL ROLLAND advises.

Malle, de Saut r w dr sw ★★★ (w sw) 89' 90' **94** 95 96' **97' 98 99** 01' 02 03' **05 06 07** 09 Beautiful Preignac CH; 50 ha, of which 28-ha for v. fine, medium-bodied SAUTERNES; also M de Malle dry white and GRAVES CH du Cardaillan.

Marbuzet St-Est r ★★ **98 99** 00' 01 02 **03 04 05'** 06 Since 2007 the 7 ha have been integrated into COS-D'ESTOURNEL. Now a second-label name for certain markets.

Margaux, Ch Marg r (w) ★★★★ 83' 85' **86' 88' 89' 90' 93 94** 95' **96' 97 98' 99** 00' 01' 02 03' 04' 05' 06' 07 08 09' 10 First Growth (91 ha); most seductive and fabulously perfumed wine of MARGAUX. Consistent since acquired by André Mentzelopoulos in 1977. Now owned and run by daughter Corinne. Only 40% of production in the *grand vin*. Pavillon Rouge (99 00' 01 02 03 04' 05' 06 08 09') is second wine. Pavillon Blanc is best white (100% Sauv Bl) of MÉDOC, but expensive (00' 01' 02 03 04' 05 06 07 08 09').

Marojallia Marg r ★★★ **99** 00' 01 02 03 04 **05'** 06 **07** 08 09' Micro-CH with 4.5 ha, looking for big prices for big, rich, beefy, un-MARGAUX-like wines. VALANDRAUD owner consults. Upmarket B&B as well. Second wine: Clos Margalaine.

Marquis-d'Alesme Marg r ★★ 89 90 95 98 00 01 04 05 07 09 10 15-ha Third Growth. Dropped "Becker" handle in 2009. Disappointing in recent yrs. Bought by CH LABÉGORCE in 2006 and improvement in 2007. To watch.

Marquis-de-Terme Marg r ★★ →★★★ 89' 90' **95 96 98 99** 00' 01 02 **03 04** 05' 06 **07** 08 09' Fourth Growth; 40 ha around AC. Better form since 2000. New manager in 2009 and richer style. Previously solid rather than elegant MARGAUX.

Martinens Marg r ★★ **98 99 00 02 03 04** 05 06 09 30 ha in Cantenac. Light, supple.

Maucaillou Mou r ★★ **98'** 00' 01 02 03 04 05 06 08 09 10 63-ha property, gd standards. Clean, fresh, value wines. Second wine: No 2 de Maucaillou.

Mazeyres Pom r ★★ **96' 98' 99** 00 01 04 **05'** 06 08 09 Consistent, if not exciting lesser POMEROL. 20 ha on sandier soils. Better since 1996. Alain Moueix, cousin of Christian of J-P MOUEIX, manages here. *See* FONROQUE.

Meyney St-Est r ★★ →★★★ 89' 90' **94 95 96** 98 00 01 02 03 04 05' 06 08 09 Big (50-ha) riverside slopes property next to MONTROSE. Rich, robust, well-structured wines. Same stable as GRAND-PUY-DUCASSE and RAYNE VIGNEAU (owned by a bank). Second label: Prieur de Meyney.

Mission-Haut-Brion Blanc, la Pe-Lé r ★★★★ 83 85' **86** 88 89' **90' 93 94** 95 96' **98'** 99 00' 01 02 03 04 05' 06 07 08 09' 10 Neighbour and long-time rival to HAUT-BRION; since 1983 in same hands. Consistently grand-scale, full-blooded, long-maturing wine; more flamboyant than HAUT-BRION. 26 ha. LA TOUR HAUT-BRION v'yd integrated from 2006. Second label: La Chapelle de la Mission. White: previously LAVILLE-HAUT-BRION; renamed la Mission-Haut-Brion Blanc in 2009.

Monbousquet St-Em r (w) ★★★ **96 98 99** 00' 01 02 03 04 05' 06 07 08 09' Substantial property on ST-EMILION's gravel plain revolutionized by new owner Gerard Pérse. Now concentrated, oaky, voluptuous wines. Classified GRAND CRU CLASSÉ in 2006. Rare v.gd white (AC BORDEAUX) from 1998. Same ownership as PAVIE and PAVIE-DECESSE.

Monbrison Marg r ★★ →★★★ 89' 90 95 96' 98 99 00 01 02 04 05' 06 08 09' 10 13 ha on fine gravel soils. Delicate, fragrant MARGAUX.

Mondotte, la St-Em r ★★★ →★★★★ 96' 97 98' 99 00' 01 02 03 04' 05' 06 07 08 09' 10 Intense, always firm, virile *garagiste* wines from 4.3 ha on ST-EMILION's limestone plateau. Same ownership as CANON-LA-GAFFELIÈRE, CLOS DE L'ORATOIRE.

Montrose St-Est r ★★★ →★★★★ 88 89' 90' 93 94 95 96' 98 99 00' 01 02 03' 04' 05' 06 07 08 09' 10 70-ha Second Growth famed for deep-coloured, forceful claret. Known as the LATOUR of ST-ESTÈPHE. Vintages 1979–85 (except 1982) were lighter. After 110 yrs in same family hands, change of ownership in 2006. Ex-HAUT-BRION director, Jean-Bernard Delmas, now managing. Environmentally conscious renovation. Second wine: La Dame de Montrose.

Moulin-à-Vent Mou r ★★ 98 00' 02 03 04 05' 06 09 A 25-ha MOULIS estate; reasonably regular quality. Supple, early-drinking.

Moulin de la Rose St-Jul r ★★ 96 98 00' 01' 02 03 04 05 06 08 09 Tiny 5-ha in ST-JULIEN; high standards. Same ownership as SÉGUR DE CABANAC in ST-ESTÈPHE.

Moulin du Cadet St-Em r p ★★ 95 96 98 00 01 03 05 09 5-ha GRAND CRU CLASSÉ v'yd on the limestone plateau, now managed by Alain Moueix (*see also* MAZEYRES). Biodynamics practised. Robust wines but more depth and finesse in 2009.

Moulinet Pom r ★★ 96 98 00 01 04 05 06 08 09 One of POMEROL's bigger CHX; 18 ha on lightish soil. DERENONCOURT consultant from 2009. Gd value.

Moulin Pey-Labrie r ★★ 96 98' 99 00' 01 02 03 04 05' 06 08 09' A leading CH in the AC. Stylish wines, Merlot-dominated with elegance and structure.

Moulin-St-Georges St-Em r ★★ 98 99 00' 01 02 03 04 05' 06 08 09' 10 Stylish and rich wine. Classed-growth level. Same ownership as AUSONE.

Mouton Rothschild Pau r (w) ★★★★ 82' 83' 85' 86' 88' 89' 90' 93' 94 95' 96 97 98' 99 00' 01' 02 03 04' 05' 06' 07 08 09' 10 85 ha (80% Cab Sauv); most exotic and voluptuous of the PAUILLAC first growths. Attains new heights from 2004. Cellars renovated in 2011. Chinese painter, Xu Lei, created 2008 artists' label; prices spiralled. White Aile d'Argent from 1991. Second wine: Le Petit Mouton from 1997. *See also* Opus One (California) and Almaviva (Chile).

Nairac Saut w sw ★★ 89 90' 95' 96' 97' 98 99 01' 02 03' 04 05' 06 07 09 10 Rich style of BARSAC; top form since 2003. Second label: Esquise de Nairac, equally rich but fresher in style.

Nenin Pom r ★★★ 95 96 98 99 00' 01 02 03 04 05 06 07 08 09' 10 LÉOVILLE-LAS-CASES ownership since 1997. Massive investment. New cellars. 4 ha of former Certan-Giraud acquired in 1999. Now a total of 34 ha. On an upward swing. Built to age. 2009 best yet. Gd-value second wine: Fugue de Nenin.

Olivier Pe-Lé r w ★★★ (r) 95 96 00 01 02 04' 05' 06 08 09' 10 (w) 98' 00 01 02 03 04' 05' 06 07 08 09 10 A 55-ha classed growth (majority red), surrounding a moated castle at Léognan. Underachiever being turned around. New investment and greater purity, expression and quality from 2002. Value at this level.

Ormes-de-Pez, les St-Est r ★★ →★★★ 96 98 99 00' 01 02 03 04 05 06 07 08 09' 10 Outstanding 29-ha; owned by LYNCH-BAGES. Dense, fleshy, needs 5–6 yrs at least.

Ormes-Sorbet, les Méd r ★★ 98' 99 00' 01 02 03' 04 05 06 08 09 Long-time leader in northern MÉDOC. 21 ha at Couquèques. Elegant, gently oaked wines that age. Consistently reliable. Second label: CH de Conques.

Palmer Marg r ★★★★ 83' 85 86' 88' 89 90 93 94 95 96' 98' 99 00 01' 02 03 04' 05' 06 07 08 09' 10 Neighbour of CH MARGAUX: a Third Growth on a par with the Super Seconds. Wine of power, delicacy and much Merlot (40%). 55 ha with Dutch, British (SICHEL family) and French owners. £7 million investment in new cellars (2010–12). Second wine: Alter Ego de Palmer.

Pape-Clément Pe-Lé r (w) ★★★ →★★★★ (r) 90' 94 95 96 98' 99 00' 01 02 03 04 05 06 07 08 09' 10 (w) 01 02 03 04 05' 07 08 09 10 Ancient PESSAC v'yd (35 ha) owned by Bernard Magrez; record of potent, scented, long-ageing if not typical reds. 2.5 ha of elegant white. Ambitious new-wave direction, oak and potency from 2000 (grapes hand-destemmed!). Also CH Poumey at Gradignan.

Parenchère, de r (w) ★★ 03 04 05 06 07 08 09 Useful AC Ste-Foy-BORDEAUX and AC BORDEAUX SUPÉRIEUR from handsome CH with 65 ha. Cuvée Raphael best.

Patache d'Aux Méd r ★★ 00 02 03 04 05' 06 07 09 43-ha property in northern MÉDOC. Gd-value, reliable largely Cab Sauv wine. *See also* LIVERSAN.

Pavie St-Em r ★★★★ 90' 94 95 96 98 99 00' 01 02 03' 04 05' 06 07 08 09' 10 Splendidly sited First Growth; 37 ha mid-slope on the *côtes*. Great track record. Bought by owner of MONBOUSQUET, along with adjacent PAVIE-DECESSE. New-wave ST-EMILION: intense, oaky, strong, mid-Atlantic; subject of heated debate.

Pavie-Decesse St-Em r ★★ 98' 99 00' 01' 02 03 04 05' 06 07 08 09' 10 3.6-ha classed growth (only 1,000 cases). Even more powerful and muscular than PAVIE.

Pavie-Macquin St-Em r ★★★ 89' 90' 94 95 96' 98' 99 00' 01 02 03 04 05' 06 07 08 09' Surprise promotion to PREMIER GRAND CRU CLASSÉ in 2006 classification. 15-ha v'yd on the limestone plateau east of ST-EMILION. Astute management and winemaking by Nicolas Thienpont of PUYGUERAUD and DERENONCOURT consultant. Powerful, structured wines that need time in bottle.

Pedesclaux Pau r ★★ 98' 99 00 02 03 04 05 06 09 Underachieving 27-ha Fifth Growth being revived and reorganized. New owner in 2009 (*see* LILIAN LADOUYS) and improvement. Supple wines with up to 50% Merlot. Watch for change.

Petit-Village Pom r ★★★ 95 96 98' 99 00' 01 03 04 05 06 07 08 09' 10 Top 11-ha property opposite VIEUX-CH-CERTAN. Lagged until 2005. DERENONCOURT consults. New cellar in 2007. Same owner (AXA Insurance) as PICHON-LONGUEVILLE since 1989. Powerful, plummy wine. Second wine: Le Jardin de Petit-Village.

Pétrus Pom r ★★★★ 75' 76 78 79' 81 82' 83 85' 86 88' 89' 90 93' 94 95' 96 97 98' 99 00' 01 02 03 04' 05' 06 07 08 09' 10 The (unofficial) First Growth of POMEROL: Merlot solo *in excelsis*. 11 ha of gravelly clay giving 2,500 cases of massively rich, concentrated wine, on allocation to the world's millionaires. Each vintage adds lustre. Long-time winemaker J-C Berrouet (44 vintages) retired in 2007. Son Olivier now at helm. Jean-François MOUEIX owner.

Peyrabon H-Méd r ★★ 00' 01 02 03 04 05 06 09' Serious 53-ha HAUT-MÉDOC estate owned by négociant (Millésima). Also La Fleur-Peyrabon PAUILLAC.

Pez, de St-Est r ★★→★★★ 95' 96' 98' 99 00 01 02 03 04 05' 06 07 08 09' 10 Outstanding ST-ESTÈPHE *cru* of 26 ha. Now more Merlot (40%) and generous and reliable in style. Bought in 1995 by ROEDERER.

Phélan-Ségur St-Est r ★★★ 89' 90' 95 96' 98 99 00' 01 02 03 04 05' 06 07 08 09' 10 Sold 22 ha to MONTROSE in 2010. Will the wine change? Now 68 ha with substantial CH. Leading player in ST-ESTÈPHE; reputation since 1988; long, supple.

Pibran Pau r ★★ 95 96 99 00' 01 03 04 05' 06 07 08 09 10 Small 17-ha property allied to PICHON-LONGUEVILLE. Classy wine with PAUILLAC drive.

Pichon-Longueville (formerly **Baron de Pichon-Longueville**) Pau r ★★★★ 86' 88' 89' 90' 93 94' 95 96 98 99 00' 01 02 03 04 05' 06 07 08 09' 10 Second Growth (73 ha) with revitalized powerful PAUILLAC wine for long ageing. Owners AXA Insurance (1987). New barrel cellar (under an artificial lake) and visitor centre in 2008. Second label: Les Tourelles de Longueville.

Pichon-Longueville Comtesse de Lalande (Pichon Lalande) Pau r ★★★★ 82' 83 85' 86' 88' 89' 90' 94 95 96 98 99 00 01 02 03' 04 05' 06 07 08 09' 10 Super Second Growth neighbour to LATOUR (87 ha). Always among the top performers; a long-lived, Merlot-marked wine of fabulous breeding, even in lesser yrs. ROEDERER owner since 2007. Sylvie Cazes (*see* LYNCH-BAGES) became new MD in 2011. Tendency in coming yrs to increase Cab Sauv. Second wine: Réserve de la Comtesse. Other property: CH BERNADOTTE.

Pin, le Pom r ★★★★ 85 86 88 89 90' 94 95 96 97 98' 99 00 01 02 04' 05' 06' 07 08 09' 10 The original of the B'X cult mini-*crus* made in a cellar not much bigger than a garage. Now a new (2011) modern winery. A mere 500 cases of 100% Merlot, with same family behind it as VIEUX-CH-CERTAN. Almost as rich as its drinkers; but prices are ridiculous.

Pitray, de r ★★ 96' 98' 00' 03 04 05 06 09' Once the best known in CASTILLON, now overshadowed by leading lights. Earthy, but value and available.

Plince Pom r ★★ 98' 99 00' 01 04 05 06 08 09 Lighter, supple wines from 9-ha.

Pointe, la Pom r ★★→★★★ 98' 99 00' 01 04 05 06 07 08 09' 10 Prominent 22-ha estate. New owner and investment (2007). ANGÉLUS owner consults. Distinct improvement in 2009. To watch.

Pontac-Monplaisir Pe-Lé r (w) ★★ 00 02 04 05' 06 07 08 09 16-ha property in PESSAC-LÉOGNAN suburbs. Attractive white; supple, so-so red. Value.

Pontet-Canet Pau r ★★★ →★★★★ 88 89' 90 94' 95 96' 98 99 00' 01 02' 03 04' 05' 06' 07 08 09' 81-ha neighbour to MOUTON-ROTHSCHILD. One of the most-improved MÉDOC estates in last 10 yrs. V. PAUILLAC in style. Only entirely biodynamic classed growth; horse ploughing. Second wine: Les Hauts de Pontet-Canet.

Potensac Méd r ★★ 95 96 98 99 00 01 02 03 04' 05' 07 08 09' Well-known 70-ha property of northern MÉDOC. Delon family of LEOVILLE-LAS-CASES; class shows. Firm, vigorous wines for long ageing. Second wine: Chapelle de Potensac.

Pouget Marg r ★★ 95 96 98' 00' 02 03 04 05' 06 07 08 09' Obscure 11-ha Fourth Growth attached to BOYD-CANTENAC. Old vines. Solid rather than elegant.

Poujeaux Mou r ★★ 90' 94' 95' 96' 98 99 00' 01 03 04 05 06 08 09' Purchased by CLOS FOURTET owner in 2007; 68 ha. CHASSE-SPLEEN the high point of MOULIS. DERENONCOURT consults. Age-worthy wines. Second label: La Salle de Poujeaux.

Premier Grand Cru Classé *See* ST-EMILION classification box, p. 104.

Prieuré-Lichine Marg r ★★★ 89' 90' 94' 95 96 98' 99 00' 01 02 03 04 05 06 07 08 09' 10 A 70-ha Fourth Growth owned by a négociant; put on the map by Alexis Lichine. V'yds v. dispersed. Advised by STÉPHANE DERENONCOURT (*see* CANON LA GAFFELIÈRE, PAVIE-MACQUIN). Fragrant MARGAUX currently on gd form. Second wine: CH de Clairefont. A gd white B'x, too.

Puygueraud r ★★ 98 99 00' 01' 02 03' 05' 06 08 09 10 Leading CH of this tiny Côtes de Francs AC. Oak-aged wines of surprising class. Gd-value Les Charmes-Godard white same owner. Special Cuvée George with Malbec (35%+) in blend. Same winemaker as PAVIE-MACQUIN and LARCISSE-DUCASSE.

Rabaud-Promis Saut w sw ★★ →★★★ 89' 90 95 96 97' 98 99 00' 01 02 03' 04 05' 06 07 09' A 30-ha classed growth at Bommes. Discreet but generally v. gd.

Rahoul Grav r w ★★ (r) 98' 00' 01 02 04 05 08 09 40-ha v'yd at Portets; Supple, Sém-dominated white (01 02 04 05' 07 08 09); red could be better.

Ramage-la-Batisse H-Méd r ★★ 98 99 00' 02 03 04 05' 07 08 09 Reasonably consistent, widely distributed HAUT-MÉDOC; 65 ha at St-Sauveur, north of PAUILLAC. Second wine: CH Tourteran.

Rauzan-Gassies Marg r ★★ 96' 98 99 00 01' 02 03 04 05' 07 08 09' 10 The 30-ha Second Growth neighbour of RAUZAN-SÉGLA that has long lagged behind it. New generation making strides but still has a way to go. Solid rather than fine.

Rauzan-Ségla Marg r ★★★★ 86' 88' 89' 90' 94' 95 96 98 99 00' 01 02 03 04' 05 06 07 08 09' 10 A Second Growth (62 ha) long famous for its fragrance; owned by owners of Chanel (*see* CANON). A great MARGAUX name right at the top, with rebuilt CH and *chais*. Second wine: Ségla.

Raymond-Lafon Saut w sw ★★★ 88 89' 90' 95 96' 97 98 99' 01' 02 03' 04 05' 06 07' 09' Sauternes estate (18 ha) acquired by former YQUEM manager (1972); now run by his children. Rich, complex wines that age. Classed-growth quality.

Rayne Vigneau Saut w sw ★★★ 89 90' 95 96 98 99 01' 02 03 05' 07 09' Large 80-ha classed growth at Bommes. Denis Dubourdieu consults. Improvement since 2006. Second label: Madame de Rayne.

Respide Médeville Grav r w ★★ (r) 99 00' 01 02 04 05' 06 07 09 (w) 00 01 02 04' 05' 07 08 09 One of the better AC GRAVES properties for both red and *white*. Same owner as GILETTE in SAUTERNES. Drink reds at around 4–6 yrs.

> **St-Emilion classification – new rules for 2012**
> A new set of rules for the 2012 edition of the ST-EMILION classification
> have been unveiled by the French appellations body, the INAO. It is
> hoped they will prevent the type of legal furore that followed the 2006
> edition, which was contested by demoted CHX. The new classification,
> now legally considered an exam rather than a competition, will be
> conducted by a commission of seven wine professionals nominated
> by the INAO, none from B'X. All candidates will be visited and the
> tastings of ten vintages (1999–2008) administered by an independent
> body (15 vintages will be tasted if promotion from GRAND CRU CLASSÉ to
> PREMIER GRAND CRU CLASSÉ is being sought). The tastings will represent
> 50% of the mark for GRAND CRU CLASSÉ status. Notoriety, management
> and terroir will make up the other 50%. There are presently 15 PREMIER
> GRAND CRU CLASSÉS and 57 GRAND CRU CLASSÉS.

Reynon r w ★★ 40 ha for fragrant white from Sauv Bl **04' 05' 06 07 08 09**; also serious red (**00 01 02 03 04' 05' 06 07 09**), too. *See also* CLOS FLORIDÈNE. Second wine (r): CH Reynon-Peyrat. Owned by Denis Dubourdieu family.

Reysson H-Méd r ★★ **00 02 03 04 05 06 08 09'** Recently replanted 49-ha HAUT-MÉDOC estate; managed by négociant CVBG-DOURTHE (*see* BELGRAVE, LA GARDE). Rich, modern style.

Ricaud, de w sw (r dr) ★★ **97 99 01' 02 03' 05 07 09** Substantial (80-ha) grower of SAUTERNES-like, age-worthy wine just across river. Red, dry white also.

Rieussec Saut w sw ★★★★ **83' 85 86' 88' 89' 90' 95 96' 97' 98 99 01' 02 03' 04 05' 06 07 09' 10** Worthy neighbour of YQUEM with 90 ha in Fargues, bought in 1985 by the (LAFITE) Rothschilds. Vinified in oak since 1996. Fabulously powerful, opulent wine. Also dry "R", now made in modern style – with less character. Second wine: Carmes de Rieussec.

Ripeau St-Em r ★★ **98 00' 01 04 05' 06 08 09** Lesser 16-ha GRAND CRU CLASSÉ on sandy soils nr CHEVAL BLANC. Lighter style. Better since 2000, but inconsistent.

Rivière, de la r ★★ **98' 99 00' 01 02 03 04 05' 06 08 09** The biggest and most impressive FRONSAC property, with a Wagnerian castle and cellars. 58 ha. Formerly big, tannic wines are now more refined. New owner in 2003, with consultant from LANGUEDOC, Claude Gros.

Rochemorin, de Pe-Lé r w ★★→★★★ (r) **98' 99 00' 01 02 04 05 06 08 09** (w) **01 02 03 04 05 06 07 08 09** An important restoration at Martillac by André Lurton of LA LOUVIÈRE: 105 ha (three-quarters red) of maturing vines. New state-of-the-art winery in 2004. Fairly consistent quality and widely distributed.

Rol Valentin St-Em r ★★★ **99 00' 01' 02 03 04 05' 06 07 08 09 10** Originally *garage*-style and size, now 7.5 ha. Wines rich, modern but balanced. New owner 2010.

Rouget Pom r ★★ **95 96 98' 99 00' 01 03 04 05 07 08 09'** Attractive old estate on the northern edge of POMEROL. 17 ha. Burgundian owners (1992). ROLLAND consults. Now excellent; rich, unctuous wines. Gd value.

Royal St-Emilion Brand name of important, dynamic growers' co-op. *See* GALIUS.

St-André-Corbin St-Em r ★★ **99 00' 01 03 04 05 08 09 09** A 22-ha estate in MONTAGNE-and ST-GEORGES-ST-EMILION. Supple, Merlot-dominated wine.

St-Georges St-Em r ★★ **95' 96 98' 00' 01 03 04 05' 08 09** Noble 18th-century CH overlooking the ST-EMILION plateau from the hill to the north. 51 ha (25% of ST-GEORGES AC). Gd wine sold direct to the public.

St-Pierre St-Jul r ★★★ **89 90' 94 95' 96' 98 99 00' 01' 02 03 04 05' 06 07 08 09' 10** Once-understated Fourth Growth (17 ha) owned by the president of BORDEAUX football club. Stylish and consistent classic ST-JULIEN. *See* GLORIA.

Sales, de Pom r ★★ 95 96 98' 00' 01' 04 05 06 08 09 Biggest v'yd of POMEROL (47 ha) on sandy/gravel soils, attached to grandest CH. Lightish wine; never quite poetry. Try top vintages. Second label: CH Chantalouette.

Sansonnet St-Em r ★★ 00' 01 02 03 04 05' 06 08 09' A small 6.8-ha plateau estate. Ambitiously run in the new ST-EMILION style (rich, fat). DERENONCOURT consulting from 2006, wines now a little more elegant.

Saransot-Dupré List r (w) ★★ 98' 99 00' 01 02 03 04 05 06 09 Small 17-ha property; firm, fleshy wines. Lots of Merlot. One of LISTRAC's band of whites (60% Sém).

Sénéjac H-Méd r (w) ★★ 99 00 01 02 03 04 05' 06 08 09' 37-ha in southern MÉDOC owned since 1999 by the same family as TALBOT. Well-balanced wines. V'yd run biodynamically by PONTET-CANET team since 2009.

Serre, la St-Em r ★★ 95 96 98' 99 00' 01 02 03 04 05 06 08 09' Small (6.5-ha) GRAND CRU CLASSÉ, on limestone plateau. Rich, stylish wines with plenty of fruit.

Sigalas-Rabaud Saut w sw ★★★ 85 86 88 89' 90 95' 96' 97' 98 99 01' 02 03' 04 05' 07 09' 10 The smaller part of the former RABAUD estate: 14 ha in Bommes; same winemaking team as LAFAURIE-PEYRAGUEY. V. fragrant and lovely. Top-ranking now. Second wine: Le Lieutenant de Sigalas.

Siran Marg r ★★→★★★ 95 96 98 99 00' 01 02 03 04 05 06 07 08 09' 10 A 40-ha property owned by the Miailhe family since 1859; Edouard runs the show today. Neighbour of DAUZAC. The wines age well and have masses of flavour.

Smith-Haut-Lafitte Pe-Lé r (w p) ★★★ (r) 90' 94 95 96 98 99 00' 01 02 03 04' 05' 06 07 08 09' 10 (w) 90 97 98 99' 00 01 02 03 04 05 06 07' 08' 09 10 Classed growth at Martillac: 67 ha. Regularly one of the stars of PESSAC-LÉOGNAN. Former ski-champion owners have vastly improved quality. Luxurious spa-hotel-restaurant also. White is full, ripe, sappy; red generous. Second label: Les Hauts de Smith. Also CH Cantelys, PESSAC-LÉOGNAN.

Sociando-Mallet H-Méd r ★★★ 89' 90' 94 95 96' 98' 99 00' 01' 02 03 04 05' 06 07 09' 10 Splendid, widely followed estate at St-Seurin. Independently minded owner celebrated 40 vintages 2009. Classed-growth quality; 85 ha. Conservative, big-boned wines to lay down for yrs. Second wine: Demoiselle de Sociando.

Soudars H-Méd r ★★ 95 96' 98 99 00' 01 03 04 05 06 09 Sister to COUFRAN and VERDIGNAN; 22 ha. Relatively traditional and regular quality.

Soutard St-Em r ★★★ 90' 94 95 96 98' 99 00' 01 03 04 05 06 07 08 09 *Potentially excellent* 27-ha classed growth on the limestone plateau. Now owned by same insurance group as LARMANDE and CADET-PIOLA. Massive investment; new cellars 2010. Finer style since 2007 (hail in 2009). Second label: Jardins du Soutard .

Suduiraut Saut w sw ★★★★ 85 86 88' 89' 90' 95 96 97' 98 99' 01' 02 03' 04 05' 06 07' 09' 10 One of the best classed-growth SAUTERNES: 90 ha with renovated CH and gardens by Le Nôtre. Owner AXA Insurance has achieved greater consistency, luscious quality. *See* PICHON-LONGUEVILLE. Second wine: Castelnau de Suduiraut. New dry wine, "S", v. promising.

Tailhas, du Pom r ★★ 95 96' 98' 99 00 01 04 05 08 09 Modest 10-ha property near FIGEAC. POMEROL of the lighter kind. Average quality.

Taillefer Pom r ★★ 95' 96 98' 00' 01 02 03 04 05' 06 08 09 11-ha v'yd on the edge of POMEROL. Astutely managed by Catherine Moueix. Less power than top estates but gently harmonious. Gd value.

Talbot St-Jul r (w) ★★★ 88' 89' 90 94 95 96' 98' 99 00' 01 02 03 04 05' 08' 09' 10 Important 102-ha Fourth Growth, for many yrs younger sister to GRUAUD-LAROSE. Wine similarly attractive: rich, *consummately charming*, *reliable* (though wobbly 2006–07). Second label: Connétable de Talbot. White: Caillou Blanc drinks well at up to 5–6 yrs. SÉNÉJAC in same family ownership.

Tertre, du Marg r ★★★ 95 96' 98' 99 00' 01 03 04' 05' 06 07 08 09' 10 Fifth

Growth (50 ha) isolated south of MARGAUX. History of undervalued fragrant (20% Cab Fr) and fruity wines. Since 1997, same owner as CH GISCOURS. Former LATOUR winemaker. New techniques and massive investment have produced a concentrated, structured wine, really humming from 2003.

Tertre Daugay St-Em r ★★★ 96 98 99 00' 01 04 05 06 07 09' 16-ha hilltop v'yd. Sister to LA GAFFELIÈRE. Escaped declassification from GRAND CRU CLASSÉ in 2006. Improvement from 2000. DERENONCOURT consulting from 2004.

Tertre-Rôteboeuf St-Em r ★★★★ 88' 89' 90' 93 94 95 96 97 98' 99 00' 01 02 03' 04 05' 06' 07 08 09' 10 A cult star (6 ha) making concentrated, dramatic, largely Merlot wine since 1985. Frightening prices. Also CÔTES DE BOURG property, Roc de Cambes of ST-EMILION classed-growth quality.

Thieuley r p w ★★ E-2-M supplier of consistent, quality AC BORDEAUX (r w); fruity CLAIRET; oak-aged Cuvée Francis Courselle (r w). Also owns Clos Ste-Anne in CADILLAC-CÔTES DE BORDEAUX.

Tour-Blanche, la Saut w sw (r) ★★★ 85 86 88' 89' 90' 95 96 97' 98 99 01' 03 04 05' 06 07 09' 10 Leading classed growth. Back on form from 1988. Sauv Bl and Muscadelle 20% of blend. Rich and powerful. Second wine: Les Charmilles de Tour-Blanche.

Tour-de-By, la Méd r ★★ 98 00 01 02 03 04 05' 06 08 09 V. well-run 74-ha family estate in northern MÉDOC with a name for sturdy but reliable wines with a fruity note. Usually gd value.

Tour-Carnet, la H-Méd r ★★ 95 96 98 99 00' 01 02 03 04 05' 06 08 09' 10 Fourth Growth (65 ha) with medieval moated fortress, owned by Bernard Magrez (see FOMBRAUGE, PAPE-CLÉMENT). Investment from 2000 has produced richer wines in more modern style. Second wine: Les Douves de Ch La Tour Carnet. Also *garage* Servitude Volontaire du Tour Carnet.

Tour Figeac, la St-Em r ★★ 90' 94' 95 96' 98' 99 00' 01' 02 04 05 06 07 08 09' 10 A 15-ha GRAND CRU CLASSÉ between FIGEAC and POMEROL. Biodynamic methods (DERENONCOURT and his wife consult). Full, fleshy and harmonious.

Tour Haut-Brion, la Pe-Lé r ★★★ 95 96' 98' 99 00' 01 02 03 04' 05' RIP from 2005 for this classed growth. The 5.05-ha v'yd has now been integrated into that of LA MISSION-HAUT-BRION. Same owner.

Tour Haut-Caussan Méd r ★★ 00' 01 02 03 04 05' 06 08 09' Well-run 18-ha property at Blaignan. Reliable. Gd value. Interests in CORBIÈRES as well.

Tour-du-Haut-Moulin H-Méd r ★★ 95 96 98 00' 02 03 04 05' 06 08 09 Family-owned 32-ha estate; intense, consistent, wines to mature.

Tour de Mons, la Marg r ★★ 96' 98' 99 00 01 02 04 05' 06 08 09' MARGAUX *cru* of 44 ha, owned by a bank. A long dull patch but recent investment and improvement. 2009 best for a while.

Tournefeuille r ★★ 00' 01' 02 03 04 05 06 07 08 09 10 18-ha property in LALANDE DE POMEROL overlooking Barbanne stream. Steady investment and improvement since 1998. Reliable.

Tour-du-Pas-St-Georges St-Em r ★★ 98 99 00' 01 03 04 05 06 09 Wine from 16 ha of ST-GEORGES-ST-EMILION owned by Pascal Delbeck. Recent investment.

Tour du Pin, la St-Em r ★★ 95 96 98 00' 01 04 05 06 08 09' 10 8 ha, formerly La Tour du Pin Figeac-Moueix but bought and renamed by CHEVAL BLANC in 2006. Unimpressive form previously, but new team turning things around. To watch.

Tour-St-Bonnet Méd r ★★ 98 99 00' 02 03 04 05 06 08 09' Consistently well-made ample northern MÉDOC from St-Christoly; 40 ha. Gd value.

Tronquoy-Lalande St-Est r ★★ 98 99 00' 02 03 04 05 06 07 08 09' Same owners as MONTROSE from 2006. Lots of Merlot and Petit Verdot; 19 ha. Definite progression. Second wine: Tronquoy de Ste-Anne. To watch.

Troplong-Mondot St-Em r ★★★ 89' 90' 94' 95 96' 98' 99 00' 01' 02 03 04 05'

06 07 08 09' 10 PREMIER GRAND CRU CLASSÉ from 2006. Well-sited 22 ha on a high point of limestone plateau. *Wines of power and depth with increasing elegance.* MICHEL ROLLAND consults. Second wine: Mondot.

Trotanoy Pom r ★★★★ 88 89' 90' 93 94 95 96 98' 99 00' 01 02 03 04' 05' 06 07 08 09' 10 A JEAN-PIERRE MOUEIX property since 1953. Only 7 ha; at best a glorious, fleshy, structured, perfumed wine. Wobbled a bit in the 1980s, but back on top form since 1989. Can occasionally rival PÉTRUS.

Trottevieille St-Em r ★★★ 89' 90 94 95 96 98 99 00' 01 03' 04 05' 06 07 08 09' 10 First Growth on the limestone plateau. Same owners as BATAILLEY and DOMAINE DE L'ÉGLISE have raised its game since 2000. Hail damage in 2009 so tiny crop. Denis Dubourdieu consults. Limited bottling of old, ungrafted Cab Fr.

Valandraud St-Em r ★★★★ 93 94 95' 96 98 99 00' 01' 02 03 04 05' 06 07 08 09' 10 Leader among *garagiste* micro-wines fulfilling aspirations to glory. Originally super-concentrated; since 1998 greater complexity. Now a selection from 10 ha; on average 15,000 bottles. Virginie de Valandraud another selection. White Blanc de Valandraud from 2003.

Verdignan H-Méd r ★★ 98 99 00' 01 02 03 04 05 06 08 09 Substantial 60-ha HAUT-MÉDOC estate; sister to COUFRAN and SOUDARS. More Cab Sauv than COUFRAN. Gd value and ageing potential.

Vieille Cure, la r ★★ 00' 01' 02 03 04 05' 06 08 09' 10 A 20-ha property, US-owned, leading in Fronsac. Accessible from 4 yrs. Reliable value.

Vieux-Ch-Certan Pom r ★★★★ 82' 83' 85 86' 88' 89 90' 94 95' 96' 98' 99 00' 01 02 04' 05' 06 07 08 09' 10 Traditionally rated close to PÉTRUS in quality, but totally different in style (30% Cab Fr and 10% Cab Sauv); authentic with plenty of finesse. 14 ha; old vines (average 40–50 yrs).

Vieux Ch St-André St-Em r ★★ 00' 01 02 03 04 05 06 08 09 Small 6-ha v'yd in MONTAGNE-ST-EMILION owned by former winemaker of PÉTRUS. Regular quality.

Villegeorge, de H-Méd r ★★ 96' 98' 99 00' 02 03 04 05 06 08 09' 20-ha property owned by Marie-Laure Lurton, sister of Henri at BRANE-CANTENAC. Classic MÉDOC style. Sister CHX Duplessis in MOULIS and La Tour de Bessan in MARGAUX.

Vray Croix de Gay Pom r ★★ 90 95 96 98' 00' 04 05 06 08 09' 10 V. small (4 ha); in the best part of POMEROL. Improvements since 2005, but still a work in progress. Sister to CH Siaurac in LALANDE DE POMEROL. DERENONCOURT consults.

Yon-Figeac St-Em r ★★ 98 99 00' 02 03 04 05 06 09 24-ha estate. V'yd restructured between 1985 and 1995. Avoided relegation from GRAND CRU CLASSÉ in 2006. Reasonably sound now but unexciting.

Yquem Saut w sw (dr) ★★★★ 79 80' 81' 83' 85 86' 88' 89' 90' 93 94 95' 96 97' 98 99' 00 01' 02 03' 04 05' 06' 07' 08 09' 10 The world's most famous sweet wine estate. 101 ha; 10,000 cases of v. strong, intense, luscious wine (3 yrs in barrel). Most vintages improve for 15+ yrs; some live 100+ yrs in transcendent splendour. Have been subtle changes under newish LVMH ownership: slightly more freshness, slightly less time in barrel. The management (same as CHEVAL BLANC) is forward-thinking, pushing prices sky-high. Also makes dry "Y" (pronounced "ygrec").

Twin peaks

Bordeaux has another brace of great vintages: 2009 and 2010. The latter is more variable, and more of a Cab Sauv vintage – but which should we buy (apart from both)? It's surprisingly simple: buy 2009 for earlier drinking, for juiciness, succulent fruit and joie de vivre; buy 2010 to tuck away for a longer time. In the case of the top growths, a very, very long time.

BORDEAUX

Italy

More heavily shaded areas are the wine-growing regions.

Abbreviations used in the text:

Ab	Abruzzo	Sar	Sardinia
Ap	Apulia	Si	Sicily
Bas	Basilicata	T-AA	Trentino- Alto Adige
Cal	Calabria	Tus	Tuscany
Cam	Campania	VdA	Valle d'Aosta
E-R	Emilia-Romagna	Ven	Veneto
F-VG	Friuli-Venezia Giulia	Umb	Umbria
Lat	Latium		
Lig	Liguria	cs	*cantine sociale*
Lom	Lombardy		
Mar	Marches		
Pie	Piedmont		

VALLE D'AOSTA · L Como · L Maggiore · Milan · **LOMBARD** · Turin **PIEDMONT** · Genoa · **LIGURIA** · *Ligurian Sea*

Is the 21st century the golden age of Italian wines? Despite being the oldest continuous wine culture on the planet, Italy in the course of its 3,000-year vinous history has experienced plenty of troughs among the infrequent peaks, and perhaps the best one can say about Italian wine's darker ages is that it has kept going. However, quality has soared in the final third of the 20th century, while volume has shrunk. As the country's wine-philosopher, the redoubtable Angelo Gaja, puts it, wine in Italy is no longer a mere commodity but a luxury, and increasingly an art form. And while Italy's wines may not yet have hit the heights that the best from her erstwhile colony Transalpine Gaul can attain, the proposition that she is capable of doing so would no longer be met with hoots of derision in wine-as-art circles. With her wealth of indigenous vine-material, her variety of geology and microclimates, her multiple latitudes and altitudes and the sheer creativity of her citizens, the potential for greatness is there in spades. Which is not to say you should approach it with awe. Turn off pre-judgements, doubts arising from complicated names, and relish its sheer entertainment value. Steer clear of bottles at look-at-me prices. Treat it as you do Italian food: to satisfy the animal in you.

Recent vintages

Amarone, Veneto & Friuli

2010 Volume on par with 2009. September rain; spells of sunshine and wind. Good for lighter wines; rain caused problems for grapes in *appassimento*.

2009 Small Valpolicella crop, superb quality. Ideal for *passito*: classic wines. Good for Prosecco, Pinot Gr, other whites. Drink from 2015 (Amarone).

2008 Textbook year for temperature and rainfall: ideal vintage conditions.
   Quantity a bit short, but classic wines of high quality. Drink from 2016.
2007 High hopes were dashed for some by hail in August. Some excellent
   wines, but very short crop. Selection needed.
2006 Outstanding, with new record for grape tonnage reserved for drying:
   30-per-cent higher than any previous vintage. Drink from 2012.
2005 Grape-drying technology saved Amarone and Recioto. Drink now.
2004 Classic, less concentrated and rich than 2003. Drink now for 20 years
   from vintage.

Campania & Basilicata

2010 Vigorous growth needed care, given which, whites were lightish with good aromas; reds were good to average; too early to say more.

2009 Wet winter, dry summer: ripe, healthy, aromatic whites, and plenty of substance and concentration (reds). Lay down (classic Aglianico/Taurasi).

2008 A dry and long summer. A classic year for Aglianico; good, too, for whites. Drink from 2013.

2007 Good to excellent quality. Drink from 2013.

2006 Rain and problems of rot in lower-lying zones, much sun and a long growing season in higher vineyards. Selection needed.

2005 Aglianico had weight, complexity and character – perhaps the finest wines of all Italy in 2005. Drink from 2012.

2004 Slow and uncertain ripening for Aglianico; has exceeded expectations. Drink now for ten years.

Marches & Abruzzo

2010 Quantity up 5% (Marches) to 15% (Abruzzo). Weather erratic, good for aroma, but also rot, with vintage rain. Difficult, some good to excellent.

2009 Wet spring, hot, dry summer. Quantity down (Verdicchio, Montepulciano); good to very good quality, esp whites. Drink from 2012 (Montepulciano).

2008 East of the Apennines weather was rainier and cooler than north and west; but vintage was fine. Some excellent wines. Drink from 2011/12.

2007 Spectacularly low crop due to heat and water shortage; but some top-quality reds. Drink from 2012.

2006 Generally positive where hail did not fall; better than 2004 and 2005, but not as good as 2003. Selection needed.

2005 Good structure for those who waited to pick. Drink now for five years.

Piedmont

2010 Cold winter, wet spring, baking July and patchy end-season. Quality correspondingly patchy, but patient growers made very good wines.

2009 Quantity up, quality good to very good. Prices on downward slide, bargain-hunt time. Drink from 2014 for ten+ years (Barolo/Barbaresco).

2008 A wet spring led to a dry, hot summer. Some great Barberas; Nebbiolos perhaps too early to judge. Drink from 2012 for ten years.

2007 Good to excellent quality for Barolo, Barbaresco and Barbera. Some classic wines. Drink from 2013 for ten+ years.

2006 Excellent Nebbiolo and Barbera. The laying-down vintage of the decade. Drink from 2014 for 20 years.

2005 Uneven for Barbera (rot) and Nebbiolo, with some good wines selling with difficulty in the current market. Drink now for five+ years.

Older fine vintages: 04 01 00 99 98 97 96 95 90 89 88. Vintages to keep: 01 99 96. Vintages to drink up: 00 97 90 88

Tuscany

2010 Poor weather at flowering reduced crop 10%. Boiling July, patchy August, September. Good fruit where carefully picked. Brunello very successful.

2009 Wettish June/July, hot, dry late summer, a sprinkle in September. All grapes healthy when picked. Quantity average, quality very good at least. Drink from 2014 (Brunello/Vino Nobile/Chianti Classico *crus*).

2008 Wet spring, very dry summer with rare and at times violent rain and hail. Mixed results with points of excellence; not necessarily for long keeping. Drink from 2012 for five years.

2007 Ideal vintage conditions made for a smaller-than-average but high-quality crop. Drink from 2013 for ten years.

2006 A year of balance, no temperature extremes, measured rainfall. Probably greatest of last 20 vintages. Drink from 2014 for 20 years.

2005 Most successful along coast and for those who picked before heavy rains. Sangiovese at every quality level imaginable; selection needed.

2004 Exceptional along coast, Montepulciano, Montalcino. Cool temperatures, but some elegant wines; beginning to drink, from 2012 for 20 years.

Older fine vintages: 01 99 97 95 90. Vintages to keep: 01 99. Vintages to drink up: 97 95 90

Aglianico del Vulture Bas DOC r dr ★★★ 01' 04 05 06 07 08 (09) (10) *Vecchio* (old) after 3 yrs, RISERVA after 5 yrs. Italy's latest-ripening quality grape, Aglianico from the slopes of spent volcano Monte Vulture, makes some of the south's finest. Top: Alovini, Basilisco, Cantine del Notaio, Lucania, Macarico, PATERNOSTER. Perhaps the best known, D'ANGELO, following a family bust-up, is now known as "Donato d'Angelo".

Alba Pie Major wine city of PIEDMONT, southeast of Turin, famous for truffles and chocolates, and home to PIEDMONT'S, if not Italy's, most prestigious wines: BAROLO, BARBARESCO, NEBBIOLO D'ALBA, ROERO, B D'ALBA and DOLCETTO D'ALBA.

Albana di Romagna E-R DOCG w dr sw s/sw (sp) ★→★★★ DYA Italy's first white DOCG, justifiably for the sweet PASSITO version, less so for the unremarkable and little-seen-abroad dry styles. Bertinoro is the commune with the best producers, inc Campodelsole, Celli, Madonia Giovanna and *Fattoria Paradiso*. ZERBINA makes perhaps the best sweet version in Scacco Matto.

Allegrini Ven ★★★ Top-quality Veronese producer; outstanding single-v'yd IGT wines (La Grola, La Poja), AMARONE and RECIOTO. Also joint owner of Poggio al Tesoro in BOLGHERI and, since 2009, Poggio San Polo in MONTALCINO (TUSCANY).

Altare, Elio Pie ★★★ Pioneering producer of short-maceration BAROLO. Look for BAROLO Arborina, BAROLO Brunate, LANGHE DOC Arborina (NEBBIOLO), Larigi (BARBERA), La Villa, VDT L'Insieme and DOLCETTO D'ALBA.

Alto Adige T-AA DOC r p w dr sw sp ★★→★★★★ The ex-Austrian, largely German-speaking province of Bolzano, known as Alto Adige or SÜDTIROL, has had phenomenal success in Italy and abroad with its mtn-fresh, minerally whites; less so with reds, except for the odd outstanding Pinot N. Several outstanding cooperatives and many small-to-medium private companies of real quality.

Ama, Castello di Tus ★★★ One of the best and most consistent modern CHIANTI CLASSICO estates, nr Gaiole. La Casuccia and Bellavista are top single-v'yd wines. Gd IGTS, CHARD and MERLOT (L'Apparita).

Amarone della Valpolicella Ven DOCG r ★★→★★★★ 90' 95 97 98 00 01 03' 04 06' 07 (08) (09) (10) Used to be called Recioto della Valpolicella Amarone. Relatively dry version of RECIOTO DELLA VALPOLICELLA from air-dried VALPOLICELLA grapes; concentrated, fairly long-lived. (For producers *see* box, p. 138.) Older vintages are hard to come by but tend to dry out beyond 20 yrs. DOCG on the market soon, following a long battle.

Anselmi, Roberto Ven ★★★ Producer at Monteforte in SOAVE who, some yrs ago, abandoned the DOC rather than accept absurd new rules. Now sells wines under IGT brand names like Capitel Croce and Capitel Foscarino (dry) and I Capitelli PASSITO (sweet). Cellars flooded in Nov 2010 rains.

Antinori, Marchesi L & P ★★→★★★★ V. influential Florentine house of highest repute, owned by Piero A, now increasingly leaving management to his three daughters and oenologist Renzo Cotarella. Famous for CHIANTI CLASSICO (Tenute Marchese Antinori and *Badia a Passignano*), Umbrian *(Castello della Sala)*, and

PIEDMONT (PRUNOTTO) wines, but esp SUPER TUSCANS TIGNANELLO and SOLAIA. Also estates in MAREMMA (Fattoria Aldobrandesca), MONTEPULCIANO (La Braccesca), MONTALCINO (Pian delle Vigne), in ASTI (for BARBERA), in FRANCIACORTA for sparkling (*Montenisa*) and in APULIA (Vigneti del Sud). V.gd DOC BOLGHERI Guado al Tasso.

Apulia The heel of the Italian boot, historically a bulk producer, increasing in quality and value. Best DOC: BRINDISI, CASTEL DEL MONTE, MANDURIA (PRIMITIVO DI), SALICE SALENTINO. Producers: ANTINORI, Botromagno, Candido, Cantele, Cantine Paradiso, Castel di Selva, Co-op Due Palme, Conti Zecca, Coppadoro, La Corte, Li Veli, D'Alfonso del Sordo, Azienda Monaci (formerly Masseria Monaci), Michele Calò, RACEMI, RIVERA, Rubino, *Rosa del Golfo*, TAURINO, Valle dell'Asso, VALLONE.

Argiano Tus Avant-garde BRUNELLO estate where Hans Vinding-Diers also makes CAB/MERLOT/SYRAH blend Solengo and smooth 100%-SANGIOVESE Suolo.

Argiano, Castello di Tus aka Sesti. Astronomer Giuseppe Maria Sesti turns out classy biodynamic BRUNELLO and Bordeaux-influenced *Terra di Siena*.

Argiolas, Antonio Sar ★★→★★★ Top Sardinian producer making excellent CANNONAU, NURAGUS, *Vermentino*, Bovale. Red IGTS Turriga (★★★) and Korem are among Italy's best reds, as is Cerdena among whites and Angialis among stickies.

Arneis Pie w ★★→★★★ DYA Fine peachy/appley white from around ALBA. Two quality denominations: ROERO DOCG and LANGHE DOC. Best: Correggia, BRUNO GIACOSA, Malvirà, Angelo Negro, PRUNOTTO, Sorilaria, VIETTI.

Asti Pie DOCG w sw sp ★→★★★ NV Piedmontese sparkler, known in past as Asti Spumante, from the Muscat grape. Producers are usually more interested in low prices than high quality, making DOCG status questionable. *See also* MOSCATO, BARBERA. The rare top producers inc BERA, Cascina Fonda, CONTRATTO, Dogliotti-Caudrina, Vignaioli di Santo Stefano.

Avignonesi Tus ★★★ Noble MONTEPULCIANO house, best known for long-aged VIN SANTO and *Occhio di Pernice* (★★★★), also VINO NOBILE from high-density, bush-trained v'yds planted to ancient *settone* system. RISERVA Grandi Annate is top red.

Azienda agricola/agraria An estate (large or small) making wine from own grapes.

Badia a Coltibuono Tus ★★→★★★★ CHIANTI CLASSICO; specializing in RISERVAS, though today the top wine is 100% SANGIOVESE BARRIQUE-aged SUPER TUSCAN "Sangioveto".

Banfi (Castello or Villa) Tus ★★→★★★ MONTALCINO CANTINA of major US importer of Italian wine. Huge plantings on lower-lying southern slopes at MONTALCINO, inc in-house-developed clones of SANGIOVESE; also CAB SAUV, MERLOT, SYRAH, PINOT N, CHARD, SAUV BL, PINOT GR. SUPER TUSCAN French-grape blends like Cum Laude and Summus tend to work better than somewhat over-extracted BRUNELLOS.

Barbaresco Pie DOCG r ★★→★★★★ 88 89' 90' 95 96' 97 98 99' 00 01 04 06' 07 08' (09) (10) Classic Piedmontese red, 100% NEBBIOLO, like BAROLO, boasting similar levels of complex aroma and flavour but with less power, more elegance. Minimum 2 yrs' ageing, 1 in wood; at 4 yrs becomes RISERVA.

Barbera Northwest Italy's most-planted red variety, dominant in PIEDMONT, Lombardy and COLLI PIACENTINI, and used for blends throughout Italy, indeed the world. High acidity, low tannin and distinctive cherry fruit are defining characteristics.

Ten top Barbarescos

Here are ten outstanding examples of BARBARESCO, worth hunting down, especially at this moment of depressed prices:

Cantina del Pino (Ovello); Castello di Neive (Riserva Santo Stefano); Castello di Verduno (Rabajà); GAJA (Barbaresco); GIACOSA BRUNO (Asili Riserva); Marchesi di Gresy (Camp Gros); Paitin (Vecchie Vigne); PRODUTTORI DEL BARBARESCO (Ovello); Rocca Albino (Brich Ronchi); BRUNO ROCCA (Rabajà).

> **Ten top Barberas**
> Most of the best are from the Piedmontese DOCS of BARBERA D'ASTI
> and BARBERA D'ALBA; occasional examples of excellence from elsewhere.
> **Barbera d'Alba** B d'Alba: BOGLIETTI (Vigna dei Romani); CLERICO
> (Trevigne); PRUNOTTO (Pian Romualdo); Gianni Voerzio (Ciabot della
> Luna); ROBERTO VOERZIO (Pozzo dell'Annunziata)
> **Barbera d'Asti** B d'Asti: BRAIDA (Bricco dell'Uccellone); COPPO (Pomorosso);
> Perrone (Mongovone); CS Vinchio Vaglio (Vigne Vecchie) LANGHE:
> ALTARE (Larigi).

Capable of diverse characters from BARRIQUED and serious to semi-sweet and frothy. Main varietal incarnations are as B D'ALBA, where it plays second fiddle to NEBBIOLO, and B D'ASTI, where it is principal red grape. *See* BRAIDA. *See also* box above for best.

Barco Reale Tus DOC r ★★ 06 07 08 09 (10) DOC for junior wine of CARMIGNANO. *See* CAPEZZANA.

Bardolino Ven DOC r p ★→★★ DYA Pale, summery, slightly bitter Lake Garda red. Bardolino CHIARETTO (v. pale rosé) arguably more suitable style. Best inc Buglioni, Cavalchina, *Guerrieri Rizzardi*, Le Fraghe, Montresor, Pantini, ZENATO, Zeni.

Barolo Pie DOCG r ★★★→★★★★ 88' 89' 90' 95 96' 97' 98' 99' 00 01' 04' 05 06' 07' (08') (09') (10') Italy's greatest red, 100% NEBBIOLO, from the eponymous village south of ALBA or any of 10 others (or parts thereof). The finest combine power and elegance, crisp tannin and perfume, and must be 3 yrs old before release (5 for RISERVA), of which 2 in wood. From 1995 to 2001 Barolo enjoyed a run of seven fine-to-excellent vintages, a feat repeated between 2004 and 2010. *See* box, p. 114 for top producers, divided between traditionalists (long maceration, large oak barrels) and modernists (shorter maceration, often aged in BARRIQUE).

Barolo Chinato Pie A "medicinal" wine made from BAROLO, alcohol, sugar, herbs, spices and the bark of the Peruvian cinchona tree. Invented by Giuseppe CAPPELLANO, whose heirs are still the best producers.

Barrique This 225-litre barrel, mainly but not necessarily of French oak, has been the major weapon of the internationalists in Italy and the *bête noire* of the traditionalists, who reject its smoky, vanilla tones in favour of the neutrality of the larger BOTTE.

Basciano Tus ★★ Producer of gd DOCG CHIANTI RÙFINA and IGT wines.

Bellavista Lom ★★★ FRANCIACORTA estate with convincing Champagne-style wines (Gran Cuvée Franciacorta is top). Also Satèn (a *crémant*-style sparkling). TERRE DI FRANCIACORTA DOC and Sebino IGT Solesine (both CAB SAUV/MERLOT blends). Vittorio Moretti has expanded into Tuscan MAREMMA, VAL DI CORNIA (Petra), MONTEREGIO.

Bera, Walter Pie ★★→★★★ Small estate making top-quality MOSCATO wines (MOSCATO D'ASTI, ASTI), also fine reds (B D'ASTI, BARBARESCO, LANGHE NEBBIOLO).

Berlucchi, Guido Lom ★★ Italy's biggest producer of sparkling METODO CLASSICO.

Bersano Pie ★→★★ Historic house in Nizza Monferrato; BARBERA D'ASTI Generala, BAROLO Badarina, most PIEDMONT DOC wines inc BARBARESCO, MOSCATO D'ASTI, ASTI.

Bertani Ven ★★→★★★ Well-known quality wines from Verona, esp traditional AMARONE and VALPOLICELLA Valpantena Secco Bertani.

Bianco di Custoza Ven DOC w (sp) ★→★★ DYA Fresh white from Lake Garda, made from an eclectic mix of grapes, inc SOAVE'S GARGANEGA and PIEDMONT'S CORTESE. Gd: Cavalchina, Le Tende, Le Vigne di San Pietro, Montresor, Zeni.

Biondi-Santi Tus ★★★★ Octogenarian Franco Biondi-Santi continues at his Greppo estate to make BRUNELLO DI MONTALCINO in a highly traditional manner, as did his father Tancredi and his grandfather Ferruccio, aiming in best yrs at wines capable of lasting 100 yrs. The 2004 RISERVA (★★★★) might just do it.

Bisol Ven *Top brand of Prosecco*.

Boca Pie *See* GATTINARA.

Boglietti, Enzo Pie ★★★ Dynamic young producer of La Morra in BAROLO zone. Top modern-style BAROLO (Arione, Case Nere), B D'ALBA (Vigna dei Romani, Roscaleto).

Bolgheri Tus DOC r p w (sw) ★★→★★★★ Arty walled village on TUSCANY's Tyrrhenian coast giving its name to an increasingly stylish, and expensive, group of SUPER TUSCANS mainly based on Bordeaux varieties with a bit of SYRAH, and even the odd drop of SANGIOVESE, thrown in. The big names are here: SASSICAIA (original inspirer of the cult), ANTINORI (at Guado al Tasso), FRESCOBALDI (at ORNELLAIA), GAJA (at CÀ MARCANDA), ALLEGRINI (at Poggio al Tesoro), Folonari (at Campo al Mare), plus the odd local in LE MACCHIOLE and MICHELE SATTA.

Bolla Ven ★★ Historic Verona firm for SOAVE, VALPOLICELLA, AMARONE, RECIOTO. Today owned by powerful GRUPPO ITALIANO VINI.

Bonarda Lom DOC r ★★ 06 07 08 09 (10) Soft, fresh FRIZZANTE and still red from OLTREPÒ PAVESE, from Croatina grape; don't confuse with Piedmontese Bonarda.

Borgo del Tiglio F-VG ★★★→★★★★ Nicola Manferrari is among Italy's outstanding white-winemakers, his COLLIO FRIULANO Ronco della Chiesa and Studio di Bianco being especially impressive. Rosso della Centa is one of Italy's top MERLOTS.

Boscarelli, Poderi Tus ★★★ Small estate with v.gd VINO NOBILE DI MONTEPULCIANO Nocio dei Boscarelli and SUPER TUSCAN blend Boscarelli.

Botte Large barrel, anything from 6–250 hl, usually between 20–50, traditionally of Slavonian but increasingly of French oak. To traditionalists, the ideal vessel for ageing wines in which an excess of oak aromas is undesirable.

Brachetto d'Acqui Pie DOCG r sw (sp) ★★ DYA Sweet, sparkling red with enticing Muscat scent. Elevated DOCG status is disputed by some.

Braida Pie ★★★ The late Giacomo Bologna's estate; top B D'ASTI (Bricco dell'Uccellone, Bricco della Bigotta, Ai Suma).

Bramaterra Pie *See* GATTINARA.

Breganze Ven DOC r w sp★→★★★ (r) 01 02 03 04 06 07 08 (09) (10) Major production area for PINOT GR, also gd Vespaiolo (still and sparkling while, sticky TORCOLATO) and PINOT N and CAB. Top producers MACULAN and Beato Bartolomeo.

Brindisi Ap DOC r p ★★ 04 05 06 07 08 (09) (10) (r) DYA (p) Smooth NEGROAMARO-based red with MONTEPULCIANO, esp from VALLONE, Due Palme, Rubino. ROSATO can be among Italy's best.

Brolio, Castello di Tus ★★→★★★ Historic estate, CHIANTI CLASSICO's largest, now thriving again under RICASOLI family after foreign-managed decline. *V.gd* CHIANTI CLASSICO and IGT Casalferro.

Brunelli, Gianni Tus ★★★ Small-scale producer of elegant, refined BRUNELLO DI MONTALCINO. Not to be confused with others in MONTALCINO called Brunelli. Now run by Gianni's widow, Laura.

Ten Top Barolos (in alphabetical order)

Here are ten outstanding examples of Italy's greatest wine, all from v'yds in the central communes of BAROLO, Castiglione Falletto, Monforte d'ALBA and Serralunga:

Cavallotto (Bricco Boschis Vigna San Giuseppe); ALDO CONTERNO (Granbussia); GIACOMO CONTERNO (Monfortino); Bartolo MASCARELLO (BAROLO); Giuseppe MASCARELLO (Monprivato); Massolino (Vigna Rionda); Giuseppe Rinaldi (Brunate-Le Coste); SANDRONE (Cannubi Boschis); PAOLO SCAVINO (Bric dël Fiasc); VIETTI (Lazzarito).

Brunello di Montalcino Tus DOCG r ★★★→★★★★ 85' 87 88 90' 93 95 97 99' 00 01 03 04' 06' (07) (08'), (09') (10) With BAROLO, Italy's most celebrated red: high-flavoured, tannic, long-lived. Minimum 4 yrs' ageing, after 5 yrs RISERVA. Purists fight to maintain the 100% varietal (Brunello) law, against suicidal moves to allow a small percentage of other grapes (read CAB, MERLOT, SYRAH). They shall not pass!

Brunellopoli Tus BRUNELLO DI MONTALCINO is supposed to be 100% SANGIOVESE, but in 2008 a few high-profile producers were accused of inc other grapes in the blend. The drama has gone quiet now, but falling prices suggest MONTALCINO's not out of the woods.

Burlotto, Commendatore G B Pie ★★★ Fabio Alessandria turns out beautifully crafted and defined PIEDMONT varietals, esp BAROLO Cannubi and Monvigliero, the latter's grapes being crushed by foot.

Bussola, Tommaso Ven ★★★★ Leading producer of AMARONE, RECIOTO and RIPASSO in VALPOLICELLA. Stunning AMARONE Vigneto Alto and RECIOTO TB.

Ca' dei Frati Lom ★★★ The best producer of DOC LUGANA, also v.gd dry white blend IGT Pratto, sweet Tre Filer and red IGT Ronchedone.

Ca' del Bosco Lom ★★★★ No 1 FRANCIACORTA estate owned by giant PINOT GR producer SANTA MARGHERITA, but still run by founder Maurizio Zanella. **Outstanding Classico-method fizz**, esp Annamaria Clementi (Italy's Dom Pérignon) and Dosage Zero; also excellent Bordeaux-style red Maurizio Zanella, Burgundy-style PINOT N Pinero and CHARD.

Ca' Marcanda Tus BOLGHERI estate created by GAJA since 1996. Focus on international varieties: CAB SAUV, MERLOT, CAB FR, SYRAH.

Ca' Viola Pie Play-on-words name of home estate of influential PIEDMONT-based consultant Beppe Caviola. Classy DOLCETTO and BARBERA-based wines.

Ca' Vit T-AA (Cantina Viticoltori) Group of co-ops nr Trento. Massive production, best being sparkling Graal.

Caberlot Mellow, flavoury red from crossing of CAB FR and MERLOT claimed to be unique to the v'yds of Bettina Rogosky at her Il Carnasciale estate in the Arezzo hills of TUSCANY. Sold only in magnum.

Cabernet Franc Increasingly preferred to CAB SAUV by Italy's internationalists. Much of what was thought in northeast Italy to be CAB FR was actually Carmenère.

Cabernet Sauvignon Has played a key role in the renaissance of Italian red wine (eg. SASSICAIA). Particularly influential in TUSCANY as a lesser partner for SANGIOVESE. Now losing ground to indigenous blenders as well as CAB FR.

Cafaggio, Villa Tus ★★★ V. reliable CHIANTI CLASSICO estate with excellent IGTS San Martino (SANGIOVESE) and Cortaccio (CAB SAUV).

Caiarossa Tus ★★★ Riparbella in the northern MAREMMA is starting to attract serious winemakers for its combination of altitude and proximity to the sea. This international project (Dutch owner Jelgersma from Bordeaux, French winemaker Dominique Génot with Australian background) is turning out some v. classy reds (Pergolaia, Caiarossa) plus v. tasty Caiarossa Bianco.

Calatrasi Si ★→★★★ Prolific producer of gd IGT D'Istinto and Terre di Ginestra ranges.

Campania The playground of the Romans is today a region of lively interest. Excellent native grapes (Falanghina, FIANO, GRECO, Coda di Volpe [w]; AGLIANICO, Piedirosso [r]), volcanic soils and cool v'yds on high slopes add up to gd potential being progressively realized. Most interesting wines tend to be varietal, but classic DOCGS inc FIANO D'AVELLINO, GRECO DI TUFO and TAURASI, with newer areas emerging such as Sannio (DOC) and Beneventano (IGT). Gd producers inc Caggiano, Cantina del Taburno, Caputo, Colli di Lapio, D'Ambra, De Angelis, Benito Ferrara, FEUDI DI SAN GREGORIO, GALARDI, LA GUARDIENSE, MASTROBERARDINO, Molettieri, MONTEVETRANO, Mustilli, Terredora di Paolo, Trabucco and VILLA MATILDE.

The best of Brunello -- top ten and the rest
Any of the below should provide a satisfying BRUNELLO DI MONTALCINO
experience, but I have put a star next to the ten I think best:
Pieri Agostina, Altesino, ARGIANO, ARGIANO (CASTELLO DI), Baricci, BIONDI-
SANTI ★, Gianni BRUNELLI ★, Camigliano, La Campana, Campogiovanni,
Canalicchio di Sopra, Canalicchio di Sotto, Caparzo, CASANOVA DI NERI,
CASE BASSE ★, CASTELGIOCONDO, Cerbaiona ★, Ciacci Piccolomini, COL
D'ORCIA, Il Colle, Collemattoni, Corte Pavone, Costanti, Eredi FULIGNI,
La Fuga, La Gerla, Lambardi, LISINI ★, La Magia, La Mannella,
Marroneto, Mastrojanni ★, Oliveto, SIRO PACENTI, Palazzo, Il Paradiso
di Manfredi, Pertimali, Pian dell'Orino★, PIEVE DI SANTA RESTITUTA, La
Poderina, Le Potazzine, IL POGGIONE ★, POGGIO ANTICO, Poggio di Sotto ★,
Salvioni-Cerbaiola ★, Uccelliera, Val di Suga, Valdicava.

Cannonau di Sardegna Sar DOC r dr (p) Cannonau, alias Grenache, is the staple red
grape of Sardinia, making strong soft reds, esp in southeast, but also varietally
or blended elsewhere, as reflected by Cannonau di Sardegna DOC. Best: ARGIOLAS,
CONTINI, Giuseppe Gabbas, Jerzu, Loi, Sedilesu.

Cantalupo, Antichi Vigneti di Pie ★★→★★★ Top GHEMME wines, esp single-v'yd
Breclemae and Carellae.

Cantina A cellar, winery or even a wine bar.

Capezzana, Tenuta di ★★★ Tuscan estate of the prolific Contini Bonacossi family.
Gd BARCO REALE, excellent CARMIGNANO (esp Villa di Capezzana, Trefiano). V.gd
Bordeaux-style red, Ghiaie Della Furba and an old-style TREBBIANO white.

Capichera Sar ★★★ V gd if high-priced producer of VERMENTINO DI GALLURA, esp
VENDEMMIA *tardiva*. Excellent red Mantèghja from Carignano grapes.

Cappellano Pie ★★★ The late Teobaldo Cappellano was one of the "characters"
of BAROLO, devoting part of his v'yd in *cru* Gabutti to ungrafted NEBBIOLO vines
(Pie Franco). Excellent BAROLOS of a highly traditional style; also BAROLO CHINATO,
invented by an ancestor.

Caprai Umb ★★★→★★★★ Large, very high-quality, market-leading, experimentalist
producer in Umbria's MONTEFALCO. Superb DOCG *Montefalco Sagrantino*, esp 25
Anni, v.gd DOC ROSSO DI MONTEFALCO.

Capri Cam DOC r p w ★→★★ Legendary island with widely abused name. Only
interesting wines are from La Caprense.

Carema Pie DOC r ★★→★★★ 99 00 01 03 04' 06' 07 (08) (09) (10) Elegant NEBBIOLO
red from lower Alpine slopes on Aosta border. Best: Luigi Ferrando.

Carignano del Sulcis Sar DOC r p ★★→★★★ 04 06 08 (09) (10) Mellow but intense
red from SARDINIA's southwest. Best: Terre Brune, Rocca Rubia from CS DI SANTADI.

Carmignano Tus DOCG r ★★★ 90' 95 97' 99 00 01 02 04 06 07 08 (09) (10)
Region west of Florence. SANGIOVESE plus CAB FR, CAB SAUV make distinctive red.
Best: Ambra, CAPEZZANA, Farnete, PIAGGIA, Le Poggiarelle, Pratesi.

Carpenè-Malvolti Ven Leading brand of PROSECCO and other sparklers at Conegliano.

Carricante Principal grape of ETNA *bianco*, now making important return.

Cartizze Ven Famous, frequently too expensive and too sweet, DOC PROSECCO of
supposedly best subzone of Valdobbiadene.

Casanova di Neri Tus ★★★ Modern BRUNELLO DI MONTALCINO, highly prized Cerretalto
and Tenuta Nuova, plus Petradonice CAB SAUV and v.gd ROSSO DI MONTALCINO.

Case Basse Tus ★★★★ Eco-geek Gianfranco Soldera claims to make the definitive
BRUNELLO; many lovers of the traditional style agree. V. expensive and rare.

Castel del Monte Ap DOC r p w ★→★★ (p w) DYA 04 06 07 08 09 (10) (r) Dry,
fresh, well-balanced wines of mid-APULIAN DOC. Gd Pietrabianca and excellent

Bocca di Lupo from Vigneti del Sud (ANTINORI). V.gd Le More from Santa Lucia. Interesting new reds from Cocevola, Giancarlo Ceci. *See also* RIVERA.

Castelgiocondo Tus ★★★ FRESCOBALDI estate, second-largest in MONTALCINO. Gd IGT MERLOT Lamaïone.

Castell' in Villa Tus ★★★ V.gd CHIANTI CLASSICO estate in Castelnuovo Berardenga.

Castellare Tus ★★→★★★ CHIANTI CLASSICO producer. First-rate SANGIOVESE-based IGT I Sodi di San Niccoló and updated CHIANTI, esp RISERVA Vigna Poggiale. Also Poggio ai Merli (MERLOT) and Coniale (CAB SAUV).

Castello Castle. (*See* under name – eg. SALA, CASTELLO DELLA.)

Castelluccio E-R ★★→★★★ Quality SANGIOVESE varietals from Romagna: IGT Ronco dei Ciliegi, Ronco delle Ginestre. Excellent SANGIOVESE/CAB SAUV blend Massicone.

Catarratto Si Prolific white grape found all over SICILY, esp in west in DOC Alcamo.

Caudrina-Dogliotti Romano Pie ★★★ Top MOSCATO D'ASTI: La Galeisa and Caudrina.

Cavicchioli E-R ★→★★★ Large producer of LAMBRUSCO and other sparkling wines: Lambrusco di Sorbara Vigna del Cristo is best. Also TERRE DI FRANCIACORTA.

Cecchi Tus ★→★★ Large-scale bottler and producer of CHIANTI CLASSICO, RISERVA, IGT.

Cerasuolo Ab DOC p ★ ROSATO version of MONTEPULCIANO D'ABRUZZO. Worth trying.

Cerasuolo di Vittoria Si DOCG r ★★ 04 05 06 07 08 (09) (10) Southeast Sicily, medium-bodied red from Frappato and NERO D'AVOLA: PLANETA, Valle dell'Acate, Cos.

Ceretto Pie ★★→★★★ Leading producer of BARBARESCO (Bricco Asili), BAROLO (Bricco Rocche, Brunate, Prapò), LANGHE ROSSO Monsordo and ARNEIS.

Cerro, Fattoria del Tus ★★★ Estate owned by insurance giant SAI, making v.gd DOCG VINO NOBILE DI MONTEPULCIANO (esp *cru* Antica Chiusina). Also owns La Poderina (BRUNELLO DI MONTALCINO), Colpetrone (MONTEFALCO SAGRANTINO) and the 1,000-ha northern MAREMMA estate of Monterufoli.

Chardonnay Has thrived in northern Italy since the 19th century, esp in northeast (TRENTINO-ALTO ADIGE, FRIULI-VENEZIA GIULIA). More recently seen in high-quality wines from TUSCANY (ISOLE E OLENA Collezione de Marchi), Umbria (CASTELLO DELLA SALA's Cervaro) and as far south as SICILY (PLANETA).

Chianti Tus DOCG r ★→★★★ For centuries the local wine of Florence and Siena, fresh, fruity, uncomplicated. Seven 20th-century-created subzones aim higher: RÚFINA (★★→★★★), Colli Fiorentini (★→★★★), Montespertoli can make CLASSICO-style RISERVAS. Montalbano, Colli Senesi, Aretini, Pisani are generally less serious.

Chianti Classico Tus DOCG r ★★→★★★★ 97' 99 01 04' 06' 07' 08 (09') (10) The historic CHIANTI zone was allowed to add CLASSICO to its name when the CHIANTI area was extended to most of central Tuscany in the early 20th century. Covering all or part of nine communes, the land is hilly and rocky, with altitudes between 250–500 m. Chianti Classico must consist of 80–100% SANGIOVESE, with an optional 20% of "other grapes" (usually CAB SAUV or MERLOT), which makes the same sense as adding SANGIOVESE to claret.

Chiaretto Ven Rosé (the word means "claret") produced esp around Lake Garda. *See* BARDOLINO.

Chiarlo, Michele Pie ★★→★★★ Gd PIEDMONT producer (BAROLOS Cerequio and Cannubi, B D'ASTI, LANGHE and MONFERRATO ROSSO). Also BARBARESCO.

Ciabot Berton Pie ★★★ Small La Morra grower; classy BAROLOS at modest prices.

Ciliegiolo Tus Grape, native to Tuscan MAREMMA, from which SANGIOVESE is probably derived. Traditionally a blender, now increasingly used varietally to great effect by Rascioni e Cecconello and Sassotondo.

Cinque Terre Lig DOC w dr sw ★★ Dry white from obscure grapes grown in steep, rocky tourist paradise on Riviera coast. Sweet version is called SCIACCHETRÀ.

Cirò Cal DOC r (p w) ★→★★★ Strong red from CALABRIA's main grape, Gaglioppo; light white from GRECO (DYA). Best: Caparra, Ippolito, *Librandi* (Duca San Felice ★★★), San Francesco (Donna Madda, Ronco dei Quattroventi), Santa Venere.

Classico Term for wines from a restricted area within the limits of a DOC. By implication (and often practice), the best of the district. *See also* METODO CLASSICO.

Clerico, Domenico Pie ★★★ Established modernist BAROLO producer, esp *crus* Percristina and Ciabot Mentin Ginestra. Also NEBBIOLO/BARBERA blend Arte.

Coffele Ven ★★★ Grower with some of the finest v'yds in SOAVE CLASSICO, making steely, minerally wines of classic concept. Try *cru* Cà Visco.

Col d'Orcia Tus ★★★ 3rd-largest, top-quality MONTALCINO estate owned by Francesco Marone Cinzano. Best wine: BRUNELLO RISERVA Poggio al Vento.

Colli Bolognesi E-R DOC r w ★★ DOC name for rarely seen varietal wines, excluding those from the otherwise ubiquitous SANGIOVESE and TREBBIANO. Terre Rosse, the pioneer, now joined by Bonzara (★★→★★★) and others. *Colli* = hills.

Colli del Trasimeno Umb DOC r w ★→★★★ (r) 04 05 06′ 07′ 08 (09) (10) Lively white wines from nr Perugia, but gd reds as well. Best: Duca della Corgna, La Fiorita, Pieve del Vescovo, Poggio Bertaio.

Colli Euganei Ven DOC r w dr s/sw (sp) ★→★★★ DYA DOC southwest of Padua. Red, white and sparkling are pleasant, rarely better. Best producers: Ca' Lustra, La Montecchia, Speaia, VIGNALTA.

Colli Orientali del Friuli F-VG DOC r w dr sw ★★→★★★★ Hills east of Udine. Zone similar to COLLIO but less experimental. Top producers include Meroi Davino, Miani, Moschioni, LIVIO FELLUGA, Rosa Bosco, Ronco del Gnemiz. Sweet wines from VERDUZZO or PICOLIT grapes can be amazing (Cos, Dri).

Colli Piacentini E-R DOC r p w ★→★★ DYA DOC inc traditional GUTTURNIO and Monterosso Val d'Arda among 11 varieties, French and local, grown south of Piacenza. Gd fizzy MALVASIA. Most wines FRIZZANTE. Gd producers: Montesissa, Mossi, Romagnoli, Solenghi, La Stoppa, Torre Fornello, La Tosa.

Colline Novaresi Pie *See* GATTINARA.

Collio F-VG DOC r w ★★→★★★★ Important quality zone on border with Slovenia. Esp known for complex, sometimes deliberately oxidized whites, which may be vinified on skins in earthenware vessels/amphoras in ground. Some excellent, some shocking blends from various French, German and Slavic grapes. Numerous gd-to-excellent producers inc BORGO DEL TIGLIO, La Castellada, Castello di Spessa, MARCO FELLUGA, Fiegl, GRAVNER, Renato Keber, LIVON, Aldo Polencic, Primosic, Princic, Russiz Superiore, *Schiopetto*, Tercic, Terpin, Venica & Venica, VILLA RUSSIZ, Zuani.

Colterenzio CS (or Schreckbichl) T-AA ★★→★★★ Pioneering quality leader among ALTO ADIGE co-ops. Look for: Cornell line of selections; Lafoa CAB SAUV and SAUV BL; Cornelius red and white blends.

Conterno-Fantino Pie ★★★ Two families joined to produce excellent modern-style BAROLO Sori Ginestra and Vigna del Gris at Monforte d'ALBA. Also NEBBIOLO/BARBERA blend Monprà.

Conterno, Aldo Pie ★★★★ Legendary grower of BAROLO at Monforte d'ALBA. V.gd CHARD Bussiadoro, BARBERA D'ALBA Conca Tre Pile. Best BAROLOS are made traditionally: Gran Bussia, Cicala, Colonello. LANGHE Favot is a modern BARRIQUE-aged version of NEBBIOLO.

Conterno, Giacomo Pie ★★★★ Iconic grower of super-traditional BAROLO at Monforte d'ALBA, Giacomo's grandson Roberto now carrying on father Giovanni's work. Two BAROLOS: Cascina Francia and Monfortino, long-macerated to age for yrs.

Contini, Attilio Sar ★→★★★ Famous Sardinian producer of Sherry-like, *flor*-affected VERNACCIA DI ORISTANO. Best is vintage blend Antico Gregori.

Contratto Pie ★★ At Canelli (owned by GRAPPA-producing family Bocchino); makes v.gd B D'ASTI, BAROLO, SPUMANTE, ASTI (De Miranda), MOSCATO D'ASTI.

Contucci Tus ★★→★★★ Millennial producer of traditional-style VINO NOBILE, a sight of whose cellar at MONTEPULCIANO *vaut le detour*.

Who makes really good Chianti Classico?
CHIANTI CLASSICO is a seriously large zone with hundreds of producers, so picking out the best is tricky. Top ten get a ★.
AMA ★, ANTINORI, BADIA A COLTIBUONO ★, Bibbiano, Le Boncie, Il Borghetto, Bossi, BROLIO, Cacchiano, CAFAGGIO, Capannelle, Capraia, Carobbio, Casaloste, Casa Sola, CASTELLARE, CASTELL'IN VILLA, Le Cinciole, Collelungo, Le Corti, Mannucci Droandi, FELSINA ★, Le Filigare, FONTERUTOLI, FONTODI★, ISOLE E OLENA ★, Lilliano, Il Molino di Grace, MONSANTO ★, Monte Bernardi, Monteraponi ★, NITTARDI, NOZZOLE, Palazzino, Paneretta, Petroio-Lenzi, Poggerino, Poggiolino, Poggiopiano, Poggio al Sole, QUERCIABELLA ★, RAMPOLLA, Riecine, Rocca di Castagnoli, Rocca di Montegrossi ★, RUFFINO, San Fabiano Calcinaia, SAN FELICE, SAN GIUSTO A RENTENNANO ★, Savignola Paolina, Selvole, Vecchie Terre di Montefili, Verrazzano, Vicchiomaggio, VIGNAMAGGIO, Villa La Rosa ★, Viticcio, VOLPAIA ★.

Copertino Ap DOC r (p) ★★★ 06 07 08 (09) (10) Smooth, savoury red of NEGROAMARO from the heel of Italy. Azienda MONACI and CS Copertino are gd producers.

Coppo Pie ★★→★★★ Top producers of B D'ASTI (Pomoroso, Riserva della Famiglia). Also excellent CHARD Monteriolo and sparkling RISERVA del Fondatore.

Cordero di Montezemolo-Monfalletto Pie ★★→★★★ Historic maker of gd BAROLO, also making fine B D'ALBA and CHARD.

Cortese di Gavi Pie *See* GAVI. (Cortese is the grape.)

Cortona Tuscan DOC contiguous to MONTEPULCIANO'S VINO NOBILE. Various red and white grapes, best results so far from AVIGNONESI's Desiderio, a Bordeaux blend, and first-rate SYRAH from Luigi d'Alessandro, Il Castagno, *La Braccesca*.

Corzano & Paterno, Fattoria di Tus ★★★ Dynamic CHIANTI Colli Fiorentini estate. V.gd RISERVA, red IGT Corzano, and outstanding VIN SANTO.

CS, Cantina Sociale Cooperative winery.

Curtefranca Lom *See* TERRE DI FRANCIACORTA.

D'Angelo Bas ★★★ Donato d'Angelo is the new name of the producer hitherto known officially as "Casa Vinicola d'Angelo". A wine bought under the old name risks not being made by the long-established wizard of AGLIANICO DEL VULTURE. A complex family matter (dispute), but buyers need only remember to seek the whole name, "Donato d'Angelo", as producer.

Dal Forno, Romano Ven ★★★★ V. high-quality VALPOLICELLA, AMARONE and RECIOTO grower whose perfectionism is the more remarkable for the fact that his v'yds are outside the CLASSICO zone.

Di Majo Norante Mol ★★→★★★ Lone star of Molise, south of Abruzzo, with v.gd Biferno *rosso*, Ramitello, Don Luigi Molise Rosso Riserva and Molise AGLIANICO Contado, white blend Falanghina-GRECO Biblos and MOSCATO PASSITO Apianae.

DOC/DOCG Quality wine designation: *see* box, p. 139.

Dolcetto Pie ★→★★★ Many of PIEDMONT's dry red gluggers are made with this user-friendly grape whose varietal name figures in numerous denominations. Capable, occasionally, of explosive depth. Best versions labelled as Dolcetto di DOGLIANI, Dolcetto di Diano d'ALBA or Dolcetto d'ALBA.

Donnafugata Si r w ★★→★★★ Well-crafted Sicilian wines of Contessa Entellina DOC: top reds are Mille e Una Notte and Tancredi; top whites Chiaranda and Vigna di Gabri. Also v. fine MOSCATO PASSITO DI PANTELLERIA Ben Rye.

Duca di Salaparuta Si ★★ Vini Corvo. Once on the list of every *trattoria*, Corvo has slipped in an age when diners seek something less middle-road. Duca Enrico (r) and Valguarnero (w) are fairly successful attempts to address this situation.

Elba Tus r w (sp) ★→★★★ DYA The island's white, based on Ansonica and TREBBIANO, can be v. drinkable with fish. Dry reds are based on SANGIOVESE. Gd sweet white (MOSCATO) and red (*Aleatico*). Top producers: Acquabona and Sapereta.

Enoteca Wine library; also wine shop or restaurant with extensive wine list. There is a national *enoteca* at the *fortezza* in Siena.

Est! Est!! Est!!! Lat DOC w dr s/sw ★ DYA Simple white from Montefiascone, north of Rome. Trades on the improbable origin of its name. Best is FALESCO.

Etna Si DOC r p w ★★→★★★ (r) 01 04 05 06 07 08 (09) (10) Wine from volcanic slopes and often considerable altitude. Once widely planted, Etna v'yds went into steep decline during the 20th century, but new investment has brought a flurry of planting and some excellent wines, not dissimilar to fine burgundy; based on NERELLO MASCALESE (r) and CARRICANTE (w). Gd producers: Barone di Villagrande, Benanti, Il Cantante, Cottanera, Terre Nere, *Passopisciaro*, Nicosia, Russo.

Falchini Tus ★★→★★★ Producer of gd DOCG VERNACCIA DI SAN GIMIGNANO (Vigna a Solatio and oaked Ab Vinea Doni); top Bordeaux blend Campora and SANGIOVESE-based Paretaio. Riccardo Falchini, one of the founders of SAN GIMIGNANO quality wine, died in 2010; succeeded by his half-American children, led by Michael.

Falerno del Massico Cam ★★→★★★ DOC r w ★★ (r) 01 03 04 06 07 08 Falernum was the best-known wine of ancient times, probably sweet white. Today elegant red from AGLIANICO, fruity dry white from Falanghina. Best: VILLA MATILDE, Amore Perrotta, Felicia, Moio, Trabucco.

Falesco Lat ★★→★★★ Estate of Cotarella brothers, v.gd MERLOT Montiano and CAB SAUV Marciliano (both ★★★). Gd red IGT Vitiano and DOC EST! EST!! EST!!!

Fara Pie *See* GATTINARA.

Farnese Ab ★★ Gd-quality supplier of the Abruzzi's favourites, esp MONTEPULCIANO D'ABRUZZO, Colline Teramane, RISERVA Opis, white Pecorino, red Edizione.

Faro Si DOC r ★★★ 00 01' 04' 06' 07' 08 (09) (10) Intense, elegant red from NERELLO MASCALESE and Nerello Cappuccio grown in the hills behind Messina. Palari, the major producer, administered the kiss of life when extinction seemed likely.

Fazi-Battaglia Mar ★★ Well-known producer of VERDICCHIO, best known for amphora-bottle Titulus (2.8 million bottles). Also Massaccio, Le Moie, San Sisto. Owns Fassati (VINO NOBILE DI MONTEPULCIANO).

Felluga, Livio F-VG ★★★ Consistently fine COLLI ORIENTALI DEL FRIULI wines, esp PINOT BL Illivio, *Pinot Gr*, SAUV BL, TOCAI, PICOLIT and MERLOT/REFOSCO blend Sosso.

Felluga, Marco F-VG ★★→★★★ The prolific brother of Livio owns a négociant house bearing his name, plus Russiz Superiore in COLLIO DOC, Castello di Buttrio in COLLI ORIENTALI DOC.

Felsina Tus ★★★ Ex-teacher Giuseppe Mazzocolin has run this now-established CHIANTI CLASSICO estate for 30 years, producing classics such as DOCG RISERVA Rancia and IGT Fontalloro, both 100% SANGIOVESE as well as consistent CHIANTI CLASSICO and a superior CAB SAUV Maestro Raro. Felsina also controls Castello di Farnetella in Colli Senesi.

Ferrari T-AA ★★→★★★ TRENTO-based maker of best METODO CLASSICO wines outside of FRANCIACORTA. Giuli Ferrari is top *cru*.

Feudi di San Gregorio Cam ★★→★★★ Much-hyped producer, with DOCG TAURASI, DOCG FIANO, *Falanghina*, GRECO DI TUFO. Red IGT Serpico and Patrimo (MERLOT), white IGT Campanaro. Also has estates in Basilicata and APULIA.

Fiano di Avellino Cam DOCG w ★★→★★★ DYA Fiano is rapidly becoming the emblematic quality white grape of southern Italy, planted successfully in Molise, APULIA, Calabria and SICILY as well as in CAMPANIA, its birthplace. Can yield intense aromas of hazelnuts, honey. Best: Caggiano, Caputo, FEUDI DI SAN GREGORIO, Grotta del Sole, LA GUARDIENSE, MASTROBERARDINO, San Paolo, Vesevo, Villa Raiano.

Fiorita, la Umb Lamborghini family property nr Lake Trasimeno, with touchstone SANGIOVESE/MERLOT blend Campoleone.

Florio Si Historic quality producer of MARSALA. Best wine: MARSALA Vergine Secco Baglio Florio. Best name: Terre Arse (burnt lands)

Folonari Ven Ambrogio Folonari and son Giovanni split off from brothers and cousins at RUFFINO to create their own house. They continue to make Cabreo (a CHARD and a SANGIOVESE/CAB SAUV Pareto), wines of NOZZOLE (inc top CAB SAUV Pareto), BRUNELLO DI MONTALCINO La Fuga, VINO NOBILE DI MONTEPULCIANO Gracciano Svetoni, plus wines from BOLGHERI, MONTECUCCO and COLLI ORIENTALI DEL FRIULI.

Fontana Candida Lat ★★ One of the biggest producers of FRASCATI. Single-v'yd Santa Teresa stands out. *See also* GRUPPO ITALIANO VINI.

Fontanafredda Pie ★★→★★★ Large-scale producer of PIEDMONT wines on former royal estates, inc BAROLO Serralunga (150,000 bottles) and BAROLO *crus* La Delizia and La Villa, also ALBA docs and sparklers dry and sweet.

Fonterutoli Tus ★★★ Historic CHIANTI CLASSICO estate of the Mazzei family at Castellina with space-age new CANTINA. Notable are *Castello di Fonterutoli* (dark, oaky CHIANTI), IGT Siepi (SANGIOVESE/MERLOT). The Mazzei family also owns Tenuta di Belguardo in MAREMMA, gd MORELLINO DI SCANSANO and IGT wines.

Fontodi Tus ★★★→★★★★ Giovanni Manetti runs this outstanding family estate at Panzano, making one of the absolute best straight CHIANTI CLASSICOS, RISERVA Vigna del Sorbo as well as a classic pure SANGIOVESE, IGT Flaccianello. IGTS PINOT N and SYRAH "Case Via" are among the best of those varietals in TUSCANY.

Foradori ★★★ Elizabetta Foradori makes *v. gd Teroldego Rotaliano DOC* and excellent Teroldego IGT Granato, white IGT Myrto. Interesting wines from Ampeleia estate in MAREMMA, esp IGT Kepos from various southern Rhône varieties not inc SYRAH.

Fossi, Enrico Tus ★★★ Enterprising Tuscan producer specializing in international varietals: MERLOT, CAB SAUV, SYRAH, PINOT N, Gamay, Malbec, SAUV BL, CHARD, RIES, PINOT BL and SANGIOVESE.

Franciacorta Lom DOCG w sp (p) ★★→★★★★ Italy's major production zone for top-quality Champagne-style wines. Best: Barone Pizzini, BELLAVISTA, CA' DEL BOSCO, Castellino, Cavalleri, Gatti, Uberti, Villa. Also v.gd: Contadi Gastaldi, Monte Rossa, Il Mosnel, Ricci Curbastri. For still (w and r), *see* TERRE DI FRANCIACORTA.

Frascati Lat DOC w dr sw s/sw (sp) ★→★★ DYA Best-known wine of Roman hills: should be limpid, golden, tasting of whole grapes. Most is disappointingly neutral today: look for Castel de Paolis, Conte Zandotti, Villa Simone, or Santa Teresa from FONTANA CANDIDA. The sweet version is known as Cannellino.

Freisa Pie DOC r dr sw s/sw fz (sp) ★→★★★ Two distinct styles: frivolous, maybe FRIZZANTE, maybe sweetish; or serious, dry and tannic for ageing (so follow BAROLO vintages). Best of serious producers: Brezza, Cigliuti, CLERICO, ALDO CONTERNO, COPPO, Franco Martinetti, GIUSEPPE MASCARELLO, Parusso, Pecchenino, Pelissero, Sebaste, Trinchero, VAJRA, VOERZIO.

Frescobaldi Tus ★★→★★★★ Ancient noble family, leading CHIANTI RÚFINA pioneer at NIPOZZANO estate (look for *Montesodi* ★★★), also BRUNELLO from CASTELGIOCONDO estate in MONTALCINO. Sole owners of LUCE estate in MONTALCINO and ORNELLAIA in BOLGHERI. V'yds also in MAREMMA, Montespertoli and COLLIO.

Friulano F-VG ★→★★ Grape aka Sauvignonasse or Sauvignon Vert. This is now the name for ex-TOCAI FRIULANO, which may no longer appear on labels due to pressure from Hungary. Makes fresh, pungent, subtly floral white in COLLIO, ISONZO and COLLI ORIENTALI. Gd producers inc BORGO DEL TIGLIO, LIVIO FELLUGA, LIS NERIS, Pierpaolo Pecorari, Ronco del Gelso, Ronco del Gnemiz, Russiz Superiore, SCHIOPETTO, LE VIGNE DI ZAMÒ, VILLA RUSSIZ. The new name for ex-TOCAI from Veneto, by the way, is "Tai".

Friuli-Venezia Giulia F-VG The northeast region on the Slovenian border. Several

DOCS, inc ISONZO, COLLIO and COLLI ORIENTALI. Gd reds, but considered the home of Italy's most adventurous whites.

Frizzante Semi-sparkling, eg. MOSCATO D'ASTI and most PROSECCO.

Fuligni Tus ★★★ V.gd producer of BRUNELLO and ROSSO DI MONTALCINO.

Gaja Pie ★★★★ Old family firm at BARBARESCO under direction of Angelo Gaja. High quality, even higher price. BARBARESCO is the only Piedmontese DOCG Gaja makes after down-classing his *crus* Sorì Tildìn, Sorì San Lorenzo and Costa Russi as well as BAROLO Sperss to LANGHE DOC so that he could blend small proportions of BARBERA in with NEBBIOLO. CHARD (Gaia e Rey), CAB SAUV Darmagi. Acquisitions elsewhere in Italy: Marengo-Marenda estate (BAROLO), commercial Gromis label; Pieve di Santa Restituta in MONTALCINO; CA' MARCANDA in BOLGHERI.

Galardi Cam ★★★→★★★★ Producer of Terra di Lavoro, a highly touted blend of AGLIANICO and Piedirosso, in north CAMPANIA nr FALERNO DEL MASSICO DOC.

Gancia Pie Once-famous ASTI house, also dry sparkling, now lives mainly on past glory.

Garda Ven DOC r p w ★→★★ DYA (w p) **06** 07 08 (09) (10) (r) Catch-all DOC for generally early-drinking wines of various colours from provinces of Verona in Veneto, Brescia and Mantua in Lombardy. Gd producers are Cavalchina, Zeni.

Garganega Ven Principal white grape of SOAVE and Gambellara.

Garofoli Mar ★★→★★★ Quality leader in the Marches, specializing in VERDICCHIO (Podium, Macrina, Serra Fiorese) and ROSSO CONERO (Piancarda, Grosso Agontano).

Gattinara Pie DOCG r ★★→★★★ 95 96' 97' 98 99' 00 01' 04' 06 07' (08) (09) (10) Best-known of a cluster of northern Piedmontese DOC/GS based on NEBBIOLO; best producers inc: Travaglini, Antoniolo, Bianchi, Nervi, Torraccia del Piantavigna. Similar DOC(G)s of the zone: GHEMME, BOCA, BRAMATERRA, COLLINE NOVARESI, Costa della Sesia, FARA, LESSONA, SIZZANO; none of which, sadly, measure up to BAROLO/BARBARESCO at their best.

Gavi Pie DOCG w ★→★★★ DYA At (rare) best, subtle dry white from CORTESE. Best: Castellari Bergaglio, Franco Martinetti, Toledana, Villa Sparina, Broglia, Cascina degli Ulivi, Castello di Tassarolo, CHIARLO, La Giustiniana, Podere Saulino.

Ghemme Pie DOCG *See* GATTINARA

Giacosa, Bruno Pie ★★→★★★★ Considered Italy's greatest winemaker by some, this brooding genius suffered a stroke in 2006, but goes on working, crafting outstanding traditional-style BARBARESCOS (Asili, Santo Stefano) and BAROLOS (Falletto, Rocche di Falletto). Top wines were not sold from 2006 vintage despite its quality (which he alone disputes). Also makes a range of fine reds (DOLCETTO, NEBBIOLO, BARBERA), whites (ARNEIS) and an amazing METODO CLASSICO Brut.

Grappa Pungent, potent spirit made from grape pomace (skins, etc., after pressing), can be anything from disgusting to inspirational. What the French call "*marc*".

Grasso, Elio Pie ★★★→★★★★ Top BAROLO producer (*crus* Vigna Chiniera, Casa Mate); v.gd BARBERA D'ALBA Vigna Martina, DOLCETTO D'ALBA and CHARD Educato.

Grave del Friuli F-VG DOC r w ★→★★ (r) **06** 07 08 09 (10) Largest DOC of FRIULI-VENEZIA GIULIA, mostly on plains, giving important volumes of underwhelming wines. Exceptions inc Borgo Magredo, Di Lenardo, Plozner, Ronco Cliona, Villa Chiopris, San Simone.

Gravner, Josko F-VG ★★★ Controversial COLLIO producer, believing in maceration on skins and long ageing in wood or amphora for whites. His wines are either loved for their complexity or loathed for their oxidation and phenolic profile. Expensive and hard to find.

Grechetto Umbrian white grape (Pulcinculo in TUSCANY); more flavour than TREBBIANO, often used in blends or solo in ORVIETO and other parts of Umbria. Look for Barberani, Bigi, CAPRAI, Cardeto, Colli Amerini, FALESCO, Palazzone.

Greco Various white "Grecos" (of Greek origin?) exist in southern Italy, not always related, eg. GRECO DI TUFO different from Greco of CIRÒ. Also Greco Nero.

Greco di Tufo Cam DOCG w (sp) ★★→★★★ DYA One of the best whites denominations of the south: fruity, slightly citric in flavour and at best ageworthy. V.gd examples from Caggiano, Caputo, Benito Ferrara, *Feudi di San Gregorio*, LA GUARDIENSE, Macchialupa, MASTROBERARDINO (Nova Serra and Vignadangelo), Vesevo, Villa Raiano.

Gresy, Marchesi di (Cisa Asinari) Pie ★★★ Consistent, sometimes inspired producer of traditional-style BARBARESCO (*crus* Gaiun and Camp Gros). Also v.gd SAUV BL, CHARD, MOSCATO D'ASTI, B D'ASTI.

Grevepesa Tus CHIANTI CLASSICO co-op – quality slowly rising.

Grignolino Pie DOC r ★ DYA lively light red of PIEDMONT'S ASTI zone, for drinking young. Best: BRAIDA, Marchesi Incisa della Rocchetta. Also Grignolino del Monferrato Casalese DOC (Accornero, Bricco Mondalino, La Tenaglia).

Gruppo Italiano Vini (GIV) Complex of co-ops and wineries, biggest v'yd-holders in Italy; estates inc Bigi, BOLLA, Ca'Bianca, Conti Serristori, FOLONARI, FONTANA CANDIDA, Lamberti, Macchiavelli, MELINI, Negri, Santi, Vignaioli di San Floriano. Has also expanded into south: SICILY and Basilicata.

Guardiense, la Cam ★★ This dynamic co-op, 1,000 grower-members, 2,000 ha v'yd, is turning out better-than-average whites and reds at lower-than-average prices under the technical direction of Riccardo Cotarella.

Gutturnio dei Colli Piacentini E-R DOC r dr ★→★★★ DYA BARBERA/BONARDA blend from the hills of Piacenza. Producers: Castelli del Duca, La Stoppa, La Tosa.

Haas, Franz T-AA ★★★ ALTO ADIGE producer; v.gd PINOT N, LAGREIN and IGT blends.

Hofstätter T-AA ★★★ ALTO ADIGE producer of top PINOT N. Look for Barthenau Vigna Sant'Urbano, LAGREIN, CAB SAUV/Petit Verdot, Gewurz.

Indicazione Geografica Tipica (IGT) *See* box, p. 139.

Insolia Sicilian white grape; aka Inzolia; on Elba, TUSCAN coast, Ansonica.

Ischia Cam DOC (r) w ★→★★ DYA Island off Naples, own grape varieties (eg. Forastera, Biancolella) mainly sold to tourists. Top: D'Ambra (Biancolella Frassitelli, Forastera Euposia). Also gd: Il Giardino Mediterraneo, Pietratorcia.

Isole e Olena Tus ★★★ →★★★★ Top CHIANTI CLASSICO estate run by astute Paolo de Marchi, with fine red IGT Cepparello. V.gd VIN SANTO, CAB SAUV, CHARD and L'Eremo SYRAH. Also own Sperino in Lessona (*see* GATTINARA).

Isonzo F-VG DOC r w ★★★ This gravelly plain of Friuli Isonzo is a multi-DOC area covering numerous red and white varietals and blends, but the stars are mostly white, scented and structured, like VIE DI ROMANS' Flors di Uis, or LIS NERIS' Fiore de Campo. Also gd: Borgo Conventi, Pierpaolo Pecorari, Ronco del Gelso.

Jermann, Silvio F-VG ★★→★★★ Famous estate with v'yds in COLLIO and ISONZO: top white blend Vintage Tunina, oak-aged blend Capo Martino and CHARD "Were dreams, now it is just wine" (*sic*).

Kante, Edi F-VG ★★→★★★ Leading light of FRIULI's Carso; fine DOC CHARD, SAUV BL, MALVASIA; gd red Terrano.

Lacrima di Morro d'Alba Mar DYA Curiously named Muscatty light red from a small commune in the Marches, no connection with ALBA or La Morra in PIEDMONT. Gd producers: Mancinelli, MONTE SCHIAVO.

Lacryma (or Lacrima) Christi del Vesuvio Cam r p w dr (sw fz) ★→★★ DOC Vesuvio wines based on Coda di Volpe (w) and Piedirosso (r). Alas, despite the romantic name, Vesuvius comes nowhere nr Etna in the quality stakes. Caputo, De Angelis and MASTROBERARDINO produce uninspired wines.

Lageder, Alois T-AA ★★→★★★ Top ALTO ADIGE producer. Most exciting wines are single-v'yd varietals: *Sauv Bl Lehenhof*, PINOT GR Benefizium Porer, CHARD Löwengang, Gewürz Am Sand, PINOT N Krafuss, LAGREIN Lindenberg, CAB SAUV Cor Römigberg. Also owns Cason Hirschprunn for v.gd IGT blends.

Lago di Corbara Umb r ★★ 05 06' 07' 08 (09) (10) Relatively recently created DOC to include quality reds of the ORVIETO area. Best from Barberani (Villa Monticelli) and Decugnano dei Barbi.

Lagrein T-AA DOC r p ★★→★★★ 01 03 04' 06' 07' 08 (09) (10) Deep-hued ALTO-ADIGE varietal with slightly bitter finish, rich, plummy fruit (r), with bright, minerally tones (p). Best growing zone: Gries, suburb of Bolzano. Best producers: Colterenzio co-op, Gojer, Gries co-op, HAAS, HOFSTÄTTER, LAGEDER, Laimburg, Josephus Mayr, Thomas Mayr, MURI GRIES, NALS MARGREID, Niedermayr, Niedrist, St-Magdalena, Terlano co-op, TIEFENBRUNNER.

Lambrusco E-R DOC (or not) r p w dr s/sw ★→★★ DYA Once extremely popular fizzy red from nr Modena, mainly in industrial, semi-sweet, non-DOC version. Sometimes vinified *blanc de noirs*. Best is *secco*, bottle-fermented or in tank. DOCs: L Grasparossa di Castelvetro, L Salamino di Santa Croce, L di Sorbara. Best: Bellei, Caprari, Casali, CAVICCHIOLI, Graziano, Lini Oreste, Medici Ermete (esp Concerto), Rinaldo Rinaldini, Venturini Baldini.

Langhe Pie The hills of central PIEDMONT, home of BAROLO, BARBARESCO, etc. DOC name for six Piedmontese varietals plus blends *bianco* and *rosso*. Those wishing to blend other grapes with NEBBIOLO (GAJA), can up to 15% under "Langhe Nebbiolo".

Latisana F-VG DOC r w ★→★★ (r) DOC for 13 varietal wines from 80 km northeast of Venice. Best wine is FRIULANO (ex-TOCAI). Try wines of Grandi e Gabana.

Lessona Pie *See* GATTINARA.

Librandi Cal ★★★ Top producer pioneering research into Calabrian varieties. V.gd red CIRÒ (*Riserva Duca San Felice* is ★★★), IGT Gravello (CAB SAUV/Gaglioppo blend), Magno Megonio (r) from Magliocco grape and IGT Efeso (w) from Mantonico grape. Other local varietals in experimental phase.

Liguria Lig The Italian Riviera is rocky, but viticulture is rewarding: most wines sell to sun-struck tourists at fat profits. Main grapes: VERMENTINO (w) and DOLCETTO (r), but don't miss CINQUE TERRE's SCIACCHETTRÀ or red Ormeasco di Pornassio.

Lis Neris F-VG ★★★ Top ISONZO estate for gd whites, esp PINOT GR, CHARD (Jurosa), SAUV BL (Picol), FRIULANO (Fiore di Campo), plus blends Confini and Lis. Also v.gd Lis Neris Rosso (MERLOT/CAB SAUV) and sweet white Tal Luc (VERDUZZO/RIES).

Lisini Tus ★★★→★★★★ Historic estate; fine, age-worthy BRUNELLO, esp RISERVA Ugolaia.

Livon F-VG ★★→★★★ Substantial COLLIO producer, also some COLLI ORIENTALI wines such as VERDUZZO. Expanded into the CHIANTI CLASSICO and MONTEFALCO DOCGS.

Loacker T-AA ★★→★★★ Biodynamic (and homeopathic) producer of ALTO ADIGE wines, installed in TUSCANY and making fine BRUNELLO and ROSSO DI MONTALCINO under the Corte Pavone label, plus gd MORELLINO DI SCANSANO Valdifalco.

Locorotondo Ap DOC w (sp) ★ DYA Thirst-quenching dry white from APULIA's Verdeca and Bianco d'Alessano varieties, much quaffed *in situ* by vacationing *trulli*-seekers, little sought back home.

Luce Tus ★★-★★★ FRESCOBALDI is sole owner of this marketing exercise of the great hyperbole and the high price, having bought old original partner Mondavi. The eponymous wine is a SANGIOVESE/MERLOT blend designed for Russian oligarchs.

Lugana DOC w (sp) ★→★★ DYA white of southern Lake Garda, main grape Trebbiano di Lugana (= VERDICCHIO). Dry and sappy. Best: CA' DEI FRATI, ZENATO, Zeni.

Lungarotti Umb ★★→★★★ Leading producer of TORGIANO, with cellars, hotel and museum nr Perugia. Star wine DOCG RISERVA *Rubesco*. Gd IGT Sangiorgio (SANGIOVESE/CAB SAUV), Aurente (CHARD), Giubilante. Gd MONTEFALCO SAGRANTINO.

Macchiole, le Tus ★★★→★★★★ Eugenio Campolmi's widow, Cinzia, continues his fine work with CAB FR (Paleo Rosso), MERLOT (Messorio), as well as SYRAH (Scrio).

Maculan Ven ★★★ Excellent CAB SAUV (Fratta, Ferrata), CHARD (Ferrata), MERLOT (Marchesante) and TORCOLATO (esp RISERVA Acininobili).

Malvasia Ancient grape of Greek origin planted so widely for so long that various sub-varieties often bear little resemblance to one another: can be white or red, sparkling or still, strong or mild, sweet or dry, aromatic or neutral. Best is probably sweet **Malvasia delle Lipari**, from islands off SICILY.

Mancini, Fattoria Mar ★★ Family estate on the sea nr Pesaro. Remarkable PINOT N (r and w), fresh white Albanella and strange Ancellota red called Blu.

Manduria (Primitivo di) Ap DOC r s/sw ★★→★★★ Primitivo, so named because it is an early ripener, came from Croatia, as did California's Zinfandel, which has similar DNA. Deep-hued, smooth with firm acidity, its many producers include Cantele, DE CASTRIS, RACEMI and CS Manduria.

Marchesi di Barolo Pie ★★ Historic, perhaps original BAROLO producer, in commune of BAROLO, making *crus* Cannubi and Sarmassa and other ALBA wines.

Maremma Southern coastal area of TUSCANY, esp province of Grosseto. DOCS inc MONTEREGIO, MORELLINO DI SCANSANO, LA PARRINA, Pitigliano, SOVANA (Grosseto). Attracting interest and investment for potential demonstrated by wines. Maremma Toscana IGT now increasingly used by top producers, rather than DOCS, which tend to diminish perceived value.

Marsala DOC w sw SICILY'S once-famous fortified wine (★→★★★), invented by Woodhouse Bros from Liverpool in 1773. An excellent apéritif, but used mostly in inferior versions for zabaglione. Dry ("virgin") sometimes made by the *solera* system, must be 5 yrs old. Top: FLORIO, Pellegrino, Rallo. *See also* VECCHIO SAMPERI.

Marzemino Trentino T-AA DOC r ★→★★ 06 07 08 09 (10) Pleasant everyday red, fruity and slightly bitter. Esp from Bossi Fedrigotti, CA' VIT, De Tarczal, Gaierhof, Letrari, Longariva, Simoncelli, E Spagnolli, Vallarom.

Mascarello Pie The name of two top producers of BAROLO: Bartolo Mascarello, of BAROLO (deceased), whose daughter Maria Theresa continues her father's highly traditional path; and Giuseppe Mascarello, of Monchiero, whose son Mauro makes superior, traditional-style BAROLO from the great Monprivato v'yd in Castiglione Falletto. Beware other Mascarellos.

Masi Ven ★★→★★★ Exponent/researcher of VALPOLICELLA, AMARONE, RECIOTO, SOAVE, etc., inc fine Rosso Veronese Campo Fiorin and AMARONE-style wines from FRIULI and Argentina. V.gd barrel-aged red IGT *Toar*, from Corvina and Oseleta, also Osar (Oseleta). Top AMARONES Mazzano and Campolongo di Torbe.

Massa, la Tus ★★★ Giampaolo Motta is a Bordeaux-lover making increasingly claret-like IGT wines, with a Tuscan accent (La Massa, Giorgio Primo), from CAB SAUV, MERLOT and SANGIOVESE, at his fine estate in CHIANTI CLASSICO, which denomination he has abandoned.

Masseria Monaci Ap ★★→★★★ Estate of Severino Garofano, for decades the oenologist behind the continuing rise of quality wine in APULIA'S SALENTO. Characterful NEGROAMARO (Eloquenzia, Simpotica), superb late-picked Le Braci, also Uva di Troia (Sine Pari) and AGLIANICO (Sine Die).

Mastroberardino Cam ★★→★★★ Historic producer of mountainous Avellino province. Quality torch-bearer for Italy's south during dark yrs of mid-20th century. Top *Taurasi* (look for Historia Naturalis and Radici), also FIANO DI AVELLINO More Maiorum and GRECO DI TUFO Nova Serra.

Melini Tus ★★ Major producer of CHIANTI CLASSICO at Poggibonsi, part of GIV. Gd quality/price: CHIANTI CLASSICO Selvanella, RISERVAS La Selvanella and Masovecchio.

Merlot Grown today throughout Italy, used varietally and to blend with SANGIOVESE *et al*, officially or otherwise. Traditional and prolific in northeast, though quality is generally better from TUSCANY. World-class Tuscans include Masseto (ORNELLAIA), Redigaffi (TUA RITA), Messorio (LE MACCHIOLE), l'Apparita (Castello di Ama), Lamaione (CASTELGIOCONDO).

Metodo classico or **tradizionale** Italian for "Champagne method".

Mezzacorona T-AA ★→★★ Massive TRENTINO co-op with a wide range of gd technical wines, esp TEROLDEGO ROTALIANO Nos and METODO CLASSICO Rotari.

Monferrato Pie DOC r p w sw ★→★★★ Hills between river Po and Apennines; wines of mostly everyday-drinking style rather than of serious intent.

Monica di Sardegna Sar DOC r ★→★★ DYA Mainstay of Sardinian light, dry red.

Monsanto Tus ★★★ Esteemed CHIANTI CLASSICO estate, esp for Il Poggio (first single-v'yd CHIANTI CLASSICO) and IGTS Fabrizio Bianchi (SANGIOVESE) and Nemo (CAB SAUV).

Montalcino Tus Small town in Siena province, famous for concentrated, expensive BRUNELLO and more approachable, better-value ROSSO DI MONTALCINO.

Monte Schiavo Mar ★★→★★★ Switched-on, medium-size producer of VERDICCHIO and MONTEPULCIANO-based wines at various quality levels, owned by world's largest manufacturer of olive-oil processing equipment, Pieralisi. V'yd holdings also in ABRUZZO, APULIA and SICILY.

Montecarlo Tus DOC r w ★★ DYA (w) White-, increasingly red-, wine area nr Lucca, TUSCANY. Producers: Buonamico (red IGTS Cercatoja Rosso, Fortino), Carmignani (v.gd red IGT For Duke), red IGTS of La Torre, Montechiari, Fattoria del Teso.

Montecucco Tus DOC between Monte Amiata and Grosseto, increasingly trendy as MONTALCINO land prices ineluctably rise. Look for CASTELLO DI POTENTINO (Sacromonte), also Begnardi, Ciacci Piccolomini, Colli Massari, Fattoria di Montecucco, Villa Patrizia. Much investment by the likes of FOLONARI, MASI, Pertimali, Riecine, Talenti.

Montefalco Sagrantino Umb DOCG r dr (sw) ★★★→★★★★ Super-tannic, powerful, long-lasting wines, until recently thought potentially great, today undergoing re-evaluation owing to difficulty of taming the phenolics without denaturing the wine. Traditional bittersweet PASSITO version might be better suited to the grape profile, though little market. Gd: Adanti, Antonelli, Paolo Bea, Benincasa, CAPRAI, Colpetrone, LUNGAROTTI, Tabarrini, Terre de' Trinci.

Montepulciano Tus Deep-coloured red grape dominant in ABRUZZO, important along Adriatic coast (MARCHE to APULIA). Also name of famous Tuscan town, unrelated.

Montepulciano d'Abruzzo Ab DOC r p ★★→★★★ 04' 05 06 07' 08 09 (10) (r) Highly popular, full-flavoured red and zesty, savoury pink (CERASUOLO) of generally excellent value from the Adriatic region opposite Rome. Production dominated by co-ops, gd ones inc Casal Thaulero, Citra, Miglianico, Roxan, Tollo. Some excellent privates, inc Cornacchia, Contesa, Illuminati, Marramiero, Masciarelli, Contucci Ponno, Pepe, La Valentina, VALENTINI, Zaccagnini.

Montepulciano, Vino Nobile di Tus *See* VINO NOBILE DI MONTEPULCIANO.

Monteregio Tus DOC nr Massa Marittima, MAREMMA, gd SANGIOVESE and CAB SAUV (r) and VERMENTINO (w) wines from MORIS FARMS, Tenuta del Fontino *et al.* Big-name investors (ANTINORI, BELLAVISTA, Eric de Rothschild, ZONIN) have invested in the relatively low land prices, but DOC yet to establish itself market-wise. To try.

Montescudaio Tus DOC r w ★★ DOC between Pisa and Livorno. Best: SANGIOVESE or SANGIOVESE/CAB SAUV blends. Try Merlini, Poggio Gagliardo, La Regola, Sorbaiano.

Montevertine Tus ★★★★ Radda estate. Non-DOCG but classic CHIANTI-style wines. IGT *Le Pergole Torte* a fine, pioneering example of pure, long-ageing SANGIOVESE.

Montevetrano Cam ★★★ Iconic CAMPANIA AZIENDA, owned by Silvia Imparato, Riccardo Cotarella consults. Superb IGT Montevetrano (CAB SAUV, MERLOT, AGLIANICO).

Morellino di Scansano Tus DOC r ★→★★★ 04' 05 06 07' 08 (09) (10) The "little black one"of the MAREMMA's Scansano zone is in fact SANGIOVESE. The wine has garnered a reputation for being light and easy-drinking, but it is also capable of considerable weight and presence. Happily the excess oak of earlier years is being toned down. For producers *see* box, p. 131.

Moris Farms Tus ★★★ One of the first of the new-age producers of TUSCANY's MAREMMA, with MONTEREGIO and *Morellino di Scansano* DOCS and VERMENTINO IGT. Top *cru* is the now iconic IGT Avvoltore, a rich SANGIOVESE/CAB SAUV/SYRAH blend. Moris is an old Spanish name.

Moscato Family of fragrant, fruity grapes, inc Moscato Bianco/di Canelli (used in ASTI and MONTALCINO), Moscato Giallo (T-AA, Ven, etc.), Moscato d'Alessandria (SICILY, PANTELLERIA) and Moscato Rosa, making a diverse range of wines: sparkling or still, light or full-bodied, white or pink, but always sweet.

Moscato d'Asti Pie DOCG w sw sp ★★→★★★ DYA Similar to DOCG ASTI, but usually better grapes; lower alcohol, sweeter, fruitier, often from small producers. Best DOCG MOSCATO: L'Armangia, BERA, BRAIDA, Ca'd'Gal, CASCINA FONDA, Cascina Pian d'Oro, Caudrina, Il Falchetto, Forteto della Luja, *Di Gresy*, Icardi, Isolabella, Manfredi/Patrizi, Marino, La Morandina, Marco Negri, Elio Perrone, Rivetti, Saracco, Scagliola, VAJRA, Vietti, Vignaioli di Sante Stefano.

Müller-Thurgau Variety of some interest in T-AA and FRIULI. Top producers: LAGEDER, Lavis, POJER & SANDRI, Zeni. TIEFENBRUNNER's Feldmarschall from 1,000-metre-high v'yd in ALTO ADIGE is possibly the best dry Müller-Thurgau in the world.

Murana, Salvatore Si ★★★ V.gd MOSCATO and PASSITO DI PANTELLERIA.

Muri Gries T-AA ★★→★★★ Monastery in the Bolzano suburb of Gries famous for LAGREIN; traditional and still top producer of ALTO ADIGE DOC. Esp *cru* Abtei-Muri.

Nals Margreid T-AA ★★→★★★ Small but quality-oriented co-op making mountain-fresh whites (esp PINOT BL Sirmian).

Nebbiolo The best red grape of PIEDMONT, possibly of Italy, used in BAROLO, BARBARESCO and other wines of the northwest (eg. Lombardy's VALTELLINA), though so far unsuccessful elsewhere in the wine world.

Nebbiolo d'Alba Pie DOC r dr ★★→★★★ 04 06 07 08 09 (10) Two styles: full and complex, similar to BAROLO/BARBARESCO; and light, fruity and fragrant. Top examples of former from PIO CESARE, GIACOSA, G MASCARELLO, FONTANAFREDDA, PRUNOTTO, SANDRONE, VAJRA.

Negroamaro APULIAN "black bitter" red grape with potential for both high quality or high volume. *See* BRINDISI, COPERTINO and SALICE SALENTINO.

Nerello Mascalese Si Medium-coloured, characterful Sicilian red grape capable of making *wines of v considerable elegance*, once widespread in northeast SICILY, recently rediscovered by the excellent Palari in Messina (FARO DOC) and growers on the upper slopes of ETNA.

Nero d'Avola Si Dark-red grape of southeast SICILY now used throughout the island at quality levels from sublime to industrial.

Nipozzano, Castello di Tus ★★★ FRESCOBALDI estate in RÚFINA east of Florence making excellent CHIANTI RÚFINA RISERVAS Nipozzano and, esp, *Montesodi*.

Nittardi Tus ★★→★★★ Reliable source of high-quality, modern-style CHIANTI CLASSICO produced by oenologist Carlo Ferrini with German proprietor Peter Femfert.

Nozzole Tus ★★→★★★ Famous estate owned by Ambrogio and Giovanni FOLONARI, in heart of CHIANTI CLASSICO. V.gd "Nozzole", excellent Cab Sauv "Pareto".

Nuragus di Cagliari Sar DOC w ★★ DYA Lively, uncomplicated Sardinian wine from Nuragus grape.

Oasi degli Angeli Mar Benchmark all-MONTEPULCIANO wines from small producer in southern Marches; lush and mouthfilling.

Occhio di Pernice Tus A type of VIN SANTO made predominantly from black grapes, mainly SANGIOVESE. AVIGNONESI's is definitive. Also an obscure black variety found in RÚFINA and elsewhere.

News from the hills

Anyone looking for a new discovery should consider Langhe Nebbiolo. Lighter than Barolo, this wine is bright and succulent, with dark kirsch fruit and some attractive grip – it's good value and utterly drinkable. Surprise your friends.

Oddero Pie ★★→★★★ Well-known La Morra estate for gd-value BAROLO (look for Mondoca di Bussia, Rocche di Castiglione and Vigna Rionda).

Oltrepò Pavese Lom DOC r w dr sw sp ★→★★★ 14 lightish wines from Pavia province, most named after grapes. Sometimes v.gd PINOT N and SPUMANTE. Gd growers: Anteo, Barbacarlo, Casa Re, Castello di Cigognola, cs Casteggio, Le Fracce, Frecciarossa, Monsupello, Mazzolino, Ruiz de Cardenas, Travaglino, Vercesi del Castellazzo, La Versa co-op.

Ornellaia Tus ★★→★★★★ 95 97 98 99 00 01' 04' 05 06' 07'08 (09) (10) Famous estate nr BOLGHERI founded by Lodovico ANTINORI, who sold to FRESCOBALDI/ Mondavi consortium, now owned solely by FRESCOBALDI. Top wines are of French grapes and method in dense modern style: BOLGHERI DOC Ornellaia, IGT Masseto (MERLOT). BOLGHERI DOC Le Serre Nuove and IGT Le Volte also gd.

Orvieto DOC w dr sw s/sw ★→★★★ DYA The classic Umbrian white, from the ancient spiritual centre of the Etruscans. Wines comparable to Vouvray (France) from tufaceous soil. *Secco* version is most popular today, *amabile* is more traditional. Sweet versions from noble rot (*muffa nobile*) grapes can be superb, eg. Barberani's Calcaia. Other gd producers Bigi, Cardeto, CASTELLO DELLA SALA, Decugnano dei Barbi, La Carraia, Palazzone.

Pacenti, Siro Tus ★★★ Beautifully made, modern-style BRUNELLO and ROSSO DI MONTALCINO from a small, caring producer.

Pantelleria Si Windswept, black (volcanic) earth island off Sicilian coast; superb stickies from MOSCATO d'Alessandria grapes. PASSITO versions are particularly dense/intense. Look for: Abraxas, Colosi, De Bartoli, DONNAFUGATA, MURANA.

Parrina, La Tus DOC r w ★★ Large estate nr Argentario Peninsula in southern MAREMMA making Parrina Bianco from TREBBIANO/CHARD and Parrina Rosso from SANGIOVESE and French grapes.

Pasqua, Fratelli Ven ★→★★ Massive producer and bottler of Verona wines: VALPOLICELLA, AMARONE, SOAVE. Also BARDOLINO and RECIOTO.

Passito Wine, often sweet, from grapes dried on trays under the sun (south Italy), or indoors on trays or hanging vertically (north Italy). Best-known styles: VIN SANTO (TUSCANY), VALPOLICELLA/SOAVE, AMARONE/RECIOTO (Veneto). *See* MONTEFALCO, ORVIETO, TORCOLATO.

Paternoster Bas ★★→★★★ Top AGLIANICO DEL VULTURE, esp Don Anselmo.

Pecorino Ab IGT Colli Pescaresi w ★★→★★★ Not a cheese but alluring dry white from a recently nr-extinct variety. Gd: Contesa, Franco Pasetti, FARNESE.

Pelaverga Pie *See* VERDUNO.

Petit Verdot Bordeaux vine catching on in Italy, esp among internationalists, mainly for blending. Casale del Giglio in Latium makes interesting varietal.

Piaggia Tus Outstanding producer of CARMIGNANO RISERVA, IGT Il Sasso and superb CAB FR Poggio dei Colli.

Piave Ven DOC r w ★→★★ DYA (w) 06 07 08 09 (10) (r) Volume-producing DOC on plains northwest of Venice for red and white varietals. CAB SAUV, MERLOT and Raboso reds can all age. Gd examples from Duca di Castelanza, Loredan Gasparini, Molon, Villa Sandi.

Picolit F-VG DOC w sw s/sw ★★→★★★ 04 05 06 07 08 09 (10). Somewhat mythical sweet white from COLLI ORIENTALI DEL FRIULI, might disappoint those who can a) find it and b) afford it. Gd from LIVIO FELLUGA, Meroi, Perusini, Specogna, VILLA RUSSIZ, Vinae dell'Abbazia. Apparently not related to black Picolit Neri, grown in GRAVE DEL FRIULI around Spilimbergo.

Piedmont (Piemonte) With TUSCANY, the most important Italian region for top-quality wine. Turin is the capital, ASTI and ALBA the wine centres. No IGTs allowed. Piemonte DOC is lowest denomination. *See* BARBARESCO, BARBERA, BAROLO, DOLCETTO, GRIGNOLINO, MOSCATO, ROERO.

Piemonte DOC r w (sp) ★→★★ PIEDMONT's catch-all DOC (no IGT in PIEDMONT), covering basic reds, whites, SPUMANTES and FRIZZANTES, grapes inc BARBERA, BONARDA, BRACHETTO, Cortese, GRIGNOLINO, CHARD, MOSCATO.

Pieropan Ven ★★★ No 1 producer of SOAVE; the house that kept the quality flag flying when all others yielded to low-cost, volume production in the lean years of 20th century. *Crus* La Rocca and Calvarino considered best SOAVE can offer.

Pieve di Santa Restituta Pie ★★★ GAJA estate for a Piedmontese interpretation of BRUNELLO DI MONTALCINO.

Pinot Bianco (Pinot Bl) Potentially excellent grape; many DOC wines in the northeast, esp high sites in ALTO ADIGE ★★★. Best ALTO ADIGE growers: Colterenzio, HOFSTÄTTER, *Lageder*, NALS MARGREID, Niedrist, TERLANO, Termeno. Gd COLLIO ★★→★★★: Renato Keber, Aldo Polencic, Russiz Superiore, SCHIOPETTO, VILLA RUSSIZ. Best COLLI ORIENTALI ★★→★★★: La Viarte, Zamò & Zamò. Masut da Rive (ISONZO).

Pinot Grigio (Pinot Gr) World-popular varietal white: medium-low acidity, broadly appealing fruit. Has given birth to countless copycats, not to say fraudulent versions. *Caveat emptor*. *The real thing can be excellent*, usually dry (unlike Alsace's residual sugar Pinot Gr), *full-bodied and velvety*; and not cheap. Try Sanct Valentin from SAN MICHELE APPIANO (AA) or Gris from LIS NERIS (FRIULI ISONZO).

Pinot Nero (Pinot N) Planted in much of northeast Italy. DOC and some quality in Lombardy (CA' DEL BOSCO's Pinero), ALTO ADIGE (co-ops of Caldaro, COLTERENZIO and NALS MARGREID, HAAS, Haderburg, HOFSTÄTTER, LAGEDER, Laimburg, NIEDERMAYR, San Michele Appiano, Termeno), OLTREPÒ PAVESE (Frecciarossa, Ruiz de Cardenas). Not bad in FRIULI (LE DUE TERRE, Masut da Riva); gets worse as you head south.

Pio Cesare Pie ★★→★★★ Long-established ALBA producer; BAROLO and BARBARESCO in both modern (BARRIQUE) and traditional (large-cask-aged) versions. Also the ALBA range, inc whites (eg. GAVI). Particularly gd NEBBIOLO D'ALBA.

Planeta Si ★★→★★★ Top SICILIAN estate: Segreta *bianco* blend, Segreta *rosso*; outstanding *Chard*, CAB SAUV, FIANO, MERLOT, NERO D'AVOLA (Santa Cecilia).

Podere Small Tuscan farm, once part of a big estate.

Poggio Means "hill" in Tuscan dialect. "POGGIONE" means "big hill".

Poggio Antico Tus ★★★ Admirably consistent, top-level BRUNELLO DI MONTALCINO.

Poggione, Tenuta Il Tus ★★★ V. reliable estate for BRUNELLO considering large volume; also ROSSO DI MONTALCINO.

Pojer & Sandri T-AA ★★→★★★ Gd TRENTINO producers of red, white and SPUMANTE.

Poliziano Tus ★★★ MONTEPULCIANO estate. Federico Carletti makes superior VINO NOBILE (esp Asinone) and gd IGT Le Stanze (CAB SAUV/MERLOT).

Pomino Tus DOC r w ★★★ (r) 04 06 07 08 (09) (10) Fine red and white blends (esp Il Benefizio). Virtually a FRESCOBALDI exclusivity.

Potentino, Castello di Tus ★★ English eccentric Charlotte Horton takes on the might of what she calls "Mort-alcino" at this medieval redoubt on the slopes of TUSCANY's eerie Monte Amiata. V.gd SANGIOVESE *Sacromonte*; better Piropo.

Prà Ven ★★★ Excellent SOAVE CLASSICO producer, esp *cru* Monte Grande and new Staforte, six mths in steel tanks on lees with mechanical *bâtonnage*.

Produttori del Barbaresco Pie ★★→★★★ One of Italy's earliest and best co-ops, making excellent traditional straight BARBARESCO as well as *crus* Asili, Montefico, Montestefano, Ovello, Pora, Rio Sordo.

Prosecco A recent change in the law, prompted by the need to protect the name like the Champenois, means "Prosecco" is no longer a grape but only a wine derived from the Glera grape grown in specified DOC/DOCG zones (IGT no longer permitted) of the Veneto and FRIULI-VENEZIA GIULIA. May be still, SPARKLING or FRIZZANTE (usually the last). *See* box, p. 130.

Prunotto, Alfredo Pie ★★★→★★★★ Traditional ALBA company modernized by ANTINORI in 1990s; run by Piero's daughter Albiera. V.gd BARBARESCO (Bric

Turot), BAROLO (Bussia), NEBBIOLO (Occhetti), B D'ALBA (Pian Romaldo), B D'ASTI (Costamiole) and MONFERRATO ROSSO (Mompertone, BARBERA/SYRAH blend).

Puglia *See* APULIA.

Pupille, Le Tus ★★★ Top producer of MORELLINO DI SCANSANO (look for Poggio Valente), excellent IGT blend Saffredi (CAB SAUV/MERLOT/SYRAH/Alicante).

Querciabella Tus ★★★★ Top CHIANTI CLASSICO estate with IGT *crus* Camartina (SANGIOVESE/CAB SAUV) and barrel-fermented CHARD/PINOT BL Batàr. Recent purchases in Radda and MAREMMA have increased production of CHIANTI CLASSICO and added Mongrana (SANGIOVESE plus CAB SAUV and MERLOT) to the portfolio. Palafreno, now 100% MERLOT, is one of best of its type.

Quintarelli, Giuseppe Ven ★★★★ Arch-traditionalist, artisan producer of sublime VALPOLICELLA, RECIOTO and AMARONE. Octogenarian Bepi's daughter and children are taking over, altering nothing.

Racemi Ap ★★ Various v'yds/wineries grouped under the Racemi name and run by the enterprising Gregory Perrucci. Based in MANDURIA, making special Primitivos inc: Dunico, Giravolta, Sinfarosa Zinfandel, Vigna del Feudo and Felline. Also, look out for obscure varietals Ottavianello (Cinsault) "Dedalo" and Susumaniello "Sum".

Rampolla, Castello dei Tus ★★★ CAB SAUV-loving estate in Panzano, CHIANTI CLASSICO. Top wines: IGTS Sammarco and d'Alceo. International style CHIANTI CLASSICO.

Recioto della Valpolicella Ven DOC r s/sw (sp) ★★★→★★★★ Potentially stunning, rich, cherry-chocolaty red from VALPOLICELLA grapes dried on trays up to six mths.

Recioto di Soave Ven DOCG w sw (sp) ★★★→★★★★ 07 08 (09) (10) SOAVE made from selected half-dried grapes: sweet, fruity, slightly almondy; sweetness is cut by high acidity. Outstanding from ANSELMI, COFFELE, Gini, PIEROPAN, Tamellini, often v.gd from Ca' Rugate, PASQUA, PRÀ, Suavia, Trabuchi.

Refosco (dal Peduncolo Rosso) F-VG r ★★ 04 05 06 07 08 09 (10) Dark, gutsy red of rustic style. Best from COLLI ORIENTALI DOC, Moschioni, Le Vigne di Zamo, *Volpi Pasini*: gd from LIVIO FELLUGA, Miani and from Dorigo, Ronchi di Manzano, Venica, Ca' Bolani and Denis Montanara in Aquileia DOC.

Regaleali Si *See* TASCA D'ALMERITA.

Ribolla F-VG DOC w ★→★★ DYA Acidic but characterful northeastern white. The best comes from COLLIO. Top estates: Il Carpino, La Castellada, Damijan, Fliegl, GRAVNER, Primosic, Radikon, Tercic.

Ricasoli Historic Tuscan family, 19th-century proposers of CHIANTI blend. The main branch occupies the medieval CASTELLO DI BROLIO. Related Ricasolis own Castello di Cacchiano and Rocca di Montegrossi.

The best of Prosecco

PINOT GR is so last year! This year the buzz in Italian wine circles is all about PROSECCO, that charming if effete sparkler that suddenly seems to have caught on. Some may call it insubstantial, but the PROSECCO-makers themselves take it seriously enough to change the laws and shunt IGT production up to DOC, DOC up to DOCG. Nor, you will not be astonished to learn, have they forgotten to shunt the price up, too. **Valdobbiadene-Conegliano** is the heartland of PROSECCO country, surrounded by the lesser mere DOC zones. Off-dry is normal, truly dry (brut) is rare. Sweetest are called Superiore di CARTIZZE. A growing number of producers boarding the gravy train include: Adami, Biancavigna, BISOL, Bortolin, Canevel, CARPENÈ-MALVOLTI, Case Bianche, Col Salice, Le Colture, Col Vetoraz, Nino Franco, Gregoletto, La Riva dei Frati, Ruggeri, Zardetto.

Tuscan coast
Recent years have seen a rush to establish v'yds in an area not
historically noted for its fine (or indeed any) wines, the coast of
TUSCANY, ie. the provinces of Pisa, Livorno and Grosseto. Much use
is made of international grapes like the CAB brothers, MERLOT, SYRAH,
Petit Verdot, but native varieties like SANGIOVESE, Ciliegiolo and Alicante
are increasingly being used. Here is a selection of the best:
Argentiera, Belguardo (Mazzei), CÀ MARCANDA (GAJA), CAIAROSSA, CASTELLO
DEL TERRICCIO, Colle Massari, Guado al Tasso (ANTINORI), Gualdo del
Re, LE MACCHIOLE, LE PUPILLE, Michele SATTA, Montepeloso, MORIS FARMS,
ORNELLAIA (FRESCOBALDI), Poggio al Tesoro (ALLEGRINI), Tenuta San Guido
(SASSICAIA), TUA RITA.

Riesling (Ries) The great German is of little interest today in Italy, with the possible
exception of one or two producers in ALTO ADIGE (HOFSTÄTTER, NIEDRIST) and in
FRIULI-VENEZIA GIULIA (Ronco del Gelso, VIE DI ROMANS). The version of VAJRA in
PIEDMONT is surprisingly successful.

Ripasso Ven VALPOLICELLA re-fermented on RECIOTO or AMARONE grape skins to make a
complex, longer-lived wine. V.gd: BUSSOLA, Castellani, DAL FORNO, QUINTARELLI, ZENATO.

Riserva Wine aged for a statutory period, usually in casks or barrels.

Rivera Ap ★★ Reliable winemakers at Andria in APULIA. ★★★ CASTEL DEL MONTE
Il Falcone RISERVA (r). V.gd Nero di Troia-based Puer Apuliae.

Rivetti, Giorgio (La Spinetta) Pie ★★★ Fine MOSCATO D'ASTI, excellent BARBERA,
interesting IGT Pin, series of super-concentrated, oaky BARBARESCOS. Now owner
of v'yds both in the BAROLO and the CHIANTI Colli Pisane DOCGS. Early vintages of
Barolo along lines of Barbaresco.

Rocca, Bruno Pie ★★★ Admirable modern-style BARBARESCO (Rabajà) and other ALBA
wines, also v. fine B D'ASTI.

Rocche dei Manzoni Pie ★★★ Modernist estate at Monforte d'Alba. Oaky BAROLO
(esp Vigna d'la Roul, Cappella di Stefano, Pianpolvere), *Bricco Manzoni* (pioneer
BARBERA/NEBBIOLO blend), Quatr Nas (LANGHE).

Roero Pie DOCG r ★★ 96 97' 98' 99' 00 01' 04' 05 06' 07' (08') (09) (10)
Potentially serious, occasionally BAROLO-level NEBBIOLOS from the LANGHE hills
across the Tanaro from ALBA. Best: Almondo, Buganza, Ca' Rossa, Cascina
Chicco, Correggia, Funtanin, Malvirà, Monchiero-Carbone, Morra, Pace,
Pioiero, Taliano, Val di Prete. *See also* ARNEIS.

Ronco Term for a hillside v'yd in northeast Italy, esp FRIULI-VENEZIA GIULIA.

Rosato Rosé; also CHIARETTO, esp around Lake Garda; and CERASUOLO, from Abruzzo;
and Kretzer, from ALTO ADIGE.

Rosato del Salento Ap p ★★ DYA From nr BRINDISI. Sturdy NEGROAMARO-based wine
from a zone that has specialized in rosé. *See* COPERTINO, SALICE SALENTINO.

Rosso Conero Mar DOCG r ★★→★★★ 01' 03' 04 05 06' 07' (08) (09) Some of
Italy's best MONTEPULCIANO (the grape, that is): GAROFOLI's Grosso Agontano,
Moroder's Dorico, MONTE SCHIAVO's Adeodato, TERRE CORTESI MONCARO's Nerone
and Vigneti del Parco, Le Terrazze's Sassi Neri and Visions of J. Also gd: Casato,
FAZI-BATTAGLIA, Lanari, Leopardi Dittajuti, Malacari, Marchetti, Piantate Lunghe,
Poggio Morelli, UMANI RONCHI.

Rosso di Montalcino Tus DOC r ★★→★★★ 06' 07' 08 (09) (10) DOC for earlier
maturing wines from BRUNELLO grapes, from younger or lesser v'yd sites.
Current fierce debate as to whether the 100% SANGIOVESE requirement should
be relaxed.

Rosso di Montefalco Umb DOC r ★★→★★★ 01' 03 04' 05 06' 07' 08 (09) (10)

SANGIOVESE/Sagrantino blend, often with a splash of softening MERLOT. For producers, *see* MONTEFALCO SAGRANTINO.

Rosso di Montepulciano Tus DOC r ★★ **04 05 06** 07 08 (09) (10) Junior version of VINO NOBILE DI MONTEPULCIANO, growers similar. Seen much less than ROSSO DI MONTALCINO, probably because of confusion with MONTEPULCIANO D'ABRUZZO, with which it has nothing in common.

Rosso Piceno Mar DOC r **06** 07 08 (09) (10) Gluggable MONTEPULCIANO/SANGIOVESE blend from southern half of Marches, SUPERIORE from restricted classic zone nr Ascoli, much improved in recent yrs and v.gd value. Best: Aurora, Boccadigabbia, Bucci, Fonte della Luna, Montecappone, MONTE SCHIAVO, Saladini Pilastri, TERRE CORTESI MONCARO, Velenosi Ercole, Villamagna.

Ruffino Tus ★→★★★ The venerable CHIANTI-producing firm of Ruffino has, for nearly a century now, been in the hands of the FOLONARI family. The days of plain CHIANTI, however, are over and this branch of the family, like their cousins (*see* FOLONARI), have been busy acquiring new Tuscan estates. At last count they were up to seven, of which three in CHIANTI CLASSICO inc Santedame (top wine Romitorio), one in MONTALCINO (Greppone Mazzi) and one in MONTEPULCIANO (Lodola Nuova). They also own Borgo Conventi in FRIULI.

Rúfina Tus ★★★ Important northern subregion of CHIANTI. Best wines from Basciano, CASTELLO DI NIPOZZANO (FRESCOBALDI), Castello del Trebbio, Colognole, Frascole, Lavacchio, SELVAPIANA, Tenuta Bossi, Travignoli. Villa di Vetrice/Grati do old vintages, sometimes aged 20 yrs+ in oak barrels or concrete vats.

Sala, Castello della Umb ★★→★★★ ANTINORI estate at ORVIETO. Campogrande is the regular white. Top wine is a splendid ***Cervaro della Sala***, oak-aged CHARD/Grechetto. Muffato della Sala was a pioneering example of an Italian botrytis-influenced dessert wine. PINOT N also creditable.

Salento Ap The tip of Italy's heel, this flat peninsula, baking but breezy between two seas, boasting great expanses of old vines and older olive trees, has long been known for robust reds and ripe *rosato*s, mainly based on NEGROAMARO. There are several DOCs, most superfluous, which is perhaps why IGT Salento is catching on.

Salice Salentino Ap DOC r ★★→★★★ **04 06** 07 08 (09) (10) Best-known of SALENTO's NEGROAMARO-based DOCs, made famous by long-established firms like Leone de Castris, Candido, TAURINO, Apollonio and VALLONE. RISERVA after 2 yrs.

San Felice ★★→★★★ Important historic Tuscan grower owned by Gruppo Allianz. Fine CHIANTI CLASSICO, RISERVA Poggio Rosso from estate in Castelnuovo Berardenga. Famous for Vitiarium, experimental v'yd for obscure varieties: excellent Pugnitello (IGT from the eponymous grape) a first result. Gd IGT Vigorello (first SUPER TUSCAN, from 1968) and BRUNELLO DI MONTALCINO Campogiovanni.

San Gimignano Tourist-overrun Tuscan town famous for its towers and dry white VERNACCIA DI SG DOCG, often overpriced and overvalued but occasionally convincing as a wine if not as a *vin de terroir*. There are some gd SANGIOVESE-based reds made under DOC San Gimignano. Producers inc FALCHINI, Cesani, Guicciardini Strozza, Montenidoli, Mormoraia, Il Palagione, Panizzi, Podera del Paradiso, Pietrafitta, Pietrasereno, La Rampa di Fugnano.

San Giusto a Rentennano Tus ★★★→★★★★ Top CHIANTI CLASSICO estate owned by Martini di Cigala family, cousins of RICASOLI. Outstanding SANGIOVESE IGT Percarlo and sublime VIN SANTO ("Vin San Giusto").

San Guido, Tenuta Tus *See* SASSICAIA.

San Leonardo T-AA ★★★ Top TRENTINO estate, run by Marchesi Guerrieri Gonzaga, consultant Carlo Ferrini. Main wine is Bordeaux blend ***San Leonardo***, sometimes called the "SASSICAIA of the north". Also v. promising MERLOT Villa Gresti.

San Michele Appiano T-AA Top ALTO ADIGE co-op, esp for whites. Look for PINOT BL

Schulthauser and Sanct Valentin (★★★) selections: CHARD, PINOT GR, SAUV BL, CAB SAUV, PINOT N, Gewurz.

Sandrone, Luciano Pie ★★★ Exponent of modern-style ALBA wines with deep, concentrated BAROLO Cannubi Boschis and Le Vigne, DOLCETTO, B D'ALBA and NEBBIOLO D'ALBA.

Sangiovese (Sangioveto) Principal red grape of west-central Italy, with a reputation of being v. difficult to get right, but sublime and long-lasting when it is. Recently and currently the subject of enormous research and experimentation, new clones are yielding more reliable fruit. Dominant in CHIANTI, VINO NOBILE, BRUNELLO DI MONTALCINO, MORELLINO DI SCANSANO and various fine IGTS. Also in Umbria generally (eg. MONTEFALCO ROSSO and TORGIANO RISERVA) and across the Apennines in Romagna and the Marches. Not so clever in the warmer, lower-altitude v'yds of the Tuscan coast, nor in other parts of Italy despite its near ubiquity.

Sangiovese di Romagna Mar DOC r ★★→★★★ Often well-made and v.gd value from La Berta, Berti, Calonga, Ca' Lunga, Cesari, Drei Donà, Paradiso, San Patrignano, Tre Monti, Trere (E-R DOC), Zerbina; IGT Ronco delle Ginestre, Ronco dei Ciliegi from CASTELLUCCIO.

Sant'Antimo Tus DOC r w sw ★★→★★★ A Romanesque abbey and catch-all DOC for (almost) everything produced in the MONTALCINO zone that isn't BRUNELLO DOCG or ROSSO DOC.

Santa Maddalena (or St-Magdalener) T-AA DOC r ★→★★ DYA Curious light red from SCHIAVA grapes grown on v. steep slopes behind ALTO ADIGE capital, Bolzano. Gd producers inc: CS St-Magdalena (Huck am Bach), Gojer, Josephus Mayr, Hans Rottensteiner (Premstallerhof), Heinrich Rottensteiner.

Santa Margherita Large Veneto (Portogruaro) merchant, famous for decent but overpriced PINOT GR. Also owns: Torresella (Veneto), Kettmeir (ALTO ADIGE), Lamole di Lamole and Vistarenni (TUSCANY) and CA' DEL BOSCO (Lombardy).

Santadi Sar ★★★ SARDINIA's, and one of Italy's, best co-ops, esp for CARIGNANO-based reds Terre Brune, Grotta Rossa and Rocca Rubia (all DOC CARIGNANO DEL SULCIS). Also whites *Vermentino Villa Solais* and Villa di Chiesa (VERMENTINO/CHARD).

Sardinia (Sardegna) Sar The Med's second-biggest island produces much decent and some v.gd wines, eg. Turriga from ARGIOLAS, Arbeskia and Dule from Gabbas, VERMENTINO of CAPICHERA, CANNONAU RISERVAS of Jerzu and Loi, VERMENTINO and CANNONAU from Dettori and the amazing flor-affected VERNACCIA of CONTINI. Best DOCS: VERMENTINO di Gallura (eg. Canayli from Cantina Gallura) and CARIGNANO DEL SULCIS (Terre Brune and Rocca Rubia from SANTADI).

Sartarelli Mar ★★★ One of top VERDICCHIO DEI CASTELLI DI JESI producers (Tralivio); outstanding, rare Verdicchio Vendemmia Tardiva (Contrada Balciana).

Sassicaia Tus r ★★★★ 85' 88' 90' 95' 97 98' 99 01' 04' 05 06 07' (08) (09) (10) A CAB (SAUV and FR) made on First Growth lines by Marchese Incisa della Rocchetta at TENUTA San Guido in BOLGHERI, Sassicaia has today been fully accepted by the international market as one of the world's top prestige and investment wines, up there with the likes of Latour and Pétrus (France) and Grange (Australia). Some might think it a shame that a CAB should be regarded as Italy's finest, but overall, Sassicaia's effect on the image of BOLGHERI, of the Tuscan coast, of SUPER TUSCANS and high-quality Italian wines generally has been extremely positive.

Satta, Michele Tus ★★★ Virtually the only BOLGHERI grower to succeed with 100% SANGIOVESE (Cavaliere). BOLGHERI DOC red blends Piastraia, SUPERIORE I Castagni.

Sauvignon Blanc Wine-lovers who don't think of Italy in connection with high-quality Sauv Bl should try cooler-climate examples: ALTO ADIGE (Voglar from Peter Dipoli), ISONZO (Piere from VIE DI ROMANS and PIEDMONT (Viridis from BURLOTTO).

Scavino, Paolo Pie ★★★ Modernist BAROLO producer of Castiglione Falletto, esp *crus* Rocche dell'Annunziata, Bric del Fiasc, Cannubi and Carobric. Gd BARBERA LANGHE Corale.

Schiava T-AA High-yielding red grape of ALTO ADIGE, used for light reds such as Lago di Caldaro, SANTA MADDALENA, etc. Known locally as Vernatsch.

Schioppetto, Mario F-VG ★★★→★★★★ Legendary late COLLIO pioneer with spacious modern winery. V.gd DOC SAUV BL, *Pinot Bl*, TOCAI, IGT blend Blanc de Rosis, etc. Recent offerings inc wines from COLLI ORIENTALI v'yds.

Sciacchetrà Lig *See* CINQUE TERRE.

Scolca, la Pie ★★ Famous GAVI estate for gd GAVI and SPUMANTE.

Sella & Mosca Sar ★★ Major Sardinian grower and merchant; v. pleasant Torbato (w) and light, fruity VERMENTINO Cala Viola (DYA). Gd Alghero DOC Marchese di Villamarina (CAB SAUV), Tanca Farrà (CANNONAU/CAB SAUV). Port-like Anghelu Ruju.

Selvapiana Tus ★★★ With possible exception of more famous NIPOZZANO estate of FRESCOBALDI, generally considered the no 1 CHIANTI RÚFINA estate. Best wines are RISERVA Bucerchiale and IGT Fornace, but even basic CHIANTI RÚFINA is a treat. Also, under the Petrognano label, some fine red DOC POMINO.

Settesoli, CS Si ★→★★ Co-op with nearly 7,000 ha, run by PLANETA family; giving SICILY a gd name with reliable and well-priced varietals (*Nero d'Avola*, SYRAH, MERLOT, CAB SAUV, CHARD, Grecanico, Viognier, blends) under Mandrarossa label.

Sforzato Lom *See* VALTELLINA.

Sicily The Mediterranean's largest island has been hailed for its creative approach to winemaking, using both native grapes (NERO D'AVOLA, NERELLO MASCALESE, Frappato, INZOLIA, Grecanico, Grillo) and international varieties. Wisely, the IGT Sicilia is widely used, avoiding obscure DOCs like Contea di Sclafani and Contessa Entellina. To seek out: Benanti, Ceusi, Colosi, Cos, De Bartoli, DONNAFUGATA, DUCA DI SALAPARUTA, Fazio, Firriato, Foraci, Gulfi-Ramada, Il Cantante, Morgante, MURANA, Pellegrino, PLANETA, Rapitalà, Romeo del Castello, Santa Anastasia, SETTESOLI, Spadafora, TASCA D'ALMERITA, Terre Nere.

Sizzano Pie *See* GATTINARA.

Soave Ven DOC w (sw) ★→★★★ 08, 09 10 Famous, still underrated. From CLASSICO zone, can be intense, mineral, v. fine, quite long-lived. When labelled SUPERIORE is DOCG; best CLASSICO producers shun the "honour", sticking to DOC. Sweet RECIOTO can be superb. Best: Cantina del Castello, La Cappuccina, Ca' Rugate, Cecilia Beretta, COFFELE, Dama del Rovere, Fattori, Gini, Guerrieri-Rizzardi, Inama, Montetondo, PIEROPAN, Portinari, PRÀ, Sartori, Suavia, Tamellini, TEDESCHI.

Solaia Tus r ★★★★ 85′ 90′ 95′ 97′ 99′ 01′ 04 06 07′ (08) (09) (10) Potentially magnificent if somewhat massive CAB SAUV/SANGIOVESE blend by ANTINORI made to the highest Bordelais specifications and requiring yrs of laying down.

Sorì Pie Term for a high south-, southeast-, or southwest-oriented site in PIEDMONT.

Sovana Tus MAREMMA DOC; inland nr Pitigliano. Look for SANGIOVESE, Ciliegiolo from Tenuta Roccaccia, Pitigliano, Ripa, Sassotondo, Malbec from ANTINORI.

Spanna Pie Local name for NEBBIOLO in various north PIEDMONT zones. *See* GATTINARA.

Spumante Sparkling. What used to be called Asti Spumante is now just ASTI.

Südtirol T-AA The local name of German-speaking South Tyrol ALTO ADIGE.

Super Tuscan From the '70s Tuscan wines underwent rapid improvement, often involving a dollop or more of Bordeaux grapes in the blend and barrique ageing. Then SANGIOVESE needed help, now no longer. Those so-called "Super Tuscans" that had established themselves in the market by the millennium held on. The rest are increasingly viewed as overpriced and irrelevant.

Superiore Wine with more ageing than normal DOC and 0.5–1% more alcohol. May indicate a restricted production zone, eg. ROSSO PICENO Superiore.

Syrah The Rhône's great grape has become popular in TUSCANY and SICILY, mainly as a blender. Il Bosco from d'Alessandro or Case Vie from FONTODI are gd examples.

Tasca d'Almerita Si ★★★ Historic SICILIAN producer owned by noble family in Palermo province. Gd IGT red, white and ROSATO Regaleali; v.gd NERO D'AVOLA *Rosso del Conte*; impressive CHARD and CAB SAUV.

Taurasi Cam DOCG r ★★★ 95 97′ 98 99 00 01′ 04′ 05 06 07′ (08) (09) (10) CAMPANIA's historic and most celebrated red, one of Italy's outstanding wines, though requiring bottle age and not easy to appreciate. RISERVA after 4 yrs. V.gd from Caggiano, Caputo, Colli di Lapio, FEUDI DI SAN GREGORIO, MASTROBERARDINO, Molettieri, Terredora di Paulo.

Taurino, Cosimo Ap ★★★ Best-known producer of Salento-APULIA when Cosimo was alive, v.gd SALICE SALENTINO, VDT Notarpanoro, and IGT Patriglione Rosso.

Tedeschi, Fratelli Ven ★★→★★★ Long-established producer of VALPOLICELLA, AMARONE, RECIOTO. Gd IGT Capitel San Rocco red.

Tenuta An agricultural holding (*See* under name – eg. SAN GUIDO, TENUTA.)

Terlano T-AA w ★★→★★★ DYA ALTO ADIGE Terlano DOC applies to one white blend and eight white varietals, esp PINOT BL and SAUV BL. Best: CS Terlano (Pinot Bl Vorberg, capable of remarkable ageing), LAGEDER, Niedermayr, Niedrist.

Teroldego Rotaliano T-AA DOC r p ★★→★★★ TRENTINO's best indigenous variety; serious, full-flavoured wine from vines mainly on the flat Campo Rotaliano. *Foradori* is top, also gd: Dorigati, Endrizzi, MEZZACORONA's RISERVA Nos, Zeni.

Terre Cortesi Moncaro ★★★ Marches co-op, making wines that compete with the best of the region at v. modest prices: gd VERDICCHIO DEI CASTELLI DI JESI (Le Vele), ROSSO CONERO, RISERVA (Nerone) and ROSSO PICENO SUPERIORE (Campo delle Mura).

Terre da Vino Pie ★→★★★ Association of 27 PIEDMONT producers; 4,500 ha, most local DOCS. BARBERA specialists: B D'ASTI La Luna e I Falò Croere. Also gd: BAROLO Essenze, BARBARESCO La Casa in Collina.

Terre di Franciacorta Lom DOC r w ★★ 06 07 08 09 (10) (r) DYA (w) So named to distinguish table wines from sparkling FRANCIACORTA DOCG. The red is an unusual blend of CAB SAUV, BARBERA, NEBBIOLO, MERLOT. Less adventurous whites from CHARD, PINOT GR. Alternative name: Curtefranca. Best producers: *see* FRANCIACORTA.

Terriccio, Castello del Tus ★★★ Large estate south of Livorno: excellent, v. expensive Bordeaux-style IGT Lupicaia, v.gd IGT Tassinaia. Impressive new IGT Terriccio, an unusual blend of mainly Rhône grapes.

Tiefenbrunner T-AA ★★→★★★ Medium-sized grower-négociant situated at a quaint Teutonic castle (Turmhof) in southern ALTO ADIGE village of Entiklar. Christof T has taken over from father Herbert (winemaker since 1943) making a wide range of mtn-fresh white and well-defined red varietals, French, Germanic and local, esp 1,000-metre-high *Feldmarschall* (*see* MÜLLER-THURGAU) and Linticlarus range CHARD/LAGREIN/PINOT N.

Tignanello Tus r ★★★★ 95 97′ 98 99′ 00 01′ 04′ 06′ 07′ 08 (09) (10) SANGIOVESE/CAB SAUV blend, BARRIQUE-aged, the wine that put SUPER TUSCANS on the map, created by ANTINORI's great oenologist Giacomo Tachis in the early 1970s.

Tocai F-VG *See* FRIULANO.

Torcolato Ven Sweet wine from Breganze; Vespaiolo grapes are laid on mats or hung up to dry for months (as RECIOTO DI SOAVE). Best producers: MACULAN, CS Beato Bartolomeo.

Torgiano Umb DOC r p w (sp) ★★ and **Torgiano, Rosso Riserva** DOCG r ★★→★★★ 97 99 00′ 01′ 03 04 06 07′ 08 (09) (10) Gd to excellent CHIANTI-style red from Umbria, dominated by LUNGAROTTI's Rubesco. Vigna Monticchio Rubesco Riserva outstanding in vintages such as 1975, 1979, 1985; keeps many yrs.

Traminer Aromatico T-AA DOC w ★★→★★★ DYA (German: Gewürz) Pungent white with all the aromatics of the Alsace versions minus the residual sugar. Best from its birthplace Tramin (Italian: Termeno), notably CS Termeno and HOFSTÄTTER. Other gd producers inc co-ops Caldaro, Colterenzio, Prima & Nuova,

---

The Maremma: beside the seaside

Names to look for in the Maremma (for IGT): Ampeleia, Belguardo, La Carletta, Casina, Col di Bacche, Fattoria di Magliano, Lhosa, La Marietta, Marsiliana, Monteti, MORIS FARMS, Montebelli, La Parrina, Poderi di Ghiaccioforte, Poggio Argentiera, Poggio Foco, Poggio al Lupo, Poggio Paoli, Poggio Verrano, Rascioni e Cecconello, Rocca di Frasinello, San Matteo, Sassotondo, La Selva, Solomaremma, Suveraia.

For Morellino di Scansano: Belguardo, La Carletta, Fattoria di Magliano, Mantellasi, Masi de Mandorlaia, MORIS FARMS, Podere 414, Poderi di Ghiaccioforte, Poggio Argentiera, Poggio al Lupo, Poggio Paoli, LE PUPILLE, Roccapesta, San Matteo, La Selva, Cantina di Scansano, Terre di Talamo and Vignaioli del Morellino di Scansano..

SAN MICHELE APPIANO, TERLANO plus Abbazia di Novacella, HAAS, Kuenhof, LAGEDER, Laimberg, NALS MARGREID, Niedermayr.

Trebbiano Principal white grape of TUSCANY, found all over Italy in many different guises. Rarely rises above the plebeian except in TUSCANY's VIN SANTO. Some gd dry whites under DOCS Romagna or Abruzzo. Trebbiano di Soave or di Lugana, aka VERDICCHIO, is only distantly related.

Trebbiano d'Abruzzo Ab DOC w ★→★★ DYA Mostly inexpensive white: gd acidity, neutral flavour; rises to considerable heights from a master like Valentini.

Trentino T-AA DOC r w dr sw ★→★★★ DOC for 20 wines, most named after grapes. Best: CHARD, PINOT BL, MARZEMINO, TEROLDEGO. Provincial capital is Trento.

Trinoro, Tenuta di ★★★★ Individualist Tuscan red wine estate, pioneer in DOC Val d'Orcia between MONTEPULCIANO and MONTALCINO. Early vintages of Bordeaux blend Trinoro caused great excitement, then the price shot up. Le Cupole adds Lazio's Cesanese and Puglia's Uva di Troia to the Bordeaux mix. Andrea Franchetti also has v'yds on Mt Etna.

Tua Rita Tus ★★→★★★★ The first producer to establish Suvereto as the new BOLGHERI in the 1990s. Producer of possibly Italy's greatest MERLOT in Redigaffi, also outstanding Bordeaux blend *Giusto di Notri*. *See* VAL DI CORNIA.

Tuscany (Toscana) The focal point of Italian wine's late 20th-century "renaissance", with experimental wines like the SUPER TUSCANS and modernized classics like CHIANTI, VINO NOBILE and BRUNELLO.

Umani Ronchi Mar ★★→★★★ Leading Marches producer, esp for VERDICCHIO (Casal di Serra, Plenio), ROSSO CONERO Cumaro, IGTS Le Busche (w), Pelago (r).

Vajra, G D Pie ★★★ Producer of immaculate BAROLO, BARBERA, DOLCETTO and Freisa in the red department as well as RIES in the white. Recently purchased Luigi Baudana estate in Serralunga.

Val di Cornia Tus DOC r p w ★★→★★ 00 01' 04' 05 06' 07 08 (09) (10) DOC south of BOLGHERI. SANGIOVESE, CAB SAUV, MERLOT, SYRAH and MONTEPULCIANO. Look for: Ambrosini, Jacopo Banti, Bulichella, Gualdo del Re, Incontri, Montepeloso, Petra, Russo, San Michele, Tenuta Casa Dei, Terricciola, TUA RITA.

Valdadige T-AA DOC r w dr s/sw ★ The name (in German: Etschtaler) for simple wines of the valley of the Adige – from ALTO ADIGE through TRENTINO to northern VENETO.

Valentini, Edoardo Ab ★★★→★★★★ Edoardo's son Francesco continues tradition of long-macerated, non-filtered, hand-bottled MONTEPULCIANO, CERASUOLO, TREBBIANO D'ABRUZZO. Quality unpredictable but potentially outstanding.

Valle d'Aosta DOC r p w ★★ Regional DOC for some 25 Alpine wines, geographically or varietally named, inc Premetta, Fumin, Blanc de Morgex et de La Salle,

Chambave, Nus Malvoisie, Arnad Montjovet, Torrette, Donnas, Enfer d'Arvier. Tiny production, wines rarely seen abroad.

Valle Isarco Eisacktal, T-AA DOC w ★★ DYA ALTO ADIGE Valle Isarco is the DOC for seven Germanic varietal whites made along the Isarco (Eisack) River northeast of Bolzano. Gd Gewürz, MÜLLER-THURGAU, RIES and Silvaner. Top producers: Abbazia di Novacella, Eisacktaler, Kuenhof.

Vallone, Agricole Ap ★★ →★★★ Large-scale private v'yd-holder in APULIA'S SALENTO peninsula, excellent gd-value BRINDISI rosso/ROSATO Vigna Flaminio, best-known for its AMARONE-like semi-dried-grape wine Graticciaia. Vigna Castello is a classy addition to the range.

Valpolicella Ven DOC r ★→★★★★ 00 01 03 04 05 06 07 08 09 (10) (SUPERIORE) Complex denomination, inc everything from light quaffers with a certain fruity warmth through stronger SUPERIORES to AMARONES and RECIOTOS of ancient lineage. Bitter cherry the common flavour. Best tend to come from CLASSICO subzone.

Valtellina Lom DOC r ★→★★★ DOC for tannic but elegant wines: mainly from Chiavennasca (NEBBIOLO) in northern Alpine Sondrio province. V.gd SUPERIORE DOCG from Grumello, Inferno, Sassella, Valgella v'yds. Best: Caven Camuna, Conti Sertoli-Salis, Fay, Nera, Nino Negri, Plozza, Rainoldi, Triacca. *Sforzato* is the most concentrated type of Valtellina; similar to AMARONE.

Vecchio Samperi Si ★★★ MARSALA Vergine/old from famous estate. Best is barrel-aged Ventennale, a blend of young and v. old vintages. Owner Marco de Bartoli also makes top DOC MARSALAS and outstanding PASSITO Bukkuram at his winery on the island of PANTELLERIA.

Vendemmia Harvest or vintage.

Venegazzu Ven ★★★→★★★★ Iconic Bordeaux blend from east Veneto producer Loredan Gasparini. Even more prestigious is the *cru* Capo di Stato (being originally created to be served at the table of the president of the Italian Republic).

Verdicchio dei Castelli di Jesi Mar DOC w (sp) ★★→★★★ DYA Versatile white wine from nr Ancona: light and quaffable; sparkling; structured, complex, long-lived (esp RISERVA, min 2 yrs old). Also CLASSICO. Best: Accadia, Bonci-Vallerosa, Brunori, Bucci, Casalfarneto, Cimarelli, Colonnara, Coroncino, FAZI-BATTAGLIA, Fonte della Luna, GAROFOLI, Laila, Lucangeli Aymerich di Laconi, Mancinelli, Montecappone, MONTE SCHIAVO, Santa Barbara, SARTARELLI, TERRE CORTESI MONCARO, UMANI RONCHI.

Verdicchio di Matelica Mar DOC w (sp) ★★→★★★ DYA Similar to above, smaller, less-known, longer-lasting. Esp Barone Pizzini, Belisario, Bisci, La Monacesca, Pagliano Tre, San Biagio.

Verduno Pie DOC r ★★ DYA Pale red similar to GRIGNOLINO, from Pelaverga grape

---

Top ten white varieties

When people think of Italian wine they tend to think of reds, perhaps by association with red-friendly foods like pizza, pasta, *bistecca fiorentina*, etc. But don't forget that long Mediterranean coastline, east and west, and the fish and seafood it provides in abundance. There are white varieties galore to accompany the myriad dishes that invariably differ from province to province. Here are ten to try (in geographical order) with one example of excellence for each: PIEDMONT – ARNEIS (GIACOSA); ALTO ADIGE – TRAMINER (CS Tramin); Veneto – GARGANEGA (SOAVE PIEROPAN); FRIULI – FRIULANO (BORGO DEL TIGLIO); Marche – VERDICCHIO (Bucci); Umbria – GRECHETTO (Barberani); Abruzzo – PECORINO (Contesa); SARDINIA – VERMENTINO (CAPICHERA); CAMPANIA – FIANO (MASTROBERARDINO); SICILY – Carricante (ETNA Bianco Benanti).

grown only in commune of Verduno. Gd: Bel Colle, BURLOTTO, Alessandria and CASTELLO DI VERDUNO.

Verduno, Castello di Pie ★★★ Husband/wife team Franco Bianco, with v'yds in Neive, and Gabriella Burlotto, with v'yds in Verduno, turn out v.gd Barbaresco Rabaja and Barolo Monvigliero with winemaker Mario Andrion.

Verduzzo Colli Orientali, F-VG DOC w dr sw s/sw ★★→★★★ Full-bodied white from indigenous variety. Ramandolo is well-regarded subzone for sweet wine. Top: Dario Coos, Dorigo, Giov Dri, Meroi. Superb LIS NERIS sweet VDT Tal Luc.

Vermentino Lig w ★★ DYA One of Italy's most characterful white grapes, whether made light/dry or *robust*, grown throughout western LIGURIA and SARDINIA, increasingly along Tuscan coast, in SARDINIA and spreading inland to Umbria. Seek, in LIGURIA: Lambruschi, Lupi; in TUSCANY: San Giusto, SATTA; *see* VERMENTINO DI GALLURA.

Vermentino di Gallura Sar DOCG w ★★→★★★ DYA *Best dry white of Sardinia*, stronger and more intensely flavoured than DOC Vermentino di Sardegna. Esp from CAPICHERA, CS di Gallura, CS del Vermentino, Depperu.

Vernaccia di Oristano Sar DOC w dr (sw fz) ★→★★★ 90' 93' 97' 00' 01 04 06 07 (08) (09) Sardinian *flor*-affected wine, like light Sherry, a touch bitter, full-bodied. SUPERIORE 15.5% alcohol, 3 yrs of age. Top: CONTINI.

Vernaccia di San Gimignano Tus *See* SAN GIMIGNANO.

Vie di Romans F-VG ★★★→★★★★ Gianfranco Gallo has built up his father's ISONZO estate to top FRIULI status. Excellent ISONZO CHARD, PINOT GR Dessimis, SAUV BL Piere and Vieris (oaked), MALVASIA/RIES/TOCAI blend called Flors di Uis.

Vietti Pie ★★★ Long-serving producer, at Castiglione Falletto, of characterful PIEDMONT wines, inc BARBARESCO Masseria, B D'ALBA Scarrone, B D'ASTI la Crena. Mainly, *textbook Barolos*: Lazzarito, Rocche, Brunate, Villero.

Vigna (or vigneto) A single v'yd, generally indicating superior quality.

Vignalta Ven ★★ Top producer in COLLI EUGANEI nr Padova (Veneto); v.gd COLLI EUGANEI CAB SAUV RISERVA and MERLOT/CAB SAUV blend Gemola.

Vignamaggio Tus ★★→★★★ Historic, beautiful and v.gd CHIANTI CLASSICO estate nr Greve. Leonardo da Vinci is said to have painted the *Mona Lisa* here.

Vigne di Zamò, le F-VG ★★★ First-class FRIULI estate. PINOT BL, TOCAI, Pignolo, CAB SAUV, MERLOT and Picolit from v'yds in three areas of COLLI ORIENTALI DEL FRIULI DOC.

Villa Matilde Cam ★★★ Top CAMPANIA producer of FALERNO ROSSO (Vigna Camarato) and *bianco* (Caracci), PASSITO Eleusi.

Villa Russiz Lom ★★★ Impressive white DOC COLLIO Goriziano: v.gd SAUV BL and MERLOT (esp "de la Tour" selections), PINOT BL, PINOT GR, TOCAI, CHARD.

Valpolicella: the best

Verona's VALPOLICELLA zone, the best of whose v'yds are on the final slopes of the Alps before descending to the vast plain of the Po Valley, is one of Italy's most classic and ancient, with texts testifying to the making of PASSITO wines going back 2,000 years. Whether it's AMARONE, RECIOTO, RIPASSO or plain VALPOLICELLA, whether DOC or IGT, these producers make good-to-great wine. The crème de la crème are indicated by ★: Accordini Stefano ★, Serego Alighieri, ALLEGRINI ★, Begali, BERTANI, BOLLA, Boscaini, Brigaldara, BRUNELLI, BUSSOLA ★, Ca' la Bianca, Campagnola, Ca' Rugate, Castellani, Corteforte, Corte Sant'Alda, CS Valpantena, Cantina Valpolicella, Valentina Cubi, DAL FORNO ★, Guerrieri-Rizzardi, MASI, Mazzi ★, Nicolis, QUINTARELLI ★, Roccolo Grassi ★, Le Ragose, Le Salette, Speri ★, TEDESCHI ★, Tommasi, Venturini, VIVIANI★, ZENATO, Zeni.

What do the initials mean?
Denominazione di Origine Controllata (DOC)
Controlled Denomination of Origin, cf. AC in France.
Denominazione di Origine Controllata e Garantita (DOCG)
"G" = "Guaranteed". Italy's highest quality designation.
Indicazione Geografica Tipica (IGT)
"Geographic Indication of Type". Broader and more vague than DOC, cf. Vin de Pays in France.
Denominazione di Origine Protetta/Indicazione Geografica Protetta (DOP/IGP) "P" = "Protected". The EU seems to want these designations to take over from DOC(G)/IGT in the long term but for now you're much more likely to encounter DOC(G) or IGT, occasionally both.

Vin Santo or Vinsanto, Vin(o) Santo Term for certain strong, usually sweet wines made from PASSITO grapes, usually TREBBIANO, MALVASIA and/or SANGIOVESE in TUSCANY ("Vin Santo"), Nosiola in TRENTINO ("Vino Santo"). Tuscan versions can be extremely variable, anything from quasi-dry and Sherry-like to sweet and v. rich. May spend 3–10 unracked yrs in small barrels called *caratelli*. AVIGNONESI's is legendary; plus CAPEZZANA, CORZANO & PATERNO, Fattoria del Cerro, FELSINA, Frascole, ISOLE E OLENA, Rocca di Montegrossi, San Gervasio, San Giusto a Rentennano, SELVAPIANA, Villa Sant'Anna, Villa di Vetrice. *See also* OCCHIO DI PERNICE.

Vino Nobile di Montepulciano Tus DOCG r ★★→★★★ 99' 00 01' 04' 05 06' 07' 08 (09) (10) Historic SANGIOVESE (here called Prugnolo Gentile) from the town (as distinct from ABRUZZO's grape) MONTEPULCIANO, often tough with drying tannins, but complex and long-lasting from best producers: AVIGNONESI, Bindella, BOSCARELLI, La Braccesca, La Calonica, Canneto, Le Casalte, CONTUCCI, Dei, Fattoria del Cerro, Gracciano della Seta, Gracciano Svetoni, Icario, Nottola, Palazzo Vecchio, POLIZIANO, Romeo, Salcheto, Trerose, Valdipiatta, Villa Sant'Anna. RISERVA after 3 yrs. Well-priced relative to BRUNELLO.

Vivaldi-Arunda T-AA ★★→★★★ Winemaker Josef Reiterer makes top ALTO ADIGE sparkling wines. Best: Extra Brut RISERVA, Cuvée Marianna.

Viviani Ven ★★★ Claudio Viviani continues to demonstrate how modern-style a wine VALPOLICELLA, and AMARONE, can be. V.gd CLASSICO SUPERIORE Campo Morar, better RECIOTO La Mandrella, outstanding AMARONE Casa dei Bepi, Tulipano Nero.

Voerzio, Roberto Pie ★★★→★★★★ BAROLO modernist. Top, v. expensive single-v'yd BAROLOS: Brunate, Cerequio, Rocche dell'Annunziata-Torriglione, Sarmassa, Serra; impressive B D'ALBA.

Volpaia, Castello di Tus ★★→★★★ V.gd CHIANTI CLASSICO estate at Radda. SUPER TUSCANS Coltassala (SANGIOVESE/Mammolo), Balifico (SANGIOVESE/CAB SAUV).

Zenato Ven ★★ V. reliable for GARDA wines, VALPOLICELLA, SOAVE, AMARONE, LUGANA.

Zerbina, Fattoria E-R ★★★ Leader in Romagna; best sweet ALBANA DOCG (Scacco Matto), v.gd SANGIOVESE (Pietramora), BARRIQUE-aged IGT Marzieno.

Zibibbo Si ★★ sw dr Local PANTELLERIA name for Muscat of Alexandria. Best from: MURANA, De Bartoli.

Zonin ★→★★★ One of Italy's biggest private estates, based at Gambellara. DOC and DOCG VALPOLICELLA. Also in ASTI, APULIA, CHIANTI CLASSICO, SAN GIMIGNANO, FRIULI, SICILY and Virginia (USA).

Zuani Lom ★★★ Small COLLIO estate owned by Patrizia, daughter of MARCO FELLUGA. Superior white blends Z Zuani (oaked) and Z Vigne.

Germany

Abbreviations used in the text:

Bad Baden
Frank Franken
M-M Mittelmosel
M Rh Mittelrhein
M-S-R Mosel-Saar-Ruwer
Na Nahe
Pfz Pfalz
Rhg Rheingau
Rhh Rheinhessen
Sachs Sachsen
Würt Württemberg

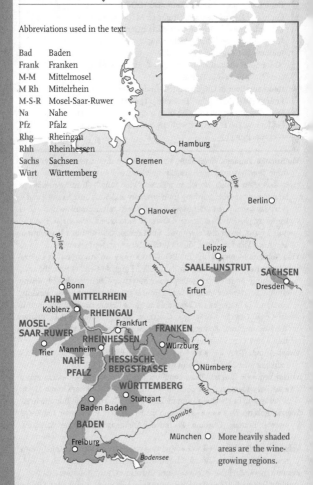

More heavily shaded areas are the wine-growing regions.

I have been calling for a Riesling Renaissance for nearly half my life – and I'm getting on a bit. German wine is first and foremost about Riesling, the greatest and most versatile wine grape of all. White-wine grape, at least; but no, there isn't a red-wine grape that's anything like as versatile. But until now it continues to be a hard sell. Has something changed? Sales figures say yes. Tasters say yes. An astonishing run of good vintages (climate change at its most positive) has given good growers confidence to raise their game, especially to enter the world competition for full-on, dry, dinner-worthy wines. This is the success story of the past few years. Growers have re-earned the respect of their own wealthy domestic market by reviving their traditional style of fully fermented dry wines. The USA is catching on, the UK more hesitantly (still looking for the old sweet styles), but the direction is clear. Germany is bidding for a thoroughly modern market in thoroughly classic wines – and across a much wider spectrum, of both grapes and regions, than the classic Riesling tradition. The national catastrophe that followed Germany's suicidal wine law of 1971 is now 40 years old. Why does the British public find it so hard to forgive and forget? The top echelon of producers, united by the VDP association, is making individual wines to the ultimate quality standards. Not to follow them and their new ideas is wanton waste.

LUXEMBOURG

It doesn't hurt to think of Luxembourg as a halfway-house between Germany and France – in wine terms, at least. Its Rieslings in particular seem half German, half French in style: typically, they remind one of an old-school Alsace Riesling on the nose, while the palate might have the lightness and the sweet-and-sour notes of an off-dry Nahe wine. Even if most of the 1,270 hectares of vines along the *Moselle Luxembourgeoise* are grown within a radius of only 25 miles from Germany's most legendary Riesling vineyard, the Scharzhofberg, the wines are quite different. First, Luxembourg's vintners grow more Rivaner (Müller-Thurgau, 27%), Auxerrois (14%) and Pinot Gris (14%) than Riesling (12%). Secondly, the soil is different: no slate, but a patchwork of Trias soils (deep Keuper, red sandstone, and shell limestone).

Luxembourg's wine law doesn't differentiate between dry and off-dry styles. Most of Luxembourg's whites have not only strong acidity, but also a more or less accentuated sweetness. Depending on vintage, producer's style, and variety, many of these wines appear to be rather *halbtrocken* or *feinherb* than *trocken*, in the German definition of these terms. Luxembourg produces a lot of sparkling wine, too. Crémant de Luxembourg can be anything from refined to rustic, cheaper versions typically tasting extra-dry even if labelled brut. The best (look for Montmollin Brut from Duhr Frères, Brut 2007 from Clos de Rochers, Brut 2007 from Bernard-Massard, or Brut Tradition from Sunnen-Hoffmann) can be v.gd value.

There is no lack of well-trained and ambitious wine-growers in Luxembourg. Among the best known are Château de Schengen (aromatic, mineral Pinot Gris), Cep d'Or (good Pinots, both white and red), Clos de Rochers (full-bodied single-vineyard Riesling from Grevenmacher and Ahn, as well as intense Riesling Vin de Glace), Duhr Frères/Clos Mon Vieux Moulin (noteworthy Gewürztraminer Fût 13, v.gd Pinot Noir Fût 2, and lovely Riesling Äiswäin (aka Icewine), Gloden & Fils (traditionally crafted, rich Schengen Markusberg Riesling), Schumacher-Knepper (seriously dry, aromatic Wintringer Felsberg Riesling Fût 35), Sunnen-Hoffmann (well-structured Riesling from Remerschen and Wintrange, organic farming). Other good producers include: Caves St-Martin, Mathis Bastian, Mme. Aly Duhr, Charles Decker, Schlink-Hoffeld. Domaines Vinsmoselle is a union of co-ops, with wines that are mostly made in a more commercial style. Good premium label: François Valentiny.

Recent vintages

Mosel-Saar-Ruwer

Mosels (including Saar and Ruwer wines) are so attractive young that their keeping qualities are not often enough explored. But well-made Ries wines of Kabinett class gain from at least five years in bottle and often much more: Spätlese from five to 20, and Auslese and Beerenauslese anything from ten to 30 years. As a rule, in poor years the Saar and Ruwer make sharp, lean wines, but in good years, which are increasingly common, they can surpass the whole world for elegance and thrilling, steely "breeding".

2010 A difficult vintage, marked by diseases, and only half of an average crop. A lot of deacidifcation went on, but in the successes both sugar and acidity levels were exceptionally high – comparable to 1990.

2009 Uneven flowering, so a small crop (20% below average); outstanding quality. A dry, sunny September and cool, sunny October meant plenty of magnificent Spätlesen and Auslesen with perfect acidity. The dry wines have a rare balance of power and finesse. Keep the best to great maturity.

2008 Early flowering. A classic cool summer with rain and sun. A cool September slowed down ripeness and kept acidity high. Wet October. Not a vintage for Auslesen, but Kabinetts and Spätlesen can be fine and elegant. Drink or keep.

2007 Good quality with high acidity levels in beautiful Kabinetts – good quantity, too. Some botrytis at the end of harvest. Drinking beautifully.

2006 The best growers achieved very high ripeness and vibrant acidity, but ruthless selection means that quantities are low. Drink.

2005 Very high ripeness levels, but with far better acidity than, say, 2003. Exceptional, especially in the Saar. Drink or keep.

2004 A humid summer led growers to fear the worst, but the vintage was saved by a glorious autumn. A fine year to drink.

2003 Some great sites suffered from drought, while less-esteemed cooler sites often fared better. Despite some sensational Trockenbeerenauslesen, considerable variation in quality. Not to keep.

2002 It is a small miracle how Riesling grapes survived one of the wettest harvests on record to give ripe, succulent, lively wines (mostly Kabinett and Spätlese), attractive drunk young or mature (now).

2001 Golden October resulted in the best Mosel Riesling since 1990. Saar and Ruwer less exciting but still perfect balance. Lots of Spätlesen and Auslesen to drink or keep.

2000 Ries stood up to harvest rain here better than most other places. Dominated by good QbA and Kabinett. Auslesen rarer, but exciting.

1999 Excellent in Saar and Ruwer, lots of Auslesen; generally only good in the Mosel due to high yields. Best drank well young and could age further.

1998 Astonishingly good results in the Middle Mosel; the Saar and Ruwer were less lucky, with mostly QbA. Plenty of Eiswein. Drink.

1997 Consistently fruity, elegant wines. Great Auslesen in Saar and Ruwer.

1996 Variable, with fine Spätlesen and Auslesen from top sites. Many Eisweins.

1995 Excellent vintage, mainly of Spätlesen and Auslesen of firm structure and long ageing potential. Drink.

1994 Another good vintage, many Auslesen and botrytis wines still tasting good.

1993 Small, excellent vintage: lots of Auslesen/botrytis; near-perfect harmony. Now wonderful to drink.

Fine older vintages: 90 89 88 76 71 69 64 59 53 49 45 37 34 21

Rheinhessen, Nahe, Pfalz, Rheingau

Even the best wines can be drunk with pleasure when young, but Spätlese and Auslese Ries gain enormously in character by keeping. Rheingau wines tend to be longest-lived, improving for 15 years or more, but best wines from the Nahe and Pfalz can last as long. Rheinhessen wines usually mature sooner, and dry Franken and Baden wines are generally best at three to six years.

2010 For the first time in a decade, grapes had difficulty ripening. Late flowering, hot June, and cool rainy conditions in late summer and at harvest made uneven quality and a low crop (40% below average). Some decent wines in Baden and Franken.

2009 A year of ups and downs. Early flowering, wet summer. But dry weather in July quelled mildew. Sun in September and October brought high degrees of maturity and surprisingly low acidity. For the first time since 2003, authorities allowed acidification. Excellent wines, especially dry.

2008 Difficult vintage: good quantity, uneven quality. Wet summer favoured mildew. Rainy September and October made picking dates difficult. Some good (and age-worthy) late-harvest wines, Rheingau especially. Very welcome: alcohol levels are down to around 12% in dry wines.

2007 Those who waited to pick until October had ripe grapes with cool nights conserving good acidity levels. However, dry wines are maturing faster than expected. Drink most.

2006 A nightmare: heavy October rains and atypical high October temperatures destroyed a promising crop. Top estates managed small quantities of fair middleweight wines. Most should be drunk now.

2005 The summer was warm but not too dry. A very fine autumn led to high ripeness levels, accompanied by excellent acidity and extract. A superb year. Drink or keep.

2004 Ripe, healthy grapes throughout the Rhine. A big crop; some dilution, though not at top estates.

2003 Very hot weather led to rich wines in the Rheingau; many lack acidity. The Pfalz produced superb Ries. Red wines fared well everywhere. Drink.

2002 Few challenge the best from 2001, but very good for both classic Kabinett/Spätlese and for dry. Excellent Pinot N. Drink.

2001 Though more erratic than in the Mosel, an exciting vintage for both dry and classic styles; excellent balance. Drink or keep.

2000 The farther south, the more harvest rain, the Pfalz catching the worst. However, all regions have islands of excellence. Drink.

1999 Quality was average where yields were high, but for top growers an excellent vintage of rich, aromatic wines with lots of charm to drink soon.

1998 Excellent: rich, balanced wines, many good Spätlesen, Auslesen: excellent ageing potential. Rain in Baden, Franken. But a great Eiswein year.

1997 Very clean, ripe grapes gave excellent QbA, Kabinett, Spätlese in dry and classic styles. Little botrytis, so Auslesen are rare.

1996 An excellent vintage, particularly in the Pfalz and the Rheingau, with many fine Spätlesen. Great Eiswein. Drink.

1995 Variable, but some excellent Spätlesen and Auslesen maturing well – like the 1990s. Weak in the Pfalz due to harvest rain.

1994 Good vintage, mostly Qualitätswein mit Prädikat, with abundant fruit and firm structure. Some superb sweet wines.

Fine older vintages: 93 90 83 76 71 69 67 64 59 53 49 45 37 34 21

Achkarren Bad (r) w ★★→★★★ Village on the KAISERSTUHL, known esp for opulent GRAUBURGUNDER kept in balance by minerality. ERSTE LAGE v'yd: Schlossberg (volcanic soil). Best: DR. HEGER, Michel, SCHWARZER ADLER, St Remigius, and co-op.

Adelmann, Weingut Graf Würt ★★→★★★ Estate based at the idyllic Schaubeck castle in WÜRTTEMBERG. The specialties are subtle red blends (notably Vignette), RIES (look for ERSTE LAGE Süßmund), and the rare Muskattrollinger.

Ahr ★★→★★★ 97 99 03 05 06 07 08 09 (10) South of Bonn. Minerally, elegant SPÄTBURGUNDER and FRÜHBURGUNDER, previously renowned for their lightness. Recently more ripeness on the valley's slate soils: now wines regularly exceed 14% – unfortunately. Best producers: Adeneuer, DEUTZERHOF, Kreuzberg, MEYER-NÄKEL, Nelles, STODDEN.

Aldinger, Weingut Gerhard Würt ★★★ One of WÜRTTEMBERG's leading estates: dense LEMBERGER and SPÄTBURGUNDER, complex Sauv Bl. Gd RIES, too.

Amtliche Prüfungsnummer (APNr) Official test number, on every label of quality wine. Used to discern AUSLESE lots a producer has made from the same v'yd.

Assmannshausen Rhg r ★→★★★ 93 96 97 98 99 01 02 03 04 05 07 08 09 (10) Craggy RHEINGAU village known for its cassis-scented, age-worthy SPÄTBURGUNDERS from slate soils. ERSTE LAGE v'yd: Höllenberg. Growers inc: KESSELER, Robert König, WEINGUT KRONE and the state domain.

Auslese Wines from selective harvest of super-ripe bunches, in many yrs affected by noble rot (*Edelfäule*) and correspondingly unctuous in flavour. Dry Auslesen are often too alcoholic and clumsy for me.

Ayl M-S-R (Saar) w ★→★★★ 90 93 95 96 97 99 01 02 03 04 05 07 08 09 All Ayl v'yds are known since 1971 by the name of its historically best site: Kupp. Such are German wine laws. Growers inc: BISCHÖFLICHE WEINGÜTER, *Lauer*.

Bacharach M Rh w (r) ★ →★★★ 96 97 01 02 03 04 05 07 08 09 Main wine town of MITTELRHEIN. Racy, austere RIES, some v. fine. Classified as ERSTE LAGE: Hahn, Posten, Wolfshöhle. Growers inc: BASTIAN, JOST, RATZENBERGER.

Baden 90 97 03 05 07 08 09 (10) Huge southwest area of scattered v'yds best known for the Pinots, and pockets of RIES, usually dry. Best areas: KAISERSTUHL, ORTENAU. Pinot N now more balanced, graceful than of yore.

Badische Bergstrasse Bad Small district of north BADEN, surrounding the city of Heidelberg. Gd RIES and SPÄTBURGUNDER. Best producer: Seeger.

Badischer Winzerkeller Bad Germany's (and Europe's) biggest co-op, produces almost a quarter of BADEN's wine: dependably unambitious, and in decline.

Bassermann-Jordan Pfz ★★★ 90 96 97 99 01 03 04 05 07 08 09 (10) MITTELHAARDT estate, under new ownership since 2003, with 49 ha of outstanding v'yds in DEIDESHEIM, FORST, RUPPERTSBERG, etc. Winemaker Ulrich Mell excels at producing majestic dry RIES and lavish sweet wines, too.

Bastian, Weingut Friedrich M Rh ★★ 6 ha BACHARACH estate. Racy, austere RIES with MOSEL-like delicacy, esp from the Posten v'yd (ERSTE LAGE).

Becker, Friedrich Pfz ★★★ Renowned estate in the municipality of SCHWEIGEN (southern PFALZ), 18 ha, specializing in refined, barrel-aged SPÄTBURGUNDER. Some of Becker's v'yds actually lie across the state border, in Alsace.

Becker, J B Rhg ★★ →★★★ The best estate at WALLUF specializing in old-fashioned, cask-aged (and long-lived) dry RIES and SPÄTBURGUNDER.

Beerenauslese (BA) Luscious sweet wine from exceptionally ripe, individually selected berries concentrated by noble rot. Rare, expensive.

Bercher Bad ★★★ KAISERSTUHL estate; 25 ha at Burkheim, consistently excellent GRAUBURGUNDER (try 09 Feuerberg GROSSES GEWÄCHS and give it 5 yrs of age), CHARD and SPÄTBURGUNDER.

Bergdolt, Weingut Pfz ★★★ South of Neustadt, this 24-ha estate produces v. fine WEISSBURGUNDER (from the Mandelberg v'yd), as well as gd RIES and SPÄTBURGUNDER.

German vintage notation

The vintage notes after entries in the German section are given
in a different form from those elsewhere in the book.
Two styles of vintage are indicated:
Bold type (eg. **99**) indicates classic, ripe vintages with a high
proportion of SPÄTLESEN and AUSLESEN; or, in the case of red wines,
gd phenolic ripeness and must weights.
Normal type (eg. 98) indicates a successful but not outstanding vintage.
German white wines, esp RIES, have high acidity and keep well, and
they display pure-fruit qualities because they are unoaked. Thus
they can be drunk young for their intense fruitiness, or kept for
a decade or two to develop more aromatic subtlety and finesse.
This means there is no one ideal moment to drink them –
which is why no vintages are specifically recommended for
drinking now.

Bernkastel M-M w ★→★★★★ 90 94 95 96 97 98 01 02 03 04 05 06 07 08 09
(10) The senior wine town of the MITTELMOSEL; the epitome of RIES. ERSTE LAGE:
Doctor (rare, and sometimes overpriced), Lay. Top growers: Kerpen, LOOSEN,
PAULY-BERGWEILER, PRÜM, Studert-Prüm, THANISCH (both estates), WEGELER.

Bernkastel (Bereich) M-M Avoid. Inc all the MITTELMOSEL. Wide area of deplorably
dim quality and superficial flowery character. Mostly MÜLLER-THURGAU.

Bischöfliche Weingüter M-S-R ★★ Famous though underperforming estate with
cellars at Trier, uniting cathedral's v'yds with those of three other charities,
the Friedrich-Wilhelm-Gymnasium, the Bischöfliches Priesterseminar and
the Bischöfliches Konvikt. Owns 130 ha of top v'yds, esp in SAAR and RUWER.
Management changes in 2007 and 2010 make it difficult to predict what
direction the estate will take. Let's hope upwards.

Bocksbeutel Inconvenient flask-shaped bottle used in FRANKEN and north BADEN.

Bodensee Bad Idyllic district of south BADEN, on Lake Constance. Dry wines are
best drunk young. RIES-like MÜLLER-THURGAU a specialty, and light but delicate
SPÄTBURGUNDER. Top village: Meersburg.

Boppard M Rh ★→★★★ 90 97 01 02 03 04 05 07 08 09 (10) Important wine town
of MITTELRHEIN with best sites all in amphitheatre of vines called Bopparder
Hamm (ERSTE LAGE). Growers: Toni Lorenz, Matthias Müller, August Perll,
WEINGART. Unbeatable value for money.

Brauneberg M-M w ★★★★ 88 89 90 93 94 95 96 97 98 99 01 02 03 04 05 06 07
08 09 (10) Top M-S-R village nr BERNKASTEL (304 ha): excellent full-flavoured RIES.
ERSTE LAGE v'yds Juffer, Juffer-Sonnenuhr. Growers: F HAAG, W HAAG, PAULINSHOF,
RICHTER, SCHLOSS LIESER, THANISCH.

Breuer, Weingut Georg Rhg ★★★→★★★★ Family estate in RÜDESHEIM (24 ha) and
RAUENTHAL (7.2 ha), giving superb dry RIES. V. fine SEKT and SPÄTBURGUNDER, too.
Pioneering winemaker Bernhard Breuer died in 2004; now his daughter
Theresa is in charge, and maintains high quality.

Buhl, Reichsrat von Pfz ★★★ Historic PFALZ estate, 60 ha, newly organic. Bought in
2005 by businessman Achim Niederberger, who also owns BASSERMANN-JORDAN
and DR. DEINHARD/VON WINNING. Modern style, fruit-driven RIES, mostly dry, from
v'yds in DEIDESHEIM, FORST, and RUPPERTSBERG.

Bürgerspital zum Heiligen Geist Frank ★★→★★★ Ancient charitable estate. 110
ha. Traditionally made whites (SILVANER and RIES) from outstanding v'yd sites in
and around WÜRZBURG. Monopoly Stein-Harfe comprises the best parcels in the
famous ERSTE LAGE v'yd Stein.

Germany's quality levels

The official range of qualities and styles in ascending order is:

1 Deutscher Tafelwein: sweetish light wine of no specified character. Will now disappear from the market.

2 Landwein: dryish Tafelwein with some regional style.

3 Qualitätswein: dry or sweetish wine with sugar added before fermentation to increase its strength, but tested for quality and with distinct local and grape character. Don't despair.

4 Kabinett: dry or dryish natural (unsugared) wine of distinct personality and distinguishing lightness. Can occasionally be sublime.

5 Spätlese: stronger, often sweeter than Kabinett. Full-bodied. Today many top SPÄTLESEN are TROCKEN or completely dry.

6 Auslese: sweeter, sometimes stronger than SPÄTLESE, often with honey-like flavours, intense and long-lived. Occasionally dry and weighty.

7 Beerenauslese (BA): v. sweet, sometimes strong, intense. Can be superb.

8 Eiswein: from naturally frozen grapes of BA or TBA quality: concentrated, sharpish and v. sweet. Some extreme, unharmonious.

9 Trockenbeerenauslese (TBA): intensely sweet and aromatic; alcohol slight. Extraordinary and everlasting.

Bürklin-Wolf, Dr. Pfz ★★★ →★★★★ Dynamic PFALZ family estate, known for its age-worthy RIES. 85 ha in FORST, DEIDESHEIM, RUPPERTSBERG and WACHENHEIM, inc many ERSTE LAGE sites. The full-bodied dry wines from these are truly individual. Now biodynamic.

Busch, Weingut Clemens M-S-R ★★ →★★★ Family-run biodynamic property, 10 ha. Since 1985, Busch works on the steep Pündericher Marienburg v'yd in lower MOSEL. His best RIES (dry and sweet) are labelled for different-coloured slate soils: Fahrlay, Falkenlay, Rothenpfad, Raffes.

Castell'sches Fürstlich Domänenamt Frank ★→★★★ Historic 65-ha princely estate in FRANKEN. Entry level in a rather popular style, but single-v'yd SILVANER, RIES, RIESLANER, dry and sweet, and the increasingly renowned SPÄTBURGUNDER are traditionally crafted. Superb monopoly v'yd *Casteller Schlossberg.*

Chardonnay Grown throughout Germany, 1,170 ha. Often neutral or overoaked; only best convince: BERCHER, BERGDOLT, HUBER, JOHNER, REBHOLZ, DR. WEHRHEIM, WITTMANN.

Christmann Pfz ★★★ 16-ha estate in Gimmeldingen, making rich, dry RIES and SPÄTBURGUNDER from ERSTE LAGE v'yds, notably Königsbacher Idig. Biodynamic farming. Steffen Christmann is president of the VDP.

Christoffel, J J M-M ★★ →★★★ Tiny domain in ÜRZIG, 4 ha. *Classic, elegant Ries.* Since 2001 leased to Robert Eymael of MÖNCHHOF.

Clüsserath, Ansgar M-S-R ★★ →★★★ 5-ha family estate led by young Eva Clüsserath-Wittmann. Remarkably age-worthy, dry RIES from TRITTENHEIMER Apotheke: delicate and mineral without being tart.

Clüsserath-Weiler, Weingut M-S-R ★★★ Helmut Clüsserath and his daughter Verena produce classic RIES from top TRITTENHEIMER Apotheke and the rare Fährfels v'yd, 6 ha. Steadily improving quality.

Crusius, Dr. Na ★★ →★★★ 18-ha family estate at TRAISEN, NAHE. Vivid and age-worthy RIES from Bastei and Rotenfels of Traisen and SCHLOSSBÖCKELHEIM.

Dautel, Weingut Ernst Würt ★★★ A reliable source of WÜRTTEMBERG's red specialties, esp LEMBERGER. 12 ha.

Deidesheim Pfz w (r) ★★ →★★★★ 90 96 97 01 02 04 05 07 08 09 (10) Largest top-quality village of the PFALZ (405 ha). Richly flavoured, lively wines.

ERSTE LAGE v'yds: Grainhübel, Hohenmorgen, Kalkofen, Kieselberg, Langenmorgen, Paradiesgarten. Top growers: BASSERMANN-JORDAN, Biffar, BUHL, BÜRKLIN-WOLF, CHRISTMANN, DEINHARD, MOSBACHER, VON WINNING.

Deinhard, Dr. Pfz ★★★ Fine 35-ha estate owned by Achim Niederberger (*see* BASSERMANN-JORDAN and BUHL). Since 2008 a brand of the newly established VON WINNING estate, but continuing to produce PFALZ RIES of classical style.

Deutzerhof, Weingut Ahr ★★→★★★ 10-ha estate producing concentrated barrique-aged SPÄTBURGUNDER. Fine quality, alarming prices.

Diel, Schlossgut Na ★★★→★★★★ Fashionable 22-ha estate; pioneered ageing GRAUBURGUNDER and WEISSBURGUNDER in barriques. Its traditional *v'yd-designated Ries* is often exquisite. Also serious SEKT.

Dönnhoff, Weingut Hermann Na ★★★★ 90 94 95 96 97 98 99 00 01 02 03 04 05 06 07 08 09 (10) 20-ha leading NAHE estate with magnificent RIES at all quality levels from NIEDERHAUSEN, Oberhausen, SCHLOSSBÖCKELHEIM. Dazzling EISWEIN.

Dornfelder Red grape making deep-coloured, usually rustic wines. Plantings have doubled since 2000 to an astonishing 8,100 ha.

Duijn, Jacob Bad ★★→★★★ Former sommelier/wine merchant, now BADEN wine-grower specializing in spicy, tannic SPÄTBURGUNDER from steeply sloping granite v'yds in the Bühler Valley, ORTENAU. 7 ha.

Durbach Bad w (r) ★★→★★★ 01 02 03 04 05 07 08 09 Village with 314 ha of v'yds, of which Plauelrain is ERSTE LAGE. Top growers: Graf Metternich, LAIBLE, H Männle, Schloss Staufenberg. KLINGELBERGER (RIES) is the outstanding variety.

Egon Müller zu Scharzhof M-S-R ★★★★ 83 85 88 89 90 93 94 95 96 97 98 99 01 02 03 04 05 06 07 08 09 (10) Top SAAR estate of 8 ha at WILTINGEN, the v'yds rising steeply behind the Müllers' manor house. Its rich and racy SCHARZHOFBERGER RIES in AUSLESEN vintages is among the world's greatest wines, sublime, honeyed, immortal; best are given gold capsules. *Kabinetts* seem feather-light but keep 5+ yrs. Gallais is a second 4-ha estate in WILTINGER Braune Kupp; gd quality, but the site is less exceptional.

Einzellage Individual v'yd site. Never to be confused with GROSSLAGE.

Eiswein Made from frozen grapes with the ice (ie. water content) discarded, producing v. concentrated wine in flavour, acidity and sugar – of BA ripeness or more. Alcohol content can be as low as 5.5%. V. expensive. Outstanding Eiswein vintages were 1998, 2002, 2004, and 2008.

Ellwanger, Weingut Würt ★★→★★★ Jürgen Ellwanger pioneered oak-aged red wines in WÜRTTEMBERG. Today aided by his sons, who continue to turn out sappy but structured LEMBERGER, SPÄTBURGUNDER and Zweigelt.

Emrich-Schönleber Na ★★★→★★★★ Monzingen. 16 ha, known for classical, precise, reliable RIES. Werner Schönleber has a knack for both dry and botrytized sweet.

Erden M-M ★★★ 88 89 90 93 95 96 97 98 99 01 02 03 04 05 06 07 08 09 (10) Village adjoining ÜRZIG: noble, full-flavoured, vigorous wine (more herbal and

---

New EU terminology

Germany's part in the new EU classification involves, firstly, abolishing the term *Tafelwein* in favour of plain *Wein*, and secondly, changing LANDWEIN to "ggA" – *geschützte geographische Angabe* or "Protected Geographical Indication". QUALITÄTSWEIN and QUALITÄTSWEIN MIT PRÄDIKAT will be replaced by "gU": *geschützte Ursprungsbezeichnung*, or Protected Designation of Origin. The existing terms – SPÄTLESE, AUSLESE and so on – will be tacked on to gU where appropriate; the rules for these styles won't change. The old designations will continue until the end of 2011, except for that of *Tafelwein*, which won't be used after December 2010.

mineral than the wines of nearby BERNKASTEL and WEHLEN but equally long-living). Classified as ERSTE LAGE: Prälat, Treppchen. Growers inc: J J CHRISTOFFEL, Erbes, LOOSEN, Lotz, Meulenhof, MÖNCHHOF, WEINS-PRÜM.

Erste Lage V'yd site of exceptional quality, classified according to criteria set up by the top wine-growers' association VERBAND DEUTSCHER PRÄDIKATSWEINGÜTER (VDP). On labels, *Erste Lage* sites are marked with a grape logo with a "1" next to it. A producer's best dry wine from an *Erste Lage* site is called GROSSES GEWÄCHS or ERSTES GEWÄCHS. Off-dry or sweet wines from *Erste Lage* v'yds display the logo, but are not called GROSSES or ERSTES GEWÄCHS.

Erstes Gewächs Translates as "first growth". Only RHEINGAU v'yds. *See* ERSTE LAGE.

Erzeugerabfüllung Bottled by producer. Being replaced by GUTSABFÜLLUNG, but only by estates. Co-ops will continue with *Erzeugerabfüllung*.

Escherndorf Frank w ★★→★★★ 97 01 02 03 04 05 06 07 08 09 (10) Important wine village, ERSTE LAGE steep slope: Lump. Best for SILVANER and RIES. Growers inc: Michael Fröhlich, JULIUSSPITAL, H SAUER, R SAUER, Egon Schäffer.

Feinherb Imprecisely defined traditional term for wines with around 10–20 g of sugar per litre. Favoured by some as a more flexible alternative to HALBTROCKEN. Used on label by, among others, Kerpen, VON KESSELSTATT, M MOLITOR.

Forst Pfz w ★★→★★★★ 90 96 97 01 02 03 04 05 07 08 09 (10) MITTELHAARDT village with 175 ha of Germany's best v'yds. Ripe, richly fragrant, full-bodied but subtle wines. ERSTE LAGE v'yds: Jesuitengarten, Kirchenstück, Freundstück, Pechstein, Ungeheuer. Top growers inc: Acham-Magin, BASSERMANN-JORDAN, BÜRKLIN-WOLF, DR. DEINHARD/VON WINNING, MOSBACHER, WOLF.

Franken (Franconia) Region of distinctive dry wines, esp *Silvaner*, mostly bottled in round-bellied flasks (BOCKSBEUTEL). The centre is WÜRZBURG. *Bereich* names: MAINDREIECK, MAINVIERECK, STEIGERWALD. Top producers inc: BÜRGERSPITAL, CASTELL'SCHES FÜRSTLICH DOMÄNENAMT, FÜRST, JULIUSSPITAL, LÖWENSTEIN, RUCK, H SAUER, STAATLICHER HOFKELLER, STÖRRLEIN, WIRSCHING.

Franzen, Weingut Reinhold M-S-R ★→★★ From Europe's steepest v'yd, Bremmer Calmont, the Franzen family makes reliable, sometimes exciting, dry RIES and EISWEIN. Owner Ulrich Franzen died 2010 in a terrible work accident.

Frühburgunder An ancient mutation of Pinot N, found mostly in the AHR but also in FRANKEN and WÜRTTEMBERG, where it is confusingly known as Clevner. Lower acidity and thus more approachable than Pinot N.

Fuder Traditional RIES cask with sizes from 500–1,500 litres depending on the region. Unlike a barrique, a *fuder* is used for many years. Traditionalists use the cask for fermentation, giving individuality to each *fuder's* wine.

Fürst Frank ★★★→★★★★ 18-ha estate in Bürgstadt making some of the best wines in FRANKEN, particularly Burgundian SPÄTBURGUNDER (arguably Germany's finest), full-flavoured RIES, and oak-aged WEISSBURGUNDER.

Gallais, Le M-S-R *See* EGON MÜLLER ZU SCHARZHOF.

Gewürztraminer (or Traminer) Highly aromatic grape, specialty of Alsace, also impressive in Germany, esp in PFALZ, BADEN, SACHSEN.

Graach M-M w ★★★→★★★★ 88 89 90 93 94 95 96 97 98 99 01 03 04 05 07 08 09 (10) Small village between BERNKASTEL and WEHLEN. ERSTE LAGE v'yds: Domprobst, Himmelreich, Josephshof. Top growers inc: Kees-Kieren, von KESSELSTATT, LOOSEN, M MOLITOR, J J PRÜM, S A PRÜM, SCHAEFER, SELBACH-OSTER, WEINS-PRÜM. All currently threatened by proposed *Autobahn*.

Grans-Fassian M-S-R ★★★ Fine MOSEL estate, 10 ha, known for steely, elegant RIES from v'yds in TRITTENHEIM, PIESPORT, LEIWEN and Drohn. EISWEIN a specialty.

Grauburgunder (or Grauer Burgunder) Both synonyms of RULÄNDER or Pinot Gr: grape giving soft, full-bodied wine. Best in BADEN (esp KAISERSTUHL) and south PFALZ. 4,480 ha planted.

> **Beware of Bereich and Grosslage**
> *Bereich* means district within an *Anbaugebiet* (region). *Bereich* on a
> label should be treated as a flashing red light. The wine is a blend
> from arbitrary sites within that district. Do not buy. The same holds
> for wines with a GROSSLAGE name, though these are more difficult to
> identify. Who could guess if "Forster Mariengarten" is an EINZELLAGE
> or a GROSSLAGE?

Grosser Ring M-S-R Group of top (VDP) MOSEL-SAAR-RUWER estates, whose annual
Sept auction at Trier sometimes sets world-record prices.

Grosses Gewächs Translates as "great/top growth". This is the top dry wine from
a VDP-classified ERSTE LAGE v'yd, except in the RHEINGAU, which has its own ERSTES
GEWÄCHS classification.

Grosslage A collection of secondary v'yds with supposedly similar character – but
no indication of quality.

Gunderloch Rhh ★★★ →★★★★ 90 96 97 99 01 02 03 04 05 07 08 09 (10) At this
NACKENHEIM estate Fritz Hasselbach makes some of the finest RIES on the entire
Rhine, esp at AUSLESE level and above. Also owns Balbach estate in NIERSTEIN.

Gutedel Bad German name for the ancient Chasselas grape, grown in south BADEN
(MARKGRÄFLERLAND). Fresh, but neutral white wines.

Gutsabfüllung Estate-bottled. Term for genuinely estate-bottled wines.

Haag, Weingut Fritz M-S-R ★★★★ 88 89 90 94 95 96 97 98 99 01 02 03 04 05
06 07 08 09 (10) BRAUNEBERG's top estate, run for decades by MITTELMOSEL veteran
Wilhelm Haag and now by his son Oliver. MOSEL RIES of crystalline purity for long
ageing. Haag's other son, Thomas, runs SCHLOSS LIESER estate.

Haag, Weingut Willi M-S-R ★★ 6 ha BRAUNEBERG estate. Old-style RIES, AUSLESEN.

Haart, Reinhold M-S-R ★★★ →★★★★ Best estate in PIESPORT and Wintrich. Refined,
aromatic wines capable of long ageing. Minerally and *racy copybook Mosel Ries*.

Haidle, Karl Würt ★★ →★★★★ 19-ha family estate in Stetten, WÜRTTEMBERG, specializing
in graceful RIES from high-altitude Pulvermächer v'yd (ERSTE LAGE).

Halbtrocken Medium-dry (literally semi-dry), with 9–18 g of unfermented sugar
per litre. Popular category, often better balanced than TROCKEN. *See* FEINHERB.

Hattenheim Rhg w ★★ →★★★★ 90 97 01 02 03 04 05 07 08 09 (10) Famous 202-
ha wine town, though not all producers achieve potential. ERSTE LAGE v'yds are
Mannberg, Nussbrunnen, Pfaffenberg, Schützenhaus, Wisselbrunnen and,
most famously, STEINBERG. Estates inc: Barth, Knyphausen, Lang, LANGWERTH VON
SIMMERN, RESS, SCHLOSS SCHÖNBORN, STAATSWEINGUT.

Heger, Dr. Bad ★★★ →★★★★ 97 99 03 05 07 08 09 (10) 20-ha estate of KAISERSTUHL
in BADEN producing minerally whites from v. steep slopes in ACHKARREN and
IHRINGEN (esp GRAUBURGUNDER, WEISSBURGUNDER, RIES, and SILVANER). Recently more
SPÄTBURGUNDER, with a refined parcel selection "Häusleboden". Wines from
rented v'yds under Weinhaus Joachim Heger label.

Hessische Bergstrasse w (r) ★★ →★★★ 90 93 95 96 97 98 99 01 02 03 04 05
07 (08) Small wine region (436 ha), north of Heidelberg. Pleasant RIES from
STAATSWEINGÜTER, Simon-Bürkle and Stadt Bensheim.

Heyl zu Herrnsheim Rhh ★★ Leading NIERSTEIN estate, bought by Detlev Meyer
(2006). 12 ha. Now part of ST-ANTONY estate. Monopoly site Brudersberg GROSSES
GEWÄCHS can be excellent, most entry-level wines disappointing.

Heymann-Löwenstein M-S-R ★★★ Family-run estate in Lower MOSEL nr Koblenz,
16 ha, specializing in spontaneously fermented, terroir-minded RIES, dry and
sweet, from picturesque terraces in the steep slope Uhlen and Röttgen v'yds.
Löwenstein has inspired other WINNINGEN growers to adopt his style.

Hochheim Rhg w ★★ →★★★★ 90 93 95 96 97 98 01 03 04 05 07 08 09 (10) 242-ha wine town 24-km east of main RHEINGAU area, once thought of as best on Rhine. Rich and distinctly earthy RIES from ERSTE LAGE v'yds: Domdechaney, Hölle, Kirchenstück. Growers inc: Himmel, Königin-Victoriaberg, KÜNSTLER, SCHLOSS SCHÖNBORN, STAATSWEINGUT, Werner.

Hock Traditional English term for Rhine wine, derived from HOCHHEIM.

Hoensbroech, Weingut Reichsgraf zu Bad ★★ Top KRAICHGAU estate. Look for dry WEISSBURGUNDER from Michelfelder Himmelberg, a v'yd on calcareous loess soils.

Hohenlohe-Oehringen, Weingut Fürst zu Würt ★★ Noble 17-ha estate in Oehringen, WÜRTTEMBERG. Bone-dry RIES and structured LEMBERGER.

Hövel, Weingut von M-S-R ★★ →★★★ Fine SAAR estate at Oberemmel (Hütte is 4.8-ha monopoly) and in SCHARZHOFBERG. In some vintages erractic quality.

Huber, Bernhard Bad ★★★ Leading estate of Breisgau area of BADEN; powerful long-lived SPÄTBURGUNDER, MUSKATELLER and burgundian-style WEISSBURGUNDER, CHARD.

Ihringen Bad r w ★ →★★★ 97 99 01 03 04 05 07 08 09 (10) Justly celebrated village of the KAISERSTUHL, BADEN. Historically a SILVANER stronghold, now better known for SPÄTBURGUNDER and GRAUBURGUNDER. The superb Winklerberg v'yd is steep terraces on volcanic soils. Stupidly, the law permits wines from a loess plateau to be sold under the same name. Top growers: DR. HEGER, Konstanzer, Pix, Stigler.

Iphofen Frank w ★★ →★★★ 90 97 01 03 04 05 06 07 08 09 (10) Village in FRANKEN's STEIGERWALD area, renowned for RIES, SILVANER, RIESLANER. First Class v'yds: Julius-Echter-Berg, Kronsberg. Growers: JULIUSSPITAL, RUCK, WIRSCHING, Zehntkeller.

Jahrgang Year – as in "vintage".

Johannisberg Rhg w ★★ →★★★★ 89 90 93 95 96 97 99 01 04 05 07 08 09 (10) A classic RHEINGAU village with superlative long-lived RIES. ERSTE LAGE v'yds: Hölle, Klaus, SCHLOSS JOHANNISBERG. GROSSLAGE (avoid!): Erntebringer. Top growers: JOHANNISHOF, SCHLOSS JOHANNISBERG, PRINZ VON HESSEN.

Johannishof Rhg ★★ →★★★ JOHANNISBERG family estate, 20 ha. Johannes Eser produces intense RIES in a modern style, rather fruit-driven than minerally.

Johner, Karl-Heinz Bad ★★ →★★★ 17-ha estate at Bischoffingen; specializing in New World-style SPÄTBURGUNDER and oak-aged WEISSBURGUNDER, CHARD, GRAUBURGUNDER.

Josephshöfer M-S-R ERSTE LAGE v'yd at GRAACH, the sole property of KESSELSTATT. Harmonious, berry-flavoured RIES, both dry and sweet. Like its neighbours, threatened by planned Autobahn.

Jost, Toni M Rh ★★★ Leading estate of the MITTELRHEIN: 14 ha, mainly RIES, in BACHARACH (sharply mineral wines). Since 2009, the excellent ERSTE LAGE Hahn is a monopoly of Jost's. He also runs a second estate at WALLUF in the RHEINGAU.

Juliusspital Frank ★★★ Ancient WÜRZBURG religious charity with 170 ha of top FRANKEN v'yds. Consistently gd quality. Look for its *dry Silvaners* (they age well) and RIES and its top white blend called BT.

Kabinett See "Germany's quality levels" box, p. 146.

Kaiserstuhl Bad Outstanding BADEN district, with notably warm climate and volcanic soil. Villages inc: ACHKARREN, Burkheim, IHRINGEN, Jechtingen, Oberrotweil. Renowned for Pinots (r w) and some surprising RIES and Muscat.

Kanzem M-S-R (Saar) w ★★★ 93 94 95 96 97 99 01 02 03 04 05 06 07 08 09 (10) Small neighbour of WILTINGEN. ERSTE LAGE v'yd: Altenberg. Growers inc: BISCHÖFLICHE WEINGÜTER, OTHEGRAVEN, Vereinigte Hospitien.

Karlsmühle M-S-R ★★★ Small estate with two Lorenzhöfer monopoly sites making classic RUWER RIES. Consistently excellent quality.

Karthäuserhof M-S-R ★★★★ 90 93 95 97 99 01 03 04 05 07 08 09 (10) Outstanding RUWER estate of 19 ha at Eitelsbach with monopoly v'yd Karthäuserhofberg. Easily recognized by bottles with only a neck label. Admired for both polished TROCKEN wines and magnificent AUSLESEN.

Kasel M-S-R (Ruwer) w ★★ →★★★ 90 99 01 03 05 07 08 09 (10) Stunning flowery and well-ageing RIES. ERSTE LAGE v'yds: Kehrnagel, Nies'chen. Top growers: Beulwitz, BISCHÖFLICHE WEINGÜTER, KARLSMÜHLE, KESSELSTATT.

Keller, Weingut Rhh ★★ →★★★★ Deep in unfashionable southern RHEINHESSEN, the Kellers show what can be achieved with scrupulous site selection. Superlative, crystalline GROSSES GEWÄCHS RIES from Dalsheimer Hubacker and expensive RIES blend from different v'yds called G-Max. Astonishing TBA and SPÄTBURGUNDER.

Kesseler, Weingut August Rhg ★★★ 21-ha estate making fine SPÄTBURGUNDER reds in ASSMANNSHAUSEN and RÜDESHEIM. Also v.gd classic-style RIES.

Kesselstatt, von M-S-R ★★★ Largest private MOSEL estate, 650 yrs old. Run for two decades by the quality-obsessed Annegret Reh-Gartner. Some 38 ha in MOSEL-SAAR-RUWER of consistently high quality, eg. JOSEPHSHÖFER, PIESPORTER Goldtröpfchen, KASELER Nies'chen and SCHARZHOFBERGER. In 2009: delicious, inexpensive village-level wines – dry WILTINGER RIES QUALITÄTSWEIN is unbeatable value for money.

Kiedrich Rhg w ★★ →★★★★ RHEINGAU village linked inseparably to the WEIL estate. Other growers (eg. Hessen, Knyphausen) own only small plots here.

Klingelberger Bad ORTENAU (BADEN) term for RIES, esp at DURBACH.

Kloster Eberbach Rhg Glorious 12th-century Cistercian abbey in HATTENHEIM, famous for its appearance in the film *Name of the Rose*. Now the label of the STAATSWEINGÜTER with a string of great v'yds in ASSMANNSHAUSEN, RÜDESHEIM, RAUENTHAL, etc. Coasting for years, now up for it with a brand-new winery.

Knebel, Weingut M-S-R ★★★ WINNINGEN is the top wine village of the lower MOSEL and Knebel shows how its sites can produce remarkable RIES in all styles.

Knipser, Weingut Pfz ★★★ →★★★★ Leading family estate in PFALZ, and one of the most serious and reliable in all Germany, 40 ha. Brothers Werner and Volker specialize in barrique-aged SPÄTBURGUNDER and other reds such as St-Laurent (*see* Austria), Syrah and Cuvée X (a Bordeaux blend). Dry RIES can be exceptional.

Koehler-Ruprecht Pfz ★★ →★★★★ 97 99 01 02 03 05 07 08 09 Outstanding Kallstadt grower. Bernd Philippi's winemaking is entirely traditional, delivering v. long-lived, dry RIES from Kallstadter Saumagen. Outstanding SPÄTBURGUNDER and gd barrique-aged Pinot varieties under the Philippi label.

Kraichgau Bad Small district southeast of Heidelberg. Top growers: Burg Ravensburg, HOENSBROECH, Hummel.

Krone, Weingut Rhg ★★ →★★★ 4-ha estate in ASSMANNSHAUSEN, with some of the best and oldest v'yds in the ERSTE LAGE Höllenberg. Famous for richly perfumed, full-bodied and age-able SPÄTBURGUNDER. Now run by WEGELER, and considerable investments are underway.

Kruger-Rumpf, Weingut Na ★★ →★★★ Most important estate of Münster, NAHE, with charming, but not superficial RIES.

Kuhn, Philipp Pfz ★★★ Talented and reliable producer in Laumersheim. Dry RIES are rich and harmonious, even at QBA level. Barrel-aged SPÄTBURGUNDER combine succulence, power and complexity.

Kühn, Weingut Peter Jakob Rhg ★★★ Excellent estate in OESTRICH. Kühn's obsessive v'yd management (now biodynamic) and his individualistic methods in the cellar (ie. an almost red wine-like vinification for the whites) bring about non-conformist but exciting RIES wines full of character.

Künstler, Franz Rhg ★★★ 25-ha estate in HOCHHEIM run by the uncompromising Gunter Künstler. Produces superb dry RIES, esp from ERSTE LAGE v'yds Hölle and Kirchenstück; also excellent AUSLESE.

Laible, Weingut Andreas Bad ★★★ 7-ha DURBACH estate. Limpid, often crystalline dry RIES from Plauelrain v'yd as well as SCHEUREBE and GEWÜRZ. Andreas Sr now joined by son Andreas Jr. Younger brother Alexander founded an estate of his own – with wines that deserve to be followed.

> **Result!**
> Germany has an ambitious football team of top growers that
> regularly plays teams of foreign producers, or chefs, or politicians.
> Yes, really. The usual formation of the so-called "Wein-Elf" is: the
> defensive backfield, Michael Gutzler of RHEINHESSEN, known for refined
> SPÄTBURGUNDER and brilliant tackling; Hansjörg REBHOLZ, with bone-dry
> positional play; Geisenheim-based wine merchant Nedjelko Mrcela.
> The list of midfielders is particularly impressive: Gunter KÜNSTLER and
> the SPREITZER brothers form an unsuperable RHEINGAU phalanx, while
> Philipp WITTMANN and Armin DIEL stay on the wings. The strikers:
> Tim Fröhlich, of the SCHÄFER-FRÖHLICH estate, a dynamic talent called
> "the turbo"; IHRINGEN steep-slope grower Andreas Stigler, a player of
> demoralizing endurance, and veteran wine-writer Rudi Knoll. Guess
> what will be poured after the match?

Landwein *See* "Germany's quality levels" box, p. 146.

Langwerth von Simmern, Weingut Rhg ★★→★★★ Famous Eltville family estate,
advocating traditional winemaking, 30 ha. Top v'yds: Baiken, Mannberg
(monopoly), MARCOBRUNN. Since Georg Freiherr Langwerth von Simmern took
over in 1996, back on form, and still improving. Stunning 2009 Marcobrunn
ERSTES GEWÄCHS – try to get hold of it!

Lauer, Weingut Peter M-S-R ★★→★★★ The SAAR village of AYL lacked conscientious
growers, until in the early 2000s Florian Lauer began exploring its subtleties
with a range of v.gd parcel selections.

Leitz, J Rhg ★★★ Fine RÜDESHEIM family estate for rich but elegant dry and sweet RIES,
36 ha. Since 1999, Johannes Leitz has gone from strength to strength.

Leiwen M-M w ★★→★★★ 93 97 98 99 01 02 03 04 05 07 08 09 (10) ERSTE LAGE:
Laurentiuslay. Village neighbouring TRITTENHEIM. GRANS-FASSIAN, CARL LOEWEN,
Rosch, SANKT URBANS-HOF have put these once overlooked v'yds firmly on the map.

Lemberger Red grape variety imported to Germany and Austria in the 18th century
from Hungary, where it is known as Kékfrankos. Deep-coloured, moderately
tannic wines; a specialty from WÜRTTEMBERG.

Liebfrauenstift-Kirchenstück Rhh A walled-in 13.5-ha v'yd in Worms producing
flowery RIES renowned for its harmony. Producers: Gutzler, Schembs. Not to be
confused with Liebfraumilch, which is a cheap and tasteless imitation.

Lieser M-M w ★★ 97 01 02 03 04 05 07 08 09 (10) Once-neglected v'yds between
BERNKASTEL and BRAUNEBERG. Best v'yd: Niederberg-Helden. Top: SCHLOSS LIESER.

Loewen, Carl M-S-R ★★→★★★ Enterprising grower of LEIWEN on MOSEL making
ravishing AUSLESE from town's classified ERSTE LAGE Laurentiuslay site, and from
Thörnicher Ritsch, a v'yd Loewen rescued from obscurity.

Loosen, Weingut Dr. M-M ★★→★★★★ 93 95 96 97 01 02 03 04 05 07 08 09 (10)
MITTELMOSEL at its very best: 18-ha estate producing complex and sublime RIES
from old vines in BERNKASTEL, ERDEN, GRAACH, ÜRZIG, WEHLEN. Reliable Dr. L Ries,
from bought-in grapes. Restless Ernie Loosen also leases WOLF in the PFALZ since
1996. Joint-venture RIES from Washington State with Chateau Ste Michelle, and,
recently, a new Pinot N project in Oregon.

Lorch Rhg w (r) ★→★★★ 90 97 99 01 02 03 04 05 07 08 09 Village in the
extreme west of the RHEINGAU, vis-à-vis the MITTELRHEIN capital BACHARACH. Now
re-discovered by dynamic producers. Minerally, austere RIES and SPÄTBURGUNDER.
Best growers: Fricke, Johanninger, von Kanitz, KESSELER, Ottes.

Löwenstein, Fürst Frank ★★★ Top 30-ha estate. Tangy, savoury SILVANER and mineral
RIES from historic Homburger Kallmuth, v. dramatic slope with 12 km of stone

walls in the v'yd. Also owns a 22-ha RHEINGAU estate in Hallgarten. In 2010 Prince Carl Friedrich Löwenstein died in a car crash; his widow has taken over.

Lützkendorf, Weingut Saale-Unstrut ★→★★ Leading SAALE-UNSTRUT estate, 9 ha. Best are usually the elegant, bone-dry SILVANER and WEISSBURGUNDER.

Maindreieck Frank District name for central FRANKEN, inc WÜRZBURG.

Mainviereck Frank District name for western FRANKEN. Best-known are the SPÄTBURGUNDER v'yds of Bürgstadt and Klingenberg.

Marcobrunn Rhg Historic RHEINGAU v'yd in Erbach; potentially one of Germany's v. best. Contemporary wines scarcely match this v'yd's past fame.

Markgräflerland District south of Freiburg, BADEN. Typical GUTEDEL wine can be refreshing when drunk v. young.

Maximin Grünhaus M-S-R (Ruwer) w ★★★★ 88 89 90 93 95 96 97 98 99 01 03 05 07 08 09 (10) Supreme RUWER estate of 31 ha at Mertesdorf. Owner Dr. Carl von Schubert is now joined by his daughter Anna Helene. Wines, dry and sweet, continue to be miracles of delicacy, subtlety and longevity. And there is more to come: Recently, 1 ha of PINOT N was planted.

Meyer-Näkel, Weingut Ahr ★★★→★★★★ 15 ha. Fine SPÄTBURGUNDERS in Dernau, Walporzheim and Bad Neuenahr exemplify modern, oak-aged (but nevertheless minerally) AHR valley reds.

Mittelhaardt The north-central and best part of the PFALZ, inc DEIDESHEIM, FORST, RUPPERTSBERG, WACHENHEIM, largely planted with RIES.

Mittelmosel The central and best part of the MOSEL, inc BERNKASTEL, PIESPORT, WEHLEN, etc. Its top sites are (or should be) entirely RIES.

Mittelrhein Northern, dramatically scenic Rhine area popular with tourists. BACHARACH and BOPPARD are the most important villages of this 465-ha region. Delicate yet steely RIES, underrated and underpriced. Many gd sites lie fallow.

Molitor, Markus M-M ★★★ With 38 ha of outstanding v'yds throughout the MOSEL and SAAR, Molitor has, since 1995, become a major player in the region. Magisterial sweet RIES, and acclaimed (if earthy) SPÄTBURGUNDER.

Mönchhof, Weingut M-M ★★ From his manor house hotel in ÜRZIG, Robert Eymael makes fruity, stylish RIES from ÜRZIG and ERDEN. Erdener Prälat usually the best wine. Also leases J J CHRISTOFFEL estate.

Mosbacher, Weingut Pfz ★★★ Fine 18-ha estate for some of best GROSSES GEWÄCHS RIES of FORST. Wines are traditionally aged in big oak casks.

Mosel-Saar-Ruwer 9,030-ha region between Trier and Koblenz; inc MITTELMOSEL, RUWER and SAAR. 60% RIES. From 2007 wines from the three regions can be labelled simply as Mosel.

Moselland, Winzergenossenschaft M-S-R Huge co-op at BERNKASTEL, inc Saar-Winzerverein at WILTINGEN, and, since 2000, a major NAHE co-op, too. Its 3,290 members, with a collective 2,400 ha, produce 25% of MOSEL-SAAR-RUWER wines (inc classic-method SEKT). Little is above-average.

Müller-Catoir, Weingut Pfz ★★→★★★ 90 93 96 97 98 99 01 05 08 09 (10) Since the 1970s, this outstanding Neustadt estate has bucked conventional wisdom using non-interventionist winemaking. The footsteps of retired director Hans Günter Schwarz are big: new team is struggling to catch up with previous fame.

Müller-Thurgau Fruity, early ripening, usually low-acid grape; most common in PFALZ, RHEINHESSEN, NAHE, BADEN and FRANKEN; was 21% of German v'yds in 1998, but 14% today. Easy-to-drink wines, nothing more.

Muskateller Ancient aromatic white grape with crisp acidity. A rarity in the PFALZ, BADEN and WÜRTTEMBERG, where it is mostly made dry.

Nackenheim Rhh w ★→★★★★ 90 97 01 03 04 05 06 07 08 09 (10) NIERSTEIN neighbour also with top Rhine terroir (red shale); similar best wines (esp ERSTE LAGE Rothenberg). Top growers: GUNDERLOCH, Kühling-Gillot.

Nahe Tributary of the Rhine and a high-quality wine region with 4,155 ha. Balanced, fresh, clean (and often inexpensive) RIES, at its best with MOSEL-like minerality and PFALZ-like fruit. EISWEIN a growing specialty.

Neckar River with many of WÜRTTEMBERG's finest v'yds, mainly between Stuttgart and Heilbronn.

Neipperg, Graf von Würt ★★→★★★ Noble estate in Schwaigern: elegant dry RIES and robust LEMBERGER. MUSKATELLER up to BA quality a specialty. A scion of the family, Count Stephan von Neipperg, makes wine at Château Canon la Gaffelière in St-Emilion (Bordeaux) and elsewhere.

Niederhausen Na w ★★→★★★★ 90 97 98 99 01 02 03 04 05 07 08 09 (10) Neighbour of SCHLOSSBÖCKELHEIM. Graceful, powerful RIES. ERSTE LAGE v'yds: Hermannsberg, Hermannshöhle. Growers: CRUSIUS, DÖNNHOFF, Gutsverwaltung Niederhausen-Schlossböckelheim, Mathern.

Nierstein Rhh w ★→★★★★★ 90 97 01 03 04 05 07 08 09 (10) 526 ha. Famous but treacherous village name. Beware GROSSLAGE Gutes Domtal: a supermarket deception. Superb ERSTE LAGE v'yds: Brudersberg, Hipping, Oelberg, Orbel, Pettenthal. Ripe, aromatic, rich wines, dry and sweet. Try Gehring, Guntrum, HEYL ZU HERRNSHEIM, Kühling-Gillot, Manz, ST-ANTONY, Strub.

Obermosel (Bereich) M-S-R District name for the upper MOSEL above Trier. Wines from the Elbling grape, generally uninspiring unless v. young.

Ockfen M-S-R (Saar) w ★★→★★★ 90 93 95 96 97 01 02 03 04 05 07 08 09 (10) Village that brings about sturdy, intense SAAR RIES from ERSTE LAGE v'yd Bockstein. Growers: Dr. Fischer, Weinhof Herrenberg, OTHEGRAVEN, SANKT URBANS-HOF, WAGNER, ZILLIKEN.

Oechsle Scale for sugar content of grape juice.

Oestrich Rhg w ★★→★★★ 90 97 01 02 03 04 05 07 08 09 (10) Big village; variable, but some splendid RIES. ERSTE LAGE v'yds: Doosberg, Lenchen. Top growers: August Eser, PETER JAKOB KÜHN, Querbach, SPREITZER, WEGELER.

Oppenheim Rhh w ★→★★★ 90 97 01 03 04 05 07 08 09 (10) Town south of NIERSTEIN; spectacular 13th-century church. ERSTE LAGE Kreuz and Sackträger. Growers inc: Heyden, Kühling-Gillot, Manz. The younger generation is starting to realize the full potential of these sites.

Ortenau Bad w (r) District around and south of Baden-Baden. Gd KLINGELBERGER (RIES) and SPÄTBURGUNDER, mainly from granite soils. Top villages: DURBACH, Neuweier, Waldulm.

Othegraven, Weingut von M-S-R ★★→★★★ In the past decade Dr. Heidi Kegel has restored the fame of this historic KANZEM, SAAR estate with its superb ERSTE LAGE v'yd Altenberg. In 2010 she handed the property over to German TV star Günther Jauch, who is a member of the von Othegraven family. Operationally, things seem to remain unchanged.

Palatinate English for PFALZ.

Paulinshof, Weingut M-M ★★ 8-ha estate, once monastic, in Kesten and BRAUNEBERG. Unusually for the MITTELMOSEL, the Jüngling family specializes in TROCKEN and HALBTROCKEN wines, as well as fine AUSLESEN.

Pauly-Bergweiler, Dr. M-M ★★→★★★ Fine BERNKASTEL estate. V'yds there (best: alte Badstube am Doctorberg) and in most other villages of the MITTELMOSEL, 18 ha.

The renaissance of big casks

New oak has never really been fashionable for German RIES, luckily, though vanilla did become popular in Pinots of all colours. Now growers are turning back to big (and old) casks, both for fermentation and for ageing. They underline the fruit, but don't cover it.

Formerly renowned second label, Peter Nicolay, has disappeared from both domestic and some export markets (eg. UK).

Pfalz Usually balmy 23,500-ha v'yd region south of RHEINHESSEN. The MITTELHAARDT area is the source of full-bodied, often dry RIES. The more southerly SÜDLICHE WEINSTRASSE is better suited to the Pinot varieties (r w). Biggest RIES area after MOSEL-SAAR-RUWER.

Piesport M-M w ★→★★★★ 90 93 94 96 **97** 99 01 02 03 04 05 07 08 09 (10) Tiny village with famous vine amphitheatre: at best glorious, rich, aromatic RIES. Great First Class v'yds: Goldtröpfchen, Domherr. Treppchen far inferior. GROSSLAGE: Michelsberg (mainly MÜLLER-THURGAU; avoid). Esp gd are GRANS-FASSIAN, Joh Haart, R HAART, Kurt Hain, KESSELSTATT, SANKT URBANS-HOF.

Portugieser 2nd-rate red-wine grape, mostly grown in RHEINHESSEN and PFALZ, now often used for WEISSHERBST. 4,350 ha in production.

Prädikat Special attributes or qualities. *See* QMP.

Prinz von Hessen Rhg ★★★→★★★★ Glorious wines of vibrancy and precision from this historic Johannisberg estate.

Prüm, J J M-S-R ★★★★ 71 76 83 88 89 90 94 95 96 **97** 99 01 02 03 04 05 06 07 08 09 (10) Legendary 22-ha WEHLEN estate with v'yds there, in GRAACH and BERNKASTEL. Delicate but long-lived wines with astonishing finesse and distinctive character. Long lees ageing makes the wines hard to taste when young, but they can age up to 30 yrs. Dr. Manfred Prüm now joined by daughter Katharina.

Prüm, S A M-S-R ★★→★★★ 90 97 01 02 03 04 05 07 08 09 If WEHLEN neighbour J J PRÜM is resolutely traditional, Raimond Prüm works in a more popular style. Sound, if sometimes inconsistent, wines from WEHLEN and GRAACH.

Qualitätswein bestimmter Anbaugebiete (QbA) Middle quality of German wine, with sugar added before fermentation (cf. French *chaptalization*), but controlled as to areas, grapes, etc. Its new name: gU (*see* box, p. 147) is little improvement.

Qualitätswein mit Prädikat (QmP) Top category, for all wines ripe enough not to need sugaring (KABINETT to TBA).

Randersacker Frank w ★★→★★★ 97 01 02 03 04 05 07 08 09 (10) Leading village south of WÜRZBURG for distinctive dry wine, esp SILVANER. ERSTE LAGE v'yds: Pfülben, Sonnenstuhl, Teufelskeller. Top growers inc: BÜRGERSPITAL, JULIUSSPITAL, STAATLICHER HOFKELLER, SCHMITT'S KINDER, STÖRRLEIN, Trockene Schmitts.

Ratzenberger M Rh ★★ Estate making racy dry and off-dry RIES in BACHARACH; best from ERSTE LAGE v'yds: Posten and Steeger St-Jost. Gd SEKT, too.

Rauenthal Rhg w ★★→★★★★ 97 98 99 01 02 03 04 05 07 08 09 (10) Supreme village on inland slopes: spicy, complex RIES. ERSTE LAGE v'yds: Baiken, Gehrn, Nonnenberg, Rothenberg, Wülfen. Top growers: BREUER, KLOSTER EBERBACH, LANGWERTH VON SIMMERN.

Rebholz Pfz ★★★→★★★★ Top SÜDLICHE WEINSTRASSE estate for decades, 19 ha, known for its bone-dry and long-lived wines (MUSKATELLER, GEWÜRZ, burgundian-style CHARD and SPÄTBURGUNDER). Outstanding RIES GROSSES GEWÄCHS from the Kastanienbusch v'yd (red shale).

Regent New dark-red grape suited for organic farming and enjoying considerable success in southern wine regions. 2,180 ha are now planted. Plum-flavoured, tannic wines of little complexity.

Ress, Balthasar Rhg ★★ 42-ha estate based in HATTENHEIM. Gd estate RIES, and basic Von Unserm label (r w) can offer gd value.

Restsüsse Unfermented grape sugar remaining in (or in cheap wines added to) wine to give it sweetness. Ranges from 3 g/l in a TROCKEN wine to 300 in a TBA.

Rheingau Best v'yd region of Rhine, mainly west of Wiesbaden. 3,125 ha. Classic, substantial RIES, yet on the whole recently eclipsed by brilliance elsewhere and hampered by some underperforming, if grand, estates. Controversially, one-third of the region is classified since 2000 as ERSTES GEWÄCHS, subject to regulations that differ from those created by the VDP for GROSSES GEWÄCHS.

Rheinhessen Germany's largest region, 26,440 ha between Mainz and Worms. Much dross, but inc top RIES from NACKENHEIM, NIERSTEIN, OPPENHEIM, etc. Remarkable spurt in quality in formerly unknown areas, from growers such as KELLER and WITTMANN in the south and WAGNER-STEMPEL in the west.

Richter, Weingut Max Ferd M-M ★★ ·★★★ Reliable MITTELMOSEL estate, at Mülheim. Esp gd RIES KABINETT and SPÄTLESEN, full and aromatic. Wines from purchased grapes carry a slightly different label.

Rieslaner Cross between SILVANER and RIES; known for low yields and difficult ripening, now a rarity (less than 50 ha). Makes fine AUSLESEN in FRANKEN and PFALZ.

Riesling The best German grape: fragrant, fruity, racy, long-lived. Only CHARD can compete as the world's best white grape.

Ruck, Weingut Johann Frank ★★→★★★ Reliable and spicy SILVANER and RIES from IPHOFEN in FRANKEN'S STEIGERWALD district. Traditional in style.

Rüdesheim Rhg w ★★ ·★★★★ 90 93 96 97 98 01 02 03 04 05 07 08 09 (10) Rhine resort with outstanding ERSTE LAGE v'yds; the three best (Roseneck, Rottland and Schlossberg) are called Rüdesheimer Berg. Full-bodied wines, fine-flavoured, often remarkable in off yrs. Best growers: BREUER, JOHANNISHOF, KESSELER, LEITZ, RESS, SCHLOSS SCHÖNBORN, STAATSWEINGÜTER.

Ruländer (Pinot Gr) Now more commonly known as GRAUBURGUNDER.

Ruppertsberg Pfz w ★★→★★★ 90 97 01 02 03 04 05 07 08 09 Southern village of MITTELHAARDT. Classic PFALZ RIES from ERSTE LAGE sites Gaisböhl, Reiterpfad, Spiess. Growers: BASSERMANN-JORDAN, Biffar, BUHL, BÜRKLIN-WOLF, CHRISTMANN, DR. DEINHARD.

Ruwer M-S-R 90 97 01 02 03 04 05 07 08 09 (10) Tributary of MOSEL nr Trier. V. fine, delicate but highly aromatic and remarkably long-lived RIES both sweet and dry. A string of warm summers has helped ripeness. Best growers: Beulwitz, KARLSMÜHLE, KARTHÄUSERHOF, KESSELSTATT, MAXIMIN GRÜNHAUS.

Saale-Unstrut 03 05 07 08 09 Climatically challenging region of 685 ha around confluence of these two rivers at Naumburg. The terraced v'yds of WEISSBURGUNDER, SILVANER, GEWÜRZ, RIES and SPÄTBURGUNDER have Cistercian origins. Quality leaders: Böhme, Born, Gussek, Kloster Pforta, LÜTZKENDORF, Pawis.

Saar M-S-R 90 93 94 95 96 97 98 99 01 02 03 04 05 07 08 09 (10) Hill-lined tributary of the MOSEL south of RUWER. Climate differs considerably from MITTELMOSEL: v'yds are 50–100 m higher in altitude. The most brilliant, austere, steely RIES of all. Villages inc: AYL, KANZEM, OCKFEN, SAARBURG, Serrig, WILTINGEN (SCHARZHOFBERGER). Many fine estates here, often at the top of their game.

Saarburg M-S-R Small town in the SAAR valley, Rausch v'yd is one of the best of the region. Best growers: WAGNER, ZILLIKEN.

Sachsen 03 05 07 08 09 (10) A region of 462 ha in the Elbe Valley. MÜLLER-THURGAU still dominates, but WEISSBURGUNDER, GRAUBURGUNDER, TRAMINER and RIES give dry wines with real character. Best growers: Vincenz Richter, SCHLOSS PROSCHWITZ, Schloss Wackerbarth, Martin Schwarz, Zimmerling.

Salm, Prinz zu Owner of Schloss Wallhausen in NAHE; Villa Sachsen in RHEINHESSEN. Lovely 2009 collection at Schloss Wallhausen: dry RIES QBA "vom roten Schiefer".

Salwey, Weingut Bad ★★★ Leading estate at Oberrotweil, 40 ha. GRAUBURGUNDER (best: Eichberg) and SPÄTBURGUNDER (best: Kirchberg) are textbook KAISERSTUHL wines, full-bodied and structured for prolonged ageing. Specialties are RIES and WEISSHERBST from high-altitude v'yds in the Glottertal (Black Forest). Wolf-Dietrich Salwey died Jan 2011; son Konrad continues.

Sankt Urbans-Hof M-S-R ★★★ New star based in LEIWEN, PIESPORT and OCKFEN. Limpid RIES of impeccable purity and raciness from 33 ha. Stunning 2008 collection.

Sauer, Horst Frank ★★★→★★★★ The finest exponent of ESCHERNDORF's top v'yd Lump. Racy, straightforward dry SILVANER and RIES, and sensational TBA. 15 ha.

Sauer, Rainer Frank ★★★ Rising family estate at ESCHERNDORF (*see* H SAUER). Rich and powerful RIES and SILVANER (mainly dry), but with good balance. 10 ha.

Schaefer, Willi M-S-R ★★★ The finest grower of GRAACH (but only 4 ha). Classic pure MOSEL RIES, rewarding at all quality levels. Of the powerful 2009 vintage, Schaefer managed to produce a little miracle: a GROSSES GEWÄCHS (Himmelreich) of only 11.5 degrees of alcohol. Breathtaking delicacy.

Schäfer-Fröhlich, Weingut Na ★★★ Increasingly brilliant RIES, dry and nobly sweet, from this 12-ha estate in Bockenau.

Scharzhofberg M-S-R (Saar) w ★★★★ 71 83 88 89 90 93 94 95 96 97 98 99 01 02 03 04 05 07 08 09 (10) Superlative v'yd: a rare coincidence of microclimate, soil and human intelligence brings the perfection of RIES, best in AUSLESEN. Top: BISCHÖFLICHE WEINGÜTER, EGON MÜLLER, VON HÖVEL, VON KESSELSTATT, VAN VOLXEM.

Scheurebe Pfz Grapefruit-scented grape of RIES parentage and gd potential, esp used in PFALZ. Excellent for botrytis wine (BA, TBA).

Schloss Johannisberg Rhg w ★★→★★★ 90 94 95 96 97 98 99 01 02 03 04 05 07 08 09 (10) Famous RHEINGAU estate of 35 ha, 100% RIES, owned by Henkell (Oetker group). Improved v'yd management under new director starts to pay off.

Schloss Lieser M-M ★★★ 10-ha estate owned by Thomas Haag, from FRITZ HAAG estate, making pure, racy RIES from underrated Niederberg Helden v'yd in LIESER, as well as from best sites in BRAUNEBERG.

Schloss Neuweier Bad ★★★ Leading producer of dry RIES in BADEN, from the volcanic soils nr Baden-Baden. Particularly successful in 2008 and 2009, eg. Schlossberg *alte Reben* (old vines) or Mauerberg GROSSES GEWÄCHS.

Schloss Proschwitz Sachs ★★ A resurrected princely estate at Meissen in SACHSEN, 59 ha, which leads former East Germany in quality, esp with dry WEISSBURGUNDER and GRAUBURGUNDER. A great success.

Schloss Reinhartshausen Rhg ★★→★★★★ Famous estate, 80 ha in Erbach, HATTENHEIM, KIEDRICH, etc. Was property of Prussian royal family, now in private hands.

Schloss Saarstein, Weingut M-S-R ★→★★★ 90 97 01 03 04 05 07 08 09 (10) Steep but chilly v'yds in Serrig need warm yrs to succeed but can deliver steely, minerally and long-lived AUSLESE and EISWEIN.

Schloss Schönborn Rhg ★★→★★★ 50-ha RHEINGAU estate, based at HATTENHEIM. Full-flavoured wines, variable, but excellent when at their best. The Schönborn family also owns a 28-ha estate at Schloss Hallburg in FRANKEN.

Schloss Vaux Rhg ★★→★★★ Superior SEKT manufacturer, specializing in bottle-fermented RIES and SPÄTBURGUNDER from top RHEINGAU sites (eg. STEINBERG or ASSMANNSHÄUSER Höllenberg). The company does not own v'yds itself, but purchases wine from leading estates (mainly from VDP members).

Schloss Vollrads Rhg w ★★ 90 97 01 03 05 07 08 09 (10) One of the greatest historic RHEINGAU estates, now owned by a bank. RIES in a popular and accessible style, but the estate's full potential has yet to be rediscovered.

Record-breaking 2009s
The VDP's 2010 auctions saw German 2009s selling for astonishing prices. EGON MÜLLER'S SCHARZHOFBERGER KABINETT "old vines" fetched 52 – add 40–50% for an approximate retail price. FRITZ HAAG'S BRAUNEBERGER Juffer-Sonnenuhr SPÄTLESE No 16 cost 364 a bottle, remarkable for a Spätlese. And a dry RHEINHESSEN RIES – a double magnum (3 litres) of KELLER'S G-Max label – sold for 3,998. For that you could get nearly 80 bottles of MÜLLER'S KABINETT.

> **Warm, warmer – but not too warm**
> The predictions of the so called Huglin Index – a measure of the
> impact of warmth on grape varieties – show that even in 2050,
> the RHEINGAU will be more suited to growing RIES than, from a
> meteorological point of view, the Adelaide Hills or the Clare
> Valley are today. Furthermore, Professor Hans R Schultz has started
> a series of experiments designed to slow down the ripening process
> in warmer conditions. De-leafing looks promising if done above the
> fruit zone, leaving the shoot tips intact. It makes the v'yd look pretty
> strange, but it can reduce the alcohol in a RIES from 13.5% to 12.5%,
> without significant loss of flavour compounds.

Schlossböckelheim Na w ★★ →★★★★ **90 97 01 02 03 04 05 07 08 09** (10) Village
with top NAHE v'yds, inc First Class Felsenberg, In den Felsen, Königsfels,
Kupfergrube. Firm yet delicate wine that ages well. Top growers: *Crusius*,
DÖNNHOFF, Gutsverwaltung Niederhausen-Schlossböckelheim, SCHÄFER-FRÖHLICH.

Schmitt's Kinder Frank ★★ →★★★ Uncompromising TROCKEN wines from
RANDERSACKER's best v'yds. 18 ha. Textbook FRANKEN SILVANER and RIES. Gd barrel-
aged SPÄTBURGUNDER and sweet SCHEUREBE, too.

Schnaitmann, Weingut Würt ★★ →★★★ Although this new WÜRTTEMBERG star makes
gd RIES and Sauv Bl, its reputation rests on a complex range of full-bodied red
wines from a range of varieties. Best: Simonroth R SPÄTBURGUNDER.

Schneider, Cornelia and Reinhold Bad ★★ →★★★ 7-ha family estate in Endingen,
KAISERSTUHL. Age-worthy SPÄTBURGUNDER; old-fashioned, opulent RULÄNDER.

Schoppenwein Café (or bar) wine, ie. wine by the glass.

Schwarzer Adler, Weingut Bad ★★ →★★★ Fritz Keller makes top GRAU-, WEISS-, and
SPÄTBURGUNDER on 55 ha at Oberbergen, KAISERSTUHL. A firm opponent of residual
sugar in Pinot. Now engaged in producing wine for a discount chain.

Schwarzriesling This grape, with 2,360 ha, is none other than the Pinot Meunier of
Champagne. In WÜRTTEMBERG a light-bodied red.

Schwegler, Albrecht Würt ★★★ Small estate known for unusual yet tasteful red
blends such as Granat (Merlot, Zweigelt, LEMBERGER and other varieties); 2 ha
only, but worth looking for.

Schweigen Pfz r w ★★ **97 99 01 02 03 04 05 07 08 09** Southern PFALZ village. Best
growers: FRIEDRICH BECKER, Bernhart, Jülg.

Sekt German sparkling wine, but v. variable in quality. Bottle fermentation not
mandatory; cheap examples may be produced in a pressure tank. Even for
notable growers, mostly only a by-product. Sekt specialists: Raumland, SCHLOSS
VAUX, Wilhelmshof.

Selbach-Oster M-M ★★★ Scrupulous 20-ha ZELTINGEN estate among MITTELMOSEL
leaders. Also makes wine from purchased grapes: estate bottlings are best.

Silvaner 3rd-most-planted German white grape variety, with 5,260 ha and thus 5%
of the surface. Best examples in FRANKEN, where Silvaner's lovely plant/earth
flavours and dry minerally taste reach perfection. Worth looking for as well in
RHEINHESSEN and KAISERSTUHL (esp IHRINGEN).

Sonnenuhr M-S-R Sundial. Name of several v'yds, esp First Class sites at WEHLEN
and ZELTINGEN currently threatened by road-building.

Spätburgunder (Pinot N) Germany's best red grape; steadily improving quality,
but most still underflavoured or overoaked. Best are excellent (eg. FÜRST, HUBER,
KNIPSER, MAYER-NÄKEL, etc.). Allegedly, Charles the Fat first brought Pinot N from
Burgundy to the shores of Lake Constance (BODENSEE) in 884.

Spätlese Late harvest. One better (riper, with more alcohol, more substance and usually more sweetness) than KABINETT. Gd examples age at least 7 yrs, often longer. TROCKEN Spätlesen, often similar in style to GROSSES GEWÄCHS, can be v. fine with food.

Spreitzer, Weingut Rhg ★★★ Andreas and Bernd Spreitzer produce RHEINGAU RIES from 17 ha, mainly in OESTRICH. Deliciously racy wines, vinified with patience and devotion to detail.

St-Antony, Weingut Rhh ★★ 28-ha NIERSTEIN estate with exceptional v'yd portfolio. Quality was uneven in recent yrs, but new owner (same as HEYL ZU HERRNSHEIM) aims at turning things around.

Staatlicher Hofkeller Frank ★★ The Bavarian state domain. 120 ha of the finest FRANKEN v'yds with spectacular cellars under the great baroque Residenz at WÜRZBURG. Quality sound but rarely exciting.

Staatsweingut (or Staatliche Weinbaudomäne) The state wine estates or domains. Some have been privatized in recent yrs.

Steigerwald District in east FRANKEN. V'yds lie at altitude but bring powerful SILVANER and RIES. Look for: CASTELL'SCHES FÜRSTLICH DOMÄNENAMT, RUCK, Weltner, WIRSCHING.

Steinberg Rhg w ★★★ 90 97 99 01 02 03 04 05 07 08 09 (10) Famous 32-ha HATTENHEIM walled v'yd, a German Clos de Vougeot, planted by Cistercian monks 700 yrs ago. Now a monopoly of KLOSTER EBERBACH. 2007 dry RIES "aus dem Cabinetkeller" ("from the cabinet cellar") is a positive step (though pricey).

Steinwein Wine from WÜRZBURG's best v'yd, Stein. Goethe's favourite, too.

Stodden, Weingut Jean Ahr ★★★ A new star. Burgundy enthusiast Gerhard Stodden crafts richly oaky SPÄTBURGUNDER. First-rate since 1999, but v. pricey.

Störrlein & Krenig, Weingut Frank ★★→★★★ Sterling dry, expressive SILVANER and RIES from RANDERSACKER; fine GROSSES GEWÄCHS from Sonnenstuhl v'yd.

Südliche Weinstrasse District name for south PFALZ. Quality improved hugely in past 25 yrs. *See* FRIEDRICH BECKER, BERGDOLT, REBHOLZ, SCHWEIGEN, DR. WEHRHEIM.

Tauberfranken Underrated district of northeast BADEN: FRANKEN-style wines from limestone soils, bone-dry and distinctly cool-climate in style.

Thanisch, Weingut Dr. M-M ★★→★★★ BERNKASTEL estate, inc part of the Doctor v'yd. This famous estate was divided in the 1980s, but the two confusingly share the same name: Erben Müller-Burggraef identifies one; Erben Thanisch the other. Similar in quality but the latter sometimes has the edge.

Traisen Na w ★★★ 90 97 01 02 03 04 05 07 08 09 Small village inc ERSTE LAGE v'yds Bastei and Rotenfels, RIES of concentration and class from volcanic soils. Top growers: CRUSIUS, von Racknitz.

Traminer *See* GEWÜRZTRAMINER.

Trier M-S-R Great wine city of Roman origin, on MOSEL, between RUWER and SAAR. Big charitable estates have cellars here among splendid Roman remains .

Trittenheim M-M w ★★ ›★★★ 90 97 01 02 03 04 05 07 08 09 (10) Attractive south MITTELMOSEL light wines. Only best plots in ERSTE LAGE v'yd Apotheke deserve that classification, unfortunately the site has a lot of flat land, too. Growers inc: ANSGAR CLÜSSERATH, Ernst Clüsserath, CLÜSSERATH-WEILER, GRANS-FASSIAN, Milz.

Trocken Dry. Trocken wines have a max 9 g unfermented sugar per litre. Quality has increased dramatically since the 1980s, when most were tart, even sour. Most dependable in PFALZ and all points south.

Trockenbeerenauslese (TBA) Sweetest, most expensive category of German wine, extremely rare, with concentrated honey flavour. Made from selected shrivelled grapes affected by noble rot (botrytis). Half-bottles a good idea.

Trollinger Pale red grape variety of WÜRTTEMBERG; identical with south Tyrol's Vernatsch; mostly overcropped but locally v. popular.

Ürzig M-M w ★★★★ 83 90 93 94 95 96 97 98 99 01 02 03 04 05 07 08 09 (10) Village on red sandstone and red slate, famous for firm, full, spicy wine unlike other MOSELS. ERSTE LAGE v'yd: Würzgarten. Growers inc: Berres, CHRISTOFFEL, LOOSEN, MÖNCHHOF, PAULY-BERGWEILER, WEINS-PRÜM. Threatened by an unneeded *Autobahn* bridge 160 metres high.

Van Volxem, Weingut M-S-R ★★ →★★★ SAAR estate revived by brewery heir Roman Niewodniczanski since 1999. V. low yields from top sites (SCHARZHOFBERG, KANZEM Altenberg) result in ultra-ripe dry (or slightly off-dry) RIES. Atypical but impressive.

Verband Deutscher Prädikats und Qualitätsweingüter (VDP) Pace-making association of premium growers. Look for its eagle insignia on wine labels, and ERSTE LAGE logo on wines from classified v'yds. President: Steffen CHRISTMANN.

Vollenweider, Weingut M-S-R ★★★ Daniel Vollenweider from Switzerland has, since 2000, revived the Wolfer Goldgrube v'yd nr Traben-Trarbach. *Excellent Ries*, but v. small quantities.

Wachenheim W ★★★ 90 97 01 02 03 04 05 07 08 09 (10) PFALZ village with 340 ha of v'yds, a little less prestigious than its MITTELHAARDT neighbours. First Class v'yds: Belz, Gerümpel, Goldbächel, Rechbächel. Top growers: Biffar, BÜRKLIN-WOLF, Karl Schäfer, WOLF.

Wagner-Stempel, Weingut Rhh ★★★ 16-ha estate, 50% RIES, nr NAHE border in obscure Siefersheim. Recent yrs have provided excellent wines, both GROSSES GEWÄCHS and nobly sweet.

Wagner, Dr. M-S-R ★★ 9-ha estate with v'yds in SAARBURG and OCKFEN. Traditional methods: all wines ferment and age in FUDER casks.

Walluf Rhg W ★★★ 90 96 97 98 99 01 02 03 04 05 07 08 09 (10) Neighbour of Eltville. Underrated wines. ERSTE LAGE v'yd: Walkenberg. Growers: J B BECKER, JOST.

Wegeler M-M ★★→★★★ Important family estates in RHEINGAU (OESTRICH) and MITTELMOSEL (BERNKASTEL), altogether 73 ha, plus a stake in the famous KRONE estate of ASSMANNSHAUSEN. Wines of high quality in gd quantity, even the "Geheimrat J" brand maintains v. high standards. The Wegelers owned the merchant house of DEINHARD until 1997.

Wehlen M-M W ★★★ →★★★★ 90 93 94 95 96 97 99 01 02 03 04 05 07 08 09 (10) BERNKASTEL neighbour with equally fine, somewhat richer wine. ERSTE LAGE: SONNENUHR. Top growers: Kerpen, KESSELSTATT, LOOSEN, MOLITOR, J J PRÜM, S A PRÜM, RICHTER, Studert-Prüm, SELBACH-OSTER, WEGELER, WEINS-PRÜM. V'yds threatened by *Autobahn* project.

Wehrheim, Weingut Dr. ★★★ In warm SÜDLICHE WEINSTRASSE Pinot varieties and CHARD as well as RIES ripen fully. Full-bodied wines, but with a firm mineral core.

Weil, Weingut Robert Rhg ★★★→★★★★ 90 96 97 01 02 03 04 05 07 08 09 (10) Outstanding estate in KIEDRICH; owned since 1988 by Suntory of Japan. Superb EISWEIN, TBA, BA; entry-level wines more variable. Recently another ERSTE LAGE beside famous Gräfenberg was approved: Turmberg, 3.7 ha. And another single v'yd will appear on the labels: Klosterberg. Estate has grown to 75 ha.

Weingart, Weingut M Rh ★★★ Outstanding estate at Spay; 11 ha v'yds in BOPPARD. Refined, minerally RIES, superb value, both dry and sweet.

Weingut Wine estate.

Weins-Prüm, Dr. M-M ★★★ Small estate; based at WEHLEN. 4 ha of superb v'yds. Scrupulous winemaking from owner Bert Selbach, who favours a taut, minerally style.

Weissburgunder (Pinot Bl) Increasingly popular for TROCKEN wines that exhibit more burgundian raciness than German CHARD; now 3,730 ha. Best from southern PFALZ and from BADEN. Also much used for SEKT.

Weissherbst Pale-pink wine, sometimes botrytis-affected and occasionally even BA, made from a single variety, often SPÄTBURGUNDER. Worth trying.

Wiltingen M-S-R W ★★→★★★★ 90 95 96 97 99 01 03 04 05 07 08 09 (10) Heart of the SAAR. 320 ha. Beautifully subtle, austere wine. Famous SCHARZHOFBERG is the best of a trio of ERSTE LAGE sites, inc Braune Kupp and Gottesfuss. Top growers: BISCHÖFLICHE WEINGÜTER, EGON MÜLLER, KESSELSTATT, VAN VOLXEM.

Winning, von Pfz New DEIDESHEIM estate, inc former DR. DEINHARD. The von Winning label is used for top wines from DR. DEINHARD v'yds. First vintage 2008 – and a success: *Ries of great purity* and terroir expression, slightly influenced by 10–20% oak fermentation. A label to watch.

Winningen M-S-R w ★★ →★★★ Lower MOSEL town nr Koblenz; excellent dry RIES and TBA. ERSTE LAGE v'yds: Röttgen, Uhlen. Top growers: HEYMANN-LÖWENSTEIN, KNEBEL, Kröber, Richard Richter.

Wirsching, Hans Frank ★★★ Estate in IPHOFEN. Dry RIES and *Silvaner*, powerful and long-lived. 72 ha above all in ERSTE LAGE v'yds: Julius-Echter-Berg, Kronsberg.

Wittmann, Weingut Rhh ★★★ Since 1999 Philipp Wittmann has propelled this 25-ha organic estate to the top ranks in RHEINHESSEN. Crystal-clear, minerally, dry RIES from QBA to GROSSES GEWÄCHS RIES and magnificent TBA.

Wöhrwag, Weingut Würt ★★ →★★★ Just outside Stuttgart, this 20-ha estate makes succulent reds, but above all elegant, dry RIES and brilliant EISWEIN.

Wolf J L Pfz ★★ →★★★ Estate in WACHENHEIM leased long-term by Ernst LOOSEN of BERNKASTEL. Dry PFALZ RIES with a MOSEL-like finesse. Sound and consistent rather than dazzling.

Württemberg Vast area in the south, 11,520 ha, little known outside Germany. Mostly standard wines for local consumption, but ambitions now rising, esp with concentrated, fruit-driven reds (LEMBERGER, Samtrot, SPÄTBURGUNDER). Experiments inc Sauv Bl and dark new crossings bred by Weinsberg research station. RIES (mostly TROCKEN) tends to be rustic, although the Remstal area close to Stuttgart can have refinement.

Würzburg Frank ★★ →★★★★ 93 97 01 02 03 04 05 07 08 09 (10) Great baroque city on the Main, centre of FRANKEN wine: fine, full-bodied, dry RIES and esp SILVANER. ERSTE LAGE v'yds: Innere Leiste, Stein, Stein-Harfe. Growers: BÜRGERSPITAL, JULIUSSPITAL, STAATLICHER HOFKELLER, Weingut am Stein.

Zehnthof, Weingut Frank ★★ Wide-ranging wines, notably SILVANER and Pinot varieties. Typically cask-fermented, from Luckert family's 12-ha estate in Sulzfeld, FRANKEN.

Zell M-S-R w ★ →★★★ 90 97 01 02 03 04 05 07 08 09 (10) Best-known lower MOSEL village, esp for awful GROSSLAGE: Schwarze Katz (Black Cat). RIES on steep slate gives aromatic wines. Top growers: S Fischer, Kallfelz.

Zeltingen M-M w ★★ →★★★★ 90 93 95 96 97 98 99 01 02 03 04 05 06 07 08 09 Top but sometimes underrated MOSEL village nr WEHLEN. Lively, crisp RIES. ERSTE LAGE v'yd: SONNENUHR. Top growers: M MOLITOR, J J PRÜM, Schömann, SELBACH-OSTER.

Ziereisen, Weingut Bad ★★ →★★★ Carpenter and ex-co-op member Hans-Peter Ziereisen turned winemaker. A full palette from BADEN: dry Pinot whites, minerally Gutedel Steingrüble and Syrah. But best are the SPÄTBURGUNDERS from various small v'yd plots with dialect names: Schulen, Tschuppen, Rhini.

Zilliken, Forstmeister Geltz M-S-R ★★★ →★★★★ 93 95 96 97 01 02 03 04 05 07 08 09 (10) Former estate of Prussian royal forester with 11 ha at SAARBURG and OCKFEN, SAAR. Produces intensely minerally *Ries from Saarburg Rausch*, inc superb AUSLESE and EISWEIN with excellent ageing potential.

Spain & Portugal

Abbreviations used in the text:

Alel	Alella	RB	Rioja Baja
Alen	Alentejo	Set	Setúbal
Alg	Algarve	Som	Somontano
Alic	Alicante	Tej	Tejo
Bair	Bairrada	U-R	Utiel-
Bei	Beiras		Requena
Bul	Bullas		
Can	Canaries	Res	*reserva*
Cat	Catalunya		
Cos del S	Costers del Segre		
Dou	Douro		
El B	El Bierzo		
Emp	Empordà-Costa Brava		
Gal	Galicia		
La M	La Mancha		
Lis	Lisboa		
Mad	Madrid, Vinos de		
Mall	Mallorca		
Min	Minho		
Mont-M	Montilla-Moriles		
Mur	Murcia		
Nav	Navarra		
Pen	Penedès		
Pri	Priorat		
Rib del D	Ribera del Duero		
R Ala	Rioja Alavesa		
R Alt	Rioja Alta		

Spain, with as many vines as any country in Europe but rather modest traditions, has learned (since the EU flooded the country with money) to restrict crops, ripen healthy grapes and follow modern norms – with some extraordinary results. She has nothing like the variety of grapes or climates as Italy and a limited palette of white wines, but spins extraordinary variations on the basic theme of structured, aromatic, oak-aged Tempranillo, coined in Rioja. Bordeaux grapes do wonderfully well in the north, especially Catalonia and Navarra. The Duero and Priorat make unique contributions. Rioja has had a turbulent time and is a more ticklish purchase than in the past, but with higher peaks than ever. Explore; real disappointments are rare.

Portugal has the advantages of an oceanic climate, and a mad medley of grapes, so no need for the international brigade. Many of its best wines are blends. There is pressure to copy the global trend for mono-varietal wines by singling out a handful of native grapes for international stardom. The hot favourites, red Touriga Nacional and white Alvarinho, are now being widely planted. But there's resistance elsewhere; in Bairrada the grubbing-up of the top red variety Baga has prompted leading producers to form Baga Friends to promote it. Expect tannins, more or less intelligently handled, and remember the best reds need time to settle.

More heavily shaded areas are the wine-growing regions.

MADEIRA (off west coast of Africa)

Funchal

SPAIN

Recent vintages

Navarra

2010 A cool spring with late frosts and hail was rescued by a late harvest with good ripening.

2009 A generous vintage; hot summer rescued by late rains. Garnacha flourished. Enjoy relatively young.

2008 Wet spring, late harvest. Slow ripening produced elegance, with selection.

2007 Long, dry summer produced some very good wines.

2006 Young wines good. Weather favoured the professionals.

2005 Exceptional vintage: deep colour; full flavours; sweet, powerful tannins.

2004 Good, intense wines for those who picked late and selectively.

2003 As in 2002, mixed. The best are already mature.

2002 The best are good, but drink now.

Penedès

2010 A cool year generally, though with a hot, early summer in Priorat. Long, even ripening points to fresher, more aromatic wines.

2009 A fresh year even given the hot weather; overall, a high-quality vintage. Priorat suffered some heat spikes.

2008 Heavy spring rains and cool vintage. Quality depends on the producer.

2007 A textbook year – one of the best in the past 50 years.

2006 Very good acidity and alcohol levels. The vintage is officially "excellent". Some baked wines.

2005 The hardest drought of the past 50 years, but thanks to cold summer nights quality was excellent though some Priorat, Montsant disappoint.

2004 A memorable year for red wines.

2003 Rains in August, then cool nights and sunny days in September resulted in a great vintage.

2002 Despite summer rains, a good September delivered good quality.

2001 Frosts reduced the yield but warm summer produced very good wines.

Ribera del Duero

2010 Early frosts reduced crop, heavy summer rains but fruit quality was excellent. Growers are expecting an outstanding vintage.

2009 The very hot summer risked hot, baked fruit but the early autumn rains helped, and top producers have very high-quality wines.

2008 Risk of rot: cool summer, frosts in September. Quality through selection.

2007 Most disastrous vintage for a decade. Damp spring then sunless summer.

2006 A hot vintage; a number of wines are ready.

2005 Overshadowed by quality of 2004, but some good wines.

2004 A fine year. Good-quality wines and a plentiful harvest.

2003 Best wines have good colour and alcohol but low acidity. Poor are baked.

2002 A large harvest of only moderate quality.

2001 Medium-sized harvest of excellent quality; ready to drink.

Rioja

2010 Spring rain; hot, dry summer; autumn rain. Yields are 10% down for reds and 5% for whites compared with 2009, promising good concentration.

2009 Hot summer suggested a repeat of 2003, but was rescued by rain. Rioja Alta and Baja stand out.

2008 Classic style wines; best are fresh and aromatic, a little lower in alcohol.

2007 A small crop. Satisfactory but not exceptional.

2006 Wines are fragrant, fresh, many ready to drink.

2005 Sits in the shadow of 2004, but many excellent wines.

2004 Outstanding vintage.

2003 Top wines sublime but most already past their prime, given hot summer.

2002 The best are still delicious; the run-of-the-mill have already peaked.

2001 An exceptional year. Many wines to drink now. The best still have some years ahead.

Aalto, Bodegas y Viñedos Rib del D r ★★★→★★★★ 00 01 02 03 04' 05 06 Glam estate (1999) in RIBERA DEL DUERO. Fine pedigree: co-founder Mariano García is ex-VEGA SICILIA and also owns MAURO, Maurodos. Two muscular wines; top wine is PS.

Abadía Retuerta r ★★→★★★ 04 05 06 07 08 Leading non-DO winery next door to RIBERA DEL DUERO. Tempranillo, Cab Sauv, Merlot and Syrah in gd-value Rívola; spicier Selección Especial; pure Tempranillo Pago Negralada; sumptuous Syrah Pago la Garduña.

Albariño Gal Spain's smartest, priciest indigenous white variety of RÍAS BAIXAS. Best: Castrocelta, Martín Códax, PALACIO DE FEFIÑANES, PAZO DE SEÑORANS. RAIMAT'S Viña

24 from COSTERS DEL SEGRE proves Albariño's potential in different terroir. Some creations are pretty callow. DYA unoaked styles.

Albet i Noya Pen r p w sp ★★→★★★04 05 06 07 08 09 (10) Leader in organics. Wide portfolio with gd CAVA.

Alicante Alic r w sw ★→★★★★ 04 05 06 07 08 09 Not just a holiday spot – also one of the hot spots for Monastrell, proving there is more to Spain than Tempranillo. Reds better than whites, inc Enrique Mendoza, Bernabé Navarro, ARTADI's El Sequé, Sierra Salinas. Outstanding sweet Moscatels, esp GUTIÉRREZ DE LA VEGA, Primitivo Quiles; historic sweet Monastrell FONDILLÓN.

Alión Rib del D r ★★★01 02 03 04 05 06 Launched in 1991 next door to, but never the poor relation of, VEGA SICILIA. Rather, Alión is the French cousin, 100% Tinto Fino (Tempranillo) in Nevers oak: inky, dense, spicy.

Allende, Finca R Alt r w ★★★→★★★★ 01 02 04' 05 06 07 08 One of the great names of the new RIOJAS. In this town-centre BODEGA in Briones, Miguel Ángel de Gregorio's focuses on single-v'yd Tempranillo. *Tinto is floral, spicy*; single v'yd Calvario is bold and balanced; Aurus is sumptuous. Fine, oak-influenced Rioja Blanco 08. Also Finca Coronado, LA MANCHA.

Artadi Bodegas y Viñedos R Ala r ★★★→★★★★ 96 98 00 01 04' 05 06 07 Top modern RIOJAS: complex Viñas del Gaín; powerful single-v'yd El Pisón; spicy, elegant Pagos Viejos. V.gd El Sequé (r) ALICANTE, and Artazuri (r, DYA p) NAVARRA.

Baigorri, Bodegas R Ala r w ★★★ 04 05' 06 07 08 09 Spectacular winery producing pricey, new-wave RIOJA with primary black fruits, bold tannins and upbeat oak. Glossy Garage wins the prizes. Best value: CRIANZA.

Barón de Ley RB r p w ★→★★ 05 06 07 Gd modern wines made in one-time Benedictine monastery. Most interesting is 7 Viñas (r), blend of seven varieties.

Báscula, La Alic, Rib del D, Rio r w sw ★★ Young wine company run by South African winemaker Bruce Jack and UK MW Ed Adams, tracking down quality and diversity: eg. Turret Fields, JUMILLA; Catalan Eagle (organic), Terra Alta.

Berberana, Bodegas Rio r w p ★ Popular juicy RIOJAS, part of BODEGAS UNIDAS group.

Beronia Rio r w p ★★ 04 05 06 07 08 09 Finally, much improved. This RIOJA house owned by GONZÁLEZ BYASS has refreshed the cellar and bought new, clean barrels. A great advance for the red; also gd ROSADO.

Bierzo r w ★→★★★ 03 04 05 06 07 08 09 V. fashionable DO luring outside winemakers to reveal potential of local red MENCÍA (aromatic, tannic) and white Godello. Best: Bodegas Peique, Bodegas Pittacum, Castro Ventosa, Dominio de Tares, DESCENDIENTES DE J PALACIOS, Gancedo, Luna Berberide, Raúl Pérez.

Binissalem Mall r w p★★ 05 06 07 08 09 Tiny but best-known MALLORCA DO northeast of Palma. Mainly reds: Mantonegro, Biniagual, Binigrau, Macía Batle.

Bodega Spanish term for (i) a wineshop; (ii) a concern occupied in the making, blending and/or shipping of wine; and (iii) a cellar.

Briones R Alt Small RIOJAN hilltop town nr HARO, peppered with underground cellars. Producers inc FINCA ALLENDE, Miguel Merino; has one of the most comprehensive wine museums in the world, owned by DINASTÍA VIVANCO.

Bullas ★→★★ 04 05 06 07 08 09 Small, high (400–800 metres), dry Murcia DO tries hard in excessively Mediterranean climate. Best: Chaveo from Bodega Monastrell.

Calatayud ★→★★★ 05 06 07 08 09 Improving mountainous Aragón DO specializing in brooding GARNACHA, often from old vines, sometimes blended with Syrah. Best: Bodegas Ateca (*see* JORGE ORDÓÑEZ), El Jalón, El Escocés Volante (Scots MW Norrel Robertson), Lobban, Virgén de la Sierra (Cruz de Piedra).

Campo de Borja r w p ★→★★★ 06 07 08 09 Aragón DO making excellent, great-value DYA modern, juicy GARNACHAS and Tempranillos, eg. *Bodegas Aragonesas*. For more complexity, try Tres Picos GARNACHA 07 from Bodegas Borsao. Top wine: Alto Moncayo's Aquilón.

Canary Islands Can (Islas Canarias) r w p ★→★★ Has an astonishing nine DOS. Quality is mixed but at best highly enjoyable; occasionally stunning dessert Malvasías and Moscatels. Many native varieties (white Listán and Marmajuelo, black Negramoll and Vijariego). Be adventurous.

Cariñena r w p ★→★★ 03 04 05 06 07 08 09 Unexciting Aragón DO. Two leading producers are Bodegas Añadas and Bodegas Victoria.

Castell del Remei Cos del S r p w ★★ →★★★ 03 05 06 07 08 09 Picturesque restored 18th-century estate. Gd white blends; v.gd vanilla and red-cherry Gotim Bru, elegant, spicy 1780, and powerful Oda.

Castilla y León r w p ★→★★★ 06 07 08 09 One of subregions that sprang out of catch-all DO Castilla-La Mancha. Many promising and established producers. DOS inc Arribes, BIERZO, CIGALES, Tierra de León, Tierra del Vino de Zamora, plus quality region Valles de Benavente. Red grapes inc MENCÍA, Juan Garcia, Prieto Picudo, Tinta del País (Tempranillo); whites Doña Blanca. Gd dry ROSADO.

Castillo de Ygay R Alt r ★★★★ 64 70 89 91 94 96 97 98 99 01 05 Legendary, long-lived top wines from MARQUÉS DE MURRIETA, esp GRAN RESERVA Especial.

Castillo Perelada, Vinos y Caves del Emp r p w sp ★→★★★ 04 05 06 07 08 09 Large estate with hotel and improving range of wines. Gd CAVAS, modern reds inc Ex Ex Monastrell, Finca Garbet Syrah. Rare solera-aged Garnatxa de l'Empordà.

Catalunya Cat r w p 04 05 06 07 08 09 Vast young (2004) DO covering the whole Catalan area, still suffering growing pains in terms of defining itself. Top names inc some of the biggest: ALBET I NOYA, FREIXENET, JEAN LÉON and TORRES.

Cava Spain's traditional-method fizz is made mainly in PENEDÈS – but not exclusively; most produced in or around San Sadurní de Noya. Dominated by FREIXENET and CODORNÍU. Quality is often higher, with a price tag to match, from Agustí Torelló, Castell Sant Antoni, CASTILLO PERELADA, GRAMONA, JUVÉ & CAMPS, MARQUÉS DE MONISTROL, Mestres, PARXET, Raimat, Recaredo (biodynamic), Sumarroca. Best drunk young. Revisit Cava: many producers are undergoing a quality transformation.

Cérvoles, Celler Cos del S r w ★★→★★★ 03 04 05 06 07 08 09 High mountainous estate north of PRIORAT making concentrated reds from Cab Sauv/Tempranillo/GARNACHA and powerful, creamy, lemon-tinged, barrel-fermented Blanc.

Chacolí/Txakoli w (r, p) ★★ DYA The Basque wine. Split into three DOS: Àlava, Guetaria, Vizcaya. All make fragrant DYA but often quirkily sharp, *pétillant* whites, locally poured into tumblers from a height. Historic Chueca family owned Txomin Etxaniz rounds off the aggression of the primary Hondarribi Zuri (w) with 15% of low-alcohol Hondarribi Beltza. Other top name: Ameztoi.

Chivite, Bodegas Julián Nav r w p sw ★★→★★★ 04 05 06 07 08 09 Historic NAVARRA BODEGA. Popular range Gran Feudo, esp ROSADO and Sobre Lias (*sur lie*). Excellent *Colección 125* range, inc serious burgundian Chard, delicate botrytis Moscatel. PAGO wine of beautfiul Arínzano estate still finding its feet. Also owns Viña Salceda in RIOJA (v.gd Conde de la Salceda).

Cigales r p (w) ★→★★★ Small, high-altitude DO north of Valladolíd. Produces commercial DYA reds, and more complex old-vine Tempranillo. Top wines: voluptuous César Príncipe; more restrained Traslanzas; also Valdelosfrailes.

Clos Mogador Pri r ★★★→★★★★ 01 02 03 04 05 06 07 08 René Barbier is one of PRIORAT's pioneers, and godfather to the younger generations of winemakers. Clos Mogador GARNACHA blend (impressive, built to last). Second wine: Manyetes. Exceptionally interesting spicy, fragrant, honeyed Clos Nelin white blend.

Codorníu Pen sp ★★→★★★★ One of the two largest CAVA firms, owned by the Raventós family, rivals to FREIXENET, favouring non-indigenous varieties, esp Chard. Best: gd vintage, Reina Maria Cristina, v. dry Non Plus Ultra, and pale, smoky Pinot N. Also owns the gradually improving Raimat in COSTERS DEL SEGRE, as well as the once-great but now slumbering Bilbainas in RIOJA.

Spanish fizz sees red

Spain's answer to sparkling Shiraz is called La Pamelita. From Lobban Wines – remember this – it's not CAVA. It can only be Vino Espumoso de Calidad, as it's the wrong colour: from this yr it will be made from Shiraz grown in CALATAYUD. The winemaker is Scottish-born Pamela Lobban whose time in the Australian wine trade inspired the choice.

Compañía Vinícola del Norte de España (CVNE) R Alt r w p ★→★★★ Famous RIOJA BODEGA; former benchmark, now again improving. Top quality are elegant Imperial and supple Viña Real. *See also* CONTINO.

Conca de Barberà Cat w r p 04 05 06 07 08 09 Small Catalan DO once purely a feeder of quality fruit to large enterprises, now has some excellent wineries, inc the biodynamic Escoda-Sanahuja. Top TORRES wines Grans Muralles and Milmanda both produced in this DO.

Condado de Haza Rib del D r ★★★ 03 04 05 06 Pure Tinto Fino aged in American oak. Second wine of Alejandro Fernández's PESQUERA and unfairly overlooked.

Consejo Regulador Organization for the control, promotion and defence of a DO. Quality as inconsistent as wines: some bureaucratic, others enterprising.

Contino, Viñedos del R Ala r ★★★★ 01 03 04 05 06 07 First single v'yd of RIOJA (1973), part of CVNE group. Jesus Madrazo makes exceptional long-lasting reds with scrupulous attention. Fine balsamic GRACIANO (a fine example of the variety), RESERVA and impressive Viña del Olivo.

Costers del Segre Cat r w p sp ★★→★★★ 03 04 05 06 07 08 09 DO scattered around city of Lleida (Lérida), with rising reputation from its excellent producers. Top producers: Castell d'Encus, CASTELL DEL REMEI, CÉRVOLES, Raimat, TOMÁS CUSINÉ.

Criado y embotellado por... Spanish for "Grown and bottled by...".

Crianza Literally "nursing"; the ageing of wine. New or unaged wine is *sin crianza* or JOVEN. Rules vary, but in general *crianza* must be at least 2 yrs old (with 6 mths–1 yr in oak) and must not be released before the 3rd yr. *See* RESERVA.

Cusiné, Tomás Cos del S r w ★★★ 04 05 06 07 08 09 The man behind CASTELL DEL REMEI and CELLER CÉRVOLES, on his own since 2003. Individual, stylish wines, inc Tempranillo blend Vilosell, and original ten-variety white blend Auzells.

Denominación de Origen (DO), Denominación de Origen Protegida (DOP) European legislation has been slow to filter down to member countries and their bottle labels. Spain is still in transition: what were former Denominación de Origen (DO) and DO Calificada are now grouped as DOP along with the single-estate PAGOS. The lesser ranking of VCPRD is on the way to becoming VCIG, Vinos de Calidad de Indicación Geográfica.

Dominio de Valdepusa Madr r w ★★★ 04 05 06 07 Enterprising UC Davis graduate Carlos Falcó, Marqués de Griñon, was first Spaniard to cultivate Syrah and Petit Verdot, and to introduce drip irrigation and a scientific approach to v'yd management. Valdepusa nr Mentrida is a PAGO. The varietals, also inc Cab, Graciano, are savoury and v. concentrated; try approachable Summa and top wine Emeritus. At El Rincón makes wine in VINOS DE MADRID DO.

Empordà-Ampurdán Cat r p w ★→★★★ 04 05 06 07 08 09 Small, fashionable DO nr French border, not far from the site of celebrated El Bulli restaurant. Best wineries: CASTILLO PERELADA, Celler Marti Fabra, Pere Guardiola. The curious will be tempted by the playful and experimental Espelt, growing any number of varieties, though with variable results. Stick to the reds.

Enate Som r p w ★★★ 04 05 06 07 08 09 Leading producer, with gd DYA Gewürz and barrel-fermented Chard, gd if somewhat overpowering Syrah, but round, satisfyingly balanced, mature Cab/Merlot Especial Reserva.

Espumoso Sparkling wine, not made according to traditional method, unlike CAVA.

Finca Farm or estate (eg. FINCA ALLENDE).

Fondillón Fabled ALICANTE wine, made from ripe Monastrell grapes matured in oak for long periods to endure sea voyages. Still made in small quantities by eg. GUTIÉRREZ DE LA VEGA, Primitivo Quiles.

Freixenet, Cavas Pen w p sp ★★ ⇢★★★ Huge CAVA firm owned by the Ferrer family. Rival of similarly enormous CODORNÍU. Best-known for frosted black-bottled Cordón Negro and standard Carta Nevada. Strongly supported by advertising. Also controls Castellblanch, Conde de Caralt and Segura Viudas, and owns major Bordeaux négociant Yvon Mau.

Galicia Galic Rainy northwestern corner of Spain producing some of Spain's best whites (*see* RÍAS BAIXAS, MONTERREI, Ribeira Sacra, RIBEIRO and VALDEORRAS).

Garnacha Traditional workhorse vine now being recognized as part of Spain's heritage. New generation of winemakers is seeking out very old vines across central and northern Spain. Rising regions inc VINOS DE MADRID, CALATAYUD.

Generoso Term for fortified wine.

Graciano One of the traditional components of RIOJA. Revised as a single varietal, esp by CONTINO.

Gramona Pen r w sw sp ★★ ⇢★★★ Substantial family firm making impressive range of wines based on serious research. Gd DYA Gewürz, spicy Xarel-lo-dominated Celler Batle, sweet wines, inc Icewines and impressive Chard/Sauv Bl Gra a Gra Blanco Dulce. Top cavas Imperial Gran Reserva, III Lustros.

Gran Reserva (GR) *See* RESERVA.

Gutiérrez de la Vega, Bodegas Alic r w sw ★⇢★★★ 02 05 06 07 Small estate founded by opera-loving former general in 1978. Expanding range all branded Casta Diva, with excellent, fragrant sweet whites made from Moscatel. Historic Monastrell sweet red, FONDILLÓN.

Hacienda Monasterio, Bodegas Rib del D r ★★⇢★★★ 01 02 03 040 05 06 07 Cult winemaker Peter Sisseck's involvement has resulted in excellent Tinto Fino/Cab/Merlot blends. Currently a delicious, expressively fruity *tinto*, approachable CRIANZA and elegantly round, complex RESERVA.

Haro R Alt Spiritual and historic centre of the Rioja Alta. Though growing, still infinitely more charming and intimate than commercial capital Logroño; home to LÓPEZ DE HEREDIA, MUGA, LA RIOJA ALTA, RODA, among others.

Huerta de Albalá r ★★⇢★★★ 06 07 Ambitious new (2006) Andalusian estate in foothills of Sierra de Grazalema, blending Syrah, Merlot, Cab Sauv and local Tintilla de Rota. V. promising, small-production Taberner No 1 with dense fruit and expressive French oak; gd Taberner.

Inurrieta, Bodega Nav r p w ★★⇢★★★ 04 05 06 07 08 09 High-tech estate nr Falces. Gd French-oaked Norte Cab/Merlot and lively DYA Mediodía ROSADO. Top wine: Altos de Inurrieta. Promising production of GRACIANO and experiments with other varieties not yet permitted by DO.

Jaro, Bodegas y Viñedos del Rib del D r ★⇢★★★ 04 05 06 07 08 Founded in 2000 by a member of the Osborne (Sherry) family. Best: intense, minerally Chafandín, seriously expensive, opulent, black-fruit-scented Sed de Caná.

Joven (vino) Young, unoaked wine. *See also* CRIANZA.

Jumilla Mur r (p w) ★⇢★★★ 05 06 07 08 09 Arid, apparently unpromising DO in mts north of Murcia, now discovered by ambitious modern winemakers. Best-known for dark, fragrant Monastrell. Also gd Tempranillo, Merlot, Cab, Syrah, Petit Verdot. Wines do not generally age. Gd producers: Agapito Rico, Casa Castillo, Casa de la Ermita, influential Juan Gil, Luzón, Valle del Carche, El Nido, Silvano Garcia.

Juvé & Camps Pen w sp ★★★ 05 06 07 Family firm making top-quality CAVA from free-run juice. Reserva de la Familia is the stalwart, with top-end GRAN RESERVA and Milesimé Chard Gran Reserva.

La Mancha r p w ★→★★ Largest wine-growing region in Spain; has long been striving to improve its reds, which are mainly Cencibel-based (Tempranillo). Best producer is undoubtedly Finca Antigua, of MARTÍNEZ BUJANDA in RIOJA, succeeding with international varieties: Syrah, Merlot, Cab Sauv, Petit Verdot.

León, Jean Pen r w ★★★ 04 05 06 07 Small firm; TORRES-owned since 1995. Gd, oaky Chards, expressive Merlot and high-priced super-*cuvée* Zemis.

López de Heredia R Alt r w p sw ★★ →★★★★ 64 81 85 87 88 89 95 96 97 98 99 01 02 03 04 Picturesque, old family BODEGA in HARO that still ferments everything in wood and oak-ages in old casks. Medium-intense Bosconia and delicate, ripe *Tondonia*. Fascinating *blanco* and *rosado* are released with a decade of age.

Madrid, Vinos de r p w ★→★★ Altitude, temperature extremes, old GARNACHA vines – all contribute to growing quality of Vinos de Madrid DO, formerly a bulk-wine producer. Go-ahead names inc: Bernabeleva, working with Raúl Pérez making interesting burgundian and top GARNACHA Viña Bonita. Also Marañones, Gosálbez-Ortí run by a former Iberia pilot, Jeromín, Divo, Viñedos de San Martín (part of ENATE group) and El Regajal.

Málaga Once-famous DO now all but vanished in the face of rocketing real-estate values. One large, super-commercial firm remains: Málaga Virgen with Moscatels and PXs. Winemaking has been revived here by former Young Turk TELMO RODRÍGUEZ with a clear, subtle, sweet white *Molino Real Moscatel*, and more recently by JORGE ORDOÑEZ's portfolio of sweet wines.

Mallorca r w ★→★★★ 05 06 07 08 09 Contrary to appearances, with the celebrities and their floating gin palaces, Mallorca is now v. serious about winemaking, and the results are high fashion in Barcelona. Plenty of interest in Anima Negra, tiny Sa Vinya de Can Servera, Hereus de Ribas, *Son Bordils, Can Vidalet*. Also 4 Kilos, Biniagual. Reds are a blend of traditional varieties (Mantonegro, Callet, Fogoneu) plus Cab, Syrah and Merlot. Whites (esp Chard) are improving fast. *See also* BINISSALEM, PLÁ I LLEVANT.

Marqués de Cáceres, Bodegas R Alt r p w ★★→★★★ 01 04 05 06 07 08 09 Well-known name in RIOJA, introduced French methods to the wineries. Fading brilliance at present although Gaudium and GRAN RESERVA stand out.

Marqués de Griñón R Alt RIOJA brand owned by BERBERANA. No longer any connection with the Marqués – *see* DOMINIO DE VALDEPUSA.

Marqués de Monistrol, Bodegas Pen r p sw sp ★→★★ Old BODEGA now owned by BODEGAS UNIDAS. Gd, reliable CAVA; once-lively, modern reds no longer so lively.

Marqués de Murrieta R Alt r p w ★★★ →★★★★ 98 02 03 04 05 06 07 08 Historic BODEGA at Ygay near Logroño, growing all its own grapes, still winning acclaim today. Most famous for its magnificent CASTILLO DE YGAY GRAN RESERVA. Best value is the dense, flavoursome RESERVA with excellent acid balance; most striking is the intense, modern red Dalmau. Capellania is the complex, textured white.

Marqués de Riscal R Ala r w (p) ★★★ 01 02 03 04 05 06 07 08 09 Don't be put off by the exhibitionist hotel by Frank Gehry of Guggenheim Bilbao fame. Quality continues to improve. Gd light reds and powerful black Barón de Chirel Reserva made with some Cab Sauv. A pioneer in RUEDA (since 1972) making fragrant DYA Sauv Bl and vibrant, lively Verdejo/Viura blend.

Martínez Bujanda, Familia La M, Rio r w p ★→★★ Commercially astute business working across a number of wineries plus making private-label wines. Most attractive are *Finca Valpiedra*, charming single estate in RIOJA; Finca Antigua in LA MANCHA. New project in RUEDA.

Mas Gil r w ★★★→★★★★ 04 05 06 07 08 09 PRIORAT estate making fresh, spicy, herbal Viognier/Roussanne/Marsanne Clos d'Agón Blanc; delicious, modern, deeply flavoured Cab/Syrah/Merlot/Cab Fr Clos d'Agón Negre as well as lesser-seen Clos Valmaña duo.

Mas Martinet r ★★★→★★★★ 01 02 03 04 05 06 07 Boutique PRIORAT pioneer, producer of excellent Clos Martinet. Second wine: Martinet Bru. Now run by second generation, inc influential winemaker Sara Pérez.

Mauro, Bodegas r ★★★ 01 03 04 05 06 07 New-wave BODEGA in Tudela del Duero where Mariano Garcia of AALTO and formerly VEGA SICILIA makes serious, reliable non-DO reds. Mauro now with a touch of Syrah; best is the pricey, Old-World-meets-New Vendimia Seleccionada though top *cuvée* is actually the powerful Terreus (03). Sister winery: Maurodos in TORO.

Mencía ★→★★★ Rising-star red; too scarce ever to challenge Tempranillo but aiding the rapid rise of Bierzo. It's aromatic, with steely tannin, and acidity can be tough. Shines with a good producer.

Monterrei Galic w ★→★★★ DYA Small but growing DO in Ourense, south-central GALICIA, making full-flavoured aromatic whites from Treixadura, Godello and Doña Blanca, showing there is more to Galicia than ALBARIÑO. Best is Gargalo.

Montilla-Moriles w sw ★→★★★ Medium-sized DO in south Córdoba once best known for Fino styles but now concentrating on dessert wines made from PX (Pedro Ximénez). Some are dark, unctuous, often bittersweet; others young and honeyed. Until recently TORO ALBALÁ was virtually the only player, but Alvear and Pérez Barquero are now also serious.

Montsant Cat r w (p)★→★★★ 04 05 06 07 08 09 PRIORAT's closest neighbour is building its own reputation, with lower prices. Fine GARNACHA *blanca*, esp from Acústic. Cariñena and GARNACHA deliver dense, balsamic, minerally reds: Celler de Capçanes, Celler el Masroig, Can Blau, Étim, Joan d'Anguera and Mas Perinet all offer impressive, individual wines.

Muga, Bodegas R Alt r w p (sp) ★★★→★★★★ 98 00 01 03 04 05 06 07 08 09 Family firm in HARO, known for some of RIOJA's most spectacular and balanced reds. Gd barrel-fermented DYA Viura reminiscent of burgundy; gd dry, salmon-coloured ROSADO; reds finely crafted and highly aromatic. Best are wonderfully fragrant GRAN RESERVA Prado Enea; warm, full and long-lasting *Torre Muga*; expressive and complex Aro; and dense, rich, structured, full-flavoured Selección Especial.

Navarra r p (w) ★★→★★★ 04 05 06 07 08 09 Extensive DO east of RIOJA. Once known for ROSADO, most of its BODEGAS now produce v.gd mid-priced Tempranillo/Cab Sauv blends, often livelier than those of its more illustrious neighbour RIOJA – despite often higher yields. Up-and-coming names include Garcia Burgos, Pago de Larrainzar, Tandem. Navarra is at last trying to improve its ROSADOS and regain lost ground. Best producers: Alzaña, ARTADI's Artazu, JULIÁN CHIVITE, INURRIETA, Nekeas, OCHOA, OTAZU, Pago de Cirsus, Señorío de Sarría.

Ochoa Nav r w p sw sp ★→★★ Ochoa father made major technical contribution to growth of NAVARRA. Ochoa children now join in to return the brand to its former glory. Gd Tempranillo; excellent ROSADO; sweet Moscatel; fun, Asti-like sparkling.

Ordoñez, Jorge US-based Spaniard, imports top Spanish wines. Invests in Spanish v'yds, specializes in reinvigorating forgotten regions, eg. CALATAYUD, MÁLAGA, RUEDA.

Otazu, Bodegas r ★★★ NAVARRA estate awarded PAGO status in 2009, with a blend of Tempranillo, Merlot and Cab Sauv.

Pago de Carraovejas Rib del D r res ★★★ 01 03 04 05 06 07 Founded 1988, quality still excellent and unable to satisfy demand. Top wine: v.gd Cuesta de las Liebres.

Pago, Vinos de *Pago* is v'yd or area of demarcated size. Term now has legal status roughly equivalent to French Grand Cru. Four *pagos* in CASTILLA-LA MANCHA: Dehesa del Carrizal, DOMINIO DE VALDEPUSA, Manuel Manzeneque's Finca Éez and the Sánchez Militerno family's Pago Guijoso; three in NAVARRA: Prado Irache, CHIVITE's Pago de Arinzano, and Otazu. Anomalous because many distinguished estates, obvious Vinos de Pago, do not have the legal status, inc L'Ermita, PINGUS, Calvario (FINCA ALLENDE), Viña del Olivo and TORRES properties.

Palacio de Fefiñanes w ★★★★ DYA Oldest BODEGA of RÍAS BAIXAS – first bottled wines in 1927. Standard *cuvée* remains one of the finest, most delicate pure ALBARIÑOS. Two superior styles: creamy but light-of-touch, barrel-fermented version 1583 (yr the winery was founded); and a super-fragrant, pricey, lees-aged, mandarin-orange-scented III.

Palacios, Álvaro Pri r ★★→★★★★ 00 01' 03 04 05 06 07 Continues to charm and surprise. Exceptional, individual wines from distinctive *llicorella* (slate) soils, from GARNACHA mainly. Les Terrasses can be drunk soonest; Finca Dofí has a dark undertone of Cab Sauv, Syrah, Merlot, CARIÑENA. Super-pricey L'Ermita is powerfully and dense from low-yielding GARNACHA.

Palacios, Descendientes de J El B r ★★★ Young biodynamic producer Ricardo Pérez, nephew of ÁLVARO PALACIOS, impresses with MENCÍA – fine young *Petalos* 08, plus serious Villa de Corullón and Las Lamas grown on schist soils.

Palacios, Rafael Galic w ★★★ Small estate producing exceptional wine from old Godello vines in the Bibei Valley. Rafael – ÁLVARO PALACIOS' younger brother – is devoted to white wines. Two distinct styles, both DYA: As Sortes is intense, toasty, citrus-fruity and white-peachy with v. gd acidity, a fine expression of Godello; Louro do Bolo.

Palacios Remondo, Bodegas RB r w ★★→★★★ 04 05 06 07 08 09 Proving that his skills are not just in PRIORAT, ÁLVARO PALACIOS has revved up his family winery (1945). Complex, oaked white Plácet (07), with citrus, peach and fennel; and super-fruity, unoaked, red, La Vendimia; organic, smoky, red-fruit flavoured La Montesa; and big, mulberry-flavoured, GARNACHA-dominated Propiedad.

Parxet Alel p w sp ★★→★★★ DYA Small CAVA producer valiantly competing with real-estate agents from Barcelona. Zesty styles include Cuvée 21, excellent Brut Nature, fragrant Titiana Pinot N and expensive dessert version Cuvée Dessert. Best-known for refreshing, off-dry Pansà Blanca and still white Marqués de Alella. Concentrated Tionio from outpost in RIBERA DEL DUERO.

Pazo de Señorans Galic w ★★★ DYA Exceptionally fragrant ALBARIÑOS from a benchmark RÍAS BAIXAS BODEGA.

Penedès Cat r w sp ★→★★★★ 04 05 06 07 08 09 Demarcated region west of Barcelona best-known for CAVA. As a result, still some confusion over identity esp since arrival of extensive CATALUNYA DO. Best: ALBET I NOYA, Can Rafols des Caus, GRAMONA, JEAN LEÓN, TORRES.

Pesquera Rib del D r ★★★★ 94 95 04 05 06 07 Alejandro Fernández was the creative force behind modern RIBERA DEL DUERO and is still a benchmark. Satisfying CRIANZA and RESERVA, and excellent, mature, well-seasoned Janus for those who can afford the price tag. *See also* CONDADO DE HAZA.

Pingus, Dominio de Rib del D r ★★★★ 01 03 04 05 06 Peter Sisseck's star continues to shine in RIBERA DEL DUERO. Production at Pingus may be tiny but there's plenty of demand for biodynamic Pingus, with its intense black fruit, fresh herbal overtones and subtle oak and tannins, made for cellaring; second label *Flor de Pingus* is more floral fruit. "Psi" is the latest project, and oak takes a step down.

Plá i Llevant Mall r w ★→★★★ 04 05 06 07 08 09 11 wineries comprise this tiny DO in MALLORCA. Aromatic whites and intense, spicy reds. Best: Toni Gelabert, Jaime Mesquida, Miguel Oliver and Vins Can Majoral.

Priorat/Priorato Cat r w ★★→★★★★ 01 04 05 06 07 08 Isolated enclave renowned for *llicorella* (slate) soils and terraced v'yards. Revived by René Barbier and others. The pioneer wineries – inc CLOS MOGADOR, MAS MARTINET, ÁLVARO PALACIOS – remain consistently gd, showing characteristic minerally purity. Recent temptation to create overextracted, overconcentrated, overpriced wines at last abandoned in favour of better balance. Other top names inc: Val-Llach, Cims de Porrera, Clos Erasmus, Clos de l'Obac, Clos Nelin, Clos i Terrasses. New arrivals inc: Ferrer-Bobet, TORRES, Dits del Terra (the project of South African Eben Sadie).

Remelluri, La Granja R Ala r w ★★→★★★ Beautiful mountainous estate making pedigree RIOJA reds from its own 105 ha. TELMO RODRIGUEZ started at his family property where he created the intriguing DYA white made from six different varieties. The future looks promising as he is returning to run it with his sister.

Remírez de Ganuza, Bodegas Fernando R Ala r w ★★→★★★ 04 05 06 07 08 09 Boutique winery taking a modern approach to Tempranillo-based wines.

Reserva Gd-quality wine matured for long periods. Red *reservas* must spend at least 1 yr in cask and 2 yrs in bottle; *gran reservas*, 2 yrs in cask and 3 yrs in bottle. Thereafter, many continue to mature for yrs. Many producers now eschew RESERVA/CRIANZA regulations, preferring clear vintage declaration.

Rías Baixas Galic w (r) ★★→★★★★ DYA GALICIAN DO increasing in global reputation and production. Founded on the ALBARIÑO variety, in five subzones: Val do Salnés, O Rosal, Condado do Tea, Soutomaior and Ribera do Ulla. The best are outstanding: Adegas Galegas, As Laxas, Castro Baroña, Fillaboa, Coto de Xiabre, Gerardo Méndez, new kid on the block Viña Nora, PALACIO DE FEFIÑANES, Pazo de Barrantes, Quinta do Lobelle, Santiago Ruíz, Terras Gauda, La Val and Valdamor. Growing interest in increased lees-ageing and barrel ageing.

Ribeiro w (r) ★→★★★ DYA GALICIAN DO in western Ourense. Whites are relatively low in alcohol and acidity, made from Treixadura, Torrontés, Godello, Loureiro, Lado. Top producers: VIÑA MEÍN, Lagar do Merens. Also specialty sweet, Tostado.

Ribera del Duero r p ★★→★★★★ 01 02 03 04 05 06 07 08 09 Fashionable, still-expanding DO east of Valladolíd, with almost 250 wineries. Tinto Fino (Tempranillo) holds sway. Some Cab, Merlot. A handful of outstanding wineries but fame of VEGA SICILIA still dominates, and there is much confusion of styles. Best producers: AALTO, ALIÓN, Astrales, CONDADO DE HAZA, HACIENDA MONASTERIO, Pago de los Capellanes, PAGO DE CARRAOVEJAS, Pérez Pascuas Hermanos, PESQUERA, PINGUS, VALBUENA. *See also* VDT ABADÍA RETUERTA and MAURO. Others to look for: Balbás, Bohórquez, Dehesa de los Canónigos, O Fournier, Hermanos Sastre, Tinio (*see* PARXET) and Vallebueno.

Rioja r p w sp ★→★★★★ 64 70 75 78 81 82 85 89 91 92 94 95 96 98 01 04 05 06 07 08 09 To the chagrin of producers elsewhere, Rioja continues to overshadow the rest of Spain. Yet no one could accuse it of being monotone. A few wineries, notably LA RIOJA ALTA and LÓPEZ DE HEREDIA, continue to make exceptional old-fashioned styles; there are the pedigree traditionalists such as CONTINO, MARQUÉS DE MURRIETA, MUGA, Marqués de Vargas, PALACIOS REMONDO and the Eguren family's Sierra Cantabria; others, such as FINCA ALLENDE, ARTADI, BAIGORRI, RODA, the Eguren family's Señorío de San Vicente and Tobia are producing more energetic styles. There are also many brands: the vigorous but basic Viña Pomal of formerly revered Bilbaínas, top-seller Campo Viejo, the now-reviving CVNE, the smooth reds of Faustino, the ever-reliable FAMILIA MARTÍNEZ BUJANDA wines. There are lots of v. reliable, consistent producers who simply make gd wine, such as the v. drinkable Luis Cañas. Thankfully Rioja whites are looking up at last as producers may now substitute Chard, Sauv Bl and Verdejo for the dull Viura.

Rioja Alta, Bodegas La r w (p sw) ★★★★ 81 95 97 00 01' 02 03 Discover traditional RIOJA. Delicate, mature, in four RESERVA styles. Alberdi is light and cedary with overtones of tobacco and redcurrants; Ardanza riper, a touch spicier but still elegant, boosted by lovely GARNACHA; the excellent, tangy, vanilla-edged GRAN RESERVA 904 and the fine, multilayered Gran Reserva 890, aged 6 yrs in oak. Also owns RÍAS BAIXAS Lagar de Cervera.

Roda, Bodegas R Alt r ★★★★ 00 01' 03 04' 05' 06 Ambitious modern BODEGA with impressive cellar making serious modern RESERVA reds from low-yield Tempranillo, backed by strong R&D. Three wines: Roda, Roda I and Cirsión. Also try outstanding Dauro olives from the same owners.

Rueda w ★★ →★★★ Small but ever-growing DO south of Valladolíd; Spain's most modern, crisp DYA whites from indigenous Verdejo, Sauv Bl, Viura and blends thereof. Barrel-fermented versions remain fashionable though less appealing. Best: Alvarez y Diez, *Belondrade*, François Lurton, MARQUÉS DE RISCAL, Naia, Ossian, José Pariente, Palacio de Bornos, Javier Sanz, SITIOS DE BODEGA, Veracruz and Vinos Sanz. New entry Unzu from JULIÁN CHIVITE López of NAVARRA family.

Sandoval, Finca Manchuela, La M ★★★ 02 03 05 06 07 Victor de la Serna is on form: his Finca Sandoval (Syrah/Monastrell/Bobal) is a wine of impressive balance, dark fruits, soft tannins, herbal notes and bright acid; second wine Salia (Syrah/GARNACHA/Bobal) altogether simpler but half the price.

Sitios de Bodega ★★ →★★★ Fifth-generation winemaker Ricardo Sanz and siblings left father Antonio Sanz's Palacio de Bornos to set up their own winery in 2005. Excellent DYA RUEDA whites (Con Class and Palacio de Ménade). Associated BODEGAS Terna, from its base in La Seca, produces interesting, high-quality reds from other regions, inc Spain's first sweet Tempranillo: La Dolce Tita VDT.

Somontano r w p ★★ →★★★ 04 05 06 07 08 09 Cool-climate DO in Pyrénéan foothills east of Zaragoza has failed so far to fulfil expectations. Much of the problem is reliance on international varieties, which reduces regionality. Opt for Merlot, Gewürz, or Chard. Best producers: ENATE, VIÑAS DEL VERO with its top property Secastilla, recently acquired by GONZÁLEZ BYASS (*see* Port, Sherry & Madeira); interesting newcomers, inc the space-age BODEGAS Irius and Laus.

Tares, Dominio de El B r w ★★★ 04 05 06 07 08 Up-and-coming producer whose dark, spicy, purple-scented *Bembibre and Cepas Viejas* proves what can be done with MENCÍA in Bierzo. Sister winery VDT Dominio dos Tares makes a range of wines from the interesting black Prieto Picudo variety: the simple Estay, more muscular Leione and big, spicy Cumal.

Telmo Rodríguez, Compañía de Vinos r w sw ★★ →★★★ Enthusiastic seeker of old vines, winemaker Telmo Rodríguez now sources and makes a wide range of excellent DO wines from all over Spain, inc MÁLAGA (Molina Real Moscatels), RIOJA (Lanzaga and Matallana), RUEDA (Basa), TORO (Dehesa Gago, Gago and Pago la Jara) and *Valdeorras* (DYA Gaba do Xil Godello). Now returning to REMELLURI in RIOJA – look for rise in quality.

Toro r ★ →★★★★ 04 05 06 07 08 09 Unstoppably fashionable DO in Zamora province, west of Valladolíd. 40 wineries do their best with local Tinta de Toro (acclimatized Tempranillo). Some continue to be rustic and overalcoholic but others are boldly expressive. Try Maurodos, with fresh, black-fruit-scented Prima and glorious old-vine San Román, as well as VEGA SICILIA-owned Pintia. Glamour comes with Numanthia, Teso la Monja. Also recommended: Domaine Magrez Espagne, Pago la Jara from TELMO RODRÍGUEZ, Quinta de la Quietud, Sobreño.

Toro Albalá Mont-M ★★ →★★★ Antonio Sánchez is known for his eccentric wine museum and his remarkable old PXs. The Don PX is made from sun-dried grapes, barrique-aged for a minimum of 25 yrs. Black, with flavours of molasses, treacle, figs, it ages indefinitely. Current vintage is 1979, yet the 1910 was only recently released. Look out for un-aged, amber-coloured DYA Dulce de Pasas, tasting of liquid raisins and apricots.

Torres, Miguel Pen r p w sw ★★ →★★★★ 01 04 05 06 07 08 09 Spain's best-known family wine firm. Properties in Chile and California. Continues to reinvent and renew itself. Currently, most informed producer about environmental issues. Makes some of the best wines from commercial to single-vy'd: ever-reliable DYA CATALUNYA Viña Sol, grapey Viña Esmeralda, PENEDÈS Sauv Bl/Parellada *Fransola*.

SPAIN

> **Where did the oak go?**
> Once upon a time RIOJA could always be identified by its vanilla
> sweetness, from long ageing in American oak barrels. Then producers
> recognized the greater status of French oak internationally and liked
> its effects. So all across the region cellars flaunted row upon row of
> brand-new oak. The result? Cedar – and sawdust – prevailed over
> the fruit. Similarly in newer regions, such as Priorat. Producers had
> to begin by putting their wine in new barrels. However the yrs have
> passed, the barrels are older and milder, the vines are older, too, with
> more concentrated fruit. And perhaps the growers are older, too,
> and have enough confidence in their wines not to need to flaunt
> the oak. The happy result is that Spain has calmed down and is
> reaching a pleasing equilibirum.

Best reds inc: classic CATALUNYA Gran Sangre de Toro; fine Penedès Cabernet
Mas la Plana; balanced, old-style Reserva Real (06). Its CONCA DE BARBERÀ duo
(*Milmanda* – one of Spain's finest Chards – and **Grans Muralles** multiblend
of local varietals) is stunning, and JEAN LEÓN has v.gd offerings, too. The range
continues to expand with workmanlike offerings from RIBERA DEL DUERO (Celeste)
and RIOJA (Ibéricos), gd PRIORAT (Salmos). The indefatigable Miguel Torres
(father) speaks of retirement – will son or winemaker daughter take the helm?

Unidas, Bodegas Umbrella organization controlling MARQUÉS DE MONISTROL, and the
BERBERANA brand, as well as workman-like RIOJA Marqués de la Concordia and
Durius from RIBERA DEL DUERO. Controls MARQUÉS DE GRIÑÓN RIOJA brand.

Utiel-Requena r p (w) ★→★★ Satellite region of VALENCIA starting to forge its own
identity by virtue of excellent Bobal variety, but hampered by its size (more than
40,000 ha), which has made it primarily a feeder for the industrial requirements
of nearby VALENCIA. Promising wines from Vicente Gandía, Alvares Nölting.

Valbuena Rib del D r ★★★★ 99 00 01 02 03 04 05 From the same stable as VEGA
SICILIA but sold when just 5 yrs old. Best at about 10 yrs; some prefer it to its elder
brother. For a more modern take on RIBERA DEL DUERO, *see* ALIÓN.

Valdeorras w r ★→★★★ GALICIAN DO in northwest Ourense fighting off its co-op-
inspired image by virtue of its DYA Godello: a highly aromatic and nationally
fashionable variety, also grown in nearby BIERZO. Best producers: Godeval, RAFAEL
PALACIOS, A Tapada, TELMO RODRÍGUEZ.

Valdepeñas r (w) ★→★★ 05 06 07 08 09 Big DO nr Andalucían border. V.gd-value
lookalike RIOJA reds, made primarily from Cencibel (Tempranillo) grape. One
producer shines: Félix Solís; *Viña Albali* brand offers real value.

Valencia r w p ★ 05 06 07 08 09 Big exporter of table wine. Primary source of
budget fortified sweet Moscatel. Most reliable producer: Murviedro.

Vega Sicilia Rib del D r ★★★★ 60 62 68 70 81 87 89 90 91 94 95 96 98 99
Spain's most prestigious BODEGA, even though not in the prestige zone of RIOJA.
Winemaking distinguished by meticulous care. Wines are deep in colour, with
an aromatic cedarwood nose, intense and complex in flavour, finishing long.
Controlled, elegant Único is aged for 6 yrs in oak; RESERVA Especial spends up to
10 yrs in barrel, then declared as NV. *See also* VALBUENA, ALIÓN, Pintia in TORO and
Oremus Tokaji, Hungary).

Vendimia Vintage.

Viña Literally, a v'yd.

Viña Meín w ★★★ Small estate, in a gradually emerging GALICIAN DO, making two
DYA exceptional whites of same name: one in steel and one barrel-fermented;
both from some seven local varieties.

Viñas del Vero Som r p w ★★ →★★★ 04 05 06 07 08 09 Improving winery, acquired by GONZÁLEZ BYASS (*see* Sherry). Top wines: Blecua and Secastilla, from GARNACHA.

Vino de la Tierra (VDT) Table wine of superior quality made in a demarcated region without DO. Covering immense geographical possibilities, this category inc many prestigious producers who are non-DO by choice in order to be freer of often inflexible regulation and produce the varieties they want. Currently all is uncertain as Spain discovers how best to manage the new wine categories.

Vivanco, Dinastia R Alt r w ★★ Major family-run commercial BODEGA in BRIONES, with some interesting single-varietal wines. *Wine museum is worth the detour.*

PORTUGAL

Recent vintages

2010 Wet winter, hot dry summer resulted in good quality and quantity. Bairrada had another excellent year. In Alentejo, may have been too hot.

2009 A good year overall. Bairrada and Lisboa excellent. Heat spikes in the Douro, Tejo and Alentejo made for big wines with high alcohol.

2008 Almost uniformly excellent; especially Bairrada and Alentejo. Low yields, slow ripening and ideal harvest gave fruit intensity, balance and aroma.

2007 Aromatic whites and well-balanced reds with round tannins.

2006 Forward reds with soft, ripe fruit and whites with less acidity than usual.

2005 Powerful reds; the Douro's finely balanced reds shine.

2004 A cool summer but glorious September and October. Well-balanced reds.

2003 Hot summer: ripe, early-maturing wines, especially Bairrada and south.

Adega A cellar or winery.

Afros Min w sp r ★★★ Intense LOUREIRO and Vinhão (r) VINHO VERDE from Portugal's first biodynamically certified estate.

Alenquer Lis r w ★★ →★★★ 04 05 06 07 08 09' 10 Sheltered DOC making gd reds just north of Lisbon. Estate wines from PANCAS and MONTE D'OIRO lead the field.

Alentejo r (w) ★ →★★★★ 02 03 04' 05 06 07' 08' 09 10 Huge, southerly DOC divided into subregions with own DOCS: Borba, Redondo, Reguengos, PORTALEGRE, Evora, Granja-Amareleja, Vidigueira, Moura. VINHO REGIONAL Alentejano preferred by many top estates. A reliably dry climate makes rich, ripe reds: key international varieties inc Syrah, Alicante Bouschet and recently Petit Verdot. Gd whites from Antão Vaz, blended with ARINTO, VERDELHO and Roupeiro. Established players CARMO, CARTUXA, CORTES DE CIMA, ESPORÃO, MOUCHÃO, MOURO, JOÃO PORTUGAL RAMOS and ZAMBUJEIRO have potency and style. Of the new guard, MALHADINHA NOVA, dos Grous and Dona Maria impress. Names to watch: SÃO MIGUEL and do Rocim, Monte da Ravasqueira, Terrenus, Fita Preta and QUINTA do Centro. Best co-ops are at Borba, Redondo and Reguengos.

Algarve r w p sp ★ →★★ Southern coast VINHO REGIONAL; DOCS include Lagos, Tavira, Lagoa and Portimão. Crooner Cliff Richard's Adega do Cantor and Quinta do Morgado are at the vanguard of a shift from quaffers to quality wine. Names to watch: Monte da Casteleja and Quinta do Frances.

Aliança, Caves Bair r w sp p res ★★ →★★★ Large firm with four estates in BAIRRADA, inc QUINTA das Baceladas making gd reds and classic-method sparkling. Also interests in BEIRAS (Casa d'Aguiar), ALENTEJO (Quinta da Terrugem), DÃO (Quinta da Garrida) and the DOURO (Quatro Ventos).

Alorna, Quinta de Tej r w p ★ →★★ DYA Appealingly zippy, ARINTO-driven whites, creamy rosé and gd reds from indigenous and international varieties.

Alvarinho Min Emerging as Portugal's, as well as VINHO VERDE's, leading white grape. Best are fragrant, fruity and age-worthy VINHO VERDE from Monção and Melgaço subregions. Elsewhere, fruity single varietal wine or adds lift to blends. Known as Albariño in neighbouring Galicia.

Ameal, Quinta do Min w sp sw ★★★ DYA Leading LOUREIRO VINHO VERDE by ANSELMO MENDES, inc age-worthy oaked Escolha, Special Late Harvest, ARINTO ESPUMANTE.

Aragonez Alen Successful red grape (Spain's Tempranillo) in ALENTEJO for varietal wines. *See* TINTA RORIZ.

Arinto White grape. Makes v.gd, aromatic, citrus-driven wines in BUCELAS, and features countrywide, often adding welcome zip to blends, esp in ALENTEJO.

Aveleda, Quinta da Min w r p ★→★★ DYA Reliable estate-grown VINHO VERDE from the Guedes family, inc big-selling brand *Casal García*. Less traditional are Charamba (DOURO) and Follies (VINHO VERDE, BAIRRADA), also new Follies "Grande" top tier and AVA crisp, white table wine.

Azevedo, Quinta do Min w ★★ DYA SOGRAPE's v.gd estate LOUREIRO-led VINHO VERDE.

Bacalhoa, Quinta da Set r ★★★ 01 02 03 04 05 06 07 08 Estate nr SETÚBAL. Elegant, mid-weight Cab Sauv/Merlot blend made by BACALHOA VINHOS. Fleshier Palaçio de Bacalhoa (more Merlot). Gd new white Bordeaux blend (ALVARINHO).

Bacalhoa Vinhos Alen, Lis, Set r w sw sp p ★★→★★★ Owned by Berardo Group, which owns QUINTA DO CARMO and significant holdings in CAVES ALIANÇA and SOGRAPE. Broad, accomplished range, inc BACALHOA, Berardo Reserve Familiar, JP, Serras de Azeitão, Só, Catarina, Cova da Ursa and v.gd Setúbal Moscatel (SETÚBAL/ PENÍNSULA DE SETÚBAL), Loridos (Estremadura) and TINTO DA ANFORA (ALENTEJO).

Bágeiras, Quinta das Bair r w sp ★★★→★★★★ (GARRAFEIRA r) 01' 03 04' 05' 24 ha estate established in 1990 by Màrio Sérgio Alves Nuno. Stunning GARRAFEIRA, red (Baga) and white are traditionally crafted and v. age-worthy, as is RESERVA red. Fine zero *dosage* sparkling wines, too.

Bairrada r sp p w ★→★★★★ 99 00 01 03' 04 05' 06 07 08' 09' 10' Central Atlantic-influenced DOC. Traditional strengths are sparkling wines and austere, age-worthy reds made from the Baga grape. New regulations allowing for different varieties have improved approachability of reds but endangered Baga plantings. Top Baga specialists include Casa de Saima, CAVES SÃO JOÃO, LUÍS PATO, Quinta de Foz de Arouce, Sidónia de Sousa and QUINTA DAS BÁGEIRAS. Leading modernists inc: CAMPOLARGO and Quinta do Encontro.

Barca Velha Dou r ★★★★ 81 82 85 91' 95' 99 00 Portugal's most famous red was created in 1952 by FERREIRA. It is made only in exceptional years in v. limited quantities. Intense, complex with a deep bouquet, it forged the DOURO's reputation for stellar wines. Distinguished, traditional style (aged several yrs before release). Second wine known as *Reserva Ferreirinha*.

Beira Interior Bei ★ Isolated DOC nr Spain's border. Huge potential from old and elevated v'yds; QUINTAS do Cardo, dos Currais and Oscar Almeida impress.

Beiras ★→★★★★ VINHO REGIONAL covering DÃO, BAIRRADA and granite ranges of central Portugal. Used by innovative producers such as LUÍS and FILIPA PATO.

Branco White.

Brejoeira, Palácio da Min w ★★ Traditional ALVARINHO VINHO VERDE from prestigious estate facing increasing competition, but it holds its own.

Brito e Cunha, João Dou r w ★★→★★★ 04 05 Young gun Brito e Cunha makes intense, elegant, mineral DOURO reds from QUINTA de San José, esp the RESERVA. The more widely sourced Azéo, esp the Reserva (w and r), is also v.gd.

Bucelas Lis w ★★ DYA Tiny DOC north of Lisbon focused on ARINTO ("Lisbon Hock" in 19th-century England). QUINTAS da Romeira, da Murta make tangy, racy wines.

Cabriz, Quinta de Dão r w p ★★→★★★ 03 04 05 06 07 08 Owned by DÃO SUL; modern, fruity, fresh but characterful wines, with gd Dão typicity. Flagship Four C is v.gd.

Cadaval, Casa Tej r w ★★ 05' **06 07** 08 Blends include gd-value Padre Pedro and showy RESERVA, Marquêsa de Cadaval. Pioneer of French varietal reds inc Pinot N, but old-vine TRINCADEIRA easily the best.

Campolargo Bair r w sp ★→★★★ 06 07 08 09 10' Large estate, until 2004 sold grapes to ALIANÇA. Gd innovative reds, mostly blends incorporating native varieties, Bordeaux varieties, also Pinot N. Diga Petit Verdot is promising as is new DÃO red made by Alvarão Castro (*see* SAES).

Carcavelos Lis br sw ★★★ Minute DOC west of Lisbon. Hen's-teeth sweet apéritif or dessert wines average 19% alcohol and resemble honeyed MADEIRA.

Carmo, Quinta do Alen r w p ★★→★★★ 03 04' 05 06 07' 50 ha, once co-owned by Rothschilds (Lafite), now owned by BACALHOA VINHOS. Fresh white and polished reds with Cab Sauv have Bordeaux restraint. Second wine: Dom Martinho.

Cartuxa, Adega da Alen r w sp ★★→★★★★ The move from 17th-century cellars to a state-of-the-art winery in 2007 increased quantity and quality. Traditionally styled flagship Pêra Manca white and red (95 97 98 **01 03** 05' 07) impress; Foral de Evora is gd-value second wine. More fruit-forward is well-made Scala Coeli red from non-local grapes. New sparkling and ALVARINHO are work in progress.

Carvalhais, Quinta dos Dão r p w sp ★★★ (r) 01 **03 04 05** 06 SOGRAPE's principal DÃO brand: eponymous single-estate wines, inc flagship Unico, v.gd Encuzado (w). Volume Duque de Viseu *marque* is made from estate and bought-in grapes.

Casal Branco, Quinta do Tej r w ★★→★★★ Large family estate. Gd entry-level wines blend local CASTELÃO and FERNÃO PIRES with others. Flagship Falcoaria range focuses on old-vine, local varieties, esp Reserva red (03 04' 05' 07).

Castelão Set Planted throughout south Portugal, esp in PENÍNSULA DE SETÚBAL. Nicknamed PERIQUITA. Firm, raspberryish reds develop figgish, tar-like quality.

Chocapalha, Quinta de Lis r p w ★★→★★★ (r) 04 05 06 07' Fine, modern estate. TOURIGA NACIONAL, TINTA RORIZ underpin rich reds, Cab Sauv is sinewy. Gd unoaked Sauv Bl, ARINTO, ARINTO-blend and fine oaked Chard/native white blend.

Chryseia Dou r ★★★→★★★★ 03' **04 05'** 06 07 08' V. successful partnership of Bordeaux's Bruno Prats and SYMINGTON FAMILY ESTATES; dense yet elegant from Port varieties now sourced from dedicated v'yds at QUINTAS de Perdiz and DE RORIZ, Chryseia's new home. V.gd second wine: *Post Scriptum* (05' **06 07** 08).

Churchill Estates Dou r w p (03 **04 05** 06 07 08) Fast-expanding range from Port shipper Churchill, now inc a white. Well-made reds inc RESERVA, Grande Reserva, single-varietal TOURIGA NACIONAL (and rosé), single-estate Quinta da Gricha.

Colares Lis r w ★★ Tiny DOC west of Lisbon. Coastal sandy soils account for its heritage of ungrafted Ramisco (r) and Malvasia (w) vines, giving tannic reds and oxidative whites. Biggest producer is Adega Regional de Colares (a co-op). Rising stars: newcomers Fundação Oriente and Stanley Ho are making well-structured but more contemporary styles.

Consumo (vinho) Ordinary (wine).

Cortes de Cima Alen r w ★★★ (r) 03 04 05 06 07 08' (w) DYA Vidigueira estate owned by Danish family. Heady, fruit-driven, single-variety wines, inc pioneering but pricey Syrah, Incognito. Homenagem a Hans Christian Andersen is better value. RESERVA (a blend) is most refined; new Petit Verdot v. promising. Unoaked Chaminé and Courela are gd quaffers.

Crasto, Quinta do Dou r w ★★→★★★★ (r) **01'** 02 **03'** 04 05' 06 07' 08 (w) DYA Impressive old-vine blends inc the single-v'yd Vinha da Ponte (98 00' 01 **03 04** 07') and María Theresa (00' 03' **05' 06 07**) made only in top yrs, also v.gd value-for-money RESERVA. Gd varietal wines occasionally made (TOURIGA NACIONAL, TINTA RORIZ). New Crasto Superior hails from youthful DOURO Superior v'yd. Xisto is joint-venture red with Jean-Michel Cazes from Bordeaux. Also Port.

Dão r w p ★★→★★★ 00' 01 02 03' **04 05** 06 07' 08' Established DOC in central

Portugal. Once rustic, now structured, elegant reds and whites come into own with food. Once dominated by co-ops, quality-focused producers large and small have improved consistency and calibre, esp DÃO SUL and QUINTAS MAIAS, DE PELLADA, DOS ROQUES and DE SAES. Rising stars: Vinha Paz and QUINTAS da Bica, da Falorca and do Corujão. New VINHO REGIONAL: Terras do Dão.

Dão Sul Dão r w ★★→★★★★ Dynamic DÃO-based venture. Impressive range with international appeal, inc QUINTA CABRIZ, CASA DE SANTAR and Quinta dos Grilos (DÃO), Sá de Baixo and das Tecedeiras (DOURO), do Encontro (BAIRRADA), do Gradil (LISBOA) and Herdade Monte da Cal (ALENTEJO). Quirky collaborations inc Homenagen (with LUÍS PATO); Dourat (DOURO TOURIGA NACIONAL/Spanish GARNACHA) and Pião (DÃO TOURIGA NACIONAL/Italian Nebbiolo). Latest venture is VINHO VERDE, made with QUINTA de Lourosa.

Denominacão de Origem Controlada (DOC) Demarcated wine region controlled by a regional commission. *See also* VINHO REGIONAL.

DFJ Vinhos r w p ★→★★ Mostly volume brands for export from TEJO and LISBOA, inc Pink Elephant rosé, Segada (r w), Manta Preta (r) and Bela Fonte DYA. Premium labels inc Grand'Arte (also sourced from the DOURO, DÃO and ALENTEJO) and QUINTA do Rocio, an unusual red blend, which includes Grenache.

Doce (vinho) Sweet (wine).

Douro Dou r w p sw ★★→★★★★ 00' 01 02 03' 04' 05' 06' 07' 08' Famous for Port and now world-class sumptuous, powerful red wines, the best with a sinewy, mineral core, and surprisingly fine whites of burgundian depth and complexity. Look for BARCA VELHA, CHRYSEIA, QUINTA DO CRASTO, NIEPOORT, QUINTA DO POIERA, VALE DONA MARIA, VALE MEÃO and WINE & SOUL. Names to watch: JOÃO BRITO E CUNHA, Conceito, Terrus and QUINTAS Nova, da Romaneira and de Tourais. VINHO REGIONAL is Duriense.

Duas Quintas Douro Dou r w ★★★ 01 02 03' 04 05 06 07' 08 Rich reds from Port shipper RAMOS PINTO, inc v.gd RESERVA, Collection, outstanding but pricey Especial.

Duorum Dou r ★★ →★★★ "From two" in Latin, Duorum combines the skills of leading oenologists JOÃO PORTUGAL RAMOS and Jose Maria Soares Franco, who oversaw BARCA VELHA for 27 years. Castelo Melhor is new 250 ha v'yd in DOURO Superior. Meantime, grapes for modern, fruit-led table wines, "Tons", COLHEITA and RESERVA, sourced from old, elevated v'yds. V.gd vintage Port too.

Esporão, Herdade do Alen w r sw ★★→★★★ 03 04 05 06 07' 08' Big quality estate (600 ha; new organic trial of 80 ha). Monte Velho, Alandra and Vinha da Defesa brands showcase ALENTEJO's ripe fruit. Quatro Castas, new improved (lower production) single-varietal range, Esporão RESERVAS, Private Selection (r w), GARRAFEIRA and flagship Torre do Esporão offer increasing depth and complexity. Recently acquired Quinta das Murças in the DOURO – 2008 is first trial vintage.

Espumante Sparkling. Best from BAIRRADA, DOURO (esp Vértice) and now VINHO VERDE.

Falua Tej r p w JOÃO PORTUGAL RAMOS' state-of-the-art venture. Well-made export brands inc entry-level Monte de Serra followed by Tagus Creek, inc RESERVA, which blends indigenous and international varieties. Tãmara and Conde de Vimioso are more traditional premium styles.

Feital, do Quinta Min w ★★★ 07' 08' Young Galician winemaker Marcial Dorado makes characterful VINHO VERDE. Lees-aged in old oak with partial malolactic, Dorado ALVARINHO is powerful and textured. Auratus, a blend of ALVARINHO and Trajadura is also v.gd.

Fernão Pires Tej White grape making aromatic, ripe-flavoured, slightly spicy whites in TEJO. (Known as María Gomes in BAIRRADA.)

Ferreira Dou r w ★→★★★★ SOGRAPE-owned Port shipper making gd to v.gd DOURO wines under Casa Ferreirinha labels: Esteva, Vinha Grande, Quinta de Leda, RESERVA Especial Ferreirinha and BARCA VELHA.

Fonseca, José María da Lis r p w dr sw sp res ★★→★★★ Historic family-owned estate. Pioneer of SETÚBAL fortified Moscatel and, with old vintages, a leader in this field. Volume branded wines such as LANCERS and PERIQUITA. Colecção Privada label continues innovation, esp unique Moscatel Roxo rosé. Other brands: Montado, Terras Altas (DÃO), Quinta de Camarate, Pasmados, Vinya, Privada Domingos Soares Franco and flagships FSF, Domini/Domini Plus (DOURO) and Hexagon.

Gaivosa, Quinta de Dou r w ★★★→★★★★ 01 03 04 05' 06 07 08' Leading estate nr Régua. Characterful range includes textured old-style Branco da Gaivosa white and concentrated old-vine red varietals (v.gd TOURIGA NACIONAL) and blends from different terroir, inc Abandonado, Quinta das Caldas, Vinha de Lordelo, RESERVA Pessoal, Vale da Raposa.

Garrafeira Label term: merchant's "private reserve", aged for min 2 yrs in cask and 1 yr in bottle, often much longer. Once most merchant's reds were called this.

Lagoalva, Quinta da Tej r w p ★★ 05' 06 07 08 Go-ahead estate, making modern, fresh wines. Gd use of Portuguese (esp Alfrocheiro) and international varieties (esp Chard, Sauv Bl, Syrah). Second label: Monte da Casta.

Lancers p w sp ★ Semi-sweet (semi-sparkling) rosé, widely shipped to the USA by JOSÉ MARÍA DA FONSECA. Rosé Free is alcohol-free.

Lavradores de Feitoria Dou r w ★★→★★★ 18 small quality-conscious estates blending from across the three DOURO regions. Labels: Meruge, Três Bagos. Sauv Bl v.gd. Reds can be oaky.

Lisboa VINHO REGIONAL on west coast, formerly Estremadura. DOCS: ALENQUER, Arruda, BUCELAS, CARCAVELOS, COLARES, Encostas d'Aire, Obidos, Torres Vedras. Wines can be pedestrian but QUINTAS DA CHOCAPALHA and esp DO MONTE D'OIRO reveal potential. Newcomers to watch: QUINTAS de Sant'Ana (promising Ries, ALVARINHO, Pinot N and gd Portuguese red blends) and do Pinto (Rhône white varieties).

Loureiro Min Best VINHO VERDE grape variety after ALVARINHO: delicate, floral whites.

Madeira w r ★→★★★ Famous for its eponymous fortified dessert and apéritif wines, Portugal's Atlantic island also makes unfortified wine (Terras Madeirenses VINHO REGIONAL and Madeirense DOC). Made by leading winemakers Rui Reguinga and Francisco Albuquerque (of Blandy's), Primeira Paixão VERDELHO is v.gd, but most is for quaffing.

Maias, Quinta das Dão ★★→★★★ (r) 01 03 04 05' 06 07' 08' (w) DYA Sister of QUINTA DOS ROQUES. Benchmark Jaen and DÃO's only VERDELHO; Flor das Maias (2005; 2007) is showy TOURIGA NACIONAL-dominated blend.

Malhadinha Nova, Herdade da Alen r p w sw ★★★ 03' 04 05 06 07' 08' Young vines but mature, quality-focused approach: v.gd big, spicy reds and rich, oak-aged white from ALENTEJO's deep south. Flagship is Marias da Malhadinha but muscular Malhadinha Tinto gives plenty of bang for buck. New Petit Manseng sweetie.

Mateus Rosé p sp (w) ★ World's bestselling, medium-dry, lightly carbonated rosé table wine from SOGRAPE. Original is Portuguese but international versions hail from France (Shiraz) and Spain (Tempranillo).

Mendes, Anselmo Min w sp sw ★★→★★★★ Acclaimed VINHO VERDE winemaker who consults widely, inc at QUINTAS DO AMEAL and DE GAIVOSA. Eponymous ALVARINHO-focused range, inc Contacto, Muros Antigos and Muros de Melgaço. Oak-aged Curtimenta and a new single-parcel ALVARINHO (yet to be named) show immense depth and concentration.

Messias r w ★→★★★ Large BAIRRADA-based firm; interests in DOURO (inc port). Old-school reds best.

Minho Min River between north Portugal and Spain, and VINHO REGIONAL. A number of leading VINHO VERDE producers prefer to use VR Minho.

Monte d'Oiro, Quinta do Lis r w ★★★→★★★★ (Res) 01' 03 04' 05 06' 07' Rhône fan José Bento dos Santos has benefited from Maison Chapoutier's (*see* France) vine cuttings and consultancy – easily Portugal's best producer of Syrah, inc Homenagem Antonio Carqueja; the RESERVA and an as yet unnamed wine made exclusively from Chapoutier cuttings. Madrigal Viognier is also v.gd as is second wine, Lybra. Chapoutier is joint-venture partner for Bento & Chapoutier's velvety Ex Aequo Syrah/TOURIGA NACIONAL (06 07').

Mouchão, Herdade de Alen r w ★★★ **99 00 01 03'** 05' Leading traditional estate. Intense, fragrant wines realize full potential of the Alicante Bouschet grape. *Flagship Tonel 3–4*, exceptional yrs only, has great complexity and persistence. Ponte das Canas is a contemporary blend of Alicante Bouschet with TOURIGAS NACIONAL and Franca and Shiraz; Dom Rafael gd value.

Mouro, Quinta do Alen r ★★★→★★★★ **98 99** 00 04' 05' 06' Fabulous, structured, terroir-driven reds, mostly ALENTEJO grapes, though single-varietal TOURIGA NACIONAL and Cab Sauv also made. Dry-farmed, low yields, concentrated, supple wines. Flagship Mouro Gold made in exceptional yrs (99 00 02 05 06').

Murganheira, Caves ★ Largest producer of ESPUMANTE. Now owns RAPOSEIRA.

Niepoort Dou r w p ★★★→★★★★ Family Port shipper making exceptional DOURO wines: Tiara (w), Vertente (r), Redoma (r p w, inc w Reserve) **01 03 04' 05' 06'** 07' 08', Robustus (r) 04 05, Batuta (r) **01' 03 04** 05' 07 08' and Charme (r) 02 **04 05'** 06 07' 08. Experimental Projectos range inc: a DOURO Ries, Sauv Bl and Pinot N. Collaborations with QUINTA DE PELLADA, SOALHEIRO, QUINTA DAS BÁGEIRAS, Muhr-van-der-Niepoort, Equipo Navazos, TELMO RODRIGUEZ and Raul Perez-Ultreia, plus own stunning new Spanish wine, Ladredo from Ribeira Sacra.

Noval, Quinta do Dou r ★★★ Leading AXA-owned Port house. Made first super-premium unfortified reds in 2004: Quinta do Noval and gd-value Cedro. Innovative Syrah blend Cedro shows the French variety's affinity for the DOURO, as does new 100% Syrah called Labrador – after the winemaker's dog.

Palmela Set r w ★→★★★ CASTELÃO-focused DOC (*see* PEGOS CLAROS). Can be long-lived.

Pancas, Quinta de Lis r w ★★→★★★ (r) **01 03 05'** 07 08' (w) DYA Prestigious estate nr ALENQUER. Owner since 2006, Companhia das Quintas has overhauled range. Flagship is Grande Escolha followed by RESERVA range: TOURIGA NACIONAL and Cab Sauv and Selecção do Enólogo.

Passadouro, Quinta do Dou r w Winemaker WINE & SOUL's Jorge Serôdio Borges now has a stake in this expanding operation. Recently acquired v'yds have boosted production. Superbly concentrated old-vine RESERVA (03 **04' 05'** 06 07' 08) and gd-value estate wine now joined by white and entry label "Passa" red.

Pato, Filipa Bei r w sp sw ★★★→★★★★ LUÍS PATO's dynamic daughter is a passionate advocate of local varieties and co-founded Baga Friends to protect and promote the Baga grape. Her eponymous range and gd-value Vinhos Doidos label skilfully harness the full potential of BAIRRADA's and DÃO's traditional grapes, esp Ensaios, Lokal (r) and Bossa and Nossa (w).

Pato, Luís Bair r w sp sw ★★★→★★★★ 95' **97 99 00** 01' 03' 04 05' 06 07 08' Fine, *seriously age-worthy, single-v'yd Baga*: Vinhas Barrio, Pan, Barrosa and flagship Quinta do Ribeirinho Pé Franco (ungrafted vines) lead the pack. Also v.gd are elegant Vinhas Velhas and Quinta do Ribeirinho 1st Choice (a Baga/TOURIGA NACIONAL blend). João Pato, early drinking TOURIGA NACIONAL, now joined by single-v'yd TOURIGA from Vinha Formal. Shows equal flair with whites (Vinhas Formal and Velhas). Sparkling wines, inc new InFormal range, sealed under crown cap; sweet Abafado range and Baga Rebel more straightforward. Rebel's cheeky label is squarely aimed at a younger generation. Consults at Quinta do Popa, which supplies DOURO TINTA RORIZ for TRePA Baga blend.

Pegões, Adega de Set r w p sp sw ★→★★★ Portugal's most dynamic co-op, based in up-and-coming PENÍNSULA DE SETÚBAL, thrives under winemaker Jaime Quendera.

Gd range, inc varietals and blends made from Portuguese and international varieties. Stella label and new low alcohol Nico white offer gd, clean fruit. V.gd Colheita Seleccionada red and white are exceptional value for money.

Pegos Claros Set r 03 04 05' 07 Benchmark PALMELA CASTELÃO, foot-trodden and aged min 3 yrs. GARRAFEIRA, only made in top yrs, sees another yr in barrel.

Pellada, Quinta de Dão r w p 04 05' 06 07' 08 Owned with QUINTA DE SAES by leading DÃO light Alvaro de Castro. Intense, not dense reds, inc flagship Pape (TOURIGA NACIONAL from Passarela v'yd with Pellada Baga) and Carrocel (100% TOURIGA). Primus is old-vine, textured white. A rosé has a dash of Cab Sauv.

Península de Setúbal Up-and-coming VINHO REGIONAL covering sandy plains around Sado Estuary, formerly known as Terras do Sado. Established producers inc: ADEGA DE PEGÕES, BACALHOA VINHOS and Casa Ermelinda Freitas (QUINTA da Mimosa and Leo d'Honor). Names to watch: Herdades da Comporta and Portocarro, Mala Tojo, Soberanas and QUINTAS de Catralvos and Alcube.

Periquita The nickname for the CASTELÃO grape and successful brand name and trademark of JOSÉ MARÍA DA FONSECA. Periquita Classico is original 100% CASTELÃO; red, RESERVA (and p and w) other varieties.

Poeira, Quinta do Dou r w ★★★→★★★★ (02 03' 04' 05' 06 07' 08') QUINTA DE LA ROSA's winemaker Jorge Moreira's elegant flagship red from north-facing slopes. Classy second wines, Pó de Poeira (r and w), are v.gd value for money. CS is a young vine Cab Sauv and DOURO varietal blend.

Portal, Quinta do Dou r p w sw ★★★ 00' 01 03 04 05' 06 07 08 New plantings and winery reaping dividends at former Sandeman estate. Lavishly oaked reds, inc Grande Reserva and flagship Auru contrast with v.gd delicate sweet wine and latest addition, Trevo VINHO VERDE.

Portalegre Alen r w p ★ →★★★ Northernmost ALENTEJO subregion (DOC) has strikingly different elevated v'yds on granite and schist that, together with double the rainfall, accounts for its fresh, structured wines. Gd local co-op, but names to watch: Altas Quintas, where Paulo Laureano (HERDADE DE MOUCHÃO's winemaker) consults; Terrenus, owned by consultant winemaker Rui Reguinga and QUINTA do Centro, his joint venture with English wine writer Richard Mayson.

Quinta Estate (*see* under name, eg. PORTAL, QUINTA DO).

Ramos, João Portugal Alen r w DYA Well-made range from Loios and Vila Santa to premium single-varietals and blends: QUINTA da Viçosa; v.gd Marqués de Borba Reserva (03 04 05 07). Impressive new DOURO joint venture DUORUM.

Raposeira Dou w sp ★★ Well-known fizz with native varieties and Chard made by classic method at Lamego.

Real Companhia Velha Dou r p w sw ★★→★★★ r 01' 03 04 05 06 07 08 Historic Port company and pioneer of dedicated table wine plantings, inc Chard, Sauv Bl, Sém and ALVARINHO. New technical director, POEIRA'S Jorge Moreira, to up game with new top wines. Existing brands: flagship Evel Grande Reserva, Porca de Murça, Quinta dos Aciprestes, Quinta de Cidro, Grantom and sweet Granjó from Sem. Also making Quinta de Venozelo and new DELAFORCE (*see* Port, Sherry & Madeira) wines.

Roques, Quinta dos Dão r w ★★→★★★★ (r) 01 03' 04 05 06 07' 08' V.gd age-worthy reds, esp flagship GARRAFEIRA blend and RESERVA. Less oak and older barrels account for smoother tannins and, in white Encruzado, greater freshness. Varietal wines from TOURIGA NATIONAL, TINTA RORIZ, Tinta Cão and Alfrocheiro Preto. Gd-value entry-level Correio label.

Roriz, Quinta de Dou r ★★★ 03' 04 05' 06 08' One of the great QUINTAS of the DOURO. Fine reds (and vintage Port). Now owned by SYMINGTON FAMILY ESTATES and new base for CHRYSEIA. Second wine: Prazo de Roriz.

Rosa, Quinta de la Dou r p w ★★★ 04 05' 06 07' 08' Firm, rich reds, esp RESERVA and

Quinta das Bandeiras-sourced Passagem (in partnership with winemaker Jorge Moreira) from warmer DOURO Superior. Maiden Passagem white impresses. DouROSA is gd entry level.

Rosado Rosé; there is life beyond MATEUS ROSÉ; new breed of textured, sophisticated rosés inc from NIEPOORT, QUINTA DE PELLADA, CHURCHILL.

Saes, Quinta de Dão r w ★★★→★★★★ 01 02 **03** 04 05 06' 07' 08' Alvaro Castro's other v'yd (see PELLADA), producing equally characterful and elegant wines, inc v.gd Reserva Branco and Dado/Doda – see NIEPOORT.

Sant'Ana, Quinta de ★★→★★★ English-owned estate at Mafra makes gd, clean whites (inc Ries) and a punchy crisp red, Homage to Baron G von Fürstenberg.

Santar, Casa de Dão w r ★★★ 01 02 **03** 04 05' Well-established estate now linked to DÃO SUL making welcome comeback. Structured reds; for Encruzado whites, Burgundian approach paying dividends.

Santos Lima, Casa Lis r p w ★★ Family-owned ALENQUER company with export focus. CSL is key brand. Huge range reflects extensive v'yds, inc QUINTAS da Boavista/ das Setencostas and do Espírito Santo. New, more focused competition offers more interest (see LISBOA).

São João, Caves Bair r w sp ★★→★★★ (r sp) **95** 97 00 01 03 05 Small, traditional firm for v.gd old-fashioned wines. Reds are bottle-aged pre-release and v. age-worthy. BAIRRADA: *Frei João*, Poço do Lobo. DÃO: Porta dos Cavaleiros.

São Miguel, Herdade de Alen w r p ★★→★★★ Young go-ahead operation producing smart wines with renowned consultant Luís Duarte (also of MALHADINHA NOVAL and MOURO). Ciconia (an upfront, fruity quaffer) and slightly firmer Montinho are gd value. São Miguel labels denote serious, well-defined estate wines, esp Reserva and admirably fresh Dos Descobridores Reserva. Private Collection is showier limited edition. Makes VINHO VERDE, too.

Seco Dry.

Setúbal br sw (r w dr) ★★★ Tiny DOC south of the river Tagus. Fortified dessert wines made predominantly from the Moscatel (Muscat) grape, inc rare red Moscatel Roxo. Main producers: BACALHOA VINHOS and JOSÉ MARIA DA FONSECA. Names to watch: António Saramago and Horácio dos Reis Simões.

Sezim, Casa de Min w ★★ DYA Beautiful estate making v.gd VINHO VERDE.

Soalheiro, Quinta de Min w sp ★★★ 00 02' 03 06 07' 08' 09 ALVARINHO specialist making revelatory (age-worthy) VINHO VERDE. Warm Melgaço location brings structure, concentration and texture. Consultancy from Dirk NIEPOORT lead to old-vine Primeiras Vinhas, barrel-fermented RESERVA, new off-dry Dócil and Niepoort's own label Girosol.

Sogrape Min ★→★★★★ Portugal's largest wine concern, making VINHO VERDE (AZEVEDO, GAZELA, Morgadio da Torre), DÃO (CARVALHAIS), ALENTEJO (Herdade do Peso), MATEUS ROSÉ. Qwner of FERREIRA, SANDEMAN, OFFLEY Port and BARCA VELHA in the DOURO. Approachable multi-regional brands Grão Vasco, Pena de Pato and Callabriga from VINHO VERDE, DOURO, DÃO, ALENTEJO. Also making wine in Spain, Argentina, New Zealand, Chile.

Sousa, José de Alen r res ★★→★★★★ 03 04 05 06 07' Small firm acquired by JOSÉ MARÍA DA FONSECA; wines now slightly lighter in style but flagship Mayor is solid, foot-trodden red fermented in clay amphoras and aged in oak.

Symington Family Estates Dou r w ★★→★★★★ Ubiquitous family-run Port shipper. Since 2000 producing serious table wines, inc CHRYSEIA with Bruno Prats, Dow Val du Bomfim, Quinta do Vesúvio, Pombal do Vesúvio. Well-made Altano brand, esp RESERVA, organic red and Quinta Ataíde (varietal TOURIGA NACIONAL), hail from 140 ha Vilariça Valley v'yd in DOURO Superior; 100% certified organic.

Tejo r w Region of the Tagus. Engine-room of gd-value from CASTELÃO, TRINCADEIRA, FERNÃO PIRES raising its game with switch to poorer soils and introduction of red varieties TOURIGA NACIONAL, TINTA RORIZ, and international grapes: Cab Sauv, Syrah, Pinot N, Chard, Sauv Bl. Gd results already at, eg. QUINTA DA LAGOALVA, Pinhal da Torre and FALUA. Rising star: VALE D'ALGARES. Subregions: Almeirim, Cartaxo, Coruche, Chamusca, Tomar, Santarem. VINHO REGIONAL TEJO.

Teodósio, Caves Dom r w ★→★★★ Large TEJO producer. Brands: Serradayres, Casaleiro; top wines from Quinta de São João Batista. Also DÃO and PALMELA wines.

Tinta Roriz Major Port grape (alias Tempranillo) making v.gd DOURO wines. Known as ARAGONEZ in ALENTEJO.

Tinto Red.

Tinto da Anfora Alen r ★★→★★★ 03 04 05′ 06 07 Reliable red from BACALHOA VINHOS. Impressively rich Grande Escolha.

Touriga Nacional Top red grape used for Port, DOURO and DÃO table wines and increasingly elsewhere. Though widely touted as Portugal's lead variety, only comprises around 3% of plantings.

Trás-os-Montes HIGH INLAND DOC with subregions Chaves, Valpaços and Planalto Mirandês. VINHO REGIONAL Transmontano.

Trincadeira V.gd red grape in ALENTEJO; spicy wines. Tinta Amarela in the DOURO.

Vale d'Algares Tej r w p ★★→★★★ No-expense-spared project focusing on super-premium international and Portuguese varieties. Lead wine is an ambitiously priced but promising Viognier, which grape is blended with ALVARINHO for its 2nd-tier Selection White. Guarda Rios is the junior brand. A name to watch.

Vale Dona Maria, Quinta do Dou r w p ★★★→★★★★ 01′ 02 03′ 04′ 05′ 06 07′ 08′ Cristiano van Zeller's highly regarded QUINTA. *V.gd plush yet elegant reds*, inc CV, Casa de Casal de Loivos and new VZ white. Gd-value Van Zellers range made from bought-in fruit. Also gd Port.

Vale Meão, Quinta do Dou r ★★★→★★★★ 01′ 03 04′ 05 06 07′ 08 Once the source of BARCA VELHA. Impressively structured wines typified by high percentage of TOURIGA NACIONAL and warm, easterly location. V.gd second wine: Meandro. New v'yd at 350 metres holds good prospects.

Vallado Dou r w ★★→★★★★ (r) 03′ 04 05′ 06 07 08′ (w) DYA Family-owned DOURO estate going from strength to strength with new winery doubling capacity and new DOURO Superior v'yd planted 2011. V.gd-value sweet-fruited single-varietals inc unusual Sousão. Top wines are minerally, well-structured blends RESERVA and flagship old-vine red Adelaide (05 07 08′).

Vinho Regional Larger provincial wine regions, with same status as French Vin de Pays: Acores, Alentejano, ALGARVE, BEIRAS, Duriense, LISBOA, MINHO, TEJO, Terras Madeirenses, Terras do Dão, Terras do Sado, Transmontano. More leeway for experimentation than DOC. *See also* DOC.

Vinho Verde Min r w sp ★→★★★ DOC between river DOURO and north frontier; fresh "green wines". Large brands like Casal García usually varietal blend with added carbon dioxide – DYA. Best are single-QUINTA with natural spritz, if any, esp ALVARINHO from Monção and Melgaço (eg. ANSELMO MENDES, QUINTAS DE SOALHEIRO, do Reguengo, de Melgaço, DO FEITAL) and LOUREIRO from Lima (eg. QUINTA DO AMEAL or AFROS). Red Vinhão is an acquired taste but can be exciting (eg. AFROS).

Wine & Soul Dou r w (r Pintas) 03′ 04′ 05′ 06 07′ 08′ (w Guru) 06′ 07 08′ 09′ Imposing, increasingly elegant wines (and Port) from winemaking couple Sandra Tavares and Jorge Serôdio Borges. Second wine: Pintas Character (r). Barrel sample of new flagship single-v'yd Manuela 2009 from prized old-vine QUINTA v. promising.

Zambujeiro Alen r ★★★ 99 00 01′ 02 03 04′ 05′ 06 Swiss-owned, quality-focused estate producing powerfully structured blends from dry-farmed Portuguese varieties. Gd second wine: Terra do Zambujeiro.

Port, Sherry & Madeira

Europe's three classic fortified wines occupy mere niches today compared with their glory days, but remain unchallenged in their spheres: Sherry as the prandial stimulus, Port as the post-prandial stabilizer and Madeira for contemplation at any hour. Port has never quite gone out of fashion; Sherry has a new vogue with food; Madeira is as exotically desirable as ever. Look for new Sherry brands, ie. Equipo Navajos, cherry-picked from the best bodegas, old vintage-dated wines, and new rosé Ports, plus ancient releases, ie. Taylor's Scion, perhaps Port's first shot at the bling market. Sherry remains the wine world's best bargain. [Abbreviations: Jerez (Jer), Puerto de Santa Maria (P de SM), Sanlúcar (San).]

Recent Port vintages

Port vintages are "declared" when the wine is outstanding and meets the shippers' highest standards. In good but not quite classic years most shippers now use the names of their quintas (estates) for single-quinta wines of great character but needing less ageing in bottle. The vintages to drink now are: 1966, 1970, 1977, 1980, 1983, 1985, 1987, 1992, 1994.

2010 Warmer and drier than usual, very promising years.

2009 Single-quinta year. Hot, dry, low-yielding year favouring higher vineyards.

2008 Single-quinta year. Low-yielding, powerful wines. Stars: Noval, Vesuvio, Fonseca do Panascal, Taylor Terra Feita.

2007 Classic year, widely declared. Late but mild, dry vintage produced deep-coloured, rich but well-balanced wines. Taylor's and Vesuvio are stars.

2006 Difficult; handful of single-quinta: Vesuvio, Roriz, Barros Quinta Galeira.

2005 Single-quinta year: Niepoort, Taylor de Vargellas, Dow da Senhora da Ribeira – iron fist in velvet glove.

2004 Single-quinta year: Pintas, Taylor de Vargellas Vinha Velha, Quinta de la Rosa – balanced, elegant wines.

2003 Classic vintage year. Hot, dry summer. Powerfully ripe, concentrated wines, universally declared. Drink from 2015/2020.

2001 Single-quinta year: Noval Nacional, Fonseca do Panascal, do Vale Meão – wet year; relatively forward wines.

2000 Classic year, very fine vintage, universally declared. Drink from 2018.

1999 Single-quinta year: Vesuvio, Taylor de Terra Feita, do Infantado – smallest vintage for decades; powerful.

1998 Single-quinta year: Dow da Senhora da Ribeira, Graham dos Malvedos, Cockburn dos Canais – bullish, firm wines.

1997 Classic year. Fine, potentially long-lasting wines with tannic backbone. Most shippers declared. Drink 2015 onward.

Almacenista Small producer, typically a source of individual, complex Sherries. In Sherry's heyday boosted major producers' stocks. Now scarcer, showcased by LUSTAU. Also Vides Palo Cortado, Cuevas Jurado Manzanilla, Obregon Amontillado.

Alvear Mont-M ★★→★★★★ Largest producer; v.gd Fino-like aperitif and exceptionally sweet, raisined wines, both from PX; esp Fino CB, SOLERA 1927.

Andresen ★★→★★★ Family owned Port house making gd 20-yr-old TAWNY and grand old COLHEITAS bottled by barrel (1910' 70', 75, 82, 91', 97); first to register a white Port with age indication (10-yr-old; new 20-yr-old).

Alvaro Domecq Jer ★★→★★★★ DOMECQ is one of Sherry's great families. After corporate shake-up, scion Alvaro Domecq launched brand based on SOLERAS of Pilar Aranda, said to be the oldest BODEGA in JEREZ. In 2007 joined boutique wine group Inveravante. Excellent 1730 label wines, inc Palo Cortado, Oloroso. Gd Fino La Janda. Also one of the best Sherry vinegars.

Barbadillo, Antonio San ★→★★★★ The former bishop's palace in SANLÚCAR is appropriate for the town's largest producer. Makes a locally v. popular budget white wine from PALOMINO but also some of SANLÚCAR's finest Sherries. Reliquia range is costly but outstanding, esp Palo Cortado and Oloroso. Solear Manzanilla is a local favourite at *feria*. Also Príncipe Amontillado, Obispo Gascón Palo Cortado, Cuco Dry Oloroso, Manzanilla EN RAMA, with seasonal *sacas*.

Barbeito Shipper of finely honed Madeiras, no added caramel. Single-cask COLHEITAS, exceptional 20- and 30-yr-old Malvasia and VERDELHO/BUAL blend. Bright, citrus COLHEITAS (Malvasia 2000, BOAL 2001) and stylish FRASQUEIRA (SERCIAL 1978', 1988, BOAL 1982, VERDELHO 1981). At the top of its game.

Barros Almeida Large Port house with several brands (inc Feist, Feuerheerd, KOPKE) owned by Sogevinus: excellent 20-yr-old TAWNY and COLHEITAS (78' 96'); VINTAGE PORTS on the up; aged white Ports (Very Old Dry White, 1935 COLHEITA).

Barros e Sousa 3rd-generation artisanal producer; hand-bottled, stencilled tiny output of 100% CANTEIRO-aged Madeira; rare vintages (Terrantez 1979, VERDELHO 1983), Bastardo Old Res, gd 10-yr-old and unusual 5-yr-old Listrao blend. No export.

Blandy Best-known name of the MADEIRA WINE COMPANY, thanks to popular 3-yr-old Duke ranges. Short ferments produce rich house style. Vast lodge houses visitor centre and over 8,000 hl of premium wines. Fine old vintages (eg. BUAL 1964, 1968,' 1977' VERDELHO 1968 and SERCIAL 1966). Recent innovations include COLHEITAS (MALMSEY 1992, 2001, BUAL 1991 Single Harvest 1977) and Alvada, a moreish blend of BUAL and Malvasia.

Borges, HM Family Madeira company. V.gd 10-yr-olds, fruity COLHEITAS (SERCIAL 1995, MALMSEY 1998) and vintages, esp SERCIAL 1977, 1979, BUAL 1977. Limited production Malvasia 40-Year-Old celebrates Funchal's 500th anniversary.

Bual (or Boal) Classic Madeira grape: tangy, smoky, sweet wines; not as rich as MALMSEY. Perfect with cheese and lighter desserts.

Burmester Small Sogevinus-owned Port house behind innovative Gilbert's G-Porto label. Best-known for fine, soft, sweet 20- and 40-yr-old TAWNY and COLHEITAS (55' 89); vintage improving (07'). Solid age-dated white Ports.

Cálem Sogevinus-owned Port house. Velhotes is the main brand. V.gd COLHEITAS (89, 2000); VINTAGE PORTS returning to form (03' 05 07). Very Old Special Reserve Tawny marks 150th anniversary. New rosé Port features braille label.

Canteiro Method of naturally cask-ageing the finest Madeira in warm, humid lodges (warehouses). Creates subtler, more complex wines than ESTUFAGEM.

Churchill 82 85 91 94 97 00 03 07 Independent family-owned Port shipper founded in 1981. Increased elegance derives from focus on TOURIGA NACIONAL and Touriga Franca. V.gd traditional LBV. Quinta da Gricha is the single-QUINTA Port (99 00 01 03' 04 05' 06 07). Benchmark aged WHITE PORT, also v.gd 10-yr-old white, 10-yr-old and new 20-yr-old TAWNY, now in 50cl bottles.

Cockburn Having acquired its assets in 2006, SYMINGTON FAMILY ESTATES in 2010 also bought this ancient Port brand. Popular Special Reserve Ruby. New-look 50cl bottles for white and age-dated TAWNY. Dry house style for VINTAGE PORTS: 63 67 70 75 83' 91 94 97 00 03' 07'. Gd TOURIGA NACIONAL-dominated single-QUINTA wines from Quinta dos Canais (98 01' 05' 06 07' 08).

Colheita Vintage-dated Port or Madeira of a single yr, cask-aged at least 7 yrs for Port and 5 yrs for Madeira. Bottling date shown on the label.

Cossart Gordon Top-quality label of MADEIRA WINE COMPANY; higher, cooler v'yds and longer ferment makes drier style than BLANDY. Best-known for Good Company brand. Also 5-yr-old RESERVES, COLHEITAS (SERCIAL 1991 *Bual* 1995, 1997, Malvasia 1996, 1998, Harvest 1999), old vintages (1977 Terrantez, 1908, 1961 BUAL).

Croft C17 Port shipper now part of Fladgate; reintroduced foot-treading for the much-improved 2003 VINTAGE PORT. Vintages: 60' 63' 66 70 75 77 82 85 91 94 00 03' 07. Lighter Quinta da Roêda. Indulgence, Triple Crown, Distinction most popular brands. "Pink", a pioneering ROSÉ PORT, prompted change of rules to allow rosés; popular cocktail ingredient or served chilled, on ice.

Croft Jerez Jer A Pale Cream Sherry owned by GONZÁLEZ BYASS.

Crusted Style of Port usually blended from several vintages, bottled young and aged so it throws a deposit, or "crust", and needs decanting.

Delaforce Now owned by Real Companhia Velha, which launched a table wine range in 2010. Fladgate still produces the Ports. Curious and Ancient 20-yr-old TAWNY and *Colheitas* (64 79 88) *are jewels*; VINTAGE PORTS are improving: 63 66 70' 75 77 82 85 92' 94 00 03. Single-QUINTA wines from Quinta da Corte.

Delgado, Zuleta San ★★ Historic (1774) SANLÚCAR firm. Manzanilla La Goya is a classic: powerful with freshness. Amontillado Viejo has bold, salty appeal.

Dios Baco Jer ★→★★ Family-owned BODEGA. V.gd Imperial VORS Palo Cortado.

Domecq Jer ★★→★★★★ One of the historic names in Sherry. Now after corporate upheaval owned by OSBORNE. The wines have fortunately survived the dramas. Outstanding collection of VORS.

Douro Rising in Spain as the Duero, this river flows through Port country, lending its name to the region: divided into the Cima (Upper) Corgo and Douro Superior, home of the best Ports, and the Baixo (Lower) Corgo. Also a table wine region.

Dow Brand name of Port house Silva & Cosens. Belongs to SYMINGTON FAMILY ESTATES; drier style than other producers in group. V.gd range, inc CRUSTED, 20- and 30-yr-old TAWNIES, single-QUINTAS Bomfim and, since 1998, v.gd da Senhora da Ribeira; vintage: 63 66 70 72 75 77 80 83 85' 91 94 97 00' 03 07'.

Emilio Hildago Jer ★★★→★★★★ Exceptional small family BODEGA. Unusually all wines except PX start with ageing under FLOR. Excellent La Panesa single v'yd Fino, Marques de Rodil Palo Cortado, El Tresillo 1874 Amontillado, Privilegio Palo Cortado from 1860 SOLERA, and v.gd Santa Ana PX 1861.

En rama Sherry bottled from the butt without filtration or cold stabilization, hence fragile, hence unpopular with some producers and retailers. Becoming fashionable (eg. González Byass launched Tío Pepe En Rama in UK in 2009). Prized by aficionados for its purity. The *saca*, or withdrawal, is when the FLOR is most abundant, in spring and autumn. Keep it in the fridge, drink up quickly.

Equipo Navazos ★★★★ "Virtual" Sherry BODEGA (no physical premises); created by a group of specialists who bottle individual butts from SOLERAS in top BODEGAS. Numbering of bottles starts at 1, eg. Bota (butt) no 1. Rapidly built reputation for highest quality: La Bota de Amontillado NPI no 5; La Bota de Palo Cortado no 21; impressive Cream, La Bota no 21. Look for more "virtual BODEGAS" in the future.

Estufagem Bulk process of slowly heating, then cooling, cheaper Madeiras to attain characteristic scorched-earth tang; less subtle than CANTEIRO process, though shift to lower temperatures has improved freshness .

Ferreira Leading Portuguese-owned Port shipper belonging to Sogrape. Best-selling brand in Portugal. Structured, rich, spicy RESERVE (Don Antónia), 10- and 20-yr-old TAWNIES, Quinta do Porto and *Duque de Bragança*. Early-maturing vintages: 66 70 75 77 78 80 82 83 85 87 90 91 94 95' 97 00 03 07'.

Flor Spanish word for "flower": refers to the layer of *Saccharomyces* yeasts that live on top of Fino/Manzanilla Sherry in a butt kept 5/6 full. By keeping oxygen at bay, it ensures freshness. Amontillados and some Olorosos begin as Finos under *flor* before the *flor* dies naturally or with the addition of fortifying spirit. *Flor* grows a thicker layer nearer the coast at PUERTO DE SANTA MARÍA and SANLÚCAR.

Fonseca Guimaraens Port shipper; belongs to Fladgate. Bin 27 and organic Terra Prima RESERVE RUBIES and sumptuous yet structured vintages (the latter now only estate grapes) among best: Fonseca 63' 66' 70 75 77' 80 83 **85'** 92 94' 97 00' 03' 07. Impressive, earlier-maturing Fonseca Guimaraens and single-QUINTA Panascal made when no classic declaration, inc 2008.

Frasqueira The official name for "vintage" Madeira from a single yr. Exceptionally intense wines bottled after at least 20 yrs in wood. Date of bottling compulsory; the longer in cask, the more concentrated and complex.

Garvey Jer ★→★★ One of the great old names of JEREZ, now also giving its name to the holding company of the BODEGAS (inc Teresa Rivero, VALDIVIA, ZOILO RUIZ-MATEOS – private-label Sherries) owned by the RUIZ-MATEOS family. Garvey San Patricio Fino a classic; also *Tío Guillermo* Amontillado, age-dated 1780 line.

González Byass Jer ★★★→★★★★ After lavishly celebrating 175 years in JEREZ in 2010, the family is looking forward with enthusiasm. One of the best Finos: *Tío Pepe*, recently joined by impressive EN RAMA bottlings. V. high standard: Viña AB Amontillado, 1847, Matúsalem Oloroso, Apóstoles Palo Cortado, outstanding, ultra-rich Noë PX. Extensive interests in brandy (Soberano, Lepanto); table wines: Finca Moncloa (Tierra de Cádiz), Altozano (Tierra de Castilla), Vilarnau (Cava), Beronia (RIOJA), Viñas del Vero and Secastilla (SOMONTANO). Also owns CROFT.

Gould Campbell Port shipper belonging to SYMINGTON FAMILY ESTATES. Gd-value, full-bodied VINTAGE PORTS 70 77' **80 83 85' 91 94** 97 00 03' 07.

Gracia Hermanos Mont-M ★ In same group as PÉREZ BARQUERO and Compañia Vinícola del Sur; gd-quality MONTILLAS (esp Tauromaquia Amontillado, PX).

Graham One of Port's greatest names, belonging to SYMINGTON FAMILY ESTATES. V.gd range: Six Grapes RESERVE RUBY, LBV, TAWNY (RESERVE) to excellent yr-aged TAWNIES and some of richest, sweetest VINTAGE PORTS 63 66 70' 75 77' 80 83' 85' 91 **94'** 97 00' 03' 07'. V.gd single-QUINTA vintage: dos Malvedos.

Gran Cruz Like Justino, owned by La Martiniquaise, the single biggest Port brand. Mostly light, inexpensive TAWNIES. New ROSÉ PORT.

Grupo Estévez Jer Energetic, expanding family business; extensive quality interests in JEREZ and SANLÚCAR, inc LA GUITA, Gil Luque, MARQUÉS DEL REAL TESORO, VALDESPINO.

Guita, La San ★→★★★ *Esp fine Manzanilla*. Owned by GRUPO ESTÉVEZ.

Gutiérrez Colosía P de SM ★→★★★ Family-owned former ALMACENISTA, now selling direct to public. Excellent old Palo Cortado.

Harvey's Jer ★→★★★ Major producer, affected by corporate storms and confusion of range changes. Now with Beam Global. Famed for Bristol Cream (icon of CREAMS); most VORS wines show briskness of old age, but PX is exceptional.

Henriques & Henriques Independent Madeira shipper uniquely with own v'yds (11 ha), supplying 15% of production. Breezy, extra-dry apéritif Monte Seco, otherwise rich, well-structured wines, inc outstanding 10- and 15-yr-olds, new 20-yr-old Malvasia and Terrantez, v. fine RESERVES, "Single Harvest" COLHEITAS, vintage and SOLERA wines (SERCIAL 1964, Terrantez 1976, Malvasia 1954, BUAL 1954, 1980, Century Malmsey-Solera 1900).

Herederos de Argüeso San ★★→★★★★ One of SANLÚCAR's top Manzanilla producers with v.gd San León and exceptional, dense and salty *San León Reserva* and youthful Las Medallas; and the still youthful VORS Amontillado Viejo.

Hidalgo La Gitana San ★★★→★★★★ Old (1792) family Sherry firm, fronted by the indefatigable Javier Hidalgo, with flagship Manzanilla La Gitana. The intense and savoury single-v'yd aged *Pastrana Manzanilla Pasada* is in impressive contrast to today's fashion for ultra-pale youthful Manzanilla. Also fine Oloroso, lovely Palo Cortado and treacly PX, v.gd VORS range.

Jerez de la Frontera Centre of Sherry industry, between Cádiz and Seville. "Sherry" is a corruption of the name, pronounced "hereth". In French, Xérès.

Sherry styles

Manzanilla Fashionably pale, dry Sherry: fresh green-apple character; a popular, unchallenging introduction to the flavours of Sherry. Matured (though not necessarily grown) in the humid, maritime conditions of SANLÚCAR DE BARRAMEDA where the FLOR grows more thickly, and the wine is said to acquire a salty tang. Drink cold and fresh from a newly opened bottle. Do not keep. Eg. HEREDEROS DE ARGÜESO, San León Reserva.

Manzanilla Pasada Manzanilla aged longer than most; v. dry, complex; eg. HIDALGO LA GITANA's single-v'yd Manzanilla Pasada Pastrana.

Fino Dry, weightier than Manzanilla; 3 yrs min age (as Manzanilla). Eg. GONZÁLEZ BYASS Tío Pepe. Serve as Manzanilla. Do not keep.

Amontillado A fino in which the layer of protective yeast FLOR has died, allowing the wine to oxidize, creating more complexity. Naturally dry. Eg. VALDESPINO Tío Diego. Commercial styles may be sweetened.

Oloroso Not aged under FLOR. Heavier when young, matures to nutty intensity. Naturally dry. May be sweetened with PX and sold as *dulce*. Eg. DOMECQ Río Viejo (dry), LUSTAU Old East India (sweet). Keeps well.

Palo Cortado V. fashionable. Traditionally, a wine that had lost its FLOR – between Amontillado and Oloroso. Today, often blended to create the style. Often difficult to identify with certainty, though some suggest it has a keynote "lactic" or "bitter butter" note. Dry, rich, complex: worth looking for. Eg. BARBADILLO Reliquía, GUTIÉRREZ COLOSÍA.

Cream A blend sweetened with grape must, PX, and/or Moscatel for a cheaper, medium-sweet style. Unashamedly commercial. Eg. HARVEY'S Bristol Cream, CROFT Pale Cream. Tailor-made for the UK market.

Pedro Ximénez [PX] Raisined sweet, dark Sherry from partly sun-dried PX grapes (MONTILLA grapes; wine made in JEREZ DO). Unctuous bargain. Sip with ice-cream. Overall, the world's sweetest wine. Eg. REY FERNANDO DE CASTILLA Antique, EMILIO HIDALGO Santa Ana 1861, VALDESPINO Toneles.

Moscatel Aromatic appeal, around half sugar of PX. Eg. LUSTAU Emilín. Unlike PX not required to be fortified. Permitted to be called "Jerez".

VOS/VORS A relatively new category of vintage-dated Sherries: some of the treasures of the JEREZ bodegas. Exceptional quality and maturity at relatively low prices. Wines assessed by carbon dating to be more than 20 yrs old are called VOS (Very Old Sherry/Vinum Optimum Signatum); those over 30 yrs old are VORS (Very Old Rare Sherry/Vinum Optimum Rare Signatum). Also 12-yr-old and 15-yr-old examples. Applies only to Amontillado, Oloroso, Palo Cortado, PX. Eg. VOS Hidalgo Jerez Cortado Wellington. Some VORS wines can be bitter or attenuated and maybe softened with PX – occasionally producers can be over-generous with the PX.

Añada (Vintage) Declared vintage; counters tradition of vintage-blended SOLERA. Formerly private bottlings now winning public accolades. Eg. LUSTAU Sweet Oloroso Añada 1990.

Justino Largest Madeira shipper, wholly owned (with GRAN CRUZ Ports) by La Martiniquaise. Gd 10-yr-old, TINTA NEGRA COLHEITA (**1995, 1996**), Terrantez Old Reserve NV, Vintage. CANTEIRO-aged TINTA NEGRA from certified organic grapes in works. Also makes Madeira under the Broadbent label, inc v.gd Terrantez 1978.

Kopke Oldest Port house (1638), now owned by BARROS ALMEIDA. Jewels inc wood-aged style, esp 40-yr-old TAWNY, new 30-yr-old WHITE PORT, COLHEITAS (66 **80' 87 89**). VINTAGE PORTS (inc single-QUINTA Quinta São Luiz) mostly early-maturing but some v.gd (83 85 87 89 91 94 97 00 03 04 05' 07). Gd new rosé (relatively dry).

Krohn Port shipper; gd 20- and 30-yr-old TAWNY and excellent COLHEITAS (61' 64 67' 68 78 82 83' 87' 91), some dating back to 1800s. VINTAGE PORTS on the up (07'), inc single-QUINTA do Retiro Novo.

Lagar Shallow granite "paddling pool" in which Port and even some Madeira (BARBEITO) is trodden by foot – or, these days, increasingly by robot.

LBV (Late Bottled Vintage) Port from a single year kept in wood for twice as long as VINTAGE PORT (around 5 yrs) so ready to drink on release; larger volumes, robustly fruity, but less powerful and complex than vintage. No need to decant, except for unfiltered wines that can age for 10 yrs or more – worth seeking out (CHURCHILL, FERREIRA, NIEPOORT, QUINTA do Nova, QUINTA DO NOVAL, SMITH WOODHOUSE, WARRE).

Leacock Volume label of the MADEIRA WINE COMPANY; sweet, rich house style. Main brand is St John, popular in Scandinavia. Older vintages inc: 1927, 1963 SERCIAL, 1914 BUAL and SOLERA 1808 and 1860.

Lustau Jer ★★★→★★★★ This Sherry house gathers awards for extensive *range of excellent individual wines*. Pioneer in ALMACENISTA Sherries, inc: Manzanilla Amontillado Jurado, Palo Cortado Vides. Other v.gd Sherries inc: East India Solera, Moscatel Emilín. Latest top-quality release is vintage sweet Oloroso, beginning with Añada 1990. Owned by the Caballero group.

Madeira Wine Company Formed 1913 by two firms as Madeira Wine Association, subsequently to include all 26 British Madeira companies. Now run by Blandy family and SYMINGTON FAMILY ESTATES partnership, it accounts for over 50% of bottled Madeira exports. Principal brands are BLANDY, COSSART GORDON, LEACOCK and Miles, each of which have retained their individual house style. Blandy and Cossart Gordon lead the pack. All except basic wines CANTEIRO-aged.

Malmsey (Malvasia Candida) The sweetest and richest of traditional Madeira grape varieties; dark-amber and honeyed, yet with Madeira's unique sharp tang; perfect match for rich fruit and chocolate puddings.

Marqués del Real Tesoro Jer ★ Fine Tío Mateo Fino. Part of GRUPO ESTÉVEZ.

Martinez Gassiot Owned by SYMINGTON FAMILY ESTATES, known for excellent rich and pungent Directors 20-yr-old TAWNY. Gd-value, age-worthy vintages in drier, traditional style: 63 67 70 75 82 85 87 91 94 97 00 03 07.

Montecristo Mont-M Brand of popular MONTILLAS by Compañía Vinícola del Sur.

Montilla-Moriles Andalucian DO nr Córdoba. Montilla owes its growing reputation to the quality of its sun-dried super-sweet PX grapes, some with long ageing in SOLERA. Top: ALVEAR, GRACIA HERMANOS, PÉREZ BARQUERO, BODEGAS TORO ALBALÁ. Important source of PX for use in DO JEREZ, to make up shortfall in JEREZ iself.

Niepoort ★★★ Small family run Port house; sensational table wines. Consistently fine (63 66 70' 75 77 78 80 82 83 87 91 92 94 97 00' 03 05' 07); unique *garrafeira* (aged in demijohns, current release is 77'), Broadbent, new single-v'yd Pisca and Secundum, designed for earlier drinking. Exceptional TAWNIES and COLHEITAS. Benchmark Dry White, also 10-yr-old white. New CRUSTED Port bottled in 2007.

Noval, Quinta do French-owned (AXA) historic Port house. Perfumed, elegant yet structured VINTAGE PORT; around 2.5 ha of ungrafted vines make small quantity of extraordinarily intense, slow-maturing Nacional – not always made in classic declared yrs (eg. 62' 80 82 85 87). Also v.gd age-dated TAWNY and COLHEITAS. Vintages: 62 63 66 67 70 75 78 82 85 87 91 94' 95 97' 00' 03' 04 07' 08'. Second vintage label: Silval. Recent additions inc: early-drinking Noval Black RESERVE RUBY and v.gd single-estate, unfiltered LBV.

Offley Brand name belonging to Sogrape. Gd, accessible range, inc Duke of Oporto volume label, Baron de Forrester age-dated TAWNY and Boa Vista Vintage: 63 66 67 70 72 75 77 80 82 83 85 87 89 94 95 97 00' 03 07. New ROSÉ PORT.

Osborne P de SM ★→★★★★ Wine business. Sherries inc Fino Quinta, Coquinero Fino Amontillado. Recent acquisition by parent company Caballero Group is

Domecq, its exceptional VORS wines now appear under the Osborne label – Amontillado 51-1a, **Sibarita Oloroso**, Capuchino Palo Cortado, Venerable PX. Table wines: Tierra de Cádiz, VDT Castilla, RIOJA, RUEDA and RIBERA DEL DUERO. Port: declared VINTAGE PORTS in 95 97 00' 03' 07. (Fladgate making Ports since 2005).

Palomino White grape used to make all Sherries except Moscatels and PX. Bland in character, the SOLERA ageing gives it identity.

Paternina, Federico Jer ★★→★★★★ Owned by Marcos Eguizábal from RIOJA, of the historic Banda Azul producer. He acquired the traditional cellars of Díez Hermanos together with three VORS wines: the excellent and unique **Fino Imperial**, Victoria Regina Oloroso and Vieja Solera PX.

Pereira d'Oliveira Vinhos Family owned. Gd basic Madeira range. 15 yr-old wines upwards CANTEIRO-aged. Traditionally styled COLHEITAS (BOAL 1983, 1988, Malvasia 1987, Terrantez 1988); vintages (labelled RESERVA), bottled on demand from cask dating back to 1850 (1937, 1971 SERCIAL, 1966 VERDELHO, 1958, 1968 BUAL).

Pérez Barquero Mont-M ★★→★★★★ A leader in revival of MONTILLA PX Fine Gran Barquero Fino, Amontillado, Oloroso; v.gd La Cañada PX.

Pilar Plá/El Maestro Sierra Jer ★→★★★★ Owned by JEREZ's grandest dame Pilar Plá Pechovierto, widow of a direct descendant of the ALMACENISTAS who started up in 1832. V. popular locally. Gd Fino and 12 and 15 yr-old Amontillado and Oloroso.

Poças Family-run Portuguese Port firm; v.gd TAWNIES and COLHEITAS (67' **86'** 94). Gd LBV and recent vintages (97 00' 03 04 05' 07'). Single-QUINTA from Quinta de Santa Bárbara. Gd table wines, too.

Puerto de Santa María, El The former port of Sherry, one of three towns forming the "Sherry Triangle". Production now in serious decline; remaining BODEGAS inc former ALMACENISTA GUTIÉRREZ COLOSÍA, OSBORNE, TERRY. Puerto's Finos are considered lighter than those of JEREZ, not as "salty" as SANLÚCAR.

Quarles Harris One of oldest Port houses (1680), owned by SYMINGTON FAMILY ESTATES. Mellow vintages, often v.gd value: **63** 66 70 75 77 80 83 85 91 94 97 00' 03 07.

Quevedo New Port brand courting a 30-something audience via social media and forward styles of WHITE, RUBY, VINTAGE (07', 08) and ROSÉ.

Quinta "Estate", traditionally denotes VINTAGE PORTS from shipper's single v'yds; declared in gd but not exceptional yrs. Increasing number make Port from top vintages. Rising stars: BARROS ALMEIDA, DUORUM, PASSADOURO, Romaneira, Tedo, Whytingham's VALE MEÃO, VALE D MARIA, WINE & SOUL's Pintas.

Ramos Pinto Dynamic Port house owned by Champagne house Louis Roederer; gd wines, too. Outstanding single-QUINTA (de Ervamoira) and TAWNIES, inc: de Ervamoira (10-yr-old), do Bom Retiro (20-yr-old), 30-yr-old. Rich, sweet, mostly early-maturing vintages. Exceptional celebratory 100-yr-old TAWNY, 2009.

Reserve/Reserva Premium Ports, mostly RESERVE RUBY but some res TAWNY, bottled without a vintage date or age indication but better than basic style.

Rey Fernando de Castilla Jer ★★ •→★★★★ Small BODEGA showing impressive revival under new ownership with v. fine Sherries and brandies. Excellent Antique Amontillado, Oloroso and PX, outstanding Antique Palo Cortado. All qualify as age-dated, though BODEGA prefers to avoid the system. Classic range at a lower price, inevitably less exciting than the Antique wines.

Rosa, Quinta de la V.gd, structured single-QUINTA Port, gd TAWNY, COLHEITA (table wines, too) from Bergqvist family. Look for 94 95 00 03' 04 05' 07'.

Rosé Port Officially recognized in 2009, prompted by CROFT's pioneering "Pink" (now trademarked), recommended served chilled, on ice or in a cocktail.

Royal Oporto Real Companhia Velha's main Port brand (it also now owns QUINTA de Ventozelo and DELAFORCE). Gd TAWNIES, COLHEITAS (53' 77) and recent VINTAGE PORTS, foot-trodden since 1997. New ROSÉ PORT.

Rozès Port shipper owned by Champagne house Vranken alongside São Pedro das Aguias. Popular in France. DOURO Superior single-QUINTA do Grifo, acquired 2004, shows promise. New ROSÉ PORT.

Ruby Youngest, cheapest Port style: simple, sweet; best labelled RESERVE.

Ruiz-Mateos, Zoilo Jer Family business with strong but fluctuating influence on Sherry. The BODEGAS of the original holding company Rumasa (formed from family name) were expropriated by the government in 1983. Relaunched Nueva ("new"), Rumasa created GARVEY group, inc SANDEMAN, VALDIVIA, Teresa Rivero. Early 2011 faces financial crisis, which threatens BODEGAS.

Sanchez Romate Jer ★★→★★★★ Family firm (1781). Best-known in Spanish-speaking world, esp brandy Cardenal Mendoza. V. fine, nutty Amontillado NPU, excellent VORS Amontillado and Oloroso La Sacristía de Romate, unctuous Sacristía PX.

Sandeman Jerez ★→★★★★ Another company that has seen corporate changes since founder George Sandeman set up twin establishments in Oporto and JEREZ in 1790. Fine wines in the cellars, inc Royal Esmeralda VOS Amontillado and *Royal Ambrosante VOS* Oloroso and PX. V'yds, stocks, BODEGA owned by RUIZ-MATEOS.

Sandeman Port Lightest of SOGRAPE brands with gd aged TAWNIES, esp 20-yr-old. Vintage elegant but until recently patchy; new winery at Quinta do Seixo has produced the goods in 2007 (63 66 70 75 77 94 97 00 03 07'). Second label: seductive Vau Vintage (97' **99** 00).

Sanlúcar de Barrameda One of the three towns of the "Sherry Triangle" at the mouth of the river Guadalquivir. Low-lying, the strong maritime influence encourages FLOR growth. Young Manzanillas typically show delicate apple fruit. The sea is said to give the wines a salty character, more obvious on older wines such as HIDALGO's Manzanilla Pasada Pastrana.

Santa Eufemia, Quinta de Family Port estate with v.gd old TAWNIES. Stunning 10-, 20- and 30-yr-old aged WHITE PORTS in 50cl bottles.

Sercial Madeira grape for the driest of the island's wines. Supreme apéritif or try with smoked salmon canapés.

Silva, C da Port shipper. Mostly inexpensive RUBIES and TAWNIES, but gd ROSÉ PORT, aged TAWNIES and COLHEITAS (52) under Dalva label. New Golden White COLHEITA WHITE PORTS (52' 63) are very complex.

Smith Woodhouse Port firm founded 1784. Firmly focused on limited-production high quality: gd unfiltered LBV and some v. fine vintages: 63 66 70 75 77' 80 83 85 91 94 97 00' 03 07. Occasional single-estate wines from QUINTA da Madelena.

Solera System used in ageing Sherry and, less commonly now, Madeira. Consists of topping up progressively more mature butts or barrels with slightly younger wine of same sort from next stage, or *criadera*. The object is continuity in final wine, maintaining vigour of FLOR in Fino and Manzanilla SOLERAS. Minimum age for a Fino or Manzanilla is 3 yrs in SOLERA.

Symington Family Estates ★★→★★★★★ Long-established, forward-looking, family run Port shippers and partner in the MADEIRA WINE COMPANY. Easily the DOURO's largest vineyard owner with 27 QUINTAS totalling over 2,300 acres. Spectacular portfolio inc: COCKBURN, DOW, GOULD CAMPBELL, GRAHAM, MARTINEZ GASSIOT, QUARLES HARRIS, Quinta de Roriz, SMITH WOODHOUSE, VESÚVIO and WARRE. For table wine: Altano, CHRYSEIA, DOW and VESÚVIO *marques*.

Tawny Style of Port that implies ageing in wood (hence tawny in colour), though many basic tawnies are little more than attenuated RUBIES. Look for wines with an indication of age: 10-, 20-, 30-, 40-yr-old or RESERVE.

Taylor, Fladgate & Yeatman (Taylor's) ★★→★★★★★ One of the best-known Port shippers, highly rated for rich, long-lived VINTAGE PORTS (63 66 70 75 77' 80 83 85 92' 94 97 00' 03' 07'). Member of Fladgate Partnership, with CROFT and FONSECA GUIMARAENS. V.gd range, inc RESERVE, LBV, aged TAWNIES. QUINTAS Vargellas and Terra Feita make impressive single-QUINTA VINTAGE PORT, esp rare Vargellas Vinha

Velha (95 97 00 04 07') from 70+-yr-old vines. Rarer still, Scion, a limited-edition bottling of two recently discovered pipes of pre-phylloxera TAWNY dating back to the 1850s (a third was said to have been acquired by Winston Churchill).

Terry, S A P de SM ★→★★ Sherry BODEGA dominating the entrance to EL PUERTO DE SANTA MARÍA; part of Beam Brands.

Tinta Negra Until recently called Tinta Negra Mole. Madeira's most planted (r) grape; workhorse, mainstay of cheaper Madeira. Coming into its own in COLHEITAS.

Toro Albalá, Bodegas Mont-M One of the top MONTILLA producers; v. fine Don PX.

Tradición Jer ★★→★★★ Small, serious BODEGA making VOS and VORS wines from an art-filled cellar in JEREZ's old town.

Urium Jer Newest (2009) BODEGA on the block, its brash and bold gold labels at odds with JEREZ's discretion. Owner is newcomer Alonso Ruiz, businessman from Huelva, with oenologist daughter Rocio. Wines are named Mons Urium: range covers aged VORS, plus Fino EN RAMA and Manzanilla Pasada.

Valdespino Jer ★★→★★★★ Famous JEREZ BODEGA producing Inocente Fino from the esteemed Macharnudo v'yd. Notably Inocente is fermented in American oak not stainless steel, and is aged longer than usual in a SOLERA that has ten stages, or *criaderas*. Tío Diego is terrific dry Amontillado, *Coliseo* even better; also vibrant, youthful SOLERA 1842 Oloroso VOS; remarkable, aged Toneles Moscatel.

Valdivia Jer ★★→★★★★ Recent BODEGA. V.gd 15-yr-old Sacromonte Amontillado, gd Oloroso. Former home of RUIZ-MATEOS family, acquired by GARVEY group (2008).

Vale D Maria, Quinta do Gd-value, beautifully elegant, forward, single-QUINTA VINTAGE PORT (00 01 02 03 05 07) and gd unfiltered LBV.

Verdelho Traditional Madeira grape for medium-dry wines; pungent but without the austerity of SERCIAL. Gd aperitif. Increasingly popular for table wines.

Vesúvio, Quinta do 19th-century Port estate restored to former glory by SYMINGTON FAMILY ESTATES; remains only estate where grapes are still foot-trodden by man. VINTAGE PORT: 91 92 94 95' 96' 97 98 99 00' 01 03' 04 05' 06 07' 08'. Exceptional 2007 vintage saw the release of a new vintage Port, Capela, and the first table wines. A tiny amount of COLHEITA is also made for family and guests.

Vila Nova de Gaia City across the river DOURO from Oporto and traditional home to the major Port shippers' lodges. Increasingly Port is aged in the DOURO in new air-conditioned lodges.

Vintage Port Classic vintages are the best wines declared in exceptional yrs by shippers between 1 Jan and 30 Sept in the 2nd yr after vintage. Bottled without filtration after 2 yrs in wood, the wine matures v. slowly in bottle, throwing a crust or deposit – always decant. Modern vintages broachable earlier but best will last more than 50 yrs. Single-QUINTA vintage Ports also drinking earlier. As for the old stuff, in 2009, 1,000 bottles of 200-yr-old Port salvaged off the coast of Brazil were pronounced suitable for consumption.

Warre Oldest of British Port shippers (since 1670); owned by SYMINGTON FAMILY ESTATES since 1905. Fine, elegant, long-maturing vintage wines, gd RESERVE, vintage character (Warrior), excellent unfiltered LBV; 10- and 20-yr-old TAWNY Otima. Single-QUINTA VINTAGE from Quinta da Cavadinha. Vintages: 63 66 70' 75 77' 80 83 85 91 94 97 00' 03 07'.

White Port Port from white grapes, occasionally sweet (*lagrima*) but mostly off-dry (driest labelled Dry). Apéritif straight or drunk long with tonic and fresh mint. Altogether more serious are new (since 2006) age-designated 10-, 20-, 30-, or 40-yr-old styles and COLHEITAS eg. C DA SILVA's Dalva Golden White.

Williams & Humbert Jer ★→★★★★ Traditional Sherry BODEGA. Once a famous name, now much involved in making private label wines. Dry Sack (Amontillado) is bestseller. V.gd old wines: *Dos Cortados PC*, Solera Especial VOS PC.

Switzerland

Abbreviations used in the text:

Aar Aargau
Ber Bern
Gris Grisons
Neu Neuchâtel
Schaff Schaffhausen
Thur Thurgau
Tic Ticino
Vd Vaud
Val Valais
Zür Zürich

SWITZERLAND

Even though wine has been made on these hills since the Romans were here, Switzerland is better known for its chocolate, cheese, banks and watches. Most Swiss wine is consumed in the country and the Swiss do little to promote their wines abroad. The trend towards local, indigenous grape varieties still holds strong. The biggest wine region, the Valais, offers more than 60 different vines, such as Heida, Humagne Rouge, Cornalin, Petite Arvine or Humagne Blanche. On the other hand almost a third of the country's vineyard is planted with Pinot Noir. The signature grape of Switzerland is still Chasselas.

Recent vintages

2010 A classic vintage. Very elegant, but less quantity then 2009.
2009 One of the best of recent years.
2008 Difficult year with lots of rain. Quality okay but not tops.
2007 Reds are less opulent than 2006. Whites are superb.
2006 Very promising and being compared to 2005.

Aigle Vd r w ★★→★★★ Well-known for elegant CHASSELAS and supple PINOT N.
Amigne Traditional VALAIS white grape, esp of Vétroz. Total planted: 43 ha. Full-bodied, tasty, often sweet but also bone-dry. Best: ANDRÉ FONTANNAZ ★★ 07' 08 09' 10 or JEAN-RENÉ GERMANIER, CAVE LES RUINETTES.
AOC Compulsory since Jan 1, 2008, for all regions; each region has different rules.
Arvine Old VALAIS white grape (also Petite Arvine): dry and sweet, elegant, long-lasting wines with salty finish. 154 ha planted. Producers: CHAPPAZ, John et Mike Favre, SIMON MAYE & FILS, Domaines des Muses, ROUVINEZ VINS, PROVINS.

Auvernier Neu r p w ★★→★★★ Old wine village. Try: Caves du Château d'Auvernier.

Bachtobel, Schlossgut Thur ★★★→★★★★ 07' 08' 09' 10 Johannes Meier has been running this top estate since 2008. V.gd PINOT N, RIES and Sauv Bl.

Badoux, Henri Vd w ★★ Big producer of commercial wines. Try Chasselas Aigle les Murailles (classic lizard label), Yvorne Petit Vignoble and red AIGLE.

Bern Capital; French- and German-speaking canton. Best villages: La Neuveville, Ligerz, Schafis, Schernelz and Twann. Chasselas, PINOT N and Müller-T.

Bielersee Ber r p w ★→★★ 08 09' 10 Wine region on northern and western shore of the Bielersee (dry, light CHASSELAS, PINOT N, Müller-T and *spécialités*, such as Chard, Pinot Gr, Sauv Bl, Malbec, Zweigelt). Best producers: Andrey Weinbau, Domaine du Signolet, Schernelz Village.

Blauburgunder German name for PINOT N; aka Clevner. Rosé to heavily oaked reds. Switzerland's main red variety, cultivated in all six wine regions. Limited editions are the trend: from Maienfeld or Tête de Cru Staatskellerei from ZÜRICH.

Bovard, Louis Vd w ★★★ Classical interpretation of CHASSELAS. V.gd Dézaley. Family business for ten generations.

Bündner Herrschaft Gris r p w ★★★→★★★★ Best German-Swiss wine region. Top villages: Fläsch, Jenins, Maienfeld, Malans, Zizers. BLAUBURGUNDER ripens esp well due to warm *Föhn* wind, cask-aged v.gd. Also Chard, Müller-T, Completer. Best: Cicero Weinbau ★★, Davaz ★★, Weingut Donatsch ★★, FROMM ★★★, GANTENBEIN ★★★★, Manfred Meier ★★, Weingut Annatina Pelizzatti ★★, Scadenagut ★★, Schloss Salenegg ★★, Weinbau von Tscharner ★★. 07' 08 09' 10. Switzerland's best BLAUBURGUNDER is from here.

Chablais Vd r w ★★→★★★ Wine region at the upper end of Lake GENEVA, inc villages AIGLE, Bex, Ollon, Villeneuve, YVORNE.

Champagne Vd The Swiss village continues to fight against the French wine-growing area that forbids everybody else to use the name "Champagne" on the label. They have to call the wines Libre-Champ.

Chanton, Josef-Marie and Mario Val ★★★ Terrific *Valais spécialités*: HEIDA, Lafnetscha, Himbertscha, Hibou, Plantscher, Resi, Gwäss.

Chappaz Val ★★★ Marie-Thérèse Chappaz of FULLY is the queen of sweet wine. Outstanding PETITE ARVINE and Marsanne Blanche Grain Noble ConfidenCiel.

Chasselas (Gutedel in Germany.) Main white variety. Neutral flavour, takes on local character: elegant (GENEVA); refined, full (VAUD); exotic, racy (VALAIS). Called FENDANT in VALAIS. Makes almost a third of Swiss wines but increasingly replaced. New DNA researches of Dr. José Vouillamoz show VAUD as origin of the grape. Best: CDC (Clos, Domaines & Château), Domaine des Muses, Domaine Henri Cruchon, Philippe Gex, Raymont PACCOT.

Château Maison Blanche Vd w ★★ Best in the area, making one CHASSELAS.

Cicero Weinbau Gris w r ★★★ Thomas Mattmann represents the new generation in the GRISONS. Wonderful PINOT N (esp Der Mattmann) and Sauv Bl.

Cornalin Val ★★→★★★ 07 08 09' 10 Local VALAIS *spécialité*. Original name Rouge du Pays, wrongly called Cornalin, since the Cornalin du Valais and the Cornalin from Aosta are not related. Cornalin du Valais and Humagne Rouge du Aosta are the same grape, says DNA profiler Dr. Vouillamoz. Best: JEAN-RENÉ GERMANIER, Anne-Catherine et Denis MERCIER, PROVINS VALAIS Maurice Zufferey, Vins des Chevaliers, Rouvinez Vins.

Côte, la Vd r p w ★→★★★ Largest VAUD AOC wine area between LAUSANNE and NYON. Traditional whites with elegant finesse; fruity, harmonious reds. Esp from MONT-SUR-ROLLE, Vinzel, Luins, FÉCHY, MORGES. Try Château de Luins, Bolle et Cie SA, DOMAINE LA COLOMBE.

Cruchon, Henri Vd w r ★★★ Biodynamic producer. Wonderful CHASSELAS, Sauv Bl, GAMARET and GAMAY.

Dézaley Vd w (r) ★★→★★★ Celebrated LAVAUX v'yd above Lake GENEVA. Potent CHASSELAS, develops esp after ageing. Try La Baronnie du Dézaley (12 producers).

Dôle Val r ★★→★★★ Most famous traditional red-wine blend. PINOT N and GAMAY must make 85% of the blend. Rest can be other reds from the VALAIS: full, supple, often v.gd. Lightly pink Dôle Blanche is pressed straight after harvest. Try SIMON MAYE ET FILS, PROVINS VALAIS, Gérald Besse.

Domaine la Colombe Vd w ★★★★ Family company; one of the best producers of fresh, elegant, minerally CHASSELAS; also try Réserve Pinot Gr.

Epesses Vd w (r) ★→★★★ 09' 10 LAVAUX AOC: supple, full-bodied whites. Try Luc Massy Vins.

Ermitage Val Alias Marsanne; a VALAIS *spécialité*. Concentrated, full-bodied dry white, sometimes with residual sugar. Best: Dom Cornulus, PROVINS VALAIS, Gregor Kuonen Caveau de Salquenen.

Féchy Vd ★→★★ Famous appellation of LA CÔTE, esp elegant whites. DYA.

Federweisser German-Swiss name for fresh white/rosé from BLAUBURGUNDER. Also called Weissherbst.

Fendant w ★→★★★ VALAIS appellation for CHASSELAS. The ideal wine for Swiss cheese dishes such as fondue or raclette. Try PROVINS VALAIS, Les Fils de Charles Favre, MAURICE ZUFFEREY, Adrian Mathier Nouveau Salquenen, Domaine des Muses, JEAN-RENÉ GERMANIER, Cave Mabillard-Fuchs.

Flétri/Mi-flétri Late-harvested grapes for sweet/slightly sweet wine.

Fontannaz, André Val w ★★★ Nobody understands the AMIGNE de Vétroz grape better.

Fribourg Smallest French-Swiss wine canton (115 ha, nr Jura). Try Cru de l'Hôpital, Cave de la Tour.

Fromm, Georg Gris ★★★ 07' 08 09' 10 Malans grower sold his second estate in New Zealand and focuses on outstanding BLAUBURGUNDER and Chard in GRISONS.

Fully Val r w Village nr Martigny; excellent ERMITAGE and GAMAY. Best producer: Marie-Thérèse CHAPPAZ ★★→★★★ 08 09' 10.

Gamaret Red grape. Resistant variety created in 1970; GAMAY x Reichensteiner. Try Staatskellerei Zürich, Domaine des Charmes, Cave Cidis.

Gamay Beaujolais grape; abounds in French cantons. Mainly thin wine used in blends (SALVAGNIN, DÔLE) and also more and more as a single variety. Try: Cave Corbassière, JEAN-RENÉ GERMANIER, Les Frères Dutruy.

Gantenbein, Daniel & Martha Gris 07 08 09' (10) ★★★★ Most famous growers in SWITZERLAND based in Fläsch/GRISONS. Top PINOT N from DRC clones (Burgundy), RIES with clones from Loosen (Mosel). Strong in export.

Garanoir Grape: twin of GAMARET. Found all over Switzerland, except in TICINO. Try Bujard Vins, Domaine du Centaure.

Geneva Capital, and French-Swiss wine canton; 3rd-largest. Key areas: Mandement, Entre Arve et Rhône, Entre Arve et Lac. Mostly CHASSELAS, GAMAY. Also GAMARET, Chard, PINOT N, Sauv Bl and gd Aligoté. Best: JEAN-MICHEL NOVELLE ★★★; interesting: Domaine des Charmes, Domaine Dugerdil, Domaine Les Hutins, Domaine Grand'Cour ★★.

Germanier, Jean-René Val Vétroz winemaker; Gilles Besse is in charge of this top estate. Cayas (100% Syrah) ★★★ 05' 06 07 08' (09'); Mitis (sweet AMIGNE) ★★★ 05' 06 07 08'. Also a pure CORNALIN 05' 06 07' and the PINOT N Clos du Four ★★★.

Glacier, Vin du (Gletscherwein) Val Fabled oxidized, wooded white from rare Rèze grape of Val d'Anniviers. Almost impossible to find on sale. Keep looking. If you love Sherry this is a must.

Grain Noble ConfidenCiel Val Quality label for top Swiss sweet wines. Try Domaine du Mont d'Or, Cave la Liaudisaz, Thierry Constantin, Domaine Cornulus.

Grisons (Graubünden) Mtn canton, mainly German/Swiss (BÜNDNER HERRSCHAFT, Churer Rheintal; esp BLAUBURGUNDER), part south of Alps (Misox, esp MERLOT).

> **Wine regions**
> Switzerland is officially divided into six wine regions. VALAIS, VAUD,
> GENEVA, TICINO, Trois Lacs (NEUCHÂTEL, Bienne, Vully and Jury) and
> German Switzerland, which comprises ZURICH, SCHAFFHAUSEN, GRISONS
> and Aargau. And contrary to Switzerland's reputation for making
> white wines, 60% of wines are red; mostly PINOT N.

PINOT N king, Chard v.gd. Best: GANTENBEIN, FROMM, CICERO WEINBAU, Weinbau von Tscharner, IRENE GRÜNENFELDER.

Grünenfelder, Irene Gris r ★★★ Only three wines but they're outstanding.

Heida (Païen) Old VALAIS white grape (Jura's Savagnin) also known as Païen or Traminer, 80 ha in the VALAIS. Famous v'yds in VISPERTERMINEN at 1,000+ metres. Full-bodied wine with high acidity. Best: JOSEF-MARIE CHANTON, PROVINS VALAIS. Try St Jodernkellerei, Cave de la Madeleine, ROUVINEZ VINS.

Huber Daniel Tic r ★★★ 07′ 08 09′ (10) MERLOT Montagna Magica is superb and inspiring for other growers in TICINO.

Humagne Strong native white grape (VALAIS *spécialité*), older than CHASSELAS. Humagne Rouge is not related to it, but also common in the VALAIS. Esp from Chamoson, Leytron, Martigny. Try Domaine Cornulus, Cave les Ruinettes.

Johannisberg Val Synonym for SYLVANER in the VALAIS. Try Les Fils Maye, Domaine du Mont d'or, Kellerei Leukersonne, Christophe et Antoine Bétrisey.

Lausanne Capital of VAUD. No longer with v'yds in town area, but long-time owner of classics: Abbaye de Mont, Château Rochefort (LA CÔTE); Clos des Moines, Clos des Abbayes, Domaine de Burignon (LAVAUX).

Lavaux Vd w (r) ★→★★★ Now a UNESCO world heritage site: v'yd terraces stretch 30 km along the south-facing north shore of Lake GENEVA from Château de Chillon to the eastern outskirts of LAUSANNE. Main grape: CHASSELAS. Wines named for the villages: Lutry, ST-SAPHORIN, Ollon, EPESSES, DÉZALEY, Montreux and more.

Mathier, Diego Val w r ★★★★ Top wine estate in SALGESCH/VALAIS. Try PINOT N, wide range of *spécialités*.

Mauler ★★→★★★ V.gd name for sparkling in NEUCHÂTEL, esp Cuvée Exellence.

Maye, Simon et Fils w r ★★★ VALAIS producer in St Pierre de Clages; interesting FENDANT, Païen, PINOT N and Syrah.

Mercier, Anne-Catherine et Denis Val ★★★ 07 08 09′ (10) Growers in SIERRE with outstanding CORNALIN and Syrah.

Merlot Tic Brought to the TICINO in 1907 by the scientist Alderige Fantuzzi (after phylloxera): soft to v. powerful wines. Also used with Cab Sauv. Best: Luigi ZANINI, Agriloro, Chiodi, Gialdi Vini, Cantina Kopp von der Krone, Guido Brivio.

Mont-sur-Rolle Vd w (r) ★★ DYA Important appellation. CHASSELAS is king.

Morges Vd r p w ★→★★ DYA Largest LA CÔTE/VAUD AOC with 39 communes: CHASSELAS, fruity reds.

Neuchâtel City and canton; 591 ha from Lake Neuchâtel to BIELERSEE. CHASSELAS: fragrant, lively (*sur lie*, sparkling). Gd OEIL DE PERDRIX, Pinot Gr, Chard. Try: Château Souaillon, Chantal Ritter, Château d'Auvrnier.

Non Filtré *Spécialité* available in springtime from NEUCHÂTEL, from CHASSELAS.

Novelle Jean-Michel Gen ★★★ 07 08 09′ 10 GENEVA-based, Domaine le Grande Clos. V.gd Sauv Bl, Petit Manseng, GAMAY, MERLOT, Syrah.

Oeil de Perdrix Neu PINOT N rosé. DYA esp NEUCHÂTEL's; name can be used anywhere.

Paccot, Raymond Vd ★★★ 08 09′ 10′ FÉCHY. Excellent CHASSELAS, esp Le Brez.

Petite Arvine *See* ARVINE.

Pinot Noir (Blauburgunder) *See* BLAUBURGUNDER. Try: GANTENBEIN (Fläsch); Schlossgut Bachtobel (Ottoberg); Pircher (Eglisau); Baumann Weingut (Oberhallau); Meier

(Kloster Sion); FROMM (Malans), Adrian Mathier (SALGESCH), John et Mike Favre (St Pierre de Clages), Château Souaillon (NEUCHÂTEL) ★★★ 08 09' 10.

Provins Valais Val Biggest winery (co-op) in Switzerland. Outstanding for Maître de Chais and Crus des Domaines labels, and interesting Les Titans range.

Rahm, Weinkellereien Schaff w r ★★ Big producer of commercial wines.

Riesling-Sylvaner Old name for Müller-T. Aromatic, dry white wine, good acidity. Best: Daniel Marugg, Weinbau Schwarzenbach, Weingut Schipf, Weingut Saxer, Schlossgut Bachtobel, VOLG WEINKELLEREIEN ★★ 09' 10.

Rouvinez Vins Val w r ★★★ Important producer. Try Château Lichten, CORNALIN from Montibeux, La Trémaille. Also owns Caves Orsat.

Salgesch Important wine village in the upper VALAIS. Try Adrian Mathier, Cave du Rhodan, Vins des Chevaliers, Caveau de Salquenen. Albert Mathier et Fils.

Salvagnin r ★→★★ 09' 10 GAMAY and/or PINOT N appellation. *Spécialité* from VAUD.

Schaffhausen Schaff German-Swiss canton/wine town on Rhine. BLAUBURGUNDER, Müller-T., *spécialités*. Best: Baumann Weingut, Bad Osterfingen ★★.

Schenk Europe-wide wine giant, founded and based in Rolle (VAUD). Owns firms in France (Burgundy and Bordeaux), Germany, Italy and Spain. Best address for classic-style Swiss wines.

Schwarzenbach Weinbau Zür w ★★★ Dry, crisp whites, Räuschling, Kerner, Müller-T.

Sierre Val r w ★★→★★★ Sunny resort; famous wine town. Known for FENDANT, PINOT N, ERMITAGE, Malvoisie. V.gd DÔLE. Visit Château de Villa (wine museum, *vinotheque* with largest VALAIS wine collection). Producers: Imesch Vins, Anne-Catherine et DENIS MERCIER, Domaine des Muses, Rouvinez Vins, Maurice Zufferey.

Sion r w ★★→★★★ Capital/wine centre of VALAIS. Esp FENDANT de Sion. Important producers: Charles Bonvin Fils, Les Fils de Charles Favre, Giroud Vins, PROVINS VALAIS, Robert Gilliard.

St-Saphorin Vd w (r) ★★→★★★ 09' 10 Famous LAVAUX AOC for fine light whites. Try Château de Glérolles.

Sternen, Weingut zum Aar r ★★★ V. interesting interpretation of PINOT N. Try Kloster Sion Pinot N.

Ticino Italian-speaking southern Switzerland (with Misox), growing mainly MERLOT (gd from mountainous Sopraceneri region) and *spécialités*. Try Cab Sauv (oaked Bordeaux style), Sauv Bl, Sem, Chard, MERLOT white and rosé (1,028 ha). Best producers: Guido Brivio, Chiodi, Gialdi, Daniel Huber, Werner Stucky, Luigi ZANINI, Agriloro, Christian Zündel, Tenuta Montalbano, Tamborini Carlo Eredi. All ★★→★★★ 07' 08 09' (10).

Valais (Wallis) Rhône Valley from German-speaking upper Valais to French lower Valais. Largest, most varied and exciting wine canton (30% of Swiss wine). Wide range: 47 grape varieties, plus many *spécialités*; FLÉTRI/MI-FLÉTRI wines.

Vaud (Waadt) French Switzerland's 2nd-largest wine canton; stronghold of CHABLAIS, LA CÔTE, LAVAUX, Bonvillars, Côtes de l'Orbe, Vully, CHASSELAS.

Visperterminen Val w (r) ★→★★ Upper VALAIS v'yds, esp for HEIDA. One of the highest v'yds in Europe (1,000+ metres; called Rieben). Try CHANTON, St Jodern Kellerei.

Volg Weinkellereien Zür w r ★★→★★★ Co-op that focuses on local terroirs and *spécialités*. Try Müller-T., Completer or different PINOT N.

Yvorne Vd w (r) ★★ 09' 10 Top CHABLAIS AOC for strong, fragrant wines. Try Château Maison Blanche.

Zanini Luigi ★★→★★★★ 07' 08 09' 10 Top TICINO producer with focus on MERLOT. Best are Castello Luigi and Vinattieri Ticinesi.

Zufferey, Maurice Val r ★★★ Try Syrah, HUMAGNE *rouge*, CORNALIN.

Zündel Christian Tic ★★★ 07' 08 09' (10) Grower to remember for top MERLOT.

Zürich Capital of largest canton. BLAUBURGUNDER mostly; esp Müller-T., RÄUSCHLING, Kerner. Try Ladolt, SCHWARZENBACH, Zweifel Weine, Schipfgut.

Austria

Abbreviations used in the text:

Burgen	Burgenland
Carn	Carnuntum
Kamp	Kamptal
Krems	Kremstal
Low A	Lower Austria
M Burg	Mittelburgenland
N'see	Neusiedlersee-Hügelland
S/W/SE Sty	Styria
Therm	Thermenregion
Trais	Traisental
Wach	Wachau
Wag	Wagram
Wein	Weinviertel

Austria is moving on. To begin with, ripeness was all. Now it's terroir; and regional authenticity is the buzzword. Austria may have warm summers, but the most successful wines are cool-climate ones. Even for the more substantial reds, structure, finesse and soil are more important than sheer fruit-driven oomph. It's easy to talk about terroir, but Austria seems to be putting its regulations where its mouth is. In Kremstal, Traisental, Kamptal and Wagram – along the Danube, in other words – vineyards are now divided into *Erste Lage* (first growth), *Klassifizierte Lage* (classified growth) and the rest. This is, naturally, a separate system to the DACs (*see* below), which already exist. One wouldn't want it to be too simple. The Wachau still has its own classification, based on ripeness alone, but it's starting to look a little out of date. It's location, location, location now.

Recent vintages

2010 A very difficult year; very small harvest. Hail and heavy rain: delayed flowering, coulure. Meticulous work imperative, yields down (up to 55%), de-acidification required. A few surprisingly impressive wines.

2009 An uneven year – hot early summer, July hailstorms in Vienna, cool spells, a wet September, then good late autumn. Some outstanding wines: whites (Lower Austria, Styria) and reds (Neusiedlersee, Middle Burgenland).

2008 Coolest year since 2004. Producers who took care produced some excellent results, don't discount.

2007 Good in Styria and, in Burgenland, for Blaufränkisch, Zweigelt and Pinot N. Excellent yields in Vienna, better for Grüner Veltliner than for Ries.

2006 A great year. Well-rounded and complex wines with great ageing potential. The more powerful Ries and Grüner Veltliners as well as the great reds are beginning to open up.

2005 Uneven and often unexciting, though some fine wines, especially in Lower Austria. Drink soon, also the reds.

Achs, Paul N'see r (w) ★★★ Trend-setting GOLS estate, esp reds: PANNOBILE blends, Ungerberg, BLAUFRÄNKISCH and Pinot N. Biodynamic producer (*see* below).

Alzinger w ★★★★ 99 01 03 05 06 07 08 09 10 Leading WACHAU estate: highly expressive RIES and GRÜNER VELTLINER, esp from Steinertal v'yd.

Ausbruch PRÄDIKAT wine with sugar levels between Beerenauslese and Trockenbeerenauslese. Traditionally produced in RUST.

Ausg'steckt ("Hung out") HEURIGEN are not open all yr; when they are, a green bush is hung above their doors.

Bayer r w ★★ Without v'yds of his own, Bayer buys in grapes mainly in the Middle Burgenland and makes polished, balanced reds with a BLAUFRÄNKISCH base.

Beck, Judith N'see r w ★★ Rising and accomplished biodynamic winemaker. Well-crafted reds, esp gd Pinot N and *St-Laurent*.

Biodynamism Still gaining new recruits, inc leading producers such as P ACHS, J BECK, Fritsch, Geyerhof, GRAF HARDEGG, HIRSCH, F LOIMER, Meinklang, Sepp & Maria Muster, NIKOLAIHOF, B OTT, J NITTNAUS, PITTNAUER, F WENINGER.

Blauburger Austrian red grape variety. A cross between BLAUER PORTUGIESER and BLAUFRÄNKISCH. Simple wines.

Blauer Burgunder (Pinot N) Some fine Pinot N is now being made by Austrian producers in BURGENLAND, KAMPTAL, THERMENREGION; from growers: P ACHS, J BECK, W BRÜNDLMAYER, F LOIMER, PITTNAUER, J & R PÖCKL, C PREISINGER, PRIELER, SCHLOSS GOBELSBURG, SCHLOSS HALBTURN, F WENINGER, F WIENINGER.

Blauer Portugieser Red varietal; light, fruity: drink slightly chilled when young.

Blauer Zweigelt BLAUFRÄNKISCH/St-Laurent cross. Mostly for appealingly velvety wines; also a gd *cuvée* partner. Top producers: Grassl, G HEINRICH, J NITTNAUS, PITTNAUER, J & R PÖCKL, Scheibelhofer, SCHWARZ, WINKLER-HERMADEN.

Blaufränkisch (Lemberger in Germany, Kékfrankos in Hungary). Potentially Austria's top red grape, widely planted in MITTELBURGENLAND: medium-bodied, peppery acidity, a characteristic salty note, berry aromas and eucalyptus. Often blended with Cab Sauv or ZWEIGELT. Best: P ACHS, GESELLMANN, J HEINRICH, IGLER, KOLLWENTZ-RÖMERHOF, KRUTZLER, MORIC, J NITTNAUS, PRIELER, SCHIEFER, E TRIEBAUMER, F WENINGER.

Bouvier Indigenous aromatic grape: v.gd BA and TBA, rarely dry wines.

Brandl, Günter Kamp w ★★ Small but consistently *fine Kamptal estate*, known esp for RIES and GRÜNER VELTLINER Novemberlese.

Braunstein, Birgit r w ★ Striving N'SEE-HÜGELLAND estate: *cuvée* Oxhoft.

Bründlmayer, Willi Kamp r w sw sp ★★★★ 00 01 02 03 05 06 07 08 09 10 Flagship Langenlois-KAMPTAL estate. Produces world-class RIES, GRÜNER VELTLINER, esp Ries Heiligenstein Alte Reben and GV Käferberg. Also Austria's best sparkling *méthode traditionelle*.

Burgenland Province and wine region (14,500 ha) in the east bordering Hungary. Warm climate, esp around shallow LAKE NEUSIEDL. Ideal conditions for reds and esp botrytis wines nr N'SEE. Four areas: MITTELBURGENLAND, N'SEE, N'SEE-HÜGELLAND, SÜDBURGENLAND.

Buschenschank A wine tavern, often a HEURIGE country cousin.

Carnuntum r w Dynamic region southeast of VIENNA now showing gd reds, often on St-Laurent base. Best: Glatzer, Grassl, G Markowitsch, Muhr-van der Niepoort, Netzl, PITTNAUER, Wiederstein.

Chardonnay Best when vinified with little oak, particularly in STYRIA and BURGENLAND.

Known in STYRIA as MORILLON: pronounced fruit, lively acidity, gd ageing potential. Esp W BRÜNDLMAYER, GROSS, KOLLWENTZ-RÖMERHOF, F LOIMER, Malat, E & W POLZ, W SATTLER, STIEGELMAR, M TEMENT, VELICH, F WIENINGER.

Deutschkreutz M Burg r (w) Red-wine area, esp for BLAUFRÄNKISCH.

Districtus Austriae Controllatus, DAC Austria's first appellation system (2003). Similar to France's AC and Italy's DOC, and rapidly gaining acceptance. Current DACs: KAMPTAL, KREMSTAL, LEITHABERG, MITTELBURGENLAND, TRAISENTAL, WEINVIERTEL.

Donabaum, Johann Wach w ★★ Fine grower with outstanding, well-balanced RIES and GRÜNER VELTLINER, esp Ries Offenberg.

Ehmoser Wag w ★ Small individualist producer, gd GRÜNER VELTLINER Aurum.

Erste Lage First growth, according to new v'yd classification by Traditionsweingüter Österreich, in Lower Austria, along the Danube.

Federspiel Wach Medium level of the VINEA WACHAU categories, roughly corresponding to Kabinett. Elegant, dry wines, less overpowering than the higher SMARAGD category.

Feiler-Artinger r w sw ★★★★ 95 02 03 04 05 06 07 08 09 Outstanding RUST estate with top AUSBRUCH dessert wines *often v.gd value* and red blends. Beautiful baroque house, too.

Forstreiter Krems w ★ Consistent producer, particularly gd RIES.

Furmint Rare white variety cultivated in and around RUST. Usually sweet, but dry wines undergoing renaissance: H SCHRÖCK.

Gemischter Satz Blend of (mostly white) grape varieties planted in one v'yd and vinified together. Traditional method that spreads risk; back in fashion in VIENNA and yielding gd results: Christ, WIENINGER.

Gesellmann M Burg r w ★★ Consistent and often fine producer; BLAUFRÄNKISCH and red *cuvées*: Opus Eximium.

Geyerhof Krems ★→★★ One of Austria's pioneers of organic viticulture, Ilse Mayer's estate now makes fine RIES and GRÜNER VELTLINER.

Gols N'see r w dr sw Dynamic wine commune on north shore of LAKE NEUSIEDL in BURGENLAND. Top producers: P ACHS, J BECK, GSELLMANN, G HEINRICH, A & H NITTNAUS, PITTNAUER, C PREISINGER, Renner, STIEGELMAR.

Graf Hardegg Wein r w Large estate. Viognier, Syrah, Pinot N and RIES.

Gross S Sty w ★★★★ 03 05 06 07 08 09 Outstanding and perfectionist south STYRIAN producer. Esp CHARD, Sauv Bl and his own favourite, Pinot Bl.

Grüner Veltliner Austria's flagship white grape, 37% of v'yds. Remarkably diverse: peppery, everyday styles to great complexity and surprising age ageing potential. Best: ALZINGER, W BRÜNDLMAYER, F HIRTZBERGER, HÖGL, M Huber, E KNOLL, F LOIMER, MANTLERHOF, NEUMAYER, NIGL, NIKOLAIHOF, B OTT, PFAFFL, FX PICHLER, F PRAGER, SCHMELZ.

Gsellmann, Hans N'see r w sw ★ Formerly Gsellmann & Gsellmann, in GOLS, esp well-made reds and dry whites.

Gumpoldskirchen Therm r w dr sw Famous HEURIGE village south of VIENNA, centre of THERMENREGION. Signature white varieties: ZIERFANDLER and ROTGIPFLER grapes. Best producers: Biegler, Spaetrot, ZIERER.

Heinrich, Gernot N'see r w dr sw ★★★★ 03 05 06 07 08 09 Ambitious, accomplished GOLS estate, member of the PANNOBILE group. Outstanding single-v'yd red wines.

Heinrich, Johann M Burg r w dr sw ★★★ 00 01 03 05 06 08 09 Leading producer. V.gd BLAUFRÄNKISCH Goldberg Reserve. Excellent *cuvée* Cupido.

Heurige Wine of the most recent harvest, called "new wine" for one yr.

Heurigen Wine taverns in which growers-cum-patrons serve their own wine with simple local food – a Viennese institution.

Hiedler Kamp w sw ★★★ Leading producer of concentrated, expressive wines. V.gd RIES Maximum.

Hirsch Kamp w ★★★ Searching organic producer. Esp fine Heiligenstein, Lamm and Gaisberg v'yds. Also Austria's screwcap pioneer.

Hirtzberger, Franz Wach w ★★★★ 01 03 05 06 07 08 09 Top producer with 20 ha at SPITZ AN DER DONAU. *Highly expressive, minerally Ries* and GRÜNER VELTLINER, esp from the Honivogl and Singerriedel v'yds.

Högl Wach ★ w sw Individual producer; often fine RIES and GRÜNER VELTLINER.

Horitschon M Burg Region for reds: IBY, F WENINGER.

Igler M Burg ★ r Consistent grower of reds: Ab Ericio, Vulcano.

Illmitz N'see w dr sw (r) SEEWINKEL region famous for BA and TBA. Best Angerhof, Martin Haider, KRACHER, Helmut Lang, Opitz.

Jamek, Josef Wach w ★ Traditional estate with restaurant. Not typical WACHAU style: often some residual sugar.

Johanneshof Reinisch Therm r w sw Large, consistent estate; esp gd whites.

Jurtschitsch/Sonnhof Kamp w (r) dr (sw) ★ Large, highly respected estate: reliable whites (RIES, GRÜNER VELTLINER, CHARD).

Kamptal r w Wine region, along river Kamp north of WACHAU. Top v'yds: Heiligenstein, Käferberg, Lanum. Best: K Angerer, G BRANDL, W BRÜNDLMAYER, Ehn, Eichinger, HIEDLER, HIRSCH, JURTSCHITSCH, F LOIMER, G RABL, SCHLOSS GOBELSBURG, STEININGER. Kamptal is now DAC (from 2008) for GRÜNER VELTLINER and RIES.

Kattus Vienna Producer of traditional sekt in VIENNA.

Kerschbaum M Burg r ★★★ 03 05 06 07 08 09 BLAUFRÄNKISCH specialist, individualist and often fascinating wines.

Klassifizierte Lage Second, or classified, growth, according to the new classification system of v'yds by the Traditionsweingüter, in Lower Austria, along the Danube.

Klosterneuburg r w Main wine town of Donauland. Rich in tradition, with a wine college founded in 1860. Best: Stift Klosterneuburg, Zimmermann.

KMW Abbreviation for Klosterneuburger Mostwaage ("must level"), the unit used in Austria to measure the sugar content in grape juice.

Knoll, Emmerich Wach w ★★★★ 00 01 03 05 06 07 08 09 Outstanding traditional estate in Loiben. *Delicate, fragrant Ries, complex Grüner Veltliner*, part from Loibenberg, Schütt.

Kollwentz-Römerhof r w dr (sw) ★★★★ 03 05 06 07 08 09 Pioneering producer nr Eisenstadt: Sauv Bl, CHARD, Eiswein. Also renowned for *fine reds: Steinzeiler*.

Kracher N'see w dr (r sw) ★★★★ 95 00 01 02 03 04 05 06 07 08 Top-class ILLMITZ producer specializing in botrytized PRÄDIKATS (dessert); barrique-aged (Nouvelle Vague), others in steel (Zwischen den Seen); gd reds since 1997. Now run by Gerhard Kracher.

Kremstal w (r) Wine region esp for GRÜNER VELTLINER and RIES. Top: Buchegger, Malat, S MOSER, NIGL, SALOMON-UNDHOF, Stagård, WEINGUT STADT KREMS.

Krug Therm r w sw Well-made, international-style wines, esp full-bodied Pinot Gr and red *cuvées*.

Krutzler S Burg r ★★★ 03 06 07 08 09 Leading producer of outstanding BLAUFRÄNKISCH, esp Perwolff.

Lackner-Tinnacher ★ Fine SÜD-OSTSTEIERMARK estate; fragrant MORILLON, MUSKATELLER.

Leithaberg N'see V'yd hill on the northern shore of LAKE NEUSIEDL; also a lively group of producers successfully redefining regional terroir-based style. Now a DAC.

Loimer, Fred Kamp w ★★★→★★★★ Thoughtful and ambitious producer, with 31-ha estate, 50% GRÜNER VELTLINER; also RIES, CHARD, Pinot Gr, v.gd Pinot N. Leading exponent of biodynamic winemaking.

Mantlerhof w ★★ KREMSTAL producer with a well-considered, traditional approach. Gd Roter Veltliner.

Mayer am Pfarrplatz w Viennese producer and HEURIGE now in new ownership, with marked improvement in the wines.

Mittelburgenland r dr (w sw) Region on Hungarian border concentrating on BLAUFRÄNKISCH (also DAC); increasingly fine. Producers: BAYER, Gager, GESELLMANN, J HEINRICH, IBY, IGLER, KERSCHBAUM, Wellanschitz, F WENINGER.

Moric M Burg ★★★ Outstanding benchmark BLAUFRÄNKISCH wine made by Roland VELICH from old vines in several MITTELBURGENLAND villages, vinified according to site. Stylistically a beacon.

Morillon Name given in STYRIA to CHARD.

Moser, Lenz Austria's largest producer, based in Krems.

Moser, Sepp Krems r w sw Consistent RIES, GRÜNER VELTLINER.

Muhr-van der Niepoort Carn w r ★ Rising winery in the CARNUNTUM region. Yes, Niepoort as in Port. Well-judged reds, esp BLAUFRÄNKISCH.

Müller, Domaine W St Individualist producer, with international outlook, esp Sauv Bl and CHARD.

Muskat-Ottonel Grape for fragrant, often dry whites, interesting PRÄDIKATS.

Muskateller Rare, aromatic grape for v. fragrant, dry whites, esp in STYRIA. Top: GROSS, F HIRTZBERGER, LACKNER-TINNACHER, FX PICHLER, E & W POLZ, W SATTLER.

Neuburger Indigenous white grape that has long been neglected; mainly in the WACHAU (elegant, flowery), THERMENREGION (mellow, ample-bodied) and north BURGENLAND (strong, full). Best from J BECK, DOMÄNE WACHAU, F HIRTZBERGER.

Neumayer Trais w ★★★ Top estate; powerful, focused, dry GRÜNER VELTLINER and RIES.

Neumeister SE Sty w ★★★ Pioneering, driven producer, esp fine Sauv Bl and CHARD.

Neusiedlersee N'see r w dr sw Region north and east of N'SEE. Best: P ACHS, J BECK, G HEINRICH, KRACHER, J NITTNAUS, J & R PÖCKL, STIEGELMAR, J UMATHUM, VELICH.

Neusiedlersee (Lake Neusiedl) Burgen V. shallow lake on Hungarian border. Warmth and autumn mists encourage botrytis. *See* next entry.

Neusiedlersee-Hügelland r w dr sw Region west of LAKE NEUSIEDL based around Oggau, RUST and Mörbisch on the lake shores, and Eisenstadt in the Leitha foothills. Best: B BRAUNSTEIN, FEILER-ARTINGER, Kloster am Spitz, KOLLWENTZ-RÖMERHOF, PRIELER, Schandl, H SCHRÖCK, Schuller, Sommer, E TRIEBAUMER, WENZEL.

Niederösterreich (Lower Austria) Region with 58% of Austria's v'yds: CARNUNTUM, Wagram, KAMPTAL, KREMSTAL, THERMENREGION, TRAISENTAL, WACHAU, WEINVIERTEL.

Nigl Krems w ★★★★ 03 05 06 07 08 09 The best in KREMSTAL, making sophisticated dry whites with remarkable mineral character from Senftenberg v'yd.

Nikolaihof Wach w ★★★★ 03 05 06 07 08 09 Built on Roman foundations, this impeccable estate has pioneered BIODYNAMISM in Austria. Outstanding RIES from Steiner Hund v'yd, often great ageing potential.

Nittnaus, John N'see r w sw ★★★ Searching organic winemaker. Esp elegant and age-worthy reds: Comondor.

Ott, Bernhard Low A w ★★→★★★ GRÜNER VELTLINER specialist from Donauland. Fass 4; also Der Ott and Rosenberg.

Pannobile N'see Association of youngish and ambitious N'SEE growers centred on GOLS and aiming to create great wine with regional character. Current members: P ACHS, J BECK, HANS GSELLMANN, G HEINRICH, LEITNER, J NITTNAUS, PITTNAUER, C PREISINGER, Renner.

Pfaffl Wein r w ★★★ 05 06 07 08 09 Estate nr VIENNA, in Stetten. Known for dry GRÜNER VELTLINER and RIES.

Pichler-Krutzler Wach w r ★★ This estate is a recent arrival on the scene, a marriage, literally, of two famous names. Fine, balanced wines, esp from the Wunderburg v'yds. Also reds, grown in SÜDBURGENLAND.

Pichler, Franz Xaver Wach w ★★★★ 01 02 03 05 06 07 08 09 One of Austria's finest. Intense and *iconic Ries*; GRÜNER VELTLINER (esp Kellerberg).

Pichler, Rudi Wach w ★★★ →★★★★ Outstanding, individualist producer of powerful, expressive RIES and GRÜNER VELTLINER.

Pittnauer, Gerhard N'see r w ★★★ Fine producer specializing in peaty, sappy St-Laurent wines.

Pöckl, Josef & René N'see r (sw) ★★★ Father-and-son team in Mönchhof. Fine reds, esp Admiral, Rêve de Jeunesse and Rosso e Nero.

Polz, Erich & Walter S Sty w ★★★ 03 05 06 07 08 09 V.gd large (Weinstrasse) growers; esp Hochgrassnitzberg: Sauv Bl, CHARD, Grauburgunder, WEISSBURGUNDER.

Prädikat, Prädikatswein German-inspired system of classifying wine by the sugar content of the juice, from Spätlese upwards (Spätlese, Auslese, Eiswein, STROHWEIN, Beerenauslese, AUSBRUCH and Trockenbeerenauslese). Now widely thought outdated in Austria. *See* Germany.

Prager, Franz Wach w ★★★★ 00 01 02 03 05 06 07 08 09 Pioneer, with JOSEF JAMEK, of top-quality WACHAU dry whites, now run by Toni Bodenstein. RIES, *Grüner Veltliner of impeccable elegance* and mineral structure: Wachstum Bodenstein.

Preisinger, Claus N'see r ★ Ambitious young N'SEE winemaker with stylish reds, esp Pinot N and *cuvée* Paradigma.

Prieler w r ★★★ Consistent, fine N'SEE-HÜGELLAND producer; BLAUFRÄNKISCH Goldberg.

Proidl, Erwin Krems ★★ Highly individual grower making interesting, age-worthy RIES and GRÜNER VELTLINER.

Rabl, Günter Kamp w r sw ★ Consistent grower long overshadowed by more famous colleagues. V.gd GRÜNER VELTLINER.

Riesling On its own, this always means Rhine Ries. WELSCHRIESLING is unrelated. In Austria this is one of the greatest varieties, particularly in KAMPTAL, KREMSTAL and WACHAU. Top growers: ALZINGER, W BRÜNDLMAYER, F HIRTZBERGER, HÖGL, E KNOLL, NIGL, NIKOLAIHOF, PFAFFL, FX PICHLER, F PRAGER, SALOMON-UNDHOF.

Rotgipfler Fragrant indigenous grape of THERMENREGION. With ZIERFANDLER, makes lively *cuvée*. Esp Biegler, Spaetrot, STADLMANN, ZIERER.

Rust N'see r w d r sw Historic town on the shores of LAKE NEUSIEDL, beautiful 17th-century houses testifying to centuries of wine production/trade, esp in Ruster AUSBRUCH. Top: FEILER-ARTINGER, Giefing, Schandl, H SCHRÖCK, E TRIEBAUMER, WENZEL.

Salomon-Undhof Krems w ★★★ Dynamic and fine producer: RIES, WEISSBURGUNDER, Traminer. Berthold Salomon also produces wine in Australia.

Sattler, Willi S Sty w ★★★★ 03 05 06 07 08 09 Top grower. Esp Sauv Bl, MORILLON, often grown on v. steep v'yds.

Schiefer S Burg ★★★ A classic garage producer, Uwe Schiefer has quickly reached the top with his deep, powerful BLAUFRÄNKISCH wines, esp from the Szapary and Reihburg v'yds.

Schilcher W St Rosé wine from indigenous Blauer Wildbacher grapes (sharp, dry, high acidity). A local taste, or at least an acquired one. Specialty of west STYRIA. Try: Klug, Lukas, Reiterer, Strohmeier.

Schloss Gobelsburg Kamp ★★★★ 01 02 03 05 06 07 08 09 Renowned estate run by Michael Moosbrugger. Excellent dry RIES and GRÜNER VELTLINER. A favourite: RIES and GRÜNER VELTLINER Tradition, and fine Pinot N.

Schloss Halbturn N'see r w sw ★★★ Revitalized estate creating ever-better wines with German and French winemakers. Esp *cuvée* Imperial, also Pinot N.

Schlumberger Vienna Largest sparkling winemaker in Austria. Also Loire (France).

Schmelz Wach w ★★★ Fine, often underestimated producer, esp outstanding RIES. Dürnsteiner Freiheit.

Schneider Therm Rising producer, esp succulent St-Laurent and gd Pinot N.

Schröck, Heidi r w sw ★★★ Wines of great purity and focus from a thoughtful RUST grower. V.gd AUSBRUCH. Also v.gd dry FURMINT. *See* Hungary.

Schuster r w ★→★★ N'SEE-HÜGELLAND estate. Son Hannes, the winemaker, produces fine St-Laurent.

Schwarz N'see r sw Small but classy producer, specializing in ZWEIGELT and STROHWEIN.

> **St-Laurent**
> Once an obscure also-ran, the red St-Laurent is definitely the grape
> to seek out at the moment. Earlier attempts at vinification marked
> by high alcohol and extraction were not so successful, but recently
> a spate of succulent and beguiling St-Laurents have come on the
> market. As peaty as a good malt whisky and with plenty of berry fruit
> and spice, this grape lends itself to a range of styles – from a light
> Beaujolais-like wine to deep and substantial wines for ageing.
> Look for J BECK, Fischer, PITTNAUER, Hannes SCHUSTER, J UMATHUM.

Seewinkel N'see ("Lake corner") Name given to the part of N'SEE, inc Apetlon, ILLMITZ and Podersdorf. Ideal conditions for botrytis.

Smaragd Highest category of VINEA WACHAU, similar to dry Spätlese; often complex and powerful.

Spätrot-Rotgipfler Typical blend of THERMENREGION. Aromatic and weighty wines, often with orange-peel aromas.

Spitz an der Donau w Cool WACHAU microclimate, esp from Singerriedel v'yd. Top growers: J DONABAUM, F HIRTZBERGER, HÖGL, Lagler.

Stadlmann r w sw ★★ THERMENREGION producer specializing in opulent ZIERFANDLER-ROTGIPFLER wines.

Steinfeder VINEA WACHAU category for light, fragrant, dry wines.

Steininger Kamp r w sp ★★ Grower with a range of outstanding single-varietal sparkling wines, as well as still ones.

Stiegelmar (Juris-Stiegelmar) N'see r w dr sw ★★ Well-regarded GOLS grower. CHARD, Sauv Bl. Reds: St-Laurent.

Strohwein Sweet wine made from grapes air-dried on straw matting.

Styria (Steiermark) Southernmost region of Austria. Some gd dry whites, esp Sauv Bl and CHARD, called MORILLON in Styria. Also fragrant MUSKATELLER. Includes: SÜDSTEIERMARK, SÜD-OSTSTEIERMARK, WESTSTEIERMARK (south, southeast, west Styria).

Süd-Oststeiermark w (r) STYRIAN region with excellent v'yds. Best producers: NEUMEISTER, WINKLER-HERMADEN.

Südburgenland r w Small south BURGENLAND wine region. V.gd BLAUFRÄNKISCH wines. Best: KRUTZLER, SCHIEFER, Wachter-Wiesler.

Südsteiermark w Best STYRIA region; popular whites (MORILLON, MUSKATELLER, WELSCHRIESLING and Sauv Bl). Best: GROSS, Jaunegg, LACKNER-TINNACHER, E & W POLZ, Potzinger Sabathi, W SATTLER, Skoff, M TEMENT, Wohlmuth.

Tegernseerhof w ★ WACHAU producer, newly invigorated and producing v. interesting RIES and GRÜNER VELTLINER.

Tement, Manfred S Sty w ★★★★ 03 05 06 07 08 09 Renowned estate with esp fine Sauv Bl and MORILLON from Zieregg site. International-style wines, modern reds.

Thermenregion r w dr sw Wine/hot-springs region, south of VIENNA. Indigenous grapes (eg. ZIERFANDLER, ROTGIPFLER), historically one of the most important regions for reds (esp St-Laurent, *see* box above) from Baden, GUMPOLDSKIRCHEN, Tattendorf, Traiskirchen areas. Producers: Alphart, Biegler, Fischer, JOHANNESHOF REINISCH, Schafler, Spätrot-Gebelshuber, STADLMANN, ZIERER.

Traisental 700 ha just south of Krems on Danube. Dry whites can be similar to WACHAU in style, not usually in quality. Top producers: Huber, NEUMAYER.

Triebaumer, Ernst N'see r (w) dr sw ★★★★ 01 03 05 06 07 08 09 Important RUST producer; BLAUFRÄNKISCH (inc the legendary Mariental), Cab Sauv/Merlot blend. V.gd AUSBRUCH.

Uhudler Local south BURGENLAND specialty. Wine made directly from American rootstocks, with a foxy, strawberry taste.

Umathum, Josef N'see r w dr sw ★★★ V.gd and thoughtful producer. V.gd reds, inc Pinot N, St-Laurent; gd whites.

Velich N'see w sw ★★★★ A searching, intellectual producer. Excellent burgundian-style Tiglat CHARD (01 03 06 08 09) with fine barrel-ageing. Some of top sweet wines in the SEEWINKEL.

Veyder-Malberg Wach w ★ A 2008 start-up, cultivating some of the WACHAU's most labour-intensive v'yds and producing wines of great purity and finesse.

Vienna w (r) Region in suburbs. Mostly simple wines, served to tourists in HEURIGEN. Producers on the rise: Christ, MAYER AM PFARRPLATZ, F WIENINGER, Zahel.

Vinea Wachau WACHAU appellation started by winemakers in 1983 with three categories of dry wine: STEINFEDER, FEDERSPIEL and the powerful SMARAGD.

Wachau w World-renowned Danube region, home to some of Austria's best. Top: Alzinger, J DONABAUM, Freie Weingärtner Wachau, F HIRTZBERGER, HÖGL, J JAMEK, E KNOLL, Lagler, NIKOLAIHOF, FX PICHLER, R PICHLER, F PRAGER, Schmelz, WESS.

Wachau, Domäne Wach w (r) ★★ 06 07 08 09 Important growers' co-op in Dürnstein, now back on form. V.gd GRÜNER VELTLINER and RIES.

Wagram w (r) Wine region just west of VIENNA, inc KLOSTERNEUBURG. Mainly whites, esp GRÜNER VELTLINER. Best: EHMOSER, Fritsch, Stift Klosterneuburg, Leth, B OTT, Wimmer-Czerny, R Zimmermann.

Weingut Stadt Krems Krems ★★ Co-op capably steered by Fritz Miesbauer, esp RIES and GRÜNER VELTLINER. Miesbauer also vinifies for Stift Göttweig.

Weinviertel ("Wine Quarter") w (r) Largest Austrian wine region, between Danube and Czech border. Largely simple qualities but increasingly striving for quality and regional character. Refreshing whites, esp from Poysdorf, Retz. Best: Bauer, J Diem, GRAF HARDEGG, Gruber, PFAFFL, Schwarzböck, WEINRIEDER, Zull.

Weissburgunder (Pinot Bl) Ubiquitous: gd dry wines and PRÄDIKATS. Esp J BECK, Fischer, GROSS, G HEINRICH, F HIRTZBERGER, LACKNER-TINNACHER, E & W POLZ, M TEMENT.

Welschriesling White grape, not related to RIES, grown in all wine regions: simple, fragrant, dry wines for everyday drinking.

Weninger, Franz M Burg r (w) ★★★ Top estate in Horitschon, with *fine reds, esp Blaufränkisch*, Dürrau and Merlot.

Wenzel N'see r w sw ★★★ V.gd AUSBRUCH. Son Michael makes ambitious and increasingly fine reds. Father Robert pioneered the FURMINT revival in RUST.

Wess Wach w ★ Gd winemaker, vinifying bought-in grapes, some from famous v'yds.

Weststeiermark p Small wine region specializing in SCHILCHER. Best: Klug, Lukas, DOMAINE MÜLLER, Reiterer, Strohmeier.

Wieder M Burg Exponent of the BLAUFRÄNKISCH renaissance, well-structured wines.

Wiederstein Carn One of the young generation of CARNUNTUM winemakers, Birgit Wiederstein makes understated but appealingly focused reds.

Wien *See* VIENNA.

Wieninger, Fritz Vienna r w ★★ 03 05 06 07 08 09 V.gd VIENNA-Stammersdorf grower with HEURIGE: CHARD, BLAUER BURGUNDER, esp gd GRÜNER VELTLINER, RIES.

Winkler-Hermaden SE Sty r w sw ★★★ Outstanding and individual southeast STYRIAN producer, gd Traminer and MORILLON, also one of the region's few v.gd reds, the ZWEIGELT-based Olivin.

Winzer Krems Large KREMSTAL co-op with 1,300 growers. Esp GRÜNER VELTLINER.

Zierer r w THERMENREGION producer, esp fine ROTGIPFLER.

Zierfandler (Spätrot) White variety almost exclusive to THERMENREGION. Often blended with ROTGIPFLER. Best: Biegler, Spaetrot, STADLMANN, ZIERER.

Zweigelt *See* BLAUER ZWEIGELT.

AUSTRIA

England & Wales

English and Welsh wines go from strength to strength, with sparkling wines leading the way – these wines are now winning international competitions and increased demand is fuelling planting of more vineyards. The total is now around 1,500 ha (with 45% to Chardonnay, Pinots Noir and Meunier). Only Bacchus makes world-class still wines and this variety is expanding. 2009 was an exceptional year, but many still wines are as good as they are likely to get. What needs to be understood is that English bubblies gain enormously with bottle-age (up to ten years).

Astley Worcester ★★ Wines continue to win awards and medals. Veritas 09 v.gd.

Biddenden Kent (1969) One of the UK's oldest vineyards. Zesty Bacchus 09 and spicy Ortega 09 worth trying. Also makes v.gd cider and apple juice.

Breaky Bottom E Sussex Planted in 1974 and now making only sparkling wines using Seyval Bl, Pinot N and Chard. Cuvée Brian Jordan 05 and John Inglis Hall 06 both well worth trying.

Camel Valley Cornwall ★★★ Lindo *père et fils*, Bob and Sam, continue to create great wines and win prizes. Bacchus 09, Pinot N Brut 07 and 08 excellent.

Chapel Down Kent ★★★ Still the UK's largest producer. NV Brut is the UK's best-value sparkling wine. Classy Pinot Res 04 sparkling v.gd; Bacchus 09 and Bacchus Res 09 both excellent. V.gd visitor facilities, award-winning restaurant.

Coates & Seely Hampshire Still a twinkle in its makers' eyes, but look out for this sparkler in 2011. Seely is the Englishman who runs AXA Millésimes, owner of Bordeaux's Pichon-Longueville *et al*.

Davenport ★ Organic Limney Estate 05 sparkling, Horsmonden 07 dry white well worth trying.

Denbies Surrey ★★ No longer the UK's largest v'yd. Wines continue to improve. Juniper Hill 08, Ortega 06 and Cubitt Reserve 06 sparkling well worth trying. V.gd visitor facilities.

Gusbourne Kent ★ Large new sparkling producer. Classic Blend 06 and Blanc de Blancs 06 excellent.

Hush Heath Estate Kent ★ Balfour Brut Rosé 06 excellent. Also v.gd apple juice.

Jenkyn Place Hampshire Newcomer with v.gd first release: Jenkyn Place 06.

Nyetimber W Sussex ★★★ Total v'yd area now 174 ha, making this the largest UK v'yd and with 1,000-tonne harvests in both 2009 and 2010; will soon be major player in sparkling-wine business. Huge new winery being built, probably ready for 2012. Best wines available now are Classic Cuvée 05 and Rosé 07.

Plumpton E Sussex UK's only wine college now starting to make interesting wines. Pinot N 09 best UK red. The Dean NV sparkling and Dean NV Blush sparkling both worth trying.

Ridgeview E Sussex ★★★★ Great quality, consistency and gd value keep this winery at the top of UK producers. Grosvenor Magnum Blanc de Blancs 01 and Grosvenor Blanc de Blancs 06 exceptional quality. Fitzrovia 08 best rosé so far.

Sharpham Devon ★★ Gd range of wines (and also great cheeses). V.gd 09 wines, esp Pinot N and Rosé. Estate Selection 09 also worth trying.

Stanlake Park Berkshire ★★ Large range of wines of above-average quality. Fruity Pinot Blush and soft Madeleine 09 both worth trying, also zesty Bacchus 09.

Three Choirs Glocestershire ★★ 09 Large range of gd-value wines, plus v.gd visitor facilities, hotel and restaurant. Good range of 09 wines, inc Bacchus, Siegerrebe, Rosé and Willow Brook blend.

Central & Southeast Europe

More heavily shaded areas are the wine-growing regions.

Abbreviations used in the text:

Dalm	Dalmatia		
Dob	Dobrogea	N Trsd	Northern Transdanubia
Mold	Moldova	Pod	Podravje
Mun	Muntenia & Oltenià Hills	Prim	Primorje
N Croa	North Croatia	S Pann	S Pannonia
N Hun	North Hungary	Tok	Tokaj

HUNGARY

Hungary has the proudest wine culture of Eastern Europe and has made most progress since communism. Tokaji in the north and the red wines of the south have both re-established themselves as world class – despite the economic crisis and endless rain in the summer of 2010 (particularly Tokaji). Fortunately the toxic autumn mud-spill missed the wine regions. Quality is higher than ever as a new generation of winemakers gets to grips with the potential of Hungary's native grapes and volcanic soils, and starts to seek balance over sheer power.

Alana-Tokaj Tok ★★ Promising producer with great v'yds. Also owns Németh Cellars in Mátra. Gd Muscat, FURMINT and ASZÚ.

Alföld Hungary's Great Plain makes mostly everyday wine from three districts: Hajós-Baja (Brilliant Holding, Sümegi), Csongrád (Somodi), Kunság (Frittmann is a step up for the region. Gd EZERJÓ and KÉKFRANKOS).

Aszú Botrytis-shrivelled grapes and the sweet wine made from them in TOKAJ. The wine is graded in sweetness, from 3 PUTTONYOS up to 6.

Aszú Essencia (or Eszencia) sw ★★★ 2nd-sweetest TOKAJI quality. 7 PUTTONYOS+ classification no longer used from 2010 vintage on.

Badacsony w dr sw ★★→★★★ Extinct volcano on north shore of Lake BALATON. Rich, highly flavoured white wines; esp well-made Ries and SZÜRKEBARÁT. Look for *Szeremley* and Laposa.

Balaton Region and Central Europe's largest freshwater lake. BADACSONY, Balatonfüred-Csopak (Feind, Figula, Jasdi), SOMLÓ to north. BALATONBOGLÁR, Zala (south, west).

Balatonboglár w r dr ★★·→★★★ Wine district; also progressive winery owned by TÖRLEY, south of Lake BALATON. Top: GARAMVÁRI, KONYÁRI, Légli. Budjosó improving.

Barta Tok ★★★ New producer (2007). Highest v'yd in TOKAJ. Dry FURMINT impressive, esp 07 and 09 Furmint Válogatás. Also v.gd sweet FURMINT-MUSKOTÁLY.

Bikavér N Hun r ★·→★★★ 03 05 06' 07 08 Literally "Bull's Blood". Now being revived as flagship blended red. Protected origin status in SZEKSZÁRD and EGER. At least three varieties; usually inc KÉKFRANKOS and sometimes KADARKA. Res is min of four varieties and restricted yield. Best producers for Egri Bikavér: Bolyki, Gróf Buttler, Demeter, TIBOR GÁL, Kaló Imre, Pók Tamás, ST ANDREA, Thummerer.

Bock, József S Pann r dr ★·→★★★ Leading family in VILLÁNY. Hearty reds. Best: Cab Fr-based Capella Cuvée 00 03' 06', Syrah 05' 06' 07', weighty Prestige Res 06'.

Bodrogkeresztúr Village in TOKAJ region with several up-and-coming estates, inc DERESZLA, Füleky, PATRICIUS,TOKAJI Nobilis, Puklus.

Bor "Wine": *vörös* is red; *fehér* is white; *édes* is sweet, *száraz* is dry.

Bussay, Dr w dr ★★ 06 07 08 09 Part-time doctor and impressive winemaker in Zala, southwest of Lake BALATON. Intense TRAMINI, Pinot Gr, OLASZRIZLING and Ries.

Csányi S Pann r ★·→★★ Major investment in VILLÁNY. Chateau Teleki range is best, esp velvety Cab Fr 07.

Degenfeld, Gróf Tok w dr sw ★★ 00 03 05 06 07 08 Large TOKAJ estate with luxury hotel. Dry to ASZÚ range, inc Fortissimo late harvest and Andante botrytis *cuvée*.

Demeter, Zoltán Tok ★★★·→★★★★ 07' 08' Superb dry and ASZÚ wines from own *grand cru* v'yds, esp Veres, Lapis, Szerelmi. Demeter in EGER different producer.

Dereszla Tok w dr sw ★★★ 50-ha estate owned by d'Aulan family from Champagne. V.gd ASZÚ, *flor*-matured dry SZAMORODNI. Superb dry Kabar 07', Muscat Res 03'.

Districtus Hungaricus Controllatus (DHC) Term for wines with specific protected designation of origin (PDO). Symbol is a local crocus and DHC on label.

Disznókő Tok w dr sw ★★·→★★★ 93 96' 97 99' 00' 03' 05 06 07' 08' Important TOKAJ estate, owned by French company AXA. Wines of great finesse and expressiveness. Single-v'yd Kapi 6 Puttonyos Aszú 99' is notable.

Dobogó Tok ★★★·→★★★★ 99' 00' 03' 05' 06 07' 08 One of the top small TOKAJ estates. V.gd ASZÚ and late-harvest Mylitta, wonderful Mylitta Álma (modern take on ASZÚ ESZENCIA) 05' 06' 07' and increasingly gd dry FURMINT 05 06' 07' 08 (09) and new Szerelmi Dulő 07. Pinot N since 2007.

Eger N Hun r w dr sw ★·→★★★ Fine baroque city; red wine centre of north. BIKAVÉR, also Cab Fr, Pinot N, Syrah. Whites: LEÁNYKA, OLASZRIZLING, Chard, Pinot Bl. Try: Bolyki, Gróf Buttler, DEMETER, TIBOR GÁL, Kaló Imre, ST ANDREA, Thummerer.

Essencia (or Eszencia) Tok ★★★★ 93 96 99 03 06 (09) Heart of TOKAJ: thick, syrupy, luscious, aromatic juice that trickles from trodden ASZÚ grapes. Alcohol around 2–3%; sugar can be over 800 g/l. Reputed to have medicinal properties.

Etyek-Buda N Trsd Region nr Budapest. V.gd crisp varietal whites, esp Chard, Sauv Bl, Pinot Gr, promising for Pinot N. Leading producers: Etyeki Kúria, Nyakas (Budai label), György-Villa (owned by TÖRLEY) and new Haraszthy Vallejo.

Ezerjó N Trsd Literally "thousand blessings". Hungarian local grape variety with sharp acids. Frittmann and MAURUS are making more exciting versions.

Furmint The classic grape of TOKAJ, with great flavour, acidity and potential for both great dry and sweet wines. Also grown in SOMLÓ.

Garamvári r w dr sp ★·→★★ Family-owned v'yd, St Donatus winery. Also owns *Chateau Vincent*, Hungary's top bottle-fermented sparkler. Sinai Hill Cab Sauv 03 06 is gd.

Gere, Attila S Pann r ★★★·→★★★★ Deservedly reputed family winemaker in VILLÁNY making some of country's best reds, esp rich Solus Merlot 02 03' 06' 07', intense Kopar Cuvée 00 03' 04 06' 07'. Top wine Grand Vin de Villány 03' 07'.

Hárslevelű "Linden-leaved" grape variety widely grown. Gd in SOMLÓ, EGER and important as second grape of TOKAJ. Gentle, mellow wine; peach aroma.

Heimann r ★★ Increasingly impressive family winery in SZEKSZÁRD. Best wines: Barbar blend 06 07 and Baranya Kékfrankos 07 08.

Hétszőlő Tok w dr sw ★★ Noble first-growth, 55-ha, bought by Michel Rebier of Château Cos d'Estournel (Bordeaux) in 2009. Investment should raise standards.

Hilltop Winery N Trsd r w dr ★→★★ Winery in Ászár-Neszmély; gd international varietal wines, inc Riverview and Woodcutters White from Cserszegi Fűszeres. Premium range best, esp Pinot Gr 09.

Irsai Olivér Local white cross of two table varieties making aromatic, Muscat-like wine for drinking young. Try NYAKAS, GARAMVÁRI.

Kadarka Spicy, light red, local grape (aka Gamza in Bulgaria), revived esp in SZEKSZÁRD for BIKAVÉR. Gd examples inc Gróf Buttler, HEIMANN, SAUSKA, TAKLER.

Kékfrankos aka Blaufränkisch. Most widely planted red variety. Gd light and full reds.

Királyudvar Tok w dr sw ★★★→★★★★ 99' 00' 01 02 03' 05 06' 07 08. Fine TOKAJ winery in old royal cellars at Tarcal, owned by Anthony Hwang. V.gd dry and late-harvest FURMINT, Cuvée Ilona (early bottled ASZÚ), stunning Cuvée Patricia and 6 Puttonyos Lapis Aszú.

Konyári r w dr ★★→★★★ 06 07 08 09 Father-and-son team making high-quality red and white from own estate at BALATONBOGLÁR, esp Loliense (r w), Szárhegy (w), Sessio Merlot and v.gd Pava blend. Also own new Ikon winery: value varietals.

Kreinbacher w dr ★★ 07 08 Established 2002, working organically and focusing on local grapes and esp blends. Try 08 Kőkonyha.

Leányka "Little girl". Light, aromatic white from Transylvania, aka Fetească Albă. Királyleányka or Fetească Regală: cross of F.Albă and Grasă (Kővérszőlő in TOKAJ).

Mád Tok Old commercial centre of the TOKAJ region with top v'yds and circle of Mád producers. Growers inc: ALANA-TOKAJ, BARTA, OROSZ GÁBOR, Demetervin, Gundel, ROYAL TOKAJI, SZEPSY, Tokaj Classic.

Malatinszky S Pann r w dr ★★★ 03' 04 06' 07 08 (09) Immaculate winery making characterful unfiltered Kúria Cab Fr, Cab Sauv, appealing Pinot Bleu, fine Chard. Single-v'yd, red blend Kövesföld 06 07' and white Serena from 09.

Mátra N Hun w (r) ★→★★ District in Mátra foothills. Reliable Pinot Gr, Chard, MUSKOTÁLY, Sauv Bl. Better producers inc: drummer-turned-winemaker Gabor Karner, Nemeth Cellars (*see* ALANA-TOKAJ), Szőke Mátyás and cooperative Szőlőskert (Nagyrede and Spice Trail labels).

Maurus Winery N Trsd w dr ★★ Young winemaker Ákos Kamocsay Jr is waking up sleepy MÓR. EZERJÓ, After Press Chard, Ries, TRAMINI show promise.

Megyer, Château Tok w dr sw ★★→★★★ 93 99 00 03' 05 06' 07 (08) Same ownership as CHÂTEAU PAJZOS: Jean-Louis Laborde of Château Clinet (Bordeaux). Megyer is typically lighter from cooler north of region. Quality improving, esp dry FURMINT and appealing dry Muscat.

Mézes-Mály One of TOKAJ's best *crus*. ROYAL TOKAJI, Balassa gd single-v'yd examples.

Mór N Trsd w ★→★★ Region; crisp EZERJÓ; Ries, Chard, TRAMINI. Try MAURUS WINERY.

Muskotály Tok Muscat; usually Ottonel, except TOKAJ where Sárga Muskotály is yellow Muscat or Muscat Lunel. A little is often added to TOKAJI blend. Occasionally makes a v.gd ASZÚ wine solo; try KIRÁLYUDVAR's Cuvée Patricia.

Olaszrizling Hungarian name for the Italian Ries or Welschriesling.

Oremus Tok w dr sw ★★→★★★★ 99' 00' 02 03' 05 06' 07 (08) Ancient TOKAJ v'yd of founding Rákóczi family, owned by Spain's Vega Sicilia. First-rate ASZÚ and v.gd dry FURMINT Mandolás.

Orosz Gábor Tok w dr sw ★★→★★★ 03 05 06 08 (09) 17 ha, mostly first-class TOKAJ v'yds. Best dry wines are single-vy'd FURMINT and HÁRSLEVELŰ, plus excellent ASZÚ. Bodvin is cheaper second label.

Pajzos, Château Tok w dr sw ★★→★★★ 93 99 00 02 03' 05 06' (07) (08) Bordeaux-owned TOKAJ estate with some fine, long-lived ASZÚ. *See* MEGYER.

Pannonhalma N Trsd r w dr ★★ 08 09 Region in north. Also revived historic Pannonhalma Abbey winery and v'yds dating back eight centuries. TRAMINI, Ries v.gd value. Expressive Sauv Bl, fine Pinot N and classy Hemina white blend.

Patricius Tok w dr sw ★★★ 00' 02 03' 05 06' 07 08 New quality TOKAJ estate (2000). V.gd dry FURMINT and 6 PUTTONYOS ASZÚ. Superb ASZÚ ESZENCIA Czigany 08.

Pécs S Pann w (r) ★→★★ Wine district around the city of Pécs. Known for whites, inc local Cirfandl. Pinot N esp Ebner Borhaz 08 continues to impress.

Pendits Winery Tok w sw ★★→★★★ Certified organic from 2008 and working on biodynamic lines (using horses and not machines), run by Márta Wille-Baumkauff and her sons. Luscious ASZÚ ESZENCIA 00 03, attractive Szello Cuvée 05 06 07 and pretty Dry Muscat 08.

Puttonyos Measure of sweetness in TOKAJI ASZÚ. A *puttony* is a 25-kg measure, a hod of grapes, traditionally. Number of *putts* per barrel (136 litres) of dry base wine or must determines the final richness of the wine, from 3–6 *putts* (3 putts: 60 g of sugar per litre, 4: 90 g, 5: 120 g, 6: 150 g, 7: 180 g). *See also* ASZÚ ESSENCIA, ESSENCIA.

Royal Tokaji Wine Co Tok ★★★ →★★★★ 96 99 00 03 05 06 07 09 Pioneer foreign joint venture at MÁD in 1990 (I am a co-founder). 81 ha, mainly first- or second-growth. First wines 90 91 (esp) 93 led renaissance of TOKAJI. Single-v'yd bottlings esp Betsek, MÉZES-MÁLY, Szent Tamás notable. Also well-made dry FURMINT and v.gd-value late-harvest Áts Cuvée. New winery opened 2010.

Sauska ★★→★★★★ 06 07 08 09 New immaculate winery in VILLÁNY. Beautifully balanced KADARKA, KÉKFRANKOS, Cab Fr; impressive red blends, esp Cuvée 7 and Cuvée 5. Sauska-Tokaj in old casino in TOKAJ (formerly Árvay): gd dry whites from 2009, esp Cuvée III and FURMINT Birsalmás. Édes Élet 03 is the star sweet wine.

Somló w ★★→★★★ Dramatic area on basalt slopes of extinct volcano famous for its mineral-rich age-worthy whites from local grapes: Juhfark ("sheep's tail"), OLASZRIZLING, FURMINT and HÁRSLEVELŰ. Traditionally wines are fermented in barrel by small producers such as Fekete, Györgykovács, Hollóvár and Spiegelberg, while Tornai and Kreinbacher are larger and more widely available.

Sopron N Trsd r ★★→★★★ Historic district on Austrian border overlooking Lake Fertő. KÉKFRANKOS most important, plus Cab Sauv, Syrah, Pinot N. Top producer is biodynamic *Weninger*, also try the very individual wines of Ráspi.

St Andrea N Hun r w dr ★★★ 05 06' 07 08 (09) One of most exciting winemakers in EGER; leading way in modern high-quality BIKAVÉR (Merengő, Áldás). Excellent white blends Napbor, Örökké, organic Boldogságos; v.gd HÁRSLEVELŰ and Pinot N.

Szamorodni Tok Literally "as it was born"; describes TOKAJI not sorted in the v'yd. Dry or sweet (ÉDES), depending on proportion of ASZÚ grapes present. Sweet style can offer ASZÚ character at less cost. The best dry versions are *flor*-aged; try TINON, DERESZLA or Karádi-Berger.

Szekszárd S Pann r ★★→★★★ District in south Hungary; some of country's top reds from KÉKFRANKOS, Cab Sauv, Cab Fr and Merlot. Also KADARKA being revived and BIKAVÉR. Look for: Dúzsi, HEIMANN, Mészáros, Sebestyén, Szent Gaál, TAKLER.

Szepsy, István Tok w dr sw ★★★★ 99' 00' 02 03' 05 06 07 (08) Brilliant small production of long-ageing TOKAJI ASZÚ from own winery in MÁD. Excellent single-v'yd dry wines from FURMINT, esp Urbán, Szent Tamás and Király HÁRSLEVELŰ 05 06' 07' and sweet SZAMORODNI from 03 06.

Szeremley, Huba N w dr sw ★★ 05 06 07 08 Pioneer in BADACSONY. Intense, minerally Ries, *Szürkebarát*, Kéknyelű, and appealing sweet Zeus.

Szürkebarát Literally "grey monk": Pinot Gr. Widely planted and produces high-quality dry wines and inexpensive Italian lookalikes, esp around BALATON.

Takler S Pann ★★ 03 04 05 06 07 08 Significant family producer in SZEKSZÁRD with over 70 ha, making super-ripe, supple reds. Best: Res selections of Cab Fr, KÉKFRANKOS, BIKAVÉR. Super-*cuvée* Regnum 03 well regarded locally and in USA.

Tibor Gál N Hun r w dr ★★ Winery in EGER founded by the late Tibor Gál (winemaker at Ornellaia, Tuscany). Son (also Tibor) has bought new cellars and is working hard to improve the wines. Best: single-v'yd Pinot N, BIKAVÉR and gd Viognier.

Tinon, Samuel Tok ★★→★★★ 00 01 04 r dr sw Frenchman from Ste-Croix-du-Mont, Bordeaux, in TOKAJ since 1991. Distinctive and v.gd TOKAJI ASZÚ with v. long maceration and barrel-ageing. Also superb *flor*-aged SZAMORODNI.

Tokaj Trading House Tok State-owned company, buying grapes from over 2,000 small growers plus 55 ha own vines, inc the fine Szarvas v'yd. Also called Kereskedőház, or Crown Estates. Quality is underperforming.

Tokaj/Tokaji w dr sw ★★→★★★★ Tokaj is the town; Tokaji is the wine, Tokay the old French and English name. Appellation covers 5,840 ha. *See* ESSENCIA, FURMINT, PUTTONYOS, SZAMORODNI. Also dry table wine of increasingly exciting quality.

Tolna S Pann Largest estate is Antinori-owned Tűzkő at Bátaapáti with 150 ha. Gd TRAMINI, Chard and blended red Talentum.

Törley r w dr sp ★→★★ Innovative large company. Consistent international varietals (Pinot Gr, Chard, Pinot N, Sauv Bl), also local varieties Zenit and Zefir. Major sparkling producer (esp *Törley* and Hungaria labels), inc *cuve close*, transfer and classic sparkling (Try François Rosé Brut 06). Chapel Hill is well-made, gd-value commercial brand, and György-Villa for top selections.

Tornai w dr ★★→★★★ 06 07 08 Largest producer in SOMLÓ. Family-owned. Intense dry whites (Juhfark, HÁRSLEVELŰ, OLASZRIZLING, FURMINT). Top Selection notable.

Tramini Gewurztraminer grape.

Villány-Siklós S Pann Southern wine region with two main towns. Villány makes mostly red, often good-quality Bordeaux styles. Siklós makes mostly white. High-quality producers: BOCK, CSÁNYI, ATTILA GERE, Tamás Gere, Heumann, MALATINSZKY, SAUSKA, Tiffán, WENINGER-GERE, VYLYAN, Wunderlich.

Vylyan S Pann r dr ★★→★★★ 03' 04 06' 07 (08) Run by the dynamic Monika Debreczeni. 130 ha with local and international varieties. Burgundian consultant's influence shows in stylish Pinot N. *Duennium Cuvée* (Cab Fr, Cab Sauv, Merlot and Zweigelt) is flagship red.

Weninger N Trsd r ★★→★★★ 04 06 07 08 Standard-setting winery in Balf, SOPRON, run by Austrian Franz Weninger Jr. Biodynamic (2006). Top single-v'yd *Spern Steiner Kékfrankos* 04' 06 07. Syrah, Pinot N, Frettner blend (r) also impressive.

Weninger-Gere S Pann r ★★★ Austro-Hungarian joint venture since 1992 between Franz Weninger Sr and ATTILA GERE. Cab Fr Selection excellent 00' 02 03' 04' 06' 07', gd-value Cuvée Phoenix, and fresh Rosé.

Zéta Tok A cross of Bouvier and FURMINT used by some in ASZÚ production.

BULGARIA

Bulgaria came late to the international wine market, scored a hit with Cabernet in the 1980s, then faded away. Now it's time to reassess our views. In recent years winemakers have raised their game, and there has been considerable foreign investment both of money and expertise: there is now a really good selection of quality wines. The 2010 vintage is mixed, however, due to unusual weather conditions.

Assenovgrad Thrace r ★→★★ MAVRUD and RUBIN specialists. MAVRUD 04 08.

Bessa Valley Thrace r ★★★ Stephan von Neipperg (Canon la Gaffelière, Bordeaux) and K-H Hauptmann's exciting winery nr Pazardjik, Enira and Enira Res 06. The only quality Bulgarian wine readily available in the UK.

Blueridge Thrace r w ★→★★ Large capacity DOMAINE BOYAR winery. Gd Chard, Cab Sauv.

Castra Rubra Thrace r ★★ New winery of TELISH in south. Michel Rolland advises young team. Try the Via Diagonalis and Castra Rubra 07.

Chateau de Val Danube r ★★ Small producer of distinctive quality wines: Grand Claret 03. Good Chard and Merlot Res.

Damianitsa Struma V r ★★ Winery specializing in MELNIK grape. V.gd Redark Merlot 04; Uniqato (single-variety RUBIN, MELNIK); Nomansland consistent high quality.

Dimiat Native white grape. Gd examples from BLUERIDGE and POMORIE.

Domaine Boyar Thrace Main exporter to UK, own v'yds and wineries. Best-known producer in Bulgaria. Award-winning Solitaire wines, Elenovo Merlot 06, and promising Pinot N and Cab Fr.

Dragomir Thrace r ★★ Promising new winery nr Plovdiv. Cab Sauv/Merlot brands, such as Karizma 07.

Gamza Red grape (Kadarka of Hungary); potential. Danube region. Try Novo Selo.

Karnobat Thrace r w ★★ Watch! Good Merlot 08 and fragrant Muscat-Traminer 09.

Katarzyna Thrace r w ★★★ r w Quality wines from new southeast winery. Excellent Encore Syrah 08. Question Mark 07 (stylish Cab Sauv/Merlot), Halla Merlot 07, Twin Cab Sauv 07, Contemplations Chard 08 recommended.

Khan Krum Bl Sea w ★ Gd whites, esp Chard and TRAMINER.

Korten Thrace r ★★ Boutique cellar of DOMAINE BOYAR; quality, traditional-style wines.

Leventa Danube w (r) ★★ Small new winery in Russe, particularly gd whites, esp Chard 08 and TRAMINER, also Merlot and Grand Selection 05.

Logodaj Struma V r w ★★ Blagoevgrad winery. Soetto Cab Fr 05, Nobile RUBIN 06.

Malkata Zvezhda Thrace r w ★ Promising new winery aiming for limited production of the highest quality. Enigma Merlot and Chard recommended.

Mavrud Thrace Considered best indigenous variety, v. popular at home. Age-worthy, dark, plummy wines only grown in the Plovdiv area.

Maxxima Thrace r (w) ★→★★ Full-bodied reds. Private Res 03 is recommended. Pioneer of terroir wines in Bulgaria.

Melnik Struma V Southwest village and highly prized indigenous grape variety grown throughout Struma Valley. Dense, full-bodied reds for ageing.

Miroglio, Edoardo Thrace r w ★★ Italian investor. Own v'yds at Elenovo. Merlot 06, Pinot N 06, Sauv Bl 07; Bulgaria's best fizz, Miroglio Brut Metodo Classico 05.

Misket Indigenous grape; mildly aromatic. The basis for most country whites. Sungurlare and Karlovo in the Valley of the Roses are specialists.

Oriachovitza Thrace r ★★ Long-established winery owned by Belvedere. Gd Res Cab Sauv 04. Dark, fruity reds at their best after 4–5 yrs.

Pamid Light, soft, everyday red in southeast and northwest.

Pomorie Bl Sea (Bl Sea Gold) w (r) ★ Chard and DIMIAT 09.

Rubin Bulgarian cross (Nebbiolo x Syrah); gd in blends, but gaining in favour as a single-varietal niche wine.

Sakar Thrace Southeast area noted for high-quality Merlot: Domaine Sakar Merlot 05.

Santa Sarah Thrace r (w) ★★ Pricey brand, Privat (Cab Sauv/MAVRUD) 06, Bin 41 Merlot 06.

Shumen Bl Sea r w ★ New World-style reds and whites from this Black Sea-region winery. Gd TRAMINER, v popular in Bulgaria.

Slaviantsi Thrace ★ Gd varietal whites.

Sliven, Vini Thrace r (w) ★ Everyday Merlot, MISKET, Chard.

Targovishte Bl Sea w (r) ★→★★ Winery in the east, gd for Chard, Sauv Bl, TRAMINER, and some promising new reds.

Telish Danube r ★★ Innovative winery. Gd-value, -quality; Cab Sauv 06, Merlot 06.

Terra Tangra Thrace r w ★★ Try MAVRUD 07, velvety Merlot Grand Res 06, Roto 06.

Todoroff Thrace r (w) ★→★★ High-profile winery. Boutique MAVRUD 09.

Traminer Fine whites with hints of spice. Most popular white in Bulgaria.

Villa Lyubimets Thrace r w ★→★★ V'yds in increasingly popular area for wineries, the southeast, referred to (by Bulgarians, not Burgundians) as Bulgaria's Côte d'Or. Villa Hissar is sister white label.

Yambol r (w) ★ Winery in Thracian plain, specializing in Cab Sauv and Merlot.

SLOVENIA

The viticultural jewel of south-central Europe leads in developing serious wine culture and image. Domestically, consumption of basic wines is decreasing in favour of better quality. Slovenia is gaining recognition abroad for original wines of serious international interest.

Batič Prim ★★ Organic, minimal intervention wine-grower in VIPAVA. Try Rosé 09, Pinela 08, white Zaria 07 and Rosso 06.

Bjana Prim ★★ Gd traditional-method sparklers (BRDA). Brut Rosé, Cuvée Prestige 05.

Blažič Prim ★★★ BRDA producer making excellent REBULA 09, aromatic SAUVIGNONASSE 09, Blaž Belo in top years.

Brda (Goriška) Prim District in PRIMORJE. Centre of quality with many top producers, inc BJANA, BLAŽIČ, EDI SIMČIČ, Erzetič, JAKONČIČ, Kabaj, Klinec, Kristančič, MOVIA, Prinčič, SIMČIČ, ŠČUREK, VINSKA KLET GORIŠKA BRDA, Zanut.

Burja Prim ★★ 09 new venture in VIPAVA from Primož Lavrenčič (previously co-owner of Sutor), focusing on local varieties Zelen and MALVAZIJA.

Čotar Prim ★★ Pioneer of natural winemaking from KRAS. Long-lived, distinctive wines, esp Vitovska white 07, MALVAZIJA 05, Sauv Bl 04. Reds need even longer: Teran 03, Terra Rossa 03, Cab Sauv 99.

Čurin-Prapotnik Pod ★★★★ 99' 04' 05' 06' 07 For world-class sweet wines only: fantastic Icewine (*ledeno vino*) from frozen grapes and botrytis styles from ŠIPON, LAŠKI RIZLING, Chard). Drier styles not in same league. Pioneer of private wine-growing in early 1970s. Brand is PRA-VinO.

Cviček Pos Locally popular traditional light red blend of POSAVJE. Low alcohol, high acid. Usually based on local Žametovka. Try Bajnof.

Dveri-Pax Pod ★★★ Excellent winery nr Maribor. Basic range is crisp, gd-value whites, esp Sauv Bl, ŠIPON, Ries. Admund range is single v'yd selections: try ŠIPON Ilovci 07, Sauv Bl Vagyen 07, Ries "M", MODRI PINOT 07 (08). Also superb sweet wines 05 08 (09).

Edi Simčič Prim ★★★→★★★★ Leading BRDA producer, bucking trend for maceration. V.gd Sivi Pinot 06 07, REBULA 06 07, white blend Triton Lex 07. Excellent Kozana single-v'yd Chard 05' 07'; red blend Duet Lex 02 03' 04' 05; v. expensive top-class Kolos 03' 04.

Istenič Pos ★★ NV Barbara and Miha are gd value, while Gourmet Rosé Brut 06 and Blanc de Blancs 03 are classy and increasingly elegant.

Istria Coastal district in PRIMORJE with Med climate. Known for REFOŠK and MALVAZIJA.

Jakončič Prim ★★★ V.gd BRDA producer; elegant whites and reds, esp Bela Carolina REBULA/Chard blend 04 05 06 06 07 and Rdeča (r) Carolina 99 00 06 07.

Joannes Pod ★★ Nr Maribor. Pioneer in dry wines, esp Ries 04' 05' 06' 07' 08. Also gd MODRI PINOT and Chard.

Kogl Pod ★★★ Small hilltop winery nr Ormož, dating back to 16th century. Finely crafted, elegant whites, inc Quartet blends and varietal Mea Culpa (try Auxerrois 09, late-harvest Chard 08).

Kras Prim Small, famous district on Terra Rossa soil in PRIMORJE. Best-known for TERAN but also whites, esp MALVAZIJA. Look for ČOTAR, Lisjak Boris, Renčel.

Kupljen Pod ★★ 07 08 09 Consistent dry wine pioneer nr Jeruzalem known for RENSKI RIZLING, Sauv Bl, SIVI PINOT, Chard, Pinot N. Wines age well.

Laški Rizling Welschriesling. Most-planted variety; unfashionable, esp as dry wine.

Ljutomer Ormož Pod ★ →★★★ Famous wine subdistrict in PODRAVJE, known for crisp, delicate whites and top botrytis. Much improved recently with new investment. *See* ČURIN-PRAPOTNIK, PUKLAVEC & FRIENDS, KOGL, Krainz, KUPLJEN, Miro, VERUS.

Macerated whites Recently v. popular in PRIMORJE. Whites produced with long maceration on skins for several days or weeks, usually at higher temperatures. Gives full-bodied, structured and long-lived wines, exciting if done well.

Malvazija Prim *See also* Croatia section. Different strain to Mediterranean Malvasia. Most important white in Slovenian ISTRIA: Malvazija by VINAKOPER is gd value. Also v.gd from Pucer z Vrha, Montemoro, SANTOMAS, ROJAC, Bordon, Korenika & Moškon. Also grown in VIPAVA and KRAS.

Marof Pod ★★ →★★★ 07 08' 09' Exciting new winery in Prekmurje raising image of the district. DYA classic range: v.gd LAŠKI RIZLING Bodonci, RENSKI RIES; barrel-fermented Breg Chard, Sauv Bl, single-v'yd Cru Chard and Blaufränkisch.

Mlečnik Prim ★★★ 05 06 in VIPAVA making natural, macerated oak-aged whites.

Modra Frankinja ★ →★★ Austria's Blaufränkisch; gd examples emerging in PODRAVJE.

Modri Pinot ★★ →★★★ Pinot N. Potentially Slovenia's best red, esp BRDA and VIPAVA.

Movia Prim ★★★ →★★★★ High-profile biodynamic winery run by charismatic Aleš Kristančič. Winemaking is extreme with v. long oak ageing, but excellent results, esp Veliko Belo (w) 93 96' 99' 00' 01' 02 03' 04' 05 and Veliko Rdeče (r) 93 96' 97' 00' 01' 02 03. V.gd MODRI PINOT 02' 03' 04' 05. Lunar (REBULA) 05' 06' 07 08 and sparkling Puro are distinctive, and split opinion.

Penina Quality sparkling wine made by either *charmat* or traditional method. Lots of styles available. Look for RADGONSKE GORICE, ISTENIČ, BJANA, Medot, MOVIA.

Pinela Rare local grape from VIPAVA. Try Guerila, Štokelj.

Podravje Pod Region in northeast. Recent investment has raised standards. Now gd fresh, mineral whites, increasingly fine reds – mostly Pinot N, MODRA FRANKINJA.

Posavje Pos Traditional region in southeast. Gd Prus, Šturm (sw), ISTENIČ (sp).

Primorje Prim Region in southwest from the Adriatic to BRDA. Currently most forward-looking Slovenian wine region for both reds and whites. Aka Primorska.

Ptujska Klet Pod ★★ →★★★ Winery in Ptuj producing v.gd crisp, modern whites, esp Sauv Bl, Ranfol, Pinot Gr under Pullus label since 2007. Excellent "G" wines and lovely Renski Rizling TBA 08'.

Puklavec & Friends Pod ★★ 09 Former Jeruzalem Ormož co-op now renamed after new owner. 600 ha own v'yds and 600 ha under contract, nr dramatic hilltop town of Jeruzalem. Crisp whites DYA, esp Furmint, Sauv Bl, Ries and great-value blend Terrace.

Radgonske Gorice Pod ★ Well-known co-op producing best-selling Slovenian sparkler Srebrna ("silver") Penina, classic-method Zlata ("golden") Penina, and legendary *demi-sec* Traminec with black label.

Rebula Prim Traditional white variety of BRDA, Very high quality potential, both in MACERATED and classical vinifications. Aka Ribolla Gialla in Italy.

Quality wines

Take a deep breath. *Vrhunsko vino z zaščitenim geografskim poreklom*, or *Vrhunsko vino ZGP*, is the term for top-quality AOP wines (*see* box p. 89), and *Kakovostno vino ZGP* for quality wines. *Deželno vino PGO* is used for IGP wines. For quality sweet wines, descriptions are: Pozna Trgatev (Spätlese), Izbor (Auslese), Jagodni Izbor (Beerenauslese), Suhi Jagodni Izbor (Trockenbeerenauslese or TBA). (*See* German chapter for definitions of terms in brackets.) Ledeno Vino is Icewine, Slamno Vino is straw wine from semi-dried grapes, Penina is natural sparkling wine.

Refošk Prim ★→★★ High-acid, local red, genetically distinct from Italy's Refosco. Teran is cousin in KRAS. Try: Bordon, Korenika & Moškon, ROJAC, SANTOMAS, Steras.

Renski Rizling Pod Ries. Floral, fruity, or minerally (ageing potential). DVERI-PAX, PUKLAVEC & FRIENDS, JOANNES, KUPLJEN, MAROF, PJUTSKA KLET, VALDHUBER, VERUS, Valcl.

Rojac Prim ★★ High-quality organic producer. Try Renero 05 (09) as new take on REFOŠK. Also Stari d'Or blend 06 08, Malvazija 09, Syrah in future.

Rumeni Muškat Yellow Muscat, or Muscat Blanc à Petits Grains.

Santomas Prim ★★★ In ISTRIA with French consultant. Some of the country's best REFOŠK and Refošk/Cab Sauv blends. Antonius 99 03 04 (06), Grande Cuvée 03 04 05. Mezzoforte 07 is v.gd value.

Sauvignonasse White grape, aka Friulano, previously Tocai, mostly in BRDA.

Šcurek Prim ★★→★★★ V. reliable BRDA producer. DYA varieties Beli Pinot (Pinot Bl), Chard, REBULA. Interesting traditional blends: Stara Brajda white 07 08, red 05 06 07. Also premium red Up 04 05 06, unusual rare Pikolit 06.

Simčič, Marjan Prim ★★★★ 00 02 03 04 06 07 08 Excellent BRDA producer. Gd varietal whites, esp SIVI PINOT, SAUVIGNONASSE, REBULA. Chard and Sauv Bl Selekcija impress and age well. Teodor Belo (w) and Merlot-based Teodor Rdeče (r) are superb and MODRI PINOT is elegant. V.gd single-v'yd range Opoka from 2006, esp notable Sauv Bl 07. Sweet Leonardo is great 03 04 05.

Šipon Pod AKA Furmint. Up-and-coming dry, crisp, delicate white. DVERI-PAX, VERUS, KUPLJEN, Miro, Krainz, PUKALVEC & FRIENDS, Valcl. Also excellent for botrytis.

Sivi Pinot Pod Pinot Grigio; much more character and body than in neighbouring Fruili Venezia-Giulia. Fine aromatics in PODRAVJE.

Štajerska Slovenija Pod Important wine district since 2006 that encompasses practically whole PODRAVJE region.

Steyer Pod ★★ Noted for Traminer in all possible styles. Sweet Vaneja 03 impresses.

Tilia Prim ★★→★★★ Young couple from VIPAVA produce bright, modern DYA SIVI PINOT, Sauv Bl and local Zelen. Also v.gd macerated Rebula Grace 08 and fine, elegant MODRI PINOT 06 07 08'.

Valdhuber Pod ★★★ Dry wine pioneers. Top (dry) Traminec; v.gd Sauv Bl.

Verus Pod ★★★ 07' 08' 09 Young team, distinctive white varietals, esp v.gd Furmint, Sauv Bl, Pinot Gr, Ries. Pinot N planned from 2010.

Vinakoper Prim ★★ Large company with own v'yds in ISTRIA. Gd-value Capris line: Plemenito (r) 05, REFOŠK 08; premium Capo d'Istria Cab Sauv 04 06.

Vinska Klet Goriška Brda Prim ★→★★★ 06 07 08 09 Immensely improved big winery. Mostly varietals, often excellent value, esp DYA Quercus whites SIVI PINOT, Pinot Bl. Bagueri (higher quality); top selection A+ (r w) impressive.

Vipava Valley noted for cool breezes in PRIMORJE. BATIČ, BURJA, Guerila, Štokelj, MLEČNIK, Sutor, TILIA. Vipava 1894 co-op ★ has premium brand Lanthieri ★★.

Zanut Prim ★★ Amazingly expressive Sauv Bl 09; single-v'yd Merlot Brjač 03 06'.

Zlati Grič Pod ★→★★New investment nr Maribor; 75 ha, New Zealand winemaker.

CROATIA

Croatia is a fascinating wine country with many unique grapes and terroirs to explore. It's divided into Coastal (Primorska Hrvatska) and Inland (Kontinentralja Hrvatska). Locally, it's the big, high-alcohol reds from the coast that command high prices, though sales are being hurt by the economic crisis. But, Istria is leading the way in raising Croatia's international profile, with its close cooperation between winemakers and its intriguing and very drinkable Malvazijas and Terans.

Agrokor ★→★★ 07 08 Major group; over 30% of Croatian wine market, six wineries inc Agrolaguna, Belje, Istravino, Iločki Podrumi, Mladina. Best: Belje (v.gd Belje Merlot), Goldberg (GRAŠEVINA, Chard); Iločki (GRAŠEVINA, Traminac Icewine).

Babić Dalm Dark native red from north DALMATIA, grown in stony seaside v'yds nr Šibenik. Exceptional quality potential. Try Gracin.

Badel 1862 Dalm ★→★★★ One of biggest wine producers, surprisingly gd. Best: Ivan Dolac (Svirče), DINGAČ (Vinarija Dingač). Duravar range is reliable and v.gd for sweet wines esp GRAŠEVINA.

Bodren N Croa ★★→★★★ 07 08 Small producer with superb range of sweet wines inc Chateau Bezanec Chard, Sivi Pinot and Ries.

Crljenak Almost extinct indigenous grape identified recently by DNA testing as the original Zinfandel.

Dalmatia Dalm Dramatic rocky coast; grower's paradise. Strong, full wines (r w).

Dingač Dalm 03' 04' 05' 06 07 Appellation on Pelješac Peninsula for PLAVAC MALI. Partially dried grapes give robust, full-bodied and often expensive reds. Look for: Bura, Kiridija, Lučić, Matuško, Miličić, SAINTS HILLS, Vinarija Dingač.

Enjingi, Ivan N Croa ★★→★★★ Producer of v.gd sweet botrytis and dry whites, esp v.gd Venje blend from Požega. Also try GRAŠEVINA, esp Kasna Berba (06).

Grape varieties Croatia has a wealth of indigenous grapes including red BABIĆ (try Gracin), Borgonja (a clone of Gamay), Bogdanuša (from HVAR – goes into PROŠEK), Debit (try Bibich Lučica), Gegić (try Boškinac), Grk (try GRGIĆ), Maraština and Zelenac (aka Austria's Rotgipfler – try KRAUTHAKER). Almost extinct CRLJENAK turns out to be Zinfandel and parent of PLAVAC MALI, while native Štajerska Belina (aka Gouais Blanc) is parent of Chard. Traminac is Gewurz, Pinot Crni is Pinot N.

Graševina N Croa Welschriesling. Best in SLAVONIJA. Try Adžić, Belje, ENJINGI, Galić, KRAUTHAKER, KUTJEVO, Mihalj, Zdjelarević. Dry to intensely sweet botrytis styles.

Grgić Dalm ★★→★★★ A famous Napa Valley producer in retirement. PLAVAC MALI and rich POŠIP on Pelješac Peninsula.

Hvar Beautiful island in mid-Dalmatia: v'yds for PLAVAC MALI, inc Ivan Dolac. Producers: Carić, Plančić, ZLATAN OTOK, Svirče, TOMIĆ (Bastijana winery).

Istria [Ist] N Adriatic Peninsula. MALVAZIJA is main grape. Gd Cab Sauv, Merlot, TERAN. Benvenuti, Clai, Coronica, Degrassi, Kozlović, MATOŠEVIĆ, ROXANICH, TRAPAN.

Korta Katarina Dalm ★★★ New, v. promising small producer with 6 ha. POŠIP 06 07 08 is excellent and v.gd PLAVAC MALI 06 07, esp Reuben's Res.

Krauthaker, Vlado ★★★ 06 07 08 09 Top dry and sweet whites from KUTJEVO, esp Chard Rosenberg, dry GRAŠEVINA Mitrovac, sweet Izborna Berba. Gd Sauv Bl.

Kutjevo N Croa Name shared by a town in SLAVONIJA, centre of GRAŠEVINA and ★★→★★★ Kutjevo Cellars. Look for De Gotho Chard 07 08, GRAŠEVINA 08 and Traminac Icewine 07.

Malvazija Most important grape in ISTRIA. Malvazija Istarka, genetically distinct from other Mediterranean Malvasia. Often vinified in light, sharpish style to drink young; good examples from Arman Franc, Benvenuti, Coronica, Degrassi, Kozlović, Malić and TRAPAN. Also rich, full-bodied versions with maceration and barrel ageing: Clai Sveti Jakov, Kabola Amfora, Kozlović Santa Lucia, MATOŠEVIĆ Alba Robinia, ROXANICH Antica Malvazija, TRAPAN Uroboros.

Matošević ★★→★★★ 05 08 09 Pioneering producer, head of ISTRIAN producers' association. Benchmark MALVAZIJA in several styles. V.gd Grimalda (r w).

Plavac Mali Croatia's top red grape, related to Zinfandel. Potential for high quality and ageing, but can be alcoholic and dull. Well-regarded producers: Baković, Bura, Duboković, Mendek (esp Selekcija), Miličić, Mrgudić Marija, Svirče, Matuško, Miloš, Frano, Lučič, ZLATAN OTOK, TOMIČ, KORTA KATARINA.

Pošip Best DALMATIAN white, mostly on island of Korčula.

Postup Dalm Famous v'yd designation northwest of DINGAČ. Medium-to-full red from PLAVAC MALI. Donja Banda, Miličić, Mrgudić Marija, Vinarija Dingač noted.

Prošek Dalm *Passito*-style dessert wine from DALMATIA, made from dried local grapes Bogdanuša, Maraština, Prč. Look for Hectorovich from TOMIČ.

Roxanich Ist ★★→★★★ 06 07 New organic producer. Powerful, intriguing whites; characterful reds, esp TERAN Ré, Superistrian Cuvée and surprisingly gd Merlot.

Saints Hills Ist ★★→★★★ New high-profile producer (2008), Michel Rolland consults. V.gd Nevina MALVAZIJA-based white blend 09. DINGAČ 08 already promising.

Slavonija N Croa Subregion in north for white. Look out for ADZIČ, Belje, ENJINGI, KRAUTHAKER, KUTJEVO, Zdjelarević. Famous for its oak, too.

Teran Indigenous red grape related to Refošk (*see* Slovenia), only in ISTRIA. increasingly exciting and drinkable: Arman Franc, Benvenuti, Coronica, ROXANICH.

Tomič Dalm ★★→★★★ dr sw 03 04 05 06 07 Owner of Bastijana winery on island of Hvar. V.gd barrique PLAVAC MALI, PROŠEK Hectorovich from dried grapes.

Trapan, Bruno Ist ★★→★★★ Rising star. Some of Croatia's most exciting MALVAZIJAS inc aged Uroboros 08 (09) and young Ponente 09. Pioneer with Syrah in Istria.

Vrhunsko vino A fairly rigorous designation for high-quality wines.

Zlatan Otok Dalm ★★→★★★ Zlatan Plavac Grand Cru 03' 04' 05' 06 07 constantly among top Croatian reds. POŠIP 08 is charming; ZLATAN PLAVAC 07 approachable and appealing.

Zlatan Plavac Dalm *Grand cru* designation for PLAVAC MALI. Usually v. high alcohol.

BOSNIA & HERZEGOVINA, SERBIA, MONTENEGRO, MACEDONIA

Virtually unknown for wine, these countries have a range of local grapes and wine styles to explore. Modern winemaking is giving a real boost to quality, though luckily without losing local identity. Bosnia and Herzegovina have plummy red Blatina (try Hercegovina Produkt) and grapey white Žilavka grapes plus ripe Vranac (try Vinarija Vukoje and Tvrdoš Monastery). Serbia's WOW winery is forward-looking (especially Sauv Bl, Pinot Gr, Chard Barrique); Radovanovioć (Cab Res) and Aleksandrović also impress; try Trijumf white 08 09 and Pinot N-based Trijumf Noir 08, also Vizija Frankovka. Montenegro's vineyards are confined to the coastal strip and the basin of Lake Skadar: 13 Jul Plantaže is the biggest producer and still state-owned, also look for first private winery Milenko Sjekloća (decent Vranac). In Macedonia wine accounts for 17–20% of GDP, making the country v. reliant on wine; most is exported to Germany and elsewhere, but there's an increasing focus on quality. Promising wineries include Cekorov, Chateau Kamnik, Dalvina, Fonko, Pivka, Popova Kula, Skovin and Tikveš.

CZECH REPUBLIC & SLOVAK REPUBLIC

Czech Republic

The Czech Republic has two wine regions, Bohemia and Moravia – most of the wine is in Moravia (not to be confused with Moldova). The annual consumption per capita is around 19 litres, and the country produces only a third of what it drinks, the rest being imported (mostly in bulk) for blending, all the more so after an abysmal vintage such as 2010. The market is dominated by two German-owned bottlers and blenders producing still and sparkling wines made largely from such imports. But huge numbers of small vineyard owners have existed here for centuries, and they are still luring city folk to their picturesque cellars with their artisan style of wine production.

Some are now high-class boutique establishments or medium-sized concerns with stainless-steel and French oak barrels. Wines are mostly bottled by varietal. New appellation VOC Znojmo is the first step to denominating a specific place (rather than just indicating must-weight levels at harvest) on the label. It is likely to be followed soon by the subzone of Pálava.

Bohemia Just 700 ha in two demarcated subregions following the banks of the river Elbe north of Prague, notably Mělník, Žernoseky, Roudnice, and also around the capital (Gröbovka, Salabka). Notable producers: Bettina Lobkowicz (Mělník), Vilém Kraus III (Mělník). Also kosher wines from Chrámce nr Most. Two giants, Bohemia Sekt and Soare, bestride sparkling-wine production.

Moravia Far larger surface with almost 19,000 ha in four demarcated subregions in the southeast corner of the country. Small progressive producers: Stapleton-Springer (Bořetice), Dobrá Vinice (Nový Šaldorf), Osička (Velké Bílovice), Reisten (Pavlov). Medium-sized wineries: Tanzberg (Mikulov), Sonberk (Pouzdřany), Spielberg (Archlebov). Reliable well-established larger concerns: Vinselekt-Michlovský (Rakvice), Znovín (Znojmo), Vinné sklepy Valtice, Valihrach (Krumvíř), F Mádl (Velké Bílovice), Baloun (Velké Pavlovice). Icewine and straw wine are highly sought after and expensive. Moravia also has sparkling wine, esp the renewed Sekt Domaine label of the late Jan Petrák, and Tanzberg.

Slovak Republic

Six wine regions stretching from the Carpathians along the foothills of the Tatra mountains right up to the small enclave of Tokaj in the east abutting the famous Hungarian region. Classic regional and international varieties. Mostly consumed locally but much bulk wine heads for the Czech Republic. Leading producers: Château Béla (Mužla) with Egon Müller's involvement (*see* Germany), Janoušek (Pezinok), Mrva & Stanko (Trnava), Karpatská Perla (Šenkvice), Masaryk (Skalica) and Tokaj's JJ Ostrožovič. Recently opened Elesko is a state-of-the-art mega-facility in Modra in the west of the country, with investment from abroad and New Zealand advice.

ROMANIA

Romania's 186,000 ha make it one of the biggest grape-growers in Europe, and EU grants are still going into replanting and renovating vineyards. Better fruit as a result and more modern winemaking mean continually improving wines, especially in small-to-medium commercial wineries. The large and unfussy domestic market has not helped quality, though tastes move towards reds and dry whites, supporting top-end projects. There's more focus on exports, too, as producers learn to work together, and exchange rates have become more favourable, so we might even see more Romanian wine outside her borders.

Băbească Neagră Mold Traditional "black grandmother grape" of MOLDOVA; light body and ruby-red colour.

Budureasca Mun ★ 270 ha largely replanted vines (formerly Carpathian winery). Decent wines from own v'yds so far under Budureasca and Origini labels. Brit Stephen Donnelly consults.

Carl Reh Mun ★★ →★★★ 06 07 08 09 German-owned winery with 190-ha v'yd. Val Duna and River Route are export labels for gd varietal range, esp Pinot Gr. V.gd reds in Oltenia Profunda range, esp La Cetate, Caloian, Crama Oprisor Cab Sauv and Smerenie. Top Arta si Vin wines include fine red blend Fragmentarium.

Cotnari Mold Region in northeast with gd botrytis conditions. Famous for over 500 yrs for medium to sweet GRASĂ, FETEASCĂ ALBĂ, TĂMÂIOASĂ and dry Frâncuşă.

Cotnari Winery Mold ★ 1,200 ha in COTNARI region, v. popular locally. Styles typically semi-dry to semi-sweet from local grapes. Can be long-lived; v.gd collection wines.

Cramele Recaş Ban r w dr ★★→★★★ 06 07 08 09 British/Romanian firm. A further 120 ha planted in 2010 plus two new cellars. Quality better than ever, esp Sole Chard, Solo FETEASCĂ REGALĂ, Solo Quinta white, La Putere FETEASCĂ NEAGRĂ. Frunza label for excellent-value modern varietals, Also V, Castle Rock, Terra Dacica labels. V.gd super-premium Cuvée Uberland red blend 06 07 08.

Davino Winery Mun ★★→★★★ 04 05 06 07 08 Premium producer with 68 ha in DEALU MARE. V.gd Dom Ceptura (r w). Also Alba Valahica FETEASCĂ ALBĂ and Purpura Valahica FETEASCĂ NEAGRĂ 06. Flagship blend is Flamboyant 03' 06'.

Dealu Mare Mun (Dealul Mare) "The Big Hill". Important, well-situated area in southeastern Carpathian foothills. Some of Romania's best reds, esp FETEASCĂ NEAGRĂ, Cab Sauv, MERLOT, PINOT N. Whites from TĂMÂIOASĂ.

Dobrogea Dob Bl Sea region. Inc DOC regions of MURFATLAR, Badabag, Sarica Niculitel. Famous for sweet, late-harvest Chard and now for full-bodied reds.

DOC Denumire de Origine Controlata: the Romanian term for AOP wines. Sub-categories inc DOC-CMD for wines harvested at full maturity, DOC-CT for late-harvest wines and DOC-CIB for noble harvest wines. *Vin cu indicaţie geografică* is term for IGP category.

Domeniile Sahateni Mun ★→★★ 70 ha estate in DEALU MARE. Anima label for varietals, inc decent Merlot 08, Artizan 08 09 for white and red blends

Domeniile Viticole Franco Române Mun ★→★★ Frenchman Denis Thomas set up this organic estate in DEALU MARE to make fine PINOT N. Crai Nou organic range.

Domeniul Coroanei Segarcea Mun ★★ Former royal estate and southernmost winery in Oltenia resurrected by former cardiologist and her husband. Replanted since 2004 and much improved quality recently, esp aromatic whites, inc TĂMÂIOASĂ, Sauv Bl. Also gd FETEASCĂ NEAGRĂ 08.

Drăgăşani Region in Oltenia south of Carpathians. Traditional (white: Crâmposie Selectionată; reds: Novac, Negru de Drăgăşani) and international varieties.

Fetească Albă Romania's second-most-planted white *vinifera* grape with gentle Muscat aroma. Same as Hungary's Leányka. Can be high quality with care.

Fetească Neagră "Black maiden grape" with potential as showpiece variety. Needs low yields in v'yd, but can give deep, full-bodied wines with character.

Fetească Regală A cross of FETEASCĂ ALBĂ with GRASĂ (Hungary's Királyleanyka).

Grasă Local Romanian grape whose name means "fat". Prone to botrytis and v. important grape in COTNARI. Grown as Kövérszölö in Hungary's Tokaj region.

Halewood Romania Mun ★→★★ British-owned company with new focus on replanted regional v'yds and higher quality, esp since 2009 vintage. Best wines: Hyperion FETEASCĂ NEAGRĂ, Cab S 06 08. Also v.gd from 09: La Catina PINOT N, Scurta Viognier and TĂMÂIOASĂ, FETEASCĂ ALBĂ DEALU MARE.

Jidvei Trans ★ Expensively modernized winery with 2,100 ha, mostly replanted, in subregion of the same name in TRANSYLVANIA. One of biggest players in domestic market, sound whites at best.

Merlot Romania's most widely planted red. Probably arrived in early 18th century.

Moldova Mold (Moldovia) Largest region northeast of Carpathians. Borders Republic of Moldova. DOC areas: Bohotin, COTNARI, Huşi, Iaşi, Odobeşti, Coteşti, Nicoreşti.

Muntenia and Oltenia Hills Mun Major region in south: DOC areas of DEALU MARE, Dealurile Olteniei, DRĂGĂŞANI, Pietroasa, Sâmbureşti, Stefaneşti, Vanju Mare.

Murfatlar Dob Area with v'yds in DOBROGEA nr Bl Sea; v.gd Chard, Pinot Gr and Cab Sauv. Subregions are Cernavoda and Megidia.

Murfatlar Winery Dob ★→★★ Largest producer on domestic market. V.gd labels Trei Hectare (FETEASCĂ NEAGRĂ, Cab Sauv, Chard) and Ferma Nouă (MERLOT, Sauv Bl). Also v.gd oak-aged sweet fortified Lacrima lui Ovidiu.

Pinot Noir Grown for 100 yrs+, originally as sparkling base. Several producers believe Romania's terroir is ideal; newer plantings of French clones show real promise.

Prince Štirbey Mun w r dr sw ★★→★★★ 06 07 08 09 20-ha estate in DRĂGĂŞANI returned to Austrian-Romanian noble family (Kripp-Costinescu). V.gd local Crâmposie Selectionată (w), FETEASCĂ REGALĂ Genius Loci (w) 07, sweet TĂMÂIOASĂ ROMÂNEASCĂ. Has revived local red varieties, v.gd Novac and Negru de Drăgăşani.

Regions Romania's wine traditions are old and proud. Six key wine regions: Banat (west); Crişana & Maramures (northwest); Dobrogea (southeast), close to the Bl Sea, noted for Chard, Sauv Bl and now for ripe reds. MOLDOVA borders the republic of the same name to the northeast. Transylvania (hilly centre) is known for crisp, aromatic whites, while Oltenia & Muntenia (south) is best regarded for full-bodied reds.

Riesling, Italian Widely planted Welschriesling, sold locally as Ries.

Senator Mold ★ Newcomer based in Odobeşti with 900 ha in MOLDOVA, Banat and Danube Delta. Whites sound, esp Varius Sauv Bl 09. Reds could improve.

SERVE Mun r w dr ★★→★★★ 03' 06' 07 08 Founded by the late Corsican Count Guy de Poix, based in DEALU MARE. Terra Romana range is excellent, esp *Cuvée Charlotte* 03' 06' 07 and Cuvée Amaury white.

Tămâioasă Românească White "frankincense" grape. Belongs to Muscat family.

Transylvania Trans Cool mtn plateau in centre of Romania. Mostly producing whites with gd acidity from FETEASCĂ ALBĂ, FETEASCĂ REGALĂ, Muscat, Traminer, Italian Ries. Promising PINOT N.

Vinarte Winery Mun ★★→★★★ 03 05 06 07 08 Italian investment for three estates: Villa Zorilor in DEALU MARE, Castel Bolovanu in DRĂGĂŞANI, Terase Danubiane in Vanju Mare. Best: Soare Cab, Prince Matei Merlot, Swallowtail FETEASCĂ NEAGRĂ.

Vincon Vrancea Winery r w dr sw ★ One of Romania's largest producers with 2,150 ha in Vrancea, plus DOBROGEA and DEALU MARE.

Vinia Mold r w dr sw ★ One of Romania's largest wineries at Iaşi. Major producer of COTNARI wines. Also whites and light reds.

Vinterra ★ Dutch/Romanian venture reviving FETEASCĂ NEAGRĂ; also sound PINOT N, MERLOT. Black Peak is brand name.

Vitis Metamorfosis Mun r w ★★ High-profile joint venture between Italy's historic Antinori family and British-owned Halewood. First release is 07 Cantus Primus Cab Sauv. Gd Vitis Metamorfosis white blend and MERLOT launched 09.

WineRo Dob r ★★ New premium estate owned by Stephan von Niepperg of Canon-la-Gaffelière (Bordeaux), Dr. Hauptmann, Marc Dworkin. Same team owns/runs Bulgaria's Bessa Valley. First release is appealing, juicy Alira Merlot 09. To watch.

MALTA

Malta's vineyards cannot supply the island's entire consumption, and tourism tends to take precedence when it comes to land use. Much of the wine on sale here is made locally from grapes imported from Italy. Real Maltese wine is subject to Demoninazzjoni ta' Origini Kontrollata (DOK) rules, in line with EU practices. Traditional, indigenous grapes are white Girgentina and red Gellewza, but international grapes are also grown. Antinori-backed Meridiana is in the lead: excellent Maltese Isis and Mistral Chards, Astarte Vermentino, Melquart Cab Sauv/Merlot, Nexus Merlot, *outstanding Bel Syrah* and premium Celsius Cab Sauv Res. Volume producers of note: Delicata, Marsovin, Camilleri.

Greece

The big news in Greece, and not just in wine, is the severe economic crisis affecting all parts of Greek society. On the plus side, if there is one, this is an opportunity to re-evaluate habits and strategies. Greek wine producers now know the only way ahead is quality and smart pricing. [Abbreviations: Peloponnese (Pelop), Central Greece (C Gr), Northern Greece (N Gr), Aegean Islands (Aeg), Cephalonia (Ceph), Attica (Att).]

Aghiorghitiko NEMEA's red grape, now planted almost everywhere, even in the north. Extemely versatile, from soft and charming to dense and age-worthy. Loves oak.

Aivalis Pelop ★★★ Boutique NEMEA producer, extracted style. Top (and pricey) wine is "4", from 120+-yr-old vines. Merlot is less successful.

Alpha Estate N Gr ★★★ Impressive estate in cool-climate Amindeo. Excellent Merlot/Syrah/XINOMAVRO blend, pungent Sauv Bl, exotic MALAGOUSIA, unfiltered XINOMAVRO (ungrafted vines). Top wine: Alpha 1 (demands ageing). ★★★★ soon?

Antonopoulos Pelop ★★★ PATRAS-based winery, with top-class MANTINIA, crisp Adoli Ghis (w), Lafon-(Burgundy)-like Anax Chard, and Cab-based Nea Dris (stunning 04 and 06). Top wine: violet-scented Vertzami/Cab Fr.

Argatia N Gr ★★★ Small KTIMA, just outside NAOUSSA, crafting tiny quantities of age-worthy XINOMAVRO in a modern vein.

Argyros Aeg ★★★ Top SANTORINI producer with exemplary VINSANTO aged 20 yrs in cask (★★★★). Exciting KTIMA white that ages for a decade, an oak-aged Vareli (w) and fragrant (dry) Aidani. Try the rare red MAVROTRAGANO.

Assyrtiko One of the v. best white grapes of the Mediterranean, balancing power, minerality, extract and high acid. Built to age.

Avantis C Gr ★★★ Boutique winery in Evia, v'yds in Boetia. Dense Syrah, Aghios Chronos Syrah/Viognier, pungent Sauv Bl, rich MALAGOUSIA, new Oneiropagida range. Top wine: Rhône-like single-v'yd Collection Syrah 03 04 05 06 07.

Biblia Chora N Gr ★★★ Polished New-World-style wines. Extremely successful Sauv Bl/ASSYRTIKO. Ovilos CS and Areti AGHIORGHITIKO are stunning. Ovilos white pushes Greek oaked whites to a new level.

Boutari, J & Son ★→★★★ Producers in several appellations. Excellent-value wines, esp *Grande Reserve Naoussa*, popular MOSCHOFILERO. Top SANTORINI Kalisti Res, Skalani (r) from CRETE and Flliria (r) from GOUMENISSA. Try the sweet red Liatiko.

Cair Aeg Large co-op winery in RHODES specializing in sparkling (esp rosé), but Pathos still range (r w) is v.gd value.

Carras, Domaine N Gr ★→★★ Estate at Sithonia, Halkidiki, with its own OPAP (Côtes de Meliton). Chateau Carras 01 02 03 04 05 and MALAGOUSIA. Underperforming.

Cava Legal term for cask-aged still white and red table wines, eg. Cava Amethystos Kosta Lazaridi, Cava Hatzimihali.

Cephalonia (Kephalonia) Ceph Ionian island: excellent, floral Robola (w), emerging styles of sweet Muscat, MAVRODAPHNE.

Crete Quality improves, led by ECONOMOU, Lyrarakis, Douloufakis, MANOUSSAKIS.

Dougos C Gr ★★→★★★ From Olympus area. Interesting Rhône blends; top Methymon range, esp red Opsimo. New RAPSANI shows different approach to this OPAP.

Driopi Pelop ★★★ New venture of TSELEPOS in high NEMEA. Initial vintages are serious (esp single-v'yd KTIMA) and of the high-octane style. Tavel-like Driopi rosé.

Economou One of the great artisans of Greece; brilliant yet esoteric Sitia reds in CRETE.

Emery Aeg ★→★★★ Historic RHODES producer, specializing in local varieties. Brands Villaré (w), Grand Rosé. V.gd-value Rhodos Athiri. Sweet Efreni Muscat.

Feggites N Gr ★★ In Drama; ex-winemaker of NICO LAZARIDI. Top oaky Sauv Bl Deka.

Gaia Pelop ★★★ Top-quality NEMEA- and SANTORINI-based producer. Fun Notios range. New World-like AGHIORGHITIKO. Thought-provoking but top-class dry white Thalassitis Santorini and revolutionary *wild-ferment Assyrtiko*. Top wine: Gaia Estate (97 98 99 00 01 03 04 05 06 07). Anatolikos sweet NEMEA, dazzling Gaia S red (AGHIORGHITIKO with a touch of Syrah).

Gentilini Ceph ★★→★★★ Exciting whites inc *v.gd Robola*. New dry red MAVRODAPHNE, serious Syrah and v. complex Selection Robola.

Gerovassiliou N Gr ★★★ Perfectionist miniature estate nr Salonika. Benchmark ASSYRTIKO/MALAGOUSIA, smooth Syrah/Merlot blend, inspiring MALAGOUSIA. Complex red Avaton 03 04 05 from rare indigenous varieties. Top wine: Syrah (01 02 03 04 05). For many, the quality leader.

Goumenissa N Gr (OPAP) ★→★★ XINOMAVRO, Negoska oaked red from Macedonia, lighter than NAOUSSA. Esp Aidarinis, BOUTARI (esp Filiria), Ligas, Tatsis Bros.

Hatzidakis Aeg ★★★ Low-tech but high-class producer, redefining SANTORINI appellation, esp with *cuvées* No 15 and 17. Stunning range, bordering on the experimental. Nihteri and Pyrgos whites could age for decades. Collio meets Aegean Sea.

Hatzimichalis, Domaine Att ★→★★★ Large v'yds and merchant in Atalanti. Huge range. Greek and French varieties, many bottlings labelled after their v'yd names. Top red Kapnias CS, top white Veriki.

Helios, Domaine Att New umbrella name and new owner for SEMELI, Nassiakos and Orinos Helios wines. Excellent Nassiakos MANTINIA.

Karydas ★★★ Small estate and great v'yd in NAOUSSA; XINOMAVRO of great breeding.

Katogi-Strofilia ★★→★★★ V'yds and wineries in Attica, Peloponnese and east Epirus. Greek and French varieties. Katogi was the first premium Greek wine. Top wines: Ktima Averoff and Rossiu di Munte range.

Katsaros C Gr ★★★ Small organic winery on Mt Olympus. KTIMA red (Cab Sauv/ Merlot) has staying power. Chard gets better each year. Broad-shouldered Merlot.

Kir-Yanni N Gr ★★→★★★ V'yds in NAOUSSA and Amindeo. Vibrant Samaropetra (w); characterful Tesseris Limnes (w); complex and age-worthy Dyo Elies (r); benchmark NAOUSSA Ramnista turning towards more supple approach, making way for XINOMAVRO/Syrah blend Diaporos.

Kourtakis, D ★★ Reliable merchant: *mild Retsina*, gd NEMEA.

Ktima Estate, domaine. Term not exclusive to wine.

Lazaridi, Nico ★★→★★★ Wineries and v'yds in Drama, Kavala and Mykonos. Gd Château Lazaridis (w p r). Top wines Magiko Vouno white (Sauv Bl) and red (CS) enjoy cult status in Greece.

Lazaridis, Domaine Kostas ★★★ V'yds and wineries in Drama and Kapandriti (nr Athens, sold under the Oenotria Land label). Popular Amethystos label (white, red, rosé). Top wine: unfiltered red CAVA Amethystos CS (97 98 99 00 01 02 03 04). First Greek consultancy of Bordeaux's Michel Rolland.

Lemnos Aeg (OPAP) Aegean island: mainly co-op-made fortified dessert wines, inc delicious, lemony Muscat of Alexandria. Also some refreshing dry whites.

Greek appellations

Much in line with other EU countries, the Greek wine appellation system is changing. The quality appellations of OPAP and OPE are now fused together into POP (or PDO) category. Regional wines known as TO will now be PGE (or PGI). The base category of table wine (EO) will be phased out. However, expect the old terms to persist on labels for some time.

Lyrarakis Aeg ★★→★★★ V.gd producer from CRETE. Whites from the rare Plyto and Dafni varieties (single-v'yd versions are extraordinary), as well as a deep, complex blend of Syrah and Kotsifali.

Malagousia Rediscovered perfumed white grape, stunning in the hands of AVANTIS, GEROVASSILIOU, MATSA and several others.

Manoussakis Crete ★★★ Impressive estate from west CRETE. Rhône-inspired blends. Delectable range under Nostos brand, led by age-worthy Roussanne, Syrah.

Mantinia (OPAP) w High, central Peloponnese region. Fresh, crisp, charming *Moschofilero*. More German than Greek in style.

Matsa, Domaine Att ★★→★★★ Historic, prestigious small estate, owned by BOUTARI but run by Roxane Matsa. MALAGOUSIA is leading example of the variety.

Mavrodaphne Red, usually sweet, wine and variety, meaning "black laurel". Cask-aged Port-style/*recioto*-like, concentrated red; fortified. Specialty of PATRAS, north Peloponnese but also found in CEPHALONIA. Dry versions (eg. ANTONOPOULOS) are increasing, showing great promise.

Mavrotragano Almost extinct but now-revived red grape of SANTORINI. Top quality. Try SIGALAS, HATZIDAKIS, ARGYROS and Avaton from GEROVASSILIOU.

Mediterra (ex-Creta-Olympias) Crete ★★ Gd Cretan producer. Value Nea Ghi range, spicy white Xerolithia, red Mirabelo. Interesting Pirorago Syrah/Cab Sauv/Kotsifali blend. Excellent, v.gd-value Silenius range.

Mercouri Pelop ★★★ One of the most beautiful family estates in Europe. V.gd KTIMA red, delicious RODITIS, age-worthy CAVA. Classy Refosco dal Penducolo red, stunning sweet Belvedere Malvasia and leading dry MAVRODAPHNE.

Mezzo Aeg Sweet wine produced in SANTORINI from sun-dried grapes, usually less sweet than VINSANTO. Dispute over style – some producers (eg. SIGALAS) use the term for wine made from the red Mandilaria variety, while others (eg. ARGYROS) use the same white varieties as VINSANTO.

Mitravelas Pelop ★★→★★★ Outstanding producer in NEMEA, promising great things from AGHIORGHITIKO. GAIA-influenced winemaking style.

Moschofilero Pink-skinned, rose-scented, high-quality, high-acid, low-alcohol grape variety. Usually white wines but some pink versions as well.

Naoussa N Gr (OPAP) r High-quality region for XINOMAVRO. One of two Greek regions where a *cru* notion may soon develop (the other being NEMEA), since soil patterns and topography are extremely complex.

Nemea (OPAP) r Region in east Peloponnese; dark, spicy AGHIORGHITIKO. Each new vintage leads to new quality levels. High Nemea merits its own appellation. Koutsi is front-runner for *cru* status (*see* GAIA, HELIOS and DRIOPI).

Nemeion Pelop ★★★ A KTIMA in NEMEA, setting new pricing standards (esp Igemon) for the appellation, with wines to match. Owned by Vassiliou, an Attika producer.

Oenoforos Pelop ★★→★★★ V.gd producer with fantastic, high-altitude v'yds. Extremely elegant RODITIS Asprolithi. Also delicate white Lagorthi (Burgundian, limited release, magnum only), and nutty Chard and delicate Mikros Vorias reds and whites. Ianos is the prestige range.

Papaïoannou Pelop ★★★ If NEMEA were Burgundy, Papaïoannou would be Jayer. Classy reds (inc Pinot N and Petit Verdot); flavourful whites. A wonderful flight of NEMEAS: Ktima Papaïoannou, Palea Klimata (old vines), Microklima (a micro-single v'yd) and top-end Terroir (a super-strict, 200%-new-oaked selection).

Patras Pelop (OPAP) w White (based on RODITIS) from diverse terroir – some great parts, some average sites. Home of MAVRODAPHNE. Rio-Patras (OPE) sweet Muscat.

Pavlidis N Gr ★★★ Ambitious v'yds and winery at Drama. Gd ASSYRTIKO/Sauv Bl, v.gd ASSYRTIKO. Excellent Syrah and Tempranillo. KTIMA red recently switched from Bordeaux blend to AGHIORGHITIKO/Syrah in a masterful move. At the top tier of Drama as well as of Greece.

Pyrgakis Pelop ★★→★★★ Highly experimental KTIMA, fully capitalizing on the highest parts of NEMEA OPAP. Try the new Petit Verdot or the 24 Chardonnay.

Rapsani N Gr ★★★ Historic red from Mt Olympus. Introduced in the 1990s by TSANTALIS, but new producers, such as Liappis and DOUGOS, are moving in.

Retsina Specialty white with Aleppo pine resin added. Modern, high-quality versions, like "The Tear of the Pine" are stunning.

Rhodes Aeg Easternmost island and OPAP for red and white. Home to lemony, elegant Athiri whites. Top wines inc: CAIR (co-op) Rodos 2400 and Emery's Villare. Also some sparkling.

Roditis Pink grape grown all over Greece, usually producing white wines. Gd when yields are low. Asprolithi is top example.

Samos Aeg (OPE) w sw Island nr Turkey famed for sweet, golden Muscat. Esp (fortified) Anthemis, (sun-dried) Nectar. Rare old bottlings can be ★★★★, such as the hard-to-find "75".

Santo Aeg ★★ The all-important co-op of SANTORINI. Vibrant portfolio, with excellent Grande Res and VINSANTOS.

Santorini Aeg Volcanic island north of CRETE and OPAP (for w dr sw). Luscious VINSANTO and MEZZO, mineral-laden, bone-dry white from fine ASSYRTIKO. Oaked examples can also be v.gd. Top producers inc: GAIA, HATZIDAKIS, SIGALAS, SANTO. Try ageing everything. Possibly the cheapest ★★★★ whites around.

Semeli ★★→★★★ Estates nr Athens and NEMEA and a new winery in MANTINIA under the Nassiakos name. Value Orinos Helios (w r) and convincing, top-end Grande Res, released after 4 yrs. *See* HELIOS.

Sigalas Aeg ★★★ Top SANTORINI estate producing leading oaked Santorini Bareli. Stylish VINSANTO. Also rare, breathtaking red Mourvèdre-like Mavrotragano.

Skouras Pelop ★★→★★★ Innovative estate. First to use screwcaps on Chard Dum Vinum Sperum with most of white range following suit. Interesting Synoro (Cab Fr-dominated). Top wines: Grande Cuvée Nemea, Megas Oenos and the ultra-rare, solera-aged Labyrinth.

Spiropoulos, Domaine Pelop ★★ Organic producer in MANTINIA and NEMEA. Oaky, red Porfyros (AGHIORGHITIKO, Cab Sauv, Merlot). Sparkling Odi Panos has potential. Firm, single-v'yd Astala Mantinia.

Tetramythos Pelop ★★ Exploring the cool-climate parts of Peloponnese, a promising venture. The winery was burned in the great summer fires of 2007, but now back on form. Excellent MALAGOUSIA and Mavro Kalavritino.

Tsantalis ★→★★★ Merchant and v'yds at Agios Pavlos, Thrace and other areas. Gd red Metoxi, RAPSANI Res and Grande Res, gd-value organic Cab Sauv, excellent Avaton and cult Kormilitsa. Major force in Greek wine exports.

Tselepos Pelop ★★★ Top-quality MANTINIA producer and Greece's best Gewurz. Other wines: oaky Chard, v.gd sparkling Amalia, single-v'yd Avlotopi Cab Sauv. Top wine: single-v'yd Kokinomylos Merlot. *See* DRIOPI.

Vinsanto Aeg Sweet wine style produced in SANTORINI, from sun-dried ASSYRTIKO and Aidani. Requires long ageing, both in oak and bottle. The best and oldest vinsantos are ★★★★ and practically indestructible. *See also* MEZZO.

Voyatzi Ktima N Gr ★★ Small estate nr Kozani. Classy XINOMAVRO, startling Cab Fr sold as Tsapournakos.

Xinomavro N Gr The great diva of indigenous red grapes (name means "acidic black"). Grown in the cooler north, it is the basis for NAOUSSA, RAPSANI, GOUMENISSA, Amindeo. Top quality and able to age for decades: Greece's answer to Nebbiolo.

Zafeirakis Thess ★★→★★★ Small KTIMA in Tyrnavos, an uncharted territory for quality wine-growing. Fastidious winemaker and a much-anticipated Limniona red, the first bottling of a v. promising and rare variety.

Eastern Mediterranean & North Africa

EASTERN MEDITERRANEAN

Historically, wine regions here have been divided by religion and even war. However, this is one of the oldest wine-growing regions in the world, and in ancient times it was where wine culture took root. The wines were pretty dire until recently, but both Israel and Lebanon, after occasional sparks of quality in the past, are now taking giant steps forward. Some of the reds are justifiably gaining attention. Cyprus and Turkey are also now showing signs of wanting to make better wines.

Cyprus

The wine industry in Cyprus continues to restructure, with the aim of higher quality. Substantial EU funds are going into replanting better varieties, ie. Shiraz and Maratheftiko, while poor-quality vineyards are being grubbed up. The once significant, cheap, bulk market has declined substantially, and while local sales are having to fight imports for market share, undoubtedly quality is better than ever, led by smaller producers based at altitude in the (phylloxera-free) hills.

Ayla Mavri ★★ 08 09 Lovely sweet Muscats from semi-dried Muscat of Alexandria.
Commandaria Sweet, oxidized wine from sun-dried XYNISTERI and MAVRO, grown in 14 designated villages. Probably the wine with the longest heritage in the world, first described by the poet Hesiod in 800BC. At best, it's rich, complex and long lived. Try St John (KEO), Alasia (Loel), or the 100% XYNISTERI St Barnabas (SODAP).
ETKO r w ★→★★ 08 09 One of former Big Four, much reduced in size. Improved quality from Olympus winery (Shiraz, Cab Sauv); St Nicholas Commandaria.
Hadjiantonas ★★ Spotless new winery, making v.gd Chard 08 09 and Shiraz 07.
KEO ★ Second-largest producer; of mixed quality. St John is COMMANDARIA brand. Best wines from Mallia Estate (Ktima Keo) and Heritage label for local grapes.
Kyperounda r w dr ★★→★★★ 06′ 07′ **08** 09 Probably Europe's highest v'yd at 1,450 metres. White Petritis from barrel-aged XYNISTERI is island's best. Chard, Cab Sauv and red blend Andessitis, also v.gd.
Lefkada Rediscovered indigenous black grape variety. Higher quality than MAVRO. Usually blended, as tannins can be aggressive.
Maratheftiko Deep-coloured local grape with potential as high-quality signature red. Tricky to grow well; winemakers getting better. Single-variety plots appearing.
Mavro The most planted black grape of Cyprus. Easier to cultivate than MARATHEFTIKO, but only moderate quality. Best for rosé.
Regions Lemesos, Pafos, Larnaca, Lefkosia have regional wine status (PGI). PDOs cover COMMANDARIA, Laona-Akamas, Pitsilia, Vouni-Panayias/Ambelitis and Wine Villages of Lemesos.
SODAP r w dr ★→★★ Grower-owned co-op and island's largest producer. New winery at Stroumbi village in hills has transformed quality, esp DYA whites. Gd value. Look for Island Vines, Mountain Vines and Kamanterena labels.
Tsiakkas r w dr ★★ Banker turned winemaker with help from VLASSIDES. Makes v.gd fresh, zesty whites, esp Sauv Bl, XYNISTERI and Chard.
Vasa ★★ 03 05 06′ **07′** (08) Small but immaculate winery. Excellent MARATHEFTIKO and Mourvèdre. V.gd Chard and St Tinon red blend. VLASSIDES consults.

Vlassides ★★→★★★ 03' 04 06' 07' 08 Davis-trained Sophocles Vlassides crafts some of the island's best wines in a tiny village winery. Shiraz Res is a star and shows Cyprus's potential for exciting wines. Also v.gd Cab Sauv and MARATHEFTIKO.

Xynisteri Cyprus's most planted white grape. Can be simple and is usually DYA, but when grown at altitude makes appealing, minerally whites. KYPEROUNDA's Petritis is best. Try TSIAKKAS, VLASSIDES, ZAMBARTAS, Kolios, Aes Ambelis, K&K Vasilikon.

Zambartas ★★→★★★ 07 08 09 (10) Father and Australian-trained son run new winery making exciting Cab Fr/LEFKADA rosé, v.gd Shiraz/LEFKADA red, 100% MARATHEFTIKO and attractive XYNISTERI/Sem.

Israel

A chronic shortage of water, a lack of rain and a hot climate are coped with by drip-feed irrigation, canopy management and higher-altitude vineyards. The viticulturists are up to the minute and most wineries have the latest technology. The winemakers are dynamic and internationally trained. The red wines, esp Bordeaux blends, Shiraz, old-vine Carignans and Petite Sirahs, seem to be improving each year. The best wines produced in Israel for 2,000 years. [Abbreviations: Galilee (Gal), Golan (Gol), Judean Hills (Jud), Lower Galilee (L Gal), Negev (Neg), Samson (Sam), Shomron (Shom); Upper Galilee (Up Gal).]

Agur Jud r ★→★★ Characterful boutique. Well-integrated Kessem Bordeaux blend.

Alexander Gal r (w) ★ Cab Sauv is incredibly oaky, full-bodied, but well-made.

Avidan Jud r (w) ★→★★ The interesting Prio blend is gently spicy and leathery.

Barkan-Segal Gal, Sam r w ★★ Israel's second-largest winery, owned by Israel's largest brewery. Gd-value wines. Specializes in Pinotage and Israeli vine Argaman (under Segal label). Barkan Altitude reds are high-quality.

Binyamina Gal, Sam r w ★→★★ Aromatic Gewurz (s/dr sw). Cave is best red.

Carmel Up Gal, Shom r w sp ★★→★★★ Founded in 1882 by a Rothschild. Strong v'yd presence in Upper Galilee. Elegant Limited Edition (03 04' 05 07'). Award-winning Kayoumi v'yd Shiraz. Excellent old-vine Carignan and Petite Sirah. New Mediterranean-style blend. Well-balanced Cab Fr. Luscious Gewurz dessert.

Château Golan Gol r (w) ★★→★★★ Beautiful winery. Geshem (r w) are Mediterranean blends to follow. Flavourful Syrah.

Chillag Gal r ★★ Elegant Merlot and rare, full-bodied Petite Sirah.

Clos de Gat Jud r w ★★★ Classy estate with big, blowsy wines. The spicy, powerful Sycra Syrah (04' 06 07) and buttery Chard are superb.

Dalton Up Gal r w ★★ Aromatic, wild-yeast Viognier. Flagship is rich, dark Matatia.

Domaine du Castel Jud r w ★★★★ Family estate in Jerusalem mts. Consistently top performer with critics. Characterful, supple Grand Vin (03 04' 05 06' 07 08). Petit Castel great value. Outstanding "C" Blanc du Castel.

Ella Valley Jud r w ★★ Exquisite Chard. Huge Petite Sirah. Intense blend "E".

Flam Jud r (w) ★★→★★★ Family winery. Fine Cab Sauv, tight Merlot, earthy, herbal Syrah Cab. Classico gd value. New crisp, fragrant rosé.

Galil Mtn Up Gal r w ★→★★ Yiron firm blend. Fruity Pinot N. Owned by YARDEN.

Galilee Gal Quality region in north, esp higher altitude Upper Galilee [Up Gal].

Golan Heights Gol Volcanic plateau at an elevation of up to 1,200 metres.

Gvaot Shom r w ★★ Gd reds. Also innovative Chard/Cab Sauv blend.

Judean Hills Jud Mountainous region on the way to Jerusalem.

Kosher Means "pure". For Jews observing dietary laws. Not all Israeli wineries are kosher, but the best happen to be, so quality is not affected.

Lewinsohn Gal r w ★★ Quality *garagiste* in a garage! Creamy Chard.

Margalit Gal r ★★★ Father-and-son team making wines in a more elegant style, in particular Bordeaux blend Enigma (06 07' 08) and *Special Reserve*.

> **Old-vine paradise**
> Newly planted varieties are contributing to a quality revolution in the
> eastern and southern Mediterranean. However, there are as many
> old-vine v'yds in this area as anywhere. The new desire to make
> quality wines from low-yielding, old-bush vines is throwing up some
> interesting surprises. Look out for old-vine Carignans from Israel and
> Tunisia, Cinsault from Lebanon, Grenache and Syrah from Morocco.

Negev Neg Desert region in the south of the country.

Pelter Gol r w (sp) ★★→★★★ Tight, well-made reds. Trio gd value. V.gd Cab Fr.

Psagot Jud rw★→★★ Improving winery. Best: single-v'yd Cab Sauv.

Recanati Gal r w ★★ Showing more elegance lately. Excellent Special Res.

Samson Sam Region, inc the Judean plain and foothills, southeast of Tel Aviv.

Saslove Up Gal r (w) ★★ Father/daughter team; new winery; complex reds.

Sea Horse Jud r (w) ★→★★ Idiosyncratic *garagiste*. Exotic blends from unusual varieties.

Shomron Shom Region with v'yds around Mt Carmel and Zichron Ya'acov.

Shvo Up Gal New v'yd-led winery. High expectations. Watch this space.

Tabor L Gal r w sp ★→★★ Growing fast. Aromatic Sauv Bl. New sparkling wines.

Teperberg Jud, Sam r w ★ Efrat reborn. Malbec and Meritage are juicy reds.

Tishbi Jud, Shom r w ★ Deep Bordeaux blend from Sde Boker in desert, best yet.

Tulip Gal r (w) ★★ Winery workers are people with special needs. Excellent Shiraz blend and Syrah Res. Powerful wines, but great value.

Tzora Jud r w ★★→★★★ Big improvements. Misty Hills: fine blend, gd ageing potential.

Vitkin Jud r w ★★ Small winery. V.gd Carignan and Petite Sirah.

Yaffo Jud r w ★→★★★ Unsung winery, with elegant Cab and Chard.

Yarden Gal ★★★ Large winery producing six million bottles. Best wines under Yarden label. Cab Sauv consistently gd. Rare Bordeaux blend Katzrin (96 00' 03 04') and much-heralded Rom (06) are flagship wines. Outstanding Blanc de Blancs, Heights Wine dessert. New sparkling rosé. Also Gamla, Golan labels.

Yatir Jud, Neg r (w) ★★★→★★★★ Rich, velvety, concentrated Yatir Forest (02 03' 04 05' 06 07) outstanding. Edgy Shiraz, mouthfilling Cab Sauv and powerful Petit Verdot. Fragrant Viognier. Owned by CARMEL.

Lebanon

Since the civil war the number of wineries here has multiplied by six. Many new wineries are producing small quantities of hand-crafted wines, not just in the Bekaa Valley. Quality is on the rise. Interesting times for Lebanese wine.

Chateau Belle-Vue r ★★ Le Chateau and La Renaissance are top-notch reds.

Château Ka r w ★ Basic range promising, esp the white from Chard, Sauv, Sem.

Chateau Kefraya r w ★★→★★★ Spicy, minerally *Comte de M* (01' 02 04) from Cab, Syrah and Mourvèdre. Fruity, easy-drinking Les Bretèches. Refreshing rosé.

Château Khoury r w★ Young winery. Pioneer in Lebanon of Alsace varieties.

Chateau Ksara r w ★★→★★★ 150 yrs old but still progressive. Excellent-value wines. Res du Couvent has mouthfilling flavour. Top of range Troisième Millénaire (03' 04 05). Le Souverain of interest – from Cab Sauv and Arinarnoa.

Château Marsyas r ★→★★ Grand launch of new winery. First wines promising.

Chateau Musar r (w) ★★★ Unique, long-lasting Cab Sauv/Cinsault/Carignan red (95' 96' 99 00' 01 02 03). Legendary to some (1979 still splendid); past its best to others. Fruity Hochar red. Oaky white from indigenous Obaideh and Merwah.

Chateau Nakad r w ★ Traditional winery; Chateau des Coteaux red is spicy and oaky.

Clos St Thomas r w ★★ Gd quality, deep, silky red wines. Les Emirs great value.

Domaine de Baal r w ★★Promising start for new winery with organic v'yd.

Domaine des Tourelles r w ★→★★ Old winery reborn. Elegant Marquis des Beys.

Domaine Wardy r w ★→★★ New-World-style Private Selection. Crisp, fresh whites.

Heritage r w ★ Easy-drinking, fruity wines like Le Fleuron and Nouveau.

Ixsir Ambitious newcomer. One to watch.

Karam ★→★★ Promising boutique from Jezzine, south Lebanon. Cloud 9 gd value.

Massaya r w ★★ Silver Selection red is a complex Rhône-style blend showing sun and spice of Lebanon. Classic series with screwtop represents great value.

Turkey

International expertise, clever use of indigenous varieties and a desire to improve are producing interesting results. A new interest in exports. Grapes to look for are Kalecik Karasi, juicy and spicy; and the classic blend of Öküzgözü and Boğazkere. Main developments are in the Marmara region.

Boğazkere Tannic, indigenous red variety. Produces full-bodied wines.

Büyülübağ r (w) ★★ Hope for the future. New boutique winery. Good Cab Sauv.

Corvus r w ★★→★★★ Boutique winery on Bozcaada island. Corpus is powerful.

Doluca r w ★→★★ Large winery. Karma label blends local and classic varieties.

Kavaklidere r w sp ★→★★ Large winery in Ankara. Turkish variety specialists.

Kayra r w ★→★★ Reincarnation of state enterprise Tekel. Promising Shiraz.

Likya r w ★ New Mediterranean winery nr Anatalya.

Narince White variety. Can produce fresh, fruity wines.

Öküzgözü Soft, fruity local red variety. Often blended with BOGAZKERE.

Sarafin r w ★→★★ Good Cab Sauv and Sauv Bl. Brand owned by DOLUCA.

Sevilen r w ★Fumé Blanc with great acidity. Good Shiraz.

Turasan r w ★ Situated in volcanic rock of Cappodocia.

NORTH AFRICA

New investors are making North Africa a place of interest again. Algeria has most potential, but falls behind because of religion and politics. Progress in Tunisia and particularly in Morocco. Most interesting are old-vine Carignans, newly planted Syrahs and traditional *vin gris*.

Castel Frères Mor ★ Owner of Sahari, Meknes and Boulaoune facilities. Gd-value brands like Bonassia, El Baraka, Halana, Larroque and Mayole.

Celliers de Meknes, Les Mor r p w ★→★★★ Dominates Moroccan market. Modern facility Château Roselane. Gd-value Riad Jamil Carignan.

Ceptunes Tun r w ★ Promising winery using classic varieties.

Domaine Atlas Tun r w ★ Austrian-Tunisian joint venture. Gd Carignan and Syrah.

Domaine Neferis Tun r p w ★→★★ Calastrasi joint venture. Selian Carignan best.

Kurubis Tun r w sp ★ Producers of traditional-method sparkling wine.

Les Deux Domaines Mor r ★★→★★★ Depardieu and Bernard Magrez joint venture. Magrez Kahina and Depardieu Lumière are powerful Syrah/Grenache blends.

Sahara Vineyards Egy w ★ Project by big producer, Gianaclis, to upgrade wines.

Thalvin Mor r p w ★→★★ Gd whites. Tandem: spicy Syrah with Alan Graillot (Rhône).

Val d'Argan Mor r p ★ Organically grown v'y'ds nr Essaouira on west coast.

Vignerons de Carthage Tun r p w ★ Best from UCCV co-op: Clipea Chard, Kelibia dry Muscat and Magon Magnus red. Encouraging foreign partners.

Vins d'Algerie Alg r ★ OCNC marketing company. Top blend: Cuvée du President. Wines named after regions: Mascara, Medea and Tlemcen.

Volubilia Mor ★★ r p w Promising new joint venture. Excellent *vin gris*.

Asia & Old Russian Empire

ASIA

China Foreign investment is pouring into China, trying to take advantage of what the whole wine world regards as its greatest potential market. Château Lafite has a joint venture in Shandong; Stephan von Niepperg of Bordeaux and Bulgaria (*see* Bessa Valley) has another. France's Pernod Ricard is involved in Domaine Helan Mountain, and Spain's Torres with Grace Vineyards (its Symphony brand has won plaudits) and Silver Heights (a gd Bordeaux blend). Around 220 producers make some 725 million litres of wine, with large brands such as Dynasty, China Great Wall and Changyu Pioneer accounting for 40% of the industry. Around 90% of Chinese wine consumption is red and Cab Sauv dominates new plantings, making mostly thin, tart, unripe wines that are pleasant neither with Chinese food nor alone. Qverall quality is still low, but smaller artisan winemaking operations such as Catai and Huadong are showing signs of real quality.

India's wine industry could hardly be said to be flourishing: a glut of local wine has meant that many wineries in Maharashtra have closed or reduced production, and grape prices have fallen. Lavish subsidies had encouraged unrealistic expansion, and the industry needs to rebalance. Wine is an expensive form of alcohol here, appealing only to wealthier classes who aspire to Western trappings of success. There is clear evidence that quality wine can be made, particularly in Nashik, nr Mumbai, and at Karnataka, south of Goa. Cab Sauv, Merlot, Syrah and Pinot N for reds; Chenin Bl, Sauv Bl, Chard and Ries for whites. Interestingly, the red/white split is about 50/50. The most notable names are Chateau Indage, Grover Vineyards and Sula Vineyards, creating consistent wines of strong varietal character.

Japan Surprisingly to most people, Japan has been making wine for over 135 yrs. Nearly all of it has been drunk locally, though since 2010 small parcels of Japanese wine have been exported to Britain and elsewhere. Locally, supermarkets dominate the cheaper end of the market (about 50% of total Japanese wine market sells at less than 900 Yen – the same price as a bottle of Heineken in a bar), with department stores and wine shops selling top-end wines, especially for gifts. Well-priced local wines are beginning to compete with global brands. This is being helped by Japanese wines gaining in quality, often supported by international winemakers such as Denis Dubourdieu and Bernard Magrez. The fact is that good wine is being made in Japan despite a climate of high humidity and consistent rainfall during the growing season, and fertile yet acidic soils. The search for new regions continues but seems to be hampered by poor spring conditions. The most dynamic winemaking industry is still centred in the horticultural prefectures (regions) of Yamanashi and Hokkaido, with the indigenous Koshu grape being Japan's point of difference. It is *vinifera* and its history dates back many hundreds of years, making lightly aromatic whites – most being perfectly pleasant but unremarkable. Since 2009, however, gold medals have been given each year to Koshu in international wine competitions. Other local wines are mostly from hybrid varieties: Muscat Bailey A, Black Queen and Yama Sauvignon. Chard, Cab Sauv and Merlot are minor varieties in small microclimates. It is impossible to know whether these traditional varieties are authentic – local laws allow up to 95% imported wine must to be blended with a small fraction of local wine and still be called "Wine of Japan".

The industry continus to be driven by the large brewery companies Mercian, Sapporo and Suntory, but there are about 250 producers in all. Consistency is still an issue for winemakers, but look for Grace Wines, Katsunuma Winery, Obuse, Haramo and Takahata Wines.

OLD RUSSIAN EMPIRE

Crimea may still be mistakenly called a Russian wine region; Georgian Saperavi might be unfamiliar to most wine-lovers, but international curiosity about winemaking in the former Soviet Union is on the up. Good modern wines can be found in all countries, although winemakers need to address consistency. Many are made with familiar grapes; in the future differences will be created by the use of exciting local varieties, especially in Georgia. A new wave of small producers is emerging.

Georgia Winemaking for over 7,000 yrs; ancient methods, ie. fermentation in clay vats *(kwevris)*, still exist, but are gradually being supplanted by modern methods. (Kwevris are becoming cult in some circles.) There are around 500 indigenous grape varieties. Most popular: red Saperavi (intense, structured) and white Rkatsiteli (lively, refreshing). There are five defined areas. Of around 50,000 ha total, 70% is produced in Kakheti (southeast). Producers: Tbilvino, Telavi Wine Cellar, Teliani Veli, Shumi, Askaneli. Foreign investors have developed, among others, GWS (Pernod Ricard), Vinoterra and Pheasant's Tears. In small producers, look for Chandrebi, Glakhuna, Khetsuriani, Metekhi, Schuchmann.

Moldova Just about everybody makes wine here, and there is lots of potential, but so far results are patchy. European grapes are widely used, with gd results for Chard, Sauv Bl, Pinot Gr, Merlot, Cab Sauv. Quality leaders: Acorex Wine Holding, Vina ria Bostavan (DAOS range), Château Vartely (Traminer, Merlot), Dionysos Mereni (Carlevana Res range, late-harvest, Icewine Ries), DK Intertrade, Vina ria Purcari (Negru de Purcari), Lion Gri (sparkling, Sauv Bl, Merlot), Cricova (sparkling).

Russia There are 65,000 ha of v'yds in the southwest of the country. The Krasnodar region, with plantations close to the Black Sea coast, leads in production. European and local cold-resistant varieties are grown; Aligoté is particularly exciting, also big improvements with Chard, Sauv Bl, Merlot, Pinot N. Vinodelnya Vedernikoff successfully experiments with local white Sibirkovy, red Krasnostop and Tsimliansky. Premium ranges are offered by Chateau le Grand Vostock (Cuvée Karsov, Chêne Royal), Fanagoria (Cru Lermont), Myskhako (Grand Reserve). Quality sparkling wines are now revived by Abrau-Durso (Premium and Imperial ranges), Tsimlianskiye Vina (esp original red sweet Tsimlianskoye), Villa Victoria.

Ukraine The Odessa region dominates grape-growing and wine production, but Crimea has better quality potential, yet to be realized in full. Traditionally the best wines were modelled on Sherry, Port and Madeira – and Champagne – historic producers, such as Massandra, Magarach and Solnechnaya Dolina, have kept great cellars. Gd examples of fortified styles are made by Massandra, Koktebel, Dionis. Novy Svet and Artyomovsk Winery produce traditional-method sparkling wines. Inkerman and Odessavinprom are known for dry wines. New names to watch: Veles (Kolonist brand), Guliev Wines.

North America

WASHINGTON
OREGON
IDAHO
NEVADA
CALIFORNIA
COLORADO
WISCONSIN
MICHIGAN
PENNSYLVANIA
OHIO
MISSOURI
VIRGINIA
NEW ENGLAND
NEW YORK/
NEW JERSEY
GEORGIA
TEXAS

NORTH COAST Mendocino Sierra Foothills
Anderson Redwood Valley
Valley
Clear Lake
Clear Lake
Sonoma Coast
Northern
Sonoma
Sonoma Carneros
Valley
Sacramento
Napa Valley
Lodi
El Dorado
Shenandoah V
Amador
Calaveras
CENTRAL
VALLEY

Santa Cruz
Mountains

NEVADA

Lake Tahoe

Sacramento

San Francisco

Livermore Valley

Santa Clara Valley

Monterey *Salinas*

San Joaquin

O Fresno

Carmel Valley Arroyo Seco CENTRAL COAST
Santa Lucia
Highlands San Lucas

Pacific Ocean

Paso Robles

CALIFORNIA

NORTH AMERICA

San Luis Obispo
Edna Valley/Arroyo GV
Santa Maria Valley
Santa Barbara
Santa Rita Hills
Santa Ynez Valley

Santa Barbara

Abbreviations used in the text
(*see also* Principal Vineyard
Areas p.232, p.247):

O Los Angeles

Ct	Connecticut
Id	Idaho
Mont	Monterey, Ca
Mend	Mendocino, Ca
NJ	New Jersey
San LO	San Luis Obispo, Ca
Santa Cz Mts	Santa Cruz Mountains, Ca
Sierra F'Hills	Sierra Foothills, Ca
Tex	Texas
Vir	Virginia
Y Car	Yamhill-Carlton, Or

CALIFORNIA

California wine just won't stand still. Just when you think you have it in focus, something pops up just outside the frame. The root of this variety might be that California wine was in the beginning a family affair, and to a certain extent still is. Despite corporate inroads, it isn't unusual to find multi-generation winemakers and growers. A family feud might split the business, but chances are the kids are back striking out on their own with their own ideas. Californians are innovators, looking over the horizon for something new: sometimes the results are good, sometimes not so good. But it keeps it interesting.

Principal vineyard areas

There are hundreds of AVAs in California, some key, some insignificant. Below are the key AVAs mentioned in the text. *See also* box, p. 256.

Alexander Valley (Alex V) Sonoma. Warm region in upper RRV. Gd Sauv Bl nr river; Cab Sauv, Zin on hillsides.

Anderson Valley (And V) Mendocino. Cool Pacific fog and winds follow Navarro River inland; Ries, Gewürz, Pinot N; Zin on benchlands above river.

Arroyo Seco Monterey Warm AVA; gd Cab Sauv, Chard.

Carneros (Car) Napa, Sonoma. Cool AVA at north tip of San Francisco Bay. Pinot N, Chard; Merlot on warmer sites. V.gd sparkling wine.

Dry Creek Valley (Dry CV) Sonoma. Outstanding Zin; Sauv Bl, Cab Sauv and Zin on hillsides above valley floor.

Edna Valley (Edna V) San Luis Obispo. Cool Pacific winds; minerally Chard.

Howell Mtn Napa. Classic Napa Cab Sauv from steep hillside v'yds.

Mt Veeder Napa. High mtn v'yds for Chard, Cab Sauv.

Napa Valley (Napa V) Napa. Cab Sauv, Merlot, Cab Fr. Look to sub-AVAs for meaningful, terroir-based wines. Note Napa V is an area within Napa.

Oakville (Oak) Napa Prime Cab Sauv territory.

Paso Robles (P Rob) San Luis Obispo. Excellent Zin, Rhône varietals; Cab.

Red Hills Lake County. Promising for Cab Sauv, Zin on cooler hillsides.

Redwood Valley Mendocino. Warmer inland region; Zin, Cab Sauv, Sauv Bl.

Russian River Valley (RRV) Sonoma. Cool Pacific fog lingers; Pinot N, Chard, Zin on benchland.

Rutherford (Ruth) Napa. Outstanding Cab Sauv, esp hillside v'yds.

Saint Helena Napa. Lovely balanced Cab Sauv; v.gd Sauv Bl.

Santa Lucia Highlands (Santa LH) Monterey. Higher elevation; Pinot N, Syrah, Rhônes.

Santa Maria Valley (Santa MH) Santa Barbara. Coastal cool; Pinot N, Chard, Viognier.

Sta Rita Hills (Sta RH) Santa Barbara. Excellent Pinot N; for legal reasons calls itself Sta rather than Santa.

Santa Ynez (Santa Y) Santa Barbara. Rhônes, Chard, Sauv Bl the best bet.

Sonoma Coast (Son Coast) Sonoma. V. cool climate; edgy Pinot N.

Sonoma Valley (Son V) Sonoma. Gd. Chard, v.gd. Zin; excellent Cab Sauv from Sonoma Mountain (Son Mtn) sub-AVA. Note Sonoma V is an area within Sonoma.

Spring Mtn Napa. Terrific Cab Sauv; v.gd Sauv Bl.

Stags Leap (Stags L) Napa. Classic Cab Sauv; v.gd Merlot.

Recent vintages

Its size and wide range of microclimates make it impossible to produce a one-size-fits-all vintage report for California. Its climate is not as consistent as its "land of sunshine" reputation suggests. Although grapes ripen regularly, they are often subject to spring frosts, sometimes a wet harvest time and (too often) drought. The following vintage assessment relies most heavily on evaluation of Cab Sauv from North Coast regions. For Chard, the best vintages are: 07 08 09.

2010 A very difficult year. Wet spring, cool summer, harvest rain – below-average crop. Picking of some red varieties continued into November. Quality uncertain. Cab Sauv could be good if handled right.

2009 A superb growing season; ample winter and spring rainfall assured even growth. Red and white wines show good balance and ageing potential.

2008 September heat led to early harvest; most grapes picked two to three weeks earlier than normal. Concern acid levels are low. Uneven quality.

2007 Rains in late September and October meant that results were mixed, especially for Cab Sauv on the North Coast.

2006 Above-average. Good Pinot N, Chard. Cab Sauv improving with age.

2004 Some of the early promise has faded. Wines for short-term consumption.

2003 A difficult year all around. Overall, spotty.

2002 The growing season was cool, and quality superior.

2001 Excellent Cab Sauv. Drink in the next year or two.

Abreu Vineyards Napa V ★★★ 03 05 06 Massive Cab Sauv with ageing potential.

Acacia Car ★★★ (Pinot N) 05 06 07 Carneros pioneer in Chard and Pinot N, featuring single-v'yd wines. Also an excellent Viognier.

Alban Vineyards Edna V ★★→★★★ Got into Rhône game early. Excellent Viognier. Grenache, Roussanne, Marsanne also top. Most grapes from Santa B.

Alma Rosa Santa RH ★★★ Richard Sanford, a master Pinot N whizz, is making lovely Pinot N and Chard from organic v'yds at his new winery. Also v.gd Pinot Gr and Vin Gris from Pinot N.

Altamura Vineyards Napa V ★★★ 00 01 02 03 04 05 06 08 Cab Sauv is outstanding, with a firm structure and deep flavours; also a gd Sangiovese.

Amador Foothills Winery Sierra F'hills ★★→★★★ Top Zin and a bright, zingy Sauv Bl. Katie's Côte, new bottling of Rhône varieties, is a winner.

Andrew Murray Santa B ★★★ Rhônes around the clock here. Outstanding Viognier and Roussanne among the whites and a solid Syrah.

Araujo Napa V ★★★★ 00 02 03 04 05 06 08 Powerful but never over-the-top cult Cab Sauv made from historic Eisele v'yd.

Artesa Car ★★→★★★ Owned by the Raventós family of Spain (Codorníu). Artesa wines are sourced from estate v'yds and other Northern California v'yds. Best shot here is the Carneros Chard. Also a gd Tempranillo.

Arthur Earl Santa B ★★★ Artisan bottlings of mostly Rhône varietals, splashing out with an occasional Italian plus a fine Zin.

Aubin Cellars ★★→★★★ An ambitious selection of wines from v'yds from central California to Washington. Pinot N and Syrah can be v.gd.

Au Bon Climat Santa B ★★★→★★★★ Owner Jim Clendenen listens to his private drummer, with outstanding results; ultra-toasty Chard, flavourful Pinot N, light-hearted Pinot Bl. Vita Nova label (Bordeaux varieties), Podere Olivos (Italianates). See QUPÉ.

Babcock Vineyards Santa Y ★★★ V.gd Pinot N, Chard and Sauv Bl from cool-climate v'yds nr the Pacific. Grand Cuvée Pinot N is outstanding.

Balletto RRV ★★★ Look for outstanding estate Chard and single-v'yd Pinot N. Also a cheerful dry rosé Pinot N and a v.gd Pinot Gr.

Barnett Vineyards Napa V ★★★ Sources grapes from several v'yds; range of v.gd to outstanding wines. Carneros Chard a treat, as is the spicy Tina Maria Pinot N (RRV). Also Spring Mtn Merlot from estate-grown, steeply terraced vines.

Beaulieu Vineyard Napa V ★★→★★★ **00 03** 05 06 07 Not the jewel it was when André Tchelistcheff was setting the style for Napa Cab Sauv more than half a century ago, but still worth looking out for, esp the Georges de Latour Private Reserve Cab Sauv. Decent budget wines under the Beaulieu Coastal label.

Beckman Santa B ★★→★★★ The focus here is on Rhône varietals with a California punch. Purisima Mtn V'yd red, a blend of Grenache and Syrah, is a gd example of Beckman's gutsy approach. Also a gd Sauv Bl.

Benessere Napa V ★★→★★★ Basic Sangiovese a winner. Super-Tuscan-style blend called Phenomenon can be outstanding.

Benovia Son V ★★★ Silky and balanced cool-climate Chard has a rich, creamy centre that is pure yummy.

Benziger Family Winery Son V ★★★ A leader in biodynamic movement. Top bottlings are estate-grown Cab Sauv, Merlot, Sauv Bl.

Beringer Blass Napa ★→★★★ (Cab) **00** 01 03 05 07 A Napa classic, now owned by Foster's. Single-v'yd Cab Sauv Reserves can sometimes be over the top, but otherwise worthy of ageing. Velvety, powerful Howell Mtn Merlot one of the best. Look for Founder's Estate bargain bottlings. Also owns CHÂTEAU ST JEAN ★★→★★★, ETUDE, Meridian ★, ST CLEMENT ★★★, STAGS' LEAP WINERY ★ and Taz, a brawny ★★ Pinot from Santa B.

Boeger Central V ★★→★★★ Mostly estate wines; attractive Merlot, Barbera, Zin and Meritage. More understated than many in SIERRA FOOTHILLS and always reliable.

Bogle Vineyards Central V ★→★★ Major grower in the Sacramento Delta, the Bogle family makes an attractive line of consistently gd and affordable wines. Look especially for the Old Vine Zin.

Bokisch Lodi ★★→★★★ The focus is on Spanish varieties at this family estate from the Lodi AVA. Garnacha, Albariño and Tempranillo show gd varietal character. Tempranillo esp impressive.

Bonny Doon Santa Cz Mts ★★★→★★★★ Original Rhône Ranger Randall Grahm has slashed production, selling off his budget brands to concentrate on single-v'yd biodynamic wines with v.gd results. The flagship *Le Cigare Volant* is better than ever. Also attractive Sangiovese and Dolcetto under the Ca'Del Solo label.

Bonterra *See* FETZER.

Bouchaine Vineyards Car ★★→★★★ Chard; juicy but serious single-v'yd Pinot N.

Brander Vineyards Santa Y ★★★ Focus on Sauv Bl, consistently one of best in state.

Bronco Wine Company Founded by Fred Franzia, nephew of Ernest GALLO. Franzia sources inexpensive Central Valley grapes for his well-known Charles Shaw Two Buck Chuck brand. Also fields other labels, inc Napa Creek and Napa Ridge. Quality is not the point: Franzia is selling wine as a popular beverage.

Buehler Napa ★★→★★★ Winery has had ups and downs but is looking v.gd of late. The estate Cab Sauv is brambly with good structure. Also look for an outstanding Zin from Napa grapes and a v.gd Chard from RRV fruit.

Buena Vista Car ★★★ Sonoma's most historic winery now focuses on Chard and Pinot N from Carneros estate.

Burgess Cellars Napa V ★★★ (Cab) 03 05 07 Cab Sauv from Howell Mtn grapes is splendid, sleek and powerful while remaining balanced.

Cain Cellars Napa V ★★★→★★★★ 03 05 07 One of NAPA's jewels, with consistent bottlings of Cain Five, a supple and elegant red wine based on Cab Sauv and its four Bordeaux cousins, from Spring Mtn grapes.

Cakebread Napa V ★★★→★★★★ **01 02** 03 05 06 07 Quality improving with each vintage; Cab Sauv shows great balance and harmony. Also a gd Sauv Bl.

Calera ★★★★ 07 08 09 Josh Jensen fell in love with Pinot N while at Oxford. He makes three supple, fine Pinot Ns named after v'yd blocks in the dry hills of San Benito, inland from Monterey: Reed, Seleck and Jensen; also intense Viognier.

Carter Cellars Napa V ★★★ Hossfeld V'yds Red Blend is the best of a batch of solid Cab Sauv-based blends: good mouthfeel with a layering of spice and black pepper, and bold fruit with a big finish that stops happily well short of jammy.

Caymus Napa V ★★★→★★★★ oo oi 05 06 07 The Special Selection Cab Sauv is consistently one of California's most formidable: rich, intense, slow to mature. Also a regular bottling, balanced and a little lighter. Gd Chard from Mer Soleil in Monterey, inc an unoaked Chard called Silver.

C Donatiello RRV ★★→★★★ Newcomer producing gd Chard and Pinot N from selected organic v'yds in cool growing regions. Floodgate Pinot N esp attractive.

Ceago Vinegarden Lake ★★→★★★ Jim Fetzer, well settled into his biodynamic ranch on Clear Lake in Lake County, produces v.gd Sauv Bl and Cab Sauv.

Ceja Vineyards Napa ★★→★★★ One of a few California wineries owned by former Mexican v'yd workers. Cab Sauv, Carneros Chard top the list.

Cesar Toxqui Cellars Mend ★★★ Toxqui came north from Mexico when he was 16, and landed his first job at FETZER V'YDS. Makes a tiny amount of Pinot N from organic v'yds in Lake and Mendocino counties – superb and worth the search.

Chalk Hill Son ★★→★★★ Cab Sauv with ageing potential; buttery Chard.

Chalone Mont ★★★ Historic mtn estate on rare limestone above Salinas Valley in Monterey. Marvellous flinty Chard and rich, intense Pinot N.

Chappellet Napa V ★★★ oi 03 05 06 07 08 Serious, age-worthy Cab Sauv, *esp Signature label*. Pleasing Chard; gd Cab Fr, Merlot. Dry Chenin Bl is one of best.

Charles Krug Napa V ★★→★★★ Historically important; on the up under 3rd generation of (the other) Mondavi family. Attractive Sauv Bl and a v.gd Cab Sauv.

Château Montelena Napa V ★★★ →★★★★ (Chard) 07 08 09 (Cab) 99 00 oi 03 05 06 Historic winery has avoided the fruit-bomb Cab Sauv trend. Balanced wines capable of at least a decade of ageing; also one of the rare age-worthy Chards.

Château St Jean Son ★★→★★★ Sonoma standout has gone through many changes since Richard Arrowood days, but still produces reliable Sauv Bl, Chard and a gd red blend, Cinq Cépages, made from the five Bordeaux red varieties.

Chimney Rock Stags L ★★★→★★★★ (Cab) 97 99 00 oi 03 05 07 Elegant, understated Cab Sauv; capable of long ageing.

Christopher Creek Son ★★→★★★ The estate Petite Sirah from RRV grapes revived faith in the variety. Try the lean and brambly Cab Sauv and a honeyed Viognier.

Claiborne & Churchill Santa B ★★★ The focus here is Alsace with a consistently top-rated Ries, v.gd Pinot Gr and Gewürz.

Clark-Clauden Napa V ★★★→★★★★ Balanced and elegant Cab Sauv with focused fruit and lasting wrap-around flavours. A much *underrated* producer.

Clavo Cellars P Rob ★★→★★★ Veteran grower Neil Roberts' venture into winemaking is a grand success. Collusion, his Bordeaux red blend, is a deeply flavoured, powerful wine with a touch of finesse. The Syrah is v.gd, as is the Zin.

Cliff Lede Stags L ★★★ Outstanding new producer of balanced, elegant Cab Sauv. The wines are built to age, featuring bright minerality backed by dark black-cherry fruit and a rich but supple intensity.

Clos du Bois Son ★★→★★★ Large-scale producer of quaffable everyday wines, single-v'yd Cab Sauv (Briarcrest) and Calcaire Chard can be v.gd.

Clos du Val Napa V ★★→★★★ Consistently elegant Cab Sauvs that are among the best ageing candidates in the state. *Chard is a delight* and a Sem/Sauv Bl blend called Ariadne is a charmer.

Cobb Wines Son ★★→★★★ Father-son team makes excellent Pinot N from Son Coast v'yds. The Coastlands V'yd bottling is three-star quality, with bright fruit and true varietal character.

Conn Creek Napa V ★★★ oi 03 05 06 07 V.gd Cab Sauv from several Napa V v'yds; elegant wines with gd structure and long ageing potential.

Constellation ★→★★★ Owns wineries in California, NY, Washington State, Canada, Chile, Australia, NZ. Produces 90 million cases annually, selling more than any other wine company in the world. Once a bottom-feeder, now going for the top. Bought ROBERT MONDAVI at end of 2004 and also owns FRANCISCAN V'YD, Estancia, Mount Veeder, RAVENSWOOD, Simi, among others.

Corison Napa V ★★★★ 95 96 97 99 00 01 02 05 06 07 Cathy Corison is a treasure of a winemaker. While many in Napa V follow the $iren call of overextracted, powerhouse wines delivering big numbers from critics but no satisfaction in the glass, Corison continues to make flavoursome, *age-worthy Cab Sauv.*

Cornerstone Cellars Howell Mtn ★★★ 00 01 02 03 05 07 Celia Mayzczek consults, impressive Cab Sauv, with a focus on harmony and balance. Also look for Stepping Stone label featuring small lots of wine from select Napa V v'yds.

Cuvaison Napa V ★★★ (Cab) 00 01 02 05 Gd to sometimes v.gd Chard, Merlot, Syrah from Carneros. Impressive Cab Sauv from Mt Veeder.

Dalla Valle Napa V ★★★ 00 01 03 05 06 07 Hillside estate with a cult following for Maya, a Cab Sauv-based, deeply extracted wine that is slow to develop.

Dashe Cellars Dry CV ★★★ It's all about Zin here, with several single-v'yd bottlings every year. Classic Dry CV style – balanced and layered with black raspberry, clove and black pepper. Should develop in the bottle over 5–10 yrs.

David Arthur Vineyards Napa V ★★→★★★ 01 03 04 05 07 Classic Napa V Cab Sauv, balanced and bright on the palate; also gd Sauv Bl.

David Bruce Santa Cz Mts ★★★ Legendary mtn estate is still on top of the game with powerful, long-lasting Chard and superb Pinot N.

Davis Bynum Son ★★★ Bynum pioneered often superb single-v'yd Pinot N in the RRV. Chard: lean, minerally, silky mouthfeel. Owned by Rodney Strong V'yds.

Dehlinger Son ★★★★ (Pinot) 06 07 08 09 Outstanding Pinot N from estate RRV v'yd. Also gd Chard and Syrah.

Del Carlo Dry CV ★★→★★★ New winery from the Teldeschi family, long-time growers in Dry CV. Terrific Zin from century-old vines; Cab Sauv has intense black cherry and blueberry fruit with the structure to age 8–10 yrs.

Delicato Vineyards ★→★★★ One-time Central Valley jug producer has moved upscale with purchase of Monterey v'yds and several new bottlings from Lodi. Watch this brand for gd quality at everyday price.

De Loach Vineyards Son ★★ Owned by Boisset Wines US, De Loach offers gd to v.gd *single-v'yd Chard,* Pinot N and Zin from mostly RRV sites at a reasonable price.

Derbrès Son ★★★ Elegant, nuanced Chard and Pinot N from cool-climate v'yds in Carneros and RRV. The Pinot N is aromatic with gd acidity; Chard is balanced with a rich, full mouthfeel and a touch of spice.

Diamond Creek Napa V ★★★★ 91 94 95 99 00 01 03 06 Austere, stunning cult Cabs from hilly v'yd nr Calistoga go by names of v'yd blocks: Gravelly Meadow, Volcanic Hill, Red Block Terrace. Wines age beautifully. One of Napa's jewels.

Domaine Carneros Car ★★★ Showy US outpost of Taittinger in Napa V, Domaine

---

A Central Coast winner

California's Central Coast seems to have it all. There are Chard, Syrah and other Rhône varietals, both red and white, as well as some excellent Zins. Add Sauv Bl to that list. It is a food-friendly choice, esp with the spicy flavours of Asian-inspired dishes becoming more popular in the USA. It can be made in a variety of styles – from the grassy boxwood styles to wines showing tropical-fruit flavours backed by subtle spices. Among newer producers look esp for JUSTIN, VINA ROBLES and WRATH VINEYARDS.

Carneros echoes austere style of its parent in Champagne (*see* France), but with a delicious dollop of California fruit. Vintage Blanc de Blancs v.gd. La Rêve the luxury *cuvée*. Still Pinot N and Chard also impressive.

Domaine Chandon ★★→★★★ Napa V branch of Champagne house. Look for the NV Res called Etoile, esp the rosé.

Dominus Estate Napa V ★★★★ 97 99 01 02 05 06 07 08 Christian Moueix of Pomerol makes red Bordeaux blend that is slow to open but ages beautifully.

Donkey & Goat ★★★ One of the trendy "urban wineries" that have sprung up in the San Francisco Bay Area. Hard to find but worth a search, esp two bottlings of Syrah: one from El Dorado (Sierra F'hills), other from old vines in Mendocino.

Donum Estate Car ★★★ Pinot N only, worth seeking out. Sleek and supple with a silky mouthfeel and long, wrap-around finish. Flirting with four stars.

Dry Creek Vineyard Dry CV ★★ V. impressive new line of Zin from old vines and heritage vines. Sauv (Fumé) Bl set standard for California for decades. Still impressive. Pleasing Chenin Bl; gd Zin.

Duckhorn Vineyards Napa V ★★★→★★★★ Known for dark, tannic, almost plummy-ripe, single-v'yd Merlots (esp Three Palms) and Cab Sauv-based blend Howell Mtn. New winery in Anderson V for Golden Eye Pinot N, robust style more akin to Cab Sauv. Makes a Zin/Cab Sauv blend in Paraduxx, a second Napa V winery.

Dunn Vineyards Howell Mtn ★★★★ 91 95 97 99 01 03 06 07 Owner Randy Dunn makes superb and *intense Cab Sauv* from Howell Mtn, which ages magnificently; milder bottling from valley floor. One of a few Napa V winemakers to resist the stampede to jammy, lush wines to curry wine critics' favour.

Dutcher Crossing Dry CV ★★ Fairly complex Cab Sauv with a splash of Syrah shows bright fruit and a long finish, marred by a little heat from high alcohol. Decant.

Dutton-Goldfield Son ★★★ Winemaker-grower duo crafting outstanding Pinot N and Chard from top cool-climate sites; modern California classics.

Eberle San LO ★★→★★★ Gary Eberle offers a solid Cab Sauv and a range of Rhône styles, most in a muscular but balanced idiom. New is an outstanding Viognier.

Edmunds St John ★★→★★★ Steve Edmunds and wife Cornelia St John are dedicated to Rhône varieties. From leased space in Berkeley they make outstanding wines chosen from a jumble of California v'yds. The line-up changes from vintage to vintage but is always worth a look, esp the treatment of Grenache.

Edna Valley Vineyard Edna V ★★★ Much improved in past few vintages; v.gd Chard, crisp and fruity, *lovely Sauv Bl*, impressive Syrah.

Elke Vineyards And V ★★→★★★ Elegant, silky Pinot N in the Diamond Series; starter Pinot N with forward fruit under Mary Elke label from Mendocino v'yds.

Envy Cellars Napa V ★★★→★★★★ A new venture from ace winemaker Nils Venge; welcome addition to the Napa line-up. Surprisingly, Venge, who made his name with Cab Sauv, is focused on Petite Sirah: stunning Vaca Mtn, dark fruit balanced with peppery spice. Nord V'yd is v.gd with a lighter hand on the fruit.

Etude *See* BERINGER BLASS.

Failla Napa V ★★→★★★ Winery on the Silverado Trail in Napa V, gaining a reputation for Son Coast and RRV Pinot N and Chard.

Far Niente Napa V ★★★ (Cab) 00 01 03 05 07 Opulence is the goal in both Cab Sauv and Chard from luxury Napa V estate. Can go over the top.

Ferrari-Carano Son ★★→★★★ Wines from this showcase estate in Dry CV have been erratic in recent yrs. Cab Sauv is slow to open. Merlot is reliable and sometimes v.gd. Pinot N and a gd Gewürz.

Fetzer Vineyards Mend ★★→★★★ A leader in the organic/sustainable-viticulture movement, Fetzer has produced consistent-value wines from least-expensive range (Sundial, Valley Oaks) to brilliant Res wines. Also owns BONTERRA v'yds (all organic grapes) where *Roussanne and Marsanne are stars*.

CALIFORNIA

Ficklin Vineyards Madera ★★★ Lush and delicious Port-style dessert wines made from the classic Portuguese varieties.

Firestone Santa Y ★★ Pioneer offers excellent Sauv Bl and lively off-dry Ries.

Flora Springs Wine Co Napa V ★★★ Best are two Meritage wines, red Trilogy and white Soliloquy, made from v'yds above valley floor. Juicy Merlot worth a look.

Flowers Vineyard & Winery Son ★★★ Intense, terroir-driven Pinot N, Chard from v. cool-climate vines. Has won early critical acclaim; clearly a winery to watch.

Fontanella Mt Veeder ★★→★★★ Solid Cab Sauv and Zin. Top hand right now is the Cab Sauv, showing excellent balance with intriguing coffee-blueberry flavours.

Foppiano Son ★★→★★★ One of the grand old families in California wine. You can count on the Zin every time, but look esp for Petite Sirah, better known as "petty sir" among the California rearguard.

Forman Vineyard Napa V ★★★★ 00 01 03 05 07 Winemaker who found fame at STERLING in 1970s now makes his own v.gd Cab Sauv and Chard from mtn v'yds.

Fortress Wines Lake ★★★ A new producer with an emphasis on Petite Sirah and Sauv Bl from mtn fruit. Keep an eye on Fortress, a California rising star.

Foxen Santa MV ★★★ Foxen has a way with Pinot N and Chard that is hard to beat. My current favourite is the Tinaquaic V'yd Chard, showing brilliant fruit and a delicious lean structure. A splendid wine.

Franciscan Vineyard Napa V ★★★ Quality has been maintained under CONSTELLATION ownership, esp the top-of-the-line wines such as the graceful red Magnificat and the Cuvée Sauvage Chard. Gd budget wines under Estancia label.

Freeman RRV ★★★ Freeman has developed a cult following with outstanding cool-climate Pinot N (Akiko's Cuvée from Son Coast) and RRV Pinot N.

Freemark Abbey Napa V ★★★→★★★★ Historic and currently underrated but consistent producer of *stylish Cab Sauv to age*. Single-v'yd Sycamore and Bosché bottlings often reach ★★★★.

Frog's Leap Ruth ★★★→★★★★★ 00 01 02 03 05 07 Small winery, as charming as its name (and T-shirts) suggests. Lean, *minerally Sauv Bl*, toasty Chard, spicy Zin. Supple and delicious Merlot, Cab Sauv. Converting to organic and biodynamic with recent wines showing more depth and intensity. Not a coincidence.

Gainey Santa B ★★★ Best bet from this top Central Coast producer is the Pinot N from Bien Nacido fruit. Chard also worth a look.

Gallo, E & J ★→★★ With a history of cheap jug wines, California's biggest winery is an easy target for wine snobs. Gallo has done more to open up the American palate to wine than any other winery. Gallo's 1960s Hearty Burgundy was a groundbreaking, popular wine. Still makes basic commodity wines, but has also created an imposing line of regional varieties, such as Anapauma, Marcellina, Turning Leaf and more: all modest quality but predictable and affordable.

Gallo Sonoma Son ★★→★★★ Coastal outpost of Central Valley giant sources grapes from several Sonoma v'yds. Cab Sauv can be v.gd, esp the single-v'yd. Chard also better than average. A gd Pinot Gr under the McMurray label.

Gary Farrell Son ★★★ Well established with some of the best Pinot N and Chard from the RRV over the yrs. Also look for Zin, Chard and a v.gd Sauv Bl. Encounter, a new red Bordeaux blend, is v.gd.

Geyser Peak Son ★★→★★★ A sometimes underrated producer of toasty Chard, powerful Cab Sauv, juicy Shiraz. A recent focus on Sauv Bl is welcome.

Gloria Ferrer Car ★★★ Built by Spain's Freixenet for sparkling wine, now making spicy Chard, silky Pinot N from Carneros fruit. Bubbly quality remains high.

Grace Family Vineyard Napa V ★★★★ 99 00 01 03 05 06 07 Stunning Cab Sauv for long ageing. One of the few cult wines that may actually be worth the price.

Greenwood Ridge And V ★★→★★★ Engaging off-dry, perfumed Ries. Reds, esp Cab Sauv and Pinot N, from cool-climate v'yds also v.gd.

Grgich Hills Cellars Napa V ★★★ Solid producer of supple Chard (that can age); balanced, elegant Cab Sauv; jammy, ripe Zin from Sonoma grapes and gd Sauv Bl in minerally style.

Groth Vineyards Napa V ★★★★ 97 99 00 01 05 06 07 Estate Cab Sauv a solid four-star, with big, wrap-around flavours made for ageing.

Hall Napa V ★★★→★★★★ Kathryn Hall's family has been growing wine grapes in Mendocino for almost four decades. She bought historic Bergfeld winery in Napa in 2005; the new winery was designed by architect Frank Gehry. There is a stunning Diamond Mtn District Cab Sauv (★★★★) and a v.gd St Helena Bergfeld Cab Sauv. The minerally Sauv Bl is delicious.

Handley Cellars ★★★ Winemaker Mila Handley makes excellent Chard, Gewürz, Pinot N from Anderson V v'yds. V.gd Sauv Bl, Chard from Dry CV; small amount of intense sparkling.

Hanna Winery Son ★★★ Has been reaching for four-star status for yrs. Recent vintages of Cab Sauv and well-made Sauv Bl are excellent.

Hanzell Son ★★★★ (Chard) 07 08 09 (Pinot N) 03 05 07 08 Pioneer (1950) small producer of outstanding terroir-driven Chard *and Pinot N* from estate vines. Always gd; quality level has risen sharply in the past few yrs. Deserves to be ranked with the best of California.

Harlan Estate Napa V ★★★ 99 00 01 03 06 07 Concentrated, sleek, cult Cab Sauv from small estate commanding luxury prices.

Harney Lane Winery Lodi ★★ Rising star. Best is the Lizzie James Old-Vine Zin; also look out for the Tempranillo and a delicious Albariño.

Harrison Clarke Santa Y ★★→★★★ All about Syrah and Grenache. Estate Syrah is worth seeking out, and the Grenache has rich flavour profile and mouthfeel.

Hartford Court Son ★★★ Part of KENDALL-JACKSON's Artisans & Estates group. V.gd single-v'yd Pinot Ns; tight, coastal-grown Chard; wonderful old-vine RRV Zins.

HdV Wines Car ★★★ *Complex and layered Chard* with a minerally edge from grower Larry Hyde's v'yd in conjunction with Aubert de Villaine of DRC (*see* France).

Heitz Cellar Napa V ★★★ 01 03 05 07 History-making, deeply flavoured, minty Cab Sauv from Martha's V'yd. Bella Oaks and newer Trailside V'yd rival but can't match Martha. Some feel quality has slipped in recent vintages.

Heller Estate Mont ★★ *Gd organic Cab Sauv* and a charming Chenin Bl.

Hess Collection, The Napa V ★★→★★★★ Owner and art collector Donald Hess uses winery visiting area as a museum. Cab Sauv from Mt Veeder v'yds step up to new quality level; Chard crisp and bright; Hess Select label v.gd value.

Hobbs, Paul ★★★ Hobbs divides his time between Argentina and California. His RRV Pinot N is lush and silky; the Chard (RRV), is creamy with a gd bit of oak. The Napa V Cab Sauv is supple with hints of bitter chocolate; gd structure.

Honig Napa V ★★★ Big jump in quality after switching to organic farming. V.gd Cab Sauv in classic Napa V style and seriously delicious Sauv Bl lead the parade.

Iron Horse Vineyards RRV ★★★ Family estate producing gd bubbly. Chard from RRV is v.gd and there is an above-average Cab Sauv from Alexander V v'yds.

Jade Mountain Napa V ★★→★★★ V.gd Rhône-style wines, esp Syrah, Mourvèdre.

Jessie's Grove Lodi ★★ Old Zin vines work well for farming family's venture.

Joel Gott Napa V ★★★ 3rd generation Joel Gott selects grapes from top Napa v'yds to make incredibly gd Zin and powerful, age-worthy Cab Sauv, among other wines.

Jordan Alex V ★★★★ (Cab) 98 99 00 01 02 05 Rob Davis makes balanced, elegant wines. Age-worthy, Bordeaux-style Cab Sauv; minerally, Burgundian Chard.

Jorian Hill Santa Y ★★★ Outstanding Rhône-inspired wines; organic hillside v'yds. BEEspoke is a powerful yet elegant Grenache/Syrah blend; Viognier is brilliant.

Joseph Phelps Napa V ★★★★ (Insignia) **97 99 00** 01 03 05 06 07 08 A true Napa "first growth"; Phelps Cab Sauv, esp Insignia and Backus, always nr the top.

CALIFORNIA

California on the cheap

A bottle of Napa Cab Sauv for under $5. Well, not quite, but close. There has been a recent surge in inexpensive California-produced wines packaged in bag-in-box, Tetra Pak and even faux-wood barrels; forget about the bottles. Grapes for products such as Three Thieves Cab Sauv Tetra Pak are sourced from AVAs in Napa and other premium coastal regions. The Black Box brand also has some Napa Cab in its blend. De Loach V'yds, owned by Boisset USA, is offering a ten-gallon wine bag packed inside a wooden barrel to restaurants. The wine inside is Pinot N from the RRV AVA. Roll out another barrel of premium Pinot, bartender.

Joseph Swan Son ★★★ Long-time RRV producer of intense Zin and classy Pinot N capable of ageing in the 10-yr range.

Joyce Vineyards ★★ Artisan producer of unfined, unfiltered wines of gd varietal character. Cab Sauv is flirting with ★★★. Merlot v.gd.

Justin Santa B ★★★ Splendid proprietary red blends: structure and ageing potential. Top is Isosceles (Bordeaux blend) with layers of fruit; Savant is a biodynamic, bold, spicy Syrah/Cab Sauv. Also try the Justification, elegant Cab Sauv Res.

J Vineyards Son ★★★ Creamy, rich Brut sparkling wine is one of state's best. Also look for v.gd Pinot N and Pinot Gr from RRV v'yds.

Kendall-Jackson ★★→★★★ Legendary market-driven Chard, Cab Sauv. Even more noteworthy for the development of a diversity of wineries under the umbrella of Kendall-Jackson's Artisans & Estates (*see* HARTFORD COURT, STONESTREET).

Kent Rasmussen Winery Car ★★★ Crisp, lingering Chard and delicious Pinot N. Ramsay is an alternative label for small production lots.

Kenwood Vineyards Son ★★→★★★ Single-v'yd Jack London Cab Sauv (01 03 05 07 08), Zin (several) the high points of a consistent line. Sauv Bl is reliable value.

Kistler Vineyards RRV ★★★ A dramatic change of direction here: more subtle Chard and Pinot N also showing more restraint.

Korbel ★ Largest US producer of classic-method fizz with focus on fruit flavours. Recently added an organic bottling. Take along on your next picnic.

Kunde Estate Son V ★★★ Solid producer and noted grower; elegant, understated Chard, flavourful Sauv Bl, peachy Viognier and silky Merlot. All estate-bottled.

La Jota Howell Mtn ★★★ Long-lived Cab Sauv and Merlot from hillside v'yds. Cab Fr v.gd recently with a spicy richness and a long, complex finish.

Lamborn Howell Mtn ★★★ V'yd planted on historic 19th-century site. Big, juicy Zin, Cab Sauv from this cult winery.

Landmark Son V ★★→★★★★ Four stars for intense Chard from Bien Nacido V'yd (Santa MV): deep, lemon zest and dried fruit. Detour Pinot N (Son Coast grapes).

Lane Tanner Santa B ★★★ Owner-winemaker makes v. personal, superb single-v'yd Pinot N that reflects its terroir with a quiet, understated elegance.

Lang & Reed Napa V ★★★ Specialist focusing on delicious Loire-style Cab Fr.

Laurel Glen Son V ★★★★ 99 00 01 03 05 06 09 Floral, long-lived Cab Sauv from steep v'yd on Son Mtn. Mid-priced Counterpoint label is gd quality at a reasonable price; budget Reds label offers exceptional value.

Lohr, J ★★→★★★ Large winery with extensive v'yds; v.gd Paso Robles Cab Sauv Seven Oaks. Recent series of Meritage-style reds best yet. Also Cypress.

Long Meadow Napa V ★★★ Elegant, silky Cab Sauv better with each vintage. Lively *Graves-style Sauv Bl* a winner as well. V'yd is organically farmed.

Longoria Santa B ★★★ Veteran winemaker Rick Longoria is on to a good thing with the recent launch of Albariño and Tempranillo, which remain true to Spanish origins while taking on New World accent. Centrepiece, however, is the Santa Rita Hills Chard, balanced and supple with yummy spice and tropical fruit.

Louis M Martini Napa ★★→★★★ History-making, age-worthy Cab Sauv, Zin. On down-slide for several yrs. On way back up after GALLO purchase (2002). Recent Cab Sauv showing v. well, esp Monte Rosso V'yds and Alexander V bottlings.

Lucas ★★→★★★ One of Lodi's rising stars, try the Zin and Chard.

L'Uvaggio ★★→★★★ Former ROBERT MONDAVI winemaker Jim Moore specializes in Italian varieties. An outstanding Barbera leads the way; also look for Vermentino from Lodi and a rosé from Santa B. Can't go wrong here.

MacPhail Son ★★★ Pinot N specialist offering intense wines from select v'yds on Son Coast and in Anderson V. Wines are silky and luscious.

Marimar Torres Estate RRV ★★★★ (Chard) 06 07 08 09 10 (Pinot N) 03 05 06 07 08 09 Several bottlings of Chard, Pinot N from Don Miguel estate v'yd in Green Valley. Chard is complex and sometimes edgy, with gd ageing potential. Acero Don Miguel Chard is unoaked and *a lovely expression of Chard fruit*. Pinot N from the Doña Margarita v'yd is intense and surprisingly rich for young vines. V'yds now farmed organically and moving towards biodynamics.

Markham Napa V ★★★ Underrated producer of elegant Merlot and solid Cab Sauv.

Martinelli RRV ★★★ Family growers from fog-shrouded western hills of Sonoma, famous for old-vine Jackass Hill V'yd Zin.

Mayacamas Vineyards Mt Veeder ★★★ Pioneer boutique v'yd with rich Chard and firm (but no longer steel-hard) *Cab Sauv, capable of long ageing*. Also a gd Sauv Bl.

Merry Edwards RRV ★★★→★★★★ Superstar consultant planted her own Pinot N v'yd and buys in grapes. Pinot N a "must". Also lovely, true-to-varietal Sauv Bl.

Merryvale Napa V ★★★ Best at Cab Sauv and Merlot, which have elegant balance and supple finish. Sauv Bl can be v.gd.

Mettler Family Vineyards Lodi ★★ Long-time growers now producing a sleek and tangy Cab Sauv and a powerful Petite Sirah.

Milano Mend ★★★→★★★★ Artisan producer of Zin, Cab Sauv, worth seeking out. New Hopland Cuvée, a blend of Cab Sauv and Pinot N is ★★★★ all the way.

Miner Family Vineyards Oak ★★★ Powerful and potentially long-ageing reds based on Cab Sauv are the star turn here. Look esp for the Icon bottling, a blend of Bordeaux varieties. The family also owns OAKVILLE RANCH.

Morgan Santa LH ★★★→★★★★ Top-end single-v'yd Pinot Ns, Chards. Esp fine, unoaked Chard Metallico. Estate Double L v'yd farmed organically. New Rhônish entry Côtes du Crows is charming.

Moshin Vineyards RRV ★★→★★★ Creamy, rich Chard: just a whiff of oak and long finish that echoes through the palate. Sauv Bl and Pinot N also worth a look.

Mumm Napa Valley Napa V ★★→★★★ Stylish bubbly, esp *delicious Blanc de Noirs* and a rich, complex DVX single-v'yd fizz to age a few yrs in the bottle.

Murphy-Goode Son ★★ Sauv Bl, Zin are top. Tin Roof (screwcap) line offers refreshing Sauv Bl and Chard *sans* oak.

Nalle Son ★★★ Doug Nalle makes lovely Zins from Dry CV fruit; juicy and delicious young but will also mature gracefully.

Napa Wine Company Napa V ★★★ Largest organic grape-grower in Napa V sells most of the fruit and operates a custom-crush facility for several small premium producers. Offers v.gd Cab Sauv under own label.

Navarro Vineyards And V ★★★→★★★★ Modern pioneer; Ries and Gewürz ranking with the best of the New World. Also Pinot N in two styles, homage to Burgundy (Anderson V grapes), plus a brisk and juicy bottling from bought-in grapes.

Newton Vineyards Spring Mtn ★★★→★★★★ Three tiers of wines: Bordeaux blend Icon (03 05 06 07); The Puzzle, site-specific bottlings of Cab Sauv, Merlot, Chard; fruit-forward Red Label. Elegant expressions of mtn v'yds. Age-worthy.

Nickel & Nickel ★★★ Specialist in exceptional terroir-driven single-v'yd Cab Sauv from Napa V and Sonoma.

Niebaum-Coppola Estate Ruth ★★★ "Godfather" Francis Ford Coppola has proven he is as serious about making wine as making movies. Best is Rubicon, a Bordeaux blend, but can be too jammy in some vintages; Edizione Pennino concentrates on delightfully old-fashioned Zin. Coppola also owns the Château Souverain winery in Sonoma and is expanding production.

Oakville Ranch Oak ★★★ This estate on the Silverado Trail (owned by the MINER FAMILY) produces consistently gd Cab Sauv and a creamy Chard.

Ojai Santa B ★★★ Former AU BON CLIMAT partner Adam Tolmach makes range of v.gd wines, esp Syrah and other Rhônes.

Opus One Oak ★★★ With a lot of in-and-out yrs at Opus, the wines rarely lived up to the hype for this red Bordeaux blend. But, the past few vintages, beginning with 2004, are showing well with the wines harmonious and balanced.

Pahlmeyer Napa V ★★★ Producer of tannic Cab Sauv and more supple Merlot.

Paloma Vineyard ★★→★★★ Merlot specialist from high-elevation v'yds on mostly lava-based soils. The wines have a gd structure, with layers of fruit and hints of chocolate. Drink now or let them age a decade.

Parducci Mend ★★→★★★ Reliable, gd-value from historic winery. Recent vintages have raised quality. New release of True Grit Petite Sirah is a great example of why this orphan variety is getting new respect and attention in California.

Patianna Vineyards RRV ★★★ Biodynamic v'yds farmed by Patty FETZER. Also sources grapes from organic v'yds in Mendocino. Lovely Sauv Bl, v.gd Syrah.

Paul Dolan Mend ★★★ Pioneer of organic and biodynamic farming when he was winemaker at FETZER, Dolan's own brand offers outstanding Zin, Syrah, Cab Sauv, Chard and Sauv Bl from organic, biodynamic North Coast v'yds.

Pedroncelli Son ★★ Old hand in Dry CV producing bright, elbow-bending Zin, Cab Sauv and a solid Chard.

Peltier Station ★★ →★★★ The Schatz family has been growing wine grapes in Lodi for over 50 yrs. Now making its own wines, and the results are gd to outstanding. Look esp for the refreshing Viognier and a yummy Zin.

Periano ★★ Gd example of the new look of Lodi wines. Esp Barbera, brilliant Viognier and v.gd Chard.

Peter Michael Winery Son ★★★→★★★★ Complex Chard from Howell Mtn in a powerful style; more supple Alexander V bottling. Cab Sauv on the tight side.

Philips, R H Central V ★→★★ The only winery in the Dunnigan Hills AVA makes a wide range of wines. Excellent job with Rhône varieties under the EXP label and gd-value Toasted Head Chard.

Philip Togni Vineyards Spring Mtn ★★★→★★★★ 00 01 03 05 97 98 Veteran winemaker makes v. *fine long-lasting Cab Sauv*.

Pine Ridge Napa V ★★★ Tannic and concentrated Cab Sauvs from several Napa V AVAs. The just off-dry Chenin Bl is a treat.

Preston Dry CV ★★★ Lou Preston is a demanding terroirist; icons such as Zin and marvellous Barbera. His Sauv Bl is delicious; several gd Rhône varietals.

Pride Mountain Spring Mtn ★★★ Well-known for Bordeaux blends, Pride has moved into the front for Merlot bottlings. There is typical mtn fruit, dominated by black cherry and a touch of chocolate. Wines are built for age.

Quady Winery Central V ★★ →★★★ Imaginative Madera Muscat dessert wines, inc: famed orangey Essensia, rose-petal-flavoured Elysium and Moscato d'Asti-like Electra. A recent addition, Vya Vermouth, is an excellent apéritif.

Quintessa Napa V ★★★→★★★★ Homage-to-Bordeaux blend, from a biodynamic estate on the Silverado Trail, developed by the Huneeus family of Chile. The wines show great finesse and balance, improving with each vintage.

Quivira Dry CV ★★★ Focus on classic and v. drinkable Zin; also a range of delicious Rhône varietals. V'yds farmed biodynamically.

Qupé Santa B ★★★ Never-a-dull-moment cellar-mate of AU BON CLIMAT. *Marsanne*, Pinot Bl, Syrah are all well worth trying.

Radio-Coteau Son ★★★ V.gd Pinot N with a little Syrah from cool-climate v'yds on the Sonoma Coast. There's a lot to like: Son Coast La Neblina Pinot N leads the charge. It has enough structure to keep for 5–8 yrs, but tastes gd young.

Rafanelli, A Son ★★★→★★★★ Extraordinary Dry CV Zin from this family estate. The Zin will age, but it's so delightful when young, why bother?

Ramey Wine Cellars RRV ★★★→★★★★ V.gd single-v'yd Cab Sauv from Napa V, and rich and complex Chard from cooler v'yds, esp the Hudson V'yd Napa V-Carneros. Don't pass on the intense and complex Son Coast Syrah.

Ravenswood ★→★★ Joel Peterson pioneered single-v'yd Zin. Later he added a budget line of Sonoma and Vintners Res Zin and Merlot. Now owned by CONSTELLATION.

Raymond Vineyards and Cellar Napa V ★★★ 01 03 05 07 09 Family v'yds; balanced, understated Cab Sauv, potential for long-term ageing, esp Generations blend.

Ridge Santa Cz Mts ★★★★ 99 00 01 03 05 07 08 Founder and wine master Paul Draper continues to work his magic here. Supple and harmonious *Montebello Cab Sauv* from estate is superb. Also outstanding single-v'yd Zin from Sonoma, Napa V, Sierra F'hills and Paso Robles. Most Zin has gd ageing potential. *Outstanding Chard* from wild-yeast fermentation often overlooked.

Robert Craig Vineyard Napa V ★★ Cab Sauv with gd structure, attractive spice and fruit. Long, balanced finish. The Affinity blend is top.

Robert Keenan Winery Napa V ★★★ Supple, restrained Cab Sauv, Merlot; also Chard from estate v'yds on Spring Mtn.

Robert Mondavi ★→★★★★ Brilliant innovator, now owned by CONSTELLATION, has wine at all price/quality ranges. Top: Napa V Reserves, Napa V appellation series (Carneros Chard, Oakville Cab Sauv, etc.), Napa V (basic). Lower end: various Central Coast wines and Robert Mondavi-Woodbridge from Lodi. V. top wines holding their quality level, but mid-ranges seem to be slipping.

Rochioli Vineyards & Winery RRV ★★★ Long-time grower sells most fruit to other top Pinot N producers, but holds back enough to make lovely, complex Pinot N under his own label, esp the Special Cuvée Pinot N. Also v.gd Sauv Bl.

Roederer Estate And V ★★★★ Branch of Champagne house. Supple, elegant house style. Easily one of the top three sparklers in California and hands-down the best rosé. Luxury *cuvée* L'Ermitage is superb.

Rosenblum Cellars ★★→★★★ Makes a wide range of Zins and Rhône varietals from v'yds up and down the state. Quality varies but always above-average.

Rusack Santa B ★★→★★★ Rusack offers exceptional quality ranging from Sauv Bl to Syrah to Grenache, but it is the Chard that offers not only great quality but good value. Good fruit plus structure plus finish.

Saddleback Cellars Napa V ★★★→★★★★ 01 05 06 07 08 Nils Venge is a legend in Napa V. Lush Zin, long-lived Cab Sauv. In some vintages, a super Sauv Bl.

St Clement Napa V ★★★→★★★★ 99 00 01 03 05 06 07 (Cab Sauv) Long-time Napa producer has a new life under BERINGER BLASS ownership, with a turn towards terroir-based wines. Supple, long-lived Oroppas, a Cab Sauv-based blend, is the go-to wine here. Merlot and Chard also outstanding.

St Francis Son ★★★ 00 01 03 05 06 07 Deep and concentrated Cab Sauv from single v'yds. Look for the Wild Oak V'yd Chard finished with a nod to Burgundy. The old-vine Zin is super.

Saintsbury Car ★★★→★★★★ Outstanding Pinot N, denser than most from Carneros and can take a few yrs of bottle age. Chard is full-flavoured, nicely balanced. Garnet Pinot N, made from younger vines, is a light-hearted quaff.

Sanford ★★ Founder Richard Sanford was one of the first to plant Pinot N in Santa B, but wines have hit a rough patch under new owners.

Santa Cruz Mountain Vineyard ★★→★★★ Wines of strong varietal character from estate grapes, inc v.gd Pinot N, exceptional Cab Sauv: concentrated, age-worthy.

Sattui, V ★★ King of direct-only sales (ie. winery door or mail order). Wines made in a rustic, drink-now style. Reds are best, esp Cab Sauv, Zin.

Sawyer Cellars Ruth ★★★ Bradfort Meritage is outstanding and could become a superstar. Intense, upfront fruit balanced by a brambly minerality.

Sbragia Dry CV ★★★ Ed Sbragia, long-time winemaker at BERINGER BLASS, has established his own family winery. A splendid selection of single-v'yd Cab Sauv and Merlot shows him at top form. Wines show classic California character, concentrated but not over-the-top. Also a v.gd Sauv Bl from estate vines.

Schramsberg Napa V ★★★→★★★★ Sparkling wine that stands the test of time. The first to make a true *méthode traditionelle* in the state in commercial quantity. Reserve is splendid; Blanc de Noirs outstanding. Luxury *cuvée* J Schram is America's Krug. Mirabelle is second label for palate-pleasing bubbly. Now making a *v.gd Cab Sauv*, J Davies, from mtn estate vines.

Screaming Eagle Napa V Small lots of cult Cab Sauv at luxury prices for those who like that kind of thing.

Seghesio Son ★★★ Respected family winery has a double focus: Italian varietals and Zin. *The Zins are superb*, drinkable when young, new depth with age. Italians are a cut above most California efforts in that line, esp Barbera and Sangiovese.

Selene Napa V ★★★→★★★★ Mia Klein makes rich, concentrated Bordeaux-varietal wines. Hyde V'yd Sauv Bl is super; Chester V'yd red blend a must.

Sequana Son ★★→★★★★ Pinot N-only venture established by California veterans Tom Selfridge and James MacPhail (who also has his own label). Three wines, two from RRV and one from Santa LH. All feature a silky complexity and intensity.

Sequoia Grove Napa V ★★★ Estate Cab Sauvs are intense and long-lived, with the trend clearly upwards. Chard is balanced and has ageing potential most yrs.

Shafer Vineyards Napa V ★★★→★★★★ (Cab Sauv) 00 01 02 03 05 (Merlot) 05 07 08 09 Top marks for deep yet supple Cab Sauv, esp the Hillside Select, and Merlot, which is capable of several yrs of bottle-ageing.

Signorello Napa V ★★★ Concentrated and rich Cab Sauv, complex, full-bodied Chard with sometimes unresolved oak tannins. Syrah is always worth a look, as are single-v'yd Pinots N from Carneros. Looking better with each vintage.

Silverado Vineyards Stags L ★★★→★★★★ Supple Cab Sauv, lean and minerally Chard, distinctive Sangiovese.

Silver Oak ★★★→★★★★ Separate wineries in Napa and Alexander V; Cab Sauv only. Napa V can be super-concentrated, loyal following. Alexander V more supple.

Sinskey Vineyards Car ★★★ Chard with a gd acidic bite and luscious Pinot N are the highlights of this reliable estate.

Smith-Madrone ★★★ High up on Spring Mtn, the Smith brothers make *one of the state's best Ries* in an aromatic, off-dry style. V'yds are dry-farmed.

Sodaro Estate Napa V ★★★ Bill and Dawnine Dyer are the consulting winemakers at this newish winery, so don't look for cult wine knockoffs here. The Sodaro family traces its winemaking roots to 19th-century Italy, but there is nothing old-fashioned about the elegant and balanced wines being produced. Look especially for the Cab Sauv-based Felicity.

Sonoma-Cutrer Vineyards Son ★★→★★★★ Chard specialist bottling, flinty and hard-edge Chard with real bite, mostly from Son Coast v'yds.

Southwest Son ★★ Susie Selby left her MBA corporate track in Texas for the lure of California wine. She's clearly having fun, with more than a dozen wines in her portfolio. Head straight for the RRV Chard, v.gd Son County Merlot as well.

Downtown wine country

Several commercial wineries have set up shop in the San Francisco Bay Area, most of them in Oakland or Berkeley. The wineries obviously buy in grapes from v'yds around the state but the wine is made on site. It makes sense from an economic standpoint; also, the wine is made and sold where the customers are, often within walking distance. *See* listings for DONKEY & GOAT, DASHE CELLARS and ROSENBLUM CELLARS.

Spottswoode St Helena ★★★★ 97 99 00 01 03 05 06 07 *Outstanding Cab Sauv* from estate v'yd is long-lasting, balanced and harmonious. Another California "first growth". Brilliant Sauv Bl is a bonus.

Spring Mountain Vineyard ★★★→★★★★ Historic mtn estate on a winning path; excellent Cab Sauv with gd structure and depth, and outstanding Sauv Bl.

Staglin Family Vineyard Napa V ★★★ 01 03 05 07 Elegant Cab Sauv from Ruth Bench.

Stag's Leap Wine Cellars ★★★★ 99 00 01 03 05 07 Celebrated for silky, seductive Cab Sauvs (SLV, Fay, top-of-line Cask 23) and Merlots. Gd Chard is often overlooked. Holding the line for balance and harmony against the onslaught of over-the-top, super-concentrated Napa V Cabs. Now owned by partnership of Piero Antinori (*see* Italy) and CHATEAU STE MICHELLE in Washington State.

Stags' Leap Winery *See* BERINGER BLASS.

Steele Wines Lake ★★→★★★★ Jed Steele is a genius at sourcing v'yds for a series of single-v'yd wines under main label and a second label called Shooting Star. Chard can get a little oaky, but Pinot N and some specialty wines, such as Washington State Aligoté, are outstanding.

Stephen Ross Edna V ★★★ It's all about Pinot N and Chard here, a nod to Syrah and Zin. V. Burgundian approach adds complexity and interest. A true rising star.

Sterling Napa V ★★→★★★★ Napa V estate making Chard and understated single-v'yd Cab Sauv. Has never seemed to fulfil potential, despite gd v'yd sources.

Stonestreet Son ★★★ One of the stars of Jess Jackson's Artisans & Estates stable. The Alexander V Cab Sauv is a brawny but balanced wine, with layers of flavours; Chard can get too buttery but worth a look.

Stony Hill Napa V ★★★★ (Chard) 91 95 97 99 00 01 03 05 06 07 Amazing hillside Chard made in an elegant "homage to Chablis" style. Most wine sold from mailing list. Wines are v. long-lived.

Storrs Winery Santa Cz Mts ★★→★★★ Top-rated Chard from mtn v'yds leads the way. A lovely and quaffable Grenache worth a glass or two.

St-Supéry Napa ★★→★★★ Sleek and graceful Merlot; Cab Sauv can be outstanding, as is red Meritage. *Sauv Bl one of best in state.* Sources some grapes from warmer Pope Valley east of Napa V. French-owned (Skalli).

Summerland Santa B ★★★ Summerland offers several single v'yd bottlings of Pinot N, Chard, a smattering of Pinot Gris and a few other (maybe too many). But, the highlight is Chard from the Bien Nacido v'yd. Lovely, structured wine.

Sunset Gd Cab Sauv, Malbec with catchy name of Twilight Tango.

Sutter Home ★→★★★ Famous for white Zin and rustic Amador red Zin. New upscale Signature Series and Trinchero Family Estates a step up, esp Cab Sauv from Chicken Ranch v'yd.

Swanson Oak ★★★ A fine Sangiovese, somewhat surprising in California. Also reach for the Alexis Cab Sauv, it's lean and supple with ripe plum and black-cherry fruit leading to a long finish.

Tablas Creek P Rob ★★★ Joint venture between owners of Château de Beaucastel (*see* France) and importer Robert Hass. V'yd based on cuttings from Châteauneuf v'yds. Côtes de Tablas red and white are amazingly gd, as is the Tablas Creek Esprit. These are **must-drink wines for Rhônistas.**

Talbott, R Mont ★★★ Chard from single v'yds is the name of the game, with the famed Sleepy Hollow v'yd in the Santa LH at the heart. Burgundian approach.

Terra Valentine Spring Mtn ★★→★★★ Estate winery seems poised to fulfill potential as a reliable producer of top quality Cab Sauv. Look esp for Yverdon bottling.

Thomas Fogarty Santa Cz Mts ★★→★★★ Rich, complex Chard that ages fairly well. Also gd Pinot N from estate v'yds, delightful Gewürz from Monterey grapes.

Titus Vineyards Napa V ★★★ Family estate, v.gd Cab Sauv, outstanding Zin, Cab Fr.

Treana P Rob ★★ Owned by the Hope family, long-time growers. Only two wines are made: Treana Red, based on Cab Sauv, and Treana White, a blend of Viognier and Marsanne. You can't go wrong with either. They are wines made to enjoy yet offer good quality as well. Another glass, please.

Trefethen Family Vineyards Napa V ★★★ Historic family winery with record for consistency and durability. Gd off-dry Ries, balanced Chard for ageing. Cab Sauv shows increasing complexity, esp top-of-the-line Halo.

Trenza San Luis Obispo ★★→★★★ Dedicated to Spanish varieties, this new winery is off to a terrific start with a red and a white blend and a rosé, all gd. The Trenza Blanco, a blend of Albariño and white Grenache, is a real treat.

Tres Sabores Ruth ★★★ Newcomer making three different Zins all from the same organically farmed hillside v'yds. Wines are consistently balanced and elegant, emphasizing different elements of the v'yd.

Tricycle Wine Company Lake ★★ Off to a good start with classic Cab Sauv from Red Hills AVA. Keep an eye on this one.

Trinchero Napa V ★★→★★★ Long-time Napa producer is remaking its image with Cab Sauv from the Chicken Ranch V'yd in the Ruth AVA. Juicy in the opening but pick up a lingering, dried-spice and black-plum quality that is quite attractive.

Truchard ★★★ Merlot in Carneros? For sure. From the warmer north end of Carneros comes one of the flavourful, firmly built Merlots that give the AVA identity. Cab Sauv and Syrah even better, and the tangy, lemony Chard is a must-drink. New bottlings of Tempranillo outstanding, as is a Roussanne.

Valley of the Moon Son ★→★★ Reliable and gd-value elbow-benders, occasionally rising to two stars, esp Pinot Bl and Zin.

Viader Estate Napa V ★★★★ 99 00 01 03 05 06 07 08 A blend of Cab Sauv and Cab Fr from Howell Mtn hillside estate. Powerful wines, yet balanced and elegant in best yrs. This is a classic Napa V mtn red. Ages well. Also look for new series of small-lot bottlings, inc Syrah, Tempranillo.

Vina Robles San LO ★★→★★★ Gd Cab Sauv, Sauv Bl, but my favourite is what I call its everyday Red and White: bright fruit backed by pleasing acidity. White is a blend of Vermentino, Viognier, Verdelho and a drop of Sauv Bl. It won Best of Show at a major California wine competition; at around $15 it's a real bargain.

Volker Eisele Family Estate Napa V ★★★→★★★★ 97 99 00 01 03 05 07 Sleek, luscious blend of Cab Sauv and Cab Fr from the little-known Chiles V AVA. Also look for a spicy Sauv Bl.

Wente Vineyards Mont ★★ →★★★ Historic specialist in whites, *esp Livermore Sauv Bl* and Sem. New range of single-v'yd Chard has moved the quality bar higher.

Whitehall Lane Napa ★★→★★★ New releases of an elegant and balanced Cab Sauv and a zippy Sauv Bl have raised the quality bar.

Williams Selyem Son ★★★ Intense, smoky RRV Pinot N, esp Rochioli V'yds and Allen V'yds. Now reaching to Son Coast, Mendocino for grapes. Cultish favourite can sometimes turn jammy and over-concentrated.

Willowbrook Son ★★★ Single-v'yd Pinot N; wines are stylish and elegant, with bright, opening fruit and deep flavours in the middle and finish. To watch.

Wilson Vineyards Son ★★→★★★ Newcomer with an eye for Zin. The estate old-vine Ellie's V'yd is outstanding – classic Dry CV Zin. The impressive Res Zin has a rich, brambly mouthfeel.

Wine Group, The Central V The third-largest producer of wine in the world, by volume, after E & J GALLO and CONSTELLATION, offers mostly bargain wines, such as Glen Ellen, Almaden and Inglenook, as well as bag-in-box bargains, such as Franzia. The wine is drinkable, for the most part, and certainly helps balance out grape supply and demand in California and around the world.

Wrath Vineyards Mont ★★★ Grapes for the outstanding Sauv Bl, made in a grassy style, are sourced from the family's San Saba v'yd. Also a gd Chard.

Zaca Mesa Santa B ★★→★★★ Now turning away from Chard and Pinot N to concentrate on estate Rhône grapes. The Black Bear Block Syrah is one of the best in the state; also look for Z Three, a delicious blend of Syrah and Grenache, and check out the Roussanne.

Zahtila Vineyards Napa ★★★ Elegant, inviting Cab Sauv, intense Zin. To watch.

THE PACIFIC NORTHWEST

Diversity is the plot-line here. Oregon, all about Pinot Noir only a few years ago, now offers complex, lush Pinot Gris and very good Cabernet, Tempranillo and Syrah from warmer vineyards in the southern part of the state. Washington, once best known for Riesling, is now producing world-class Cabernets, Chardonnay, Syrah and maybe the best Merlot on the West Coast. The Pacific Northwest has a lot of stories to tell and they are worth hearing.

Principal viticultural areas

Applegate Valley (App V) Oregon. Warm region in south; gd Cab Sauv, Syrah.
Columbia Valley (Col V) Washington. A huge AVA inc much of southern and central Washington; Cab Sauv, Ries, Syrah, Chard, Cab Fr and more. Sub-AVAs: Horse Heaven Hills, Red Mtn, Walla Walla (Walla) and Yakima Valley (Yak V).
Umpqua Valley (Um V) Oregon. Warmer region but with cooling Pacific winds. Promising plantings of Tempranillo; Cab Sauv.
Willamette Valley (Will V) Oregon. This is Pinot N central. Several sub-AVAs have been established as Oregon growers make serious efforts to sort out terroir. Also gd Ries, Pinot Gr, Chard.

Recent vintages

Any general discussion of vintages is difficult because of the wide variation in climate over the area and the jumble of microclimates in small regions.

2010 A very difficult vintage. Summer was cool with on-off rain through harvest. Crop levels were very low (50% off in some places). Those who picked carefully may produce wines with good acidity.

2009 It was a hot growing season for both Oregon and Washington. Harvest was early, with the red wines in particular showing good fruit.

2008 Cool spring, late harvest. Growers are optimistic about the future of the young wines, some calling it vintage of the decade. Oregon Pinot N looked especially promising. Washington and Idaho near-perfect grapes.

2007 Not an easy vintage. Those who paid attention got it right.

2006 Incredible quality across the board in Oregon, Washington and Idaho.

2005 This is turning out to be an amazing vintage, if the winery paid attention. Oregon Pinot N, Washington Cab Sauv, Merlot, could be exceptional.

Oregon

Abacela V'yds Um V ★★★ V.gd Tempranillo, Dolcetto, Cab Fr. Syrah a treat.

Adelsheim Vineyard Y-Car ★★★→★★★★ 05 06 07 09 Oregon Pinot N veteran remains on top of the game with elegant Pinot N. New Dijon clone Chard, Ries, top Pinots Gr and Bl: clean, bracing.

Alexana Will V ★★★ Lynn Penner-Ash is winemaker; supple and balanced Pinot N, showing an edgy fruit balanced by gd acidity. Also try the engaging Pinot Gr.

Amalie Robert Estate Will V★★★ A promising estate, with a minerally, terroir-driven Pinot N and luscious Chard.

Amity Will V★★ →★★★ Pioneer, exceptional Ries, Pinot Bl. Pinot often rises to ★★★.

Anam Cara Cellars Will V ★★★ An extraordinary Chehalem Mts Res Pinot N, rich and deeply concentrated. Elegant estate Pinot N and delicious estate Ries.

Andrew Rich (Tabula Rasa) Will V ★★→★★★ Small lots of artisan wines, inc a supple Pinot N and exceptional Syrah.

Anne Amie Will V ★★ Gd Winemaker's Selection Pinot N, balanced and harmonious; v.gd Pinot Gr as well. Several other Pinot N bottlings vary in quality.

Antica Terra Will V ★★→★★★ Now owned by four partners, inc ex-California winemaker Maggie Harrison (Sine Qua Non). The Pinot N, made from Amity Hills fruit, is California-meets-Oregon, with rich, deep flavours.

Archery Summit Will V★★★ Powerful Pinot N bottlings from several v'yds made in a bold style that has won a loyal following.

Argyle Y-Car ★★→★★★ V.gd Ries and v. fine Pinot N lead the way; also *bargain bubbly*. Winery founded by Aussie superstar winemaker Brian Croser.

Beaux Frères Y-Car ★★★ Pinot N has more concentration than most Oregon offerings. Part-owned by critic Robert Parker.

Benton Lane Will V ★★ Delicious Pinot N, balanced and harmonious. Also v.gd Pinot Gr. If you are lucky enough to find the rosé of Pinot N, grab it.

Bergstorm Estate Will V ★★★ Consistently one of Oregon's top Pinot Ns as well a bright Pinot Gr. The estate Pinot N, certified biodynamic, is an intense wine with good mouthfeel and a long finish.

Bethel Heights Will V ★★→★★★ Deftly made estate Pinot N. *Chard one of best in state*; gd Pinot Bl, Pinot Gr.

Brandborg Cellars ★★→★★★ Wines are made from Umpqua V v'yds in southern Oregon. Pinot N and Syrah are especially worth a look and the bright and cheerful Pinot Gr makes an appealing aperitif.

Brick House Y-Car ★★★ Huge estate Pinot N. Dark and brooding; Estate Select a leaner, more balanced version.

Broadley Vineyards Will V ★★★ Several bottlings of Pinot N a year. The wines tend to be rich and powerful, with dark fruit lightly brushed with oak.

Brooks Will V ★★★ Making its name with superb organic/biodynamic Ries and Pinot N. Wines are elegant with long flavours and v.gd value. Seek these out.

Carabella Will V ★★★ Chard is outstanding: silky mouthfeel and just a touch of oak.

Chehalem Y-Car ★★→★★★ Outstanding Chard with ageing potential, as well as a new drink-me-now, no-oak Chard. V.gd Ries, Pinot Gr.

Coehlo Winery Will V ★★ Pinot N-only producer is off to a gd start with an aromatic, lively wine that shows promise for the future.

Cooper Mtn Will V ★★★★ Complex Pinot N and a rich, intense Chard. The Res Pinot N is capable of some bottle-age. Certified biodynamic v'yds.

Domaine Danielle Laurent Y-Car ★★★ Gd-to-v.gd single-v'yd Pinot N, esp the Soléna bottling. Syrah worth a glass.

Domaine Drouhin Will V ★★★→★★★★ 03 04 05 06 *Outstanding Pinot N* silky and elegant, improving with each vintage. Chard also a winner.

Domaine Serene Will V★★★★ Burgundian approach to single-v'yd Pinot N is usually well ahead of the pack. Bottled unfiltered.

Elk Cove V'yds Will V ★★→★★★ V.gd Ries, inc late-harvest. Top Pinot N.

Erath Vineyards Yam-C ★★★→★★★★ Oregon pioneer, founded 1968. V.gd Chard, Pinot Gr, Gewürz, Pinot Bl. Pinots and Ries age well.

Evesham Wood Will V ★★★ Small family winery with fine Pinot N, Pinot Gr and dry Gewürz. Pinot N leaping ahead in recent vintages. Organic.

Eyrie Vineyards Will V ★★★ Chard and Pinot Gr rich yet crisp. All wines age.

Foris Vineyards ★★ A lovely Pinot Bl and a classic red-cherry Pinot N top the list. One of the best in the south of the state.

Four Graces Will V ★★→★★★ The great strength here is an exceptional estate Pinot N offering bright, lively fruit and gd mouthfeel.

Freja Will V ★★★ Only estate-grown Pinot N. Wines are silky on the palate but with an underlying power, clearly in homage to Burgundy.

Henry Estate Um V ★★ In this warmer section of Oregon, Henry Estate makes a solid Cab Sauv and a gd Merlot. Also look for a v.gd dry Gewürz.

Ken Wright Cellars Y-Car ★★★ Highly regarded Pinot N, v.gd single-v'yd Chard.

King Estate Will V ★★★→★★★★ One of Oregon's largest wineries. Organic. Lovely, constantly improving Pinot N, outstanding Chard.

Lachini Vineyards ★★★ Upcoming producer of outstanding Pinot N and v.gd Pinot Gr. Biodynamic. New wines from v'yds in Washington's Red Mtn AVA, a Bordeaux blend and a bold Cab Sauv. Look for upcoming Ries and Albariño.

Lange Winery Y-Car ★★→★★★ Rich and silky Pinot N, backed by a v.gd Pinot Gr and excellent Chard.

Lemelson Vineyards Will V ★★★ There are seven organic v'yds here, with up to 12 bottlings of Pinot N made in some vintages. Wines tend to be elegant with bright minerality. They do give immediate pleasure but should age 5–10 yrs.

Monk's Gate Will V ★★★ Small-production Pinot N is complex and rich while maintaining balance and harmony. Worth looking for.

Montinore Will V ★★ Estate Pinot N is the flagship but save room for a spicy and inviting Pinot Gr. Borealis, a blend of Müller-Thurgau, Gewürz and Pinot Gr, is a delightful off-dry apéritif.

Oak Knoll Will V ★★ Pinot is the big story at this popular winery, with intense but balanced bottlings. Also a v.gd off-dry Ries.

Panther Creek Will V ★★★ Pinot N from several v'yds is concentrated, built to age; new is a delicious unoaked Chard.

Patricia Green Cellars Y-Car ★★★→★★★★ Exciting single-v'yd Pinot N. Wines vary in style from light, racy Pinot to bolder, concentrated; all worth a look.

Penner-Ash Y-Car ★★★→★★★★ REX HILL winemaker Lynn Penner-Ash and her husband make intense, rich Pinot N from up to six v'yds in a bolder style than many in Oregon. Also a v.gd Viognier.

Ponzi Vineyards Will V ★★★→★★★★ 03 05 06 Long-established with consistently *outstanding Pinot N* and v.gd Pinot Gr and Chard.

Quady North App V ★★→★★★ Quady has taken full advantage of the climate (warm, dry) and soils here to make outstanding Viognier and Syrah. The Flagship bottling of Syrah tops the bill.

Resonance Y-Car ★★★ Complex, delicious Pinot N from organic/biodynamic grapes.

Retour Wines Will V ★★★ Terroir-driven old-vine Pinot N is stunning, with touches of earthy spice and anise. Keep an eye on Retour.

Rex Hill Will V ★★★→★★★★ Excellent Pinot N, Pinot Gr and Chard from several v'yds. Reserve wines can hit ★★★★.

RoxyAnn ★★ Southern Oregon producer of an esp gd Viognier and excellent Pinot Gr. Claret red blend is a pleasing quaff.

> 2008 Oregon – a vintage to cherish
> It is no secret that Oregon vintners sometimes have to struggle with difficult vintages, the 2010 harvest being a case in point. Cool summers can lead to even cooler autumns and the wines are, well, difficult. So when a year like 2008 comes along, stand up and cheer. The Pinot N is across-the-board incredible. The flavours are powerful yet the wines are never in-your-face. They manage to be ripe and rounded, yet elegant as well. Best of all, they should develop in the bottle over the next decade.

Sineann ★★→★★★ Stylish wines of great intensity sourced from v'yds in Oregon and Washington. There is a terrific old-vine Zin and an astonishingly gd Merlot from Horse Heaven V'yds in Washington.

Sokol Blosser Will V ★★★→★★★★ Superb wines throughout with an esp v.gd Pinot N, Chard and Gewürz, balanced and harmonious. Syrah is a treat.

Solena Will V ★★★ There's a rich and earthy Pinot N from the estate v'yd, backed by an attractive range of wines inc: Zin, Cab Sauv and Syrah from select v'yd sites in Oregon and Washington.

Soter Y-Car ★★★ Tony Soter has moved his winemaking skills from California (ex-Etude) to Oregon and he is getting it right. *Mineral Springs Vineyard Pinot N*: a superb wine, balanced and harmonious with a long, lyrical finish.

Stoller Estate ★★★ The SV Estate Pinot N is balanced and elegant with supple fruit, the JV Estate Pinot N is riper with softer tannins. Gd Chard from estate grapes.

Torii Mor Y-Car ★★★ V.gd single-v'yd Pinot N bottlings and superior Pinot Gr.

Trisaetum Vineyards Will V ★★★ A newcomer, Trisaetum Pinot N is a bold exercise in Pinot, with a striking, cheery, spice spectrum of flavours. The Ries shows four-star promise, especially the dry Alsace-style bottling.

Tyee Wine Cellars Will V ★★ Artisan producer; v.gd Pinot N, Pinot Gr; tasty Gewürz.

Van Duzer Winery Will V ★★→★★★ Bright, fruity Pinot N, delicious Pinot Gr, from cool hillside v'yds. Steadily improving.

Willakenzie Estate Y-Car ★★★ Specialist in small lots of Pinots N, Gr, Bl, Meunier with a tiny amount of Gamay Noir. Can be outstanding and always worth a look.

Willamette Valley Vineyards Will V ★★→★★★ Gd Ries, Chard and v.gd Pinot N. New clonal selection Chard raises the quality bar.

Washington & Idaho

Abeja Walla ★★→★★★ Abeja first made a name for Cab Sauv and Chard, but the Syrah has been attracting attention recently. It shows the same balance and harmony as the Cab Sauv, with a spicy edge and lingering finish.

Alexandria Nicole Cellars Col V ★★→★★★ Artisan estate in the Horse Heaven Hills AVA; number of wines, inc Bordeaux varietals, but the Syrah draws rave reviews.

Amavi Cellars Walla ★★★ There is pure pleasure coupled with outstanding quality in Amavi wine, with the Cab Sauv and Syrah out in front. The Cab Sauv is the flagship with intense varietal type and wrap-around flavours.

Andrew Will ★★★★ 97 00 01 02 05 07 08 08 Chris Camarda sources Bordeaux varietals; outstanding single-v'yd reds: elegant, with excellent ageing potential.

Arbor Crest ★★ The top draw at this good-value winery is the Chard, followed closely by a floral Sauv Bl.

Badger Mtn Col V ★★→★★★ Washington's first organic v'yd, making gd Cab Sauv and Chard. Also a new line of "no sulfites" organic wines.

Barnard Griffin Col V ★★→★★★ Well-made Merlot, Chard (esp barrel-fermented), Sem, Sauv Bl. Top Syrah and Viognier.

Basel Cellars Walla ★★★ Newcomer off to a gd start, with Bordeaux varieties and a fine Syrah. Look esp for Merriment, a Bordeaux blend.

Bergevin Lane Walla ★★ Gd beginning for another new winery; Syrah out in front.

Betz Yak V ★★★→★★★★ Rhône varietals are the inspiration for veteran winemaker Bob Betz, esp Syrah, where many feel Betz is setting the standard for Washington. Most years there are three bottlings: Serenne (approachable), Côte Rousse and La Côte Patriarche (need time in bottle).

Brian Carter Cellars ★★→★★★ Limited production of gd to v.gd blends, inc a white blend of aromatic varietals, a Sangiovese-based "Super Tuscan", two Bordeaux blends and Byzance, a ★★★ Rhône blend.

Bunnell Cellars Col V ★★★ Rhône rules at this estate winery. Top marks for a series of single-v'yd Syrahs, a v.gd Viognier and a new Grenache.

Buty Walla ★★★ Focus on Bordeaux blends; results have been outstanding. A recent favorite is the Champoux V'yd Horse Heaven Hills Cab Sauv/Cab Fr blend. There is lovely fruit behind a perfumed nose, with a long, elegant finish.

Cadaretta Walla ★★★ A terrific Sauv Bl/Sem called SDS, a silky Syrah that has you reaching for a second glass. Expect even better things as the estate v'yds mature.

Cayuse Walla ★★ →★★★ Gd to v.gd Syrah and an outstanding Bordeaux blend made from biodynamic grapes.

Charles Smith Wines Walla Ex-rock band manager Smith has gained a cult following for jammy, concentrated Syrah and Syrah blends from mostly Col V Ries. Also bottles under the K-Wine label. Get it? K-Syrah.

Chateau Ste Michelle ★★→★★★★ Washington's largest winery; also owns COLUMBIA CREST, Northstar (top Merlot), and SNOQUALMIE, among others. Major v'yd holdings, first-rate equipment and skilled winemakers keep wide range of varieties in front ranks. V.gd v'yd-designated Cab Sauv, Merlot and Chard. Links with Loosen (*see* Germany) and Antinori (*see* Italy).

Chinook Wines Yak V ★★★ Elegant Merlot and Cab Sauv; outstanding Cab Fr and a delicious Cab Fr rosé.

Columbia Crest Col V ★★ →★★★ Cab, Merlot, Syrah, Sauv Bl all gd-value favourites.

Columbia Winery ★★★ Pioneer and still a leader, with balanced, stylish, understated single-v'yd wines. *Marvellous Syrah.*

DeLille Cellars ★★★→★★★★ 00 01 02 03 05 07 08 09 A Bordeaux specialist producing v.gd to excellent wines. New addition is Syrah, Doyenne.

Di Stefano ★★ →★★★ Best bet is Bordeaux red, inc a v.gd, elegant Cab Sauv and Cab Fr; also a bright and juicy Syrah.

Dunham Cellars Walla ★★ →★★★ Artisan producer focusing on long-lived Cab Sauv and superb Syrah and a v.gd Chard.

Forgeron Walla ★★ →★★★ Small lots of single-v'yd wines; v.gd Syrah in a juicy style and notable Roussanne and Pinot Gr.

Glacial Lake Missoula (GLM) Wine Company Yak V ★★★ Keep an eye on GLM (name from a huge lake formed by glacial melt at the end of the last ice age). Deluge, a blend of Cab Sauv and Cab Fr, is superb. It has structure for ageing, with complex layers of fruit and a long, wrap-around finish.

Glen Fiona Walla ★★ →★★★ Rhône specialist, esp Syrah/Cinsault/Counoise *cuvée.*

Gramercy Cellars Walla ★★★ A lot of buzz about this new winery and its wines, which are made by Master Sommelier Greg Harrington. Syrah is rising towards four stars; Grenache-based blend, Third Man, is v. pleasing. Keep an eye on this winery.

Hedges Cellars Yak V ★★★→★★★★ V. fine Bordeaux reds from Red Mtn AVA. Fumé is a delicious and popular blend of Chard and Sauv Bl.

Hogue Cellars, The Yak V ★ →★★ Large, reliable producer known for excellent, gd-value wines, esp Ries, Chard, Merlot, Cab Sauv.

Hyatt Vineyards Yak V ★★→★★★ Stylish Merlot is among the state's best. Seek Black Muscat Icewine when conditions are right.

Indian Creek Id ★→★★ Top wine is Pinot N, plus a v.gd Ries and gd Cab Sauv.

Januik Col V ★★★ Mike Januik, former head winemaker at CHATEAU STE MICHELLE, makes some of Washington's best Cab Sauv. Wines built to age 10–15 yrs.

Kiona Vineyards Yak V ★★→★★★ Solid wines from Red Mtn AVA, esp Cab Sauv; gd value and quality.

Lake Chelan Winery Col V ★★ A promising newcomer with range of wines, inc gd Cab Sauv, an attractive Syrah and a floral Ries.

Latah Creek ★★→★★★ Latah Creek has been around long enough (founded 1982) that it is sometimes overlooked by critics chasing the latest buzz. Truth is, some of Washington's best Merlot and Chard come from here. The wines are invariably balanced with bright fruit profiles.

L'Ecole No 41 Walla ★★★→★★★★ (Merlot) 02 04 05 06 07 09 Blockbuster but balanced reds (Merlot, Cab Sauv and super Meritage blend) with forward, age-worthy fruit. Gd barrel-fermented Sem.

Leonetti Walla ★★★→★★★★ Leonetti's bold cult Cab Sauv is a gd match for the v. fine Merlot, one of Washington's stars.

Long Shadows Col V ★★★→★★★★ Former CHATEAU STE MICHELLE CEO Allen Shoup brought together leading international winemakers to make wines from Washington grapes. Look for *Poet's Leap Ries* by Armin Diel (Germany); Cab Sauv Feather by Randy Dunn (California); glorious Syrah Sequel by John Duval (Australia).

McCrea ★★★ A Rhône pioneer making small lots of gd to v. fine Viognier, Syrah and Grenache, even a rare varietal bottling of Counoise.

Milbrandt Vineyards ★★→★★★ Long-time growers with more than 650 ha of vines in eastern Washington, the Milbrandt brothers are now producing their own wine. The Legacy Evergreen Chard is a winner, with crisp minerality; also look for Traditions bottlings, esp the Syrah.

Nicolas Cole Cellars Col V ★★→★★★ Limited bottlings of balanced and elegant Bordeaux-style reds and Rhônes that will age.

Nota Bene Cellars ★★→★★★ Amazing Bordeaux varietal reds sourced from the Red Mtn AVA and other top Washington v'yds. Wines are built to last. Worth seeking out.

Owen Roe ★★→★★★ Look for the Yak V Chard, Ries. Reds from Col V are v.gd, esp Bordeaux varieties. Gd-value wines under the O'Reilly label with a v.gd Pinot Gr.

Pacific Rim ★★→★★★ Randall Grahm first made Pacific Rim Ries at his California winery BONNY DOON in 1992. The wine became so popular that he built a winery in Washington in 2006, now in full production. Several Ries: both dry and sweet versions are super. Also *gd single-v'yd Ries*. Don't overlook the Chenin Bl.

Pend d'Oreille Id ★★→★★★ Lovely, fruit-forward Chard with bright acidity is the best choice here. Also a tasty Viognier and Merlot are worth a second or third glass.

Not your usual Chardonnay

Oregon and Washington are not normally thought of as Chard country but there are bottlings there that offer a tasty alternative to a steady diet of California Chard. In Oregon's Willamette Valley the model is clearly Burgundian, with high acids and minerality. Washington's generally warmer climate is tempered by cool nights, yielding a more rounded wine with brighter fruit. Gd examples inc: DOMAINE DROUHIN and CHEHALEM from Oregon, and OWEN ROE and LATAH CREEK from Washington.

Quilceda Creek ★★★→★★★★ 01 03 04 05 07 09 Expertly crafted *Columbia Valley Cab Sauv*. Wines are beautifully balanced to age.

Reininger Walla ★★→★★★ Small producer of gd Merlot and v. fine Syrah. Helix label features wines from throughout the state; esp gd Syrah.

Robert Karl Col V ★★→★★★ Spokane-based winery makes small lots of single-v'yd wines from Horse Heaven Hills AVA. Both Merlot and Cab Sauv can hit ★★★.

Sandhill Winery Col V ★★★ Estate-only wines from Red Mtn AVA. Outstanding Cab and Merlot; v.gd Pinot Gr. Cinnamon Teal Red Table Wine is a local favourite.

Saviah Cellars Walla ★★→★★★ V.gd Bordeaux blends from small family winery; outstanding Syrah.

Sawtooth Cellars Id ★★→★★★ Gd Cab Sauv with latest Syrah and Viognier v.gd. Recently added an excellent Roussanne.

Seven Hills Walla ★★→★★★ Known for balanced, elegant Cab Sauv and Merlot. Ciel du Cheval Bordeaux blend v.gd. Pinot Gr from Oregon grapes well received.

Snoqualmie Vineyards Col V ★★→★★★ Always a reliable producer of Cab Sauv and Merlot, among others. Quality gone up with introduction of Naked bottlings, from organically grown grapes. The luscious Naked Ries is an instant classic.

Ste Chapelle Id ★★ Pleasant, forward Chard, Cab Sauv, Merlot and Syrah. Also v.gd Ries and Gewürz in dry Alsace style. Attractive sparkling wine. Chateau Series label features gd-value wines.

Three Rivers Winery Walla ★★ A "destination" winery producing a wide range of wines. Look esp for the bold Syrah and a gulpable Grenache.

Whitman Cellars Walla ★★→★★★ Steve Lessard makes wine from more than a dozen different v'yd blocks in Walla and Red Mtn AVAs. Wines inc a v.gd Syrah, gd Cab Sauv and one of Washington's best Merlots.

Woodward Canyon Walla ★★★→★★★★ (Cab) 01 02 03 04 05 06 07 09 The winery has set the standard for *Washington Cab Sauv* and Merlot for almost 30 yrs. Often overlooked, the Chard is also excellent.

NORTHEAST, SOUTHEAST & CENTRAL

This emerging region continues to grow at a rapid pace in both number of wineries and quality, despite an otherwise sagging economy. The number of oeno-tourists is expanding: New York State wine country now receives some five million visitors annually. Every state has seen an explosion of growth. New York (NY) has a total of 289 wineries, with 34 new establishments opening their doors in the past couple of years. Growth has been particularly strong in NY in non-traditional areas, ie. the Thousand Islands and the Champlain region; even Manhattan now boasts a winery. Virginia has 190 wineries, up from last year's 157. New Jersey now has 40 wineries, and Pennsylvania 140 (up from 120). The best Eastern wines are starting to gain recognition outside their own region. Top Rieslings from NY's Finger Lakes can now compete internationally. Long Island Merlot, Syrah and Cab Franc are fulfilling their initial promise, as is Michigan's Riesling. Virginia is making notable Viognier, as well as impressive Cabernet Franc, Petit Verdot, Syrah and other Rhône grapes.

Recent vintages

Because the 2010 growing season was mostly very hot and dry, grapes were harvested up to three weeks earlier than usual in many parts. Compared to 2009 – a good vintage in some areas but suffered in others because of a damp, cold spring – 2010 is universally viewed as the vintage of the decade in the east.

Alba NJ ★★ Unique microclimate for gd Pinot N and Cab F, and excellent Ries.

Anthony Road Finger L, NY ★★★★ 08 09 10 One of the best producers in the East with exceptional Ries; fine Pinot Gr, Cab Fr/Lemberger, late-harvest Vignoles.

Barboursville Vir ★★★★ 08 09 10 Founded 1976, one of the east's oldest and best modern-era wineries. Owned by the Zonin family (*see* Italy). Outstanding Italian varieties inc Barbera and Nebbiolo, plus succulent Bordeaux-style blend, excellent Cab F, and *Malvasia*. Elegant inn and Tuscan-style restaurant.

Bedell Long I, NY ★★★ 08 09 10 One of LONG ISLAND's first serious estates, now better than ever with new owner (co-founder of New Line Cinema) and new infusion of cash. Outstanding varietally labelled wines, inc Chard, Gewürz and Cab Fr, plus a bevy of toothsome blends.

Breaux Vir ★→★★ 09 10 Hilltop v'yd, hour from Washington DC. Gd Chard, Merlot.

Chamard Ct ★→★★ Leading winery with Chard, Pinot N, Cab Fr. Southeastern New England AVA.

Channing Daughters ★★★ 09 10 LONG ISLAND's South Fork estate giving special attention to uncommon varietals such as Tocai Friulano, Pinot Bianco, Pinot Gr.

Château LaFayette Reneau Finger L, NY ★★★ 08 09 10 Scenic winery overlooking Lake Seneca, with exceptional Cabs, Merlot, Chard and Ries.

Chrysalis Vir ★★★ 09 10 Notable Viognier, Petit Manseng, Albariño, Tannat, Norton.

Debonné Vineyards L Erie ★→★★ 09 10 Largest OHIO estate winery; *vinifera* and some hybrids. Top selections: Chard, Ries, Pinot Gr and Vidal Blanc Icewine.

Ferrante Winery Harpersfield OHIO producer, since 1937, with Chard, Pinot Grigio, Gewürz, Ries, native Catawba, Icewine.

Finger Lakes Scenic region in upstate NY with over 100 wineries nestled around the lakes. Source of most of the state's wines. Among top wineries are Anthony Road, CHATEAU LAFAYETTE RENEAU, DR. KONSTANTIN FRANK, FOX RUN, HERMANN J WIEMER, HERON HILL, KING FERRY, Lakewood, LAMOREAUX LANDING, Ravines, RED NEWT, STANDING STONE and Swedish Hill.

Firelands L Erie ★→★★ 10 Venerable OHIO producer (1880). Chard, Gewürz, Pinot Gr, Cab, Icewine.

Fox Run Finger L, NY ★★ 08 09 10 One of the best wineries here; fine Ries, Chard, Gewürz, Pinot N. A café for good light fare overlooks Lake Seneca.

Frank, Dr Konstantin (Vinifera Wine Cellars) Finger L, NY ★★★★ 07 08 09 10 Pioneering estate remains a leader in the East, with *Excellent Ries*, Gewürz; gd Chard, Gruner Veltliner, Pinot N. Fine Château Frank sparkling.

Georgia Now over 12 wineries. Look for: Three Sisters (Dahlonega), Habersham V'yds and Château Élan (Braselton), which features Southern splendour with v'yds, wine and a resort.

Glen Manor Vineyards Vir ★→★★ 09 10 Flinty Sauv Bl, age-worthy Bordeaux varietals.

Hamptons, The (aka South Fork) Long I, NY Enchanting region with three wineries: Channing Daughters, Duckwalk, and Wolfer Estate.

Hermann J Wiemer Finger L, NY ★→★★★ 08 09 10 Eponymous estate founded by German-born winemaker/former owner, one of first to plant *vinifera* in NY. Superior Ries, Chard, Gewürz and gd sparkling wine.

Heron Hill Finger L, NY ★★ 09 10 Views of Lake Keuka. Notable Ries; dessert wines.

Hillsborough One of Virginia's most promising young wineries.

Horton Vir ★ 08 09 10 Pioneering producer (early 1990s); gd Viognier, Norton.

Hudson River Region NY state's first AVA. Straddles the Hudson 90 minutes' drive north of Manhattan. Flagship estate: Millbrook.

Jefferson Vir ★★ 09 10 A stone's throw from Thomas Jefferson's historic Monticello estate. Fine Pinot Gr, Viognier, Chard, Merlot, Bordeaux blend.

Keswick Vir ★★★ 09 10 Exceptional Viognier, v.gd Touriga.

King Family Vineyards Vir ★★ 09 10 Toothsome Meritage, fine Pinot Verdot, *vin de paille* style Viognier/Petit Manseng blend.

King Ferry Finger L, NY ★★ 08 09 10 V. fine Ries, Chards, Cab Fr.

Lake Erie Important grape-growing area in the eastern US; 10,117 ha along the lake shore. Inc portions of NY, PENNSYLVANIA and OHIO. Also name of a tri-state AVA with more than 60 wineries.

Lamoureaux Landing Finger L, NY ★★★★ 08 09 10 Handsome estate with some of NY's best Chard, plus gd Ries and Cab Fr.

Lenz Long I, NY ★★★ 09 10 One of leading producers in NORTH FORK AVA. V. nice sparkling wine, Chard, Gewürz, Cabs and Merlot.

Linden Vir ★★★ 08 09 10 Pioneering estate (since 1981) in mts, 100-km west of Washington DC; remains one of region's best. Superb Sauv Bl, also Cab Fr, Petit Verdot, Bordeaux-style red blends.

Long Island NY wine region extending 120 miles into the Atlantic Ocean. First *vinifera* vines planted 1973. Today 56 wineries, most of them on the NORTH FORK (three AVAs: LONG ISLAND, NORTH FORK and THE HAMPTONS), all *vinifera*. Top estates: Jamesport, Pugliese, Rafael, Sherwood House. Also Comtesse Thérèse, Martha Clara, Raphael, Shinn Estate, Sherwood House, Bouké, Clovis Point, Roanoke and Sparkling Pointe.

Maryland With 45 wineries, top estates are Black Ankle, Sugarloaf and Elk Run. Woodhall continues to produce gd Barbera. Up-and-coming stars: Bordeleau, (Chard, Viognier and Malbec), and Serpent Ridge (Cabs Sauv and Fr).

Michael Shaps/Virginia Wineworks ★★★★ 07 08 09 10 Consistent producer of superior Viognier, complex Chard, notable Petit Verdot, Cab Fr, Merlot; v. fine Bordeaux-style red blend; Raisin d'Être made from dried Petit Verdot and Cab Fr.

Michigan 85 wineries using Michigan grapes (800 ha, two-thirds *vinifera*), four AVAs. Impressive Ries, Gewürz, Pinot Gr; v.gd Cab Fr and blends in some yrs. Best: Bel Lago, Black Star, Bowers Harbor, Brys, Château Grand Traverse, Fenn Valley, Peninsula Cellars (esp dry Gewürz), Tabor Hill and L Mawby (outstanding sparkling). Up-and-coming: Chateau Chantal, Chateau Fontaine, Cherry Creek, 45 North, Lawton Ridge, Left Foot Charley, Longview, 2 Lads.

Millbrook Hudson R ★★ 09 10 Prestige estate in NY's Hudson Valley, produces Chard, Tocai Friulano, Pinot N, Cab Fr.

Missouri Winemaking continues to expand, with 92 producers in three AVAs: Augusta, Hermann, Ozark Highlands. Best wines are from Seyval Bl, Vidal, Vignoles (sweet and dry versions) and Chambourcin. The Unversity of Missouri has a new experimental winery to test techniques and grape varieties. Stone Hill in Hermann makes v.gd Chardonel (a frost-hardy hybrid of Seyval Bl and Chard), Norton and gd Seyval Bl and Vidal Blanc. Hermannhof is also drawing notice for Vignoles, Chardonel and Norton. Also notable: St James for Vignoles, Seyval, Norton; Mount Pleasant (Augusta) for rich Port-style and Norton; Adam Puchta for gd Port-style and Norton, Vignoles, Vidal Blanc; Augusta Winery for Chambourcin, Chardonel, Icewine; Les Bourgeois for gd Syrah, Norton, Chardonel, Montelle, v.gd Cynthiana and Chambourcin.

North Carolina 100 wineries, inc Biltmore, Childress, Duplin (for Muscadine), Hanover Park, Iron Gate, Laurel Gray, McRitchie, Old North State, RagApple, RayLen, Raffaldini, Rockhouse, Shelton. Top varieties: Chard, Viognier, Cab Fr.

North Fork Popular getaway destination for Manhattanites. LONG ISLAND AVA. NY AVA. Among top estates: Bedell, Jamesport, Lieb, LENZ, PALMER, PAUMANOK, PELLEGRINI, PINDAR, Raphael.

Ohio 155 wineries, five AVAs. Some exceptional Pinot Gr, Ries, Pinot N, Icewine. Top producers: DEBONNÉ, FERRANTE, FIRELANDS, Harmony Hill, Harpersfield, Henke, Kinkead Ridge, Paper Moon, St Joseph, Valley V'yds.

Palmer Long I, NY ★★ 09 10 Founded in 1986 by savvy advertising exec Bob Palmer. Notable Chard, Sauv Bl, Cab Fr, and sparkling wine.

Paumanok Long I, NY ★★★ 08 09 10 Family owned and run winery on NORTH FORK; makes quality Ries, Chard, Chenin Bl, Merlot, Cabs, and Petit Verdot.

Pellegrini Long I, NY ★★★ 08 09 10 Sophisticated winery, with classy Merlot, Chards, Cab Fr.

Pennsylvania 140 wineries. Top estates: Briar Valley (gd Chard, Cab Fr), Chaddsford (can be exceptional red blends), Allegro (Chard, Merlot), Crossing (Chard, Cab Fr, Merlot, Vidal), Pinnacle Ridge (sparkling, Bordeaux-style blend), Chambourcin), Manatawny Creek (Cabs Fr and Sauv, Bordeaux-style blend), Waltz (Chard, Cabs), LAKE ERIE's Mazza (Vidal Icewine).

Pindar Vineyards Long I, NY ★★ 09 10 LONG ISLAND's largest winery (116 ha). Wide range, inc fine Chards, Merlot, Ries, Cab Fr, v.gd Bordeaux-style blends. Visitors centre.

Pollack Vir ★★★ 07 08 09 10 Superior winery (2003), outstanding Chard, Pinot Gr, Petit Verdot, Cabs Fr and Sauv Bl, Merlot, and Bordeaux blends (r w).

RDV Vir Brand-new estate (2011) with spectacular caves and promising wines.

Red Newt Finger L, NY ★★★ 09 10 One of FINGER LAKE's best; superb Ries, outstanding Chard, Cab Fr, Merlot, Bordeaux-style blend. Fine bistro: regional cuisine.

Sakonnet Rhode I ★ 09 10 One of New England's most venerable estates, with gd Chard, Vidal Blanc and sparkling wine.

Sheldrake Point Finger L, NY ★★★ 09 10 Outstanding Ries, Gewürz, Chard. Fine bistro on shores of Lake Cayuga.

Southeastern New England An AVA running from Cape Cod through the southern coast of Massachusetts, coastal Rhode Island and coastal Connecticut. The climate is heavily influenced by its close proximity to the Atlantic Ocean. Whites and sparkling wines dominate. Leading producers: Newport V'yds, Truro V'yds, Sakonnet and Westport Rivers.

Standing Stone Finger L, NY ★★ 09 10 Excellent producer; v.gd Ries, Gewürz, Vidal, and Bordeaux-style blend.

Unionville Vineyards N Jer ★→★★ Notable Chard, Ries; fine Bordeaux-style red.

Veritas Vir ★★ 09 10 Fine Virginia producer, with stylish Brut Sparkling, Sauv Bl, Chard, Cab F and Petit Manseng.

Villa Appalaccia Vir ★★ 09 10 Nestled in the scenic Blue Ridge Mts; wines with a taste of Italy, inc Primitivo, Sangiovese, Pinot Gr, and a Malvasia Bianca blend.

American Viticultural Areas (AVAs)

The federal regulations regarding appellation of origin in the USA were established in 1977, rather late in the day and confusing as well. There are two categories. First: a straightforward political AVA that includes an entire state, ie. California, Washington, Oregon and so on. Individual counties can also be used, such as Santa Barbara or Sonoma. When the county designation is used, all grapes must come from that county. The second category is a geographical designation, such as Napa Valley or Willamette Valley within the state. These AVAs are supposed to be based on similarity of soils, weather, etc. In practice, they are inclusive not exclusive. Within the AVAs there can be further sub-appellations. For example, the Napa Valley AVA contains Rutherford and Stags Leap. When the geographical designations are used, all grapes must come from that region. A producer meeting the regulatory standards may choose a purely political listing, such as Napa, or a geographical listing, such as Napa Valley.

Virginia (Vir) 190 bonded wineries (many less than an hour's drive from Washington DC) and six AVAs. Virginia has become one of the most important wine producing states in the east. Overall quality has skyrocketed.

White Hall Vir ★★★ 09 10 This is a stylish winery nr historic Charlottesville. Fine Pinot Gr, Gewürz; commendable Petit Manseng and top Chard, Cab Fr, Cab Sauv blends.

Wisconsin Best is Wollersheim, specializing in variations of Maréchel Foch. Prairie Fumé (Seyval Bl) is a commercial success.

Wölffer Estate Long I, NY ★★★ 08 09 Fine Chard, vibrant rosé and gd Merlot from talented German-born winemaker.

THE SOUTHWEST

From the dry, arid regions of Arizona to the mountains of Colorado to the plains of Texas, the Southwest is establishing a place in the world of wine. Wine festivals, wine clubs and wine-trail promotions are drawing in aficionados, leading to an increase in the number of wineries. Texas has over 200 wineries, an increase of 30% since 2000, and ranks fifth in the USA in wine production. Colorado, approaching 100 wineries, makes rich, full-bodied wines. Arizona, often using organic, biodynamic and solar techniques, has over 45 wineries. Dick Erath of Oregon now has a winery, Cimarron, in Arizona. With a great diversity of growing conditions to work with, winemakers are experimenting with various grape varieties. Oklahoma, along with *vinifera*, grows hybrids and native American grapes. New Mexico looks to Rhône, Italian and Spanish grapes. Seek out Montepulciano, Tempranillo and Refosco.

Alamosa Tex V.gd Tempranillo; early-drinking white blends, especially Scissortail with Marsanne.

Arizona Alcantara V'yds: gd Sauv Bl, Mourvèdre. Callaghan V'yds: ★★ one of Arizona's best wineries. Look for Syrah and red blend: Claire. Cimarron: label of Dick Erath of Oregon; new, promising, exciting. Dos Cabezas: v.gd Cab Sauv, Syrah. Keeling Schaefer V'yds: gd Grenache, Syrah. Page Springs: new, promising with emphasis on Rhône-styles. Pillsbury Wine Company: filmmaker Sam Pillsbury finds success with his Arizona wines and catchy labels: Roan Red, WildChild White, Wildchild Red worth seeking out. Sonoita: a pioneer of Arizona wines with gd Syrah, Colombard, Cab Sauv.

Becker Vineyards Tex ★★ Continues with award-winning wines, esp Cab Sauv, Viognier, Res Malbec, Sauv Bl.

Brennan Vineyards Tex Excellent Viognier, v.gd Cab Sauv and Syrah.

Colorado Allis Ranch: boutique winery with focus on Rhône varietals, v.gd Two Husky Syrah. Balistreri V'ds: v.gd Merlot, Zin. Bookcliff: gd Viognier/ Ries. Boulder Creek: v.gd Viognier, Cab Sauv. Canyon Wind: v.gd Sauv Bl, Tempranillo, and IV, a red blend of Petit Verdot, Cab Sauv, Merlot, Cab Fr. Carlson Cellars: ★★ excellent Ries, v.gd Lemberger, fruit wines, esp cherry served with melted chocolate. Garfield Estates: v.gd Sauv Bl, Cab Fr, Syrah. Graystone: specializes in Port-styles, all v.gd with rich aftertaste. Guy Drew: excellent Syrah, v.gd Petit Verdot, Cab Fr. Ptarmigan: 5th largest in Colorado, has second label, Stoney Mesa, both with v. approachable wines, esp Ries, Gewürz, Merlot. Reeder Mesa: gd Cab Fr, Syrah, Land's End Red blend. Winery at Holy Cross: ★ excellent Cab Sauv, Syrah. V.gd Ries, Merlot, Cab Fr.

Duchman Tex New and promising producer, with v.gd Montepulciano, Vermentino and Dolcetto.

Fairhaven Vineyards Tex Focusing on French/American and American hybrids showing that Chambourcin and Baco Noir are well worth tasting.

Flat Creek Tex V.gd Pinot Gr, gd Mistella (dessert wine) unfermented Muscat Canelli and brandy.

Grape Creek Tex Gd Viognier, Pinot Gr, Merlot and red blends.

Haak Winery Tex ★ V.gd Malbec, Blanc du Bois; bestselling Madeira continues winning awards and praise.

Inwood Estates A worthy Texas Hill Country addition with v.gd Tempranillo and a Palomino/Chard Blend.

Kiepersol Estates Vineyards Tex V.gd Sangiovese, Syrah, Cab Sauv.

Llano Estacado Lubbock, Tex ★★ The pioneer and one of Texas' largest wineries. Gd Viviana, a white blend; v.gd Port-style and Cab Sauv.

Lone Oak Burleson, Tex. V.gd Tempranillo, gd Merlot.

McPherson Cellars Lubbock, Tex ★→★★ Created to honour Dr. Clinton McPherson, a Texas wine pioneer; well-crafted Cab Sauv, Sangiovese, Viognier, Syrah.

Messina Hof Wine Cellars Bryan, Tex ★★ Excellent Ries, esp late-harvest. V.gd Cab Sauv, Meritage (red) and Port-styles. Winemaker Paul Bonarrigo continues to charm with his red beret.

Nevada Tahoe Ridge, previously Churchill V'yds: gd Res Zin, Petite Sirah. Pahrump Valley, nr Las Vegas, is quite a showplace, with restaurant; gd Symphony, Zin.

New Mexico Amaro Winey: new with gd Dolcetto, Refosco. Black Mesa ★★, Estrella del Norte and Santa Fe V'yds all under winemaker Jerry Burd. V.gd Montepulciano, Dolcetto and, after a visit to Spain, a winning Sherry-style aged in solera. Casa Abril: small, family-owned, with promising Malbec, Tempranillo. Gruet: ★★ excellent sparkling wines just get better. Don Quixote: enterprising boutique winery and craft distillery nr Los Alamos. Wines under label Manhattan Project worth watching. Intriguing *grappa* and blue corn vodka. Wines of the San Juan: In Four Corners with gd Cab Sauv, Pale Morning Dun, blend of Ugni Bl, Chenin Bl, Muscat. Luna Rossa: ★→★★ v.gd Montepulciano and age-worthy Cab Sauv.

Oklahoma Chapel Hill, El Reno: gd Traminett, Norton. Greenfield V'yd, Chandler: gd Merlot, Sauv Bl. Nuyaka Creek, Nuyaka: tasty, but unusual fruit/berry wines, some blended with grapes; try Elderberry, Peach Mist with Chard and peaches or Baileyana, made from local native grapes. Stone Bluff Cellars, Haskell: gd Vignoles, Cynthiana, Chardonel. Oak Hills Winery, Chelsea: v.gd Catawba, Chambourcin, Seyval Bl, Traminette.

Peregrine Hill Fort Stockton, Tex Gd Chard, Pinot N.

Sunset Burleson, Tex Gd Cab Sauv and Twilight Tango Malbec.

Val Verde Tex A 4th-generation tradition. V.gd Chard, Pinot Grigio, Merlot.

Zin Valle Tex V.gd Rising Star Brut (sparkling); gd Pinot N, Gewürz.

Canada

S ome 500 producers strong, Canada grows a wide variety of grapes from coast to coast. In Ontario's Niagara Peninsula and more recently further east in Prince Edward County, Chardonnay, Riesling, Pinot Noir and Cabernet Franc are challenging Icewine's supremacy. To the west, British Columbia's Okanagan and Similkameen valleys and selected Vancouver Island sites are making equally noteworthy wines, with their future likely shaped by Pinot Gris, Merlot, Syrah and an array of aromatic white blends. Nova Scotia is showing sparkling promise.

Ontario

Cave Spring ★★→★★★ 09 (10) Benchmark Ries, especially CSV and Estate labels; burgundian-style, old-vines Chard; exceptional late-harvest and Icewines.

Flat Rock ★★★ 09 (10) Crisp, modern, cool-climate wines, screwcap. Consistently excellent Ries, Pinot N and Chard. Single-block Nadja's Ries is a standout.

Henry of Pelham ★★★ 07 09 (10) Family-run; specializing in Chard, Ries; Bordeaux-style reds, unique Baco Noir, Ries Icewine. Top label: Speck Family Reserve (SFR).

Inniskillin ★★★ 07 09 (10) Pioneer Icewine house. New era with Bruce Nicholson. Delicious Ries, Pinot Gr, Pinot N, Cab Fr; specialty Ries and Vidal Icewine.

Jackson-Triggs ★★★ 07 (10) State-of-art winery. Delaine Vineyard and Grand Res whites lead the pack with promising releases of Pinot N and Syrah.

Le Clos Jordanne ★★★★ 08 09 (10) Founded as a France-Canada joint venture making benchmark Niagara Pinot N and Chard from organic v'yds.

Stratus ★★★★ 07 (10) High-tech winery, flagship white and red multivarietal blends; excellent Icewine.

Tawse ★★★★ 07 (10) The *Wine Access* 2010 Canadian Winery of the Year, making outstanding Chard, Ries and high-quality Pinot N, Cab Fr and Merlot farmed using organic principles.

Thirty Bench Wine Makers ★★★ V.gd single-lot, old-vine Ries from 27-ha Beamsville Bench v'yd. Owner Andrew Peller, Canada's second-largest wine producer.

British Columbia

Blue Mountain ★★★★ 06 09 Long-time producer of excellent sparkling wine, and high-quality, age-worthy Pinot N, Chard and Pinot Gr.

Burrowing Owl ★★★ 06 09 Picture-perfect wine estate making excellent Chard, Cab Fr, Pinot Gr and Syrah; acclaimed boutique hotel and restaurant.

CedarCreek ★★★★ 06 09 Terrific aromatic Ries, Gewürz, Ehrenfelser and classic Northwest Merlot; plus top-end Platinum Chard, Syrah and Pinot N.

Jackson-Triggs Okanagan ★★★ 06 09 Popular, easy-drinking style with v.gd Shiraz, Meritage and outstanding Ries Icewine.

Mission Hill ★★★★ 06 08 09 Acclaimed Chard, Syrah and Legacy Series: Perpetua, Oculus, Quatrain and Compendium. Al fresco dining, good cooking.

Nk'Mip ★★★ 06 09 Part of $25m Aboriginal resort and spa. Well-made Pinot Bl, Ries and Pinot N; top picks Qwam Qwmt Pinot N and Meritage.

Osoyoos Larose ★★★★ 07 08 09 Remarkable benchmark, single-vineyard, age-worthy Bordeaux blend by Groupe Taillan and Vincor Canada. The excellent second label is Pétales d'Osoyoos.

Quails' Gate ★★★ 06 09 Family-owned estate making excellent Pinot N and Chard, aromatic Ries, Chenin Bl with cult-like following for its Old-Vines Foch.

Tantalus ★★★★ 08 09 New green facility complements one of the oldest (1927) v'yds. Non-interventionist Pinot N and Ries are the story.

South America

Abbreviations used in the text:

Aco	Aconcagua
Cata	Catamar
Casa	Casablanca
Col	Colchagua
Cur	Curicó
Elq	Elqui
Mai	Maipo
Mau	Maule
Men	Mendoza
Pat	Patagonia
Rap	Rapel
Sal	Salta
San J	San Juan
San A	San Antonio
Sant	Santiago

Recent vintages

Whites are almost without exception at their best within two years of vintage, reds within three years. The most ambitious reds (Chilean Cabernet-based wines and Syrah, Argentine Cabernets and Malbecs) will last for a decade or more, but whether they improve beyond their 5th year is debatable. Also, recent improvements mean that wines from a lesser vintage today outperform those from earlier, more favourable years (the earthquake that struck Curicó and Maule in Chile early in 2010 took place before vintage, so while some quantities were down, quality was unaffected).

CHILE

First the negative. Chile still has too many reds that are correct but soulless, offering little beyond oaky, blackcurrant-pastille flavour, made by winemakers whose clean fingernails show just how close they aren't to the soil. Now the positive. There's an ongoing search for newer, usually cooler regions, combined with a more grown-up approach to white wines. The result is increasing complexity and minerality in the best bottles. A resurrection of old vines (especially in less fashionable Maule and Itata) sees Carignan and País undergoing something of a renaissance. MOVI (Movimiento de Viñateros Indipendientes) is a new formation of boutique wineries from all over the country. Chile is divided into five viticultural zones (with subregions). North to south: Atacama

(Copiapó, Huasco), Coquimbo (Elqui, Limarí, Choapa), Aconcagua (Aconcagua, Casablanca, San Antonio), Central Valley (Maipo, Rapel, Curicó, Maule) and the South (Itata, Bío-Bío, Malleco). It's generally cooler the further south you go, but altitude and proximity to the sea also determine which grapes suit which vineyard.

Aconcagua Traditionally a warm region for sturdy reds, but new coastal plantings show potential for whites.

Almaviva Mai ★★★ Expensive, classy, claret-style red; joint venture between CONCHA Y TORO and Baron Philippe de Rothschild (Escudo Rojo red blend is also v.gd).

Altaïr Rap ★★→★★★ Ambitious joint venture: Ch Dassault (St-Emilion) and SAN PEDRO DE YACOCHUYA. Pascal Chatonnet of Bordeaux consults; *grand vin* (mostly Cab Sauv, Carmenère) complex, earthy. Second wine: Sideral, earlier-drinking.

Anakena ★→★★ Solid range. Flagship wines under ONA label: punchy Syrah, single-v'yd bottlings; Res Chard gd. Look for Viognier and ONA Pinot N.

Antiyal Mai ★★→★★★ Alvaro Espinoza's own biodynamically farmed estate; fine, complex red blend from Carmenère, Cab Sauv and Syrah. Second wine is Kuyen, also new varietal Carmenère.

Apaltagua Rap ★★→★★★ Carmenère specialist drawing on old-vine fruit from Apalta (Colchagua). Grial is rich, herbal flagship wine.

Aquitania, Viña Mai ★★→★★★ Chilean/French joint venture (Paul Pontallier and Bruno Prats [Bordeaux]); v.gd Lazuli Cab Sauv, Sol de Sol Chard (from Malleco).

Arboleda, Viña ★★→★★★ Part of the ERRÁZURIZ/CALITERRA stable, with whites from Leyda and Casablanca and reds from Aconcagua, inc polished Cab Sauv/Merlot/Carmenère blend Seña and excellent varietal Carmenère. New Marsanne/Viognier/Roussanne peachy but refined.

Aristos ★★→★★★ New label for terroir-specialist Pedro Parra and two French winemakers. Intriguing Chard and two red blends (one Bordeaux-inspired, the other a Syrah/Petite Sirah blend) augur well for the future.

Bío-Bío Promising southern region. Potential for gd whites and Pinot N.

Botalcura Cur ★★→★★★ French winemaker Philippe Debrus makes v.gd Grand Res Cab Fr and red blend Cayao; promising Nebbiolo, too.

Caliterra ★→★★ Sister winery of ERRÁZURIZ. Chard and Sauv Bl improving, reds becoming less one-dimensional, esp Tributo range and new flagship red Cenit. Bio-Sur is new organic range.

Carmen, Viña ★★→★★★ Organic pioneer; same ownership as SANTA RITA. Ripe, fresh Casablanca Chard Special Res; top late-harvest Sem. Reds even better, esp Petite Sirah and Gold Res Cab Sauv.

Casablanca Cool-climate region between Santiago and coast. Little water: drip-irrigation essential. Top-class Chard, Sauv Bl; promising Merlot, Pinot N.

Casablanca, Viña ★→★★ Originally a white specialist with fine Sauv Bl, Chard, Gewürz but super-*cuvée* Syrah-based Neblus (CASABLANCA) and Nimbus Estate Merlot (COLCHAGUA) are v.gd

Casa Marín San A ★★★ Dynamic white specialist, v.gd Gewürz and superb Sauv Bl. Syrah and Pinot N promising.

Casas del Bosque ★→★★ Elegant range, inc juicy, underrated Sauv Bl, svelte Pinot N, peppery Syrah Res and refined Cachapoal Cab Sauv.

Casas del Toqui ★→★★★ RAPEL venture by Médoc Château Larose-Trintaudon under the Las Casas del Toqui and Viña Alamosa labels. Silky top-end Leyenda red blend and Prestige Cab Sauv.

Casa Silva Col ★★ V'yds in the coastal zone of Paredones (v.gd Sauv Bl). Solid range topped by silky, complex Altura red, smoky Microterroir Carmenère and Quinta Generación Red and White. Also commendable Doña Dominga range.

CHILE

Chocalan, Viña ★★ Gentle, friendly reds, inc fragrant Gran Reserva Malbec. Also range of Malvilla whites from SAN ANTONIO.

Clos Ouvert Mau ★★ New venture; natural winemaking using old-vine fruit. Range inc: Loncomilla (Carménère), Huaso (País) and red blend Otono.

Concha y Toro Sant ★→★★★ Mammoth, quality-minded operation. Best: subtle Amelia Chard (CASABLANCA); *grippy Don Melchor Cab Sauv*; Terrunyo; Winemaker Lot single-v'yd range; and complex Carmin de Peumo (Carménère). Marqués de Casa Concha, Trio, Explorer, Casillero del Diablo v.gd value. New Gran Reserva Serie Riberas range features six wines from v'yds close to different rivers. Maycas del Limarí in the north making gd Chard; owns Fairtrade producer Viña Los Robles and Palo Alto. *See also* ALMAVIVA, CONO SUR, TRIVENTO (Argentina).

Cono Sur ★★→★★★ V.gd Pinot N, headed by Ocio. Other top releases appear as 20 Barrels selection; new innovations under Visión label (BÍO-BÍO Ries is superb). Also *dense, fruity Cab Sauv*, delicious Viognier, rose-petal Gewürz, impressive new Syrah. Second label: Isla Negra; owned by CONCHA Y TORO.

Cousiño Macul Mai ★★ Reliable Antiguas Res Cab Sauv; zesty Sauvignon Gris; top-of-the-range blend Lota is gd rather than great. Cab Sauv rosé v. refreshing.

Edwards, Luís Felipe ★★ Decent Colchagua reds (silky Res Cab Sauv, Shiraz and plump Doña Bernarda) and Leyda whites (citrus Gran Reserva Chard and tangy Marea de Leyda Sauv Bl).

Elqui Northernmost wine-producing valley, v'yds cooled by sea breezes range from 350–2,000 metres in altitude, suitable for several varieties.

Emiliana ★→★★★ Organic/biodynamic specialist involving Alvaro Espinoza (*see also* ANTIYAL, GEO WINES). Complex, Syrah-heavy "G" and Coyam almost Mediterranean-style wildness; cheaper Adobe and Novas ranges v.gd for affordable complexity.

Errázuriz ★→★★★ Complex *Wild Ferment Chard*; brooding La Cumbre Syrah; complex Don Maximiano Cab Sauv; fragrant KAI Carmenère. *See also* ARBOLEDA, CALITERRA, VIÑEDO CHADWICK.

Falernia, Viña ★★ ELQUI pioneer making Rhône-like Syrah, fragrant Carmenère, tangy Sauv Bl; complex new red blend Number One. Labels inc Alta Tierra, Mayu.

Fournier, Bodegas O ★★ Promising new venture for one of Argentina's top producers, already v'gd Leyda Sauv Bl and Centauri Red blend (MAULE).

Garcés Silva, Viña ★★→★★★ Exciting SAN ANTONIO bodega making excellent, full-bodied Sauv Bl and commendable Pinot N and Chard under Amayna label.

Geo Wines Umbrella label under which Alvaro Espinoza makes wines for several new wineries. Look for earthy Chono San Lorenzo MAIPO red blend, Ventolera Leyda Pinot N and tangy Quintay BÍO-BÍO Ries.

Hacienda Araucano ★★→★★★ François Lurton's Chilean enterprise. Complex Gran Araucano Sauv Bl (CASABLANCA), refined Carmenère/Cab Sauv blend Clos de Lolol, heady Alka Carmenère.

Haras de Pirque Mai ★★→★★★ Estate in Pirque. Smoky Sauv Bl, stylish Chard, dense Cab Sauv/Merlot. Top wine Albis (Cab Sauv/Carménère) is solid, smoky red made in joint venture with Antinori (*see* Italy).

Koyle Col ★→★★ UNDURRAGA family's new winery, making solid Syrah and Cab Sauv.

Lapostolle ★★→★★★★ Impressive French-owned, Michel Rolland-inspired winery. Gd across the board, with Sem highlight of the increasingly elegant whites, and Cuvée Alexandre Merlot and Syrah and Carmenère-based Clos Apalta pick of the reds. Classic range now renamed Casa.

La Rosa, Viña ★★ Reliable RAPEL Chard, Merlot, Cab Sauv (La Palma, La Capitana, Cornellana labels). Don Reca reds the stars and Ossa Sixth Generation red blend.

Leyda, Viña ★★→★★★ SAN ANTONIO pioneers, producing elegant Chard (Lot 5 Wild Yeasts is the pick), lush Pinot N (esp Lot 21 *cuvée* and lively rosé), tangy Garuma Sauv Bl. Now under same ownership as TABALÍ.

Limarí Northerly, high-altitude region, so quite chilly (for Chile); impressing with Syrah and Chard.

Loma Larga Casa ★★→★★★ V. classy range, with Sauv Bl, Pinot N, Cab Fr and Syrah all impressing. Second label: Lomas del Valle.

Maipo Famous wine region close to Santiago. Chile's best Cab Sauvs often come from higher, eastern subregions, such as Pirque and Puente Alto.

Martino, de ★★ →★★★ Based in west MAIPO, but with v'yds throughout Chile, best known for Carmenère, but also impressing with Cab Sauv Gran Familia, single-v'yd wines and Legado range.

Matetic San A ★★★ Decent Pinot N and Chard from exciting winery. Stars are fragrant, *zesty Sauv Bl* and spicy, berry EQ Syrah. Second label: Corralillo.

Maule Southernmost region in Valle Central. Claro, Loncomilla, Tutuven valleys.

Montes ★★→★★★★ Highlights of a first-class range are Alpha Cab Sauv, Bordeaux-blend Montes Alpha M, *Folly Syrah from Apalta* and Purple Angel – Carmenère at its most intense. Also promising new Leyda Sauv Bl and Pinot N. Experiments with v. high-density plantings – 15,000 vines/ha! – in Marchihue. Also promising Sauv Bl and Pinot N from nearby beach resort, Zapallar.

MontGras ★★→★★★ Fine limited-edition wines, inc Syrah, Zin. High-class flagships Ninquén Cab Sauv, Antu Ninquén Syrah. Gd-value organic Soleus; gentle but fine Intriga (MAIPO) Cab Sauv; excellent Amaral (Leyda) whites.

Morandé ★★ Gd-value range, inc César, Cinsault, Bouschet, Carignan. Edición Limitada range, inc a spicy Syrah/Cab Sauv, inky Malbec; top wine is Cab Sauv-based House of Morandé.

Neyen Rap ★★★ Apalta project for Patrick Valette of St-Emilion, making intense old-vine Carmenère/Cab Sauv blend. Now owned by VERAMONTE.

Odfjell ★→★★★ Red specialist with v.gd Carmenère, Carignan (from MAULE) and Aliara (a blend); other ranges Orzada and entry-level Armador.

Pérez Cruz, Viña ★★★ MAIPO winery with Alvaro Espinoza (ANTIYAL) in charge of winemaking. Fresh, spicy Syrah; aromatic Cot; stylish Quelen, Liguai red blends.

Principal, El ★★→★★★ Now thriving under new ownership, from high-altitude v'yd, all Cab/Carmenère blends: Calicanto, Memorias, El Principal.

Quebrada de Macul, Viña Mai ★★→★★★ Ambitious winery making gd Chard and v.gd Domus Aurea Cab Sauv; sister Cabs Stella Aurea and Peñalolen also tasty.

Rapel Quality region divided into Colchagua and Cachapoal valleys. Best for hearty reds, esp Carmenère and Syrah, but watch for cooler coastal subregions Marchihue and Paradones.

Ribera del Lago Mau ★★ Complex Cab Sauv Merlot and minerally Sauv Bl from Rafael Tirado under the Laberinto label.

San Antonio Coastal region west of Santiago benefiting from sea breezes; v. promising for whites, Syrah and Pinot N. Leyda is a subzone.

San Pedro de Yacochuya ★→★★★ Massive Curicó-based producer. 35 South (35 Sur) for affordable varietals; Castillo de Molina a step up. Best are 1865 Limited Edition reds, Kankana del Elqui Syrah and elegant Cabo de Hornos. Under same ownership as ALTAÏR, Viña Mar, Missiones de Rengo, Santa Helena, TARAPACÁ.

Santa Alicia Mai ★→★★★ Red specialist. Best wines: firm but juicy Millantu Cab Sauv-based flagship wine, and lithe but structured Anke Blend 1 (Cab Fr/ Petit Verdot).

Santa Carolina, Viña Sant ★★→★★★ Quality ladder goes varietal, Reserva, Barrica Selection, Reserva de Familia and new VSC Cab Sauv/Syrah/Petit Verdot blends. Syrah and Carmenère gd at all levels, new Specialties range (SAN ANTONIO Sauv Bl, LIMARÍ Chard, MAULE Carignan, MAIPO Syrah) excellent.

Santa Rita ★★→★★★★ Quality-conscious bodega, based in MAIPO, but with v'yds in many regions, now working with Aussie Brian Croser. Best: *Casa Real Cab Sauv;*

but Pehuén (Carmenère), Triple C (Cab Sauv/Cab Fr/Carmenère) and Floresta range nearly as gd.

Seña Mai *See* ARBOLEDA.

Tabalí ★★ Winery partly owned by SAN PEDRO, making refined Chard, peachy Viognier, silky Pinot N and earthy, peppery Syrah. Single-v'yd Payen Syrah, Talinay Chard and Pinot N top the range.

Tamaya, Viña Casa ★★ On the ball with Graves-like Winemaker's Selection Sauv Bl, and gd Res Carmenère and Syrah.

Tarapacá, Viña ★★ Steadily improving historic winery, now part of the VSPT group with SAN PEDRO. Top wines Tara Pakay (Cab Sauv/Syrah) and Etiqueta Negra Gran Reserva (Cab Sauv).

Torres, Miguel Cur ★★→★★★ Fresh whites and gd reds, esp sturdy *Manso de Velasco* single-v'yd Cab Sauv and Cariñena-based Cordillera. Conde de Superunda is rare top *cuvée*, also new organic range Tormenta. *See also* Spain.

Undurraga ★→★★ Historic MAIPO estate, now impressing under new ownership. Best wines are LIMARÍ Syrah and the Sauv Bls from Leyda and CASABLANCA under the TH (Terroir Hunter) label; also lively Brut Royal Chard/Pinot N sparkler and peachy Late Harvest Sem.

Valdivieso Cur ★→★★★ Major producer impressing in recent yrs with Res and single-v'yd range from top terroirs around Chile (Leyda Chard esp gd). NV red blend Caballo Loco and wonderfully spicy new Carignan-based éclat.

Vascos, Los Rap ★→★★★ Lafite-Rothschild venture moving from Bordeaux wannabe to more successful yet still elegant style. Top: Le Dix and Grande Réserve.

VC Family Estates ★→★★★ Major company with v'yds in various regions, inc over 700 ha in BÍO-BÍO, and brands Gracia de Chile, Porta, Agustinos (gd, peppery Grand Res Malbec) and Veranda, formerly a joint venture with Boisset of Burgundy, and now making v'gd Pinot N – Millerandage is top *cuvée*.

Ventisquero, Viña Col ★→★★★ Ambitious winery, whose labels inc Chilano and Yali; top wines are two Apalta reds: rich but fragrant Pangea Syrah and Carmenère/Syrah blend Vertice. Promising new Herú CASABLANCA Pinot N.

Veramonte Casa ★★ Whites from CASABLANCA fruit, red from Valle Central grapes – all gd. Top wine: Primus red blend.

Viñedo Chadwick Mai ★★★ Stylish Cab Sauv improving with each vintage from v'yd owned by Eduardo Chadwick, chairman of ERRÁZURIZ.

Viu Manent Col ★→★★ Emerging winery. Malbec-based Viu I, Carmenère-based El Incidente best. Secreto Malbec, Viognier also v.gd. Late-harvest Sem top-notch.

Von Siebenthal Aco ★★★ Swiss-owned boutique winery. V.gd Carabantes Syrah, elegant Montelig blend, fine-boned Toknar Petit Verdot and concentrated but v. pricey Carmenère-based Tatay de Cristóbal.

ARGENTINA

Currently the darling of American wine-drinkers, but are we alone in finding many reds just too much of a good thing? Expect richness and intensity from old-vine Malbec, but there should also be some fragrance and gentleness – missing in too many top-end *cuvées*. Seek out those from cooler spots, such as Tupungato, Mendoza or Neuquen and Río Negro, Patagonia. For whites, while the fragrant Torrontés can make some characterful, grapey wines in the Cafayate region of Salta, fresh young Sauvignons and Chardonnays from those cool areas would be preferable.

Achaval Ferrer Men ★★★ Super-concentrated Altamira, Bella Vista and Mirador single-v'yd Malbecs and Quimera Malbec/Cab/Merlot blends.

Alta Vista Men ★→★★★ Excellent dense, spicy *Alto* (Malbec/Cab) and trio of single-v'yd Malbecs: Alizarine, Serenade (Luján de Cuyo), Temis (Uco Valley). Also zesty Torrontés. Sister winery Navarrita makes fine Winemaker's Selection Malbec.

Altocedro Men ★★→★★★ Lightly oaked Malbec and Tempranillo are trump cards for this La Consulta (Valle de Uco) winery – blended for top wine Desnudos.

Altos las Hormigas Men ★★→★★★ Malbec specialist; impressive Bonarda, Alberto Antonini (ex-Italy's Antinori) makes the wine. Best: Viña las Hormigas Reserva.

Antucura Men ★★★ Valle de Uco bodega with beautifully balanced, spicy Cab Sauv/ Merlot blend. Second label: Calvulcura.

Argento Men ★→★★ CATENA offshoot making gd commercial wine under Libertad, Malambo and Argento labels.

Atamisque ★→★★★ Based in Tupungato; impressing with tangy reds, esp Malbec/ Merlot/Cab Sauv Assemblage. Serbal, Catalpa are lower tiers in v.gd range.

Bianchi, Valentin ★ San Rafael red specialist. Enzo Bianchi (Cab Sauv/Merlot/ Malbec) is excellent flagship. Gd-value Elsa's V'yd, inc meaty Barbera. Pithy Sauv Bl; also decent sparkling.

Bressia Men ★★→★★★ Tiny new winery already on form with classy Malbec-dominated Profundo from Agrelo and Conjuro Malbec from Tupungato.

Cabernet de los Andes Cata ★★ Promising organic (and partly biodynamic) Catamarca estate with big, fragrant, balanced reds under Vicien and Tizac labels.

Canale, Bodegas Humberto Pat ★→★★ RÍO NEGRO winery known for Sauv Bl, Pinot N (Marcus is top wine), but Merlot, Malbec (esp Black River label) better.

CarinaE Men ★★ New winery in Cruz de Piedra: rich, fragrant, elegant reds.

Catena Zapata, Bodega Men ★★→★★★★ Consistently gd range rises from Alamos through Catena and Catena Alta to flagship Nicolas Catena Zapata and Malbec Argentino, plus Adrianna and Nicasia single-v'yd Malbecs. Also joint venture with the Rothschilds of Lafite: seriously classy *Caro* and younger Amancaya; *see* ARGENTO; LUCA/TIKAL/TAHUAN/ALMA NEGRA.

Chacra Pat ★★★ Superb RÍO NEGRO Pinot N from bodega owned by Piero Incisa della Rocchetta of Sassicaia (*see* Italy), top *cuvée* Treinta y Dos from 1932 vines; also v.gd Mainqué Merlot. Wines made by the team at NOEMIA.

Chakana Men ★★ Agrelo winery; watch for joyful Malbec, Cab Sauv, Syrah, Bonarda.

Chandon, Bodegas Men ★→★★ Makers of Baron B and M Chandon sparkling; Moët & Chandon supervise; promising Pinot N/Chard blend. *See* TERRAZAS DE LOS ANDES.

Clos de los Siete Men ★★ Reliable, plump Vistaflores (Valle de Uco) blend of Merlot, Malbec, Syrah, Cab Sauv. Michel Rolland oversees winemaking (*see* DIAMANDES, MONTEVIEJO, VAL DE FLORES).

Cobos, Viña Men ★★→★★★ Ultra-rich, ultra-ripe (too ripe?) reds from Californian Paul Hobbs with the best using fruit from the Marchiori v'yd. Bramare and Felino are 2nd and 3rd tiers. Look, too, for the Marchiori & Barraud wines from two of the Cobos winemaking team.

Colomé, Bodega Sal ★★→★★★ Bodega in remote Calchaquí Valley; Hess Collection (California) owner. Pure, intense, biodynamic Malbec-based reds, lively Torrontés, smoky Tannat. Second label, Amalaya, now made in Cafayate winery.

Decero, Finca Men ★★→★★★ Lush yet elegant reds, inc a fine Petit Verdot, from the Remolinos v'yd in Agrelo.

Desierto, Bodega del ★→★★ Pioneering winery in La Pampa; promising Syrah, Cab Fr, Malbec under 25/5, Desierto Pampa labels. Paul Hobbs (Viña Cobos) consults.

DiamAndes Men Part of Clos de los Siete project, owned by Bonnie family (Château Malartic Lagravière, Bordeaux); solid, meaty Gran Reserva (Malbec/Cab Sauv).

Dominio del Plata Men ★→★★★ Two ex-CATENA winemakers make superior wines under the Crios, Susana Balbo, BenMarco, Anubis and Budini labels. Nosotros is bold Malbec/Cab Sauv flagship. BenMarco Expresivo also v.gd.

Doña Paula Men ★→★★ Luján de Cuyo estate owned by SANTA RITA (Chile). Elegant Malbec; modern fleshy Cab Sauv; tangy Los Cardos Sauv Bl; exotic Naked Grape Viognier; experiments with Verdelho, Touriga Nacional and Ancelotta.

Durigutti Men ★★ Classy Agrelo Malbec and v.gd Bonarda from two brothers who consult to several of Argentina's finest.

Etchart Sal ★★→★★★ Reds gd, topped by plummy Cafayate Cab Sauv. Torrontés also one of the best, with intriguing late-harvest Tardio.

Fabre Montmayou ★★ French-owned operation, aka Domaine Vistalba, with v'yds in Luján de Cuyo (MENDOZA) and RÍO NEGRO (sometimes labelled Infinitus); reds with a French accent esp gd. Second label Phebus; also gd-value Viñalba wines on some export markets.

Familia Schroeder Pat ★★ NEUQUÉN estate impressing with reds and whites. V.gd Saurus Select range, inc sappy Sauv Bl, earthy Merlot and fragrant Malbec.

Familia Zuccardi Men ★→★★ Dynamic estate; gd-value Santa Julia range, led by new blend Magna, better Q label (impressive Malbec, Merlot, Tempranillo), and deep yet elegant Zeta (Malbec/Tempranillo). Also gd fortified Malamado (r w).

Fin del Mundo, Bodega del Pat ★★ First winery in the province of NEUQUÉN; Malbec a speciality; top wine Special Blend is Merlot/Malbec/Cab Sauv.

Flichman, Finca Men ★★ Owned by Sogrape (Portugal), impressive Syrah. Best: Dedicado blend (mostly Cab Sauv/Syrah). Paisaje de Tupungato (Bordeaux blend), Paisaje de Barrancas (Syrah-based); decent Extra Brut (Chard/Malbec).

Foster, Enrique ★★ MENDOZA Malbec specialist, all excellent from young, fragrant Ique to powerful Edición Limitada and Terruño single-v'yd wines.

Fournier, O Men ★→★★★ Spanish-owned Valle de Uco bodega. Urban Uco v.gd entry-level range; then B Crux and Alfa Crux, both fine Tempranillo/Merlot/ Malbec blends. Also fragrant but rare Syrah. Now producing Chilean wines.

Kaikén Men ★★→★★★ Owned by Aurelio MONTES (Chile) and making user-friendly range topped by new Mai Malbec followed by Ultra Cab Sauv and Malbec.

La Anita, Finca ★★→★★★ MENDOZA estate making high-class reds, esp Syrah, Malbec and new Varúa Merlot. Intriguing whites, inc Sem and Tocai Friulano.

Lagar Carmelo Patti, El Men ★★ Tiny bodega making intense Malbec, Cab Sauv and blend Gran Assemblage.

La Riojana ★→★★ Dynamic company, currently the world's largest Fairtrade wine producer. *Raza Ltd Edition Malbec* is top wine, but quality and value at all levels.

Las Moras, Finca San J ★→★★ Chunky Tannat, chewy Malbec Reserva, solid Gran Shiraz and plump, fragrant Malbec/Bonarda blend Mora Negra.

Los Clop ★→★★ Yes, there's Malbec at this Maipu winery, but the fragrant Syrah is arguably the star turn.

Luca/Tikal/Tahuan/Alma Negra Men ★★→★★★ Classy boutique wineries owned by Nicolas CATENA's children Laura (Luca) and Ernesto (Tikal/Tahuan/Alma Negra, with the last making a sparkling Malbec). Winemaker Luis Reginato also makes excellent La Posta del Viñatero range.

Luigi Bosca Men ★★→★★★ Three quality tiers: Finca La Linda, Luigi Bosca Res and a top level that include esp gd Finca Los Nobles Malbec/Verdot and Cab Sauv/ Bouchet, plus impressive Gala blends – new Cab Fr-based Gala IV esp gd.

Lurton, Bodegas François Men ★→★★★ Juicy Piedra Negra Malbec, complex, earthy Chacayes (Malbec) head range; Flor de Torrontés more serious than most, also sweet but fresh Pasitea Torrontés/Pinot Gr, white blend Corte Friulano.

Masi Tupungato Men ★★→★★★ Enterprise for the well-known Valpolicella producer (Italy). Passo Doble is fine *ripasso*-style Malbec/Corvina/Merlot blend; Corbec is even better Amarone lookalike (Corvina/Malbec).

Melipal Men ★★ Top-class Malbec from old Agrelo v'yds; value second label, Ikella.

Mendel Men ★★★ Former TERRAZAS DE LOS ANDES winemaker Roberta de la Mota makes plummy Malbec, inc super Finca Remota from Altamira v'yd, and graceful Unus blend. Decent Sem, too.

Mendoza Men Most important province for wine (over 70% of plantings). Best subregions: Agrelo, Valle de Uco (inc Tupungato), Luján de Cuyo, Maipú.

Michel Torino Sal ★★ Rapidly improving organic Cafayate enterprise; Don David Malbec, Cab Sauv and Syrah v.gd. Altimus is rather oaky flagship.

Monteviejo Men ★★→★★★★ One of the v'yds of CLOS DE LOS SIETE, now with top-class range of reds headed by wonderfully textured Monteviejo blend (Malbec/Merlot/Cab Sauv/Syrah); Lindaflor Malbec also v.gd.

Neuquén Patagonian region to watch: huge developments since 2000, although salinity proving a problem.

Nieto Senetiner, Bodegas Men ★★ Luján de Cuyo-based bodega. Quality rises from tasty *entry-level Santa Isabel* through Reserva to top-of-range Cadus reds.

Noemia Pat ★★★→★★★★★ Old-vine RÍO NEGRO Malbec from Hans Vinding-Diers and Noemi Cinzano. J Alberto and A Lisa second labels. Also a Malbec rosé and Cab Sauv Merlot blend "2". And *see* CHACRA.

Norton, Bodega Men ★→★★★ Gd whites; v.gd reds, esp Malbec (new Privada v.gd), Malbec/Merlot/Cab Sauv blends Privada and Perdriel, Malbec-based Gernot Langes icon and new Finca La Colonia range inc. Sangiovese and Barbera.

Peñaflor Men ★→★★★ Argentina's biggest wine company. Labels inc: Andean V'yds and finer TRAPICHE, Finca las Moras, Santa Ana and MICHEL TORINO.

Poesia Men ★→★★★ Exciting Luján de Cuyo producer under same ownership as Clos l'Eglise of Bordeaux (France); stylish Poesia (Cab Sauv/Malbec), chunkier but fine Clos des Andes (Malbec) and juicy Pasodoble Malbec/Syrah/Cab Sauv blend.

Porvenir de los Andes, El Sal ★★ Cafayate estate with classy Laborum reds, inc fine, smoky Tannat. Amauta blends also gd. New venture Camino del Inca with their US importer for Tannat-based Quipu, Malbec and Torrontés.

Pulenta, Carlos Men ★★ Vistalba bodega, basic range is Tomero, upper tier has fine trio of Malbec-based reds, Vistalba Corte A, B and C. Also Progenie sparkler.

Pulenta Estate Men ★★→★★★ Luján de Cuyo winery. Gd Sauv Bl and v.gd reds. Best: Gran Corte (Cab Sauv/Malbec/Merlot/Petit Verdot), Cab Fr and Malbec.

Renacer Men ★★→★★★ Old-vine Malbec specialist, Renacer (mostly Malbec) is flagship, but most interesting wine is Enamore – an Amarone-style red made with help from Allegrini (Italy).

Riglos Men ★★ New bodega; intense, oak-infused reds from Tupungato fruit.

Río Negro Patagonia's oldest wine region; gd Pinot N, Malbec in right hands.

Rosell-Boher Men ★★ Sparkling wine specialist, using Chard and Pinot N from high-altitude Tupungato sites to rich yet never too boisterous effect .

Ruca Malen Men ★★→★★★ Promising red wine specialist with v'yds in Luján de Cuyo and the Uco Valley. Top range is Kinien, tender, floral Malbec and svelte, aromatic Don Raúl blend. New Petit Verdot rich and smoky.

Salentein, Bodegas Men ★★ Highlights are Primus Pinot N and Malbec, and Numina (Malbec/Merlot). Portillo gd for cheaper wines; also Bodegas Callia in SAN JUAN, where Shiraz is the focus.

Salta Northerly province with some of the world's highest v'yds, esp in Calchaquí Valley. Subregion Cafayate renowned for Torrontés.

San Juan Second-largest wine region, home to promising Shiraz and Tannat.

San Pedro de Yacochuya Sal ★★★ Cafayate collaboration between Michel Rolland (*see* France) and the ETCHART family. Ripe but fragrant Torrontés; dense, earthy Malbec; and powerful, stunning Yacochuya Malbec from oldest vines.

Soluna Men ★★ Ambitious new Fairtrade project making Malbec in Luján de Cuyo; top wine: fleshy Primus.

ARGENTINA

Sophenia, Finca Men ★★ Tupungato bodega. Advice from Michel Rolland (*see* France). Malbec and Cab Sauv shine; gd Altosur entry-level range; top Synthesis.

Tapiz Men ★★ Luján de Cuyo-based bodega, punchy Sauv Bl, v'gd red range topped by serious Black Tears Malbec and Reserva Selección de Barricas (Cab Sauv/Malbec/Merlot). Sister label: Zolo.

Terrazas de los Andes Men ★★→★★★ CHANDON enterprise. Three ranges: entry-level Terrazas (juicy Cab Sauv is the star), mid-price Reserva, and top-of-the-tree Afincado, inc v.gd Tardío Petit Manseng. Joint venture with Château Cheval Blanc of Bordeaux (France) making superb *Cheval des Andes* blend.

Toso, Pascual Men ★★→★★★ Californian Paul Hobbs heads a team making gd-value, tasty range, inc ripe but finely structured Magdalena Toso (mostly Malbec) and Malbec/Cab Sauv single v'yd Finca Pedregal.

Trapiche Men ★★→★★★ PEÑAFLOR premium label increasingly potent and less oaky under head winemaker Daniel Pi. Trio of single-v'yd Malbecs and Manos Malbec shine out; red blend Iscay is gd but pricey. Better value under the Oak Cask, Fond de Cave, Briquel (gd Cab Fr) and Medalla labels.

Trivento Men ★→★★ Owned by CONCHA Y TORO of Chile, making gd-value range, with Viognier standing out; also under Otra Vida label.

Val de Flores Men ★★★ Another Michel Rolland-driven enterprise close to CLOS DE LOS SIETE for compelling yet elegant (and biodynamic) old-vine Malbec.

Viña 1924 de Angeles Men ★★★ New Luján de Cuyo winery whose forte is old-vine Malbec. Top wine Gran Malbec.

Weinert, Bodegas Men ★→★★ Potentially fine reds, esp Cavas de Weinert blend (Cab Sauv/Merlot/Malbec), are occasionally spoiled by extended ageing in old oak. Own Argentina's most southerly v'yd in Chubut.

OTHER SOUTH AMERICAN WINES

Bolivia Most of Bolivia is too hot and humid for vines, but some decent Syrah, Cab, Malbec emerging from high-altitude v'yds in the southern province of Tarija, just over the border from SALTA, Argentina. Pick of small number of wineries: La Concepción, Kohlberg, Magnus, Aranjuez, Campos de Solana.

Brazil South America's third most important wine-producing country has a surprisingly European approach to wine, thanks to the arrival of Italian settlers in the 19th century. Most wines come from the Vale dos Vinhedos in the southern province of Rio Grande do Sul. With improved viticulture, wineries overcoming humidity issues. Several impressive reds (look for Merlot, Tannat, Teroldego, Nebbiolo) and some decent sparklers. Further north, continuous harvesting is possible in some equatorial v'yds. Look for Salton, Lidio Carraro, Pizzato, Dom Cândido, Amadeu (for the Geisse sparklers), Casa Valduga and the pioneering Miolo, with gd-value Aurora and Rio Sol. Most unusual wine? The Perico Winery in Santa Catarina is working on a Cab Sauv Icewine.

Peru Lima's first wine bar is now open. Viña Tacama exports some pleasant wines, esp Gran Vino Blanco; also Cab Sauv and classic-method sparkling. Chincha, Moquegua, Tacha regions making progress (serious phylloxera issue).

Uruguay Thanks to the maritime climate, Tannat thrives here, producing ripe, balanced wines, often with Merlot and Cab Sauv. Viognier also does well. Pisano wines are stylish and fine. Juanicó is equally impressive, with flagship red blend Preludio and joint venture with Bernard Magrez of Château Pape Clément to produce Gran Casa Magrez de Uruguay. Bouza is focused, elegant. Others: Ariano, Bruzzone & Sciutto, Carrau/Castel Pujol, Casa Filguera, Castillo Viejo, De Lucca, Los Cerros de San Juan, Dante Irurtia, Marichal, Pizzorno, Stagnari and Traversa.

Australia

QUEENSLAND

Abbreviations used in the text:

Ad Hills	Adelaide Hills, SA
Beech	Beechworth, Vic
Coon	Coonawarra, SA
Kang I	Kangaroo Island, SA
Lang C	Langhorne Creek, SA
Mor Pen	Mornington Peninsula, Vic
N/S Tas	North/South Tasmania
Qld	Queensland

SOUTH AUSTRALIA

NEW SOUTH WALES

Upper Hunter

Mudgee

Hunt

Darling

Clare Valley

Riverland

Mildura

Big Rivers

Orange

Griffith

Lower Hunter

Sydney

Cowra

Barossa Valley

Eden Valley

Adelaide

Adelaide Hills

McLaren

Vale/Lang C

Murray River

Murrumbidgee

Murray

Riverina

Canberra

Southern Highland

Kangaroo Island

VICTORIA

Padthaway

Rutherglen

King Valley/Beechworth/

Coonawarra

Grampians

Pyrenees

Goulburn Valley

Alpine Valleys

Heathcote/Bendigo

Macedon

Indian Ocean

Melbourne

Geelong

Yarra Valley

Mornington Peninsula

Gippsland

Swan District

WESTERN AUSTRALIA

Perth

Swan

Perth Hills

TASMANIA

Margaret River

Geographe

Great Southern

Frankland River

Hobart

Pemberton

Margaret River

Mount Barker

Denmark

Albany

N otwithstanding its informal national motto ("No worries, mate") Australia has had some in recent years. Drought, fires, floods, farmers who plant vines apparently to get rid of surplus money, massive dependence on irrigation, an inflated currency, the loss-leader strategies of supermarkets, hot competition from the Kiwis next door, not to mention cricket, have caused a good deal of rethinking. It's very different from the hubris of 20 years ago. And yet Australia's fine wines may yet take over the world. Quantity is the issue, not quality. We have seen wonderful handmade wines in so many categories; just far too many boring industrial ones.

Shiraz and Chardonnay, Cabernet and Riesling (and Semillon) will continue to be Australia's classics, but Grenache and Pinot Noir, with Sangiovese and Tempranillo in the wings, have found ideal homes, too, in Australia's extraordinary range of geology and geography. On condition we are prepared to pay fine-wine prices, Australia has more to offer than any other region of the new wine world.

Recent vintages

New South Wales (NSW)

2010 Regular heavy rain, tricky year: lighter reds but good whites (Hunter, Cowra, Orange). Hilltops, Canberra, (early-picked) Hunter best reds.

2009 Excellent vintage all over, but reds better than whites. Both rain and heat caused some damage, but Mudgee, Cowra, Hilltops and Canberra District producers excited by the results.

2008 Another record early start, good whites; torrential rain destroyed nearly all Hunter reds. Canberra reds outstanding. Coonawarra stands out.

2007 The earliest vintage ever recorded for all regions; full flavour across white and red wines. Peak Hunter red vintage.

2006 A burst of extreme heat around Christmas in some regions did no real damage. Time kind to reds.

2005 A very good to exceptional year across almost all districts, especially the Hunter, Mudgee, Orange.

Victoria (Vic)

2010 Normal transmission was resumed. Temperate vintage with no great alarms or surprises. Whites and reds should be good from most districts.

2009 Characterized by tragic bush fire. Extreme heat, drought, fire and related smoke taint. Yarra Valley worst (but not uniformly) affected. Beechworth, Goulburn Valley, Grampians, King Valley, Pyrenees, Mornington Peninsula and Sunbury reds of good, concentrated quality.

2008 Started one day later than 2007 but finished one week earlier. Reds excellent in Grampians, Mornington Peninsula, Yarra Valley.

2007 Broke the record for the earliest vintage; frost and bush-fire smoke taint hit some regions hard.

2006 One of the earliest and most compressed vintages on record; paradoxically fruit flavour came even earlier. A charmed year.

2005 Rain up to end of February was followed by a freakish three-month Indian summer, giving superb fruit.

South Australia (SA)

2010 Excellent year. Clare and Eden Valley Ries both very good. Shiraz from all major districts best since 2005. Coonawarra Cab Sauv on song.

2009 Low yields; hot vintage. Dire predictions for the state's whites but Clare Valley and Eden Valley Ries both look very good as young wines. Adelaide Hills very good for both whites and reds. Coonawarra reds excellent. McLaren Vale and Barossa Valley generally very good for Shiraz.

2008 Very early start in February turned out to create a curate's egg: excellent wines picked prior to March 6, non-fortified "Ports" for those picked after the record heatwave. Very high alcohols. Coonawarra Cab of note.

2007 Devastating frosts hit the Limestone Coast repeatedly. A dry, warm vintage favoured red wines across the board. Good at best.

2006 A great Cab year; for other reds those picked before Easter rains did best. Here, too, flavour ripeness came early.

2005 Clare Valley, Coonawarra, Wrattonbully and Langhorne Creek did best in what was a large but high-quality vintage with reds to the fore.

Western Australia (WA)

2010 Warm early before milder weather prevailed. Reds will be generally better than whites. Some caught by late rains but in general very good.

2009 Low yields, excellent quality. Mild summer. Particularly good year for Margaret River (w r), Pemberton (w). Margaret River so often experiences polar-opposite conditions to regions of the eastern states. Here so again.

2008 The best vintage for many years across all regions and all varieties; normal harvest dates.

2007 A warm quick-fire vintage made white quality variable; fine reds.

2006 Complete opposite to eastern Australia; a cool, wet and late vintage – searing whites, highly dubious reds.

2005 Heavy rain spoiled what would have been the vintage of a generation for Cab and Shiraz in the south; whites uniformly excellent.

Accolade Wines *See* CONSTELLATION.

Adelaide Hills SA Best Sauv Bl region: cool 450-metre sites in Mt Lofty ranges.

Alkoomi Mt Barker, WA r w ★★ (Ries) 01 02' **04 05'** 07' 08 (Cab Sauv) 01' 02' **04 05'** 07 A veteran of 35 yrs making fine Ries and long-lived reds.

All Saints Rutherglen, Vic r w BR ★★ Historic producer making creditable table wines; great fortifieds. Wooded Marsanne best of recent table (white) wines.

Alpine Valleys Vic Geographically similar to KING VALLEY. Similar use of grapes. Mayford the region's best producer.

Angove's SA r w (br) ★ Long-established MURRAY VALLEY family business. Gd-value white and red varietals. New organic offerings. Long Row Cab Sauv best value.

Annie's Lane Clare V, SA r w ★★ →★★★ Part of TWE. Consistently gd, boldly flavoured wines; flagship Copper Trail excellent, esp Ries and Shiraz.

Arrivo Ad Hills, SA r Arrivo has arrived. Long-maceration Nebbiolo. Sophisticated, sexy, dry rosé. Minute quantities.

Ashton Hills Ad Hills, SA r w (sp) ★★★ Fine, racy, long-lived Ries and compelling Pinot N crafted by Stephen George from 25-yr-old v'yds.

Bailey's NE Vic r w br ★★★ Rich Shiraz; magnificent dessert Muscat (★★★★); TOPAQUE. Part of TWE. V'yds grown organic. Petit Verdot a good new addition.

Balgownie Estate r w ★★ Old name for fine Cab, rejuvenated, with v. well-balanced wines, esp Cab Sauv, now with separate YARRA VALLEY arm.

Balnaves of Coonawarra SA r w ★★★ Grape-grower since 1975; winery since 1996. V.gd Chard; excellent supple, medium-bodied Shiraz, Merlot, Cab Sauv.

Bannockburn Vic r w ★★★ (Chard) 00 02' 03 04 05' 06' 08' (Pinot N) 02' 03' 04' 05' 06 07 08 Intense, complex Chard and Pinot N produced using Burgundian techniques. Winemaker Michael "Gloverboy" Glover is a whizz.

Banrock Station Riverland, SA r w ★→★★ Almost 1,600-ha property, Murray River; 243-ha v'yd; owned by CONSTELLATION. Impressive budget wines.

Barossa Valley SA Australia's most important winery (but not v'yd) area. Local specialties: v. old-vine Shiraz, Mourvèdre, Cab Sauv and Grenache.

Bass Phillip Gippsland, Vic r ★★★→★★★★ (Pinot N) 99' 02' 03 04 05' 06' 07' 09 Tiny amounts of stylish, sought-after Pinot N in three quality grades. Burgundian in style. Quality can be erratic (to say the least). Chard improving.

Bay of Fires N Tas r w sp ★★★ Pipers River outpost of CONSTELLATION empire. Makes stylish table wines and Arras super-*cuvée* sparkler. Complex Pinot N.

Beechworth Vic Cool-climate, inland region. CASTAGNA, GIACONDA, Sorrenberg and Savaterre are best-known wineries. Shiraz and Chard best.

Bellarmine Wines Pemberton, WA w (r) ★★ German Schumacher family is long-distance owner of this 20-ha v'yd: (*inter alia*) startling Mosel-like Ries at various sweetness/alcohol levels, at low prices.

Bendigo Vic Widespread region with 34 small v'yds. Some v.gd quality: BALGOWNIE ESTATE, Sutton Grange, PONDALOWIE, Bress, Harcourt Valley V'yds, Turner's Crossing and Water Wheel.

AUSTRALIA

Best's Grampians, Vic r w ★★→★★★★ (Shiraz) 97' 01' 03' 04' 05' 06 **08** Conservative old family winery; *v.gd mid-weight reds*. Thomson Family Shiraz from 120-yr-old vines is superb. Recent form excellent.

Big Rivers Zone The continuation of South Australia's Riverland, inc the Murray Darling, Perricoota and Swan Hill regions.

Bindi Macedon, Vic r w ★★★→★★★★ (Pinot N) 04' 06' 08' Ultra-fastidious, terroir-driven maker of outstanding, long-lived Pinot N and Chard.

Blue Pyrenees Pyrenees, Vic r w sp ★★ 180 ha of mature v'yds are being better utilized than before across a broad range of wines. Cab Sauv quality resurgent.

Boireann Granite Belt Qld r ★★→★★★ Consistently the best producer of red wines in Queensland (in tiny quantities).

Botobolar Mudgee, NSW r w ★★ Marvellously eccentric little organic winery.

Brand's of Coonawarra Coon, SA r w ★★ 91' **94** 96 98' 02' 03 05' 07 Owned by MCWILLIAM'S. Custodian of 100-yr-old vines; quality has struggled of late.

Bremerton Lang C, SA r w ★★ Red wines with silky-soft mouthfeel and stacks of flavour. Has thrived since sisters Lucy and Rebecca Willson took over family winery.

Brokenwood Hunter V, NSW r w ★★★ (ILR Res Sem) 03' 05' (07') (Graveyard Shiraz) 93' **97'** 98' 00' 02' 03' 05' 07' and Cricket Pitch Sem/Sauv Bl fuel sales. One of the great HUNTER names with keen followers.

Brookland Valley Margaret R, WA r w ★★★ Superbly sited winery doing great things, esp with Sauv Bl and Cab Sauv. Owned by CWA.

Brown Brothers King V, Vic r w br dr sw sp ★→★★★ (Noble Ries) **99'** 00 02' 04 05 Old family firm with new ideas. Wide range of delicate, varietal wines, many from cool mtn districts, inc Chard and Ries. Dry white Muscat is outstanding. Cab Sauv blend is best red. Extensive Prosecco plantings.

Buller Rutherglen, Vic br ★★★★ Rated for superb Rare Liqueur Muscat and the newly minted name TOPAQUE (replacing "Tokay").

By Farr/Farr Rising Vic r w ★★★ Father Gary and son Nick's own, after departure from BANNOCKBURN. Chard and Pinot N can be minor masterpieces.

Calabria Estate r w ★★ Thriving family producer of tasty bargains, esp Private Bin Shiraz/Durif. Creative, charismatic Bill C is in charge.

Campbells Rutherglen, Vic r br (w) ★★ Smooth, ripe reds and unusually elegant Merchant Prince Rare Muscat and Isabella Rare TOPAQUE (★★★★).

Canberra District NSW Both quality and quantity on the increase; altitude-dependent, site selection important. CLONAKILLA best known.

Cape Mentelle Margaret R, WA r w ★★★ Robust Cab Sauv gd, Chard better; also Zin, v. popular Sauv Bl/Sem. Shiraz on rise. Owned by LVMH Veuve Clicquot.

Capercaillie Hunter V, NSW r w ★★→★★ Sudden death of owner Alasdair Sutherland hasn't changed winning formula of supplementing local grapes with purchases from elsewhere, inc MCLAREN VALE, ORANGE etc.

Capital Wines Canberra, NSW r w ★★★ The estate's Kyeema v'yd has a history of growing some of the region's best wines. Shiraz and Ries stand-outs.

Carlei Estate Yarra V, Vic r w ★★ Winemaker Sergio Carlei sources Pinot N and Chard from cool regions to make wines of character. Largely biodynamic.

Casella Riverina, NSW r w ★ Yellow Tail phenomenon, with multimillion-case sales in the USA. Like Fanta: soft and sweet. High Aussie dollar a threat.

Castagna Beech, Vic r ★★★★ (Syrah) 01' **02' 04' 05'** 06 **08** Julian Castagna; chef/winemaker. Deserved leader of the biodynamic brigade. Shiraz/Viognier and Sangiovese/Shiraz blends v.gd. Recent Nebbiolo plantings promising.

Central Ranges Zone NSW Encompasses MUDGEE, ORANGE and Cowra regions, expanding in high-altitude, moderately cool to warm climates.

Chalkers Crossing Hilltops, NSW r w ★★ →★★★ Balanced cool-climate wines made by French-trained Celine Rousseau; esp Shiraz. Alcohol levels v. high of late.

Chambers Rosewood NE Vic br (r w) ★★ →★★★ Viewed with MORRIS as the greatest maker of sticky TOPAQUE and Muscat. Less successful table wines.

Chapel Hill r The darling of modern-day MCLAREN VALE has risen once more. Went through a flat patch from the late 1990s until 2005, but now again at high revs. Range expanding successfully.

Charles Melton Barossa V, SA r w (sp) ★★★ Tiny winery with bold, luscious reds, esp Nine Popes, an old-vine Grenache/Shiraz blend.

Clare Valley SA SA Small high-quality area 145-km north of Adelaide. Best for Ries; also Shiraz and Cab Sauv.

Clarendon Hills McLaren V, SA r ★★★ Deeply structured reds from small parcels of contract grapes around hills above MCLAREN VALE. Noted for high alcohol and over-the-top fruit intensity.

Clonakilla Canberra, NSW r w ★★★★ (Shiraz) 01' 03' 05' 06' 07' 08 **09** *Deserved leader of the Shiraz/Viognier brigade.* Ries and other wines also v.gd. May well be Australia's best auction performer.

Coldstream Hills Yarra V, Vic r w (sp) ★★★ (Chard) **02' 03** 04' 05' 06' 07 08 (Pinot N) 92' 96' **02' 04'** 06' Established in 1985 by wine critic James Halliday. Delicious Pinot N to drink young, and *Reserve to age.* V.gd Chard (esp Res), fruity Cab Sauv, Merlot. Part of TWE.

Collector Wines Canberra, NSW r ★★★ Alex McKay (ex-CONSTELLATION) is a star of the CANBERRA DISTRICT winemaking scene. His Res Shiraz shows layers of spicy, perfumed, complex flavour. CONSTELLATION should never have let him go.

Constellation Wines Australia (CWA) Name for all wines/wineries previously under HARDYS brand. Now under new ownership and renamed Accolade Wines.

Coonawarra SA Southernmost v'yds of state: home to most of Australia's best Cab Sauv; successful Chard, Ries and Shiraz.

Coriole McLaren V, SA r w ★★→★★★ (Lloyd Res Shiraz) 91' 96' 98' 02' 04' 06' To watch, esp for Sangiovese and old-vine Shiraz Lloyd Res.

Craiglee Macedon, Vic r w ★★★ (Shiraz) 96' 97' 98' 00' 02' 04' 05 06' 08 Recreation of famous 19th-century estate. Fragrant, peppery Shiraz, Chard. Low-key Aussie gem.

Crawford River Heathcote, Vic r w ★★★ John Thomson consistently produces some of Australia's best Ries from this ultra-cool region.

Cullen Wines Margaret R, WA r w ★★★★ (Chard) 00' 02' 04' 05' 07 08' **09** (Cab Sauv/Merlot) 94' 95' 98' 04' 05' 07' Vanya Cullen makes strongly structured substantial but subtle Sem/Sauv Bl, bold Chard and outstanding Cab/Merlot.

Cumulus Orange, NSW r w ★★ By far the largest v'yd owner and producer in the region. Variable quality.

Curly Flat Macedon, Vic r w ★★ (Pinot N) 03' 05' 06' Robust but perfumed Pinot N. Full-flavoured Chard. Both eminently age-worthy.

d'Arenberg McLaren V, SA r w (br sp sw) ★★ →★★★ Old firm with new lease of life; sumptuous Shiraz and Grenache, lots of varieties and wacky labels (inc The Cenosilicaphobic Cat Sagrantino).

Dalwhinnie Pyrenees, Vic r w ★★★ (Chard) 04' 05' 06' 08 (Shiraz) 99' **00 02** 04' 05' 06' 07 08 Rich Chard,Cab Sauv and Shiraz. Best PYRENEES producer.

De Bortoli r w dr sw (br) ★★→★★★ (Noble Sem) Both irrigation-area winery and leading YARRA VALLEY producer. Exc Pinot N, Shiraz and v.gd sweet, botrytized, Sauternes-style Noble Sem.

Deakin Estate Vic r w ★ Part of KATNOOK group, producing large volumes of v. decent varietal table wines. V. low-alcohol Moscato.

Devil's Lair Margaret R, WA r w ★★★ Opulently concentrated Chard and Cab Sauv/Merlot. Fifth Leg is popular second label. Ex-PENFOLDS winemaker Oliver Crawford has put a bomb under the place. Part of TWE.

Diamond Valley Yarra V, Vic r w ★★ (Pinot N) 02' 04' **05'** 06' V.gd Pinot N in significant quantities; others gd, esp Chard.

Domaine A S Tas r w ★★★ Swiss owners/winemakers Peter and Ruth Althaus are perfectionists; v.gd Sauv Bl (Fumé Blanc) and Cab Sauv.

Domaine Chandon Yarra V, Vic sp (r w) ★★ Gd sparkling wine, grapes from cooler wine regions. Owned by Moët & Chandon. Well-known in UK as GREEN POINT.

Eden Road r w ★★ New producer making wines from Hilltops, TUMBARUMBA, CANBERRA DISTRICT. V.gd Shiraz and Cab Sauv. Won Jimmy Watson Trophy 2009.

Eden Valley SA Hilly region home to HENSCHKE, Torzi Matthews and PEWSEY VALE; Ries and Shiraz of v. high quality.

Elderton Barossa V, SA r w (br sp) ★★ Old vines; rich, oaked Cab Sauv and Shiraz. Large range nowadays. Trialling organics/biodynamics.

Eldridge Estate Mor Pen, Vic ★★ Winemaker David Lloyd would drive you mad with his fastidious experimentation. Pinot N and Chard are worth the fuss.

Epis r w ★★ (Pinot N) Alec Epis is an ex-professional footballer but he grows a mighty grape. Long-lived Pinot N and elegant, low-oak Chard.

Evans & Tate Margaret R, WA r w ★★→★★ In October 2007, now owned by MCWILLIAM'S. Wine quality has remained stable during extended financial woes.

Ferngrove V'yds Gt Southern, WA r w ★★ Cattle farmer Murray Burton's syndicate has established 223 ha since 1997; v. gd Ries, Malbec, Cab Sauv.

Flametree r w ★★ Winner of Australia's most prestigious wine trophy (Jimmy Watson) in 2008. Exc Cab Sauv but Shiraz spicy and seductive.

Fosters Wine Estates (FWE) See TREASURY WINE ESTATES.

Freycinet Tas r w (sp) ★★★ (Pinot N) **96'** 00' **02'** 05' 06' 07 08 East-coast winery making dense Pinot N, gd Chard. Radenti sparkling perhaps best of all.

Geelong Vic Once-famous area destroyed by phylloxera, re-established in the mid-1960s. V. cool, dry climate. Names include BANNOCKBURN, BY FARR, Curlewis, LETHBRIDGE, Bellarine Estate, SCOTCHMANS HILL.

Gemtree V'yds McLaren V, SA r (w) ★★→★★★ Top-class Shiraz alongside Tempranillo and other exotica, linked by quality. Largely biodynamic.

Geoff Merrill McLaren V, SA r w ★★ Ebullient maker of Geoff Merrill and Mt Hurtle. Wine: mixed. TAHBILK owns 50%.

Giaconda Beech, Vic r w ★★★★ (Chard) 96' **00'** 02' 04' 05' 06' (Shiraz) **02'** 04' 06' In the mid-1980s Rick Kinzbrunner did that rare thing: walked up a steep, stony hill and came down a champion wine producer. Ranks beside LEEUWIN ESTATE as Australia's best Chard. Pinot N less successful. Funkified Shiraz the rising star. Nebbiolo shows promise.

Glaetzer Wines Barossa V, SA r ★★★ Hyper-rich, unfiltered, v. ripe old-vine Shiraz led by iconic Amon-Ra. V.gd examples of high-octane style.

Goulburn Valley Vic V. old region in temperate mid-Victoria. Full-bodied but savoury table wines. Marsanne, Cab Sauv and Shiraz specialties. TAHBILK and MITCHELTON the mainstays.

Grampians Vic Region previously known as Great Western. Temperate region in northwest of state. High quality, esp Shiraz and sparkling Shiraz.

Granite Belt Qld High-altitude, (relatively) cool region just north of Queensland/ NSW border. Esp spicy Shiraz and rich Sem.

Granite Hills Macedon, Vic r w ★★ 30-yr-old family v'yd and winery has regained original class with fine, elegant Ries and spicy Shiraz.

Grant Burge Barossa V, SA r w (br sw sp) ★★ 400,000 cases of smooth reds and whites from the best grapes of Burge's large v'yd holdings.

Great Southern WA Remote cool area; FERNGROVE and Goundrey are the largest wineries. Albany, Denmark, Frankland River, Mount Barker and Porongurup are official subregions. First-class Ries and Shiraz.

Green Point Vic *See* DOMAINE CHANDON.

Greenstone V'yd Heathcote, Vic r ★★ A partnership between David Gleave MW (London), Alberto Antonini (Italy) and Australian viticulturist Mark Walpole; v.gd Shiraz, gd Sangiovese.

Grosset Clare V, SA r w ★★★→★★★★ (Ries) 00' 02' 03 06' 07' **10** (Gaia) 90' **91' 96' 98' 99** 02' 04' 05' 06 09 Fastidious winemaker. Foremost Australian Ries, lovely Chard, Pinot N and exceptional Gaia Cab Sauv/Merlot from dry v'yd in Watervale and Polish Hill subregions.

Hanging Rock Macedon, Vic r w sp ★→★★★ (Heathcote Shiraz) 00' 01' 02' 04' 06' Has successfully moved upmarket with sparkling Macedon and Heathcote Shiraz; bread and butter comes from contract winemaking.

Hardys r w sp (sw) ★★★→★★★★ (Eileen Chard) 01' 02' 04' 05 06' 08 (Eileen Shiraz) **70'** 96' 98' 02' 04' 06' Historic company blending wines from several areas. Best are Eileen Hardy. Part of CWA.

Heathcote Vic The 500-million-yr-old, blood-red Cambrian soil has seemingly unlimited potential to produce reds, esp Shiraz, of the highest quality. Ten-year drought hasn't helped realize the promise.

Heggies Eden V, SA r w dr (sw) ★★ V'yd at 500 metres owned by S SMITH & SONS, like PEWSEY VALE with v.gd Ries and Viognier. Chard is the in-the-know tip.

Henschke Eden V, SA r w ★★★★ (Shiraz) 58' 84' 86' 90' **91'** 96' 98' 01 02' 04' 06' (Cab Sauv) 86' **88** 90' 96' 98 99' 02' 04' 06' A 120-yr-old family business known for delectable Hill of Grace (Shiraz), v.gd Cab Sauv and red blends, and gd whites, inc long-ageing Ries.

Hewitson SE Aus r (w) ★★★ Much-travelled winemaker Dean Hewitson sources parcels off v. old vines. Shiraz and varietal release from "oldest Mourvèdre vines on the planet" (esp *Old Garden*) v.gd.

Hollick Coon, SA r w (sp) ★★→★★★ Has expanded estate v'yds, most recently in WRATTONBULLY. Cab Sauv, Shiraz, Merlot. Gd restaurant with vineyard views.

Houghton Swan V, WA r w ★★→★★★ Most famous old winery of Western Australia. Soft, ripe Supreme is top-selling, age-worthy white; *a national classic.* Excellent Cab Sauv, Verdelho, Shiraz from MARGARET RIVER and GREAT SOUTHERN. Part of CWA.

Howard Park WA r w ★★★ (Ries) 97' **99'** 02' 04 05' 07' 08 09 (Cab Sauv) 88' 94' 96' **99'** 01' 05' 07' 09 (Chard) 01' 02' 04 05' 07' Scented Ries, Chard; spicy Cab Sauv. Second label: MadFish Bay is excellent value.

Hunter Valley Great name in NSW. Broad, soft, earthy Shiraz and gentle Sem that can live for 30 yrs. Produces Australia's most blatantly terroir-driven styles.

Islander Estate, The Kang I, SA r w ★★ New, full-scale development by Jacques Lurton of Bordeaux, planned as likely retirement venture. Grenache, Malbec, Cab Sauv/Shiraz/Viognier all v.gd.

Jacob's Creek (Orlando) Barossa V, SA r w sp (br sw) ★→★★★ Great pioneering company, now owned by Pernod Ricard. Almost totally focused on three tiers of Jacob's Creek wines, covering all varieties and prices.

Jasper Hill Heathcote, Vic r w ★★→★★★ (Shiraz) 85' 96' 97' 98' 99' 02' 04' 06' 09 Emily's Paddock Shiraz/Cab Fr blend and Georgia's Paddock Shiraz from dry-land estate are intense, long-lived and much admired.

Jim Barry Clare V, SA r w ★★→★★★ Some great v'yds provide gd Ries, McCrae Wood Shiraz, and richly robed and oaked The Armagh Shiraz.

John Duval Wines Barossa V, SA r ★★★ The eponymous business of former chief red-winemaker for PENFOLDS (and Grange), making *delicious Rhôney reds* that are supple and smooth, yet amply structured.

Kaesler Barossa V, SA r (w) ★★→★★★ Old Bastard Shiraz outranks Old Vine Shiraz. Wine in the glass generally gd (in heroic style), but alcohol levels often intrude.

Katnook Estate Coon, SA r w (w sw sp) ★★★ (Odyssey Cab Sauv) 91' **92' 94'** 96' 97'

AUSTRALIA

98' 00 01' 02' 05' Excellent pricey icons *Odyssey* and Prodigy Shiraz. Lavishly oaked. Standard 08 Cab Sauv gd.

Keith Tulloch Hunter V, NSW r w ★★ Ex-Rothbury winemaker fastidiously crafting elegant yet complex Sem, Shiraz, etc.

Killkanoon Clare V, SA ★★→★★★ r w Ries and Shiraz have been exc performers in shows over past yrs. In Sept 2007, acquired National Trust-ranked SEPPELTSFIELD. Luscious, beautifully crafted reds.

King Valley Vic Altitude between 155 and 860 metres has massive impact on varieties and styles. 29 wineries headed by BROWN BROS, Dal Zotto, Chrismont and PIZZINI, and important supplier to many others.

Kingston Estate SE Aus ★→★★ Kaleidoscopic array of varietal wines from all over the place, consistency and value providing the glue.

Knappstein Wines Clare V, SA r w ★★ Reliable Ries, Cab Sauv/Merlot, Shiraz and Cab Sauv. Owned by LION NATHAN. Modest performance in recent yrs.

Kooyong Mor Pen, Vic ★★★ Pinot N, Chard of power, structure, Pinot Gr of charm. Single-v'yd wines. Winemaker Sandro Moselle is a force to be reckoned with.

Lake Breeze Lang C, SA r (w) ★★ Long-term grape-growers turned winemakers, producing succulently smooth Shiraz and Cab Sauv.

Lake's Folly Hunter V, NSW r w ★★★ (Chard) 97' 99' 00' 01' 04' 05' 07' (Cab Sauv) 69' 89' 93 97' 98' 03' 05' 07' Founded by Max Lake, pioneer of HUNTER VALLEY Cab Sauv. New owners since 2000. Chard often better than Cab Sauv blend.

Langmeil Barossa V, SA r w ★★ Owns oldest block of Shiraz (planted in 1843) in world plus other old v'yds, making opulent Shiraz without excessive alcohol. Oak use could be classier.

Larry Cherubino Wines Frankland R, WA r w ★★★ Ex-HARDYS wunderkind winemaker now putting runs on the board under his own name. Intense Sauv Bl and harmonious Shiraz are causing the main excitement. Also crisp Wallflower Riesling. Spicy, specific, thoughtful styles.

Lazy Ballerina McLaren V, SA r ★★ Run by (young) viticulturist James Hook, who enjoys thumbing his nose at the big companies. Calls his winery newsletter *Wine Fight Club*. Rich, tannic, textured Shiraz; excellent value.

Leasingham Clare V, SA r w ★★ Once-important brand with v.gd Ries, Shiraz, Cab Sauv and Cab Sauv/Malbec blend. Various labels, inc individual v'yds. Lost ground of late.

Leeuwin Estate Margaret R, WA r w ★★★★ (Chard) 85' 87' 92' 97' 99' 01' 02' 04' 05' 06 07' Leading Western Australia estate. Superb, age-worthy Art Series Chard. Sauv Bl, *Ries* and Cab Sauv also gd.

Leo Buring Barossa V, SA w ★★★ 79' 84' 91' 94 98 02' 04 05' 06' 08 Part of TWE. Now exclusively Ries producer; Leonay top label, *ages superbly*. Screwcapped.

Lethbridge Vic w r ★★★ Stylish small-run producer of Chard, Shiraz and Pinot N. Reputation grows annually.

Limestone Coast Zone SA Important zone, inc Bordertown, COONAWARRA, Mount Benson, Mount Gambier, PADTHAWAY, Robe and WRATTONBULLY.

Lindemans r w ★→★★ One of the oldest firms, now owned by TWE. Low-price Bin range (esp Bin 65 Chard) now its main focus, a far cry from former glory. Lindemans COONAWARRA reds resurgent.

Lion Nathan New Zealand brewery; owns KNAPPSTEIN, MITCHELTON, PETALUMA, ST HALLETT, Smithbrook, STONIER and TATACHILLA.

Macedon and Sunbury Vic Adjacent regions, Macedon higher elevation. CRAIGLEE, GRANITE HILLS, HANGING ROCK, Bindi, Curly Flat, Epis.

Main Ridge Estate Mor Pen, Vic r w ★★ Rich, age-worthy Chard and Pinot N Peninsula pioneer Nat White boasts that the region has now made all of its mistakes "because I made them all".

Majella r (w) ★★★ ·→★★★★ Rising to the top of COONAWARRA cream. Outstanding super-premium Malleea Cab Sauv/Shiraz. V.gd Shiraz, Cab Sauv.

Margaret River WA Temperate coastal area south of Perth, with superbly elegant wines. Australia's most vibrant tourist wine (and surfing) region.

McLaren Vale SA Historic region on southern outskirts of Adelaide. Big, alcoholic, flavoursome reds have great appeal to the USA, but CORIOLE, HARDYS, WIRRA WIRRA and growing number of others show elegance as well as flavour.

McWilliam's SE Aus r w (br sw) ★★·→★★★ Still family-owned (Gallo lurking with 10% of shares) but has reinvented itself with some flair, often overdelivering. *Elizabeth Sem* the darling of Sydney, cheaper Hanwood blends in many parts of the world. Lovedale Sem so consistent and age-worthy that vintages irrelevant.

Meerea Park Hunter V, NSW r w Brothers Garth and Rhys Eather have taken nearly 20 yrs to be an overnight success. Bright-flavoured Sem, Chard, Shiraz.

Mike Press Wines Ad Hills, SA r w ★★ Tiny production, extreme value. Shiraz, Cab Sauv, Chard. No one knows how he does it, a lot would like to.

Mitchell Clare V, SA r w ★★ (Ries) 00' 01' 04 05' 06' 07 Small family winery for excellent Cab Sauv and firmly structured dry Ries.

Mitchelton Goulburn V, Vic r w (w sw) ★★ Reliable producer of Ries, Shiraz, Cab Sauv at several price points, plus specialty of *Marsanne* and Roussanne.

Mitolo r ★★★ One of the best "virtual wineries" (ie. contract v'yds, wineries, winemaker), paying top dollar for top-quality Shiraz and Cab Sauv; Ben GLAETZER winemaker. Heroic but (often) irresistible wines.

Moorilla Estate Tas r w (sp) ★★ Nr Hobart on Derwent River: v.gd Ries and Chard; Pinot N gd. Superb restaurant and world-class art gallery.

Moorooduc Estate Mor Pen, Vic r w ★★★ Stylish and sophisticated (wild yeast, etc.) producer of top-flight Chard and Pinot N. Influential.

Moppity V'yds Hilltops, NSW r w ★★ Making a name for its Res Shiraz/Viognier (Hilltops) and Chard (TUMBARUMBA). Name to watch.

Mornington Peninsula Vic Exciting wines in cool, coastal area 40-km south of Melbourne; 1,000 ha. Many high-quality boutique wineries.

Morris NE Vic br (r w) ★★·→★★★★ Old winery at RUTHERGLEN for some of Australia's greatest dessert Muscats and "Tokays/TOPAQUES".

Moss Wood r w ★★★★ (Cab Sauv) 80' 85 90' 91' 04' 05' 07' To many, the best MARGARET RIVER winery (11.7 ha). Sem, Cab Sauv, Chard, all with opulent fruit/oak flavours. *Cab Sauv* smoother than a baby's bottom.

Mount Horrocks Clare V, SA r w ★★·→★★★★ Finest dry Ries and sweet Cordon Cut Ries; *Chard best in region.* Related to GROSSET.

Mount Langi Ghiran Grampians, Vic r w ★★★★ (Shiraz) 89' 93' 96' 03' 05' 06' 08 Esp for superb, rich, peppery, *Rhône-like Shiraz*, one of Australia's best cool-climate versions. V.gd sparkling Shiraz, too. Sister of YERING STATION.

Mount Mary Yarra V, Vic w ★★★★ (Pinot N) 97' 99 00' 02' 05' 06' (Quintet) 84' 86' 88' 90' 92' 96' 98' 02' 04' 06 The late Dr John Middleton made tiny amounts of suave Chard, vivid Pinot N and (best of all) Cab Sauv blend: Australia's most Bordeaux-like "claret". All age impeccably. His family goes on.

Mudgee NSW Long-established region northwest of Sydney. Big reds, surprisingly fine Sem, full Chard. Struggled of late. Return of Robert Oatley a lifeline.

Murray Valley SA Vast irrigated v'yds. Now at the epicentre of the drought/climate-change firestorm.

Ngeringa Ad Hills, SA r w ★★ Excellent, v. perfumed, biodynamic Pinot N. Family history in cosmetics industry. In the first blush of a long wine journey.

Ninth Island Tas *See* PIPERS BROOK.

O'Leary Walker Wines Clare V, SA r w ★★★ Two whizz-kids have midlife crisis and leave Beringer Blass to do their own thing – v. well.

Orange NSW A cool-climate, high-elevation region; with lively Merlot and Shiraz, but excellent Chard.

Padthaway SA Large area developed as overspill of COONAWARRA. Cool climate; gd Chard and excellent Shiraz (Orlando).

Pannell, SC McLaren V, SA r ★★ Ex-HARDYS chief winemaker Steve Pannell now with eponymous label. Gd Shiraz and Grenache-based wines. Nebbiolo rising.

Paringa Estate Mor Pen, Vic r w ★★★★ Maker of spectacular Chard, Pinot N and Shiraz, winning innumerable trophies.

Parker Estate Coon, SA r ★★★ Small estate making v.gd Cab Sauv, esp Terra Rossa First Growth. Sister of YERING STATION since 2004. Low profile.

Paxton McLaren V, SA r ★★ Significant v'yd holder. Largely organic/biodynamic. Ripe but elegant Shiraz and Grenache.

Pemberton WA Region between MARGARET RIVER and GREAT SOUTHERN; initial enthusiasm for Pinot N replaced by Ries, Chard, Merlot, Shiraz.

Penfolds Originally Adelaide, now everywhere r w (br sp) ★★-★★★★ (Grange) 52' 53' 55' 60' 62' 63' 66' 71' **76' 78' 83'** 86' **90' 94' 96' 98'** 99' 02' 04' (05', 06') (Cab Sauv Bin 707) 64' 66' 76' 86' 90' 91' 96' **98'** 02' 04' 06' 07' Consistently Australia's best red-wine company, if you can decode its labels. Its Grange (was called Hermitage) is deservedly ★★★★. Yattarna Chard and Bin Chard comparable quality to reds. St Henri Shiraz champion of understatement.

Penley Estate Coon, SA r w ★★ Rich, textured, fruit-and-oak Cab Sauv; Shiraz/Cab Sauv blend; Chard. Rising alcohols a concern.

Perth Hills WA Fledgling area 30-km east of Perth with a larger number of growers on mild hillside sites. Millbrook and Western Range best.

Petaluma Ad Hills, SA r w sp ★★★ (Ries) 04' 05' 06' (Chard) **01' 03'** 04' 05 06' (Cab Sauv Coonawarra) 79' **90' 91' 95' 98'** 03' 05' 06' Created by industry leader Brian Croser. Reds richer from 1988 on. Fell prey to LION NATHAN in 2002.

Peter Lehmann Wines r w (w br sw sp) ★★★ Defender of BAROSSA VALLEY faith; fought off Allied-Domecq by marriage with Swiss Hess group. Consistently well-priced wines in substantial quantities. Try Stonewell Shiraz and outstanding Res Bin Sem and Ries with 5 yrs' age.

Pewsey Vale Ad Hills, SA w ★★★ ·★★★★ Glorious Ries, esp The Contours, released with screwcap, 5 yrs' bottle-age and multiple trophies.

Pierro Margaret R, WA r w ★★★ (Chard) **96'** 99' 00' 01' 02' 03 05' 06' (07') Highly rated producer: expensive, tangy Sem/Sauv Bl and v.gd barrel-fermented Chard.

Pipers Brook Tas r w sp ★★ (Ries) **99'** 00' 01' **02' 04' 06'** 07' (Chard) 00' 02' 05' 06 07' Cool-area pioneer. Gd Ries, Pinot N, *restrained Chard and sparkling* from Tamar Valley. Second label: Ninth Island. Owned by Belgian Kreglinger family.

Pirramimma McLaren V, SA r w ★★ Century-old family business with large v'yds moving with the times; snappy new packaging, the wines not forgotten.

Pizzini King V, Vic r ★★★ (Nebbiolo) 98' 02' **04** Leads the charge towards Italian varieties in Australia. Nebbiolo and Sangiovese, and blends. Difficult vintages of late but a top Australian producer.

Plantagenet Mt Barker, WA r w (sp) ★★ (r) **95** 98' 01' 03 04' 05' 07' 08' The region's elder statesman: wide range of varieties, esp rich Chard, Shiraz and vibrant, potent Cab Sauv.

Pondalowie Bendigo, Vic r ★★ Flying winemakers with exciting Shiraz/Viognier/Tempranillo in various combinations.

Primo Estate SA r w dr (w sw) ★★★ Joe Grilli's many successes include v.gd MCLAREN VALE cherry, spicy Shiraz/Sangiovese, tangy Colombard and potent Joseph Cab Sauv/Merlot.

Pyrenees Central Victoria region producing rich, often minty reds. Dalwhinnie, Taltarni, Blue Pyrenees, Mount Avoca and Dog Rock wineries all ascendant.

Redheads McLaren V, SA r ★★ Tiny "studio" for super-concentrated reds.

Richmond Grove Barossa V, SA r w ★→★★★ Offers v.gd Ries at bargain prices; other wines less impressive. Owned by Orlando Wyndham but has become faceless.

Riverina NSW Large-volume irrigated zone centred on Griffith. Its water supply will be better than the Murray Darling over next few yrs.

Robert Oatley Wines Mudgee, NSW r w Robert Oatley created ROSEMOUNT ESTATE, back when it was gd. Ambition burns anew. Initial releases weren't quite there but they are fast improving. Single-v'yd Shiraz v.gd.

Rockford Barossa V, SA r w sp ★★→★★★★ Small producer from old, low-yielding v'yds; reds best, also iconic sparkling Black Shiraz.

Rosemount Estate r w A major presence in production terms but a shadow of its former self, quality-wise. Top end missing in action.

Rutherglen and Glenrowan Vic Two of four regions in the northeast Victoria zone, justly famous for weighty reds and magnificent fortified dessert wines.

Saltram Barossa V, SA r w ★★→★★★ Mamre Brook (Shiraz, Cab Sauv, Chard) and No 1 Shiraz are leaders. A TWE brand.

Samuel's Gorge McLaren V, SA r ★★ Justin McNamee has hair like Sideshow Bob (*The Simpsons*) but is making Shiraz and Tempranillo of precision and place.

Sandalford Swan V, WA r w (br) ★→★★ Fine old winery with contrasting styles of red and white single-grape wines from SWAN VALLEY and MARGARET RIVER areas.

Savaterre Beech, Vic r w ★★ (Pinot N) 02 04' 06' 08' Tough run of seasons (03 07 09) but v.gd Chard and Pinot N. Close-planted vines. Biodynamic practices. Winery a room of owner/winemaker Keppell Smith's house.

Scotchmans Hill Vic r w Makes significant quantities of Pinot N, gd Chard and spicy Shiraz.

Seppelt Vic r w br sp (w sw) ★★★ (St Peter's Shiraz) 71' 85 86' 91' 96 97' 99' 04' 05' 06 08 Now a specialist table-wine producer for FWE with a v. impressive array of region-specific Ries, Chard, Shiraz and Cab Sauv.

Seppeltsfield Barossa V, SA National Trust Heritage Winery, bought by KILLIKANOON in 2007. Stocks of fortified wines in barrels date back to 1878.

Setanta Wines Ad Hills, SA r w ★★★ The Sullivan family, first-generation Australians originally from Ireland, produces wonderful Ries, Chard, Sauv Bl, Shiraz and Cab Sauv with Irish mythology labels of striking design.

Sevenhill Clare V, SA r w (br) ★★★ Owned by the Jesuitical Manresa Society since 1851. Consistently gd wine; Shiraz and Ries can be outstanding.

Seville Estate Yarra V, Vic r w ★★★ (Shiraz) 94 97' 99' 02' 04' 05' 06' 08' Ownership changes have not affected quality of Chard, Shiraz, Pinot N.

Shadowfax Vic r w ★★→★★★★ Stylish winery, part of Werribee Park; also hotel based on 1880s mansion. V.gd Chard, Pinot N, Shiraz.

Shaw & Smith Ad Hills, SA w (r) ★★★ Founded by Martin Shaw and Australia's first MW, Michael Hill-Smith. Crisp, harmonious *Sauv Bl*; complex, barrel-fermented M3 Chard; and, surpassing them both, Shiraz.

Shelmerdine V'yds Heathcote, Vic r w ★★→★★★ Well-known family with v. elegant wines from estate in the YARRA VALLEY and HEATHCOTE.

Sirromet Qld r w A striking 100,000-case winery. Wines from 100-plus ha of estate v'yds in GRANITE BELT can be okay.

Smith, S & Sons (alias Yalumba) Barossa V, SA r w br sp (w sw) ★★→★★★ Big, old family firm with considerable verve. *Full spectrum of high-quality wines*, inc HEGGIES, PEWSEY VALE and YALUMBA. Angas Brut, a gd-value sparkling wine, and Oxford Landing varietals are now world brands. In outstanding form.

South Burnett Queensland's second region: 15 wineries and more births (and some deaths) imminent, symptomatic of southeast corner of the state.

South Coast NSW Zone NSW Includes Shoalhaven Coast and Southern Highlands.

Southcorp The former giant of the industry; now part of TWE. Owns LINDEMANS, PENFOLDS, ROSEMOUNT ESTATE, Seaview, Seppelt, WYNNS and many others.

Southern NSW Zone Inc CANBERRA, Gundagai, Hilltops, TUMBARUMBA.

Spinifex Barossa V, SA r ★★★ Small, high-quality producer of complex Shiraz and Grenache blends. Nothing over-the-top here. In the past 2 yrs it has pulled clearly ahead of the pack of most new Aussie producers.

St Hallett Barossa V, SA r w ★★★ (Old Block) **86' 90' 91' 98** 99' 01 02' 04 05' 06' Old Block Shiraz the star; rest of range is smooth, stylish. LION NATHAN-owned.

Stanton & Killeen Rutherglen, Vic r br ★★★ The sudden and untimely death of Chris Killeen in 2007 was a major blow to this fine producer of fortified and dry red wines, but his children are carrying on as the 4th generation – in gd style, too.

Stefano Lubiana S Tas r w sp ★★★ Beautiful v'yds on the banks of the Derwent River 20 minutes from Hobart. V.gd Pinot N, sparkling, Merlot and Chard.

Stella Bella Margaret R, WA r w ★★★ Labels and names shouldn't obscure quality commitment. Try Cab Sauv, Sem/Sauv Bl, Chard, Shiraz, Sangiovese/Cab Sauv.

Stonier Wines Mor Pen, Vic r w ★★ (Chard) **02 03'** 04' 05 06' 07 (Pinot N) 00' 02' 04' 05 06' 07 08' Consistently gd; Res's notable for their elegance. Owned by LION NATHAN.

Sunbury Vic *See* MACEDON AND SUNBURY.

Swan Valley WA Located 20-minutes north of Perth. Birthplace of wine in the west. Hot climate makes strong, low-acid wines; being rejuvenated for wine tourism.

T'Gallant Mor Pen, Vic w (r) Improbable name and avant-garde labels for Australia's best-known Pinot Gr producer. Quixotic acquisition by TWE.

Tahbilk Goulburn V, Vic r w ★★★ (Marsanne) **74' 82' 92'** 97' **99'** 01' 03' 05' 06' 07' (Shiraz) **68' 71' 76' 86 98'** 02 04' 05 06' Beautiful historic family estate: long-ageing reds, also Ries and some of Australia's best *Marsanne*. Res Cab Sauv outstanding; value for money ditto. Rare 1860 Vines Shiraz, too.

Taltarni Pyrenees, Vic r w ★★⋯★★★ (sp) Shiraz and Cab Sauv in best shape for yrs. Long-haul wines but jack-hammer no longer required to remove the tannin from your gums.

Tamar Ridge N Tas r w (sp) ★★ 230-plus ha of vines make this a major player in TASMANIA. 75,000 cases. Acquired in 2010 by BROWN BROTHERS. Gd Pinot N.

Tapanappa SA r ★★★ New WRATTONBULLY collaboration between Brian Croser, Bollinger and J-M Cazes of Pauillac (Bordeaux). Sky-high standards. Cab Sauv blend, Shiraz, Merlot. Surprising *Pinot N* from Fleurieu Peninsula.

TarraWarra Yarra V, Vic r w ★★★ (Chard) 02' 04' 05' 06' (Pinot N) 00' 01 02' **04'** 05' 06' Has moved from idiosyncratic to elegant, mainstream Chard and Pinot N. Standard Pinot N (formerly Tin Cows) not in same class as Reserve.

Tasmania Production continues to surge but still small. Outstanding sparkling Pinot N and Ries in cool climate, Chard, Sauv Bl and Pinot Gr v.gd, cool-climate styles, in great demand.

The Chardonnay irony

Australian wine is greatly indebted to Chard (it was its *entrée* to the world) but it's also the cause of its greatest irony. For all the emphasis and attention on Australian red wine, it's Chard that is arguably the grape Australia grows best. The problem is that when Chard was the main face of Australian wine, it was generally made in a heavy, buttery, busty style. As food styles turned lighter and spicier, it seemed out of place. Now that tastes have moved to fresher, lower-oaked wine styles, Australian Chard has finally got its act together. Racy, complex examples abound.

Tatachilla McLaren V, SA r w ★★ Significant production of nice whites and gd reds. Acquired by LION NATHAN in 2002.

Taylors Wines Clare V, SA r w ★★ Large-scale production led by Ries, Shiraz, Cab Sauv. Exports under Wakefield Wines brand (trademark issues with Taylor's of Oporto) with much success.

Ten Minutes by Tractor Mor Pen, Vic r w ★★★ Amusing name and sophisticated packaging, rapidly growing under owner Martin Spedding. Sauv Bl, Chard, Pinot N are all v.gd.

Teusner Barossa V, SA r ★★★ Old vines, clever winemaking, pure fruit flavours. Leads a BAROSSA VALLEY trend towards "more wood, no good". All about the grapes.

Topaque Vic Iconic fortified Australian (Rutherglen) wine Tokay gains a new name: Topaque. Don't confuse with topic or, worse, toupée. Name change the result of EU negotiations.

Torbreck Barossa V, SA ★★★ r (w) Most stylish of the cult wineries beloved of the USA; focus on old-vine Rhône varieties led by Shiraz. Rich, sweet, high alcohol; a sip goes a long way. Maker of Australia's most expensive new-release wine.

Torzi Matthews Eden V, SA r ★★ Rich, stylish Shiraz. Lower-priced wines generally better. Torzi Schist Rock Shiraz difficult to say, politely, after a glass or two.

Treasury Wine Estates (TWE) New name of the merged Beringer Blass and SOUTHCORP wine groups. Dozens of brands in Australia that come and go like mushrooms after rain. Penfolds and Wynns the jewels in the crown. Name changed, to widespread ridicule, in 2010.

Trentham Estate Vic (r) w ★★ 60,000 cases of family-grown and -made, sensibly priced wines from "boutique" winery on Murray River; is building diversified portfolio from distinguished Victoria regions. Popular tourist spot.

Tumbarumba Cool-climate NSW region nestled in the Australian Alps. Sites between 500 and 800 metres above sea level. Chard the star. Mandatory to add "cha-cha-cha" after saying "Tumbarumba".

Turkey Flat Barossa V, SA r p ★★★ Fine producer of rosé, Grenache and Shiraz from core of 150-yr-old v'yd. Top stuff; controlled alcohol and oak (and price).

Two Hands Barossa V, SA r ★★ Cult winery with top Shiraz from PADTHAWAY, MCLAREN VALE, Langhorne Creek, BAROSSA VALLEY and HEATHCOTE stuffed full of alcohol, rich fruit, oak and the kitchen sink.

Tyrrell's Hunter V, NSW r w ★★★★ (Sem) 99' 00' 01' 05' 07' (Vat 47 Chard) 00' 02 04 05' 07' Australia's greatest maker of Sem, Vat 1 now joined with a series of individual v'yd or subregional wines, one or more of which will stand out in any given vintage, hence the unusual vintage ratings for the Sems. Vat 47, Aus's first Chard, continues to defy the climatic odds, albeit in a different style from LAKE'S FOLLY. Excellent old-vine 4 Acres Shiraz, too.

Upper Hunter NSW Established in early 1960s; irrigated vines (mainly whites), lighter and quicker-developing than Lower Hunter's.

Vasse Felix Margaret R, WA r w ★★★ (Cab Sauv) 97 98 99' 01 04' 05' 07 08 With CULLEN, pioneer of MARGARET RIVER. Elegant Cab Sauv for mid-weight balance. Generally resurgent. Chard on rapid rise.

Voyager Estate Margaret R, WA r w ★★★ 35,000 cases of estate-grown, rich, powerful Sem, Sauv Bl, Chard, Cab Sauv/Merlot. New star of MARGARET RIVER, to follow.

Wendouree Clare V, SA r ★★★★ Treasured maker (tiny quantities) of powerful and concentrated reds, based on Shiraz, Cab Sauv, Mourvèdre and Malbec. Immensely long-lived, so much so that any wine less than 20 yrs old is unlikely to have reached maturity.

West Cape Howe Denmark, WA r w ★★ The minnow that swallowed the whale in 2009 when it purchased 7,700-tonne Goundrey winery and 237 ha of estate v'yds. V.gd Shiraz and Cab Sauv blends.

Willow Creek Mor Pen, Vic r w ★★★ Impressive producer of Chard and Pinot N. Ex-STONIER winemaker Geraldine McFaul recently took the helm.

Wilson Vinyard Clare V, SA r w ★★ Stylish Ries from CLARE VALLEY and adjoining Polish Hill River; Hand Plunge Shiraz and Cab Sauv often of gd quality.

Wirra Wirra McLaren V, SA r w (w sw sp) ★★★ (RSW Shiraz) 98' 99' 02' 04' 05' 06' 07' (Cab Sauv) 97' 98' 01' 02' 04' 05' 06' High-quality wines making a big impact. RSW Shiraz has edged in front of Cab Sauv; both superb. The Angelus Cab Sauv now Dead Ringer in export markets.

Wolf Blass Barossa V, SA r w (br sw sp) ★★ (Cab Sauv blend) 90' 91' 96' 98' 02' 04' 05 06' Now swallowed up by TWE. Not the noisy player it once was.

Woodlands Margaret R, WA r (w) ★★★ 7 ha of 30+-yr-old Cab Sauv among top v'yds in region, plus younger but still v.gd plantings of other Bordeaux reds.

Wrattonbully SA Important grape-growing region in LIMESTONE COAST ZONE for 30 yrs; profile lifted by recent arrival of TAPANAPPA and Peppertree.

Wynns Coon, SA r w ★★★★ (Shiraz) 55' 63 86' 90' 91' 94' 96' 98 99' 02 04' 05' 06' 09' (Cab Sauv) 57' 60' 82' 85' 86' 90' 91' 94' 96' 98' 00 02 04' 05' 06 07 08 Foster's-owned COONAWARRA classic. Ries, Chard, Shiraz and *Cab Sauv* are all v.gd, esp *John Riddoch Cab Sauv* and Michael Shiraz. In top form. Recent single-v'yd releases add more lustre.

Yabby Lake Mor Pen, Vic r w ★★★ Joint venture between movie magnate Robert Kirby, Larry McKenna and Tod Dexter. Quality on sharp rise since winemaker Tom Carson arrived. Single-site Pinot N and Shiraz are excellent.

Yalumba Barossa V, SA r w br sp (w sw) ★★→★★★ 162 years young. Family firm showing considerable verve. Full spectrum of high-quality wines, from budget to elite old-vine, single-v'yd. In outstanding form. Also HEGGIES, PEWSEY VALE, Jansz and Oxford Landing under Hill Smith Family V'yds.

Yarra Burn Yarra V, Vic r w sp ★★ Estate making Sem, Sauv Bl, Chard, sparkling Pinot N/Chard/Pinot Meunier. Acquired by HARDYS in 1995. Bastard Hill Chard and Pinot N legitimate flag-bearers.

Yarra Valley Vic Historic area nr Melbourne. Growing emphasis on v. successful Pinot N, Chard, Shiraz and sparkling.

Yarra Yarra Yarra V, Vic r w ★★★ Recently increased to 7 ha, giving greater access to fine Sem/Sauv Bl and Cab Sauv, each in classic Bordeaux style.

Yarra Yering Yarra V, Vic r w ★★★★ (Dry Reds) 80' 81' 82' 83 84 85' 90' 91' 93' 94 97' 99' 00 01 02' 04' 05' 06' 08 Best-known Lilydale boutique winery. Esp racy, powerful Pinot N; deep, herby Cab Sauv (Dry Red No 1); Shiraz (Dry Red No 2). Luscious, daring flavours in red and white. Much-admired founder/owner Bailey Carrodus died in 2008. Acquired in 2009 by KAESLER.

Yellow Tail NSW *See* CASELLA.

Yering Station/Yarrabank Yarra V, Vic r w sp ★★ On site of Victoria's first v'yd; replanted after 80-yr gap. Yering Station table wines (Res Chard, Pinot N, Shiraz, Viognier); Yarrabank (esp fine sparkling wines in joint venture with Champagne Devaux).

Yeringberg Yarra V, Vic r w ★★★ (Marsanne) 91' 92 94' 95 97 98 00 02' 04 05 06' (Cab Sauv) 77' 80 81' 84' 88' 90 97' 98 00' 02 04 05' 06' 08' Dreamlike historic estate still in the hands of founding family. Makes small quantities of v. high-quality Marsanne, Roussanne, Chard, Cab Sauv and Pinot N.

Zema Estate Coon, SA r ★★ One of the last bastions of hand-pruning in COONAWARRA. Powerful, straightforward reds.

New Zealand

Abbreviations used in the text:

Auck	Auckland
B of P	Bay of Plenty
Cant	Canterbury
C Ot	Central Otago
Gis	Gisborne
Hawk	Hawkes Bay
Marl	Marlborough
Mart	Martinborough
Nel	Nelson
Wair	Wairarapa
Waih	Waiheke Island
Waip	Waipara

New Zealand wine has never been cheaper or more plentiful. Half of the country's wineries have not raised their prices for at least five years; a third have *lowered* their prices. Export volumes are growing, and in the UK, New Zealand's white wines sell for 40% more than the average price of any bottle, but over the past decade their inflation-adjusted price has been on a steady decline. Many producers are starting to feel that New Zealand, as a small-scale producer, should shift its focus to the top end of the world's wine markets. Several marketing alliances have been formed to push the export of high-end wines. Marlborough (60% vineyard area) and Sauvignon Blanc (50+%), continue to dominate the country's output. Other key varieties are Pinot Noir (15%), Chardonnay (12%), Pinot Gris (5%), Merlot (4%). In 2010, nearly one million cases of Pinot Noir were exported (139,000 cases in 2003), as producers launched a host of second-, third- and fourth-tier labels for cash-strapped consumers. Syrah (rare and mostly in Hawke's Bay, Waiheke Island) is the latest star.

Recent vintages

2010 Low-cropping year. Aromatic, strongly flavoured Marlborough Sauv Bl with firm acidity. Hawke's Bay predicts outstanding Chard.

2009 A dry autumn. Intense, zingy Marlborough Sauv Bl; concentrated, ripe Hawke's Bay reds. Central Otago frosty and cool, with variable Pinot N.

2008 Warm growing season, heavy autumn rains in Marlborough led to below-average quality; early-picked fared best. Variable quality in Hawke's Bay.

Akarua C Ot ★★ Respected producer; powerful, rich Res Pinot N (09'), crisp Chard, intense Ries, full-bodied, spicy Pinot Gr. Supple, charming 2nd-tier Pinot N (09').

Allan Scott Marl ★★ V.gd Ries (from vines up to 30 yrs old), elegant Chard, tropical fruit-flavoured Sauv Bl; sturdy, spicy Pinot N. Recent focus on single-v'yd, organic and sparkling wines, typically full of interest.

Alpha Domus Hawk ★★ V.gd Chard and Viognier. Concentrated, Bordeaux-style reds, esp savoury Merlot-based The Navigator, and notably dark, rich Cab Sauv-based The Aviator. Top wines labelled AD.

Amisfield C Ot ★★ Impressive, fleshy, smooth Pinot Gr; tense, minerally Ries (dry and sweet); stylish, intense Sauv Bl; and floral, complex Pinot N (Rocky Knoll is Rolls Royce model). Lake Hayes is lower-tier label.

Ara Marl ★★ Huge v'yd in Waihopai Valley; Sauv Bl, Pinot N. Top wines: Resolute; Composite v.gd. Dry, minerally wines. 3rd-tier Pathway wines gd value.

Astrolabe Marl ★★ Label part-owned by WHITEHAVEN winemaker Simon Waghorn. Intense, harmonious, large-volume Voyage Sauv Bl. Discovery Awatere Valley Sauv Bl is more herbaceous. 2nd label: Durvillea.

Ata Rangi Mart ★★★ Small, highly respected winery. *Outstanding Pinot N* (05 06' 07 08 09) is one of NZ's greatest, cellaring well for a decade, and v.gd young-vine Crimson Pinot N. Rich, concentrated Craighall Chard and Lismore Pinot Gr.

Auckland Largest city in NZ. Nearby wine districts are Henderson, Huapai, Kumeu (long-established) and newer (since 1980s) Matakana, Clevedon, Waiheke Island. Variable but often classy Bordeaux-style reds, bold, ripe Syrah (esp gd on Waiheke) and underrated, often stylish Chard.

Auntsfield Marl ★★ Excellent wines from site of the region's first v'yd, planted in 1873, uprooted in 1931 and replanted by the Cowley family in 1999. Strong, tropical-fruit-flavoured Long Cow Sauv Bl; fleshy, peachy, rich Cob Cottage Chard; sturdy, dense, firm Hawk Hill Pinot N.

Awatere Valley Marl Major subregion, with few wineries but huge recent plantings. Slightly cooler and drier than the larger WAIRAU VALLEY, with racy, herbaceous, minerally Sauv Bl and scented, often slightly leafy Pinot N.

Babich Hend ★★ →★★★ Mid-size family firm (1916); quality, value. HAWKE'S BAY, MARLBOROUGH v'yds. Refined, slow-maturing Irongate Chard (07', **08**); elegant Irongate Cab/Merlot/Cab Fr (single-v'yd). Ripe, dry MARLBOROUGH Sauv Bl big seller (rich Individual V'yd Cowslip Valley). Mid-tier Winemaker's Reserve.

Bald Hills C Ot ★★ Bannockburn v'yd with crisp, dry Pinot Gr; floral, full-bodied, slightly sweet Ries and generous, savoury, complex Pinot N.

Bell Hill Cant ★★★ Tiny, elevated v'yd on limestone soil, inland from Waipara, owned by Marcel GIESEN and Sherwyn Veldhuizen. Strikingly rich, fine Chard and gorgeously scented, powerful, velvety Pinot N. Second label: Old Weka Pass.

Bilancia Hawk ★★ Small producer of classy Syrah (inc brilliant hill-grown La Collina) and rich Viognier, Pinot Gr (Reserve is richer, sweeter.) La Collina White is new blend of Viognier and Gewürz (powerful apricot and spice flavours).

Blackenbrook Nel ★★ Small winery; excellent whites, esp perfumed, rich Gewürz, Pinot Gr. Punchy Sauv Bl; fleshy, supple Res Pinot N. St Jacques is second label.

Borthwick Wair ★★ Lively, tropical-fruit-flavoured Sauv Bl; rich, dryish Ries; peachy, toasty Chard and deeply coloured, perfumed, muscular Pinot N.

Brancott Marl ★ →★★★ Brand formerly used by PERNOD RICARD NZ in USA, as a substitute for MONTANA; now replacing the MONTANA brand worldwide.

Brightwater Nel ★★ Impressive whites, esp crisp, flavour-packed Sauv Bl, pure, medium-dry Ries, rich, gently sweet Pinot Gr. Top wines label: Lord Rutherford.

Brookfields ★★ Excellent "gold label" Cab Sauv/Merlot; gd Chard, Pinot Gr, Gewürz and Syrah (esp powerful, spicy Hillside Syrah). Dense Sun-Dried Malbec (09).

Cable Bay Waih ★★ Mid-sized producer with tight, refined Waiheke Chard; outstanding Res Syrah, bold yet stylish; and spicy, savoury Five Hills red (mostly Merlot and Malbec). Subtle, finely textured MARLBOROUGH Sauv Bl.

Canterbury NZ's 4th-largest wine region; almost all top v'yds are in warm, sheltered Waipara district. Sauv Bl is most heavily planted, but greatest success with Ries and Pinot N. Emerging strengths in Gewürz and Pinot Gr.

Carrick C Ot ★★ Bannockburn winery with crisp, flavourful whites (Pinot Gr, Sauv Bl, Chard), excellent Ries (dry, medium and sweet) and densely packed Pinot N, built to last. Drink-young style Unravelled Pinot N is also sturdy and rich.

Central Otago C Ot (r) 09 10 (w) 09 10 Cool, relatively low rainfall, mountainous region (now NZ's 5th-largest) in southern South Island. Scented, crisp Ries and Pinot Gr; Pinot N notably perfumed and silky, with intense character and plenty of drink-young charm. Promising, Champagne-style sparkling.

Chard Farm C Ot ★★ Rich, citrous, medium Ries; fleshy, oily Pinot Gr; perfumed, midweight, supple Pinot N. Also light, smooth Rabbit Ranch Pinot N.

Cheviot Hills Cant New subregion in the South Island, north of Waipara in north CANTERBURY, pioneered by Mt Beautiful. Vibrant, intense Sauv Bl, Ries.

Church Road Hawk ★★→★★★ PERNOD RICARD NZ winery with deep HAWKE'S BAY roots, now also making savoury, complex Central Otago Pinot N (09). Rich, refined Chard and elegant, distinctly Bordeaux-like Merlot/Cab Sauv. Top-flight Res wines; prestige claret-style red TOM (02' 07'). Mid-priced Cuve range is superb quality and value. Magnificent new TOM Chard (06').

Churton Marl ★★ Subtle, complex, finely textured Sauv Bl; fragrant, spicy, v. harmonious Pinot N (esp The Abyss – oldest vines, greater depth.)

Clearview Hawk ★★→★★★ Hedonistic, lush, super-charged Res Chard; impressive oak-fermented Res Sauv Bl; dark, rich Res Cab Fr, Enigma (Merlot-based), Old Olive Block (Cab Sauv blend).

Clifford Bay Marl ★★ AWATERE VALLEY producer. Scented, intense Sauv Bl is best, with pure, racy gooseberry and lime flavours. Now linked to VAVASOUR.

Clos Henri Marl ★★→★★★ Established by HENRI BOURGEOIS (*see* France). Delicious, weighty, rounded Sauv Bl (grown in stony soils and partly barrel-fermented), vibrant, supple Pinot N (clay soils.) Second label (based on soil type): Bel Echo. Third label (based on young vines): Petit Clos.

Cloudy Bay Marl ★★★ Large-volume Sauv Bl (weighty, dry, finely textured, since 2010, inc minor % of barrel-ageing), Chard (robust, complex, crisp) and Pinot N (floral, supple) all classy. Pelorus vintage-dated sparkling (toasty, rich) and v. elegant, Chard-pred NV. Rarer Gewürz, Late Harvest Ries, barrel-aged, medium-dry Ries, and Te Koko (oak-aged Sauv Bl) now the greatest wines. Owned by LVMH.

Constellation New Zealand Auck ★→★★ NZ's second-largest wine company, was Nobilo Wine Group, now owned by US-based Constellation Brands. Nobilo MARLBOROUGH Sauv Bl (fresh, ripe, tropical fruit) is now biggest-selling Sauv Bl in USA. Superior varietals labelled Nobilo Icon (weighty, ripely herbaceous Sauv Bl esp impressive); v.gd Drylands Sauv Bl. *See* KIM CRAWFORD, MONKEY BAY, SELAKS.

Cooper's Creek Auck ★★ Extensive range of gd-value wines from four regions. Excellent Swamp Res Chard; v.gd Sauv Bl, Ries; Merlot, top-value Viognier; debut Grüner Veltliner 2008 (NZ's first). SV (Select V'yd) range is mid-tier.

Corbans Auck ★→★★★ Former PERNOD RICARD NZ brand, sold in 2010 to brewer Lion Nathan (owner of WITHER HILLS) and its joint venture partner Indevin. Best: Cottage Block; Private Bin. Quality from basic to outstanding (esp v. refined, complex, creamy Cottage Block Hawke's Bay Chard).

Craggy Range Hawk ★★→★★★ Mid-sized winery, MARTINBOROUGH and HAWKE'S BAY v'yds. Restrained Sauv Bl, stylish Chard, Pinot N; strikingly dense, ripe Merlot (esp Sophia) and Syrah (esp majestic Le Sol) from GIMBLETT GRAVELS. Most recent reds are best (more supple, refined.) Cheaper regional blends label Wild Rock.

Delegat's Auck ★★ Large, fast-expanding company, still controlled by brother-and-sister team, Jim and Rosé Delegat. V'yds and other big wineries in HAWKE'S BAY and MARLBOROUGH. Res Chard and Cab Sauv/Merlot offer v.gd quality and value. Hugely successful OYSTER BAY brand.

Delta Marl ★★ Owned by consultant winemaker Matt Thomson, UK importer

David Gleave and others. Vibrant, tropical fruit-flavoured Sauv Bl and floral, silky Pinot N. Top label: Hatter's Hill (richer, more new oak).

Destiny Bay Waih ★★★ Expat Americans; expensive, lush, silky Bordeaux-style reds. Flagship is substantial, deep, savoury Magna Praemia (mostly Cab Sauv).

Deutz Auck ★★★ Champagne company; fine sparkling from MARLBOROUGH by PERNOD RICARD NZ. NV: lively, yeasty, intense. Vintage Blanc de Blancs: finely focused, citrous, piercing (NZ's most awarded bubbly). Rosé: crisp, yeasty, strawberryish.

Distant Land Auck ★→★★ New export brand from old family winery, Lincoln. Best: crisp MARLBOROUGH Sauv Bl; scented, rich MARLBOROUGH Pinot Gr.

Dog Point Marl ★★ Grower Ivan Sutherland and winemaker James Healy (both ex-CLOUDY BAY) make unusually complex, oak-aged Sauv Bl (Section 94), Chard and Pinot N (one of MARLBOROUGH's greatest.) Also limey, smooth, unoaked Sauv Bl.

Dry River Mart ★★★ Small winery, now US owner, but founder Neil McCallum involved. Elegant, long-lived Chard, Ries, Pinot Gr, Gewürz; gorgeous late-harvest whites; floral, v. sweet-fruited, age-worthy Pinot N (03' **05 06**' 07 08).

Elephant Hill ★★ German-owned, coastal v'yd and winery at Te Awanga, first vintage 2007. Sophisticated wines, inc v. pure Viognier, rich, vibrant Chard, and deliciously floral, supple Syrah.

Escarpment Mart ★★ Sturdy, Alsace-like Pinot Gr, fleshy, soft Chard and complex, concentrated Pinot N from Larry McKenna, ex-MARTINBOROUGH V'YD. Top label: Kupe. Single-v'yd reds launched from 2006. The Edge: drink-young range.

Esk Valley Hawk ★★→★★★ Owned by VILLA MARIA. Some of NZ's most voluptuous Merlot-based reds (esp Winemakers Res 06' 07'), excellent Merlot/Malbec Rosé (one of NZ's best), v.gd Chard, Chenin Bl, MARLBOROUGH Sauv Bl. Flagship red: The Terraces (supercharged, single-v'yd blend from Malbec, Merlot, Cab Fr).

Fairhall Downs Marl ★★ Single-v'yd wines from elevated site. Weighty, dry Pinot Gr; full-flavoured Chard; racy Sauv Bl; perfumed Pinot N. Second label: Torea.

Felton Road C Ot ★★★ Star winery in warm Bannockburn area. Bold, graceful Pinot N Block 3 and 5, and light, intense Ries (dry and medium); excellent Chard and regular Pinot N. Superb Cornish Point Pinot N from nearby v'yd.

Forrest Marl ★★ Mid-size winery with wide range. Gd Sauv Bl and Ries; gorgeous botrytized Ries; flavour-crammed HAWKE'S BAY Newton/Forrest Cornerstone (Bordeaux red blend). Distinguished flagship range John Forrest Collection. Popular low-alcohol Ries under The Doctors' label.

Foxes Island Marl ★★ Smallish producer of rich, smooth Chard, finely textured Sauv Bl and elegant, supple Pinot N. Gd, large-volume Sauv Bl and Pinot N under Seven Terraces and Fox Junior brands.

Framingham Marl ★★ Owned by Sogrape (Portugal). Superb whites: intense, zesty Ries (esp rich, medium Classic) and lush, sl sweet Pinot Gr, Gewürz. Subtle, dry Sauv Bl. Scented, silky Pinot N. New F Series (rare, "innovative" wines).

Fromm Marl ★★★ Swiss-founded; now less tannic, more charming reds. Sturdy, long-lived Pinot N, esp under Fromm V'yd (firmly structured) and Clayvin V'yd (rich, elegant) labels. Also unusually stylish, citrous, minerally Clayvin Chard. Earlier-drinking La Strada range also v.gd, inc deliciously fruity, supple Syrah.

Gibbston Valley C Ot ★★ Pioneer winery. Strength is Pinot N, esp rich, complex CENTRAL OTAGO regional blend and robust, exuberantly fruity Res (09'). Racy whites, esp zingy, flavour-packed Ries and scented, full-bodied, dry Pinot Gr.

Giesen Cant ★→★★ German family winery. Bulk of production is fresh, tangy MARLBOROUGH Sauv Bl. Also weighty, concentrated The Brothers Sauv Bl and commanding, barrel-fermented The August Sauv Bl.

Gimblett Gravels Hawk Defined area (over 800 ha planted) with v. free-draining soils, noted for rich, ripe Bordeaux-style reds (mostly Merlot-predominant) and fragrant, vibrant Syrah. Best of both are world-class.

Gisborne Gis (r) 09' 10' (w) 09' 10' NZ's 3rd-largest region. Abundant sunshine and rain, with fertile soils. Key strength is Chard (typically deliciously fragrant, ripe and soft in its youth, but the best mature well). Excellent Gewürz and Viognier; Merlot and Pinot Gr more variable.

Gladstone Wair ★→★★ Tropical Sauv Bl; weighty, partly oak-aged Pinot Gr; supple Pinot N under top label, Gladstone; 12,000 Miles is lower-priced brand.

Greenhough Nel ★★→★★★ One of region's top producers, with immaculate and deep-flavoured Ries, Sauv Bl, Chard, Pinot N. Top label: Hope V'yd (incl complex, creamy Chard and rich, mushroomy Pinot N).

Greystone Waip ★★ Emerging star with classy whites (Ries, Gewürz, Pinot Gr – all rich, finely textured); fast-improving Chard and Sauv Bl; promising Pinot N.

Greywacke Marl ★★ New label of Kevin Judd, ex-CLOUDY BAY, launched from 2009. Named after a soil type. Tight, elegant, lingering Sauv Bl, fleshy, generous Pinot Gr, rich, gently sweet Ries and lovely late-harvest Gewürz.

Grove Mill Marl ★★ Attractive whites, inc v.gd, punchy, ripe Sauv Bl and slightly sweet Pinot Gr, Ries. Reds less exciting. Gd-value lower-tier Sanctuary brand. First winery to earn carboNZero certification.

Hans Herzog Marl ★★★ Established by Swiss immigrants. Power-packed, classy, long-lived Merlot/Cab Sauv (region's greatest), Montepulciano, Pinot N, sturdy, dry Viognier and Pinot Gr; rich, oak-aged Sauv Bl. Hans brand in Europe, USA.

Hawke's Bay (r) 07' 09' 10' (w) 07 10' NZ's 2nd-largest region. Long history of winemaking in sunny, warm climate; shingly and heavier soils. Full, rich Merlot and Cab Sauv-based reds in gd vintages; Syrah a fast-rising star; powerful Chard; ripe, rounded Sauv Bl (suits oak); NZ's best Viognier.

Highfield Marl ★★ Japanese-owned with light, intense Ries, citrous, mealy Chard, immaculate Sauv Bl and generous, savoury Pinot N. Elstree sparkling variable lately; can be almost Champagne-like.

Hunter's Marl ★★→★★★ Pioneering winery (since 1982) with intense, immaculate, fully dry Sauv Bl. Fine, delicate, gently oaked Chard. Excellent sparkling (MiruMiru), Ries, Gewürz; light, elegant Pinot N. All gd value.

Isabel Estate Marl ★→★★ Family estate; formerly outstanding Pinot N, Sauv Bl (09 best for yrs), Chard; lately less exciting. Crisp, dryish Pinot Gr; strong, dry Ries.

Jackson Estate Marl ★★ Rich, ripe Sauv Bl is consistently outstanding; attractive, gently oaked Chard and sweet-fruited, supple Pinot N (esp top-tier, v. deep, finely textured Gum Emperor Pinot N).

Johanneshof Marl ★→★★ Small, low-profile winery with outstandingly perfumed, lush, gently sw Gewürz (one of NZ's finest). Other wines more variable.

Jules Taylor Marl ★★ Jules Taylor and George Elworthy produce a growing volume of intense Ries; weighty, creamy Pinot Gr; rich, complex Chard; conc'd Sauv Bl.

Julicher Mart ★★ Small, consistently excellent producer of tangy, dryish Ries and generous, plummy, spicy, complex Pinot N. (99 Rows gd-value second label.)

Kim Crawford Hawk ★★ Part of US-based CONSTELLATION empire. Easy-drinking wines, inc rich, oaky Gisborne Chard; fresh, plummy Merlot; scented, strong-flavoured MARLBOROUGH Sauv Bl. Top range label, SP (Small Parcel).

Kumeu River Auck ★★→★★★ Rich, refined Kumeu Estate Chard (08') single-v'yd Mate's V'yd Chard even more opulent. Both among NZ's greatest. Weighty, floral Pinot Gr; sturdy, earthy Pinot N; ripe, tropical, dry MARLBOROUGH Sauv Bl. Second label: Kumeu River Village.

Lake Chalice Marl ★★ Small producer; vibrant, creamy Chard; incisive, slightly sweet Ries; v.gd-quality Sauv Bl (esp The Raptor). Platinum premium label.

Lawson's Dry Hills Marl ★★→★★★ Weighty wines with intense flavours. Unusually complex Sauv Bl and opulent Gewürz, Pinot Gr. Dry, toasty, bottle-aged Ries. New top-end range from 2009: The Pioneer.

Lindauer Auck ★★ Huge-selling sparkling brand – esp bottle-fermented, low-priced Lindauer Brut – sold in 2010 by PERNOD RICARD NZ to Lion Nathan.

Mahi Marl ★★ Stylish, complex, mostly single-v'yd wines from Brian Bicknell, ex-SERESIN winemaker. Finely textured, full-of-personality Sauv Bl, Chard, Pinot N.

Man O' War Auck ★★ Largest v'yd on Waiheke Island, owned by Spencer family. First planted 1993, but wines only now distributed widely. Dense, Bordeaux-style reds (esp Ironclad) and powerful, spicy, firm Dreadnought Syrah.

Margrain Mart ★★ Small winery with firm, concentrated Chard, Ries, Pinot Gr, Gewürz and Pinot N, all of which reward bottle-ageing. Classy new sparkling: La Michelle – biscuity, smooth, v. dry.

Marlborough (r) 09' 10' (w) 09' 10' NZ's largest region by far at top of South Island. Warm, sunny days and cold nights give aromatic, crisp whites. Intense Sauv Bl; fresh, limey Ries (inc recent wave of low-alcohol wines); v. promising Pinot Gr, Gewürz; Chard leaner, more appley than HAWKE'S BAY. High-quality sparkling and botrytized Ries. Pinot N underrated, top wines among NZ's finest.

Martinborough Mart (r) 08' 09 10 (w) 09 10 Small, high-quality area in south WAIRARAPA (foot of North Island). Warm summers, dry autumns, gravelly soils. Success with several white grapes (incl MARLBOROUGH-like Sauv Bl) but renowned for sturdy, rich, long-lived Pinot N.

Martinborough V'yd Mart ★★★ Distinguished small winery; one of NZ's top Pinot N (06' 07'), spicy, complex. Rich Chard, intense Ries, concentrated Pinot Gr. Also single-v'yd Burnt Spur, drink-young Te Tera ranges (top-value Pinot N).

Matua Valley Auck ★→★★ Producer of NZ's first Sauv Bl in 1974. Once prestigious, family-run producer, now owned by Treasury Wine Estates (Foster's) with v'yds in four regions. GISBORNE (esp Judd Chard), HAWKE'S BAY and MARLBOROUGH wines; most offer pleasant, easy-drinking. Shingle Peak Sauv Bl top value.

Mills Reef B of P ★★→★★★ Preston family makes impressive wines from HAWKE'S BAY grapes, incl fine Chard. Top Elspeth range inc dense, rich Bordeaux-style reds and Syrah. Res range reds also impressive and outstanding value.

Millton Gis ★★→★★★★ Region's top winery: certified organic. Hill-grown single-v'yd Clos de Ste Anne range (Chard, Viognier, Syrah, Pinot N) is v. concentrated, full of personality. Rich, long-lived Chenin Bl is NZ's finest (honeyed in wetter yrs; pure and long-lived in drier yrs). Classy, gd-value Riverpoint V'yd Viognier.

Misha's C Ot ★★ Large v'yd at Bendigo, owned by Misha and Andy Wilkinson. First vintage 2008. Consistently classy Gewürz, Pinot Gr, Ries (medium Limelight and medium-dry Lyric), savoury, complex Pinot N.

Mission Hawk ★★ NZ's oldest wine producer (1851), first sales in the 1890s, still run by Catholic Society of Mary. Solid, inc gd varietals: creamy-smooth Chard

---

Hot off the presses

Think New Zealand wine – think punchy, zesty Sauv Bl or more recently, enticingly floral and supple Pinot N. Of the hundreds of brand-new labels released in the past year, most were based on Sauv Bl, Pinot Gr, Pinot N or Syrah. However, there is rising interest in other grape varieties – Arneis, Grüner Veltliner, Verdelho, Sauvignon Gris, Tempranillo, Dolcetto and Montepulciano. The hot new wine style is sparkling Sauv Bl. Mount Riley in 2000 was the country's first winery to put bubbles in Sauv Bl, but until recently attracted few imitators. Suddenly, sparkling Sauvs are everywhere. A convenient way to shift surplus stocks of Sauv Bl, the wines are typically fresh and simple, with tropical-fruit flavours, crisp and lively.

and fruit-driven Syrah are top value. Res range includes gd Bordeaux-style reds, Syrah and Chard. Top label: Jewelstone (v. classy, concentrated Chard).

Monkey Bay ★ CONSTELLATION NZ brand, modestly priced and v. popular in the USA. Easy-drinking Chard; crisp, herbaceous Sauv Bl; light Pinot Gr; fruity Merlot.

Montana Auck ★→★★★ Former key brand of PERNOD RICARD NZ, replaced in 2010 by Brancott Estate. Top wines are Letter Series (eg. "B" Brancott Sauv Bl). Res range v. gd quality and value. Biggest-selling varietals inc: crisp, grassy MARLBOROUGH Sauv Bl (annual production one million cases); fresh, fruit-driven Gisborne Chard; floral, smooth, easy-drinking South Island Pinot N.

Morton Estate B of P ★→★★★ Mid-size producer with v'yds in HAWKE'S BAY and MARLBOROUGH. Refined Black Label Chard. White Label Chard and Premium Brut gd and top value; ditto Viognier and Pinot Gr. Reds less exciting.

Mount Riley Marl ★★ Fast-growing. Punchy, gd value, dry Sauv Bl; finely textured Pinot Gr; easy-drinking Pinot N. Top range is Seventeen Valley.

Mt Difficulty C Ot ★★ Quality producer in Bannockburn area. Best-known for v. refined, intense Pinot N (Roaring Meg drinking early; Single V'yd Pipeclay Terrace is dense, lasting). Classy whites (Ries, Pinot Gr); full-flavoured rosé.

Mud House Cant ★★ Large, fast-expanding WAIPARA-based winery. Brands inc: Mud House (top range is Swan); Hay Maker (lower tier); Waipara Hills. Punchy, vibrant MARLBOROUGH Sauv Bl is classy and top value; intense, racy Waipara Ries.

Muddy Water Waip ★★→★★★ Small, v. high-quality producer with beautifully intense Ries (among NZ's best), minerally Chard and savoury, subtle, notably complex Pinot N (esp Slowhand, based on oldest, low-yielding vines).

Nautilus Marl ★★ Small, v. reliable range of distributors Négociants (NZ), owned by S Smith & Sons (Australia). Top wines: stylish Sauv Bl (released with bottle age); savoury Pinot N; classy sparkler. Mid tier: Opawa. Lower tier: Twin Islands.

Ned, The Marl ★★ Latest venture of Brent Marris, ex-WITHER HILLS. Full-flavoured, vibrant Sauv Bl, lively, dryish Pinot Gr, and berryish, supple Pinot N. New brand: Marisco – classy, incisive, dry Sauv Bl.

Nelson (r) 09 10 (w) 09 10' Small, steadily expanding region west of MARLBOROUGH; climate is wetter but equally sunny. Clay soils of Upper Moutere hills and silty Waimea plains. Strengths in aromatic whites, esp Ries, Sauv Bl, Pinot Gr, Gewürz; also gd (sometimes outstanding) Chard and Pinot N.

Neudorf Nel ★★★ A top smallish winery. Powerful yet elegant Moutere Chard (07, 08, 09') is one of NZ's greatest; superb, v. savoury Moutere Pinot N (esp Home Vineyard.) Sauv Bl, Pinot Gr and Ries also top-flight.

Ngatarawa Hawk ★★→★★★ Mid-sized. Top Alwyn range, inc powerful Chard, dark, generous Merlot/Cab and honey-sweet Noble Harvest Ries. Mid-range Glazebrook also excellent. Stables range: gd value.

No. 1 Family Marl ★★ Family-owned company of Daniel Le Brun, ex-Champagne but MARLBOROUGH-based since 1980. Specialist in sparkling wine, esp refined, tight-knit, NV Blanc de Blancs, Cuvee No 1.

Nobilo Marl *See* CONSTELLATION NZ.

Obsidian Waih ★★ V. stylish Bordeaux blend ("The Obsidian"), Viognier, Chard and Syrah under top brand Obsidian. Gd-value Waiheke reds (inc Merlot, Syrah and Montepulciano) under 2nd-tier Weeping Sands label.

Olssens C Ot ★★ Consistently attractive Pinot N, from first Bannockburn v'yd. Smooth, rich Jackson Barry Pinot N is mid-tier; top wine is bold Slapjack Creek Res Pinot N. Whites solid but less exciting.

Oyster Bay Marl ★★ From DELEGAT'S, this is a marketing triumph, with sales exceeding 1.5 million cases (inc the no 1 white wine spot in Australia.) Vibrant, elegant, fruit-driven wines, mostly from Sauv Bl, Chard and Pinot N.

Palliser Mart ★★→★★★ One of the area's largest and best wineries. Superb, tropical

Sauv Bl, excellent Chard, Ries, Pinot Gr, bubbly, Pinot N. Top wines: Palliser Estate. Lower tier: Pencarrow (great value but not always MARTINBOROUGH).

Pask, C J Hawk ★★ Mid-size winery, extensive v'yds in GIMBLETT GRAVELS. Syrah, Cab Sauv and Merlot-based reds consistently impressive and fine value; Chard, too. Top Declaration range less convincing.

Passage Rock Waih ★★ Powerful, densely coloured, opulent Syrah (esp Res, Waiheke's most awarded wine). Gd Bordeaux-style reds, whites solid.

Pegasus Bay Waip ★★★ Family-owned producer with distinguished range: taut, cool-climate Chard; complex, oaked Sauv Bl/Sem; v. rich, zingy Ries, lush, silky Pinot N (esp old-vine Prima Donna). Second label: Main Divide (gd value).

Peregrine C Ot ★★ Crisp, cool-climate, concentrated whites and beautifully rich, silky Pinot N (a regular show-stopper.) Saddleback Pinot N esp gd value.

Pernod Ricard NZ Auck ★→★★★ NZ wine giant, formerly MONTANA. Sold Corbans and LINDAUER brands in 2010 and dropped MONTANA brand in favour of Brancott Estate. Wineries in AUCKLAND, HAWKE'S BAY and MARLBOROUGH. Extensive co-owned v'yds for MARLBOROUGH whites, inc: top-value MONTANA Sauv Bl. Strength in sparkling, esp DEUTZ MARLBOROUGH CUVÉE. Elegant CHURCH ROAD reds, quality Chard. Other key brands: STONELEIGH (Sauv Bl) and Triplebank (vibrant, racy AWATERE VALLEY wines). Camshorn is gd Waipara Ries and Pinot N.

Puriri Hills Auck ★★ Silky, seductive Merlot-based reds from Clevedon. Rich, plump Res, with more new oak. Classy, blended "Pope" (one-third Carmenère).

Pyramid Valley Cant ★★ Tiny v'yd at Waikari, inland from Waipara. Mike Weersing makes two estate-grown, floral Pinot Ns (Angel Flower, Earth Smoke), showing strong personality; classy Growers Collection wines from other regions.

Quartz Reef C Ot ★★ Small, quality producer with crisp, citrous, dry Pinot Gr; deep, spicy Pinot N (Bendigo Estate V'yd esp concentrated); yeasty, lingering, Champagne-like sparkler (vintage esp gd).

Rippon V'yd C Ot ★★ Stunning v'yd on shores of Lake Wanaka. "Feminine" Mature Vine Pinot N. Jeunesse Pinot N from younger vines; complex Tinker's Field Pinot N (from oldest vines). Slowly evolving whites, inc steely, appley Ries.

Rockburn C Ot ★★ Crisp, racy Chard, Pinot Gr, Gewürz, Ries, Sauv Bl. Supple, rich Pinot N is best and an emerging star. Lively rosé from Pinot N: Stolen Kiss.

Sacred Hill Hawk ★★ ·★★★ Mid-size producer, partly Chinese-owned. Distinguished Riflemans Chard (powerful but refined, from cool, elevated site). Dark, rich, long-lived Brokenstone Merlot, Helmsman Cab/Merlot and Deer Stalkers Syrah from GIMBLETT GRAVELS. Punchy MARLBOROUGH Sauv Bl. Other brands: Gunn Estate, Wild South (gd value MARLBOROUGH range).

Saint Clair Marl ★★→★★★ Large, family-owned producer with extensive v'yds. Highly acclaimed Sauv Bl, esp impressive, great-value regional blend and exceedingly intense Wairau Res. Fragrant Ries, easy Chard and plummy, early-drinking Merlot. Rich Res Chard, Merlot, Pinot N. Bewildering array of 2nd-tier Pioneer Block wines (inc nine Sauv Bls). Vicar's Choice is lower tier.

Seifried Estate Nel ★★ Region's biggest winery. Known initially for aromatic, crisp, medium-dry Ries and Gewürz; now also producing gd-value, often excellent Sauv Bl and Chard. Best wines: Winemakers Collection (inc freeze-concentrated Sweet Agnes Ries.) Old Coach Road is 3rd tier. Plain reds.

Selaks Marl ★·★★ Now a brand of CONSTELLATION NZ. Moderately priced, fruit-driven MARLBOROUGH whites under Premium Selection label. Top: Founders Res. Emerging mid-tier, Winemaker's Favourite, offers excellent quality/value (esp rich, creamy Chard and pungent, nettley Sauv Bl.)

Seresin Marl ★★→★★★ Medium-sized producer, by NZ film producer Michael Seresin. V. stylish, rich Sauv Bl (certified organic), Chard, Pinots N and Gr, Ries; 2nd tier: Momo (gd quality/value). Overall, complex, finely textured wines.

Sileni Hawk ★★ Architecturally striking winery with extensive v'yds and classy Chard, Merlot and MARLBOROUGH Sauv Bl. Top wines: rare EV (Exceptional Vintage), then a range with individual names (inc lush, concentrated The Lodge Chard), followed by Cellar Selection (satisfying, easy-drinking Merlot.) Rich, smooth MARLBOROUGH Sauv Bl (esp The Straits).

Spy Valley Marl ★★→★★★ High-achieving, extensive v'yds. Sauv Bl, Chard, Ries, Gewürz, Pinot Gr, Merlot/Malbec, Pinot N all v.gd and priced right. Superb top selection: Envoy (inc subtle Chard, Mosel-like Ries). Second label: Satellite.

Staete Landt Marl ★★ Dutch immigrants, producing v. refined Chard, Sauv Bl and Pinot Gr, and graceful, supple Pinot N. Promising Viognier and Syrah.

Stonecroft Hawk ★★→★★★ Small winery. NZ's first serious Syrah (since 1989), more Rhône than Australia. Outstanding Chard, v. rich Old Vine Gewürz, fresh, light Zinfandel in dry yrs. New ownership since 2010.

Stoneleigh Marl ★★ Owned by PERNOD RICARD NZ. Impressive, large-volume MARLBOROUGH whites (inc punchy, tropical-fruit Sauv Bl, generous, slightly sweet Pinot Gr, refined, medium-dry Ries and creamy-smooth Chard) and fast-improving, savoury Pinot N. Top wines: Rapaura Series.

Stonyridge Waih ★★★ Boutique winery. Famous for exceptional, Cab Sauv-based blended red, Larose (00' **04' 05'** 06 07 08' 09, 10'). Airfield is little brother of Larose. Also powerful, dense Rhône-style blend Pilgrim and super-charged Luna Negra Malbec. Second label: Fallen Angel.

Te Awa Hawk ★★ US-owned estate v'yd, with reputation for refined Chard and Bordeaux-like, Merlot-based reds. New, premium Kidnapper Cliffs range (v. classy Chard; highly concentrated, silky Ariki – mostly Merlot; bold, peppery Pinotage; v. elegant Syrah.) Now linked to DRY RIVER.

Te Kairanga Mart ★→★★ One of district's largest wineries; chequered history of early quality issues and lately financial problems. Strategy is to focus on MARTINBOROUGH for Pinot N, with other varieties purchased from elsewhere. Moderately complex Estate Pinot N is gd value; Estate Ries is strong, tangy.

Te Mata Hawk ★★★→★★★★ Prestigious, old winery (1895). Fine, powerful Elston Chard; super-stylish Coleraine (Merlot/Cab Sauv/Cab Fr blend) (98' 00 02 04 05' 06' 07', 08); Awatea Cabs/Merlot also classy and more forward. Bullnose Syrah among NZ's finest. Woodthorpe range for early drinking (v.gd and great-value Chard, Sauv Bl, Gamay Noir – NZ's only – Merlot/Cab, Syrah/Viognier).

Te Whau Waih ★★→★★★ Tiny v'yd/restaurant. Beautifully ripe, complex Chard and savoury, earthy, complex, mostly Cab Sauv blend The Point (05', **07**, 08'). Now also outstanding Syrah and deep, dry rosé.

TerraVin Marl ★★ Weighty, dry, tropical Sauv Bl (Single V'yd more oak), but real focus is rich, firmly structured, complex Pinot N, esp Hillside Res.

Tohu ★★ Maori-owned venture with extensive v'yds. Punchy Sauv Bl (Mugwi Res is oak-aged); strong, medium-dry Ries; citrous, creamy, unoaked Chard; moderately complex Pinot N, all from MARLBOROUGH; scented, weighty NELSON Pinot Gr.

Trinity Hill Hawk ★★→★★★ Innovative winery with firm, concentrated reds (Bordeaux-style The Gimblett is rich, refined) and top-flight HAWKE'S BAY Chard. Exceptional Homage Syrah – scented, muscular, dense. V. promising Tempranillo. Scented, soft, rich Pinot Gr and Viognier among NZ's best. HAWKE'S BAY Sauv Bl: fresh, frisky, gd value.

Two Paddocks C Ot ★★ Actor Sam Neill produces several Pinot Ns, inc Picnic (drink-young style), First Paddock (more herbal style from cool Gibbston district), Last Chance (riper style from warmer Alexandra district).

Unison Hawk ★★→★★★ Dark, spicy, flavour-crammed blends of Merlot, Cab Sauv, Syrah. Selection label is oak-aged the longest. Also fragrant, fleshy, flavour-rich Syrah and "serious" dry rosé. New owners since 2008.

Vavasour Marl ★★ Based in AWATERE VALLEY. Immaculate, intense Chard and pure, nettley, racy Sauv Bl; promising Pinot N and Pinot Gr. Vavasour AWATERE VALLEY is top label; Vavasour Redwood Pass and Dashwood are regional blends (aromatic, vibrant Sauv Bl is top value). Linked to Goldwater and CLIFFORD BAY.

Vidal Hawk ★★→★★★ Part of VILLA MARIA. Distinguished Res Chard and Res Merlot/ Cab Sauv. Mid-priced Merlot/Cab Sauv is great value. Top Syrahs (Res and Soler) outstanding. Excellent MARLBOROUGH Sauv Bl, Ries and Pinot N. Strength in Viognier (fine value East Coast and rich, rounded Res).

Villa Maria Auck ★★→★★★ NZ's largest family-owned wine company, VIDAL and ESK VALLEY. Top ranges: Res (express regional character) and Single V'yd (reflect individual sites); Cellar Selection: mid-tier (less oak) is often v.gd; 3rd-tier Private Bin wines can be excellent and gd value (esp Ries, Sauv Bl, Gewürz, Pinot Gr, Pinot N). Brilliant track record in competitions. Thornbury brand: rich, soft Merlot and perfumed, supple Pinot N.

Vinoptima Gis ★★→★★★ Small Gewürz specialist, owned by Nick Nobilo (ex-NOBILO Wines). Top vintages (06) are pricey but full of power and personality. Also gorgeous Noble Late Harvest.

Voss Mart ★★ Small, respected producer of Pinot N (perfumed, weighty, silky); dryish, citrous Ries, and Res Chard (lush, creamy, complex).

Waimea Nel ★★ One of region's best white-wine producers. Punchy, ripe Sauv Bl, rich, softly textured Pinot Gr (top awards), gd Ries (Classic is honeyed, medium-style). Reds solid but less exciting. Top range: Bolitho SV. Spinyback range: DYA.

Waipara Hills Cant ★★ Now a brand of MUD HOUSE. Intense, ripe, racy MARLBOROUGH Sauv Bl, top-flight Waipara Ries. Equinox and Southern Cross Selection are top ranges. Next tier: Soul of the South.

Waipara Springs Cant ★★ Small producer of lively, cool-climate Ries (dry and medium), Sauv Bl and Chard; impressive top range: Premo (inc finely fragrant, concentrated Pinot N from district's oldest Pinot N vines).

Wairarapa NZ's 6th-largest wine region. *See* MARTINBOROUGH. Includes GLADSTONE sub-region in the north (slightly higher, cooler, wetter.) Driest, coolest region in North Island: strength in whites and Pinot N (full-bodied, spicy, savoury.)

Wairau River Marl ★★ Intense, racy Sauv Bl; full-bodied, rounded Pinot Gr; softly mouthfilling Gewürz, promising Viognier; light, gently sweet Summer Ries; finely crafted Pinot N. Res is top label.

Wairau Valley Marl MARLBOROUGH's largest and first-planted subregion, still with most of the region's wineries. Sauv Bl grown on the stony, silty plains; Pinot N on the clay-based, north-facing slopes to the south.

Waitaki Valley C Ot Emerging district in North Otago, hyped a decade ago, but plantings still small. Promising Pinot N, Pinot Gr and Ries.

Whitehaven Marl ★→★★★ Scented, pure and harmonious Sauv Bl is best; other whites (inc rich, soft Gewürz) and Pinot N: sound, easy drinking. Gallo (California) is part-owner. Top range: Greg (named after founder Greg White).

Wither Hills Marl ★★→★★★ Large producer, owned since 2002 by Lion Nathan. V. popular gooseberry/lime Sauv Bl. Rich Chard and Pinot N; latest vintages less oak-influenced. Outstandingly intense Single V'yd Sauv Bl (Rarangi: weighty, racy, long) and excellent Single V'yd Pinot N since 2007. Scented, finely poised Pinot Gr. Other brands: Shepherds Ridge, Two Tracks.

Wooing Tree C Ot ★★ Single-v'yd producer at Cromwell. Bold Pinot N (Beetle Juice Pinot N less new oak). Sandstorm Res: esp low-yielding vines, oak-aged longer.

Yealands Marl ★★ Privately owned v'yd, one of NZ's biggest, in AWATERE VALLEY. First vintage 2008. Top wines labelled Estate (Sauv Bl: punchy, herbaceous; Ries: tight, elegant, citrous; Pinot N: floral, full-bodied, supple). Other brands: Pete's Shed, Full Circle (plastic bottles).

South Africa

Abbreviations used in the text:

C'dorp	Calitzdorp	Fran	Franschhoek
Ced	Cederberg	Rob	Robertson
Coast	Coastal region	Stel	Stellenbosch
Const	Constantia	Swa	Swartland
Dar	Darling	Tul	Tulbagh
Dur	Durbanville	Wlk B	Walker Bay
Elg	Elgin	Well	Wellington

South Africa has attracted its share of foreign wine investors, including Americans, but the acquisition of two of the country's top wineries, Mulderbosch Vineyards and Tulbagh Mountain Vineyards, by a California group headed by Charles Banks (partner in top-flight Cabernet producer Screaming Eagle) could be a significant development. The USA, along with China and India, is one of the key growth markets identified by local vintners, and the rub-off from the association (albeit indirect) with America's *über* cult wine – and one of the most sought-after labels in the world – could be quite substantial. At the very least, it's yet another upbeat signal emanating from the USA, where South African wines and winemakers increasingly receive flattering comment and ratings.

Translating any good vibes into actual sales, not just in the USA but also in South Africa's traditional export markets, and indeed at home, is complicated, however, by the stubbornly strong Rand, the global economic downturn, competing alcoholic beverages and other factors. Still, there are many favourable drivers. It's widely agreed that South African quality, especially in white-wine categories, has never been better, and market forces combined with winemakers' own initiatives will see the bar raised higher still. Advancing average vine age, more rigorous site selection, science-based viticulture and the accession of a younger winemaking generation are having a positive impact today and boding well for the future. Of course, one Eagle does not a summer make, but this is not a common-or-garden bird, and the local wine community will be watching with interest.

Recent vintages

2010 "The vintage after the great 2009" is a mixed bag, later-ripening varieties (reds and whites) generally faring best. More than ever, be guided by producer's reputation rather than vintage generalizations.

2009 South Africa's 350th harvest and, serendipitously, one of its best. Stellar whites and most reds; standout Merlot.

2008 One of the more challenging harvests in recent years but also one of the coolest, yielding ripe but elegant wines with lower-than-usual alcohol.

2007 Sturdy whites for keeping; soft, easy reds for earlier drinking.

2006 The fifth sound vintage in a row.

2005 Small, thick-skinned berries; concentrated reds for keeping.

Note: Most dry whites are best drunk within two to three years.

Adoro Wines W Cape r w (sw) ★★★ Sibling to single-malt Scotch distiller The BenRiach; sophisticated red and white blends, SAUV BL, new "off-sweet" dessert Mourvèdre; all intended for food pairing.

Alto Estate Stell r (br) ★★→★★★ Montane v'yds co-owned by DISTELL, noted for age-worthy CAB SAUV (01' 02 **03** 04 05 06 07 08). New Cab Fr-based blend MPHS honours winemakers past and present.

Anthonij Rupert Wines W Cape r w ★→★★★ Evolving wine portfolio named after international businessman and brand-owner Johann Rupert's late brother. Flagship Anthonij Rupert range with emphatic reds; Cape of Good Hope old-vines bottlings; Italianate Terra del Capo trio; early-drinking Protea label.

Anwilka Stell r ★★→★★★ Partnership between KLEIN CONSTANTIA and Bordeaux's Bruno Prats and Hubert de Boüard. Flagship is SHIRAZ/CAB SAUV blend Anwilka (05 06 07 08); second wine is Ugaba.

Asara Wine Estate & Hotel W Cape r (p) w (sw) ★→★★★ Luxe German-owned tourist destination and winery nr STELLENBOSCH; best quality in Bell Tower range; flavourful quirkiness in vine-dried PINOTAGE/SHIRAZ and white CAB SAUV.

Ashbourne *See* HAMILTON RUSSELL.

Ataraxia W Cape r w ★★★ PINOT N from Kevin Grant and partners' breathtakingly situated young v'yds in Hemel-en-Aarde Ridge WARD poised to join critically acclaimed CHARD, SAUV BL and Serenity red.

Avondale Bio-LOGIC & Organic Wines Coast r (p) w (br sw sp) ★→★★★ Family-owned eco pioneer; v. gd Les Pleurs, Res and Green Duck ranges; expanding ORGANIC-certified offering includes new Viognier-scented White blend.

Axe Hill C'dorp br sw ★★★ Outstanding Port-style specialist. Restrainedly opulent Cape Vintage (mainly Touriga Nacional 01 02' **03**' 04 05' 06 07 08); solera-aged Dry White Port from CHENIN BL.

Backsberg Estate Cellars W Cape r (p) w (br s/sw sp) ★→★★★ Family enterprise with 20+ labels in five ranges, inc KOSHER. New Tread Lightly brand, locally first certified wine in lightweight PET bottles, reflects owners' eco-awareness.

Badenhorst Family Wines Coast r (p) w (sw) ★★→★★★ SWARTLAND-based "dynamic and good-looking" cousins Hein and Adi Badenhorst (latter ex-RUSTENBERG) traditionally vinify mainly Mediterranean varieties under serious but light-hearted and -textured A. A. Badenhorst and Secateurs labels.

Bamboes Bay Tiny (5 ha) maritime WARD in OLIFANTS RIVER region. Fryer's Cove first and still only winery, known for pyrotechnic SAUV BL.

Beaumont Wines W Cape r (p) w (br sw) ★→★★★ Rustic family estate; expressive CHENIN BL, PINOTAGE, varietal and blended Mourvèdre, and Bordeaux red Ariane.

Bellingham W Cape r (p) w ★→★★★ Revitalized DGB brand led by flamboyant Bernard Series (now with rare varietal Roussanne), mid-tier Legends, and easy-drinking Fusion and Blends ranges.

Beyerskloof Stell r (p w br sp) ★→★★★ South Africa's top PINOTAGE producer: ten versions of grape on offer, inc superlative varietal bottling Diesel (06 07' 08') and various CAPE BLENDS. Also classically styled Bordeaux red, Field Blend (00 01 02 **03'** 04 05).

Biodynamic Anthroposophic mode of wine-growing practised by small but expanding group, inc: REYNEKE, Glen Heatlie, Heron Ridge, The Observatory, Waterkloof, Zandvliet. *See also* ORGANIC.

Boekenhoutskloof Winery W Cape r (w sw) ★★→★★★★ Consistently excellent producer specializing in unfiltered native-yeast ferments. Spicy Syrah (01' 02' **03** 04' 05 06' 07 08); intense, minerally CAB SAUV (01' 02' **03** 04' 05 06' 07' 08'). Also fine SEM, Mediterranean-style red The Chocolate Block, and gd-value labels Porcupine Ridge and Wolftrap.

Boland Kelder Paarl r (p) w (br sw) ★→★★★ Large (23,000 tonnes), enterprising winery at PAARL, with 24 labels in five ranges, including "terroir selections" under Boland Private Cellar.

Bon Courage Estate Rob r (p) w (br) sw sp ★★→★★★ Extensive family-grown range led by Inkará reds, stylish MCC, and outstanding RIES and Muscat desserts.

Boplaas Family Vineyards W Cape r (p) w br (sp) ★→★★★ Best-known for Port styles, esp Vintage Res (99' 01 **03** 04' 05' 06' 07' 08) and Cape Tawny. Cool Bay (unfortified) range from ocean-facing vines.

Boschendal Wines Coast r (p) w sp ★★→★★★ Famous old estate showing new élan under DGB ownership. Calling cards: SHIRAZ, CAB SAUV, SAUV BL and Bordeaux/ Shiraz Grand Res. Revived emphasis on MCC.

Bot River *See* WALKER BAY.

Bouchard Finlayson Wlk B r w ★★→★★★★ V. fine PINOT N grower. Galpin Peak (01 02' **03** 04 05 07 08 09), barrel-selection Tête de Cuvée (99 01' **03'** 05' 07 09) and Unfiltered Limited Edition (07). Impressive CHARD, SAUV BL and exotic red blend Hannibal.

Breedekloof Large (12,400 ha) inland district in Breede River Valley region making mainly bulk wine for distilling and the merchant trade. Notable exceptions: Avondrood, Bergsig, Deetlefs, Mtn Oaks, Du Preez and Merwida.

Buitenverwachting Coast r (p) w (sw sp) ★★→★★★ Classy family-owned v'yds, cellar and restaurant; standout SAUV BL, Cab Fr, restrained Bordeaux blend Christine (00 01' 02 03 04 06 07), aromatic Muscat dessert "1769".

Cabernet Sauvignon Ubiquitous, but truly at home on mts around STELLENBOSCH. Top names: DE TRAFFORD, EDGEBASTON, KANONKOP, KLEINE ZALZE, LE RICHE, NEIL ELLIS, RUSTENBERG, Stark-Condé, THELEMA, VERGELEGEN, WATERFORD; elsewhere: BOEKENHOUTSKLOOF, CEDERBERG, GLEN CARLOU, SPRINGFIELD.

Cabrière W Cape (r p w sw) sp ★→★★★ NV MCC sparkling under Pierre Jourdan label (Blanc de Blancs, Cuvée Reserve); *vin doux naturel*-style apéritif from CHARD.

Calitzdorp District in KLEIN KAROO region, climatically similar to the Douro and known for Port styles. Best: AXE HILL, BOPLAAS, DE KRANS, Peter Bayly.

Camberley Wines Stell r (br sp) ★★→★★★ Fine, family-vinified SHIRAZ (inc rare sparkling version), Bordeaux blend Philosopher's Stone, PINOTAGE, new Elm Tree MERLOT.

Capaia Estate Phil r (w) ★★→★★★ German-owned winery employing top French and Austrian advisers for pair of Bordeaux blends and SAUV BL.

Cape Agulhas *See* ELIM.

Cape blend Usually a red blend with proportion of PINOTAGE. Top examples include BEYERSKLOOF, GRAHAM BECK, GRANGEHURST, KAAPZICHT, MEINERT, Post House, RAKA, REMHOOGTE, SPIER, WARWICK.

Cape Chamonix Wine Farm Fran r w (sp) ★★→★★★ Rising star. Individual and v.gd PINOT N, PINOTAGE, CHARD, SAUV BL, CHARD MCC and Bordeaux red Troika.

Cape Point Tiny (32 ha) maritime district on southern tip of Cape Peninsula. Mainly white grapes. Sole winery CAPE POINT V'YDS consistent star performer despite viticultural challenges.

Cape Point Vineyards Cape P (r) w ★→★★★★ One of South Africa's most exciting producers. Complex SAUV BL/SEM blend Isliedh, racy CHARD and thrilling SAUV BL; gd-value Splattered Toad label helps save endangered amphibians.

Cape Winemakers Guild (CWG) Independent, invitation-only association of 41 top growers. Stages benchmarking annual auction of limited premium bottlings and, via a trust, provides development aid to wineland school children, education bursaries and mentorship for just-graduated winemakers.

Cederberg WARD in remote Cederberg Mts. Just 48 ha, mainly red varieties, among highest in South Africa. Newcomer Driehoek and established star CEDERBERG PRIVATE CELLAR are sole producers.

Cederberg Private Cellar Ced r w (p sp) ★★→★★★ High-altitude minerality in intense, flavoured SHIRAZ, CAB SAUV, SAUV BL, SEM, CHENIN BL and rare varietal Bukettraube.

Chardonnay Styles from cool and lean to warm and fleshy, with a more sensitive use of oak. ATARAXIA, CAPE CHAMONIX, GROOT CONSTANTIA, HAMILTON RUSSELL, HARTENBERG, MULDERBOSCH, PAUL CLUVER, RUSTENBERG, THELEMA, VERGELEGEN, WATERFORD, THE WINERY OF GOOD HOPE, BOUCHARD FINLAYSON, JORDAN, SPRINGFIELD, DE WETSHOF; the last four also offer v.gd unwooded versions.

Chenin Blanc Many styles, from unwooded to heavily oaked off-dry. Brands worth trying: BEAUMONT, CEDERBERG, GRAHAM BECK, JEAN DANEEL, KEN FORRESTER, Lammershoek, RAATS, RIJK'S, RUDERA, SPICE ROUTE, SPIER, Springfontein, StellenRust, Teddy Hall, THE WINERY OF GOOD HOPE.

Coastal Large (32,000 ha) region, inc sea-influenced districts of CAPE POINT, DARLING, Tygerberg, STELLENBOSCH, SWARTLAND, and landlocked PAARL and TULBAGH.

Company of Wine People, The r (p) w (sw sp) ★→★★★ 2.5-million-cases-a-yr operation nr STELLENBOSCH, with 60-plus labels in 16 ranges. Best is Kumkani; also well-priced easy-drinkers in Arniston Bay, Versus and Welmoed lines.

Constantia South Africa's original fine-wine-growing area; home of the famous sweet Muscat-based wines of the 18th and 19th centuries, revived in recent yrs by GROOT and KLEIN CONSTANTIA. Other leading names: BUITENVERWACHTING, Constantia Glen, CONSTANTIA UITSIG, Eagles' Nest, STEENBERG.

Constantia Uitsig Const (r) (br sp) ★★★ Premium v'yds and tourist destination, partly black-owned. Mainly white wines and MCC, all excellent.

Dalla Cia Wine & Spirit Company Stell r w ★★→★★★ Owned by Italian *famiglia*; CAB SAUV, Bordeaux red Giorgio, lightly oaked CHARD and SAUV BL styled for food.

Danie de Wet *See* DE WETSHOF.

Darling District (2,800 ha) around eponymous west coast town; best v'yds in hilly Groenekloof WARD. Cloof, Darling Cellars, GROOTE POST, Ormonde, Tullie Family (new) bottle under own labels; most other fruit trucked out for other brands.

De Grendel Wines W Cape r (p) w (sp) ★→★★★ Hillside property overlooking Table Bay, owned by Sir David Graaff. Brisk, layered reds, whites and MCC.

De Krans C'dorp r (p) w br (sw) ★→★★★ Family v'yds noted for rich, impressive Port styles (esp Vintage Res 01 02 03' 04' 05' 06' 07 08'), fortified Muscats, and varietal bottlings of rarer grapes eg. Tempranillo, Touriga Nacional.

De Toren Private Cellar Stell r ★★★ Consistently flavourful Bordeaux blend Fusion V (02 03' 04 05' 06' 07 08) and earlier-maturing MERLOT-based blend "Z".

De Trafford Wines Stell r (p w sw) ★★★★ Exceptional boutique grower, with international reputation for bold but elegant wines. Brilliant Bordeaux/SHIRAZ blend Elevation 393 (01 03' 04 05 06 07 08), CAB SAUV (01 03' 04 05 06 07 08) and SHIRAZ. Sijnn brand showcases promising young maritime v'yds.

De Wetshof Estate Rob (r p) w (br sw) ★→★★★ Famed CHARD pioneer and exponent;

six versions, oaked and unwooded, under De Wetshof and Danie de Wet branding. Promising DeW CAB SAUV and PINOT N.

Delaire Graff Estate W Cape r (p) w (br sw) ★★→★★★ International jeweller Laurence Graff's eyrie v'yds, winery and opulent tourist destination. Evolving line-up includes stunning new CAB SAUV Res.

Delheim W Cape r (p) w (sw s/sw) ★★→★★★ Eco-minded family winery nr STELLENBOSCH. Acclaimed Vera Cruz SHIRAZ; plummy CAB SAUV Grand Res (00 01 03 04' 05 06 07').

DeWaal Wines Stell r w ★→★★★ Family estate Uiterwyk is HQ for established DeWaal and new Cape Gable brands. PINOTAGE a forte: old-vines DeWaal Top of the Hill among the best.

DGB Well-established Wellington-based producer/wholesaler; brands inc: BELLINGHAM/Bernard Series, BOSCHENDAL, Brampton and Douglas Green.

Diemersdal Estate Dur r (p) w ★★→★★★ Family firm with dynamic younger generation specializing in red blends, CHARD and SAUV BL. Exciting LAMBERTS BAY joint venture, Sir Lambert SAUV BL.

Diemersfontein Wines Well r (w) ★★→★★★ Noted for full-throttle styling, esp PINOTAGE, CHENIN BL, VIOGNIER. Empowerment brand is Thokozani.

Distell South Africa's biggest drinks company, headquartered in STELLENBOSCH. Owns many brands, spanning quality scales. Also interests in various top STELLENBOSCH wineries, inc ALTO and STELLENZICHT, and in empowerment brand Tukulu.

Dornier Wines W Cape r (p) w (sw) ★→★★★ Architectural showpiece in a sylvan valley nr STELLENBOSCH. Stylish Red and White flagships under Donatus label.

Durbanville Cool, hilly WARD (1,500 ha) known for pungent SAUV BL and MERLOT. Crop of new family boutiques, eg. De Vallei, Klein Roosboom, Kronendal, Russo, Signal Gun giving established cellars run for their money.

Durbanville Hills Dur r w ★→★★★ Maritime-cooled v'yds co-owned by DISTELL and local growers. Best are single-v'yd and Rhinofields Res ranges.

Edgebaston Stell r w ★★→★★★ Finlayson family (GLEN CARLOU fame). V.gd "GS" CAB SAUV (05 '06 07 08), SHIRAZ, CHARD; classy, early-ready reds Berry Box, Pepper Pot.

Elgin Cool upland WARD, among South Africa's fastest-growing fine-wine areas. Historically white wines, esp SAUV BL and CHARD, but increasingly recognized for reds, notably PINOT N, MERLOT and Bordeaux blends.

Elim Sea-breezy WARD (147 ha) in southernmost district, Cape Agulhas. Aromatic, elegant SAUV BL, white blends and SHIRAZ from The Berrio, Black Oystercatcher, Land's End/Hidden Valley, Lomond, Quoin Rock, Strandveld and Zoetendal.

Ernie Els Wines Stell r ★★→★★★★ South African champion golfer's wine venture. Rich, aromatic Bordeaux red Ernie Els Signature (01 02' 03 04' 05 06 07') v. pricey; new CAB SAUV and Proprietor's Syrah. V.gd Guardian Peak range.

Estate Wine Official term for wines grown, made and bottled on "units registered for the production of estate wine". Not a quality designation.

Fairview W Cape r (p) w (sw s/sw) ★→★★★★ Dynamic and innovative proprietor Charles Back. Under Fairview label, a top range of single-v'yd and "terroir-specific" wines, plus smorgasbord of blends and varietal bottlings. Goats do Roam is taunting, gimmicky standalone brand that usually overdelivers. "Goat" theme recurs in entry-level La Capra range. *See also* SPICE ROUTE.

FirstCape Vineyards W Cape r (p) w (sp) ★→★★ Founded ten years ago, now biggest-selling South African wine brand in Britain. Joint venture of five local co-ops and UK's Brand Phoenix, with inexpensive entry-level wines in half-dozen ranges.

Flagstone Winery W Cape r w (br) ★★→★★★ Medalled winery at Somerset West, now owned by Australia's CHAMP Private Equity. Idiosyncratically named labels (eg. Writer's Block PINOTAGE, The Last Word Port) in top-end Flagstone and Knockon Wood, and early-ready Stumble V'yds ranges.

Fleur du Cap W Cape r w (sw) ★★→★★★ DISTELL premium label; v.gd Unfiltered Collection and racy botrytis Noble Late Harvest in Bergkelder Selection.

Foundry, The Coast r w ★★★ MEERLUST winemaker Chris Williams and wine-partner James Reid vinify selected STELLENBOSCH and Voor Paardeberg parcels for outstanding Syrah, Viognier and Grenache Blanc.

Franschhoek Valley French Huguenot-founded district in COASTAL region. 1,400 ha, mainly SAUV BL, CAB SAUV and SHIRAZ. Many wineries (and restaurants), inc: ANTHONIJ RUPERT, BOEKENHOUTSKLOOF, Colmant, CAPE CHAMONIX, GRAHAM BECK, LA MOTTE, Lynx, Môreson, SOLMS-DELTA, Topiary.

Glen Carlou Coast r w (sw) ★★→★★★ First-rate Donald Hess-owned winery, v'yds, fine-art gallery and restaurant near PAARL. Spicy Syrah (02 03 04' 05 06 07); fine Bordeaux red Grand Classique (00 01 02 **03** 04 05 06' 07).

Glenelly W Cape r w ★★→★★★ Former Château Pichon Lalande (Bordeaux) owner May-Eliane de Lencquesaing's v'yds and state-of-the-art cellar at STELLENBOSCH. Impressive red flagships Lady May (Bordeaux) and Grand Vin (Bordeaux/SHIRAZ); promising new Glass Collection.

Graham Beck Wines W Cape r (p) w sp (br sw) ★★→★★★ Top-rank properties at ROBERTSON and STELLENBOSCH founded by late mining tycoon Graham Beck. 30+ labels, inc classy bubbles, varietal and blended reds/whites, topped by superb new Cuvée Clive MCC and Ad Honorem CAB SAUV/SHIRAZ.

Grangehurst Winery Stell r (p) ★★→★★★ Small, top red and, latterly, rosé specialist. V.gd CAPE BLEND Nikela (98 99 00 01 02 03), PINOTAGE (97 98 99 01 02 03').

Groot Constantia Estate W Cape r (p) w (br sw sp) ★★→★★★ Showy wines befitting a CONSTANTIA wine and tourism showcase. PINOTAGE, CHARD, new Res SEM/SAUV blend. Grand Constance revives tradition of world-class Muscat desserts.

Groote Post Vineyards Dar r w (sw sp) ★★→★★★ Ocean-facing property of the Pentz family. V.gd CHARD and SAUV BL Res, aromatic RIES, juicy PINOT N.

Guardian Peak See ERNIE ELS.

Hamilton Russell Vineyards (HRV) Wlk B r w ★★★→★★★★ Burgundian-style specialist at Hermanus. Fine PINOT N (01' 03' 04 05 06 07 08 09); classy CHARD. Super SAUV BL, PINOTAGE, white blend under Southern Right, Ashbourne labels.

Hartenberg Estate Stell r w ★★→★★★★ Cape front-ranker. Trio of outstanding SHIRAZ: always serious (01 02 **03** 04' 05 06 07), flagship single-site The Stork (**03** 04' 05' 06' 07) and Gravel Hill; fine MERLOT, CHARD.

Haskell Vineyards Stell r ★★★ American-owned v'yds and cellar in Helderberg foothills receiving rave notices for pair of Syrah (Pillars and Aeon) and Bordeaux red Haskell IV. Sibling brand is Dombeya.

Hemel-en-Aarde Trio of cool-climate WARDS in WALKER BAY district (Hemel-en-Aarde Valley, Upper Hemel-en-Aarde, Hemel-en-Aarde Ridge), producing outstanding PINOT N, CHARD and SAUV BL. BOUCHARD FINLAYSON, ATARAXIA, NEWTON JOHNSON and HAMILTON RUSSELL are top names.

Hermanuspietersfontein Wingerde r (p) w ★★→★★★ Leading SAUV BL and Bordeaux red specialist; creatively markets physical and historical connections with seaside resort Hermanus.

J C le Roux W Cape sp ★★ South Africa's largest sparkling-wine house, DISTELL-owned. Best are PINOT N, Scintilla (CHARD/PINOT N), and PINOT N Rosé, all MCC.

J P Bredell Wines Stell (r) br ★★★ Best-known for Port styles, esp plush Cape Vintage Res (97' 98' 00 01' 03' 07') and Late Bottled Vintage.

Jean Daneel Wines Coast r w (br sp) ★★★ Family winery at Napier; outstanding Signature Series, esp CHENIN BL, CAB SAUV/MERLOT/SHIRAZ, MCC sparkling (CHARD and new CHENIN BL).

Jordan Wine Estate Stell r (p) w ★★→★★★ Consistency, quality and value, from entry-level Bradgate and Chameleon lines to immaculate CWG Auction bottlings.

Flagship CHARD Nine Yards; Bordeaux blend Cobblers Hill (00 01 **03** 04' 05' 06 07); CAB SAUV; MERLOT; SAUV BL; RIES botrytis dessert.

Kaapzicht Estate Stell r (p) w (br sw) ★★→★★★ Family winery with internationally acclaimed top range Steytler: Vision CAPE BLEND (01' 02' **03'** 04 05' 06 07), PINOTAGE and Bordeaux red Pentagon.

Kanonkop Estate Stell r ★★→★★★★ Grand local status in the past three decades, mainly with PINOTAGE (01 02 **03'** 04 05 06 07 08), Bordeaux blend Paul Sauer (01 02 **03** 04' 05 06' 07) and CAB SAUV. Second tier Kadette now inc PINOTAGE Dry Rosé.

Kanu Wines Stell r w sw ★★→★★★ Reputation for barrel-aged CHENIN BL, Bordeaux red Keystone and botrytis CHENIN BL Kia-Ora.

Ken Forrester Wines W Cape r w sw ★★→★★★ Somerset West-based vintner/restaurateur Ken Forrester and wine-grower Martin MEINERT collaboration. Three benchmark CHENIN BL: racy, dry Ken Forrester; opulent off-dry The FMC; sumptuous botrytis "T".

Klein Constantia Estate W Cape r (p) w sw (sp) ★★→★★★ Luscious (non-botrytis) Vin de Constance (00' 01 02' 04 05 06') convincingly re-creates legendary 18th-century Constantia Muscat dessert. Also elegant Marlbrook blends, age-worthy RIES, classy SAUV BL and earlier-ready KC range. *See also* ANWILKA.

Klein Karoo Semi-arid region (2,700 ha) known for fortified, esp Port-style in CALITZDORP district. Higher-lying Tradouw, Tradouw Highlands, Outeniqua and Upper Langkloof WARDS show promise with PINOT N, SHIRAZ and SAUV BL.

Kleine Zalze Wines W Cape r (p) w ★★→★★★ STELLENBOSCH rising star with brilliant CAB SAUV, SHIRAZ, CHENIN BL and SAUV BL in Family Res and V'yd Selection ranges; many well-priced quaffers in Cellar Selection and Zalze line-ups.

Kosher Niche category served mainly by BACKSBERG, Kleine Draken and Hill & Dale/STELLENZICHT.

Krone Tul (w) sp ★★★ Fine, elegant Brut MCC, inc Borealis, Rosé and *prestige cuvée* Nicolas Charles Krone, from PINOT N/CHARD, by TWEE JONGE GEZELLEN estate.

Kumala W Cape r (p) w ★→★★ Hugely successful export label, recently acquired by Sydney-based CHAMP Private Equity, undergoing quality boost under aegis of Bruce Jack, founder of sister brand FLAGSTONE.

KwaZulu-Natal Province and demarcated Geographical Unit (*see* WARD) on country's east coast; summer rainfall; subtropical or tropical climate in coastal areas; cooler, hilly central Midlands plateau home to nascent fine-wine industry led by The Stables and Abingdon estates.

KWV W Cape r (p) w (br s/sw sw sp) ★→★★★ Formerly the national wine co-op and controlling body, today a partly black-owned listed group based in PAARL. ±40 reds, whites, sparkling, Port styles and fortified desserts in seven ranges; best are Heritage, Cathedral Cellar, Laborie, Res and Mentors.

L'Avenir Vineyards W Cape r (p) w (sp) ★→★★★ AdVini-owned v'yds and tourist hotspot nr STELLENBOSCH, vinifying South African stalwarts PINOTAGE and CHENIN BL with Gallic panache, esp in flagship Icon range.

La Motte W Cape r w (sp) ★★→★★★ Increasingly ORGANIC venture by the Rupert family, based at FRANSCHHOEK. Fine, distinctive SHIRAZ/Viognier, SAUV BL and SHIRAZ/Grenache in flagship Pierneef Collection.

Lamberts Bay West coast WARD (22 ha) close by Atlantic. Trenchant SAUV BL, promising SHIRAZ; Sir Lambert, local joint venture with DIEMERSDAL, a cracker.

Lammershoek Winery Swa r w (br sw) ★★→★★★ Traditionally vinified, deep-flavoured Rhône-style blends and CHENIN BL that epitomize SWARTLAND warmth and concentration.

Lanzerac Stell r (p) w ★★→★★★ Venerable property (inc luxury hotel) long associated with PINOTAGE (1st vintage 1959). Sister farm to LOURENSFORD.

Le Riche Wines Stell r (w) ★★★ Fine CAB SAUV-based boutique wines, hand-crafted by respected Etienne le Riche and family.

Lourensford Wine Estate W Cape r (p) w (sw sp) ★★→★★★ Sibling to LANZERAC, rejuvenated and refocused on SHIRAZ, CAB SAUV, CHARD, SAUV BL, Viognier. Best in Lourensford and "1700" ranges. Eden Crest, River Garden entry-level labels.

Lower Orange Standalone inland "super WARD" (12,000 ha) straddling the Gariep (Orange) River; hot, dry, dependent on irrigation; mainly white wines and fortified; major producer is Orange River Wine Cellars.

Meerlust Estate Stell r w ★★★★ Prestigious v'yds and cellar, probably South Africa's best-known quality red label. Hallmark elegance and restraint in flagship Rubicon (99 00 01' **03' 04** 05 06), one of Cape's first Bordeaux blends; also excellent MERLOT, CAB SAUV, CHARD and PINOT N.

Meinert Wines r (p w) ★★→★★★ Producer/consultant Martin Meinert makes two fine blends: Devon Crest (Bordeaux) and Synchronicity (Bordeaux/PINOTAGE), CAB SAUV, MERLOT, new PINOTAGE and SAUV BL.

Merlot Temperamental and site-specific, thus rarely rises to great heights as standalone. Worth seeking out, however: Amani, Bein, Dombeya, HARTENBERG, JORDAN, Shannon, SPIER, THELEMA, VEENWOUDEN, VERGELEGEN, Yonder Hill.

Méthode Cap Classique (MCC) *See* box below.

Morgenhof Estate Stell r (p) w (br sw s/sw) ★→★★★ 1692 property revitalized by Anne Cointreau (of Cognac/liqueur family). Bordeaux red The Morgenhof Estate and CHENIN BL. Gd everyday Fantail range.

Morgenster Estate Stell r (p) ★★→★★★ Prime Italian-owned wine and olive farm, advised by Bordelais Pierre Lurton (Cheval Blanc). Classic Bordeaux red Morgenster (00 01 **03** 04 05' **06'** 08); second label Lourens River Valley. Italian Collection features blends with rare-in-Cape Sangiovese and Nebbiolo.

Mulderbosch Vineyards W Cape r (p) w (sw) ★★→★★★ STELLENBOSCH v'yds and winery now owned by Terroir Capital, Screaming Eagle ex-partner Charles Banks' California-based investment group. Individualistic offerings, inc SAUV BL, just-dry and botrytis; wood-fermented CHARD; pricey CHENIN BL Small Change.

Mullineux Family Wines Swa r w sw ★★★ Rising star husband-and-wife team Chris and Andrea Mullineux, specializing in smart, generous, carefully made Rhône-style blends (r w) and CHENIN BL.

Mvemve Raats Stell r ★★★ Mzokhona Mvemve, first university-qualified black winemaker, and Bruwer RAATS vinify acclaimed Bordeaux red De Compostella.

Nederburg Wines W Cape r (p) w sw s/sw sp ★→★★★★ Among South Africa's biggest (1.4 million cases) and best-known brands, DISTELL-owned. Exceptional Ingenuity Red (05 06 07') and White; excellent Manor House label; reliable The

---

20 Years of Méthode Cap Classique

Coined exactly 20 years ago as a generic, EU-friendly alternative to the term *méthode champenoise*, Méthode Cap Classique (MCC) bottle-fermented sparkling is one of South Africa's major success stories. Originating in 1971 with a single brand – Simonsig Estate's Kaapse Vonkel – MCC as a category has effervesced to over 140 labels, with annual sales of 2.3 million bottles, representing roughly 20% of all sparkling sold locally. Of the dozen or so houses who got together in 1992 to devise the MCC name, Avontuur, BOSCHENDAL, CABRIÈRE, GRAHAM BECK, JC LE ROUX, KRONE, PONGRÁCZ, SIMONSIG and VILLIERA today continue to produce top-quality bubbles. Also highly rated are Ambeloui, BON COURAGE, Colmant, CONSTANTIA UITSIG, Silverthorn, STEENBERG, Tanzanite and WELTEVREDE. Recent debutant Topiary is one to watch.

Winemaster's Reserves, inc enduring Edelrood and Baronne reds. Inexpensive quaffers, still and sparkling. Small, sometimes stellar Private Bins for annual Nederburg Auction, inc CHENIN BL botrytis Edelkeur (02 03' 04' 05 06 07' 08 09').

Neethlingshof Estate Stell r w sw ★★→★★★ Tourist magnet co-owned by DISTELL. Best in flagship Short Story Collection (esp botrytis RIES); lovely Gewürz.

Neil Ellis Wines Coast r w ★★★→★★★★ Veteran winemaker Neil Ellis sources cooler-climate parcels for site expression. Top V'yd Selection CAB SAUV (99 00' 01 03 04' 05 06 07), Syrah, SAUV BL, PINOTAGE and sensational old-vine Grenache Noir from Piekenierskloof WARD.

Newton Johnson Vineyards W Cape r (p) w ★★→★★★ Cellar and restaurant in scenic Upper HEMEL-EN-AARDE. Outstanding PINOT N, CHARD, SAUV BL, SHIRAZ/Mourvèdre, from own and partner v'yds. Widely sourced entry-level brand Felicité.

Nitida Cellars Dur r w (sp) ★→★★★ Visitor-welcoming family winery; fresh, vital SAUV BL, SEM, white blend Coronata; rare sparkling SHIRAZ.

Olifants River West coast region. Warm valley floors, conducive to ORGANIC cultivation, and cooler, fine-wine-favouring sites in the mtn WARD of Piekenierskloof, and, nr the Atlantic, BAMBOES BAY and Koekenaap.

Organic Quality variable, but producers with track records inc: AVONDALE, Bon Cap, Groot Parys, Laibach, Mtn Oaks, Reyneke, Stellar, Tukulu, TULBAGH MTN V'YDS, Upland and Waverley. Lazanou one to watch. *See also* BIODYNAMIC.

Outeniqua *See* KLEIN KAROO.

Overgaauw Estate Stell r (p) w (br) ★→★★★ Van Velden family farm. Classic-style Bordeaux red Tria Corda; Cape's only bottling of Sylvaner.

Paarl Town and demarcated wine district around 50-km northeast of Cape Town. 14,000 ha. Diverse styles and approaches; best results with Mediterranean varieties (r w), CAB SAUV. Leading names: AVONDALE, BACKSBERG, BOLAND KELDER, BOSCHENDAL, DIEMERSFONTEIN, FAIRVIEW, GLEN CARLOU, KWV, NEDERBURG, PLAISIR DE MERLE, RUPERT & ROTHSCHILD, Schalk Burger, VEENWOUDEN, Val de Vie, VILAFONTÉ.

Paul Cluver Estate Wines Elg r w sw ★★★→★★★★ Appellation's leading winery, Cluver-family-owned; convincing PINOT N, elegant CHARD, always gorgeous Gewürz and botrytis RIES (03' 04 05' 06' 07 08' 09).

Pinot Noir Inspires a passion inversely proportionate to its less than 1% share of the national v'yd. BOUCHARD FINLAYSON, CAPE CHAMONIX, Catherine Marshall, Crystallum, Creation, DE TRAFFORD, GLEN CARLOU, HAMILTON RUSSELL, MEERLUST, NEWTON JOHNSON, Oak Valley, PAUL CLUVER, Shannon, VRIESENHOF.

Pinotage South Africa's "own" red grape in sympathetic hands is accessible, harmonious, even profound. Try ASHBOURNE, L'AVENIR, BEYERSKLOOF, CAPE CHAMONIX, Chateau Naudé, DEWAAL, DIEMERSFONTEIN, FAIRVIEW, GRANGEHURST, GROOT CONSTANTIA, KAAPZICHT, KANONKOP, SIMONSIG.

Plaisir de Merle W Cape r w ★★→★★★ Imposing DISTELL-owned cellar and v'yds nr PAARL. V. gd range headlined by outstanding Cab Fr (03' 04 05 06 07 08).

Pongrácz W Cape sp ★★ DISTELL-owned MCC brand; vintaged Desiderius and popular NV Pongrácz Brut.

Quoin Rock Winery W Cape r w (sp sw) ★★★ Classically styled wines, some featuring grapes from own Cape Agulhas v'yds. Syrah, MERLOT, white flagship Oculus, SAUV BL The Nicobar and CHARD/PINOT N MCC.

Raats Family Wines Coast r w ★★→★★★ Cab Fr and two pure-fruited CHENIN BL, oaked and u/w, vinified by STELLENBOSCH-based Bruwer Raats, also a partner in boutique-scale MVEMVE RAATS.

Raka Kl R r (p) w ★★→★★★ Powerful, personality-packed range from family winery nr Stanford; Biography SHIRAZ, Figurehead CAPE BLEND, MERLOT and Malbec.

Remhoogte Wine Estate Stell r (w) ★★→★★★ Boustred family winery best-known for trio of CAPE BLENDS. Impressive new MERLOT Res.

Reyneke Wines Stell r w ★★★ ORGANIC and BIODYNAMIC producer recently showing much-improved form, esp with Res Red (mainly SHIRAZ) and White (SAUV BL).

Riesling Obstinately unfashionable category, but BUITENVERWACHTING, DE WETSHOF, GROOTE POST, HARTENBERG, KLEIN CONSTANTIA, NITIDA, PAUL CLUVER, THELEMA, newcomer Howard Booysen and handful of passionate others press on regardless.

Rijk's Coast r w ★★→★★★ Acclaimed TULBAGH winery vinifying/marketing both as "Estate" (focused on SHIRAZ) and "Private Cellar" (varietal and blended reds/whites, notably CAB SAUV, SHIRAZ, PINOTAGE, CHENIN BL).

Robertson District Low-rainfall inland valley; 13,500 ha; lime soils; conducive climate for ORGANIC production. Historically gd CHARD, dessert styles (notably Muscat); more recently SAUV BL, SHIRAZ, CAB SAUV; many family boutiques (inc tyros AlexKia, Sumsaré); major cellars: BON COURAGE, DE WETSHOF, GRAHAM BECK, Rietvallei, ROBERTSON WINERY, Rooiberg, SPRINGFIELD, WELTEVREDE, Zandvliet.

Robertson Winery Rob r (br) w (br) sw s/sw ★→★★ Consistency and gd-value from co-op-scale winery. Best is No 1 Constitution Rd SHIRAZ; also v.gd V'yd Selection.

Rudera Wines r w (sw) ★★→★★★ Hailed for consistently excellent CHENIN BL (dry/semi-dry and botrytis), CAB SAUV, Syrah. Second label: Halala/Lula.

Rupert & Rothschild Vignerons W Cape r w ★★★ Top v'yds and cellar nr PAARL, owned by the Rupert family and Baron Benjamin de Rothschild. Impressive Bordeaux blend Baron Edmond (98 00 01 03' 04 05 07); CHARD Baroness Nadine is a deep-flavoured classic.

Rust en Vrede Estate Stell r ★★★ Strong, individual offering features pricey single-v'yd Syrah and limited-release SHIRAZ/CAB SAUV blend "1694 Classification".

Rustenberg Wines W Cape r w (sw) ★★→★★★ Prestigious family winery nr STELLENBOSCH. Flagship is single-v'yd CAB SAUV Peter Barlow (99' 01' 03 04 05 06 07). Outstanding Bordeaux blend John X Merriman; savoury Syrah; single-v'yd CHARD called Five Soldiers.

Sadie Family Wines Swa r w ★★★★ Organically grown, traditionally made Columella (SHIRAZ/Mourvèdre) (01 02' 03 04 05' 06 07' 08) a Cape benchmark. Complex, intriguing CHENIN BL-based white Palladius. Star winemaker Eben Sadie also grows the rated Sequillo Red and White with Cape Wine Master Cornel Spies.

Saronsberg Cellar Coast r (p) w (sw) ★→★★★ Growing following for Rhône varieties and blends, inc SHIRAZ and Viognier-seasoned Full Circle. Unfrivolous entry-level Provenance range.

Sauvignon Blanc South Africa's fifth most widely planted variety comes in a multitude of styles, from racy and herbaceous to sedate and tropical. Equally diverse terroirs, from coastal ELIM (The Berrio, Strandveld) and WALKER BAY (Domaine des Dieux, Robert Stanford) to craggy CEDERBERG (Driehoek, CEDERBERG PVT CELLAR) and the mtn WARDS of KLEIN KAROO (Herold, The Goose).

Saxenburg Stell r (p) w (sp) ★★→★★★ Swiss-owned v'yds, winery and restaurant. Roundly oaked reds, SAUV BL and CHARD in high-end Private Collection; flagship SHIRAZ Select (00 01 02 03' 05' 06').

Secateurs See BADENHORST FAMILY.

Semillon Enjoying renewed interest in blends, but varietal bottlings worth sampling include BOEKENHOUTSKLOOF, CEDERBERG, CONSTANTIA UITSIG, Creation, FLEUR DU CAP, GlenWood, GROOT CONSTANTIA, Landau du Val, NITIDA, Stony Brook.

Sequillo See SADIE FAMILY.

Shiraz Wins plaudits solo and in blends. Some top varietal bottlings (sometimes as "Syrah"): BOEKENHOUTSKLOOF, BON COURAGE, CEDERBERG, DE TRAFFORD, FAIRVIEW, GRAHAM BECK, HARTENBERG, Haskell, Luddite, SARONSBERG, SAXENBURG, SIMONSIG, STELLENZICHT, WATERFORD.

Signal Hill W Cape r (p) w sw ★★→★★★ French flair in lively range; widely sourced grapes, inc tiny parcels in/around Cape Town city centre.

Simonsig Wine Estate W Cape r w (sw s/sw) sp ★→★★★ Consistency and value among hallmarks of Malan family winery nr STELLENBOSCH. Extensive but serious top end, inc: Merindol Syrah (01 02' **03** 04 05 06), Red Hill PINOTAGE (01 02 **03'** 04 05 06 07'). First (31 yrs ago) with an MCC, Kaapse Vonkel.

Solms-Delta W Cape r (p) w (br sp) ★★→★★★ Delightfully different wines from historic FRANSCHHOEK estate, partly worker-owned; Amarone-style SHIRAZ Africana, sophisticated dry rosé Lekkerwijn, scented RIES blend Koloni, *pétillant* Cape Jazz SHIRAZ.

Southern Right *See* HAMILTON RUSSELL.

Spice Route Winery Swa r w ★★→★★★ Cellar owned by Charles Back (FAIRVIEW); Rhône-style reds, esp spicy Chakalaka blend; also scented Viognier. Non-Rhône offerings include v.gd CHENIN BL and PINOTAGE.

Spier W Cape r (p) w ★→★★★ Serious, multi-awarded player (1 million+ cases per annum) headquartered nr STELLENBOSCH. Flagship is brooding CAPE BLEND Frans K Smit (04 05' 06'); Spier and Savanha brands, each with tiers of quality, reflect meticulous wine-growing.

Springfield Estate Rob r w ★★→★★★ Cult winemaker Abrie Bruwer. Traditionally vinified pairs of CAB SAUV (Méthode Ancienne and Whole Berry), CHARD (Méthode Ancienne and Wild Yeast) and SAUV BL (Special Cuvée and Life from Stone), all oozing class, personality.

Stables Estate, The *See* KWAZULU-NATAL.

Steenberg Vineyards W Cape r (p) w (sp) ★★→★★★★ Top winery, v'yds and chic cellar door, known for arresting SAUV BL, SAUV BL/SEM blends and, increasingly, MCC. Fine reds include rare varietal Nebbiolo.

Stellenbosch University town and demarcated wine district (14,100 ha). Heart of the wine industry – the Napa of South Africa. Many top estates, esp for reds, tucked into mtn valleys and foothills; extensive wine tasting, accommodation and fine-dining options.

Stellenzicht Vineyards Stell r w ★→★★★ DISTELL co-owned winery and v'yds scaling Helderberg Mtn; excellent Syrah, SEM Res, PINOTAGE; standalone value brand Hill & Dale.

Swartland Increasingly acclaimed warm-climate district in COASTAL region; 11,800 ha of mainly shy-bearing, unirrigated bush vines producing concentrated, hearty wines. BADENHORST FAMILY/Secateurs, Annex Kloof, DeanDavid, LAMMERSHOEK, MULLINEUX, Orangerie, SADIE FAMILY/Sequillo, SPICE ROUTE.

Thandi Wines W Cape r (p) w ★→★★ Among original black-empowerment ventures; shareholding/land ownership for 240+ families. Best: CAB SAUV, PINOT N, CHARD.

Thelema Mountain Vineyards r w ★★→★★★★ Pioneer of South Africa's modern wine revival still top of game, with CAB SAUV (00' **03** 04 05 06 07 08), The Mint CAB SAUV (05 06' 07 08) et al. Sutherland range from ELGIN charts fresh course (eg. PINOT N, Roussanne/Viognier), rekindles old excitement.

Tokara W Cape r (p) w (sw) ★★→★★★★ Wine, food and art showcase overlooking STELLENBOSCH. V'yds also in ELGIN, WALKER BAY. Gorgeous Director's Res red and white blends; pure, elegant CHARD and SAUV BL; gd-value Zondernaam range. Winemaker Miles Mossop's proprietary label also excellent.

Tulbagh Inland district historically associated with white wine and bubbly, now also with beefy reds, some sweeter styles and ORGANIC. 1,400 ha. KRONE, RIJK'S, SARONSBERG, TULBAGH MTN V'YDS, Waverley ORGANIC.

Tulbagh Mountain Vineyards W Cape r w sw ★★★ ORGANIC winery and v'yds nr Tulbagh; Rhône styles, CHENIN BL. Exceptional naturally fermented White blend.

Twee Jonge Gezellen *See* KRONE.

Uva Mira Vineyards Stell r w ★★→★★★ Lofty Helderberg Mtn sites yielding pure, vibrant CHARD, Bordeaux/SHIRAZ blend, Syrah and SAUV BL.

Veenwouden Private Cellar Paarl r (w) ★★→★★★ Sophisticated and age-worthy MERLOT, Bordeaux-style red Classic and CHARD; characterful earlier drinking Vivat Bacchus Red and White blends.

Vergelegen W Cape r w (sw) ★★→★★★★ A great mansion, immaculate v'yds and wines, serially awarded cellar door at Somerset West; owned by Anglo American plc. Flagships are powerful single-v'yd CAB SAUV "V" (01' 03 04 05 06), lower-keyed but still sumptuous Bordeaux "Red", and minerally, oak-fermented SAUV BL/SEM "White".

Vilafonté Paarl r ★★★ California's Zelma Long (ex-Simi winemaker) and Phil Freese (ex-Mondavi viticulturalist) partnering WARWICK's Mike Ratcliffe. Two acclaimed Bordeaux blends: firmly structured Series C, fleshier Series M.

Villiera Wines W Cape r w sp (br sw) ★★ →★★★ Grier family v'yds and winery with excellent quality/value range. Cream of crop: Bordeaux red Monro; Bush Vine SAUV BL; Traditional CHENIN BL; five MCC bubblies (inc sulphur-free Brut Natural). Boutique-scale Domaine Grier nr Perpignan.

Vriesenhof Vineyards Stell r w ★★→★★★ Vinification overseen by veteran Jan Coetzee. Best: Bordeaux red Kallista, PINOTAGE-based Enthopio, PINOT N and new Grenache.

Walker Bay Small (900 ha), fast-developing and highly reputed district, with sub-appellations HEMEL-EN-AARDE, Bot River and Sunday's Glen. PINOT N, SHIRAZ, CHARD and SAUV BL are standouts; some top producers: ATARAXIA, BEAUMONT, BOUCHARD FINLAYSON, Creation, HAMILTON RUSSELL, HERMANUSPIETERSFONTEIN, NEWTON JOHNSON, Luddite, RAKA, Springfontein, Sumaridge.

Ward Geographically the smallest of the four main WINE OF ORIGIN demarcations (largest is Geographical Unit, followed by Region and District).

Warwick Estate W Cape r w ★★★ Ratcliffe family farm on STELLENBOSCH outskirts, recently more tourist cordial ("v'yd safaris", gourmet picnics). V. fine red blends Trilogy (aka Estate Res), First Lady, Three Cape Ladies; opulent CHARD.

Waterford Estate W Cape r (p) w (sw) ★★★ Classy family winery nr STELLENBOSCH with award-winning cellar door. Savoury SHIRAZ (01 02' 03 04 05 06 07 08), minerally CAB SAUV (01 02 03' 04 05 06 07) and emphatic new CHARD Res. Superb (and pricey) CAB SAUV-based flagship The Jem.

Weltevrede Estate Rob r w (br sw) sp ★→★★★ Well-crafted CHARD, SAUV BL and Syrah emphasizing diverse soils; Entheos NV CHARD/PINOT N in expanded Philip Jonker Brut MCC collection.

Wine of Origin South Africa's "AC", but without French crop yield, etc. restrictions. Certifies vintage, variety, area of origin. New opt-in "sustainability" certification additionally guarantees eco-sensitive production – grape to glass. *See also* WARD.

Winery of Good Hope, The r w (sw) ★★→★★★ First-rate Australian-French-South African joint venture. Excellent PINOT N, Gravity red blend, CHARD, Viognier under headline Radford Dale label; CAB SAUV, CHENIN BL in Vinum, Land of Hope ranges.

Zorgvliet Wines Stell r (p) w (sp) ★★→★★★ Vinous arm of luxury lifestyle group Zorgvliet Portfolio. Extensive Zorgvliet and Silver Myn ranges, inc rare varietal Tannat and new CHARD MCC.

Sorting out South Africa

For consumers, sorting out the wine styles of South Africa can be the big problem: these range from elegant to enormous, and there is no guide on the label. Cooler regions, such as ELGIN, ELIM or WALKER BAY, tend to offer lighter wines; the designation "Western Cape" is so broad as to be unhelpful, and STELLENBOSCH can make pretty well anything. Following a producer's name through its range is usually the best bet – and having this book to hand.

Wines of the
South of France

Near the Tarn Gorge – and a world away from the wine lake

Can one encompass the South of France in a few pages?
It's a vast, sprawling region, climbing the foothills of
the Pyrenees in the west and nudging Italy in the east.
It produces every style of wine, including sparkling and
fortified, and every possible quality. It used to be wine-lake
country; then the Pays d'Oc made a name for itself with
New-World-driven varietal Cabernets and Chardonnays.

But there has long been a handful of top-quality estates,
hidden up in the hills, making wines for a small band
of aficionados. Now these have multiplied. Sometimes
families which used to sell their grapes to the local
cooperative decide to go it alone; sometimes bankers and
business tycoons decide to plough their millions into
creating model estates where nothing is too much trouble,
no detail too small. The stars of today come from both
categories – and the attraction for the millionaires-turned-
vignerons is not only the beauty of the landscape but the
fact that so much of it is still undiscovered. Every square
centimetre of Bordeaux and Burgundy is known. But in
the South there are fabulous terroirs still waiting to be
noticed. Give them the attention they deserve and you'll be
rewarded with wines of complexity, depth and resonance.

For us, the consumers, the rewards are even greater. The
complications of the region are enormous, and in the next
few pages we aim to give you the background you need
to experiment with confidence. You need an open mind,
a readiness to abandon props like appellation names (not
always a guide to the best) and a liking for wines of wild,
surprising flavours. So, let's head for the sun...

Does the south of France have too many appellations, or too few? It has more than any normal person is likely to remember – well over 50 in both Languedoc and Provence – yet the region is so diverse that for appellation names to offer a reliable guide to style and terroir it would need many, many more. The 18-km (11.2-mile) valley of Maury is so varied, according to one grower, that it could usefully be divided into 15 different appellations. At the moment it has just two: Maury, for sweet Grenache (*see* p. 310) and Côtes de Roussillon for dry reds.

This is the problem with the South of France: there are few signposts to help would-be consumers. The authorities in Languedoc-Roussillon have been working on the problem, first by creating an elite level of *cru* appellations above the standard appellations, and second by creating a catch-all appellation, Languedoc, to act as a sort of dustbin below them; it covers the entire Languedoc-Roussillon area.

Probably the most outstanding *cru* is Terrasses de Larzac, tailored around some remarkable estates (Mas Jullien, Mas de l'Écriture, La Grange des Pères, Château de Jonquières, Mas de Plan de l'Om, Le Clos du Serres, Mas Cal Demoura, Causse d'Arboras, La Sauvageonne, La Pèira, La Réserve d'O, Domaine de Montcalmès, Mas des Chimères, Mas Conscience) on high and remote, sheep-cropped limestone terraces in the Coteaux de Languedoc. There are wines here of profound originality and depth – and substantial price tags.

Rocks, mountains and vines – but few signposts

These *crus* are undoubtedly good for the prestige of the region, but if prestige is involved, local politics will follow. The *cru* of Minervois la Livinière, for example, was apparently originally intended to cover just a single village, but the eventual compromise included five villages. Yet it wouldn't be the first appellation in the world to confer on its wines a faint note of fudge.

Crus are not the whole story. There are also *vins de pays*, which may be varietally focused, and fine if you want Syrah that tastes of Syrah and Cabernet that tastes of Cabernet. But they may also appear on the labels of complex, terroir-driven wines whose producers simply prefer a different grape blend to the one favoured by the authorities.

Grape varieties, as ever, are a source of contention. At one point it looked as though planting Cabernet, Syrah and Mourvèdre – the great grape of Bandol – was the way forward all over the South. Carignan, Cinsault and Grenache, the major traditional vines, seemed rustic and old-fashioned, and the appellations that insisted on a proportion of such grapes (most of them) looked equally dowdy.

Now that has changed again, and Grenache and Carignan, preferably from vines of great age and witchy gnarledness, are as modish as you can get. A better understanding of ripeness, acidity and tannins has brought them back. It is no longer a case of *vins de pays* meaning modern, and AC meaning stick-in-the-mud. Both are increasingly used as flags of convenience for producers who rely on their own reputations to sell their wines.

The great divide
Industry vs. artisans

This is the great divide in the South of France. On the one hand there are big companies, with brands that are reliable, enjoyable, easy to track down and easy to buy. At the other extreme there are small companies, maybe husband and wife and one of the children, working perhaps 15 ha and selling locally and to a few export markets. The latter doesn't have a promotional budget and is unlikely to sell its wines to supermarkets. If you find it on a shelf and happen to buy it, you have to take a guess about whether it's ready to drink, and indeed, what food to drink it with. And then next time you want it it might not be there. It's not surprising that brands do so well.

Are they necessarily a less interesting option? Not always. Most basic brands are perfectly agreeable and well made. They also often have a top echelon of estate wines that can be a big step up in quality. But where most brands suffer is in pandering to the belief of so many consumers that wines from the South of France should be cheap. They shouldn't. Yes, the plains that stretch inland from the sea were wine-lake country and can churn out large quantities of cheap wine. But what makes the region interesting to the wine-lover is its remarkable terroirs: the schist foothills, the limestone plateaux, the chalky clay of the rolling slopes; the biting winds that keep yields down, the cool nights at higher altitudes, the wild herbs of the *garrigue*. This is what

Horses for courses: both methods work well, but at different levels

terroirism is all about: the penetrating minerality of high-country wines, the invitingly open textures that come from more amenable landscapes, the sense that a wine is a reflection of a particular spot on the earth and nowhere else.

The great terroirs of the South are not yet all discovered. Not every terroir is great; when AXA Millésimes, owner of numerous top estates in Bordeaux and elsewhere, went prospecting in the South, it found that interesting terroirs tended to be on a small scale, and that larger estates had less interesting terroirs. And then terroirs have to be treated sympathetically: the grape varieties must suit the terroir, not just the market, and the grower must understand the nuances of this slope compared to that one. Growers have to be in love with their land in order to express it in the wine.

The number of good artisan growers is increasing all the time, and while we squeeze as many as we can into the French chapter of this book, there are others who deserve a mention. So here are some growers' names to conjure with (and *see also* the French chapter): Mas Belles Eaux, Dom Cabrol, Dom de Peyreficade, Léon Barral, Ch du Gravillas, Dom Les Aurelles, Ch La Dournie, Ch Cesseras, Dom de Clovallon, Dom Alain Chabanon, Dom Peyre Rose (Languedoc-Roussillon); Clos d'Alaric, Ch Roubine, Ch St-Julien d'Ailles.

The midwife of terroir
Grenache

I have stolen the title above from Marc Parcé of La Preceptorie de Centernach in Maury because there is no better way of summing up the nature of of this extraordinary grape. It's not shouty, it's not flashy and it's difficult to handle in both vineyard and winery: in temperament at least Grenache Noir reminds one of Pinot Noir. But there the resemblance ends. Grenache, historically, was one of the wine lake grapes, able to produce vast quantities of alcoholic wine. It had little flavour, colour or structure, but other grapes could lend those to a blend. Up in the southern Rhône it did rather better and was (and is) a staple in the Châteauneuf-du-Pape blend, not least because good growers there took trouble to cultivate it properly and limit its yields. In the Midi and Provence, though, it was regarded for years as part of the problem rather than as part of the solution. The solution was supposed to be Cabernet, Syrah and Mourvèdre: grapes with structure, acidity and assertive flavours.

Today's growers see it differently. With Grenache, you get out what you put in. On the right site – which can be dry and hot; it's a glutton for punishment in that respect – with yields strictly limited, and with the grapes picked at precisely the right moment, it will transmit its terroir with complete transparency. It's not a grape you can use to hide anything: as Marc put its, it forbids all trickery, all trumpery, it doesn't wear make-up and it doesn't show off. And yet it's not austere. It's showing itself to be one of the most intellectual of grapes, yet in the glass it's sleek and silky, warm and ripe and dangerously easy to drink: it may be chocolatey in youth (it's never very high in acidity) but herbal, *garrigue* notes soon develop, and leathery, earthy, spicy tones. A good Grenache can easily live for ten years or more, though simpler ones are best if drunk within five. It makes good rosé, and it also makes good fortified (*see* page 316).

So where does Grenache grow? The answer is pretty well everywhere, to some extent, in the South. Blends are the southern tradition, and it's a good team player, never seeking to dominate. It can work as a varietal, but often a touch of something else as a seasoning is a good idea. Southern French versions may not say "Grenache" on the front label and are probably blends anyway, so here are a few names we've particularly enjoyed lately (*see* also recommendations in the French chapter): Chêne Bleu, Ch de Prieuré, Dom Le Nouveau Monde, Ch de Corneilla, Ch de Flaugergues, Mas Bruguière, Doms Paul Mas, Dom Les Eminades, Dom Madeloc, Les Clos Perdus, Vignerons de Maury (Languedoc-Roussillon); Les Maîtres Vignerons de la Presqu'Ile de St Tropez, Ch de Berne, Ch Cavalier (Provence).

Grenache: treating it seriously means keeping yields down

In the pink
The rise of rosé

What is it about pink wine? From being a bit of a seasonal frivolity rosé has become a year-round staple, as likely to be offered before Sunday lunch in February as sipped with sardines in some Mediterranean café in July.

Yet rosé is the only wine to be sold primarily on its colour. Red grapes must be allowed to stain the juice only just so much before they're hustled off to be pressed. In Provence, indeed, where the preferred shade is pale or even paler, the red grapes go pretty much straight from vineyard to press.

Provence is the centre of rosé production in the South. Rosé is made everywhere, but the style of Provence tends to be the style of the South. More than 80 per cent of the wine made in Provence is pink; and so, not surprisingly, they take it very seriously. Yes, they certainly care about the colour – the rosé research station there (the only one in the world) has identified 21 typical shades of Provence rosé – but they are also busy planting different grape varieties in different climates and soils to see which vines produce which characteristics in which sites. This might not sound remarkable, but nobody else in the world is doing this for rosé. Because the way to make the best rosé is to start in the vineyard: to select your site, plant your vines and choose your picking date with rosé in mind, not red. Treat rosé as a by-product of red, as something you run off the red vats to concentrate what's left, as most of the wine world has done and some still does – and you'll get rosé that risks tasting like a by-product, with a touch of coarseness and perhaps less than perfect balance. Sound familiar?

It's a bit of a conundrum, then: a wine that to most consumers sells on its colour is benefiting from the sort of research that has always been reserved for more prestigious wines. But then Provence rosé is not cheap, and some of it is very, very expensive. The flavours are of rose, strawberry, raspberry, cherry: red fruits in the main, but also melon, lychee and even grapefruit. There might be some spice notes, and more weight in the mouth than you expect. And it's dry; bone dry. Sweetish, mawkish rosés are not the Provençal way: these wines are crisp, delicate but structured. They have a creaminess of texture that makes them good with food, too. But then anyone who has ever eaten bouillabaisse on a summer evening, watching the boats bobbing in the harbour as the sun sets over the Mediterranean, knows that already.

Check the colour: Provence rosé varies from pale to even paler

Food

The sea, the hills, the plains

It was the railways that brought prosperity to the South. Once fresh produce – the earliest possible peas, beans and asparagus; clams and mussels, octopus, sardines and mullet from the coast – could be raced to rich markets further north, life down here became (sometimes) easier. Until then, it was a matter of survival. Food evolved to deal with summer drought and winter cold, and any self-respecting store cupboard would contain sacks of several different sorts of bean, garlands of dried sausages, strings of onions, salt fish and meat, dried herbs, olives in brine and olive oil.

From there to cassoulet is but a short step, if several hours of work, and to *brandade de morue*, the salt-cod dish, which, in its deliciousness, makes redundant many of Portugal's 365 ways of cooking salt cod. The flavours of the South are powerful and pungent.

Typically one thinks of tomatoes and olives, garlic and the herbs of the *garrigue* – thyme, bay and rosemary especially, scenting a *gigot d'agneau* – and oranges and lemons giving zest to a *daube*. Ingredients change as you move from the Spanish border to the Italian: near Spain there are green olives and dried red peppers, in Provence, tapenade and anchoïade and small black Niçoise olives. But the same dishes, with innumerable local variations, appear again and again: fish stews and soups that make the best of the small, fast-growing but poorly textured Mediterranean fish; garlicky aioli and saffron; quantities of basil; truffles and wild mushrooms. And superb vegetables: purple-edged artichokes, and the aubergines and courgettes that find their way into ratatouille. In the local Michelin-starred restaurants the food is primped and polished for a high-rolling clientele, but in their original form these dishes were rich, substantial and rustic.

There's a parallel here with the wines. These, too, used to be rustic and at their best are so no longer. (And just as you can get bad food if you pick the wrong restaurant, so there's still plenty of indifferent wine if you pick the wrong producer.) Hit the right time of year and you can indulge yourself with a truffle menu, or tiny milk-fed lamb, or wild strawberries. Or, at any time, a chocolate confection with Maury or Banyuls.

Traditions can be invented, too. Tarte Tropezienne, a brioche cake filled with lavish amounts of crème patissière, is said to have been made by an expatriate Pole named Alexandre Micka who gave it to the film crew and cast of "And God Created Woman". Not good for the bikini figure, though...

The Mediterranean diet, in the markets at Aix-en-Provence and elsewhere

Keeping it sweet
Vins Doux Naturels

The fortified sweet wines of the South are unexpected: perfumed white Muscats of delicacy and finesse, and rich, resonant Grenache reds with a bite of *rancio* (*see* the French chapter) to wake up the palate. The whites should be drunk as young as possible, the reds at any age, but as old as possible is not a bad rule of thumb.

The Muscats dance – or they should. Muscat Blanc à Petits Grains has such elegance, such finesse, that the powerful, concentrated Muscat aroma becomes airy and lacy; this is Muscat de Beaumes de Venise (which is technically – yes, we know – from the Rhône) at its best. Venture outside Beaumes de Venise to Mireval, Lunel, Frontignan or St-Jean-de-Minervois and you'll probably get some of the slightly clumsier Muscat of Alexandria mixed in; the wines are good but they dance in shoes rather than barefoot. In Rivesaltes the Muscat is probably going to be all Alexandria, and the wines can be very good, but the shoes are brogues in comparison. Drink all of them either as aperitifs, like the French, or with or after dessert.

But if the whites are pretty the reds, made mostly from Grenache, can be extraordinary. They come from vertiginously steep, austerely dry and hot vineyards either on the coast (Banyuls) or further inland (Maury), and they're rich, toffeeish, with good acidity and, with age, that maderised, clean, sour tang of *rancio*. Old examples, aged for 20 or 30 years, can be astonishingly complex, deep wines. But they can be complicated to buy just because they vary so much. They can be aged in solera, or wood, or glass demi-johns, kept in conditions that are dry or humid, hot or cool, and may be sold young or with any amount of age. The older they are, the more concentrated they are. Find some old wines from Les Vignerons de Maury, Pla del Fount, Dom Madeloc, Terra Vinya, Doms de Terroirs du Sud or from the producers in the French chapter. Drink them alone, with blue cheese or some good chocolate.

Vins Doux Naturels: Grenache in bottles, left, and demi-johns

Key people
Who's who in the South

GÉRARD GAUBY   CLAUDE GROS

GÉRARD GAUBY: ROUSSILLON PERSONIFIED

It's hard to think of anyone who epitomizes the transformation of Roussillon better than Gérard Gauby. He was a, perhaps the, pioneer of the Agly valley, now one of the quality hotspots of the region, and he has led the way from the big, extracted, tannic wines of his early years to the burgundy-inspired balance and elegance of his more recent offerings.

His first vintage was 1985; before that the grapes from the five ha of family vineyards had been delivered, year after year, to the local co-op. He's built up his holdings now to some 45ha, all in the high, demanding land around the village of Calce. His 150 different parcels of vines cover almost every soil type you can think of, and he's fully biodynamic. Horses plough the vineyards and he makes his own biodynamic preparations.

CLAUDE GROS: ECLECTIC CONSULTANT

Narbonne-based Claude Gros brings his expertise to many of the best and better wines of the South; he's in demand in Bordeaux, too, and Washington State, Spain and Slovenia, but his main stamping-ground is Roussillon – he's Catalan by birth, which perhaps explains it.

Unlike some consultants, he's not associated with any particular style. La Pèira in Terrasses du Larzac bears his thumbprint, as does Thunevin-Calvet in Maury, Château de la Négly in La Clape, Mas Champart in St-Chinian, Château Puech-Haut in Fitou and many others. He also makes his own wine at Domaine de Boede, sister estate to Négly and works with American broker Jeffrey Davis at Clos des Truffiers, a wine (unlike the others) designed largely with the US market in mind.

Key people

Who's who in the South

ELOI DURRBACH   OLIVIER DECELLE

ELOI DURRBACH: PROVENÇAL PIONEER

Domaine de Trévallon is on the slopes of the Alpilles, and was
bought by his parents as a holiday base; well, it's been no holiday
for Eloi. First of all he found that Mourvèdre and Grenache
didn't ripen well there, so planted Syrah and Cabernet. Then the
authorities reduced the amount of Cabernet permitted in AC
wine there to 20%: Eloi, who uses 50% in his red, didn't budge,
and the wine became VDP des Bouches du Rhône; not the most
distinguished of monikers, but an indication of how little the
appellations of the South are a guide to the best wines.

The labels, by the way, are designed by Eloï's father, who also
roped in his friend Pablo Picasso to be Eloï's godfather.

OLIVIER DECELLE: MAURY MOGUL

Having made his money in frozen foods, Olivier Decelle headed
for the hot, dry hills of Maury to spend it. He arrived at Mas Amiel
in 1999 and set about regenerating it – and, almost by accident, set
the whole appellation on a better footing. He hired the experts he
needed, and espoused organic (now biodynamic) principles.

Maury is normally thought of as what the French make because
they can't make port, and it's generally played second fiddle to
more famous Banyuls. Decelle's mission has been to show how
richly aromatic and complex Maury can be. He also now makes
table wines, in which Grenache Noir, Gris and Blanc play major
parts. But try his Maury for a modern take on a traditional style.

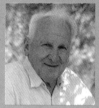

AIMÉ GUIBERT   **OLIVIER JULLIEN**

AIMÉ GUIBERT: MAS DE DAUMAS GASSAC

If at one time Aimé Guibert looked as though he was fighting a rearguard action against commercially cloned vines and synthetic vineyard treatments, now he's in the vanguard. Mas de Daumas Gassac is a homage to a landscape, a history and a culture: all the things that separate terroir wines from industrial ones. And he started back in the 1970s, when nobody except he (and Professors Enjalbert and Peynaud of Bordeaux University) believed that credible wine could be made in the Languedoc.

The reds are neither especially weighty nor especially modern, and after three or four years they close up and shouldn't be broached until they've reached seven or eight. There's a weird collection of vines here from Georgia, Armenia, Madeira, as well as Nebbiolo, Pinot Noir and Tannat, but Cabernet Sauvignon plays the biggest part in the blends – and indeed prevents it from using the newly starry AC of Terrasses de Larzac, although that is where it is.

OLIVIER JULLIEN: LARZAC LUMINARY

Olivier Jullien's Mas Jullien is up on the exposed, windswept Terrasses de Larzac, on the edge of the Cevennes. It was Jullien who gave the wine region its name; before 2005, when the borders were finally established, it was better known for its sheep, the milk of which make Rocquefort. (For Mas de Daumas Gassac, see above.)

He set up the estate in 1985, preferring to buy his own vineyards than continue the family tradition of selling grapes to the local co-op. Olivier is biodynamic, and believes in local grapes: he has Carignan, Mourvèdre, Syrah, Grenache, Cinsault for the reds, Carignan Blanc, Grenache Blanc, Chenin Blanc, Clairette, Viognier and others for the whites. His wines combine harmony with concealed power; they have weight, but they wear it lightly.

Who's who in the South

MARC PARCÉ   DANIEL RAVIER

MARC PARCÉ: REVIVING VIN DOUX NATUREL (VDN)
There are a number of Parcés in Banyuls: Marc works with his
brothers, Thierry and Pierre, and another Parcé, Jean-Michel, runs
the other star of Banyuls and Collioure, Dom du Mas Blanc.

Marc took over at Dom de la Rectorie in 1976 and has switched
its production from mainly fortified VDN to dry table wines
under the Collioure appellation, though his Banyuls Cuvée Léon
Parcé is a must-try wine. In 2001 he joined forces with other local
growers to form La Préceptorie in Maury, where he makes Côtes
de Roussillon, *vin de table* and Maury. He's a passionate advocate of
Grenache, and an equally passionate polemicist on the subject of
the reform of AOC and the role of the vigneron. Thierry is a pianist
and Pierre a photographer. The wines are rich, distinctive and deep
and approach cult status.

PEYRAUD FAMILY & DANIEL RAVIER: HEART OF BANDOL
Bandol would not be the wine it is today if it was not for the efforts
of the Peyrauds of Dom Tempier. In 1940 Lucien Peyraud married
Lucie Tempier; at their wedding Lucie's father presented Lucien
with an old bottle of Dom Tempier. It was a lightbulb moment: the
rest of his career was spent pushing for Bandol to be recognized as
a great, long-lived and complex wine, for Tempier to be recognized
as the best of Bandol and for Bandol to be based on the then
obscure Mourvèdre grape. Lucien died in 1998. His sons, Jean-
Marie and François, continued his work and retired in 2000; the
estate is now run by manager Daniel Ravier, who continues to
work the vineyards organically and continues to win plaudits.

Also available

Hugh Johnson's Wine Guide

Search thousands of wines,
vintages, winemakers, regions
and much more

A little learning...

A few technical words

The jargon of laboratory analysis is often seen on back-labels. It creeps menacingly into newspapers and magazines. What does it mean? This hard-edged wine-talk, unsympathetic as it is to most lovers of wine, is very briefly explained below.

Alcohol content (mainly ethyl alcohol) is expressed in per cent by volume of the total liquid. (Also known as "degrees".) Table wines are usually between 12.5° and 14.5°, though up to 16° is increasingly seen.

Acidity is both fixed and volatile. Fixed acidity consists principally of tartaric, malic and citric acids, all found in the grape, and lactic and succinic acids, produced during fermentation. Volatile acidity consists mainly of acetic acid, which is rapidly formed by bacteria in the presence of oxygen. A small amount of volatile acidity is inevitable and even attractive. With a larger amount the wine becomes "pricked"– to use the Shakespearian term. It turns to vinegar. Acidity may be natural, in warm regions it may also be added.

Total acidity is fixed and volatile acidity combined. As a rule of thumb, for a well-balanced wine it should be in the region of one gram per thousand for each 10° Oechsle (see above).

Barriques Vital to modern wine, either in ageing and/or for fermenting in barrels (the newer the barrel the stronger the influence) or from the addition of oak chips or – at worst – oak essence. Newcomers to wine can easily be beguiled by the vanilla-like scent and flavour into thinking they have bought something luxurious rather than something cosmetically flavoured. But barrels are expensive; real ones are only used for wines with the inherent quality to benefit long-term. French oak is classic and most expensive. American oak has a strong vanilla flavour.

Malolactic fermentation is often referred to as a secondary fermentation, and can occur naturally or be induced. The process involves converting tart malic acid into softer lactic acid. Unrelated to alcoholic fermentation, the "malo" can add complexity and flavour to both red and white wines. In hotter climates where natural acidity may be low canny operators avoid it.

Micro-oxygenation is a widely used technique that allows the wine controlled contact with oxygen during maturation. This mimics the effect of barrel-ageing, reduces the need for racking, and helps to stabilize the wine.

pH is a measure of the strength of the acidity: the lower the figure the more acid. Wine usually ranges from pH 2.8 to 3.8. High pH can be a problem in hot climates. Lower pH gives better colour, helps stop bacterial spoilage and allows more of the SO_2 to be free and active as a preservative.

Residual sugar is that left after fermentation has finished or been stopped, measured in grams per litre. A dry wine has virtually none.

Sulphur dioxide (SO_2) is added to prevent oxidation and other accidents in winemaking. Some of it combines with sugars etc and is "bound". Only the "free" SO_2 is effective as a preservative. Total SO_2 is controlled by
· law according to the level of residual sugar: the more sugar, the more SO_2 is needed.

Tannins are the focus of attention for red-winemakers intent on producing softer, more approachable wines. Later picking, and picking by tannin ripeness rather than sugar levels gives riper, silkier tannins.

Toast refers to the burning of the inside of the barrel. "High toast" gives the wine caramel-like flavours.